David Olusoga is a British-Nigerian historian, broadcaster and BAFTA award-winning presenter and filmmaker. His previous books include *The Kaiser's Holocaust* and *The World's War*. He was also a contributor to *The Oxford Companion to Black British History*.

Black and British was longlisted for the Orwell Prize, shortlisted for the inaugural Jhalak Prize and the PEN Hessell-Tiltman Prize and was a Waterstones History Book of the Year.

Praise for *Black and British*

'You could not ask for a more judicious, comprehensive and highly readable survey of a part of British history that has been so long overlooked or denied. David Olusoga, in keeping with the high standards of his earlier books, is a superb guide.'

Adam Hochschild

'A classic in every sense of the word. At last David Olusoga has painstakingly put together a history that is planted in Britain, Africa and the Americas in a way which goes clearly to show that we are all connected . . . This book should be made compulsory reading in all our schools.' The Most Reverend & Right Honourable Dr John Sentamu, Archbishop of York

'Groundbreaking'   *Observer*

'[A] comprehensive and important history of black Britain . . . Written with a wonderful clarity of style and with great force and passion. It is thoroughly researched and there are many interesting anecdotes.' Kwasi Kwarteng, *Sunday Times*

'A radical reappraisal of the parameters of history, exposing lacunae in the nation's version of its past.' Arifa Akbar, *Guardian*

'An insightful, inclusive history of black people in Britain . . . Rich in detail and packed with strong personalities, this is an important contribution to our understanding of life in the UK.'

History Revealed

'Luci   *Herald Scotland*

D0525029

Also by David Olusoga

*The Kaiser's Holocaust: Germany's Forgotten Genocide
and the Colonial Roots of Nazism*

The World's War: Forgotten Soldiers of Empire

DAVID OLUSOGA

BLACK AND BRITISH

A FORGOTTEN HISTORY

PAN BOOKS

First published 2016 by Macmillan

This paperback edition published 2017 by Pan Books
an imprint of Pan Macmillan
20 New Wharf Road, London N1 9RR
Associated companies throughout the world
www.panmacmillan.com

ISBN 978-1-4472-9976-9

5 7 9 8 6 4

A CIP catalogue record for this book is available from the British Library.

Typeset in Perpetua Std by
Palimpsest Book Production Ltd, Falkirk, Stirlingshire
Printed and bound by CPI Group (UK) Ltd, Croydon CR0 4YY

Visit **www.panmacmillan.com** to read more about all our books
and to buy them. You will also find features, author interviews and
news of any author events, and you can sign up for e-newsletters
so that you're always first to hear about our new releases.

Dedicated to the Memory of

Adesola Oladipupo Olusoga

&

Isaiah Gabriel Temidayo Olusoga

CONTENTS

LIST OF ILLUSTRATIONS

PREFACE

When I was a child, growing up on a council estate in the North-East of England, I imbibed enough of the background racial tensions of the late 1970s and 1980s to feel profoundly unwelcome in Britain. My right, not just to regard myself as a British citizen, but even to be in Britain seemed contested. Despite our mother's careful protection, the tenor of our times seeped through the concrete walls into our home and into my mind and my siblings'. Secretly I harboured fears that as part of the group identified by chanting neo-Nazis, hostile neighbours and even television comedians as 'them' we might be sent 'back'. This, in our case, presumably meant 'back' to Nigeria, a country of which I had only infant memories, and a land upon which my youngest siblings had never set foot.

At the zenith of its swaggering confidence, the National Front – the NF – made enough noise and sparked enough debate within Britain to make the idea of sending 'them' 'back' seem vaguely plausible. The fact that in the 1970s and 1980s reputable, mainstream politicians openly discussed programmes for voluntary assisted repatriation that were aimed exclusively at non-white immigrants demonstrates the extent to which the political aether had been polluted by the politics of hate. In the year of my birth the Conservative Party's General Election Manifesto contained a pledge to encourage voluntary repatriation of immigrants.[1] Today we seem to have forgotten that Enoch Powell's prediction of 'Rivers of Blood' was followed, many years later, by unsubtle calls for a mechanism to be found that might prevent the black British population from 'doubling or trebling'. In 1981 Powell suggested that people from the 'new commonwealth' might be 'happier outside of the UK', and proposed a new British Nationality Act to redefine what British citizenship meant. In my childish fearfulness such discussions translated into a deep but unspoken anxiety that a process might, feasibly, be set in train that could lead to the separation and destruction of my family.

To thousands of younger black and mixed-race Britons who, thankfully, cannot remember those decades, the racism of the 1970s and 1980s and the insecurities it bred in the minds of black people are difficult to imagine or relate to.* But they are powerful memories for my generation. I was eight years old when the BBC finally cancelled *The Black & White Minstrel Show*. I have memories of my mother rushing across our living room to change television channels (in the days before remote controls) to avoid her mixed-race children being confronted by grotesque caricatures of themselves on prime-time television. I was seventeen when the last of the touring blackface minstrel shows finally disappeared, having clung on for a decade performing in fading ballrooms on the decaying piers of Britain's seaside towns. I grew up in a Britain in which there were pictures of golliwogs on jam jars and golliwog dolls alongside the teddy bears in the toy shop windows. One of the worst moments of my unhappy schooling was when, during the run-up to a 1970s Christmas, we were allowed to bring in our favourite toys. The girl who innocently brought her golliwog doll into our classroom plunged me into a day of humiliation and pain that I still find hard to recall, decades later. When, in recent years, I have been assured that such dolls, and the words 'golliwog' and 'wog', are in fact harmless and that opposition to them is a symptom of rampant political correctness, I recall another incident. It is difficult to regard a word as benign when it has been scrawled onto a note, wrapped around a brick and thrown through one's living-room window in the dead of night, as happened to my family when I was a boy of fourteen. That scribbled note reiterated the demand that me and my siblings be sent 'back'.

---

* Sadly young black Britons today face different forms of racism and lack of opportunity, perhaps more insidious and subtle but no less damaging.

In the early twenty-first century, politicians in Whitehall and researchers in think tanks fret about the failures of ethnic-minority communities to properly integrate into British society. In my childhood the resistance seemed, to me at least, to come from the opposite direction. Many non-white people felt that while it was possible to be in Britain it was much harder to be *of* Britain. They felt marked out and unwanted whenever they left the confines of family or community. It was a place and a time in which 'black' meant 'other', and 'black' was unquestionably the opposite of 'British'. The phrase 'Black British', with which we are so familiar today, was little heard in those years. In the minds of some it spoke of an impossible duality. In the face of such hostility many black British people, and their white and mixed-race family members, slipped into a siege mentality, a state of mind from which it has been difficult to entirely escape. What drove us deeper into that citadel of self-reliance and watchful mistrust was not just racial prejudice but a wave of racial violence.

Almost every black or mixed-race person of my generation has a story of racial violence to tell. These stories range from humiliation to hospitalization. They are raw, visceral, highly personal and rarely shared beyond family circles. This oral history of twentieth-century racial violence has never been collected or collated, but it is there and it is shocking. Racial violence impacted most dramatically upon me and my family in the mid-1980s, when I was in my early teens. In 1984 my family – my mother, two sisters, younger brother and grandmother – were driven out of our home by a sustained campaign of almost nightly attacks. For what seemed like many months, but was in fact only a few weeks, we lived in darkness, as the windows of our home were broken one by one, smashed by bricks and rocks thrown from an old cemetery just across the street. As replacing the glass merely invited further attacks the windows were boarded up and we slowly disappeared into the gloom, quarantined together behind a screen of plywood. As the attacks came after dark, policemen working on a rota were dispatched to take up positions behind our front door, in the hope of catching our assailants in the act. When, after a week or so, this plan failed, no other strategy was put forward, and the barrage continued. The bricks bounced off the plywood screens with thuds that left me and my siblings shaking and screaming in our beds.

When the attacks became known at my school I was sat down one afternoon by a well-meaning but inexcusably naive teacher, who recounted to me what was evidently one of his favoured anecdotes. He told me how in the 1960s Louis Armstrong had overheard a white diner, a few tables away in a restaurant, loudly rebuking the waiters for allowing a 'negro' to eat in an establishment that served whites. At the end of his dinner, after he had presumably been mollified by the waiters, the white diner demanded his bill and was shocked to discover that it had already been paid by Armstrong. The meaning of the parable, I was informed, is that by rising above racial hatred Armstrong had won a sort of moral victory. That my teacher believed that this hackneyed yarn, of questionable provenance, was of some relevance to an embattled, angry mixed-race teenager, whose family were under regular attack, was to me – even at that age – a clear signal that we were on our own.

On a summer's evening many months later, long after my family had been delivered from our tormentors and evacuated to emergency housing, I timorously ventured back to our former home after school. I stood across the street, never finding the courage to go any closer. Constantly and instinctively I kept turning my head towards the graveyard from which the bricks and stones had come.

The windows of our former home remained boarded up, as they had been on the day we had hastily loaded up our possessions into a removal van. But a black-gloss swastika had been painted on the white front door. Thick tendrils of paint had dripped down from each arm of that horrible cross. Above and below it had been scrawled the words 'NF Won Here'. If, at that moment I had had the means to leave Britain I would have done so, immediately and with the intention of never returning. Thankfully, I was young, penniless and had nowhere to go. I stayed and life got slowly better.

Throughout those embattled years my mother, somehow, managed to maintain within our family a regime of self-education and self-improvement. It was this internal, familial micro-culture that slowly drew me to read history. I stumbled upon the subject that was to become my vocation out of a simple love of story, and because of a gung-ho fascination with the Second World War that was almost obligatory among boys of that period, whatever their racial background. Britain of the 1980s was a nation still saturated in the culture and paraphernalia of that conflict. For the white working-class community that I grew up in, the war was the most exciting and significant event ever to collide with our terraced streets and decaying factories. It had changed the lives of my white grandparents, whom I loved deeply, and I was intoxicated by the thought that German bombers had prowled the skies above my home town, and that my grandfather had scanned those skies while on watch on the roof of the Vickers Armstrong factory by the River Tyne, where he worked building tanks. I wandered into history looking for excitement. I never expected that there I would encounter black and brown people who were like me and my family. I was alerted to those stories of presence and participation by my white mother, and I stumbled across more and more stories of black British people as my interests took me further back, into the nineteenth and then the eighteenth century.

In 1986 I came across the book *Staying Power* by the British journalist Peter Fryer. It was, I believe, the first book I ever bought for myself with my own money. This history of the black presence in Britain was published in 1984, the year in which my family had been besieged in our home, and it set the racism that had so deeply affected our lives within a historical context. It allowed me to understand my own experiences as part of a longer story and to appreciate that in an age when black men were dying on the floors of police cells, my own encounters with British racism had been relatively mild. For me and for thousands of black and white people who read Fryer's book its effect was transformative. Fryer took his readers back through the centuries and introduced us to an enormous pantheon of black historical characters, about whom we had previously known nothing. Those black Britons have been with me ever since. I have visited their graves and read their letters and memoirs. They have become part of British history and in some cases part of the national curriculum. *Staying Power* remains a uniquely important book and anyone who has ever written about black history has found themselves referencing it, quoting from it or seeking out some of the myriad of primary sources it drew together. Fryer's eloquent chapters offer guidance and provide orientation through a complex and fractured history. Although not the first work of black British history its impact spread further than most, in part because its publication came at a crucial moment, three years after a wave of riots sparked by hostile policing set ablaze black neighbourhoods of London, Bristol and Liverpool.

Staying Power was part of a wider process of historical salvage. It was one of a number of pioneering books of black British history that recovered lost people, reclaimed lost events and reassessed the significance of racism in British history. Just as important were *Black and White* by James Walvin (1973) and *Black People in Britain* by Folarin Shyllon (1977). The books that came out of that wave of new research were in part an attempt to compensate for the failures and myopia of so-called mainstream history. When Fryer, Walvin and others were writing it was not unusual for books on the British eighteenth century to make no mention of slavery and the slave trade, or concentrate only on the abolition of those institutions. The presence and role of black people in the British story was all too often ignored completely or else reduced to footnotes. When black figures did appear they were often mute and passive, the victims of slavery or the beneficiaries of abolition. Black history was so poorly understood at that time that when James Walvin embarked upon his research he wrote to every county archivist in Britain asking them if they had come across any forgotten black figures in the documents they cared for. What this first wave of black history writing demonstrated was that while post-war migration had been unprecedented in scale it had not marked the beginnings of black British history. Thanks to their work it is today well understood that people of African descent have been present in Britain since the third century, and there have been black 'communities' of sorts since the 1500s.

This book and the BBC television series it accompanies are a modest attempt to build on the work of those earlier historians and to bring the histories they uncovered to new audiences. But it is also a tentative endeavour to reimagine what we mean by 'black history' and ask where its borders might be drawn. The black history of Britain is by its nature a global history. Yet too often it is seen as being only the history of migration, settlement and community formation in Britain itself. Black British history is as global as the empire. Like Britain's triangular slave trade it is a triangular history, firmly planted in Britain, Africa and the Americas. On all three continents stand its ruins and relics. Black British history can be read in the crumbling stones of the forty slave fortresses that are peppered along the coast of West Africa and in the old plantations and former slave markets of the lost British empire of North America. Its imprint can be read in stately homes, street names, statues and memorials across Britain and is intertwined with the cultural and economic histories of the nation.

This book is an experiment. It is an attempt to see what new stories and approaches emerge if black British history is envisaged as a global history and – perhaps more controversially – as a history of more than just the black experience itself. As no single work spanning so large a time frame and painted across so broad a canvas can hope to address all the nuances and complexities of each subject or specialism, my hope is that the bibliography and endnotes will direct the reader to other volumes. To keep this book to a manageable size I have also chosen to dwell only briefly on the biographies of the key figures of black history. That a modern writer is in a position to merely sketch out these biographies is because they have been so effectively fleshed out elsewhere. For this I am grateful. I have also tried to avoid areas covered exhaustively in earlier books. As historians including Peter Fryer and Hakim Adi have so vividly explored the histories of Pan-Africanism and black radicalism, I have left those histories largely untouched here. Likewise the history and the workings of plantation slavery in the British Caribbean and North America are only touched upon. Certain problems inherent within black British history are insurmountable. The list of unknowns is as long as it is frustrating. Many most significant black figures are mute, silenced by a lack of written sources. There is also a problem relating to gender. A history largely shaped by migration – both forced and voluntary – is disproportionately male. In the Atlantic slave trade, male slaves were valued more than female. Slave-ship captains who transported black children to Britain to work as servants or be sold as exotic novelties to the households of the rich preferred black boys to black girls, and it was black men not women who were cast across the empire serving in the Royal Navy. Likewise African kings and chiefs sent their sons not their daughters to schools in Liverpool and London. This creates a challenge to the historian of black British history to locate and re-present the voices of the black women.

Like anyone writing on black British history I am indebted to the works, observations, research and insights of others before me. If this book has anything in common with the pioneering works of Fryer, Walvin and others it is that it is written in the firm belief that Britain is a nation capable of confronting all aspects of its past and becoming a better nation for doing so.

INTRODUCTION

'Years of Distant Wandering'

About twenty miles upriver from Freetown, the hilly capital of Sierra Leone, is a small oval-shaped island which from a distance looks no different to any of the other small, oval-shaped islands that are irregularly dotted along the Sierra Leone River. When viewed from the water little can be seen of Bunce Island, covered as it is by a dense canopy of trees.* The shoreline is a narrow strip of coarse dark-orange sand, strewn with grey rocks, and it is only when approaching the island that any man-made structures become visible. Two small jetties, only a few metres apart, project from the western shore. One is made of concrete blocks, the other of square-cut blocks of local stone, blackened, barnacled and ancient, while on the northern tip of the island, standing at the crest of a low hill, are the ruins of a large and substantial structure, clearly visible from the shoreline despite the thick undergrowth.

That structure was built there because for a century and a half Bunce Island's location made it a perfect meeting place. The island is situated close enough to the mouth of the Sierra Leone River for the channel to still be deep enough for ocean-going ships to navigate, but is far enough upstream for the island to be easily accessible by small river craft. As Bunce also sits near the confluence with the Rokel River, it can be reached by river traffic from across a wide hinterland. This position, and the island's natural defensive qualities,

---

* At various times in its history Bunce Island has been known as both 'Bance' and 'Bence'. There is no definitive spelling.

made it the ideal location in the seventeenth century for English traders to establish a slave fortress. Three and a half centuries after it was built the ruins of the citadel remain impressive. Attacked and destroyed on six different occasions – four times by the French (1695, 1704, 1779, and 1794) and twice by pirates (1719, 1720) – the ruins are the remains of the seventh Bunce Island fortress. This litany of destruction and reconstruction is testimony to the importance of the island to the British and evidence of the outrageous profits generated by the trade in enslaved Africans.

The trees of Bunce Island, and the thick vegetation beneath them, make it difficult to imagine what the fortress looked like during its heyday. Believing that malaria was caused by miasmas that emanated from vegetation, rather than by mosquitoes, the European agents who ran commercial operations at Bunce Island had the undergrowth cut back regularly and saplings hacked down. In their day the island was a largely open space over which the great outer walls of the fortress loomed formidably. There was 'little else but iron, rock & gravel', claimed a 1773 visitor to the island.[1] The first fortress was built by the British around 1670. It was what in the seventeenth and eighteenth centuries was called a slave factory, and was one of around forty slave-trading outposts constructed along the coast of West Africa, most of them on islands in the mouths of rivers, or on promontories jutting out to sea. More than some comparable fortresses Bunce operated like a factory in the industrial sense. It was, in a way, a proto-industrial production line, along which captive Africans were bought and sold, sorted, processed, warehoused and literally branded – marking them out as human commodities, at least in the eyes of their captors. These processes were part of an organized and globalized system designed to turn captive Africans into New World slaves, a process that was completed – for those who survived the Atlantic crossing – on the plantations of the Americas during the 'seasoning', a brutal period of punishments, beatings, cultural deracination and instruction designed to break the spirit.

The 'production line' at Bunce Island moved from east to west. African captives arrived on a beach on the eastern side of the island. They were landed there by inland slave-traders who had brought them on river canoes. Some of these traders were Africans, others were from mixed-race Afro-Portuguese or Afro-English peoples, powerful coastal communities that were the offspring of European slave-traders and local women. By the time the captives arrived on the 'slave beach' they were already profoundly traumatized. Most had been seized in slave raids against their home villages. These typically took place in the early hours of the morning in order to capture people at their most disorientated. The old and very young, whose economic value was negligible and who might slow down the caravan, were murdered in front of their relatives. These killings were intended to shock those taken captive into meek submission. So effective was this tactic that European slave-traders on Bunce Island and elsewhere complained that the captives arrived in a stupor, a condition that was called 'the lethargy', but which modern psychologists would recognize as PTSD – post-traumatic stress disorder. From the slave beach the silent, sullen captives were marched up a short pathway to the Sorting Yard, an open area located directly in front of the main defensive walls of the fortress, not far from the main gate.

This clearing was where the buying and selling was done. Here the slave-traders displayed their wares – captive human beings, but also ivory, gold and camwood, from which a coloured dye was extracted. The British agents came out to meet their trading partners, bringing with them bottles of wine and rum to help lubricate the coming negotiations. In exchange for slaves and other valuable commodities the British offered glass beads, bundles of cloth, gunpowder, European metal goods, tobacco pipes, bottles of liquor and European weapons. Until a few years ago the ground of the Sorting Yard was littered with tiny glass beads and fragments of pottery that had been dropped and discarded by both buyers and sellers centuries earlier. Most of these grim souvenirs have been hoovered up by tourists who travel out to Bunce Island from Freetown, but many more relics of the trade lie beneath the soil, along with iron nails used to attach shackles and chains to African arms and legs, and broken wine bottles. It was in the Sorting Yard, during the early decades of Bunce Island's history, that the captives, once purchased, were branded with hot irons, and marked indelibly with the initials of the companies that now owned them.

When negotiations were over and sales concluded, the river canoes were loaded up with their newly acquired goods and paddled away. The captives who had been rejected by the agents were taken downstream and offered to rival traders; Bunce Island's location meant that its agents had first pick of the tens of thousands of Africans who were shipped down the Sierra Leone River during the seventeenth and eighteenth centuries. The non-human commodities bought by the traders were deposited in a large storeroom and the captives were brought up through the main gate and into the fortress itself. In a large and open space, in front of the agents' house where the Europeans lived, the men were separated from the women and children, tearing families apart, and all were marched off to special holding yards. Accessed through secure double doors, these yards were large open spaces behind walls more than three metres high. Inside were simple wooden shelters. As the slaves were now the property of the companies for whom the agents worked, it was in their economic interests to protect them from the elements. The agents understood that the longer slaves were warehoused in the holding yards the more of them became sick and died, lowering profits. They also knew that once the initial trauma of their capture subsided there was a greater risk that they might recover and combine in violent resistance. Yet the duration of their stay depended upon the arrival of slave ships seeking to make purchases.

The northern wall of the men's holding yard was also the outer wall of the agents' house. It was by all accounts a two-storey building in which the agents attempted an approximation of a genteel existence. One visitor described it as being of a 'respectable and formidable appearance . . . about one hundred feet in length, and thirty in breadth, and contains nine rooms, on one floor, under which are commodious large cellars and store rooms'.[2] The front had a full-length veranda and the main entrance was an arched doorway that opened up into a hallway in which had been built a fireplace. In a country in which temperatures almost never drop below 20 °C this was a purely decorative flourish. The faux gentility of the agents' house was undermined by the fact that the windows of the room in which they and their guests dined and drank looked directly into the men's holding yard. Today the ruins of this strange villa, far higher than the other structures on the island, look like they could come crashing down at any moment. Fallen bricks and lumps of local stone litter the ground and there are sections of wall that remain upright more out of habit than structural integrity.

The holding yard in which the women and children were imprisoned lies to the south of the men's yard and is much smaller, a reflection of the fact that the majority of the captives were men as they attracted higher prices in the slave markets of the Americas. Built into the western-facing wall of the women's holding yard is a small structure. The remains are held together by a row of three trees. Tall and thin, their finger-like roots have colonized the stonework, but the door that once opened out into the holding yard can still be passed through, and on each side of it are two small square windows. The room inside is only a few square metres in size. No similar structure was built in the men's holding yard. On the right-hand side of the door, when entered from the women's holding yard, there was, it appears, a rudimentary bathroom and to the left some sort of chamber. The historians and archaeologists who have explored Bunce Island have speculated over what its function might have been. The appalling conclusion that some of them have reached is that it was what Miss Isatu Smith, the formidable Director of the Sierra Leonean Monuments and Relics Committee, calls the 'rape house' of Bunce Island. It was one grim feature in a section of the fortress dedicated to 'recreation'. Behind the 'rape house' was an orchard which, as one late-eighteenth-century visitor to the island tells us, was planted with orange trees. This little heaven, just metres from where slave women were assaulted, was where the agents met to relax and drink. The island is strewn with broken eighteenth-century wine bottles, and written accounts of life on the island describe sumptuous dinners and heavy drinking. The agents were able to enjoy their drinks chilled as this most luxurious of slave fortresses had its own ice store. Henry Smeathman, a British botanist, whom we shall meet again in later chapters, came to Bunce Island in the 1770s. The account he left us speaks more about recreation than any other subject. While on the island as a guest of the slave agents, Smeathman spent a day playing golf on the island's two-hole golf course, the first ever built on the African continent. The players wore white cotton and were accompanied by African caddies clad in tartan loincloths made from woollen cloth imported from Glasgow. After a day's golf Smeathman joined the slave-traders for a game of backgammon, then it was time for dinner. This consisted of antelope, wild boar, river fish and ape.[3] The feast was accompanied by Madeira wine and Virginia tobacco. Another guest of the agents, who came to the island in 1791, described spending a 'day in comfort and pleasantry, under the hospitable roof of Bance Island house' and on several occasions noted how much drinking went on there.[4]

In the final hours of their captivity on Bunce Island the Africans were marched out of the holding yards, through the main gates and down a stone pathway towards the jetty. Without knowing it they were already heading westwards in the direction of the Americas, where those who survived the Middle Passage were to spend the rest of their lives. On their way to the water's edge, on a bend in the pathway, it appears that a blacksmith was stationed. There shackles were fixed to the legs of the 'slaves' – as they now unquestionably were. At the jetty they were loaded into small boats and ferried out to the ocean-going slave ships assembled in the deeper waters of the river channel. The whole operation was carried out under the gaze of a huge cannon. It is still there, blackened and encrusted to the stonework of the jetty. It was on those stone blocks that between thirty and fifty thousand Africans took their last step on the continent of their birth.

In 1808, when the slave trade was abandoned, Bunce Island's location, which had been so important and so advantageous for so many years, became a liability. The centre of British activity in Sierra Leone shifted to Freetown at the mouth of the river and although the British colonial authorities were reluctant to abandon the collection of expensive and extensive buildings, no long-term use for them could be found. The fortress was briefly converted into a barracks and training ground for locally recruited African regiments, and after that became a sawmill, where valuable African teak wood was cut and planed for use in ship-building. But in the early 1840s, with the main fortifications and the walls of the agents' house already crumbling into disrepair, the whole island was abandoned. The vegetation that had been for so long tamed now rioted across the holding yards; great trees pushed their roots into the foundations and vines and creepers spread their tendrils across the old walls.

As the island now had no economic raison d'être there was no reason to visit and few people did. Slowly consumed and concealed by the trees, the fortress was forgotten. Generations later the rumour emerged that the ruins were of a Portuguese slave factory – as the Portuguese were the first Europeans to arrive on the Guinea Coast anything conspicuously old in Sierra Leone tended to be described as Portuguese. When, in the 1970s, American archaeologists arrived on Bunce Island they were able to instantly establish the true nationality of the ruins. On the battlements that defended the northern and western edges of the fortress they came across several abandoned cannon on which, beneath the symbol of a crown, were initials 'G R' – George Rex, the cipher of the British King George III.[5]

The most dedicated of archaeologists who have worked on Bunce Island is Joseph Opala. He once described the island as the 'Pompeii' of the Atlantic slave trade. Opala linked Bunce Island to the history of the United States in a way that was both remarkable and unique. It regarded the story of the Gullah people, sometimes called the Geechee. These African American communities were formed in isolated coastal settlements in South Carolina and Georgia. Thanks to genealogical research and well-preserved records of the transportation and sale of enslaved Africans in that part of colonial North America, members of the Gullah communities are among the tiny number of African Americans who can know with some certainty which parts of Africa their ancestors came from. A handful have even been able to trace the names of their ancestors.[6] Many were people who had been sold to the owners of rice plantations in South Carolina and Georgia from the infamous slave market at Charleston in South Carolina, to which the ships that left the jetty at Bunce Island regularly travelled. After the abolition of American slavery in the 1860s, the Gullah were largely left to their own devices and were able to preserve aspects of their original African languages and cultures. When historians and archaeologists like Joseph Opala began to trace the lineage of these communities, the branches of their family trees led, time and again, to Bunce Island.

Since 1989 Bunce Island has witnessed several Gullah 'homecomings', in which members of Gullah families from South Carolina and Georgia travelled to Sierra Leone and visited the slave fortress. These visits have been raw, emotional and visceral – as well as unique. During the 1989 homecoming some Gullah people reported being so overcome they said they could 'see', not merely 'feel', their ancestors when they entered the holding yards. Most of the people who travel upriver to Bunce Island today are from the United States. Despite interruptions caused by Sierra Leone's disastrous civil war of the 1990s and more recently by the 2015 Ebola epidemic, Bunce Island has become a place of pilgrimage for African Americans. Some visitors have carved their names, the names of their home towns or simply the word 'Gullah' into the bark of the trees that have grown up around the former agents' house.

Most people who come to Bunce Island, even those with no family connection, find it an eerie and disturbing place. A few years ago a caretaker was hired to maintain the ruins, and a concrete house was built for him on the island. He found himself unable to be alone on Bunce Island at night, and took to leaving each evening and commuting to work by boat. As dusk falls and the trees begin to cast long shadows over the walls of the holding yards and the 'rape house', the urge to get on a boat and leave Bunce Island is almost irresistible. Too much has happened here for this island ever to be inhabited again, even by a solitary caretaker.

If the ghosts of the slaves perhaps linger on Bunce Island then they are not alone. The presence of the agents and the slave-traders is just as strongly imprinted. Many of what look like rocks on the beaches are in fact the heavy, concave bases of eighteenth-century wine bottles. The glass is a dark brown, its surface opaque having been ground down by two centuries of daily tides and ceaseless currents. They are in their greatest abundance on the far northern tip, directly under the fortifications, in front of the agents' house. There it is possible to pick up the remnants of a bottle that was, perhaps, thrown into the sea two centuries earlier, by a man who traded in enslaved human beings.

Bunce Island has been dramatically rediscovered. It is studied by historians, examined by archaeologists and now sacred to the Gullah people. But, at the very moment of its exhumation, it is at terrible risk. The tides and currents of the Sierra Leone River that thousands of years ago created Bunce Island are slowly destroying it. The island is being eroded away, year by year. In 2008 the fortress was placed on the World Monuments Fund's list of the world's '100 Most Endangered Sites'. It is almost as if the Sierra Leone River, a waterway on which so many thousands of Africans were transported into slavery, is trying to wipe Bunce Island off the map and wash away its own dark past. As the river eats away at its foundations, the trees continue their long offensive against the stonework. Great cracks have wrenched apart whole sections of the main defensive walls; doorways and windows are being held up only by temporary wooden supports. Sierra Leone's Monuments and Relics Commission is energetically gathering funds and securing partnership to save Bunce Island, and if that money is found it seems probable that much of it will come from the United States.

Each year more African Americans learn of Bunce Island, and more arrive to commune with their ancestors. When, in 1992, General Colin Powell visited the island he stated that there he came to see himself as an African as well as an American. 'I feel my roots here in this continent,' he told his hosts. More recently a team from the US National Park Service have carried out a survey of the island and generated a 3D model of the fortress. There have been books written and documentaries filmed about the island, and about what is known as the Gullah Connection. Bunce Island has come to be regarded as the most significant site on the African continent for the study of African American history. Yet, through all the stages of its bleak history, Bunce Island was linked umbilically to another island three thousand miles to the north.

All four of the companies that managed the fortress were British. The money made there flowed back to British investors. Even the bricks that were used to build the walls of the fortress were fired in Britain and carried to Africa in the bellies of British slave ships as ballast. Most of the men whose bones lie crumbling in the European graveyard were British-born and most of the ships that dropped anchor off Bunce Island, firing their cannon in a seven-gun salute to the agents in the fortress, had set sail from British cities: Bristol, Liverpool and London. Other ships arrived from ports in Britain's North American colonies.

Bunce Island, hidden for so many years behind a screen of trees, is an extreme example of a wider phenomenon. The history of Britain's long, complex and traumatic relationship with Africa and her peoples has been and remains largely obscured. The most difficult chapters in that history, those that record the age of slavery, were largely expunged after the 1830s. When the moral climate changed and slavery was abolished, the families and dynasties who had grown wealthy from it airbrushed it out of their family histories. Likewise the worst crimes of the age of empire, of which Africans were not the only victims, are little discussed, as the empire itself has become reduced to little more than images of explorers in pith helmets, romantic ideas of railways and the Raj and some vague notions of the spread of English values and language. But there is more to it. This is not simply a case of historical amnesia. The parts of British history in which black people were active participants, as well as those in which they were the exploited victims, have been erased and the story of the black presence in Britain remains obscure and even disputed despite more than fifty years of archival discovery and historical scholarship. In the 1990s the African American historian Gretchen Gerzina was informed by an assistant in a London bookshop that there 'were no black people in England before 1945'.[7] Around the same time a correspondent writing to the *Independent* newspaper complained of '20th-century multi-culturalists' who 'invent a spurious history for black settlement in Britain before the Fifties and Sixties.'[8] The denial and avowal of black British history, even in the face of mounting documentary and archaeological evidence, is not just a consequence of racism but a feature of racism.

On St George's Day 1961 a man who is to play a significant role in our story gave a speech that never attained the notoriety of one of his later sermons.[9] Seven years, almost to the day, before his 'Rivers of Blood' speech, the Conservative MP Enoch Powell, the former Health Minister, gave a lecture to the members of the Royal Society of St George. Formed in the 1890s and dedicated to the promotion of English history and traditions, the society still exists today and every British monarch since Queen Victoria has accepted the role of patron. Speaking a little over a year after Harold Macmillan's 'Wind of Change' speech, Powell's subject was the loss of empire and what it meant for Britain, though it was England rather than Britain that really interested him. In his own contrarian way Enoch Powell had once been an enthusiastic advocate of the British Empire. But by 1961 the Wind of Change had blown much of it away. India was gone and in Africa Ghana, Nigeria, Somalia and Sudan had followed. By the end of the year Tanganyika had become a nation rather than a colonial 'Territory' and British Cameroon and French Cameroon had been amalgamated to create the independent Republic of Cameroon. Even as Powell was delivering his speech, Queen Elizabeth II was on board the royal yacht travelling to Sierra Leone. Five days later she was in Freetown to witness the lowering of the Union flag and the birth of the Republic of Sierra Leone, marking the end of the Sierra Leone Protectorate, the territory that had been Britain's very first West African colony.

In a remarkable speech that has been largely forgotten, Enoch Powell asked what all this meant for Britain. He began by making a startling claim. He suggested that the British Empire had been unique in a way that few commentators had noted. 'There was this deep, this providential difference between our empire and those others', he suggested. What was special was 'that the nationhood of the mother country' had, according to him, 'remained unaltered through it all, almost unconscious of the strange fantastic structure built around her'. Despite having assembled the greatest empire the world had ever known, Britain had somehow remained, in Powell's word, 'uninvolved' in the whole enterprise.[10] During the colonial period a 'brief conjunction of cheap and invincible sea power with industrial potential' had allowed much of the world to be brought 'under the spell of England'.[11] But the experience had not been reciprocal. The conquered territories had not cast any similar spell over the English, and the deep, inner core of the English character and essential nature of England's national institutions had passed through four centuries of empire-building largely unchanged and unaffected.

To England, the empire had been a dream from which the nation was only now, in the post-war era, awakening. At this historic juncture, with the colonies breaking away one by one and at a disconcerting rate, England had the opportunity to rediscover her true, inner self; 'our generation', Powell claimed, 'is one which comes home again from years of distant wandering. We discover affinities with earlier generations of English who felt no country but this to be their own.'[12] Awoken from the colonial dream and home once again, the English could now commune with their distant ancestors and perhaps even revert to being the people they had been before the ships of Elizabethan and Stuart England had set off to forge the foundations of the first British Empire in the Americas and on the shores of Africa. In his most romantic passage Powell said, 'backward travels our gaze, beyond the grenadiers and the philosophers of the eighteenth century, beyond the pikemen and the preachers of the seventeenth, back through the brash adventurous days of the first Elizabeth and the hard materialism of the Tudors and there at last we find them [our English ancestors].'

Powell spoke in beautiful, elegiac prose that conjured up evocative myths of Britishness, continuity and belonging and did so with as much lyricism and eloquence as any of the famous speeches of Winston Churchill; although even Powell's most thorough biographer concedes that it was a moment in which 'the romantic took over'.[13] To thousands of colonial administrators, soldiers and their families, who were returning from former colonies and arriving 'home' to a Britain they hardly knew, it was stirring stuff; a deeply emotional appeal to romantic ethnic nationalism. But it was also a vision of England that did not match the realities of the nation as it was in the early 1960s, and a vision that required much of the history of the past four hundred years to be set aside.

At the heart of Powell's theory was the idea that despite having been for so long an imperial power, in the case of England, 'the continuity of her existence was unbroken'. This continuity had been preserved by Britain's unique and uniquely ancient institutions: the law, the monarchy and particularly Parliament. These great constants had forged what he called the 'homogeneity of England', which he believed had survived the Age of Empire essentially unaltered. This sense of continuity was sacred to Powell and he believed that in the post-colonial moment, as the 'looser connections which had linked her with distant continents and strange races fell away', it was essential to the forging of a new post-imperial nation.

By the early 1960s Powell's gaze had resolutely turned inwards, towards his ideas of English 'continuity' and 'homogeneity'. Powell was not one of those Conservatives who nursed delusions that the Wind of Change might abate, or that any significant scraps of the empire could be retained. While there were some in his nation and in his party who reconciled themselves to the loss of empire by boasting that Britain had introduced her ancient institutions to previously backward peoples, bestowing them as wondrous gifts, Powell spoke of the need for a 'clean break' from the colonial past. He regarded the invention of the Commonwealth as an institution that complicated and delayed the severing of links between the former colonizer and formerly colonized that was urgently necessary.

In a section of the speech heavy with allusions to classical antiquity – as was Powell's habit – he compared the English, as they abandoned their colonies and returned to their home islands, to the people of Athens who returned to their city in the fifth century BC after it had been sacked by the Persians. There they supposedly found, within the city, 'alive and flourishing in the midst of the blackened ruins, the sacred olive tree, the native symbol of their country'. 'So we today,' said Powell, 'at the heart of a vanished empire, amid the fragments of demolished glory, seem to find, like one of her own oak trees, standing and growing, the sap still rising from her ancient roots to meet the spring, England herself.'

Among the many problems with this analogy was that in post-war, post-colonial Britain – as opposed to fifth-century Athens – not all of the 'Persians' had gone home. The 'strange races' from 'distant continents' who had been drawn into Britain's empire over the preceding four centuries did not 'fall away'. Powell's St George's Day speech was delivered near the peak of Caribbean migration to Britain. Around sixty thousand Caribbean immigrants arrived in Britain that year and these newest arrivals joined the estimated two hundred thousand already here. By the end of the decade that community would number more than half a million.[14] While these waves of post-war migration were unprecedented in scale, they were not an historical aberration. At the end of the previous war there had been around twenty thousand black people in Britain. Before that Britain had been home to small communities of black Edwardians, black Victorians and a larger population of black Georgians. There had been black Stuarts and black Tudors and in the 1960s, across the Americas and the Caribbean, lived millions of people of African descent whose ancestors had been transplanted into the New World from their home continent by British traders. In the middle of the twentieth century, X million Africans spoke English and twenty-three of the independent nations that were to emerge on that continent from the ruins of the British Empire chose English as their official national language. The economic, commercial, linguistic, cultural and familial links between Britain, Africa and the West Indies that had been forged over four centuries did not simply 'fall away'. But the existence of these interconnections, and the presence in Britain of thousands of black people who claimed British citizenship, like the existence of a similar Asian community, was profoundly at odds with Powell's vision of a return to some pre-colonial England of village churches and Norman architecture.

Black Britons were to Powell and those like him a constant reminder of the lost empire and the connections and interconnections that had made Britain powerful. But more than that they profoundly undermined another idea that was sacred to Powell; that whiteness and Britishness were interchangeable, and always had been.[15] The idea, already current in the early 1960s, that the nation should change, adapt to the presence of black and brown Britons, denounce racism and pass anti-discrimination laws, was counter to Powell's conception of England. These ethnic outsiders, as he saw them, should not be accommodated but marginalized and ideally expelled; he called it 're-emigration', and described them as the 'immigrant-descended population'. If this was not possible then a new definition of Britishness and British citizenship had to be established, one that viewed Britishness in racial terms, something that English law had rarely done. With the exception of a couple of minor inter-war ordinances, the English common law had – in letter if not always in practice – been colour-blind. In one of his most emphatic and disturbing statements, made late in 1968 and several months after he had predicted that 'rivers of blood' would flow in British streets, Powell dismissed utterly the concept of integration and rejected the notion that it was ever possible for a non-white person born in Britain to become British in a true or meaningful sense. 'The West Indian or Indian does not, by being born in England, become an Englishman. In law he becomes a United Kingdom citizen by birth; in fact he is a West Indian or an Asian still . . . he will by the very nature of things lose one nationality without acquiring a new one. Time is running against us and them.'[16]

Powell's vision of a Britain purged of the empire, freed from the past and re-energized by a new national and racial self-consciousness was a fantasy and a dangerous one. In order to save the imagined homogeneity and continuity of England, the non-white Britons who had emigrated from what was then called the 'New Commonwealth' had to be treated differently, denied full British citizenship and ideally expelled. It was a strain of what has been called 'insular and defensive racism'.[17] A less confident credo than the racism of the high imperial period, but one that disfigured the lives of thousands of black and Asian Britons. Ultimately these beliefs led Powell throughout the 1960s and 1970s to ratchet up his rhetoric, which led ultimately to his predictions of 'rivers of blood' and 'civil war'.

Enoch Powell is remembered as the man who signed the political warrant for the racial prejudice and wave of racial violence that were unleashed against Britain's post-war black and Asian populations. What is less well remembered is that what became known as 'Powellism' was also a call – made by a scholar of the classical past – for the denial and disavowal of parts of four hundred years of history. The loss of the empire, in Powell's view, made jettisoning imperial history necessary, as only through this amputation could his vision of England as an ethnic and racial state be realized and continuity with the past ensured. Counter-intuitively it was only by turning their back on English history could the English save themselves. Yet the history that was to be jettisoned was the very history that explained where the 'immigrant-descended population' had come from, who they were, what they had been through and why they were here. When in later decades the Jamaican-born British intellectual Stuart Hall explained to his British readers that the immigrants 'are here because you were there', he was seeking to remake the connections that Powell and others had sought to break. There had been and still existed what Professor Hall called 'an umbilical connection' between Britain and the empire, and there could be 'no understanding Englishness without understanding its imperial and colonial dimensions'.[18]

Whatever else can be said about him, Enoch Powell was certainly a man who knew his history. Consequently he understood just how far backwards our collective gaze had to be directed in order to fall upon the sort of England he was looking for. But the further back that journey took him the more preposterous became his notion that people of mid-twentieth-century Britain could commune with ancestors so distant. Furthermore, each phase of the British past through which Powell asked his St George's Day audience to time-travel had the effect of reinforcing the opposite view – that the Age of Empire had been so significant and so transformative that it could not simply be excised from memory or the national story. In each of those epochs Britain's relationship with the outside world had expanded and deepened. And throughout the four imperial centuries, whose memory Powell now regarded as toxic, Africa and her people had been part of the British experience and imagination.

To take what Powell described as 'the brash adventurous days of the first Elizabeth', this was an age in which the Elizabethan imagination was fired by the idea of Africa, her supposed youth, her potential wealth and the gold that for centuries had trickled across the Sahara. But Africa's people too were a fascination. In those Tudor years, some of them – both North Africans and people from the regions below the Sahara – appeared in the midst of Elizabeth's subjects. In the same years some of the ships on which England's brash adventurers set sail headed for the coasts of Guinea and Sierra Leone, where they traded in gold, pepper, ivory and captured slaves. In 1590, one hundred and thirty-five Africans were brought to Bristol aboard a single English privateering ship. But England's explosion onto the stage of global power politics did not just lead to the arrival and settlement of Africans in England; some of these Africans became themselves players and pawns within that Age of Discovery.

There were black men on the English ships that encountered new peoples and new lands. Sir Francis Drake's mission to circumnavigate the globe in 1577 was achieved with a crew that was what we today would call inter-racial. Drake was – in fits and starts – a slave-trader, inspired by his cousin Sir John Hawkins, the infamous pioneer of the English trade. But in a way we find difficult to relate to he was capable of enslaving black people while seeing other black men as his comrades-in-arms. Among Drake's crew in 1577 were four Africans. In an earlier expedition to Panama, Drake had formed an alliance with the 'Cimaroons', mixed-race Africans who had escaped from the Spanish and intermarried with local peoples. Their local knowledge was invaluable and helped 'El Draco' capture a fleet of Spanish ships carrying silver back to Spain. A few of the Cimaroons chose to join Drake and return with him to England as part of the crew; one of them was named Diego. As is the case repeatedly throughout our story, moments like this in which African people and white Englishmen found common cause are interspersed with more tragic events. Diego died during the circumnavigation and another of the Cimaroons, a woman, was abandoned on an Indonesian island mid-voyage, while heavily pregnant.[19] While Drake was at sea, Queen Elizabeth herself was seeking to cultivate relationships with Africa. Seeking allies against Spain she entered into correspondence and traded arms with the Moroccan leader Mulay Ahmad al-Mansur. In all sorts of ways relationships with Africa and Africans appeared critical to England's survival in her existential struggle against the Catholic superpower that was Spain under Philip II.

Drake's alliance with black former slaves, who became 'black Englishmen' of sorts, and England's ambitions in the Atlantic world are perhaps hinted at in the 'Drake Jewel', which was presented to him by Queen Elizabeth in 1588. It shows the head of a black African man, carved in ivory and superimposed over that of a white European woman. Inside is a miniature of Queen Elizabeth herself. Although the jewel had many meanings it shows how the black African, perhaps in this case a black emperor, had become part of the visual culture of the age, a figure in the English imagination.[20] Drake is depicted in his most famous portrait wearing the jewel. In that image he stands beside a globe, on which the continent of Africa has been turned to face the viewer, indicating perhaps the focus of future English ambitions. Without understanding the presence and the impact of people of African descent it is impossible to fully understand the character and mindset of the Elizabethan age. Africa and her people were not only the focus of enormous excitement and curiosity, the continent came to represent a sense of limitless possibility and perhaps destiny to that expansive, mercantile, piratical, heretical England, as it exploded across the oceans during the reign of the Virgin Queen. The black face on the Drake Jewel was in that sense a perfect symbol of the age.

Even when Enoch Powell's gaze had taken him all the way back to his lost England, his imagined pre-colonial 'year zero', the isolation he sought could not be found. Sixty years before Powell spoke, a number of skeletons had been discovered near Sycamore Terrace, a nondescript street in Bootham, near York – one of Britain's most ancient settlements. As Powell gave his lecture, peppered as it was with references to classical antiquity, those skeletons were lying in anonymous storage. In 1961 the stamp of their racial origin was invisible to the archaeologists but modern isotope testing reveals to us in the early twenty-first century that some of these citizens of Roman Britain were mixed-race people of African heritage, whose families had come from the warm southern limits of that intercontinental empire. Among them was the now famed Ivory Bangle Lady.

Enoch Powell was right, there is *some* continuity in British history, but it is in large part the continuity of contact, globalism, empire, interaction, migration, alliance-building, travel, exploration, exploitation, slavery, trade and intermarriage. This is not to deny that the era through which he lived, the post-war age, was one in which the levels of immigration and integration were unprecedented, but the England he cast his gaze backwards to find had never truly existed.

Powell's appeal to an imagined past was only possible because when he gave his speech in the early 1960s two distinct processes of historical forgetting had largely removed black people from the 'island story' version of British history. In the first of those processes the chapters of British history in which the fates, status and humanity of black people had been critical and central – those dealing with British slavery and empire in Africa – had been marginalized and quarantined into historical specialisms. In the second process the story of the long presence of black people within Britain itself had been rendered almost invisible.

The most effective and remarkable of these had been the almost surgical excision of slavery and the slave trade from the histories of Britain of the seventeenth, eighteenth and nineteenth centuries. Here geography, coupled with a strong urge to focus on abolition rather than slavery, had made the process easier. The cotton plantations of the American South existed on the soil of the United States itself; British slavery took place an ocean away on the islands of the Caribbean or the plantations of the North American colonies. As a result even today many people in Britain have a more vivid image of American slavery than they do of life as it was for enslaved Africans on the British plantations of the Caribbean. Slavery for them conjures up images of cotton fields and whitewashed plantation houses at the end of long avenues of tall trees – the imagery of *Roots*, *Gone With the Wind* and *12 Years a Slave*. Fewer people find their mind's eye drawn to images of the semi-industrial process of sugar cultivation in Jamaica, Guyana or Barbados in the eighteenth century, and fewer still think of the British slave fortresses like Bunce Island through which the Africans who worked those plantations were channelled.

The second process cannot, of course, be explained by geographic distance. That process concealed not only the reality that black people were not only continually present in Britain from the sixteenth century onwards but also the fact that they played a role in many of the pivotal moments of British history. The black history of Britain and the biographies of notable black Britons run through mainstream British history like a rich but underworked seam. At times it is close to the surface, at others deeply buried. Black history is everywhere but repeatedly and often intentionally it has been misfiled, recategorized or sidelined. At times black British history is hidden in plain view.

At the very centre of our capital city stands one of the most sympathetic, humane and heroic depictions of a black Briton. The memorial in question is situated on a London intersection from which can be seen the Houses of Parliament, the Cenotaph, the National Gallery, Admiralty Arch and Buckingham Palace which is just visible through the trees at the end of the Mall. Yet the black Briton represented in this famous work of public art is almost entirely unknown and rarely commented upon, despite having been on public display for well over one and a half centuries. He can be found within one of the great brass reliefs that adorn the base of Nelson's column, four huge panels of bronze that were forged from captured French cannon. The south-facing relief is entitled *The Death of Nelson*. It freeze-frames the moment just after Nelson has been struck down by a French sniper. The admiral lies mortally wounded in the arms of his men and fellow officers. To the left of them stands a black sailor holding a musket. His head is tilted upwards as he scans the rigging of the enemy ships. The man's features are unmistakably and unambiguously African. Not only was this black seaman included in the relief, which was cast thirty-five years after the battle, he was both acknowledged and celebrated. When the reliefs were unveiled one contemporary reviewer was particularly drawn to what he called 'the figure of the negro', whom he described as 'a perfect work of art, full of character – the distended nostrils, strained eye-balls, and the firm manner in which the gun he has is clasped in his hand, clearly tell the emotions which might be supposed to occupy the mind under such circumstances'.[21] There was no suggestion in this effusive review, written near the high-water mark of British anti-slavery sentiment, that the mind of this black sailor might be inferior to that of his white comrades, or that the emotions that surged in his heart during the heat of battle might be less noble than those of Europeans.

The artist who cast the brass relief was the Irish sculptor John Edward Carew. He included this depiction of a young black sailor not out of some nineteenth-century sense of 'political correctness' or as some gesture of ethnic tokenism. The black sailor is there in bronze because men just like him were there in flesh and bone, on the ships that fought at Trafalgar. The evidence for their presence can be found in the muster books of the ships of Nelson's fleet held at the National Archives in London. These documents list the names, pay-book numbers, ages and places of birth of every man who did his duty under Admiral Nelson that day.[22] Among them are men from across Britain but also others from India, Malta, Italy and the former American colonies. There are also eighteen men listed as having been born in Africa and another hundred and twenty-three in the West Indies. One African and six West Indians are listed as serving under Nelson on HMS *Victory*. Among the Africans at Trafalgar were John Amboyne, who was twenty-seven years old and had been born in Guinea. He served as a landsman on HMS *Defiance*. George Brown, also born in Guinea, was a boy of just thirteen at the time of the battle. He fought on HMS *Colossus* alongside two other African-born shipmates, the twenty-year-old William Cully and thirty-five-year-old Jean Moncier, who had been born in Sallee in Morocco. Ordinary Seaman George Butler was twenty-six in 1805 and fought on HMS *Orion*. John Ephraim, who had been born in Africa's Calabar Coast, in what is today Nigeria, served on board HMS *Temeraire*, the 98-gun ship of the line immortalized thirty-three years later by J. M. W. Turner, who painted her being solemnly towed up the Thames by a steam-powered tug on her way to the breaker's yard. Ordinary Seaman John Cupide was a twenty-year-old African who served on HMS *Minotaur* while twenty-three-year-old African William Hughes faced the French fleet from the decks of a British warship fittingly named HMS *Africa*, which had served in the American Revolution, another war in which black men fought for Britain. We know from his service records that William Hughes was discharged from the Royal Navy's Haslar Hospital in Portsmouth on 14 January 1806, three months after the battle in which he presumably received his wounds. As far as we can tell it seems that against the odds all the Africans identified in the muster books survived the Battle of Trafalgar. After that, and like so many of the black people in our story, they fade from the official record and disappear. The sculptor John Carew might have reasonably presumed that this depiction of a black sailor, the young black man whom he had cast in bronze and affixed to a national memorial at the very centre of the imperial capital, would become similarly fixed within British historical memory. But that was to underestimate our capacity to forget and our ability to unlearn.

If the presence of black people within some of the most celebrated events of the British past can be forgotten, then it is perhaps little surprising that their involvement in other aspects of the national story has been lost or expunged. Time and again events and phenomena that we think we know and understand contain within them lost or camouflaged connections to Africa, slavery and black history.

Each year two of the most prestigious horse races in the British calendar take place at Newmarket. The Two Thousand Guinea Stakes and the One Thousand Guinea Stakes have been run each year since 1809 and 1814 respectively. The prize money paid to the winners is today far in excess of the titular sums but Newmarket's strong sense of tradition and continuity has made it perhaps the last place in twenty-first-century Britain where the guinea is still used. The guinea was a gold coin officially worth twenty-one shillings, or one pound sterling and five pence, although its value fluctuated with the price of gold. Despite being replaced by the pound in 1816 the guinea has remained a part of British national culture and business long after that date. Throughout much of the nineteenth century and even into the twentieth it was the favoured denomination for companies and professionals who provided upmarket services to the wealthy – lawyers, doctors, accountants and hoteliers. It retained strong aristocratic overtones and was widely regarded as an indicator of exclusivity and quality. It was also traditionally used in buying and selling horses, hence its continuing association with the world of horse-racing. The Newmarket bloodstock auctioneers Tattersalls still conduct their business in guineas, as they have done since their foundation in 1766. Yet the origins of the guinea and the source of the gold from which the original coins were minted have been largely forgotten. The guinea was so named because it was made from gold bought on Africa's Guinea Coast. On one side of the coins was the head of the King and on the other the symbol of an elephant and castle – the trademark of the Royal African Company.

In the late seventeenth and early eighteenth centuries the Royal African Company traded off the coast of West Africa predominantly in gold, ivory and slaves. The Royal African Company transported more Africans into slavery than any other British company in the whole history of the Atlantic slave trade. Between the 1670s and the 1730s around a hundred and fifty thousand men, women and children passed through the company's coastal fortresses on their way to lives of miserable slavery. Among those fortresses was Bunce Island. The Royal African Company was a royal chartered monopoly and as such was able to call upon the services of the Royal Navy to protect its monopoly, defend its fortresses and intercept the ships of so-called interlopers who attempted to muscle in on its trade. Protected from competition, the company was able to freely trade and thereby generate large profits for its investors. The 'Royal' in the company's title was not a mere honorific. Among the company founders were King Charles II and his brother James Duke of York, the future King James II (the man after whom New York was named), who was actively involved in its administration. His name appears among shareholders who attended company meetings and on lists of those who drew profits and dividends. Among the other share-holders was the philosopher John Locke, whose sixteenth-century ancestor had been among the very first English traders to reach the coast of West Africa. So profitable were the activities of the Royal African Company that when in 1689, after he had been deposed in the Glorious Revolution and replaced with William of Orange and his wife Queen Mary, James II dispatched a representative to London to liquidate his shares, the former king's profits amounted to £5,730,[23] and were used to help fund his comfortable exile in Paris.

Just before the Africans purchased by the agents of Bunce Island were herded into the male and female holding yards, they were taken to an area in front of the agents' house. There the company initials – 'RAC' – were branded onto their chests. At other times the company preferred to brand Africans with the letters 'DY' – for Duke of York. Literally and figuratively these were the company's 'brands' and they were intended to be indicators of quality. It was with the same intent that two centuries later Victorian lawyers and doctors issued bills to their wealthy and aristocratic clients in guineas rather than pounds sterling. The involvement of the British monarchy in the slave trade is little known today yet the Stuarts were not unique in this respect. Queen Elizabeth I had invested in the early English slave-trading expeditions of Sir John Hawkins in the 1560s, and both the pirate Hawkins and his queen profited greatly from his successful slaving missions to the coast of West Africa.

The origin of the guinea is one of numerous aspects of our collective past that have been de-tethered from their links to black history and Africa. The story of the South Sea Company and the speculative bubble that brought it down has been similarly sanitized. The South Sea Bubble is remembered today as one of the great cautionary tales of British history, an economic parable that warns of the perils of financial mismanagement and uncontrolled speculation. Reduced to historical colour, it is dutifully wheeled out by journalists and economic commentators in the aftermath of every economic crash, acting as a reminder that market crashes, booms, busts and speculative bubbles are nothing new. Few retellings of the history of the South Sea Bubble however mention the chief commodity the South Sea Company failed to profitably trade. In 1713, under a clause of the Treaty of Utrecht, Britain was awarded the 'Asiento', the right to supply slaves to the Spanish colonies in the Americas. This valuable concession was handed over to the South Sea Company. Although the causes of the company's spectacular and ruinous crash are complex and multiple, its rise and fall are rarely acknowledged or understood as part of the history of Britain's slave trade. To complete the disconnect it has also been forgotten that in the year of its implosion the honorary governor of this inept slave-trading company was another British monarch, King George I.

A different story from the same era has, in a very similar way, been stripped of its connections to Africa and slavery. The War of Jenkins' Ear is certainly the most bizarrely named of Britain's many eighteenth-century wars. It raged intermittently from 1738 to 1749, but its name is derived from a gruesome incident in 1731 which occurred when the British brig *Rebecca* was intercepted by the Spanish ship *La Isabela* off the coast of Cuba. The captain of the *Rebecca*, the English smuggler Robert Jenkins, was accused of piracy by Julio León Fandiño, the captain of the *Isabela*, who emphasized his point by cutting off Robert Jenkins' left ear. The British later added Fandiño's impromptu auriculectomy to a dodgy dossier of excuses and pretexts that was used to justify a declaration of war against Spain. It was a century later that the conflict was named by the Victorian writer and apologist for slavery Thomas Carlyle. In Spain it is known more soberly as 'La Guerra del Asiento' – the war of the Asiento, as it was fought not to avenge Robert Jenkins for the loss of an ear but over the contract to sell slaves to the Spanish colonies that had been agreed at the Treaty of Utrecht. On the eve of war in 1738, Robert Jenkins testified before Parliament and recounted the incident. In an engraving made of his day in parliament he is shown standing before the seated figure of the Prime Minister, Robert Walpole. The captain's wig is being removed to reveal his left ear, or rather its conspicuous absence. The man removing Jenkins' wig in the engraving is a black man. He wears a liveried coat, the uniform of the enslaved black servant of the mid-eighteenth century.

Thomas Carlyle, the man who gave the War of Jenkins' Ear its strange name, was the author of a common phrase which has become similarly de-tethered from its origins. Like the story of the South Sea Bubble, Carlyle's description of economics as 'the dismal science' is deployed with obvious relish by journalists and celebrity econo-mists in times of economic turbulence. Carlyle coined that term in his 1849 essay 'Occasional Discourse on the Negro Question', a near-hysterical denunciation of the humanity of black people which became an influential assault upon British anti-slavery politics. The phrase is often reused without remembering the essay from which it came. So complete was the decoupling of the phrase from Carlyle's toxic writing on race that over time an alternative genesis myth emerged. This suggested that the phrase arose from Carlyle's essays on the great eighteenth-century political demographer Thomas Malthus. This alternative origin story, being conveniently free from any association with the history of slavery and racism, has often been favoured.[24]

With black history and black people largely expunged from the mainstream narrative of British history, we have been left with a distorted and diminished vision of our national past. Black history, in one sense, is a series of unwritten chapters that together make sense of the wider history of Britain. Our understanding of Victorian Britain, for example, is incomplete without a chapter explaining how slavery – both British and American – impacted upon the Victorian imagination and shaped the national economy. Take the history of the Industrial Revolution. It is constantly replayed in our national imagination as a history of coal and iron, of factory towns and mines, and has rightly become a central feature of our national self-image. It is commemorated and perpetuated by a huge industry of working mills, heritage sites and recreated model communities, often replete with re-enactors and working steam trains and traction engines. At these sites and in our classrooms generations of Britons are transported back to those frenetic, dynamic and inventive decades when this small island became the 'workshop of the world'. Central to this history is the story of the mills of Lancashire, and the great industrial rivalry that was fought between Liverpool, the great port of the Atlantic-facing empire, and Manchester, the world's first industrial mega-city. Between them these two industrial giants dominated the global production of cotton cloth and cotton clothes and by the middle of Queen Victoria's reign the cotton industry employed almost one and a half million people. Millions more worked in ancillary industries or were dependent upon the cotton economy. What is remembered today are not these startling employment figures, or the wealth generated by cotton, but the social history of Factory Acts, child labour, spinning jennies and water-frames. Yet this is a history that is usually silent about the source of the cotton that was processed in Lancashire's 4,500 mills. The great bulk of that essential raw material came from the Mississippi Valley and the 'white gold' of the Deep South was harvested by the black hands of enslaved Africans. In the first half of the nineteenth century it was possible for slaves in the Southern states to spend most of their stolen lives producing the cotton that stoked Britain's Industrial Revolution. By the time of America's Civil War in 1861 almost two million slaves laboured in the cotton fields, and New Orleans was linked to Liverpool by a ceaseless flow of slave-produced cotton. The black men and women of the American South are the missing persons in the popular retelling of our industrial heritage. As we today lament the suffering of the Victorian mill workers we forget that many of them felt a comparable sense of sympathy for the slaves of the United States. The more educated and radical of the Lancashire mill workers were well aware that the hands which had tied the bales of cotton that arrived in their mills were those of black men and women who were the legal property of others. Any honest, comprehensive and full-blooded retelling of the history of the Industrial Revolution cannot fail to acknowledge their plight.

The list of lost connections continues and unwritten chapters goes on. The hymn 'Amazing Grace', beloved by generations of Britons, was written by the British slave-trader John Newton, whose religious conversion eventually led him to condemn the trade in which he was once enthusiastically engaged. Our alternative national anthem, 'Land of Hope and Glory', with its declaration that 'Britons never shall be slaves', has links to black history and slavery that are glaringly obvious and yet hardly noticed. Across the country, on heritage plaques and in guidebooks, the grim careers of Britain's slave-traders and slave owners are disguised behind the sanitizing euphemisms 'West India Merchant' and 'West India Planter'.

The whitewashing of British history and the wilful forgetting of slavery has now lasted almost as long as British slavery itself. We have developed what amounts to a cultural blind spot about these chapters of our past, and our collective squeamishness that prevents us from openly discussing British slavery and the darker aspects of British imperialism has rendered us unable to properly appreciate the place of black people and Africa in our national story. The importance of Africa at various junctures in British history is little examined and the presence of black people in Britain although increasingly accepted has been partially obscured by a celebration of the post-war immigration that, although welcome and positive, tends to drown out the longer more complex story.

Black history is too often regarded as a segregated, ghettoized narrative that runs in its own shallow channel alongside the mainstream, only very occasionally becoming a tributary into that broader narrative. But black British history is not an optional extra. Nor is it a bolt-on addition to mainstream British history deployed only occasionally in order to add – literally – a splash of colour to favoured epochs of the national story. It is an integral and essential aspect of mainstream British history. Britain's interactions with Africa, the role of black people within British history and the history of the empire are too significant to be marginalized, brushed under the carpet or corralled into some historical annexe.

More than any other factor it is the new demographics of Britain in the early twenty-first century that make the call for a new appreciation of black British history more pertinent. The 2011 census revealed that the fastest-growing ethnic group in Britain is people who are racially mixed, and Britain has higher levels of mixing than any nation in Europe. America's melting pot – predicted by liberal optimists in the 1960s – has failed to emerge: London, more than New York or Chicago, has become the model of an ethnically diverse and inter-mixed city. More than any other ethnic group, it is the black British population who are mixing. Today, 48 per cent of black Caribbean men and 34 per cent of black Caribbean women are in relationships with partners of a different ethnic group. We are moving to an age in which the 'black community' could end up being smaller than the mixed-race community. We might, in decades to come, be a country in which black families in which all the faces are black will be rare, or they will be the families of recent immigrants. It is too easy to be over-comforted by these statistics and there are worrying signs that testify to the resilience and persistence of racism but the change in attitudes is profound. Black and white couples, with brown babies, whose presence sparked race riots on the streets during the 1950s and were the stuff of scandal in the newspapers of the 1960s, have become one of the defining features of twenty-first-century Britain. Mixed-race Britons are a new normal, an integral part of Britain's self-image. Racial mixing is one of the great constants of this history.

The current patterns of racial mixing are different in scale but are not out of step with our longer history. The modern black populations are doing what their Elizabethan, Georgian, Victorian and Edwardian predecessors did – amalgamating and integrating. That longer, wider and deeper history helps explain the present. It sets modern trends within context and discredits the notion that the history of 'black Britain' can be understood as a separate or marginal one. Most of the black Britons whose stories were exhumed by the pioneers of black British history were men who married white women. Olaudah Equiano, James Gronniosaw, Ira Aldridge, John Blanke the trumpeter at the court of Henry VIII, Francis Barber the servant and surrogate son of Samuel Johnson, George Africanus the eighteenth-century black entrepreneur – all of them inter-married. Knowingly or unknowingly their mixed-race ancestors carry on their blood-lines.

For them and for Britain today racial mixing is not just a story of inter-racial couples and mixed-race children but of their families and extended families. Mixed-race children have cousins, grandparents, aunts and uncles. Through intermarriage and racial mixing, millions of white Britons have become part of the black British story. As the barriers between black and white break down, the divisions between so-called black history and so-called mainstream British history become unstable and unhelpful. For me there has never been a separate history exclusively about and for black people in Britain. Black British history cannot be understood solely as the history of the black experience. It has always also been the story of encounter. It is a history populated by the black Britons whose lives were recovered by the first writers of black British history, but also a history of white people, both the notorious architects of racism and slavery and of the millions of ordinary British people who, despite the ebb and flow of race and racial theory, welcomed people of African descent into their lives and their families. Black British history is everyone's history and is all the stronger for it.

ONE

'Sons of Ham'

The people of the British Isles and the people of Africa met for the first time when Britain was a cold province on the northern fringe of Rome's intercontinental, multi-ethnic and multi-racial empire. We were colonized long before we became colonizers. Among the Roman citizens who settled in Britain, and serving in its Roman garrison, were people from the empire's African provinces, as well as men and women from sub-Saharan Africa who had passed through the empire's porous borders. Imperialism was the force that brought the first Africans to Britain, just as centuries later it would take thousands of Britons to Africa. Those Afro-Romans arrived in the British Isles during the third century AD, well over a thousand years before the first English sailors reached the shores of sub-Saharan Africa in the middle years of the sixteenth century.

We know about one group of Afro-Romans who were stationed in the North of England due to two pieces of evidence. The first appeared in 1934 in the little village of Beaumont, on the banks of the River Eden in Cumbria, when an altar stone was found in the foundations of an old cottage during its demolition. Carved into it was an inscription dedicated to the god Jupiter. It was written in the stylized and abbreviated Latin that was favoured by the Roman legions, and it recorded that in the middle of the third century, at the nearby Roman fortress of Aballava, a unit 'of Aurelian Moors' had been stationed.[1]

The Aurelian Moors, probably named in honour of Emperor Marcus Aurelius, had been raised in the North African provinces of the Roman Empire, which consisted of parts of what are today the states of Libya, Tunisia and Algeria – regions that were particularly racially diverse. Their base at the fortress of Aballava was one of the strongpoints sited at the western end of Hadrian's Wall, which is occupied today by the little Cumbrian village of Burgh-by-Sands. At its centre stands the church of St Michael, the oldest parts of which were constructed from stone blocks harvested from Hadrian's Wall itself, their origins betrayed by the telltale marks and striations left by the tools of Roman masons. The inscription found in Beaumont referenced the names of two Roman emperors, Valerian and Gallienus, which allows historians to establish the approximate date of the inscription, and therefore the presence of the Roman Africans in Britain, as lying between AD 253 and AD 258. The second piece of evidence that connects the Aurelian Moors to Hadrian's Wall and the fortress of Aballava is a *Notitia Dignitatum*, a Roman register that lists the officials and dignitaries who visited the region, including a visit by the 'prefect of the numerus [unit] of Aurelian Moors, at Aballava'.

The Beaumont inscription and the *Notitia Dignitatum* are among the small number of artefacts and inscriptions that between them record the presence of Africans at various Roman sites in Britain. Most are clustered along Hadrian's Wall, the most strongly garrisoned region.[2] Much of this evidence and most of these artefacts were available to historians writing on the black presence in Britain half a century ago, and new finds are extremely rare. However, in recent years a revolution in archaeology and forensic science has brought a remarkable and unexpected expansion in what is known about the presence of people of African descent in Roman Britain.

Key discoveries relate to some two hundred human remains that were discovered in York in finds made by chance over the course of the nineteenth and twentieth centuries. When the historian Peter Fryer wrote his book *Staying Power* in 1984 he noted that among the skeletons exhumed were several 'whose limb proportions suggest that they were black Africans'.[3] Thirty years later and forensic science has confirmed what in the 1980s was a mere suspicion. The innovation that is transforming our understanding of the presence of African peoples in Roman Britain is the process of radioisotope analysis, a technique that uses oxygen and strontium isotopes to detect chemical signatures in bones and teeth. This allows archaeologists to determine where individuals originated and where they spent their childhood years. By means of these techniques, we can distinguish individuals born and brought up in hot climates from those who come from colder regions, and establish whether remains unearthed in Britain belong to locals or outsiders. This powerful new tool has enabled archaeologists to identify the patterns of mobility and migration within ancient populations; skeletons excavated decades ago are suddenly able to tell their stories. When applied to Roman remains, long ago excavated and stored in the vaults and basements of British museums and universities, isotope analysis continues to reveal new evidence for the settlement in Britain of people from Roman North Africa and beyond.

Isotope analysis has worked best when combined with craniometrics, the measuring of tiny details and proportions in the human skull. When cranial analysis was carried out by the University of Reading's Department of Archaeology a number of the two hundred or so skulls excavated in York were found to be of mixed ethnic ancestry. The remains of these citizens of Roman York were also subjected to isotope analysis, and while most of those examined displayed European ancestry, some 11 to 12 per cent proved to have been of African descent. That the remains studied came from two different burial sites, one of them used to bury poorer people and the other reserved for York's wealthier residents, suggests not only that there were significant numbers of people of North African ancestry living in Roman York, but that they moved in all levels of society.

The now famous Ivory Bangle Lady is perhaps the most significant individual to have emerged from the work on third-century York's citizens. She was discovered in 1901 in a stone sarcophagus buried in a site near to Sycamore Terrace, an everyday street in the city. On one of the shards of bone had been carved the inscription *SOROR AVE VIVAS IN DEO*, which translates as 'Hail sister, may you live in God', and suggests that she may have been a Christian. In her sarcophagus were a number of luxury grave goods: some blue glass beads, fragments of five bone bracelets, silver and bronze lockets, two yellow glass earrings, two marbled glass beads, a small round glass mirror and a blue glass perfume bottle.[4] The presence of these objects suggests that she was a woman of high social status, from the upper strata of Roman York, a settlement then known as Eboracum. The most telling of her grave goods were two bracelets, one made of jet stone, which probably came from Whitby on the north-east coast of England, the other made of African ivory.

The geographic range from which her grave goods had been drawn was, it later proved, reflective of her own ancestry. In 2009, sixteen centuries after her death, the remains of the Ivory Bangle Lady were subjected to radioisotope analysis, and precise measurements taken of her skull and skeleton. The chemical signature deposited by the food and drink she had consumed in her childhood, and the measurements of her skeleton, suggest that this high-status citizen of Roman York is likely to have been a mixed-race woman of North African descent, and that either she, or her parents or grandparents, had come from Mediterranean North Africa. She had been between eighteen and twenty-three years old when she died, although the cause of death was unclear. Her mobility across the empire is suggestive of a woman who was connected to the Roman army, as whole families moved to accompany men posted in distant provinces and York was a significant military settlement. Relocations from the provinces in North Africa to those of northern England were not unknown, and others have been recorded. Subsequent work on other remains is now demonstrating that Roman Britain was a society of far greater racial diversity than had been presumed.[5] The mobility that was a feature of the late Roman Empire may well have meant that parts of third-century Eboracum may well have been more ethnically and racially diverse than parts of York today in the twenty-first century.

Another equally remarkable discovery was recently made in the seaside town of Eastbourne, on the south coast of England. Again it involved the reassessment and analysis of remains that had been excavated decades earlier, and again an Afro-Roman woman was discovered. In 2012 local archaeologists in Eastbourne began to work their way through a collection of skeletons that had been locally excavated from the late nineteenth century up until the 1990s. One skeleton – almost complete – was stored in a box labelled 'Beachy Head', by earlier generations of archaeologists. The remains were those of a young woman, only around five feet tall and probably in her early twenties at the time of death, but there was little to indicate when she might have lived. The skeleton of the 'Beachy Head Lady', as she was dubbed, was one of twelve sent for radioisotope analysis to determine if they had been born locally. The archaeologists, led by Heritage Manager Jo Seaman, arranged for a forensic facial reconstruction to be carried out by Professor Caroline Wilkinson, a leading figure in the field. Professor Wilkinson was able to tell, merely by looking at the skull, and before she had begun the minute measurements that underpin her work, that the skull of the Beachy Head Lady was that of a sub-Saharan African. The process of radiocarbon dating placed the Lady as having lived around AD 125 to 245, and the results of the radioisotope analysis confirmed that she had spent much of her childhood in the southeast of England.

The Beachy Head Lady was therefore a second- or third-century Afro-Roman who had been brought up in the south of England and had either been born in that region or was brought there very young, possibly from Africa. The radioisotope analysis also suggested that she was well nourished in her youth, having had a diet rich in fish and vegetables, details that were encoded in the chemicals of her teeth. The facts that those teeth were in good condition, that she had enjoyed a healthy diet and was discovered laid out carefully in her grave go to suggest that in life she had not served in a lowly position, or lived as a slave. Over a millennium before the British people began their 'years of distant wandering' and empire-building the Beachy Head Lady – the first black Briton known to us – had lived and died in rural East Sussex, by the Channel coast with its white cliffs and green rolling hills.

From the fall of the Western Roman Empire in the fifth century AD to the beginning of Europe's Age of Exploration a millennium later, the British Isles, like the rest of Europe, were largely cut off from Africa and her people. The collapse of Rome marked the end of an era of extraordinary connectivity and mobility. The intercontinental pathways that had made it possible for the Ivory Bangle Lady and the Beachy Head Woman to settle in the British Isles were wiped away. In the seventh century the rise of Islam further broadened the gulf between Africa and Europe. As the Arabs expanded along the coast of North Africa the new states they created became a political, religious, military and cultural barrier spreading northward of the physical barrier of the Sahara.[6] For the next millennium contact and interchange between Africans and Europeans was mediated by the Arab traders who controlled the caravan routes across the Sahara.

Despite this, the archaeological record and a handful of archival sources reveal that there were tiny numbers of people of African heritage travelling to and living in Britain in the medieval age. Yet while, for most Britons, Africans were no longer encountered face to face as individuals, as they had been during the Roman era, this did not mean that Africans vanished beneath their mental horizon. Both the people and their continent continued to reside within the realms of myth, legend and scripture. Africa was, after all, a land of the Bible, and through the books of the Old Testament, the African continent – the Nile Valley and the land of Ethiopia in particular – remained present in the minds of medieval scholars and was discussed by the priests and monks whose cathedrals and monasteries were the great centres of learning. Just as important were the texts of the classical world, as it was through these ancient writings that medieval Europe's tiny educated elite were able to read travel accounts that described the geography of Africa and portrayals of the nature and reputed habits of her people. Medieval Europe knew that not only had the Greeks and Romans reached sub-Saharan Africa, but black people from those regions had moved north and been part of Greek and Roman societies, as both free and enslaved people.

Africans and their homelands were chronicled in the works of Homer, Herodotus, Ptolemy and Pliny, among others, as well as in pictorial form on pottery and in sculpture. The picture of Africa that educated Europeans drew from the classical texts contained much that was later demonstrated to be accurate. The first-century-BC writer Diodorus Siculus, for example, informed medieval readers that the people of Africa were 'black of colour', with 'flat noses and woolly hair'.[7] Other ancient scholars had worked out the rough shape of the continent. Yet classical texts were also prone to misdescribe both the people and the continent itself. Africa was repeatedly conflated with and confused for other poorly understood regions of the world, and there was a strong tendency within the works of the Greek and Roman writers for conjecture and myth to be given the same weight as verifiable facts. The Greek historian Herodotus offered his readers an accurate description of the people who lived to the south of the Nile, a region he himself had visited, but then went on to speculate that somewhere in Africa was a race of men who had the heads of dogs.

Of all the classical authors, it was perhaps the Roman writer Pliny the Elder who contributed most to the mystification of Africa. In the 1550s, just as the first English traders began to reach West Africa, a new popular edition of Pliny's *Summary of the Antique Wonders of the World* was published in England.[8] In one remarkable passage Pliny catalogued the many bizarre and monstrous races of mankind who resided in Africa:

> Of the Ethiopians there are diverse forms and kinds of men. Some there are towards the East, that have neither nose nor nostrils, but the face all full. Others that have no upper lip, they are without tongues, and they speak by signs, and they have but a little hole to take their breath at, by which they drink with an oaten straw . . . In a part of Africa be people called Ptoemphane, for their king they have a dog, at whose fancy they are governed . . . Towards the west there is a people called Arimaspi, that hath but one eye in their foreheads, they are in the desert and wild country. The people called Agriphagi live with the flesh of panthers and lions; and the people called Anthropophagi, which we call Cannibals, live with human flesh. The Cinamolgi, their heads are almost like to the heads of dogs.[9]

Pliny also informed his readers of the existence in Africa of the Garamantes, a people who eschewed the institution of marriage and whose men held all women in common. Just as fascinating were the Gamphasantes, who were said to never wear clothes, the Troglodytes, who lived in caves, and a race of people who walked on their hands.

Not content with the considerable assortment of bizarre peoples and array of natural wonders bequeathed to them by the classical authors, medieval European writers added their own layers of mythology, fantastical conjecture and geographic confusion. Some of these authors were men who claimed to have travelled out into the world beyond Europe. Others had stayed at home and were merely the compilers of the accounts of others. The most influential of these works tells the story of an epic journey claimed to have been undertaken by the book's supposed author. *The Travels of Sir John Mandeville* – *Mandeville's Travels*, as it is more commonly known – was originally written in French, sometime in the mid-fourteenth century (some sources suggest 1356 or 1357). It has undergone a vast amount of scholarly detective work, yet many questions remain unanswered and probably always will. The book describes a journey across central Asia, Arabia, India, the Far East and Northern Africa, and was assembled from around two dozen separate texts, variously either consulted, quoted or plagiarized (if plagiarism is the appropriate word for the way that medieval authors habitually took liberties with one another's texts when compiling their own).[10] The author of the book was said to have been a certain Sir John Mandeville, an English knight of St Albans, but modern scholars suggest that the author was in fact a Frenchman, and a number of possible candidates have been identified. More than any other book, *Mandeville's Travels* offered, or appeared to offer, answers to burning questions about the nature of the known but unreachable continents outside of Europe. The marvels of other civilizations and the wonders of the natural and supernatural worlds were laid bare. As in the writings of the classical authors, the book freely mixed elements of genuine travel writing with what to the modern eye is evidently the fantastical and the mythological. One of its interesting claims is that the world is round.

Mandeville's Travels was one of the most widely translated books of the later Middle Ages; editions appeared in several languages as it spread rapidly and widely across Latin Christendom. It is believed that alongside Marco Polo's travels, Christopher Columbus took a copy of Mandeville with him on his journey to find the Indies in 1492. The book told its readers that: 'In Ethiopia men and women, in the summertime, go together to streams and lie therein from morning till noon, all naked, because of the great heat of the sun.' In other parts of Ethiopia 'the air is so cold that . . . there is a continual frost which freezes the water so that it turns to crystals'.[11] Africa was also a region, Mandeville explains, in which diamonds littered the earth and grew to enormous sizes, yet despite these treasures the people of Africa lived in a state of almost communist equality, as 'the goods of the country are common to every man, and none of them is allowed to be richer than the others, nor does any desire to be'. Such utopian egalitarianism was possible in Mandeville's Africa because there was a limitless supply of food that could be effortlessly gathered. Even more fortunately, the rivers and streams that cut across Africa flowed with waters that were flavoured and spiced. Other natural springs were capable of curing the sick of their maladies. The Mandeville author himself claimed to have drunk from a well that was the source of eternal youth. Those who lived near it, he wrote, 'never get sick, and their appearance is always youthful'.

Something of the sense of wonder at Africa that emanates from the pages of *Mandeville's Travels* can also be seen in medieval maps. Hereford Cathedral's Mappa Mundi – literally, Map of the World – was produced around 1300, about fifty years before *Mandeville's Travels* appeared, and is the largest surviving medieval map of the world. Little about it corresponds to our modern understanding of geography or the conventions of cartography. Instead, it is an orbisculum, a map of the known earth shown in the form of a sphere, and its orientation is profoundly confusing to the twenty-first-century viewer, with Asia placed at the top of the map, rather than Europe in the north. On the Mappa Mundi, as in other medieval maps, Africa is shown as one of three known continents, a tripartite division that was an essential feature of the medieval world-view. The map depicts time as well as physical space, showing events from the Bible as well as the locations of nations. At the top, Adam and Eve are shown being expelled from the Garden of Eden, and above them the Day of Judgement has arrived: the saved are being welcomed into heaven and the damned driven en masse towards the mouth of hell. At the centre of the map – both literally and conceptually – is the city of Jerusalem, above which can be seen the crucifixion.

Whereas Europe is shown on the Mappa Mundi with its rivers and cities clearly marked and illustrated, the continents of Asia and Africa, which lay beyond the knowledge of the map's creator, are depicted as the realms of the monstrous races that Mandeville described. The monopods, a race of men with only one foot, whom Mandeville claimed to have seen in Ethiopia, are depicted in Asia. An illustration of that race shows a man sheltering from the sun beneath the shade of his single enormous foot. As well as presenting Africa as the realm of monstrous peoples, the Mappa Mundi reinforces the ancient idea that Africa was a land of such excessive heat that its residents are forced to seek shelter from the sun or have become adapted to its burning rays.

At the fringes of Africa, right on the very edge of the map and therefore of the known world, are the strangest of all the monstrous races, the Blemmyes, a people who have no heads, but faces upon their chests. On the coast of Ethiopia can be found the Marmini people, who each have four eyes with which they can gaze in four different directions simultaneously. Near them in Ethiopia are the Agriophagi of whom Pliny had spoken and whom Shakespeare would later mention in *Othello* and *The Merry Wives of Windsor*. The Agriophagi apparently lived under the rule of a cyclops king who is shown on the Mappa Mundi wearing a crown and carrying a sceptre.[12]

Both the author of *Mandeville's Travels* and the creator of the Mappa Mundi presented Africa as a land that was wondrous and profoundly different from late medieval Europe. Yet despite its riches and many natural marvels the continent was occupied by peoples that both considered savage. The cultural practices of the Africans were strange and at times unnatural. Their sexual habits ran counter to European norms and their religions were false and troubling. Yet of all the many astounding and disconcerting possibilities that *Mandeville's Travels* presented to late medieval Europeans, nothing was more startling and enticing than his claim that somewhere within Africa there lay a black Christian kingdom. The author was embellishing an already established legend that had first emerged in the twelfth century. The myth had probably begun when the crusaders, whose conquests in Palestine were being threatened by the rising power of the Saracens, heard rumours of a Christian kingdom beyond their reach in Eastern Africa, and may have encountered Christian Africans in the Holy Lands. This lost Christian kingdom was ruled over by an African king known as Prester John. Both he and his people were said to be fabulously wealthy, and within his kingdom lay many natural wonders, including the aforementioned fountain of youth.

There were many versions of the legend. In some, the kingdom of Prester John was said to be located somewhere in Asia, in others it was to be found in Ethiopia, and in some in India — which did little to pin it down on the map, as there were believed to be two Indias, India inferior and India superior, as well as two distinct and separate Ethiopias.[13] The tendency of the kingdom of Prester John to migrate around the known world over the course of innumerable retellings and reimaginings was a reflection of the medieval European tendency to conflate Africa with India, or to subsume Africa into a vague general notion of the 'Saracen' lands of Asia and the Middle East. By the fifteenth century, however, the locus of Prester John had come to rest more firmly in Africa, specifically in Abyssinia, modern Ethiopia.

The origins of this myth are obscure, but the reasons why it so appealed to the medieval mind are relatively simple. The idea that somewhere in Africa, beyond the barrier of the Islamic world, lay a black Christian kingdom raised the tantalizing prospect that an intercontinental Christian alliance might be forged. In this vision, Prester John and his African people were presented as a potential ally that could be roused to arms, perhaps thereby tipping the balance in Christendom's centuries-long conflict with Islam. The myth was, in effect, a collective act of wishful thinking, born out of growing knowledge in Europe of the enormous military and cultural power of the Islamic world.

The myth of Prester John might well have stemmed in part from the cultural shadow cast across medieval Europe by the very real Coptic Christian kingdom that did exist in Ethiopia. Separated from Europe by Islamic North Africa, Ethiopia's Christians gradually became known to Europeans during the late medieval period, and it seems possible that the reality of Coptic Ethiopia at some stage fused with the legend of Prester John. So convinced were Europeans of the existence of this African king that in 1400 King Henry VI of England dispatched a letter to him. By the fifteenth century Prester John had become firmly established as the name that Europeans ascribed to the emperors of Ethiopia, and which came as an utter surprise to them. In 1441, when a diplomatic delegation from the Ethiopian monastery in Jerusalem travelled to Italy to attend the Council of Florence, it shocked their European hosts to learn that the name Prester John meant nothing to their African co-religionists, and that the name had never been used in Ethiopia.

Yet even this was not enough to demolish the legend. When

Portuguese explorers began to make their way around the coast
of Africa in the fifteenth century, making contact with numerous
African societies, they continued to enquire about the whereabouts
of Prester John and his kingdom. The medieval myth and the tantalizing prospect of a grand pan-Christian alliance lingered on until
the seventeenth century. Prester John's mythical kingdom and the
wondrous regions described in books such as *Mandeville's Travels* may
well have been the earliest origins of the persistent notion that
somewhere in Africa lay a great and ancient 'lost kingdom'. This
trope survived well into the twentieth century, in novels by John
Buchan and Rider Haggard.

At the start of the fifteenth century, around thirty human generations
after the fall of Rome, the regions of Africa below the Sahara
remained beyond the reach of European travellers and obscured
behind a dense veil of classical and medieval mythology. So powerful
were these ideas that when, in the early fifteenth century, European
explorers did begin to inch their way around the coast of Africa,
they did so with copies of *Mandeville's Travels* in their hands, and in
the genuine hope of finding Prester John. The first European traders
and explorers were able to make those epic journeys because they
also carried with them the fruits of Islamic learning: new instruments
for navigation and books on astronomy, maths and trigonometry.

   The people who led the way were the Portuguese, the great
mariners of what became known as the Age of Discovery. Portugal's cartographers and navigators had built upon Islamic learning
and were far in advance of most of their competitors. Her shipbuilders had also risen to the challenge and crafted a vessel capable
of taking Europeans further south than they had travelled since
the age of Rome. This was the caravel, built around a rugged
internal frame. Tiny by modern standards, it was in its day the
most advanced ocean-going vessel Europeans had yet constructed,
the fifteenth- and sixteenth-century equivalent of the space shuttle.
Shallow-draughted, with two or three masts and lateen sails, it was
uniquely suited to harnessing the poorly understood winds of the
African coast and tackling its demanding shoreline. The journeys
that took Europeans out of the familiar and navigable Mediterranean

and around the Atlantic coast of Africa pushed the arts of navigation to their limits and required breath-taking courage. Mariners
ventured into regions about which almost nothing was known and
of which mythology offered ominous predictions of fatal climates
and treacherous seas.

Portugal's first base on African soil was the city of Ceuta, on
the very tip of Northern Africa in modern-day Morocco, directly
opposite Gibraltar. In 1419 King Henry of Portugal, known as
'Henry the Navigator', ordered his captains to venture around the
North African coast. Progress was painfully slow, each expedition
probing a little further than the last, testing whether the winds
were capable of returning them to Lisbon. By 1434 they had
ventured two hundred miles beyond the dreaded Cape Bojador on
the coast of modern-day Morocco. This headland that juts out into
the North Atlantic was known to the Arabs as Abu Khatar – The
Father of Danger. By breaching that barrier the Portuguese had
disproved the widely held belief that the seas to the south of Bojador
were governed by winds and currents that would make any return
to Europe impossible. In 1436 they travelled beyond Cape Blanco
on the modern border between Western Sahara and Mauritania. A
mission to the Bay of Arguin in Mauritania returned to Portugal
with gold and African slaves, and in 1441 the Portuguese dispatched
a mission to push on and find the legendary 'river of gold' that
some late medieval maps located in the region of what is today
Senegal. By the 1460s they had established a trading post on the
island of Arguin, and from that bridgehead had begun to draw out
the wealth of the African continent.

It was in many ways natural that Portugal would be the nation
that first reached out towards Africa. Like Spain, she had been
conquered by Muslim invaders from North Africa, and the legends
of Africa's gold mines and Prester John gripped imaginations in
Lisbon. But geography also played a part. Comparatively isolated,
on the far west of Europe, Portugal's ports and harbours faced not
the Mediterranean but the austere and seemingly endless Atlantic.
The ocean almost summoned her sailors and traders out into its
great expanse. But Portugal was also a nation in search of wealth,
which was needed to build up her power and fend off the attentions
of her larger neighbour, Spain. Trade with Africa might also fund

further expeditions to discover a sea route to India and access to the spice trade monopolized till now by Muslim traders into the eastern Mediterranean. While Portugal's kings and mariners were possessed by a spirit of adventure and human curiosity, her interest in Africa was motivated primarily by a clear-eyed and pragmatic search for trade. Economic considerations were always paramount.

The commodities that drew the Portuguese to Africa were dyewood, ivory (which English merchants were later to quaintly call 'elephants' teeth'), and a form of pepper from Sierra Leone, known then as 'grains of paradise'. The trade in slaves did not count for much at this stage, although both African and Berber people were captured on some of these early ventures and enslaved in small numbers. The real lure of Africa was gold. Since the age of the Byzantine Empire, Europeans had been aware that somewhere in Africa lay the source of the gold that flowed across the Sahara and into their continent, carried by Arab and Berber caravans. By traversing down the coast of Africa in their caravels the Portuguese had outflanked the desert and travelled around Islamic North Africa. African gold could now be shipped directly to Europe without passing through the intermediary hands of desert traders and Muslim merchants. Portugal had cut out the middleman.

Even before it had been fully proved, the trade in African gold was given papal approval and protection. In the 1450s, Pope Nicholas V and his successor Callixtus III took it upon themselves to issue papal bulls, edicts confirming Portugal's position as the exclusive trader along two thousand miles of African coastline. By the 1470s the mariners of Lisbon had reached the coast of modern Ghana, a land that up until its independence in 1957 retained the name it acquired in the Age of Discovery – the Gold Coast. In 1482 the Portuguese built a trade fortress there named São Jorge da Mina – Saint George of the Mine – because the Portuguese optimistically believed that their new outpost lay close to Africa's legendary gold mines. From this enclave they hoped to tap the region's prodigious wealth at source. Unbeknownst to the men who built the fortress of El Mina, the alluvial goldfields of West Africa lay many miles inland, through the then impenetrable forest belt. Neither the Portuguese nor any of their European rivals in the Age of Discovery were ever to gain access to those regions of the interior.* It would take Europeans another four centuries to finally break through the forests to the gold mines, and it was to be the British in the 1890s, rather than the Portuguese in the 1480s, who reached the mines around the city of Kumasi. Even then, and armed with the Maxim gun and the modern rifle, the British forces were decimated by disease and suffered serious losses in battle against the Ashanti people who vigorously defended their kingdom and its riches.

Nonetheless, by the end of the fifteenth century 25,000 ounces of African gold had been brought from the interior and sold to the Portuguese on the coast by African traders, thereby reaching Europe directly from Africa. In the late fifteenth and early sixteenth centuries the predecessors of the British colonialists who were to capture the gold mines of Ghana looked upon Portugal's expansion into the African world with a mixture of wonder and envy. Reports of Portuguese discoveries and trade heightened interest in Africa and its new, exotic products. Coveted and desired in London as much as in Lisbon, these commodities became markers of social distinction and signifiers of wealth and status. English merchants who saw the enormous wealth that the Portuguese had acquired through the trade in African gold sought to find other distant regions of the world where they might set up similar trades. Some of them were sorely tempted to break into the Portuguese sphere of influence on the coast of West Africa itself and grab a share of the African gold trade. In the 1530s the English sea captain William Hawkins, of Tavistock in Devonshire, sailed in quest of trade to the Guinea coast of West Africa, but his was a one-off venture. No matter how strong the draw of African gold, there were sizeable obstacles (Portugal's established relationships, the trade fortress at El Mina, and the power of the papal bulls) that deterred English mariners from ventures along the African coast.

However, the barrier imposed by the papal bull was suddenly

---

* In a further slip in the European account of Africa, the region that became known as the Gold Coast, from which the gold of the Akan peoples of the interior did flow, was conflated with the ancient kingdom of Ghana, an error that was to be compounded when the Gold Coast took the name Ghana at independence despite lying many miles distant from ancient Ghana.

and unexpectedly removed when Henry VIII married Anne Boleyn in 1534 and a year later passed the Act of Supremacy. This led, inevitably, to Henry's excommunication by Pope Clement VII. Clement's successor Paul III excommunicated the English king for a second time, and in the papal bull *Eius qui immobilis* made the judgement hereditary. With some irony it specifically mentioned Henry's sons 'born or to be born' (the issue of sons having been the root cause of Henry's break with Rome).[14] Excommunication meant that England was a heretical state, one that in theory at least was no longer subject to papal bulls. But this in itself was not inducement enough for English mariners to rush headlong for the Guinea coast of West Africa. Further encouragement was required, and some of it may well have been provided by Anthony Anes Pinteado, a Portuguese captain who had sailed the routes between Africa and the Portuguese colonies in Brazil.[15] Having fallen out of favour in Lisbon, Pinteado had travelled to England, and there offered his services.* His experience of the Guinea Coast, and the tales he may have told his English hosts of the riches to be obtained there, appear to have helped stiffen English resolve. Pinteado was appointed adviser and second-in-command in the first English expedition to the African coast that aimed to break into the Portuguese trade – that of Thomas Wyndham in 1553.

Wyndham left from Portsmouth with three ships: the *Lion*, the *Moon* and the *Primrose*. He had previously sailed with William Hawkins and was backed by a number of London merchants and, it seems, by King Edward VI, the son and heir that had finally been delivered to Henry VIII by Jane Seymour. There is some evidence to suggest that the *Moon* and the *Primrose* may have been royal vessels.[16] Giving the Portuguese a taste of what was to come, Wyndham's expedition sought plunder as well as trade. He attacked Portuguese shipping and raided their bases. As Wyndham was a seasoned pirate, such violence was part of his standard operating procedure; all that was

---

* Anthony Anes Pinteado's fall from grace in Portugal may have been connected to his faith, as he may well have been a *converso* – an Iberian Jew who had converted to Catholicism to avoid persecution, yet who remained distrusted and relegated even after accepting the Catholic faith.

unique about this aspect of his 1553 voyage was how far from home he had sailed to locate his prey.[17] Tacking along the coast of West Africa, heading towards the Gold Coast, Wyndham and Pinteado took good care to skirt the Portuguese fortress at El Mina, and during their progress were able to trade for 150 pounds of African gold. Yet despite this success, at some point in the venture the two men appear to have quarrelled; Wyndham is reported as having denounced his second-in-command as a 'whoreson Jew'.[18]

After trading on the Gold Coast, Wyndham ventured further east to the court of Benin, inland through the lagoons of modern-day Nigeria. There he traded his English goods for 80 tons of Malaguetta pepper. However, he was to be denied a glorious return to England with his cargo of gold and pepper. Ignoring the advice of the more experienced Pinteado, he extended the mission long enough for disease to sweep through the crew. He and Pinteado and around two-thirds of their men succumbed to tropical fevers and died. There were so few survivors that the Lion was abandoned, for lack of hands to sail her home. Only around forty of the original complement of 140 made it back to Plymouth. The expedition had been costly in lives but enormously profitable for its investors. Thomas Wyndham had demonstrated the potential of the African trade, albeit posthumously.

The next English expedition to make an incursion into Portugal's sphere of influence was supported by some of the same investors who had profitably backed Wyndham's fatal voyage. The new venture was led by John Lok, a member of a significant London merchant family and the great-great-great-grandfather of the great Enlightenment philosopher John Locke (the spelling evolved over the centuries).[19] Lok left for the coast of Africa in 1554 just four months after the survivors of Wyndham's expedition had returned. His three ships headed to the Gold Coast, and like Wyndham avoided the Portuguese centre of power at El Mina. Returning to England faster than Wyndham had, Lok and his men did not suffer the death toll that befell the early expedition and arrived back in Britain with a cargo of pepper, 250 tusks of ivory and most importantly gold – more than 400 pounds of it. Lok's expedition, coming so hard on the heels of Wyndham's, reaffirmed to the London merchants that the so-called Guinea trade was viable. To the Portuguese the incursions of Wyndham and Lok showed that their African monopoly was under threat and that they were unable to defend their trading rights along so extensive a coastline. Official protestations were registered in London by the envoys of the Portuguese King John III, but further English and French interlopers were inspired to organize fresh expeditions.

An account describing the voyage of John Lok tells us that in addition to their haul of ivory, pepper and gold, Lok and his men also, 'brought with them certaine blacke slaves'. These men, five in total, seem not to have been slaves, in fact, but Africans recruited to act as intermediaries and translators for future English expeditions in the hope that these would become more regular and increasingly profitable. While in London the five men were to learn English and then be returned to Africa. Here again the English were learning from the Portuguese, who as early as the 1440s had pioneered the practice of taking Africans – sometimes by force – and training them as translators. The men Lok brought to England were from Shama, a small and unremarkable fishing town that can still be found on the coast of Ghana. Their African names are not recorded, but the names that three of them adopted while in England were Anthonie, Binnie and George. We know little of their time in England, or what they made of the land from which their new trading partners had come. Richard Hakluyt, the author of *The Principal Navigations, Voyages, Traffiques and Discoveries of the English Nation* (1598), a compendium of sixteenth-century expeditions to Africa, describes them as 'tall and strong men', who were able to 'wel agree with our meates and drinkes'. Hakluyt recorded that 'The colde and moyst aire doth somewhat offend them' and noted that these 'men that are borne in hot Regions may better abide colde, then men that are borne in colde regions may abide heate'.[20] By the nineteenth century the confident belief that Africans were able to easily tolerate the cold of Europe had evaporated. By the Victorian age the prevailing view in Britain was that the climate of Europe was injurious to the health of Africans, and those arriving in Britain were encouraged to remain in the country only for short periods.

The five men from Shama were returned to Africa after just a few months in London. Three were carried back to the Gold Coast by the London merchant William Towerson in 1556, while Anthonie and Binnie stayed on in London. A description of the return of the first three to Africa, written by an English mariner, describes how when the expedition landed in the town of Hanta, not far from Shama, they discovered that the three Africans 'were well knowen, and the men of the towne wept for joy when they saw them, and demanded of them where Anthonie and Binne had bene: and they told them that they had bene at London in England, and should bee brought home the next voyage.' When the English ships reached Shama itself the three men were returned to their families and similar scenes erupted: 'wee sent our Negros on shore, and after them divers of us, and were very well received, and the people were very glad of our Negros, specially one of their brothers wives, and one of their aunts, which received them which much joy, and so did all the rest of the people . . .'[21]

The recruitment of the five men from Shama to act as translators was evidence that London merchants like Lok believed that the English might be able to permanently force their way into the Portuguese-dominated gold trade, but the English effort to train translators to work on their behalf on the coast of Africa also tells us something of the nature of the relationship that had developed between Europeans and their African trading partners. Our mental image of the British in Africa is so firmly fixed in the so-called Scramble for Africa of the late nineteenth century that we struggle to recall that when Englishmen first arrived in Africa they came not in pith helmets and khaki uniforms but in doublets and hose. The English traders who infiltrated the Portuguese trading zones in coastal West Africa in the sixteenth century did not come as colonizers but, like all other Europeans, as traders.

No other relationship would have been possible. The African peoples with whom they hoped to trade were members of societies that were neither inward-looking nor primitive. Centuries of contact with the Islamic states of North Africa and the Middle East had bound the region up with the wider world and trained its rulers in the profitable arts of long-distance trade and negotiation. The trans-Saharan trade routes had brought wealth to African societies, but also new ideas and knowledge. Islam had moved southwards with the trade caravans. There, in the lands below the Sahara, highly organized, administratively centralized empires had been formed. In modern-day Nigeria the Oyo empire had risen. To its west stood the empire of Dahomey, which dominated much of what is today the nation of Benin. The Akan peoples in whose territory lay the goldfields of the Gold Coast had taken control of much of the south and central region of what is today the state of Ghana, while the ancient empire of Benin had become the paramount power in the south of modern Nigeria. Centuries of trade and cultural contact meant that these states and empires were worldly enough to deal competently with their European trading partners in this first stage of contact. Some of the kingdoms of West Africa had, like Benin, constructed cities, and there was no question of all their populations living in straggling villages prone to seaborne incursion.

By the time the English arrived in the middle of the sixteenth century, West Africans had been trading with the Portuguese for several generations. The leaders of these kingdoms tended to welcome the English as new customers, and to such militarily powerful and administratively competent African societies the English, in these early decades, must at times have looked unimpressive – few in number, often sickly, and plainly inexperienced. Neither the English interlopers nor the Portuguese who were present in far greater numbers, and who had built permanent structures, offered a significant military threat. This is not to say that relationships between West Africans and Europeans were always peaceful. The English captain William Towerson made several expeditions to the coast of Africa in the 1550s. During his third voyage of 1558 he faced opposition from the Portuguese and found that some of the Africans he approached were openly hostile and unwilling to trade. In a portent of things to come, Towerson responded by attacking and burning an African town.[22]

Some sense of the overall balance of power between Europeans and their African trading partners comes from the accounts of the merchants themselves. The Dutch trader Pieter de Marees, who wrote of his trip to West Africa in 1602, noted that the Africans he encountered and entered into trade with had a clear understanding of the value of their commodities and very definite ideas about the types and qualities of the European goods which they were willing to accept in exchange. These were not people to be swindled, and they were quick to spot any attempt to cheat or defraud them. 'When we have brought them things they did not like,' de Marees reported, 'they have mocked us in a scandalous way.'[23] Another trader noted that the Africans he traded with used weights and measures to determine the exact value of the gold they traded and were 'very ware in theyr bargenynge, and wyl not lose one sparke of golde of any value'.[24] Thomas Wyndham had been surprised when, on meeting the Oba (King) of Benin in 1553, he discovered that the monarch 'could speake the Portugall tongue, which he had learned of a child'.

It was Benin, of all the African kingdoms with which Europeans traded in the sixteenth century, that the traders and chroniclers found most impressive. This powerful kingdom refused to permit Europeans to build trading fortresses on its territory, and the value and scale of its trade in pepper, ivory, home-grown cotton goods and other commodities impressed all visitors. The Oba, who had dispatched an ambassador to Lisbon following the arrival of the very first Portuguese explorers, ruled from Benin City. Its enormous earthen-wall defences and wide boulevards awed European visitors, as did the palace of the Oba, with its long hallways decorated with brass reliefs. Centuries later, those brass reliefs were wrenched from the walls and doors of the palace and sold to defray the costs of the punitive British expedition launched against the city in 1897. They can today be found in museums across Europe and North America, with a large collection on display in the British Museum.

In the period before the rise of the Atlantic slave trade, the societies of West Africa were in some ways at an advantage in their dealings with Europeans. This was due not just to their own cultural and military power but also to the geography of their coastline and the natural barrier of the inland forest belt. The coast of West Africa might have been built to fend off potential colonizers. Three thousand miles long, it is armoured along much of its length with an array of deadly obstacles. Powerful surf tides and steeply rising beaches make dropping anchor difficult in many places and impossible in others. Treacherous sandbanks lurk under the waters, forcing travellers in sailing vessels to keep their distance. These natural defences include the deadly Bank of Arguin, off the coast of modern

Mauritania, where in the nineteenth century the French frigate
Méduse famously ran aground, her passengers resorting to cannibalism
while adrift on a makeshift raft. Between the Sierra Leone River
and the lagoons and inlets of the Niger River, the coast of West
Africa is largely bereft of natural harbours. The few accessible anchor-
ages that do exist are far from ideal. One of the striking features
of the first age of contact between Europeans and West Africans is
how few European structures were built, and how small and scattered they were. Much of the coastline remained impenetrable and
unreachable. These geographic factors combined with the prevalence
of tropical disease and the military capacities of the West African
empires to effectively lay down the rules of engagement that Europeans and Africans were to follow until the advent of the Atlantic
slave trade.

Although the voyages of John Lok and later of William Towerson
might have proved the viability of an English trade with Africa, albeit
one forbidden by the Papacy, the English remained only minor players
in the gold trade of the sixteenth century. Seven years after John
Lok had arrived in London with the five men from Shama, John
Hawkins, a ship owner and trader from Plymouth, became the pioneer
of the English triangular slave trade. Hawkins was the younger
son of the trader William Hawkins, who had sailed to the West African
coast in the 1530s. He was also the cousin of Sir Francis Drake and
to some extent was Drake's mentor. Like the other English traders,
Hawkins was aware that Africans were being sold as slaves on the
West African coast and shipped by Spain to her colonies in the New
World. In October 1562 he set off for West Africa, arriving in the
vast harbour of the Sierra Leone River, a region which, over the
following centuries, Britain was to reshape and remake more than
perhaps any other part of the continent. Richard Hakluyt in his
Principal Navigations tells us that in Sierra Leone Hawkins 'got into
his possession, partly by the sword and partly by other means, 300
Negroes at the least, besides other merchandises which that country
yieldeth'.

  Hawkins had attacked and plundered a number of Portuguese
vessels, seizing the enslaved Africans on board. With his ships loaded

up 'with that prey he sailed over the Ocean sea unto the island of Hispaniola' (present-day Haiti and the Dominican Republic). Hawkins called at several Spanish colonies and sold his commodities, including the African captives. According to Hakluyt 'he received, by way of exchange, hides, ginger, sugars, and some pearls'. When he arrived back in England in September 1563 he had, through this one expedition, made himself a fortune and proved that English ships could break into the Spanish trade in African slaves, even though English participation in the trade was prohibited under Spanish law. He had also shown that buying and selling human beings could be as profitable as the trade in gold.

In 1564 and again in 1567 Hawkins embarked upon further slave-trading missions to the West African coast, attracting investors from the political elite of the Elizabethan court. Among those who backed his later expeditions were William Cecil, then Secretary of State, the Earls of Leicester and Pembroke and Queen Elizabeth I herself. In the hope of boosting profits and increasing the chances of success, the Queen provided Hawkins's second slave-trading mission with two of her own ships, the *Minion* and the 700-ton *Jesus of Lübeck*, a vessel that Henry VIII had bought from the German Hanseatic League – hence its Teutonic name. The second expedition was essentially a repeat of the first. Hawkins again headed for the Sierra Leone River and there went ashore 'to take the inhabitants . . . burning and spoiling their towns'. Other Africans were seized from intercepted Portuguese ships. Again, Hawkins then set sail for the New World, there selling the enslaved Africans to Spanish colonists.

This second venture proved as profitable as his first. Hawkins claimed that his personal profit stood at 60 per cent.[25] Queen Elizabeth was clearly pleased with the return on her investment, as soon afterwards Hawkins was knighted. The coat of arms he had designed for him in 1571 included an image of a female African slave.

Sir John Hawkins is often considered the initiator of the English triangular trade and the first English slave-trader. This is questionable in two ways. First, as the work of the historian Gustav Ungerer has demonstrated, other English slave-traders were active before Hawkins. As early as the 1480s Englishmen were operating from bases in Andalusia, trading in slaves and other commodities in close cooperation with their Spanish, Genoese, Florentine and Portuguese business partners.[26] Some were slave owners as well as slave-traders. While England was a relative latecomer to the slave trade and was late to acquire New World slave colonies, English merchants, operating from abroad, were active in both trades generations earlier.

The second obstacle to the idea that Hawkins's expeditions marked the beginning of an English slave trade is the fact that his missions did not represent the beginning of an unbroken pattern of slave-trading in the Atlantic, carried out by domestic merchants and mariners sailing from British ports. This is partly because Hawkins's final expedition was a disaster. In 1568, sailing in a fleet of five ships, one of them commanded by Francis Drake (not yet knighted), Hawkins was intercepted by the Spanish off Mexico – then the colony of New Spain. In the ensuing battle of San Juan de Ulúa three of the English ships, including the *Jesus of Lübeck*, and a caravel recently captured from the Portuguese, were lost. Only two English vessels made it home and the incipient triangular trade was brought to an ignominious and ruinous end. It was to be a century before it would be revived in any serious sense. In the interim, the English discovered themselves to be more adept at privateering – licensed and state-sanctioned piracy against the Spanish treasure fleets – than slave-trading.

Between Thomas Wyndham's 1553 voyage and 1565 there were nine English expeditions to the coast of West Africa, which between them involved at least twenty large ocean-going vessels and an unknown number of smaller craft. The historian Cheryl A. Fury has estimated that between a thousand and fifteen hundred men took part in these ventures, most of whom came safely back to England.[27] Wyndham, Lok and the other English traders who sailed to the coast of West Africa left England knowing little of the continent, but they and their crewmen returned with their own first-hand experiences and observations.

It might be expected that these new accounts – both verbal and literary – would overthrow and displace the image of Africa that had emerged from medieval mythology, but that is not what happened. To the modern observer one key feature of the Age of Discovery is that Europeans could continue to harbour beliefs in medieval myths even in the face of observed and verifiable reality. In the case of the English, this was because each voyage appeared to confirm rather than refute the notion that Africa was a land of mysteries and marvels. The reports of mariners who returned from the continent were rapidly adulterated with large doses of exaggeration and conjecture. Such accounts did little to dim the allure of the old myths, some of which were, if anything, reinforced by the tales told by England's mariners.

In 1555, the same year that John Lok had returned to London with the five men from Shama, two new books were published that reiterated a number of timeworn myths. *The Fardle of Facions* was a translation of a work by Johannes Boemus that blended classical accounts of Africa, including those of Pliny and Herodotus, with equally misleading medieval sources. More influential was Richard Eden's dubious translation of Peter Martyr's *The Decades of the New World*, which offered an account of the Spanish exploration and colonization of South and Central America. To this established work Eden appended accounts of the English voyages of Wyndham, Lok and others, padding out their narrative accounts of those voyages with a great deal of fantasy of his own invention. Some of Eden's additions were later incorporated into Richard Hakluyt's *Principal Navigations*, and in this way, long after English traders had encountered the real Africa and traded with real Africans, the continent continued to be described in fantastical terms. Eden's account of the journey of John Lok, for example, offered a relatively sober description of the morphology and habits of elephants. This was immediately followed, however, by a passage, apparently of Eden's devising, in which it is boldly stated that these giant creatures live for two hundred years and are continually at war with dragons, who prey upon them in order to drink their blood, which is said to be icy cold.[28]

Artefacts as well as words contributed to the mystification of Africa. On his return to London John Lok, in addition to his five African translators and his haul of gold, had brought with him the head of an elephant. This was put on display at the home of another London merchant, Sir Andrew Judde. Those who might have been willing to abandon medieval notions that Africa was a land of monsters and monstrous men might well have concluded that if elephants existed in Africa, and their remains could be viewed at the home of a London merchant, then might not some future expedition return to the city with Blemmyes, Troglodytes or the head of a dragon? If elephants were real and verifiable, then why not dragons?

Accounts of incredible animals and of the intense climatic conditions that were said to prevail in Africa were no more exciting or perplexing to the English than what they were learning in the same years about the people of Africa themselves. Human physical difference, and most importantly the blackness of African skin, posed profound challenges to the thinkers, chroniclers and philosophers of the sixteenth century. Why were Africans black? Was it – as seemed logical to many – because they had been burnt or bronzed by the extreme heat of the African sun? If that were the case, would Africans remain black if they settled in Europe? Conversely, would the skin of Europeans become blackened if they resided in Africa for long periods? Was the blackness of Africans temporary or permanent, congenital and inherited? What about children born to inter-racial couples: would they be black, white or some other hue? And what, if anything, did the black skin of the African signify?

All of these questions swirled around in the Elizabethan imagination. Although the causes of human blackness were a matter for philosophical debate, its permanence seemed to be widely appreciated. That no amount of washing could change skin colour was a truism that spawned aphorisms such as, 'To wash a blackamoor is to labour in vain'.[29] Jon Lok was one of the first to reject the hypothesis that blackness was due to the heat of Africa, concluding that the skin colour of Africans was due to 'a secret worke of nature'. Lok observed that 'throughout all Africke, under the Equinoctial line . . . the regions are extreeme hote', and there the people were indeed 'very blacke'. However he also noted that there were 'regions of the West Indies' that were equally tropical and correspondingly hot, yet the indigenous peoples of these islands (Amerindian peoples who were decimated by European conquest) were 'neither blacke, nor with curlde and short wooll on their heads, as they of Africke have, but [are] of the colour of an Olive, with long and blacke heare on their heads'. If the peoples of the West Indies lived under a sun as intense as that which burned over Africa, and yet were not as dark, then the sun alone could not explain African blackness, concluded Lok.

The English sailor George Best reached the same conclusion via a different route. In the 1580s he wrote, 'I myselfe have seen an Ethiopian as blacke as cole brought into England, who taking an English wife begat a sonne in all respects as blacke as the father was, although England were his native countrey, and an English woman his mother; whereby it seemeth that blackness proceedeth rather of some natural infection of that man, which was so strong, that neither the nature of the Clime, neither the good complexion of the mother concurring, could any thing alter and therefore, we cannot impute it to the nature of the Clime.'[30] If a mixed-race child conceived by an African man and an English woman was born with dark skin, then there had to be some other explanation for 'the Ethiopians great blackness', Best reasoned.

After determining that the cause of human blackness was not the ferocity of the African sun, George Best fell back upon religion. The explanation 'manifestly and plainly appeareth by holy scripture', he asserted. The biblical story that Best and some of his contemporaries looked to was well known in the sixteenth century, and was often discussed and deployed in the centuries that followed, but has been largely forgotten in the modern age. According to scripture, in the book of Genesis, the three sons of Noah were the progenitors of the three acknowledged races of mankind. As George Best explained, 'after the generall inundation and overflowing of the earth, there remained no moe men alive, but Noe [Noah] and his three sonnes, Sem, Cham, and Japhet, who onely were left to possess and inhabit the whole face of the earth: therefore all the land that until this day hath been inhabited by sundry descents, must needs come of the offspring either of Sem, Cham, or Japhet'.

The idea that the peoples of the world were the offspring of the three sons of Noah was one that neatly correlated with other aspects of the medieval world-view. Up until 1492 there had been only three known continents, and upon each, it was believed, resided the three races of mankind. Medieval mapmakers at times used the names of the three sons of Noah to denote the three known continents. The descendants of Cham – or Ham as he was more commonly known – were said to be the people of Africa, Asia was the home of the descendants of Sem, and Europe the land of the people born of the familial line of Japhet. This understanding of the world was reflected in another late medieval concept, that of the Three Kings or Three Wise Men who travel to Bethlehem to worship the infant Christ. In a tradition that probably began in Germany in the last decades of the fourteenth century, the youngest of the Three Kings, Balthazar, came to be depicted as a black African.[31] The Three Kings, therefore, accorded with the trinity of known continents and races. The notion that one of them was an African was referenced in a number of medieval literary texts, including *Mandeville's Travels*.[32] This tradition, which has become a familiar feature of each Christmas and nativity play, has deep medieval roots that have been largely lost and forgotten.

From the sixteenth century onwards, the legend that Africans were the 'sons of Ham' was often invoked to explain their blackness. The legend was also to have far-reaching and dismal consequences, as it was later deployed as a justification for New World slavery. According to scripture, Ham had humiliated his father, and as punishment for his transgression Noah had placed a terrible curse upon Ham's son Canaan. This curse was to be passed on to all of Canaan's descendants in perpetuity. In the relevant passage of Genesis, Canaan was condemned to become 'a servant of servants . . . unto his brethren', and that same status was to be passed down to each generation for all time.

Although neither race nor skin colour is mentioned within these passages from Genesis, at some point the story of the Curse of Ham became racialized. George Best stated that Noah had intended that all the children of Ham 'should be so black and loathsome, that it might remain a spectacle of disobedience to all the world'. Best believed that it was from 'this black and cursed' line of humanity that 'all these black Moores which are in Africa' had sprung.[33] How fast and how far that idea spread is difficult to determine, but George Best was not alone in interpreting the black skin of the African as the marker of the curse of endless servitude that Noah had imposed upon the sons of Ham. In an age in which scripture was the highest source of knowledge and explanation, this biblical story – obscure and bizarre though it may be to the modern reader – became for some the favoured explanation for the blackness of Africans.

TWO

'Blackamoors'

The mystery of human physical difference and its causes, and the exotic and at times erotic fascination with black Africans, was literally brought home to the people of Elizabethan England and Stuart Scotland as, in the later sixteenth and early seventeenth centuries, Africans themselves began to visit and settle in the British Isles. The five men from Shama who arrived with John Lok were perhaps unique in the 1550s in that they had come to England directly from Africa. While they undoubtedly fascinated those who encountered them, what marked them out as special was perhaps more their 'African-ness' than their skin colour, for we can be certain that they were not the only black people resident in the British Isles in the mid-sixteenth century. There were people of African descent arriving and settling in various parts of Britain in the period, but they were mainly concentrated in London and the southern seaports. There remained very few of them, but as the geographic horizons of England and Scotland expanded, so did their numbers. Most appear to have lived ordinary lives, marrying and raising families, and while the majority of these black Tudor Africans were domestic servants they appear not to have been enslaved. There were slaves across fifteenth- and sixteenth-century Europe, but these unfortunates were drawn from various races. Despite the biblical notion of the Curse of Ham, there was no commonly recognized or popularly understood link between the condition of slavery and the people of Africa at this time – that was to come later.[1]

It used to be the case that the study of the presence of black people in Britain during the Tudor and Stuart ages was a neglected area. This is no longer true due to the effort of several historians (Imtiaz Habib, Miranda Kaufmann, Onyeka Nubia, Marika Sherwood and others) who have scoured the archives and uncovered the identities of literally hundreds of 'black Tudors'.[2] They have been found in parish registers, in the correspondence of the wealthy, and in legal records. Through such sources we learn of the three 'blackamore maids' who were said to be under the employ of the London alderman Paul Banning in 1586, and of Bastien, who was buried in Plymouth on 10 December 1583 and described as 'a Blackmoore of Mr. Willm Hawkins', the brother of the slave-trader sir John Hawkins.[3] Eleven years later and in the same town, Mary, recorded as a 'negro of John Whites', was baptized; her father was said to be a Dutchman.[4] These tantalizing glimpses often raise more questions than they provide answers. How did Bastien come to be buried in Plymouth? Was he a slave seized from Africa by Sir John Hawkins and gifted to his brother William? What became of Mary from Plymouth? Was she a mixed-race Afro-Dutch woman living in sixteenth-century England, did she marry and have children, was she free or enslaved?

Most black Tudors probably arrived in Britain via the Iberian and Mediterranean worlds. Some were brought to Britain by their employers. The scale of contact, trade and diplomacy between Portugal and Africa had led to the emergence in Lisbon of a large population of both free and enslaved Africans, as well as an unknown number of people of mixed heritage. Together they may have made up around 20 per cent of Lisbon's population in the late sixteenth century. As England and Scotland's disputes with Spain and Portugal escalated, many of the African people who found themselves in the British Isles were men and women who had been on board captured slave-trading ships belonging to the two Iberian powers.

The records of the black presence in Tudor England and Stuart Britain that do exist tell us that most black people were in domestic service and on the lower rungs of Tudor society. The archives record their births and deaths but also their baptisms and marriages, suggesting that when given the opportunity they became integrated into the society around them. But the numbers of black Tudors are too small for us to talk of a 'black community'. There were, however, a tiny number of black Tudors upon whom the records shine a brighter light, and among them is a black man who was part of the Tudor court. His name was John Blanke, and he may well have arrived in England in 1501, as part of the entourage of Catherine of Aragon, who had come to London to marry Arthur, Prince of Wales, the elder brother of Henry VIII. Arthur died in early 1502. Seven years later Henry took his brother's widow as his wife, and acceded within days to the throne.

John Blanke makes his first appearance in the records in 1509, when a note records wages being paid to him by the court of Henry VIII. But he exists in more than just the documentary record. Incredibly he is the first black person in Britain for whom we have not just a name in the official records but also an image; we can put a face to the name. This came about because Blanke performed at the celebrations that were staged in January 1511 to mark the birth of Prince Henry, the son born to Henry VIII and Catherine of Aragon. The infant, who died ten days after his birth, was the couple's second child and the second to have been lost; a still-born daughter had been delivered in January 1510, a year and a half after Henry and Catherine had married.[5] The festivities of 1511 are recorded in the Westminster Tournament Roll, a sixty-foot illustrated vellum roll held today at the Royal College of Arms in London. John Blanke appears twice on the Roll, shown on both occasions within the procession riding a grey horse and wearing an identical liveried uniform to his five fellow royal trumpeters. Their costumes differ only in the fact that Blanke wears a turban of brown and yellow. He was recorded as having been awarded a special payment for performing at the tournament.

Even before the Westminster Tournament, Blanke had witnessed a number of the pivotal events in the grim but compelling drama that was the Tudor dynasty. He had been present at the funeral of Henry VII in the spring of 1509, at which he had worn a black mourning livery. In the summer of that same year, this time wearing clothes of a regal red, Blanke had performed at the coronation of Henry VIII. We learn from a document of 1509 that he had petitioned Henry VIII, requesting that he be awarded the job and the wages of a recently deceased fellow trumpeter. In a skilfully worded petition to the King, Blanke informed his monarch that his current rates of pay were not 'sufficient to mayntaigne and kepe hym to doo your grace lyke service as other your trompeters doo'. Promising lifelong service and loyalty, Blanke made his case for promotion and reward.[6] Another document from 1512 reveals that John Blanke was married – presumably to an English woman of whom nothing is known. The document in question records that Blanke received a wedding gift from the King.[7] 'John Blak [sic], our trompeter', a gown of violet cloth, and also a bonnet and a hat, 'to be taken of our gift against his marriage' reads the note.[8] It seems likely that Blanke, who most probably came to Britain from Spain, was given a surname that reflected that life's journey. Historians have speculated that 'Blanke' might be an example of Tudor ironic humour – a comic play on words based around *blanco* and *blanc*, meaning white in Spanish and French respectively.[9]

John Blanke's place within the Tudor court may well have been a reflection of the studied modernity to which the Tudors and the English aristocracy aspired, as by the early sixteenth century Africans had become a recognized feature of the international, outward-looking cultures of Renaissance court life and pageantry, and a fashion for black musicians had spread across Europe. The Medici dynasty in Florence was known to have employed a black trumpeter in the 1550s, and there were Africans in the court of James IV in Edinburgh. The Shrove Tuesday celebrations held in the Scottish court in 1505 involved a dance choreographed by a black drummer referred to in the records as a 'taubronar' who appears to have been a favoured member of the royal court. The Shrove Tuesday celebrations involved twelve dancers wearing black and white chequered costumes.[10]

The presence of black people in the court of the Stuart kings was in part a reflection of that nation's excursions into the Atlantic world. Scottish privateers had been unleashed by James IV to prey on Portuguese ships in which enslaved Africans, as well as gold and ivory, were being transported to Europe. Elizabeth I, like her father, is known to have employed Africans in her court. A 'Blackamoore boy' is listed in a warrant of April 1574 in which the Queen commanded a tailor to make the child a 'garcon coat . . . of white taphata' lined with 'gold and silver'.[11] Other Africans arrived in the courts of Europe as diplomats from various parts of Africa. Representatives of the kings of Congo began to make visits to Lisbon from the fifteenth century onwards, and in 1544 the nephew of the

Congolese king paid a visit to the Portuguese capital, as did the sons of other elite Congolese families who were sent to Lisbon to further their educations.

John Blanke was a man with marketable skills and talents, which enabled him to earn a (presumably) comfortable living and command a certain degree of social status. Details of his life, and the images of him that appear on the Westminster Tournament Rolls, are preserved in the archival records due to Blanke's close proximity to power. Most black Tudors were not so fortunate in life and exist only as fragmentary passing references in parish registers and other documents. Another comparatively fortunate black Tudor, about whom we know a little more, appears in the records three decades after the last mention of John Blanke. Jacques Francis, like Blanke, had a connection with the court of Henry VIII. He was a salvage diver, twenty years old and from Arguin Island, in what is now Mauritania.

Francis was a slave employed by Peter Paulo Corsi, a Venetian salvage expert, who brought him to England around 1546. Corsi and his team had been tasked by Henry VIII with salvaging guns from the wreck of the *Mary Rose*, the great Tudor flagship that had sunk in the Solent in 1545, probably after tacking too sharply with her lower gunports open. Jacques Francis was the lead diver in the salvage operation, but records of him and his time in England survive not because he was employed on such a high-profile project but because in 1547 he found himself testifying in a court of law. When Corsi was accused of illegally salvaging metals from another wreck by a group of Italian merchants, Francis was called to give testimony in defence of his master in the High Court of Admiralty. It is significant that the testimony of Francis was admitted into an English court. He was a foreigner, a non-Christian, and an African marked out by difference in skin colour. Furthermore, he was enslaved. Yet his testimony was accepted and his humanity acknowledged by the court at a time when the testimonies of thousands of white English villeins (bonded serfs) would not have been admissible in court. One of Corsi's accusers, the Venetian merchant Anthony de Nicholao Rimero, attempted to have Francis's testimony disregarded, on the grounds that he was 'a morisco born where they are not christenyd and slave to the sayd peter Paulo ym And therefore . . . no Credite nor faithe ought to be geven to his Sayenges as in other Strange Christian cuntryes hit ys to no suche slave geven.'[12] Rimero's appeals were rejected by the High Court of Admiralty.

How did the people of Elizabethan England and Stuart Scotland regard the Africans who arrived in their nations during the sixteenth and early seventeenth centuries? What rights did they accord them? Were there then, present and detectable within those societies, forms of what we today would recognize as racism? For many years historians regarded an order of the Privy Council, dating from 1596, as compelling evidence that black people were unwanted and unwelcome in Elizabethan England, and that steps were taken, with the full support and active encouragement of the state and the Queen, to remove them from the nation. The order granted Caspar Van Senden, a German merchant from Lübeck, 'lysence to take up so muche blackamoors here in this realm and to transport them into Spain and Portugall' where Van Senden intended to sell them into slavery.[13] The licence was addressed to the mayors and sheriffs of England and may have had the support of Privy Councillors, as they may have considered it a cheap way of settling a debt.

Van Senden had secured the release of eighty-nine English subjects from Spanish and Portuguese custody and had incurred costs in doing so. Rather than directly compensate him, it seems that the debt owed him by the state was to have been settled by the granting of a licence that, in theory at least, entitled him to kidnap and sell a number of black people resident in England. However, Van Senden's arrangement – initiated during a period when a number of bizarre schemes were able to acquire a degree of official backing – proved fundamentally impractical. The licence stipulated that the 'blackamoors' within the English realm, most of whom were servants, could only be deported if the permission of their masters was first secured. As no compensation was to be offered them for the loss of their servants, this was an insurmountable obstacle.

In 1601, a second and more strongly worded petition was drafted. It stated that 'the Queen's majesty, tendering the good and welfare of her own natural subjects, greatly distressed in these hard times of dearth, is highly discontented to understand the great number of Negroes and blackamoors which (as she is informed) are carried

into this realm'.[14] To address this problem the licence affirmed that
the Queen 'hath given a special commandment that the said kind
of people shall be with all speed avoided and discharged out of this
her majesty's realms; and to that end and purpose hath appointed
Casper van Senden, merchant of Lubeck, for their speedy transportation'.[15] It appears that this second licence was never issued as a
proclamation and may have been drafted by Van Senden himself.
And the merchant's plan to deport and enslave black Tudors came
to nothing.[16] Yet for decades these two documents, unearthed from
the archives and seemingly unambiguous in their content, were
(understandably) regarded by historians as strong evidence that a
policy of forced deportation targeted at black people had been
officially sanctioned, and that such a policy reflected widespread
antipathy towards Africans. In reality Van Senden's scheme was a
failed profit-making venture proposed by a foreign merchant, rather
than the smoking-gun proof of rampant racism towards black people
in Elizabeth's England.[17] This, however, is not to say that there was
no intolerance shown to black people in early modern Britain.

Elizabethan and Stuart attitudes to what we today call race were
complex, often contradictory, ever-shifting and developing. A range
of reactions towards black people, their skin colour and ethnicity,
appear to have operated concurrently. While within the everyday
English spoken in Elizabethan times the colour black was laden with
negative associations, many of the black people who appear in
sixteenth-century parish registers were evidently accepted into the
Church. Some got married – presumably to white spouses – and
had children. Their skin colour evidently did not prevent them
integrating into the society around them, and the black Tudors we
have already met, John Blanke and Jacques Francis, were able to
hold positions of relative prestige within the same society.

Similar contradictions are evident in the fact that while English
slave-traders, engaged in the enslavement and transportation of Africans, operated freely from Andalusia and occasionally from English
ports, slavery within England itself was illegal. In 1587, twenty years
after Sir John Hawkins had made a fortune carrying captured Africans
to Spain's New World colonies, a Spanish resident of England, Hector
Nuñez, filed a complaint with the Court of Requests detailing how
a black man he had purchased as a slave and brought into England

was unwilling to recognize his enslavement and 'utterly refuseth to tarry and serve'. Nuñez was exceedingly disappointed that the English common law offered him 'no remedie . . . to compel' this 'Ethiopian' to submit to his demands.[18] That strange duality in attitudes which many foreigners were to regard as an acute form of hypocrisy was to be characteristic of British attitudes towards the rights, status and humanity of Africans in later centuries.

One arena in which the complexities and contradictions within English attitudes and beliefs were played out was the Elizabethan stage. Shakespeare, like most of his educated countrymen and women, was captivated by the new accounts of Africa, Asia and the Americas that emerged during the latter years of the sixteenth century. Richard Hakluyt's bestselling *Principal Navigations* was published in 1598 – the year when Shakespeare wrote *Henry IV, Part 2* and started *Much Ado About Nothing* – and it is probable that Shakespeare read Hakluyt, conceivably the much-expanded three-volume version that emerged in 1599–1600. Shakespeare, it appears, also read the Berber author Leo Africanus's book *Geographical Historie of Africa*, published in English translation in 1600, which described the supposed habits and cultures of the people of Africa and tended to conflate the habits and appearances of the people of North Africa with those of sub-Saharan Africa. Leo Africanus is often considered to have influenced Shakespeare's characterization of Othello.[19]

Despite there being clues encoded within the plays as to what Shakespeare was reading, it is impossible to get a full sense of how he or his audiences at the Globe regarded the black Africans about whom they had read in Hakluyt, or the black people they now encountered in the capital. It would be a mistake, however, to see Shakespeare's plays through the optic of the forms of racism and racial thinking that emerged only later in the seventeenth century, when England and Scotland became more deeply involved in the Atlantic slave trade and New World slavery. It is sometimes forgotten that Shakespeare's writing career (roughly 1589 to 1613) pre-dated both the start of the English slave trade and the establishment of English colonies in the Americas. Sir John Hawkins's first slaving expedition took place just before Shakespeare's birth, and his efforts petered out while the young William was just a boy. Shakespeare's death in 1616 came three years before the traditionally accepted date for the start of slavery in the English New World. Shakespeare did live in an age in which slavery was practised by the Spanish and Portuguese in the New World, and in Mediterranean Europe, including in Italy, where many of his plays were set. Yet in sixteenth-century Europe slaves were white as well as black. Indeed one of the fears that haunted the dreams of the English was the dread of being enslaved by Barbary corsairs, slave-trading pirates from Islamic North Africa. Not only was slavery not a condition solely associated with Africans in Shakespeare's time, but ideas of race and racial difference were profoundly different from those that were to develop during the age of the Atlantic slave trade. We can, for these reasons, be certain that Shakespeare's audiences did not come to the Globe with anything resembling a modern understanding of the idea of 'race', and what was meant by the word 'race' in early modern England remains to some extent unclear, despite having been the focus of a huge amount of scholarly debate. It was a word Shakespeare did use in his plays, but only sparingly. The word 'race' did not mean to Shakespeare and his contemporaries what it means to us. It had a tendency to shift its meaning and at times overlapped with notions of purity and pedigree.

What Elizabethans and early Stuarts did understand were ideas surrounding skin colour. Shakespeare's audiences had a fascination with human blackness that was influenced by older, medieval, ideas about the meanings of the colour black and its symbolic relationship with its opposite, white. Blackness in the sixteenth and early seventeenth centuries was associated with the night, the supernatural and the diabolical. The devil was depicted as black in innumerable medieval paintings, and continued to be portrayed as such in Elizabethan and Stuart woodcuts. The blackest everyday objects were described as being 'as black as a devil', and on occasions the skin of the devil was said to be as black as that of an African. To call someone black in Shakespeare's England was to insult them, not by any linkage with race, but because the colour itself was pregnant with negative symbolism.[20]

Whiteness by contrast was the marker of purity, virginity and even divinity, concepts that were never more loaded with meaning than in the years during which a Virgin Queen who whitened her skin with lead-based make-up ruled England. Elizabeth's whiteness was flatteringly commented upon by foreign visitors. Elizabethans, therefore, quite naturally asked if the blackness of the African's skin was a marker of his or her inner character. Were Africans imbued with the negative traits associated with the colour black? Another concern stemmed from the belief that extreme heat, as was found in Africa, unbalanced the supposed four humours of the body and rendered men more volatile and vengeful – an aspect of a theory known to historians as 'geohumoralism'. Might this be true of black men born under the heat of an African sun?[21] Human blackness was therefore not merely an interesting conundrum to be debated by travellers and philosophers like George Best and John Lok, but a live and pressing issue.

The ways in which Shakespeare interpreted these ideas and intellectual currents has been the subject of a huge amount of scholarship and is too vast a subject to be addressed here. But it is clear that Shakespeare himself was fascinated by the creative possibilities inherent in the symbolic clash between black and white. On stage, black skin – albeit applied with heavy theatrical make-up – was a potentially potent visual device. Yet Shakespeare's exploration and, in *Othello*, subversion of these ideas and themes was only possible because his audience was aware of the same tensions, notions and enigmas. It was because it understood the references and stereotypes involved that Shakespeare was able to challenge and confound them.

The words that Shakespeare puts in the mouths of his black characters suggest that they too are aware of the tensions and debates around blackness, and operate in a world in which attitudes towards their skin colour might differ widely from one encounter to another. On occasion, they pre-emptively request tolerance, aware that they may meet prejudice and intolerance.[22] On other occasions, they are met with warmth and apparent acceptance to which they easily adapt. Racial intolerance was clearly present, both on the stage and in the society that was reflected on it, but such negative attitudes towards Africans were not so ubiquitous as to make other relationships and interactions between black and white people impossible or improper. Most of all in Shakespeare there is contradiction. He repeatedly reflected and refracted what must be presumed to have been a prevailing attitude of his age: that Africans were unattractive and ugly. 'Away you Ethiope,' shouts Lysander at Hermia in

A Midsummer Night's Dream, while in *Much Ado About Nothing* Claudio's love for Hero is so great that it would sustain him even if she had black skin. 'I'll hold my mind were she an Ethiope', he exclaims in Act 5. Shakespeare, however, suggests that there were those who regarded Africans as attractive. In *Two Gentlemen of Verona*, Proteus refers to 'the old saying' that 'Black men are pearls in beauteous ladies' eyes.'

Shakespeare's greatest black character, Othello, is so complex a figure that whole libraries have been written about him. *Othello* can be read as a critique of black male sexuality and as an exploration of the ideas and taboos surrounding racial mixing. Those taboos are scrutinized in some of Shakespeare's most vivid language, which played heavily on sexual ideas that evidently titillated his audiences, who after all had been informed by Hakluyt that Africans were indiscriminate in their sexual encounters and rejected the institution of marriage. But *Othello* cannot be understood only in terms of the racial attitudes of the Elizabethan age. Othello's characterization and his role in the play are also reflective of contemporary debates about Islam and the power of the sixteenth-century Ottoman Empire; the enemy Othello leaves Venice to confront are the Ottoman Turks. What is striking about the play is the depth of Shakespeare's apparent empathy for Othello even as he destroys that which he loves.

In *Principal Navigations*, Richard Hakluyt made an earnest appeal to his countrymen. Alarmed that the Spanish had such a formidable head-start in Africa, he urged Protestant England to commit its energies to establishing colonies in the New World. Unless the English staked their claim and began to draw on the riches of the Americas, Hakluyt warned, the Spanish would ultimately become too wealthy and too powerful to resist.[23] Until the establishment of the Jamestown settlement in Virginia in the early years of the seventeenth century, the English had no permanent colonies in the New World, and had played only a minor part in the Atlantic slave trade. Since the three expeditions of Sir John Hawkins in the 1560s, only a handful of English sea captains had attempted to break into the slave trade, and the few English slaving ventures that had been launched had been opportunistic, ad hoc or piratical.

If any single factor explains why all this changed, and why the fate and prosperity of the British Isles became so firmly tied to Africa, that factor would be sugar. When Englishmen did at last found viable colonies on the smaller and less significant islands of the eastern Caribbean, all of which were prudently distant from the Spanish centres of power, those early settlers discovered that more than any other crop, cane sugar had the capacity to make them rich.

Those first waves of English planters were no more pioneers of New World sugar cultivation than Sir John Hawkins had been the inventor of the slave trade. As was so often the case, in these form-ative decades the English (accompanied later by Irishmen, Scots and Jews) were copying rather than inventing; taking methods and prac-tices developed by others and applying them within their own modest colonies. From Dutch colonists in Brazil, the English borrowed the agricultural skills required to grow sugar cane and the technological knowledge to process the cane juice into sugar and molasses. The adoption of the new crop and the new technologies required to process it taught the English that sugar was inordinately profitable but demanded huge amounts of labour.

The first stages of the settlement and development of the island of Barbados, England's wealthiest West Indian possession, were achieved using white indentured servants and a small number of imported Africans. Indentured servitude was a harsh and often abusive form of apprenticeship, in which poor men and women from the British Isles sold their labour for a period of between seven and nine years. In return, they were given passage to the colonies and food and shelter during the term of service. The more fortunate were also paid wages at the end of the service and were given either a cash payment or a parcel of land upon which they could build a new life. At its best, indentured service made possible forms of social mobility that were unfeasible and almost unheard of in Britain itself. This, at least, was the theory. In ruthless frontier societies like Barbados, many servants were abused and exploited, never receiving their promised rewards and being subject to cruel punishments. Some did not survive their terms of service. Indentured servants were dispatched not just to the West Indies but also to North America, where in Virginia and Maryland English colonists had established tobacco plantations that were almost as labour-hungry as the sugar estates of Barbados. In the first half of the seventeenth century, more than half of all the immigrants who arrived in the North American colonies were indentured servants. However, as labour became more scarce in England after the Civil War, the system of indentured servitude could no longer provide the tobacco planters of Virginia, the Carolinas and Maryland or the sugar planters of Barbados with the manpower required to cultivate their estates.

In Barbados, the nature of sugar itself made the demand for an expanded and dependable source of labour especially urgent. Not only was the cultivation of sugar labour-intensive – more so than tobacco, processing the canes into sugar was time-sensitive and semi-industrial, requiring the establishment during harvesting of something akin to a production line. The fresh-cut cane had to be rapidly transported from the fields to the 'factory', where the cane juice was extracted by heavy rollers. From there it was rushed to the 'boiling house', where the juice was heated and the solution reduced, leaving the raw sugar.

The intensity of sugar production, combined with the decline in the numbers of indentured servants immigrating into the island, provided the planters of Barbados with the economic rationale for the transition towards African slavery. By the 1640s the Barbados planters were abandoning other crops in favour of sugar and were well on the way towards discarding indentured labour. By 1680 there were thirty-eight thousand slaves on Barbados. By the end of the seventeenth century there were fifty thousand. The island was being divided up among wealthy landowners as the English Caribbean entered the hands of men with the funds, credit and contacts required to become established in the sugar business.

In 1661, the sugar planters who dominated the Barbados Assembly passed the Barbados Slave Code, also known as the Barbados Slave Act, which combined a number of previously separate laws and ordinances to formalize slavery as a legally sanctioned and regulated institution. The Slave Code represented a tacit acceptance by the planters that the decline in the numbers of white servants and the booming sugar industry had made it inevitable that the island should become and remain a society in which black slaves were the majority.

In 1637 there were only two hundred Africans on Barbados out of an island population of six thousand. By 1660 the majority of

Barbadians were black Africans, and consequently much of the Slave
Code was focused on measures to prevent uprisings and revolutions
among the enslaved. Slave owners were called upon to monitor their
human property and carry out regular searches of the cabins that
they lived in, in order to prevent weapons falling into their hands.
A system of passes was instituted that required all slaves absent from
the plantations upon which they worked to have a ticket that
accounted for their absence and explained the reasons for their
journey. Those unable to produce the necessary document were to
be subjected to a 'moderate whipping'.[24]

Critically, the Barbados Slave Code drew clear distinctions
between white 'servants' and 'negro' slaves, and it used the terms
'negro' and 'slave' interchangeably. To be black on Barbados was to
be a slave. The Slave Code denounced black people as 'heathenish
brutish and an uncertain dangerous pride of people', whose nature
required that they be subject to rigorous and 'punishionary laws'.[25]
The code set out a long litany of punishments, most of them brutal
and exemplary, to which only black slaves could be exposed. Muti-
lation of the face, slitting of nostrils, branding of cheeks and foreheads
and castration were all deemed acceptable punishments for Africans.
The list of offences for which the approved punishment for black
people was death was expanded to include petty theft and the
destruction of property. When white men, even the lowliest indentured servants, committed similar crimes they were subject to far
less harsh punishments, often penalized by having their terms of
service extended by a number of years.

Most importantly, indentured servants, despite the abuse that
many endured, remained under the protection of the English
common law. They retained the right to trial by jury, which was
specifically denied to 'negroes'. The Barbados Slave Code determined
that 'brutish slaves deserve not for the baseness of the Conditions
to be tried by the legall tryall of twelve Men'.[26]

In this way and others the Slave Code divided Barbados society
along the lines of race. All white men of all classes were accorded
rights that were systematically denied to black people. The planters,
who had long held the white poor in deep disdain, especially Irish
indentured servants and the convict labourers, understood that white
racial unity was an insurance policy that might protect them in the

event of a slave rebellion. They were therefore willing to deliberately blur the distinctions of classes in order to bring racial differences into sharper relief. The Atlantic slave trade had taken Africans from numerous and widely differing cultures and ethnic groups and defined them en masse as 'negroes'. Now the pioneers of English plantation slavery, driven by their desperate desire for security, ushered all Europeans, irrespective of their ethnic or social backgrounds, into the new category of 'white'; a term that had to be explained to newly arriving Europeans who were unfamiliar with the workings of the new slave society. The model quickly spread to other islands.

The decline of Spain and Portugal in the seventeenth century opened the way for predatory rivals to stake territorial claims across the New World. The French, Dutch, Danish, Swedish and the north German states, as well as England, all jostled to obtain territories in the West Indies. For the English, the waning of Spanish power made it possible for the Barbados blueprint to be applied elsewhere. When the English Protectorate under Oliver Cromwell went to war with Spain in the 1650s, the English seized the island of Jamaica. Twenty-five times the size of Barbados, Jamaica was a vast and glittering prize. As it was cleared and parcelled out into sugar estates, the slave population soared. Many of the first and most eager English settlers on Jamaica were Barbadian planters who had the skills but not the acres to make their fortunes. The same semi-industrial processes of sugar cultivation were imported into Jamaica along with the Barbados Slave Code, which was copied almost verbatim. The Jamaican Slave Act of 1696 barely deviated from a slave act passed in Barbados eight years earlier. Where the two islands differed was that Jamaican planters proved more reluctant to execute slaves accused of petty offences. This was not because the men who ran Jamaica were more moderate or humane than their countrymen in Barbados, but because in its formative decades Jamaica struggled to secure enough black slaves to meet the demands of its booming plantation economy.

Something similar took place in the English colonies of North America. Like the settlers of Barbados and Jamaica, the tobacco farmers of Virginia and Maryland, who had clustered around the Chesapeake Bay area, had established their plantations using indentured labourers — English and Irish, both men and women. The increasing availability of African slaves meant that here again, over the course of the seventeenth century, there was a shift away from the indentured servitude of whites and towards the enslavement of growing numbers of black men and women.

In 1619, at the first English settlement of Jamestown, Virginia, '20 and odd Negroes' had been landed — an event that is often regarded as the symbolic beginning of African slavery in North America. The Africans in question were landed by the Dutch warship the *White Lion*. The vessel was on a privateering mission and had intercepted a Portuguese slave ship, the *San Juan Bautista*. The twenty Africans brought ashore at Jamestown had been taken from the hold of the Portuguese slaver and had not been trafficked directly from Africa by English traders, for the English, even now that they possessed embryonic colonies in the New World, had yet to properly enter the slave trade. The few English slave-trading missions that had taken place were at this point small-scale and ad hoc.

In 1626 two traders from London and Southampton, Maurice Thompson and Thomas Combe, arrived in the island of St Kitts with sixty enslaved Africans. Eleven years later Nicholas Crispe, a trader who had been granted a licence to transport slaves from the Guinea Coast by Charles I, had the ship *Talbot* fitted out 'to take nigers and to carry them to foreign parts'.[27] There are records of a handful of other English missions, but in the first half of the seventeenth century most English mariners had rightly concluded that privateering offered an easier route to wealth, and continued to prey upon the treasure fleets that ferried gold and silver to Spain from her New World colonies, rather than on the people of Africa's Atlantic coast. Then, within the span of a single decade, the English abandoned their earlier reticence and launched themselves wholeheartedly into the slave trade.

The restoration of the English monarchy in 1660 placed upon the throne a king who understood the potential profitability of an English slave trade that could provide the English colonists of the West Indies and North America with African captives. Charles II and his inner circle, which included the King's brother James, Duke of York, and his cousin Prince Rupert, regarded the joint-stock company as the perfect instrument with which to profitably establish such a trade. The first company to be focused upon the African trade was the Company of Royal Adventurers Trading to Africa, founded in 1660. Its charter stipulated that the company would have the 'whole, entire and only trade for the buying and selling bartering and exchanging of for or with any Negroes, slaves, goods wares and merchandises' to be found in Africa.[28] The company operated until 1667, by which time it had delivered to the English planters of the New World colonies sixteen thousand African slaves, yet was heavily in debt.

The following year a new joint-stock company, the Company of Gambia Adventures, was formed and given the right to trade to the north of the Bight of Benin. It was in 1670, under the Gambia Adventures, that the first fortress on Bunce Island was constructed. Two years later in 1672, King Charles II established the Royal African Company, which was given a huge scope of operation including the 'full power to make and declare peace and war with any of the heathen nations' that lay within its zone of operations. It also had the right to call upon the Royal Navy to search and seize the vessels of 'interlopers' – independent English traders who attempted to trade along the African coast, from Morocco to Cape of Good Hope in South Africa, over which the company claimed British monopoly rights.[29]

The Royal African Company was responsible for transporting and enslaving more Africans than any other company in British history. More than any other institution it established Britain as a key player in the transatlantic slave trade, setting her on an upward trajectory that, by the eighteenth century, would enable her to become the dominant slave-trading power in Europe. Its most significant years of operation were between 1672 and the early 1720s, during which it dispatched over five hundred expeditions to Africa. Within a decade of the Royal African Company's formation, the English share of the Atlantic trade had increased from 33 per cent to 74 per cent, mainly at the expense of the Dutch and the French.[30] Over the whole of its existence the Royal African Company dispatched into slavery around a hundred and fifty thousand African men, women and children.[31]

In a strange mirroring of the situation that had prevailed on the African coast in the 1550s and 1560s, the Royal African Company used its ships and coastal fortresses to defend its monopoly from interlopers, just as the Portuguese had attempted to do in the face of English incursions over a century earlier. In the late seventeenth century, the illegal traders were not foreigners but Englishmen, the so-called 'separate traders to Africa'. These independent merchants were men determined to break into the African trade and defy the right of Stuart monarchs to claim the entire trade for the benefit of themselves and their supporters. The Royal African Company confiscated both ships and cargoes and imprisoned the interlopers, some of whom died while incarcerated in the company's African fortresses. The historian William A. Pettigrew has chronicled how the separate traders took on what they called the 'African Monster' and launched a political campaign against the Royal African Company, demanding that access to the slave trade be made a right of all Englishmen. In their envisioning of English freedoms, the right to trade anywhere, with anyone and in any commodity was placed among those natural freedoms that the separate traders claimed had been bestowed upon all Englishmen. Stone-blind to irony, they argued, audaciously and amorally, that the right to enslave Africans was a defining feature of English freedom. Seeking to influence public opinion, they clamoured that the trade in enslaved human beings should be for the benefit of the whole country, rather than just the monarchy and the cabal that surrounded them, and energetically propagated this view through a war of pamphlets, lobbying and persuasion.

From time to time, the voices of the West Indian plantation owners and the tobacco farmers of Virginia and Maryland were raised in support of these contentions and in opposition to the monopoly of the Royal African Company.[32] For England to thrive, for her balance of trade to be healthy and for her power to be extended into the Atlantic world, the slave trade had to be deregulated and privatized, they reasoned. Without such a move, the sugar and tobacco plantations of the Americas had no viable future, and England would no longer be able to supply the nation with those highly desirable commodities. Few people disagreed with the economic case, and fewer still concerned themselves with the plight of the enslaved Africans whose commoditized bodies were placed at the centre of a debate about the nature of English freedom.

To the individual traders the Royal African Company was a tyranny. To the owners of plantations in the English West Indies its greatest failure was its inefficiency. Despite enormously increasing the English market share in the Atlantic slave trade, the company had demonstrated itself largely incapable of meeting the growing demand for enslaved Africans in Barbados and on the tobacco estates of the North American colonies. After many years of campaigning and political lobbying, the royal monopoly was weakened, and in 1712 finally abandoned. The company to which Charles II had awarded a charter to run for 1,000 years in 1672 was effectively disbanded after eighty years, finally being wound up in 1752.

Now the independent traders were turned loose upon the shores of West Africa. These private slave-traders, operating in a newly privatized and deregulated economy, between them increased the scale of the trade beyond anything the Royal African Company as a lone monopoly company had been able to achieve. Between 1673 and 1688, the years during which the Royal African Company had been able to largely enforce its monopoly, the company had managed an average of twenty-three slave-trading voyages per year. After the end of the monopoly, in the years between 1714 and 1729 the independent traders dispatched an average of seventy-seven expeditions.[33] One estimate puts the increase in the carrying capacity of the trade after the end of the royal monopoly at around 60 per cent.

The elbowing aside of the Royal African Company, precipitated in part by the fall of the Stuart monarchy itself during the Glorious Revolution of 1688, was the opening act in the era of the Atlantic slave trade and the one that we know most about. Thus began the period of the so-called 'respectable trade', in which the merchants of Bristol, Liverpool, Glasgow and other small British cities – the so-called 'outports' – vastly enriched themselves and their cities.

The effects of the end of the monopoly were felt just as acutely on the other side of the Atlantic. Finally, the plantation owners of Barbados, St Kitts, Jamaica and the North American colonies could be supplied with enslaved Africans on a scale large enough to allow for their exponential expansion and enrichment. In the tobacco-producing regions of North America, the newly secured availability of expanded numbers of enslaved 'Negro servants' allowed the plantation owners to begin to make the full and irrevocable transition away from white indentured servitude and towards the full reliance on African slavery. This transition was to be written into the laws of

Virginia in the following decades, in a series of slave laws that formalized the binary, black and white, nature of Virginia society. Like Barbados, the North American colonies became full slave societies.

The English domination of the North Atlantic slave trade led eventually to enormous and devastating transformations within the societies on the coasts of West Africa. During the same decades, the sugar economy remade the Caribbean, transforming previously rather idyllic, heavily forested islands into closely managed, highly artificial landscapes constantly being reshaped and reworked by vast armies of enslaved people whose origins lay three thousand miles away. The plantation led to new methods of management and new principles for the organization of workers. A flurry of books on estate management appeared in print. The sugar estates of the West Indies became, at this early stage, more advanced than the proto-industrial factories that were just beginning to appear in Britain.

Also appearing in Britain were the West India planters themselves. Enormously enriched, infamously ostentatious, they left the West Indies in order to express their incredible wealth upon a larger stage. They bought property, invested in land and married off their sons and daughters to the old landed aristocracy. The phrase 'as rich as a West Indian' entered common usage, and the excesses and conspicuous consumption of the returned West India planter became the subject of satire as well as the source of envy.[34]

Another side effect of the expansion in the sugar economy and the slave trade that was noted by anxious social commentators was the hundreds and then thousands of black people who were shipped into Britain by returning plantation owners and the captains of slave-trading ships. In the last decades of the seventeenth century and throughout the eighteenth century, Africans arrived as slaves and as free people in greater numbers than in any previous period. From those decades onwards, the black presence in Britain has been unbroken and continuous. The presence of these black Georgians became a recognized symbol of the burgeoning new age of globalism, prosperity and brutality.

THREE

'For Blacks or Dogs'

Not long ago – just thirty years or so – historians felt justified in complaining that the popular image of Georgian Britain was a reductive and myopic one. Most 'educated people', they grumbled, understood the Georgian past primarily through the buildings and relics it had left behind.[1] For most of the twentieth century, Georgian Britain was indeed a victim of its own historical myth, its wider history obscured behind its architectural achievement. No age before or since – including that of the fussy and over-decorative Victorians – managed to match that of the Georgians in its capacity to transpose the virtues of order, elegance and rationalism into bricks and mortar, Bath stone and stucco, silverware and furniture. The Britain they had created, with its neat city squares, tranquil, effortless churches and restrained, perfectly proportioned homes, left in its historical wake a sense of stability and even serenity that encouraged subsequent generations to view the period through the distorting prism of architecture, art and design.

Fine art further conspired to fix the gaze in that general direction. In many of the most celebrated street scenes painted by home-grown artists like Samuel Scott, and by artistic visitors to Britain like Canaletto, it is often the architecture that dominates, the streets are rendered placid and left half empty. Urban landscape paintings of the period tend to be urban only in the thinnest sense. The stench, dirt, danger and cruelty that moulded the lives of so many eighteenth-century city dwellers are all notably absent. Likewise, when the Georgians mapped their cities they captured that same sense of studied tranquillity. In Georgian maps it is always late afternoon on a summer's day. The neat lines of trees that fringe every ornate garden, frame every public building and line the major thoroughfares cast long afternoon shadows across an empty cityscape, heightening the symmetry of the street plan.

Today, however, another vision of the Georgian age fires the British imagination, that of the Georgian street, populated and alive. While we admire Georgian architecture we are now also drawn to the dark and seedy side of that hypocritical age. We are fascinated by its great nocturnal empire of wine, prostitution, blood sports, card games and vice and long to peep into the homosexual, cross-dressing underworld of the molly houses and meet the bloodied heroes of eighteenth-century Britain's bare-knuckle-boxing circuit. We find that England in Tom Jones and Moll Flanders and the art of William Hogarth, an artist who was without question one of Britain's greatest storytellers – in any medium.

Part of what draws twenty-first-century viewers to the abyssal labyrinth of the Georgian slums, the underworlds of the brothels, prisons and gin-houses, is that special frisson of excitement that comes from self-recognition. Despite being more distant from us in historical time than the age of the Victorians, Britain under the Georges seems a more authentic representation of the British as we really are, before our vices, appetites and proclivities were partially concealed behind the veneer of nineteenth-century respectability. Both nations – theirs and ours – were awash with self-destructive, orgiastic excess. Although we live in cities that are more Victorian than Georgian any tour of those cities late on a Saturday night, when the Victorian cult of respectability has been partially dissolved by a tsunami of cheap beer and hooch, reveals the British street returned to the age of Hogarth and John Bull. The early twenty-first century's binge-drinking culture is a milder version of the eighteenth-century gin craze, re-enacted with alcopops and 'two-for-one' happy hour offers. Hogarth's celebrated *Gin Lane* is an eighteenth-century rendering of scenes that can be found in the pubs, clubs and Accident & Emergency Departments of any of our larger towns. Young women brought up in our modern drinking culture have given birth to babies bearing the indelible facial stamp of foetal alcohol syndrome, the same macabre death-mask worn by the infant in the centre of frame in *Gin Lane*, as he falls from the arms of his inebriated mother.

Like us the Georgians were obsessed with fame, scandal and sex. The transient fame of today's WAGs, reality-TV stars and kiss-and-tell girls neatly mirrors the various progresses and falls of the star courtesans of Covent Garden, and the celebrated rakes who fluttered away ancient family wealth in a single season at the card tables. The final comeuppances of Hogarth's harlots and idlers are all very much in keeping with the familiar modern narrative of rise, hubris and fall, the subtext of every tabloid-enabled celebrity career. For despite the wigs, the bustling, fussy clothing and much else that is superficial and unimportant, the hypocritical, corrupt, sentimental, acquisitive, nationalistic, xenophobic, debauched, drunken, scandal-obsessed, globally-aware, riot-prone, debt-fuelled, multi-racial Britain of the late eighteenth century is instantly redolent of us.

But the kinship between the two ages runs even deeper. Both Britains – that of the late eighteenth century and early twenty-first century – were sustained by illusory, booming, bubble economies, built on the shifting sands of credit and debt. And in both most people appeared to be getting richer. Yesterday's luxuries became firmly established as today's necessities, commodities to which all but the poorest had automatic access. The eighteenth century, as much as the early twenty-first, was an era fascinated by new products, tastes and fashions. In both cases this was partly made possible by the unseen labour of foreign peoples, living and labouring in faraway lands. In the twenty-first century the shadowy figures whose plight plays on our collective conscience are the millions who toil in factories and sweat shops making our clothes and mobile phones and the impoverished Indians who construct football stadiums and fantasy towers in desert kingdoms that we visit on our holidays. In the eighteenth century the invisible enablers of everyday luxury were Africans, slaves who produced the tobacco that millions smoked in little clay pipes and snorted as snuff, and the cane sugar that in two generations went from a frivolous extravagance – added to the food of the rich in tiny quantities – to one of the main sources of calories for the poor.

The enslaved Africans who were the unwilling producers of those commodities were separated from the consumers by an ocean, and gradually by the developing idea of race. But as in the twenty-first century, the borders between 'here' and 'there' had a tendency to break down. People, money and ideas surged across the ocean, transitioning between Britain and the slave societies she had created in the Americas. Enslaved Africans were carried along on the global currents of an Atlantic economy that was anchored in three continents. Some were transported to Britain by returning plantation owners, soldiers and colonial functionaries who had grown accustomed to being waited on by enslaved servants and felt it natural that they would take their portable property – human or otherwise – home with them to Britain. Other black people were conveyed to British ports in the ships of the triangular trade, and offered for sale by the commanders of slave ships, like any other newly imported commodity. The forms of slavery that were practised in Britain were racial, in that they only applied to black people, but the picture is more complex. The story of black people in Britain during the age of the slave is not that of the transplanting of New World slavery onto British soil. Firstly, not all the black people who came to Britain in that period were slaves. Some made their own way to the centre of the empire, through their own ingenuity and tenacity; many of this group were sailors. More significantly a proportion of those who did arrive as slaves discovered that the borders between slavery and service were not nearly as well delineated in Britain as they were in the binary, slave societies of the West Indies and North America. There is evidence that some of them were able to navigate within Georgian society and to some extent and in some cases renegotiate their positions. Young enslaved children who were sold off to wealthy families sometimes spent their whole lives in service, but an unknown number came to be regarded as favoured servants rather than as human property. The most fortunate were educated by their 'owners', some were even apprenticed. The social mobility that underwrites the incredible lives of the most famous of the black Georgians – Ignatius Sancho, Phillis Wheatley, Olaudah Equiano, Francis Barber and Bill Richmond – owed much to the education and opportunities opened up for them by the well-connected families within which they were ensconced, as well as to their own remarkable talents.

While ideas of race and African inferiority developed rapidly over the period of the British slave trade, and although those ideas were energetically propagated through the writings of men like Edward

Long and Philip Thicknesse, it is not clear how influential they were among the great mass of the people. Historians have searched without great success for the black 'communities' of Georgian London – where the majority of black people were to be found – and various regions of the capital have been identified as potential sites where such communities might have gathered, but the evidence suggests that black Georgians were everywhere, scattered across London, and not limited to any district. Free or enslaved, or of some status unde-. fined by the law and unclear to them or their purported 'owners', they were numerous enough to have been a feature of city life but still unusual enough to have remained an exotic novelty, worthy of mention in the accounts of travellers and the reports of journalists. They worked as servants in the homes of the wealthy, as liveried coachmen and pageboys, highly sought after and highly visible in the fashionable streets of the rapidly expanding city. They were bandsmen in the army, sailors both free and enslaved, on merchant ships and even on ships of the triangular trade. They worked as bargemen on the Thames or as stevedores on its banks. There were black people in the bars and taverns, some of which were key meeting places for black servants living otherwise atomized lives. There were black beggars on the streets struggling to survive, sharing their misery with equally desperate white people, with whom they formed part-nerships, friendships and marriages. As there had been in the London of Shakespeare there were black prostitutes and there may have been at least one brothel in the city that made the sexual services of black women its speciality. A former slave known as Black Harriott who, one report patronizingly claimed, 'had attained a degree of politeness, scarce to be paralleled in an African female', became a famous cour-tesan before her untimely and tragic death.[2] Her career was recorded in the book *Nocturnal Revels, or the History of King's-Place and Other Modern Nunneries*, a late-eighteenth-century exposé of vice in the capital that shocked contemporary readers and detailed the sexual proclivities of a number of aristocrats.

As was the case through much of British history, black people were conscripted into the world of performance, their novelty making them attractive to impresarios; it was only later that the notion developed that black people were especially musical or gifted in dancing or singing. Georgian prints reveal that there were black performers in the hugely popular fairs. Hogarth's depiction of South-wark Fair in 1733 has a black trumpeter in the foreground, entertaining the crowd. In other various guises over two dozen black people appear in his works, some appearing in his most famous sequences – *A Harlot's Progress* and *Marriage à la Mode*.[3] Hogarth was recording his city and his nation as he saw it and as it was, chaotic, violent, consumed by class conflict and multi-racial. Black people were part of that Georgian world and for those clear-eyed enough to make the connection they were a reminder of the realm from which they had been delivered and to which the less fortunate were returned; that vast empire of sugar, slavery and misery three thousand miles away across the Atlantic.

In 1744 a notice in the *Daily Advertiser* read,

> To be sold. A pretty little Negro Boy, about nine Years old, and well limb'd. If not dispos'd of, is to be sent to the West Indies in six days Time. He is to be seen at the Dolphin Tavern in Tower Street.[4]

This advertisement for the sale of a child from a London pub was sandwiched between a listing for Scottish linen, 'of the best Fabrick and Colour', and an offer of employment for 'Two Journeymen Taylors' who might be willing to ply their trade in the West Indies. It is not unique. Historians have found around forty listings like it in English newspapers, and eight in Scottish periodicals, all from between 1709 and 1792.[5] There are without doubt others that lie as yet undiscovered. In 1709 the *Tatler* offered 'a black boy, twelve years of age, fit to wait on a gentleman'. That child could be procured from 'Dennis's Coffee-house in Finch Lane'.[6] Half a century later the *London Advertiser* carried a notice of 'a Negro boy age about fourteen years old, warranted free from any distemper' who, it was assured, 'has been used two years to all kinds of household work, and to wait on table; his price is £25, and would not be sold but the person he belongs to is leaving off business.' Those interested were casually instructed to, 'Apply at the bar of George Coffee House in Chancery Lane, over the Gate'.[7]

Although, as we shall see, some black people were able to move around within British society and integrate and assimilate with the white people they lived amongst, the reality remains that some Africans lived and died as slaves in Britain in the seventeenth and eighteenth centuries. There is still a misconception that slavery was restricted to the colonies of the Caribbean and North America, and while there is no question that the full-blooded brutality of plantation slavery was a colonial phenomenon, unfreedom and the sale of black human beings was a feature of British life between the 1650s and the close of the eighteenth century. The newspapers tell us that transactions for the sale of human beings were conducted not just from pubs but also in the thriving and fashionable coffee-houses, particularly in the key port towns of Liverpool, Bristol and London. Slaves were sold by art dealers, a few of whom appear to have carried on a profitable sideline, auctioning slaves alongside paintings, two commodities only available to the wealthy and increasingly targeted at those newly enriched by wealth from property in the West Indies, human and otherwise.[8] Black people were passed on in British wills and inherited alongside real estate and livestock. In 1701 Thomas Papillon of London left his son an enslaved man, 'whom I take to be in the nature of my goods and chattels.'[9] That Papillon felt the need to assert his claim to this enslaved man as chattel hints at some understanding on his part that the laws of England were unclear on the exact status of slaves, as they were to remain for at least another seventy years. In October 1718 the Bristol merchant Beecher Fleming evidently felt more confident about his right to leave 'my negro boy, named Tallow' to Mrs Mary Beecher, presumably his widow.[10]

The slaves listed for sale in advertisements tended to be recent arrivals, shipped in from the West Indies. A custom developed in the slave ships that plied the triangular trade that their captains were entitled to bring back a handful of slaves to sell in Britain. It was in effect a bonus that increased their personal profit from each voyage. Bristol appears to have been at the centre of this custom and there are advertisements in the seventeenth- and eighteenth-century newspapers of that city offering 'Negro' boys for sale to 'gentlemen or ladies'. *Farley's Bristol Newspaper* of 31 August 1728 included an advertisement from Captain John Gwythen who offered for sale 'a Negro man about 20 years old, well limbed, fit to serve a gentleman or to be instructed in a trade'.[11]

Other enslaved black people were brought to Britain by owners who had no intention of offering them for sale. Planters, merchants, soldiers, ships' officers and officials who had spent time in the Caribbean sometimes returned home with their domestic slaves, who had attended to them in the Americas. These returnees saw no reason to change their habits and preferred slaves to paid servants, for obvious reasons. In 1752, when Colonel Richard Bathurst from Jamaica sold his unprofitable estates he brought with him the seven-year-old slave Francis Barber, who was to become the servant and companion of Samuel Johnson. It is also certain that some of the enslaved children who were brought to Britain were the mixed-race illegitimate children of West India planters; this may have been the case with Francis Barber and Colonel Bathurst, who ensured that Francis was educated and legally freed and left him money in his will. The captains of slave ships also retained slaves, and while they were happy to augment their profits through the sale of one or two 'privilege negroes' carried to Britain on the last leg of their triangular journeys, their personal slaves, it seems, were not for sale. They remained with them even when they settled back in Britain, where they worked as their attendants and became conspicuous demonstrations of their personal wealth. A Bristol newspaper of 1746 carried a notice from one Captain Eaton offering a guinea for the capture and return of his slave Mingo, whom he had owned for eight years.[12] Eleven years later a different Bristol periodical reported that the human property of another of the city's mariners, Captain Bouchier of Keynsham, had absconded.[13]

This practice of bringing slaves into Britain to work as servants in British households raised serious concerns in certain quarters. The magistrate Sir John Fielding, half-brother to Henry Fielding, the author of *Tom Jones*, complained in 1762 of 'The immense confusion that has arose in the families of merchants and other gentlemen who have estates in the West Indies from the great numbers of Negro slaves they have brought into this Kingdom.'[14] A writer to the *London Chronicle* in 1765 calling himself 'F Freeman' complained along similar lines of the number of 'Negro and east India servants, who of late have become too abundant in this kingdom'. Why he was so affronted by the sight of black humanity in London is not clear.[15]

*

How great was the influx of black people into Britain that so worried men like Sir John Fielding? That remains the most tantalizing and intractable of the many unknowables. The size of the black British population in the age of slavery is a mystery that lies beyond the capacity of historians to solve. All we have are the estimates that were made at the time. The author of a letter to the *Gentleman's Magazine* in 1764 believed 'that the number in this metropolis only, is supposed to be near 20,000'.[16] In 1789 a concerned commentator put the black population of Britain, as opposed to just London, at around forty thousand. A correspondent writing to the *Morning Chronicle* in 1765 was of the opinion that London's black population had reached thirty thousand, while the Committee for the Relief of the Black Poor founded in 1786 concluded that there were between three and five thousand black people in the capital. In 1772 an estimate of around fifteen thousand was cited during the famous Somerset case and was, it seems, accepted as the best available estimate by the Chief Justice of England, Lord Mansfield. The Jamaican planter Edward Long, one of the fathers of British racism, of whom we shall hear more later, had earlier estimated there were as few as three thousand black people in Britain. This conservative estimate, which might well be closer to the real figure than any other tally, rather undermined Long's efforts to frighten the British public with apocalyptic visions of their nation brought to chaos by a large and rapidly expanding black community, whose unrestrained sexuality was contaminating the blood of the English; so Long later increased his estimate to between fourteen and fifteen thousand, putting it in line with the figure heard in court that same year.[17] This allowed him to demand, in his somewhat hysterical tract *Candid Reflections*, that 'some restraint should be laid on the unnatural increases of blacks imported' into Britain.[18] Anxious to establish some sense of scale to the black population that appears so vividly in newspaper advertisements, paintings, memoirs and letters, historians have tended to accept figures of between ten and fifteen thousand, but as the historian James Walvin has pointed out these figures remain estimates, perhaps little better than guesses, no matter how often they are repeated.[19]

The records are similarly mute as to where black people lived in Georgian Britain. What can be said with certainty is that the majority of black Georgians lived in London, with lesser but significant numbers in Bristol and Liverpool. There may have been clusters of black people in various districts of the capital. The St Giles' area was said to be home to a black community known as the 'St Giles' blackbirds', but the sources for this are vague.[20] There may have also been other clusters in other parts of the city in the second half of the eighteenth century, but what seems doubtful is that these clusters amounted to what we would consider communities. There is no suggestion that there were ethnic ghettos in which black people made up anything even approaching the majority of the population.

Visitors to the capital from abroad commented on the numbers of black people they saw in the city. London's reputation as a city in which black domestic slaves were common, combined with the capital's place as a node in the Atlantic economy, was so well established that when the Russian Tsarina dispatched her agents to purchase a 'number of the finest best made black boys in order to be sent to Petersburgh as attendants on her Russian Majesty' that shopping party came to London to make its purchases.[21]

The numbers question is not the only difficulty. The list of what we do not know is long. How many of the black people who came to Britain in the seventeenth and eighteenth centuries came as free people and how many as slaves? How were those who were enslaved regarded by white Britons who had never been to the Americas and were as unused to the sight of bondage as they were to the presence of Africans? Were those who lived as slaves exposed to anything like the levels of violence that was a routine feature of slavery in the colonies? How common was it for slaves in Britain to escape and seek to merge into the free black population? We can only guess at the answers through the fragmentary snapshots of individual lives that lie in official records, newspapers, court reports and other documents. However, the distance between us and them, between their world and our own, can be partially and momentarily suspended through art, as it is possible to see the faces of black Britons from the seventeenth and eighteenth centuries staring back at us, from portraits and paintings scattered across Britain, in private collections and public galleries. Black Britons can been found in formal group portraits by Reynolds and Zoffany as well as in the earthy depictions of Georgian street life produced by Hogarth. In both cases these black figures usually appear individually and in the margins; they are rarely a central figure – although Hogarth broke that rule on a few occasions. Almost all of these black figures are servants, slaves and attendants, though a tiny number of the black faces captured on canvas in the eighteenth century are those of the most celebrated, educated and fortunate black Britons who rose to prominence and had their own dedicated portraits painted.

That black servants and slaves appear in such numbers in British paintings during the age of slavery is largely due to a fashion among the rich for enslaved black children, a trend that seems to have begun in Britain some time around 1650 and largely faded by the end of the eighteenth century. It was a fashion that united some unlikely constituencies; the commanders of slave ships, returned plantation owners, colonial officials and soldiers, as well as kings and queens. Black slave boys – and they usually were boys – became prized status symbols. There were certainly some black female maids in Britain but as they were deemed less fashionable they appear less often in art. As they were paid less, female servants, of any colour, were more common and therefore a far less potent statement of wealth and conspicuous consumption. We do not know, and never will, how many were formally slaves and how many might have been regarded more as servants, nor do we fully understand how the borders between those two conditions were policed and managed, and the likelihood is that it varied enormously from family to family and from case to case, as well as over time. In formal portraits these little black boys appear alongside their masters and mistresses as human ornaments. They are usually in the margins of the painting, sometimes pushed up against the frame. Their function is to indicate that the main subject of the portrait is a woman or a man of high social standing, someone who is educated, knowledgeable and a participant, in some way, in the intoxicatingly exciting New World economy. Enslaved black servants were signifiers of what the Georgians called rank, a word that was important to them but that has lost much of the meaning it conveyed in the eighteenth century. As the historian David Dabydeen has written, 'the black existed merely

to reflect upon the white'.[22] It was an extreme form of objectifica-
tion, one that was sometimes emphasized by having these black
children pose alongside other 'products' of the tropics – exotic
fruits, monkeys, and parrots and other birds that were rare and
sought-after.

Both on canvas and in daily life the effect of owning an enslaved
black pageboy could be magnified further through costume and dress.
The clothes worn by the black boys in these paintings and described
in various documents were designed to signify the wealth and rank
of the master or mistress. The portraits show little boys and young
men – often just teenagers – in liveried coats, of reds, blues and
golden yellows, with metal buttons and neat waistcoats. Newspaper
notices for the recapture of escaped black pageboys describe the
outfits we see in the portraits – outfits which like the wearer
remained the property of the master. 'A NEGRO MAN, about 17
or 18 Years Old' who had fled from slavery in Bristol was reported
as wearing 'a brown Livery Coat lined with Red, red Buttons Holes
and Collar, red Waistcoat, a Pair of old Leather Breeches pieced at
the Knee, a black Leather Cap and a Pair of black ribbed Stockings'.[23]
The outfits depicted on canvas and described in the newspaper
notices sometimes reveal a confused jumble of exoticism, orientalism
and geographic confusion. Black slave boys appear in the paintings
wearing costumes and headdresses influenced by the styles of the
Indian and the Ottoman world, rather than anything authentically
African. A notice that offered a reward of 'five Gines [sic]' for the
return of David Marat, a seventeen-year-old runaway, described him
as wearing a 'Cloath Livery, Lin'd with Blew, and Princes-mettal
Buttons . . . with a Turbant on his Head'.[24] In some portraits the
turbans appear to be made of silk and come adorned with feathers.

Georgian portrait artists took dubious pleasure in contrasting
the skin colours between the pageboys and their mistresses to add
further layers of meaning. Black skin was generally regarded as a
useful artistic device, in portraiture and beyond, which could be
used to highlight the presumed superiority and beauty of whiteness,
in an age in which both women and men whitened their skin with
lead powder, which slowly poisoned them and ironically resulted in
the slow blackening of their skin. The inclusion of a pearl ring in
the ears of enslaved boys in some portraits was a beloved trope,

allowing portraitists to further highlight contrasts between shimmering white pearls and gleaming black skin. This fascination with contrast was so pronounced that slaves with darker complexions appear, on occasions, to have been valued more highly than those with lighter skin. The intensity of blackness was a significant draw to those who sought a black pageboy as an ostentatious accessory. An advertisement from *Williamson's Liverpool Advertiser* of 1756 read, 'Wanted immediately a Black Boy. He must be of a deep black complexion'.[25] The exoticizing effects of dark skin, liveried clothes and oriental turbans was in many cases finished off with classical names that were ascribed to these boys and young men – Caesar, Scipio and Pompey were all recorded.

In portraits of male owners these black slaves tend to be older footmen rather than pageboys, and most look like teenagers. They attend to their master's horses or offer drinks or food. A young black man in livery holds the reins of his master's horse in George Stubbs' painting *Henry Fox and the Third Earl of Albemarle Shooting at Goodwood* of 1759. Dressed in red and yellow livery he sits watching the action, alone except for the earl's dog. A young black boy wearing a silk turban and feather leads the horse of Frederick William Ernest in a Joshua Reynolds portrait of 1767, and a similarly youthful black man in exquisite livery adjusts the even grander costume of the Prince of Wales himself, in another work by Reynolds.[26] In a very masculine portrait that is now believed to be of Charles Goring of Wiston, a black pageboy in blue and red livery presents his master with the woodcock he has just shot, staring at him appreciatively and intently.

When the main subjects of eighteenth-century portraits are female, the pageboys offer their mistresses more suitably feminine items. Trays of flowers are a common device but ornate boxes of smelling salts are also popular. Elizabeth Murray, Lady Tollemache is shown in a portrait from around 1651 with a young black servant, who wears a silk shirt and a pearl earring.[27] Leaning forward he stares fixedly at his mistress' face and presents her with a bowl of flowers. Nearly a century later Elizabeth Murray's descendants commissioned a rather crowded portrait of Lady Grace Carteret, Countess of Dysart, who is painted with her child, a black servant, a cockatoo and a spaniel.[28] Little has changed. The black boy is younger than his predecessor and wears a liveried coat, but again has a pearl earring and stares at the main subjects of the portrait. He holds a cockatoo rather than a tray of flowers; the bird, like him, acts as an easily decipherable symbol of the family's links to the New World and its riches, which had considerably expanded since 1651. Everything was done to emphasize the supposed inferiority of the black person in these portraits. Not insignificantly, enslaved Africans are repeatedly pictured alongside dogs, cockatoos, monkeys and other pets. The result is that although such paintings are by definition group portraits, the black people appear in them as lonely isolated figures.

The images preserved on canvas are affected snapshots of the lives of the sitters and the pageboys, but they were representations of a living fashion and real lifestyles of conspicuous wealth and consumption, lifestyles that were broadcast through fashionable society. The ladies who sat for their portraits with black pageboys also paraded around the more fashionable parts of London with them in tow. The pageboy's day-to-day role was to attend to his mistress' whims. At the theatre they accompanied them to their box and carried their opera glasses. When entertaining at home pageboys prepared their tea and generally impressed lower-ranking visitors. Plate 2 of William Hogarth's brilliant rise and fall satire, *A Harlot's Progress*, includes an enslaved black pageboy. The child is shown attending to his mistress, Moll the country girl corrupted by city life. He carries a teapot or a kettle – it is difficult to determine which – but Moll's self-destructive debauchery makes for a chaotic rendering of this supposedly refined scene.

That Hogarth gave his 'Harlot' an enslaved pageboy hints at a problem. What was fashionable for wealthy ladies of the gentry and aristocracy was also vogue among what were called 'town misses', the high-class prostitutes of Georgian London. In 1680 an eight-page pamphlet, *The Character of a Town-Miss*, appeared. A nasty, judgemental, misogynistic little tome, it relishes in the inevitable fall and diseased ruin of a London prostitute and smugly rages against social climbing. It also identifies the black enslaved servant as one of the signifiers of the town miss, stating, 'She hath always two necessary Implements about her, a Blackamoor, and a little dog; for without these, she would be neither Fair nor Sweet'.[29] These two accessories are united again in satirical prints from the time. In one, entitled *Heyday! Is this my daughter Anne!*, a farmer's wife arrives in London and is shocked to see her daughter parading through a park wearing an extravagant flowing dress and with an enormous powdered wig, piled several feet above her head, a comically exaggerated portrayal of the attire of a lady of fashion. In a 1779 version of the same satire, published by Robert Wilkinson, Anne has a lap dog snapping at her feet, but an alternative version of 1771, by Carington Bowles, has the lap dog held in the arms of a black pageboy, presumably enslaved. He wears the customary livery coat and feathered turban.[30] Yet another version of 1774 came hand-tinted. Entitled *Be not amaz'd Dear Mother – It is indeed your Daughter Anne*, it shows the pageboy painted with the darkest complexion; his livery consists of a red waistcoat and gold-coloured coat, the feather in his turban an ostentatious pink.* The black pageboy had become firmly established as an essential accessory among the richest and the most fashionable, but also as a symbol of morally dubious extravagance and show.

Not all the black people who landed in British ports in the period of the British slave trade – from the 1660s to 1807 – were enslaved. Among the free black people were sailors, who like their white shipmates were discharged from ships in British ports – most notably Liverpool and London – and there awaited employment on another vessel. While waiting they lived around the docks and although their populations were constantly shifting and highly globalized, black seafarers might have the best claim to have organized the first geographic black 'communities' in eighteenth-century Britain. Yet even in the seafarers' districts black sailors were always a small minority. While there were slaves working on British ships in the eighteenth century some of the sailors who are recorded in Britain are known to have received wages, and so were, by definition, employed rather than enslaved.[31] Wills and other records reveal that

---

* The other, numerous follies of Anne were the subjects of a long series of satirical prints and the trope of the country girl corrupted into folly by the city was more generally a favourite of the Georgian era, as evidenced by Hogarth's *A Harlot's Progress*.

some received prize money, for taking part in the capture of enemies' ships and goods.

There was no obligation on ships' captains to record the race of sailors they recruited; some recorded their places of birth and this information can be a clue to their origins. Sometimes the names of sailors revealed them to be of African or Caribbean origin and from this the trace of their presence in Britain has been deduced. Some of the black sailors who spent time in Britain or who settled in Liverpool, Bristol or London will have worked on the slave ships of the triangular trade. Baptism records reveal that a number of black seafarers passed through Stepney in London. One local clergyman, Dr Mayo, was reported as being 'particularly kind to the Negroes and uninstructured men of colour, who, employed generally on board of ship, occasionally resided in his parish which is full of seafaring people. I suppose no clergyman in England ever baptized so many black men and mulatto'.[32]

Another group were students. The chiefs of Sierra Leone sent their sons to Britain to receive educations that would assist their families in their trading deals with Europeans. Around fifty boys, and some girls, from Sierra Leone were said to be studying in Liverpool in 1789, and there were others in Bristol, Lancaster and London. Some chiefs sent their wives as well as their children. Among the mixed-race students sent to Britain for their educations were the children, usually the sons, of British planters in the West Indies who had children with enslaved women. The most fortunate of these received the educations befitting Georgian gentlemen. One of the most remarkable cases was that of Nathaniel Wells, the favourite son of a prominent St Kitts plantation owner. Educated in Britain, in 1794 he inherited a fortune worth around £200,000 on his father's death, which included three sugar estates and the slaves who worked them. Among the slaves was his own mother, an enslaved woman who had remained the legal property of his father. Wells freed his mother and a handful of other relatives but continued as a slave owner, despite his own racial heritage. As a mixed-race man he understood that his presence in the Caribbean would be unwelcome and so never returned to St Kitts. He used his great fortune to buy a country home, the grand Piercefield House, near

Chepstow, and there he played the part of a country gentleman, becoming High Sheriff of Monmouthshire.

As well as carrying advertisements for the sale of slaves, British newspapers of the late seventeenth and eighteenth centuries carried notices reporting the escape of domestic slaves. Some historians have categorized these notices as Hue and Cry advertisements, which in theory obligated all who read them to be on the lookout for a criminal on the run.[33] In this case the 'criminal' was a slave who had stolen him- or herself away. The legal veracity of these advertisements is questionable, as was the legality of slavery in Britain, but they open a window into understanding the conditions enslaved people lived in. On 10 February 1763 an advertisement in the *Bath Chronicle* offered to 'sufficiently reward' any person willing to return 'A Negro Servant Named Gloucester' to his owner, John Stone of Chippenham. Gloucester, who was twenty-one years old and five feet six in height, was said to speak 'English tolerably well' and was identifiable by his 'light coloured Cloth Livery Coat and red waistcoat, with white Metal Buttons.' The advertisement warned that 'any person countenancing or harboring the said Black, will be prosecuted agreeable to Law'.[34] Most chillingly John Stone of Chippenham informed readers of his notice that the young man could also be distinguished by 'a long scar down the middle of his Forehead'. Repeatedly advertisements for Africans who had absconded from slavery in Britain listed the scars and disfigurements they bore on their bodies. William Jacobs 'a Negro aged 22' who escaped from his master in 1719 had 'the Mark of a cut in his Forehead'.[35] The *London Gazette* of 5 July 1715 carried a notice on behalf of Mr Pyne, the postmaster of Bristol, in which he offered a reward of two guineas and the payment of expenses for the recovery of Captain Stephen Courtney's negro, aged about twenty and who, 'having three or four marks on each temple and the same on each cheek', was easily identifiable. A few notices of rewards offered for the return of runaway slaves describe them as bearing branding marks.

The number of these notices, from the middle of the seventeenth century to the last decades of the eighteenth, suggests that some of the enslaved in Britain were marked out as human property by slave collars. These were usually brass or copper, occasionally silver, and were riveted or padlocked around the neck and could not be removed. Some carried the initials or the name of the 'owner'. In 1756 Mathew Dyer, a goldsmith on Duck Lane in Westminster, offered collars for sale as well as 'silver padlocks for Blacks or Dogs'.[36] They marked the runaway out as a slave making their recapture and return more likely. Some newspaper advertisements listed such collars as identifying features, alongside clothes and scars. In March 1685 the *London Gazette* offered a reward for the return of a fifteen-year-old boy named John White who had a silver collar fixed around his neck that bore the coat of arms and the cipher of one Colonel Kirke. The advertisement also noted that the boy had 'upon his throat a great scar'.[37] In 1691 the *London Gazette* reported that a ten-year-old boy named John Moor had run away with 'a silver collar about his neck'.[38] Four years later the same newspaper accounted that a black boy, 'about thirteen years old, run away the 8th inst. from Putney, with a collar about his neck with this inscription: "The Lady of Bromfield's black, in Lincoln's Inn Fields." Whoever brings him to Sir Edward Bromfield's at Putney, shall have a guinea reward'.[39]

Slave collars can be seen around the necks of some of the black pageboys in Georgian portraits, and the pageboy in the bottom right-hand corner in Plate 2 of Hogarth's *A Harlot's Progress* wears the full panoply of slave garb and a polished slave collar – the only element of his dress that links him to the world he had come from, the Atlantic world of slave ships, whips, manacles and plantations. In *A Harlot's Progress* Hogarth established the black pageboy as a mute witness to his owner's gradual ruin, and he is depicted alongside her other exotic 'pet' from the tropics, a small monkey. Ornate slave collars of this sort, engraved and polished, were expensive items, and might be considered a repugnant form of jewellery. Disconcertingly they are almost indistinguishable from the brass dog collars of the same period. Very few survive, unlike the rougher more utilitarian collars and shackles used on the plantations of the Caribbean and on the ships of the Atlantic trade, which were produced in vast numbers.

Newspapers in colonial North America and the Caribbean dedicated whole pages to notices of rewards for Africans who had absconded from the plantations and there was nothing unique about slaves in Britain seeking freedom through flight, but life in Britain, away from the clear black and white binary of the slave societies, must have made the possibility of freedom appear more tangible. Most black people in Britain – free or enslaved – worked in domestic service. This was the biggest sector of the employment market in the eighteenth century. There were said to be fifty thousand servants in London alone, one in thirteen of the population, and the plans and layouts of middle-class Georgian homes demonstrate that servants were the engines of domestic life. They worked in hot cellars and kitchens and slept in cold, small attics, while the rich and even the middling classes lived in the more spacious middle floors. Black slaves finding themselves working and living alongside white servants within such households will inevitably have begun to question their status and see themselves as little different from their white colleagues. Like migrants from Africa and the Caribbean in later centuries life in Britain also broke the unquestioned habit of the equating of blackness with service and whiteness with wealth and power. The sight of poor white people performing menial tasks or suffering hardships may have been an epiphany for slaves who had lived in the West Indies where even the least wealthy whites shirked any forms of service or manual labour. The magistrate Sir John Fielding believed that placing black slaves in positions comparable to those occupied by white servants lay at the root of a social problem. He complained in 1762 of the gentlemen slave owners from the West Indies who

have either, at a vast expense, caused some of these blacks to be instructed in the necessary qualifications of a domestic servant, or else have purchased them after they have been instructed: they then bring them to England as cheap servants, having no right to wages; they no sooner arrive here, than they put themselves on a footing with other servants, become intoxicated with liberty, grow refractory, and, either by persuasion of others or from their own inclinations, begin to expect wages according to their own opinion of their merits: and, as there are already a great number of black men who have made themselves so troublesome and dangerous to the families who brought them over, as to get themselves discharged, these enter into societies, and make it their business to corrupt and dissatisfy the mind of every fresh black servant that comes to England; first, by getting them christened or married, which, they inform them, makes them free.[40]

Slaves and black servants, and those who occupied some position between those two states, were isolated and preoccupied with their daily work. They were not the issue. What bothered Fielding was not the sight of liveried black coachmen and enslaved pageboys following their mistresses around fashionable parts of London but the presence in Britain of free black people, who he feared were expanding their ranks by recruiting new members from black people in service.

Two years later the *Gentleman's Magazine* warned that –

The practice of importing Negroe servants into these kingdoms is said to be already a grievance that requires a remedy, and yet it is every day encouraged . . . the main objections to their importation is, that they cease to consider themselves as slaves in this free country, nor will they put up with an inequality of treatment, nor more willingly perform the laborious offices of servitude than our own people, and if put to do it, are generally sullen spiteful, treacherous, and revengeful. It is therefore highly impolitic to introduce them as servants here, where that rigour and severity is impracticable which is absolutely necessary to make them useful.[41]

The advertisements for the return of runaways suggest that there was some determination on the part of some slave owners to reclaim their property, despite the apparent likelihood that a slave who had tasted freedom in Britain once would seek it again. Fielding could see no solution to this problem and suggested that the least damaging strategy was to allow slaves who had rejected their condition in Britain to 'go about their business', rather than return them to slavery in the West Indies. This was not because he had any sympathy with them or their plight but because he believed 'there is great reason that those blacks who have been sent back to the Plantations . . . have been the occasion of those . . . recent insurrections in the . . . West Indies. It is a species of inhumanity to the blacks themselves,' Fielding concluded, 'to bring them to a free country.'[42]

How common were Fielding's views? The records tell us little but what they do not show is any general hostility towards runaway black servants. If the image he presented, of London under the scourge of an uncontrolled and expanding black population, had much truth to it or had much impact upon the popular imagination then one might expect that white Londoners would take the opportunity to support slave owners seeking to recapture their slaves and transport them to the West Indies. There is no evidence that this happened.[43]

Those who did escape slavery in Britain, like those who were freed with no trade, education or support, lived lives that were extremely hard. Freed from slavery, most were imprisoned by poverty. Few had skills with which they might build new lives and they lived in fear of recapture and deportation to the Americas. Some of the problems they faced were not a result of their race but down to their status as aliens. Being from the West Indies, North America or in some cases Africa, they had no home parish in Britain, which meant they vanished through the already sizeable cracks in the Poor Law system, which allowed those who had fallen upon hard times to return to the parish of their birth and there receive food and assistance. Just as important they were without family, in an age in which kinship networks were often crucial to entering trades and gaining access to apprenticeships.

Even former slaves who sought to work as servants struggled to survive, as without a family they had nowhere to shelter when they were 'out of place', and in between jobs. The pathway to a trade and a steady income in Georgian Britain, for men at least, was an apprenticeship but these were often organized by the parish, which tended to preclude former or escaped slaves. There was also a problem of age; while the black population of Britain in the eighteenth century was very young, many of those who were recorded in the newspaper notices as having escaped were rather old to begin a seven-year apprenticeship.[44] Those with luck on their side or helpful contacts

did, however. John Moore of York became a freeman of that city in
1687 and a century later Bill Richmond, who was to become Britain's
first black sporting celebrity, began his independent life in Britain
serving as an apprenticed cabinetmaker; his incongruous shift to
bare-knuckle boxing came later in life. But his acceptance as an
apprentice came not after an escape from slavery but with the help
and blessing of the influential white family who had taken him under
their wing. Even former slaves who married into white families and
had the support of white friends were not immune from poverty.

The story of James Albert Ukawsaw Gronniosaw, a Nigerian who
was sold into slavery in the West Indies and North America, gives us
a first-hand account of life for a poor black man in Georgian Britain.
His 1772 biography *A Narrative of the Most Remarkable Particulars in the
Life of James Albert Ukawsaw Gronniosaw, an African Prince, As related by
himself* is especially useful as he lived not just in London but also in
Portsmouth, Colchester and Kidderminster. He was taught to read
when a domestic slave to a clergyman in New York. It was that master
who freed him in his will. Gronniosaw served in the British army
then headed to Britain, but in Portsmouth he was swindled out of
his savings. Moving to London he was assisted by a white preacher
he had known in North America and in the capital he met his English
wife Elizabeth. Together they moved out of London. Gronniosaw's
narrative was probably ghost-written but is a poignant depiction of
poverty as it existed in the late eighteenth century for people of any
colour, revealing how precarious and unstable life was. There were
periods when Gronniosaw and his wife went hungry but living among
the poor of Georgian London, Colchester and Kidderminster the
couple and their two mixed-race children seem to have encountered
little direct racial prejudice, or at least none is reported. When Gronniosaw encountered difficulties contracting his marriage to Elizabeth
it was not because of his race but because of her poverty and debts.

As the many advertisements for the sale of black boys or the
return of runaways suggest, the great majority of the black British
population were men and boys.* The historian Felicity Nussbaum

---

* As Kathleen Chater has pointed out this gender balance might be distorted by the fact
that male slaves were more likely to abscond than female.

estimates the gender balance as 80 per cent male to 20 per cent female.[45] This was about the same ratio as the slaves transported from Africa by British traders, as plantation owners, for obvious reasons, preferred male slaves and paid more for them. This meant that most black men, if they were to marry, had no option but to marry white women and it is clear from those for whom we have records that many did; Equiano married Susannah Cullen from Soham in Cambridgeshire, George Scipio Africanus married Esther Shaw from Nottingham and had seven children, only one of whom lived to adulthood. Through marriage, men like Equiano and Africanus acquired not just wives and children but extended families and greater access through those networks into British white society which allowed them to both integrate and assimilate. But marriage and assimilation did not insulate former slaves from poverty and hardship.

A factor that might well have encouraged some enslaved Africans to escape their masters was the existence in London, and to a much lesser extent in Bristol and Liverpool, of free black people in significant numbers. As black people in seventeenth- and eighteenth-century Britain were what today is called a 'visible minority', they would have been aware of one another and in a position to potentially cooperate. As well as sharing a physical, 'racial' identity they had shared experiences. Most had lost their links to Africa, if they ever had any. From the accounts of literate black Georgians, such as James Gronniosaw, Ottobah Cugoano and Olaudah Equiano, we know that some clearly had memories of their homelands and retained some knowledge of their native languages – though it must have been very rare for them to find someone with whom they could converse. More commonly black Georgians shared the mutual experiences and memories of slavery. They carried the scars – both physical and psychological – of childhoods or earlier lives spent on the plantations, or in the ships of the triangular trade. These collective experiences, as well as their shared racial identities, will naturally have drawn them together.

There is some evidence that black people living in Georgian London did cooperate and look out for one another, and stronger evidence that they sought out one another's company and came together for social occasions. Black servants in the city appear to have organized their own gatherings in taverns. The Yorkshire Stingo, a pub in Marylebone, was said to serve a largely black clientele and in 1764 the *London Chronicle* reported that 'Among the sundry fashionable routs or clubs, that are held in town, that of the Blacks or Negro servants is not the least . . . On Wednesday night last, no less than fifty-seven of them, men and women, supped, drank and entertained themselves with dancing and music, consisting of violins, French horns, and other instruments, at a public-house in Fleet-street, till four in the morning. No Whites were allowed to be present, for all the performers were Blacks.'[46]

The diary of the magistrate John Baker, who served as Solicitor-General to the island of St Kitts, the Leeward Islands, records one evening in the 1760s when he arrived at his London home to discover that his black servant, Jack Beef, had 'gone out to a ball of the Blacks'. It may well also have been the case that black servants in service to tolerant and obliging masters or mistresses may have occasionally been able to use the servants' rooms in which they worked and lodged for small gatherings of fellow black Londoners. This seems to have been the case with Francis Barber, whose relationship with Samuel Johnson was at times more akin to that of father and son than master and servant. A guest who called at Johnson's house in Gough Square, off Fleet Street, reported that 'The Doctor was absent, and when Francis Barber, his black servant opened the door to tell me so, a group of his African countrymen were sitting round a fire in a gloomy anti-room: and on their all turning their sooty faces at once to stare at me, they presented a curious spectacle'.[47]

How typical were men like Francis Barber and Jack Beef? Both enjoyed considerable freedom and were respected and valued by their employers for their talents. Francis Barber, by 1752, was a free man, and in service to an extremely liberal and accommodating employer, and was in a position to have his own guests visit him. It is highly probable that Francis Barber and Jack Beef knew one another and that they both also knew the black servant, whose name is lost, who worked for Joshua Reynolds, a member of Dr Johnson's famous club. But how typical was this group of black servants employed by members of the city's cultural elite? Barber and Beef lived in central London, with the city's infamous night life on their door step. Were they simply young black men about town, in an age when black people were still a novelty and in which long-established myths about black male sexuality were well understood? Or were they part of something we would recognize as a community?

Its seems likely that they were part of a group of black people who worked as servants to the rich – some of them formally free, some enslaved and some of undetermined status. The reports of black gatherings support this idea but how strong a sense of community might there have been between black servants who occupied such comfortable positions in the homes of the rich, and could afford to have guests call or be found out at night on their master's return, and members of London's hungry and illiterate black poor? On the same streets but in a different century, the social explorer Henry Mayhew encountered a black American who survived largely by begging. This unfortunate reported that his own brother, who was in service to 'a great gentleman in Harewood-square', was 'very proud, and I do not think would speak to me if he saw me.'[48] Georgian London was a society every bit as fixated with rank and social status as the Victorian city of the 1850s. While there was probably no exclusively black community among the poor in eighteenth-century London there is clear evidence that the black poor had formed a broader 'community' that consisted of themselves, their white wives and husbands and their mixed-race children. It is this community that was to become the focus of so much attention and effort in the 1780s, as we shall see.

Even if this 'community' of black servants and the black poor was fragmented, coming together only on rare occasions, and even then not in great numbers, reports of gatherings of black people were enough to convince some propagandists of racism that they were a threat to Britain. Or perhaps it was seen as a plausible spectre by which they hoped to whip up anti-black feeling and shore up support for slavery. These attacks slipped into the tone and the language of the immigration panics that repeatedly flare up throughout British history and are as old and established a British tradition as immigration itself.

*

Black Georgians who absconded from white masters who regarded them as chattels shared not just common experiences but the threat of recapture. Escaped black slaves could never be sure of their freedom. It is unlikely that there were professional slave-hunters in eighteenth-century London, the size of the black population was probably too small to make such a specialization viable, but there were men willing to hunt down and seize escaped slaves when paid to do so.[49] Through their efforts black men and women were kidnapped, imprisoned and returned to their masters. More disastrously, and it seems more commonly, some were sold to new owners in the Americas. Despite the warnings of men like John Fielding that slaves who had tasted freedom in Britain were a risk to the security of the sugar islands of the West Indies, the owners of slaves resident in Britain were willing to accept financial offers for their slaves and sell them back into slavery when it suited them to do so – private profit overwhelming any collective concern for the security of the plantations. Some of those who were sold to New World slave owners had not absconded, their owners had simply been offered a good price and accepted it. Sometimes slaves living in Britain were sold because their owner had gone bankrupt or died and their assets, including human property, were liquidated. The threat of being sold to West Indian planters haunted the lives of black people in Britain, in service or ostensibly living independent lives. For those in service their owners' 'chief disciplinary weapon was the ship, not the whip' suggests the historian Seymour Drescher.[50]

While slaves who had escaped and found refuge among the poor of London and the port towns were of no value to their masters they retained a residual value as a potential plantation slave if they could be traced and sold back to the Caribbean. Families who were short of money were tempted to sell black slaves, men and women whose lives had in most respects begun to look and feel very much like those of white servants, but who remained the property of their masters. Any uncertainty about the status of a black person was ended once they were shackled in a West India-bound ship. The case of John and Mary Hylas demonstrates how precarious the position of slaves in Britain was. They had arrived with separate owners around 1754 and married four years later, both sets of owners consenting to the union. But in 1766, after eight years of marriage,

Mary was kidnapped and shipped to the West Indies by her owners, the Newton family, and there she was sold. It was only with the help of the great abolitionist and campaigner Granville Sharp that John Hylas was able to go to court and successfully demand the return of his wife.

There was what the historian Seymour Drescher has called a 'deadly game of hide and seek' played out on the streets and the docks of London, Bristol and the other slave ports in the eighteenth century, as slaves struggled to avoid the attentions of their former masters who hired kidnappers to seize them and smuggle them on board ships bound for the West Indies.[51] The desperate attempts of former slaves to avoid transportation suggest that conditions of slavery in Britain, despite the evidence of violence and abuses, were still far removed from the routine brutality of plantation slavery.[52] So feared was transportation that in 1773 an escapee who had been recaptured and separated from his English wife shot himself while on a boat on the Thames, rather than face a life of slavery.[53] This tragedy was the supposed inspiration for *The Dying Negro*, an anti-slavery poem by Thomas Day and John Bicknall.* In 1790 the abolitionist Hannah More wrote to Horace Walpole describing the kidnap of a black woman in Bristol.

> I cannot forbear telling you that at my city of Bristol, during church time, the congregations were surprised last Sunday with the bell of the public crier in the streets. It was so unusual a sound on that day that the people were alarmed in the churches. They found that the bellman was crying the reward of a guinea to any one who would produce a poor negro girl who had run away because she would not return to one of those trafficking islands, whither her master was resolved to send her. To my great grief and indignation, the poor trembling wretch was dragged out from a hole in the top of a house where she had hid herself, and forced on board ship.[54]

---

* The poem was originally published as *The Dying Negro, a Poetical Epistle, supposed to be written by a black, (who lately shot himself on board a vessel in the River Thames;) to his intended Wife* (London, 1773). Some sources say the English woman was the fiancée rather than wife.

Two years later a Bristol journal reported the case of a black servant girl of many years' service who had been sold by her master for £80 Jamaica currency, and that she had been shipped to that island. 'A bystander who saw her put on board the boat at Lamplighter's Hall says, her tears flowed down her face like a shower of rain.'[55]

The reason for deportation could be petty as well as pecuniary. Pageboys who had grown too old to play their allotted role of glamorous accessory were sent back to the West Indies. The black pageboy of the Duchess of Kingston, purchased when he was five or six, was dispatched to West Indian slavery when he reached his teenage years.[56] The Duchess of Devonshire attempted to palm off her unwanted pageboy, regarded as superannuated at eleven years old, to her mother with the instruction, 'if you don't like him they say Lady Rockingham wants one'.[57]

Of those who did begin their lives in Britain as slaves – purchased from slave-ship captains, or brought over from the New World by their owners – how many of them remained enslaved? Some will have concluded that their life within the household of their master, despite being one of unfreedom, was safer and more desirable than any realistic alternative. So long as the family they were in service to were not violent and abusive, or more violent and abusive than average, then remaining with them at the very least offered a bed and food. The street might offer freedom but also starvation and danger.

Others may have formed bonds with their masters and mistresses. This is not as bizarre a notion as it might sound. Servants in the eighteenth century, particularly those who remained in service for many years, could become members of the household. Some attended church with the family and the inevitable intimacy of certain aspects of their work – helping family members dress and undress, caring for them when they fell ill – meant that in the best and most humane households servants could come to be regarded as part of an extended, informal family, and see themselves as such. Eighteenth-century guides to household management warned women of the perils of blurring the lines between servants, friends and family members. They counselled of the dangers of becoming overfriendly with servants or confiding sensitive information in them.

But even in a society as hierarchical as Georgian Britain personal affections and loyalties could and did develop between people of widely different social standing. The evidence that such bonds could cut across distinctions of race, as much as they did differences of wealth and rank, can been found in English churchyards, in the inscriptions of the headstones of black servants. St Mary's churchyard in the Henbury district of Bristol contains the wonderfully ornate, and presumably expensive, grave of Scipio Africanus, an enslaved teenage boy who was 'servant' to Charles William Howard, the 7th Earl of Suffolk. Scipio, who died in 1720, lies beneath a headstone decorated with black cherubs and an accompanying footstone inscribed with the following epitaph,

> I who was born a pagan and a slave
> Now sweetly sleep a Christian in my grave.
> What though my hue was dark my Saviour's sight
> Shall change this darkness into radiant light.
> Such grace to me my lord on earth has given
> To recommend me to my Lord in Heaven.
> Whose glorious second coming here I wait
> With saints and angels Him to celebrate.[58]

A dedication from around 1700, set into a wall at Werrington Church, a village on the border between Devon and Cornwall, celebrates the life of Philip Scipio, 'an African whose Quality might have done Honour to any Nation or Climate And Give us to See That Virtue is Confined To no Country or Complexion'.[59] The epitaph suggests that Philip Scipio's owners or employers – whichever they were or imagined themselves to be – were aware of the stereotype of Africans as disloyal, untrustworthy and innately immoral that was emerging in the eighteenth century, and regarded his virtues and qualities as a rebuttal to such notions. In the last decades of the century accounts of black slaves or servants who had performed years of loyal service, or demonstrated conspicuous skills or qualities, were deployed by the opponents of slavery to counter the spread of such stereotypes.

While there were slave owners who passed their human property on to their family in their wills there were also instances of slaves being rewarded with freedom on their master's death. Some received money or gifts in addition. Some slaves were formally freed and others regarded themselves as free, a presumption that in many cases was never formally recognized but neither was it challenged or tested by them or their 'master'. Slaves who had been baptized sometimes regarded that ceremony as marking the end of their status as chattel. As we shall see later the law, for many years, was uncertain on this point, but while the judges debated, there were black people who considered their acceptance into the Church and the Christian message as incompatible with slavery, and adjusted their view of themselves accordingly. Their owners often disagreed, as was the case with Katherine Auker, a baptized black woman who had lived in England for six years. In 1690 her master Robert Rich, who was preparing to return to Barbados, refused to release her from slavery or to allow her to find employment with another family. Indeed Rich and his wife 'tortured her and turned her out'. From Barbados they arranged for her to be imprisoned. Auker eventually went to court in Middlesex to be released from her master but was only partially successful.[60] She was granted permission to work for any master who would offer her a position but informed that she would be compelled to return to the household of Robert Rich should he return from Barbados.

An unknown number of enslaved black people in Britain in this period seem to have slipped into the very broad and vague category of 'servant', without any formal recognition or record of that transition. The fact that some black people were able to leave the household in which they were in service and work for another master, or indeed enter a different trade suggests that they occupied a position more akin to that of a servant. John Duck, a black servant to a family in Surrey, was permitted to leave their employment, get married and become an instructor in sword-fighting in London, where he passed on his skills to gentlemen and the Inns of Court.[61] John Duck was clearly not a slave.

The fashion for black servants among the rich of Georgian Britain had a number of unintended consequences. For the most fortunate, life even as a slave within the homes of the wealthiest presented opportunities. The biographies of many of the best-known black Georgian figures show that they received some education while enslaved. We have no reason to presume that this was a common, never mind universal, experience but that it happened at all shows how complicated relationships could be between people who were ostensibly slaves and people who were ostensibly slave owners. That owners of enslaved Africans elected to bestow upon some of them the gift of education – with all the potential for social mobility and advancement that it offered – is in part down to the nature of service in the eighteenth century. Servants, no matter what their race, could become more useful if they were educated, but it is highly likely that some enslaved pageboys were educated to prepare them for a future after their years in service.

One recipient of an education was George John Scipio Africanus, who may have originated in Sierra Leone and is thought to have come to Britain in 1776, where he came into the household of Benjamin Molineux of Wolverhampton. Clearly treated more as a favoured servant than an enslaved person, he was educated by the Molineux family and apprenticed in a brass foundry. After leaving service he moved to Nottingham and married an English woman called Esther Shaw, with whom he began Africanus' Register of Servants, a Georgian employment agency.[62] When the doors to education were opened, it was discovered that some black servants had natural abilities and talents. When the young Phillis Wheatley, who from the age of eight was a servant to the Wheatley family of Boston, was given lessons in English she mastered the language with a speed that was said to have amazed those around her. After rapidly learning English she took up French and Latin. The published collection of her neo-classical poetry was ecstatically received in Britain and parts of America.

It was the prospect of literacy, eagerly embraced by some enslaved Africans, which, along with luck and talent, allowed some to rise in life and become independent and self-reliant. A handful, like Phillis Wheatley, Ignatius Sancho, Olaudah Equiano, Francis Williams, James Gronniosaw and Ottobah Cugoano, became not just literate but literary. We have their voices thanks to their own determination but also because they were lucky enough to have received some education.

Ignatius Sancho, who had been born on board a slave ship in 1729, was given the gifts of literacy and learning only begrudgingly. He was brought up in Greenwich by three sisters who had no intention of educating him, fearing knowledge and access to books would render the boy unsuited for the life of service that lay ahead of him. Although the young Sancho had no reason to imagine that he would ever be permitted to live an independent life, he set out to educate himself. He was helped in that endeavour by the Duke and Duchess of Montagu, who lived locally. The couple gave the young boy books and Sancho eventually entered the Montagu household, employed as a butler after the duke's death, and there with the help of the duchess was able to throw himself into a world of learning. On her death the Duchess of Montagu left Sancho a gift of £70 and an annuity of £30. Sancho's later achievements, his published letters and musical compositions and the place he came to occupy within Georgian society were made possible by the opportunities for learning that he wrested from those around him, sometimes in the face of considerable opposition. Although he lived modestly as a shopkeeper with his wife Anne, who was also literate and literary-minded, Sancho carried on a literary correspondence with Laurence Sterne, had his portrait painted by Reynolds and was friends with a number of eminent Georgians, including David Garrick. The critical and commercial success of his own letters, published posthumously, has to be put down to his own talents, but Sancho's supposed exoticism might have added to his allure and increased his fame.

The figure whose life story encompasses the greatest extremes, ranging from slavery to privilege and flamboyant excess, was Julius Soubise, though it certainly cannot be said that Soubise used the education gifted him as wisely as Sancho. Soubise was born a slave on the island of St Kitts and brought to Britain in 1764 by a captain in the Royal Navy. That year he became the property of Catherine Hyde, the Duchess of Queensberry and cousin of the captain. A famous eccentric and socialite, Catherine Hyde occupied a central position within London high society, and cosseted in the unreal and arguably surreal world of privilege the young Soubise was both educated and indulged. The diarist Lady Mary Coke described visiting the Duchess of Queensberry at home in 1767 where she found her half dress'd & half undress'd; She was talking to her Black Boy, who indeed seems to have a very extraordinary capacity, something very uncommon; She told me She had him taught everything he had a mind to learn, She thought it better than keeping him to serve in the House; in that I think her Grace judged right, but When She told me he learnt to ride & fence, I could not help thinking those exercises too much above his condition to be useful, & wou'd only serve to give him expectations that cou'd not be answer'd.[63]

The exact nature of the 'condition' that Julius Soubise occupied is difficult to determine. Growing to adolescence he developed into an excellent equestrian and swordsman and continued to perform some of the duties that might be expected of a servant, but there appears to have been absolutely no pretence of him being a slave. In the early 1770s Soubise emerged into the social scene of Georgian London; befriending David Garrick he became an amateur actor, musician and poet. With the bills for his lavish lifestyle covered by the duchess he lived the life of the upper-class rake, spending heavily on entertaining. He appears to have developed both an entourage and a reputation as a Don Juan. This did not go unnoticed. Soubise and the duchess were satirized in popular prints and the nature of their relationship questioned. Like Anne, the fictional 'town miss' depicted in engravings of the period, the very real Julius Soubise became a symbol for the folly and hubris of London's fashionable elite – the 'macaroni' as they were known. As inevitably as if he was a character in one of Hogarth's progresses, his rise ended with a fall, both literally and metaphorically. In 1777 he was accused of raping a housemaid. To protect him the duchess sent him to India. In Calcutta he opened a successful riding school and appears to have settled down to marriage, but in 1798 he died after being thrown from a horse. It was an incredibly privileged, exciting and global life for anyone in the eighteenth century, but more so for a boy born into slavery in the West Indies.

The last decades of the eighteenth century were a period during which new racial theories were developed and stereotypes of black people refined and propagated by a pro-slavery, planter class determined to defend the slave trade and their right to own slaves. Ideas from which we are still unable to fully break free took shape in these years. Yet there appears to be a gulf between the toxicity of the theories of stereotypes being developed and propagated by those pro-slavery propagandists, men like Edward Long, and the experiences of many black Georgians in their daily lives among the white population. This is not to say that racism was not a feature of those experiences. In the fractured biographies of a number of black Georgians we can see opportunities curtailed and chances of mobility and improvement denied to them on account of their race, or sometimes because of the presumptions that others would be offended by their presence. Yet it seems that for the most part white servants did not seem to object to working alongside black people performing similar roles, whether free or enslaved. Through the biographies of many of the best-known black Georgians we can see that inter-racial marriage was a seemingly unremarkable feature of life. Olaudah Equiano, James Gronniosaw, Bill Richmond, Francis Barber all married white women; Equiano, Gronniosaw, Richmond and Barber all left mixed-race children, Equiano left his surviving daughter a small inheritance. The focus in much of the propaganda of Edward Long and others on the dangers and immorality of racial mixing, combined with the vicious cartoons that lampooned black sexuality, seem not to have convinced some people that relationships with black people should be taboo. Long's hysterical rantings about racial mixing and the comments by other writers who were disturbed by the sight of mixed-race children might be taken as evidence that what they really feared was white people who did not share their racism. That they felt the need to complain about the popularity of black men with white women again suggests that there were many people who did not share their views.

We know from the black Georgians who left us their own accounts that they did experience racism on the street. Ignatius Sancho and three of his daughters were subjected to racial abuse on a trip to the Vauxhall pleasure gardens. The extent to which this wounded Sancho is as ever difficult to tell. He routinely self-mocked in his affected literary style of the time, and made fun of his own racial identity; it is difficult to tell if this was a defence mechanism

or part of the jovial demeanour of a man who knew he was fortunate and was unashamedly happy; with a loving wife and six children
he had much to be happy about. Racism does not seem to have
been a major issue in the lives of the Sancho family. In the lives of
other black Georgians, poverty and the constant struggle to fend
it off consumed much more attention. It is plausible that in their
biographies some black Britons, Equiano, James Gronniosaw, Mary
Prince, omitted accounts of racial abuse in Britain because they
were trifling compared to the experiences they had known as slaves
in the New World, or because they wanted to express their affection for Britain and conceal their disappointments. Equiano's
biography saved its ire for the slave trade and slavery, not British
racism, but perhaps he was prioritizing and choosing his battles.
Eighteenth-century Britain was a ferociously xenophobic society in
which it was extremely unwise to appear disloyal or unpatriotic,
and black British writers tended to stress their loyalty to Britain.
Phillis Wheatley praised the King and Sancho commended Britain's
war against the North American colonists.[64]

The picture is mixed and much of it is concealed. What we can
say is that most black Georgians lived lives of constrained unfreedom
as slaves or low-ranking servants. Some were brutally treated by men
and women who regarded them as their property and as the law was
unclear on the issue they were able to make their claim real through
physical force and violence. Black Britons who rejected that predicament fell into another one, and struggled destitute on the streets,
where many lived off charity or crime, their names turning up in
the records of the courts. The lives of the most fortunate were
characterized by some degree of social mobility, with opportunities
for learning and engaging in a religious life. Those who had the time
and the security to look beyond their own needs were politically
active and culturally productive. Equiano became a full-time anti-
slavery activist and author. Ignatius Sancho never made a living from
his writing but became a genuine cultural figure; he was painted by
Thomas Gainsborough. Francis Barber may have had the same honour
– the provenance of the portrait believed to be of him is not proven.
Sancho was also the first black man known to vote in Britain. His
death in 1780 was announced in the *Gentleman's Magazine*. His obit-
uary, which was listed among those of other people deemed to be

'considerable Persons', reads 'In Charles-str. Westminster, Mister Ignatius Sancho, grocer and oilman; a character immortalized by the epistolary correspondence of Sterne.' It did not mention that he was a black man.[65] Two years later *The Letters of the Late Ignatius Sancho, An African* were published. The book drew more than twelve hundred subscribers and sold out the first edition. It was a demonstration in print of the author's learning and eloquence.

The biggest question the achievements of figures like Sancho, Wheatley, and Equiano raise is this: how were they able to live such remarkable lives, escape from slavery and navigate across societies, during the decades that saw Britain become the dominant slave-trading nation and the Atlantic slave trade carried more Africans that ever before into lives of miserable and brutal slavery?

FOUR

'Too Pure an Air for Slaves'

One day in the winter of 1765, the exact date is not known, a lawyer from Barbados named David Lisle savagely beat Jonathan Strong, his black slave. Lisle, who lived in London, was in the habit of beating the boy, but this attack was more severe than his previous assaults. He repeatedly struck Strong about the head and face with a pistol. The blows were so ferocious and so numerous that eventually the pistol broke, the metal barrel and lock separating from the wooden stock. Deprived of his weapon, Lisle cast the boy out into the filth of the Georgian street, his face a mass of open wounds. An account detailing Strong's injuries concluded that the blows he had received had 'made his head swell very greatly, and, when the swelling abated, a disorder fell on his eyes, which nearly occasioned the loss of his sight. This was followed by an ague, fever, and lameness in both feet.'[1] By modern standards Jonathan Strong was a minor, a child of around sixteen, who had been beaten almost to the point of death and then thrown into the gutter. But David Lisle believed he had committed no crime, and was never charged for his horrific attack. The legal dispute that was to rumble on for the next two years concerned not the near-fatal injuries he had inflicted upon a child but his presumed right to sell that child to another man.

It is not clear from the records how Jonathan Strong survived the hours after the attack. He surfaces next in Mincing Lane in the City of London, a street that still exists today. Strong had evidently heard of William Sharp, a doctor, whose surgery was located on that street, and who once a week tended to the injuries and maladies of the destitute and the penniless. Somehow, Strong had found his way there to seek help. It appears that it was the doctor's brother, Granville Sharp, who first saw Jonathan Strong queuing up with all the other unfortunates that morning in Mincing Lane. But even within that wretched line-up of Georgian London's lame and disfigured, Strong was a shocking sight. 'The boy seemed ready to die', Granville Sharp later commented, he 'almost lost the use of his Legs and Feet . . . and to compleat his misfortunes [was] afflicted with so violent a disorder in his Eyes that there appeared to be the utmost danger of his becoming totally blind.'[2] Strong himself tells us a little of what happened, both before and after arriving in Mincing Lane. 'I . . . went to Mr. Sharp. I could hardly walk, or see my way, where I was going. When I came to him, and he saw me in that condition, the gentleman take charity of me.'[3]

The charity that the two Sharp brothers provided to Strong possibly saved his life and almost certainly saved him from blindness. He was admitted to St Bartholomew's Hospital, and so devastating were his injuries that he remained there for four and a half months. 'All the while I was in the hospital', Strong later explained, 'the gentleman find me in clothes, shoes, and stockings, and when I come out, he paid for my lodging, and a money to find myself some necessaries, till he get me into a place.'[4] By 'place' Strong meant a job. He became a messenger boy, some sources say footman, to a Mr Baker, an apothecary, whose shop was located close to William Sharp's surgery. With the assistance of Granville and William Sharp, Jonathan Strong had not only survived his injuries but had miraculously made the transition from abused slave to apparently free man in a paid position. For the first time in his short life he was independent and could imagine a future.

That might easily have been the end of things. The story of Jonathan Strong and Granville Sharp, two unknowns whose lives became momentarily entwined, could have become merely one of those tiny historical details that are from time to time picked out by hawk-eyed scholars. But two years later, on 5 September 1767, Strong was running an errand for his employer Mr Baker when he was spotted on the street by David Lisle. The broken boy, the child he had discarded as a worthless and expended item of property, was now fit and well. Lisle must have presumed that he would never see Strong again; educated and well travelled, he was worldly enough to have known that there was a very real chance he might die from the injuries he had inflicted upon him. But the sight of the boy revived in health, awoke in Lisle his sense of ownership and entitlement and he set about scheming to recover his 'property' and profit from it.

There might not have been full-time, professional slave-hunters in the London of the 1760s but there were certainly men who could be hired to kidnap black people and bundle them into West Indies-bound ships on the Thames. In the coming years Granville Sharp would learn all the intimate details of how these abductions were arranged and executed. It was to men with these skills that Lisle now turned. After having Strong watched, he had two city officers approach him. They told Strong that someone wanted to speak to him at a nearby pub, and the boy innocently agreed to accompany them. That 'someone' was David Lisle, who had Strong imprisoned at the Poultry Compter, a small city-centre prison used to hold vagrants, debtors and other unfortunates accused of minor offences – it was so named because it was near to one of London's old poultry markets. By the 1760s the compter had become the facility in which recaptured slaves were incarcerated while their 'owners' made arrangements for them to be shipped to the West Indies and sold as plantation slaves. This was what Lisle had in mind for Strong and while he was behind bars the lawyer sold him for £30 to James Kerr, a Jamaican planter.

Again it was education that made the critical difference in shaping the life of a black Georgian. Strong had learned to read and write and he quickly dispatched a series of desperate notes. One was to Mr Baker, the apothecary; another was to Granville Sharp. Having grown used to the notion that he was the owner of his own person Strong implored Sharp to offer him 'protection from being sold as a Slave'. Rushing to the compter, Sharp demanded to see Strong but at this critical moment he did not demand that the prison master release him. Understanding where the real danger lay, he instead insisted that the prison master, 'at his own peril, [was] not to deliver him up to any person whatever, who might claim him, until he had been carried before the Lord Mayor'. Sharp then rushed off to the office of the Lord Mayor, Sir Robert Kite, and informed him, 'that a Jonathan Strong had been confined in prison without any warrant'.[5]

Sir Robert Kite agreed to summon all parties to appear before him. On 18 September, two weeks after Strong had been spotted on the street by Lisle, he was brought before the Lord Mayor in his offices at the Mansion House. Strong and Sharp were confronted by Macbean, a lawyer who was acting for James Kerr, Strong's new owner, and Captain Laird, who was the commander of the ship in which Strong was to be transported to the West Indies. David Lisle was absent.

The scene that followed starkly demonstrated the legal uncertainty over the status of slaves in Britain. The Lord Mayor could have viewed Jonathan Strong in one of two ways: as a man who despite having committed no crime had been kidnapped and imprisoned; or as an item of property who had been stolen from his legal owners by Granville Sharp. As Sharp reported in his notebook, Sir Robert Kite, 'having heard the claim, said, that "the lad had not stolen any thing, and was not guilty of any offence, and was therefore at liberty to go away"'. However, at that verdict Captain Laird turned to Jonathan Strong and 'seized him by the arm'. In a raised voice Laird informed the Lord Mayor that he was claiming the boy 'as the property of Mr. Kerr'. By this point Strong was convinced that a life of slavery awaited him and had been reduced and was weeping and shaking with fear. Sharp too was momentarily overcome by the startling abruptness of Captain Laird's actions. But amidst the shouting and the crying, the city coroner, Mr Beech, who up to that point had been a mute witness to events, 'came behind' Granville Sharp, 'and whispered in his ear the words "Charge him".' As if awoken from a stupor Sharp 'turned upon the captain, and in an angry manner said, "Sir, I charge you for an assault." On this, Captain Laird quitted his hold of Jonathan's arm, and all bowed to the Lord Mayor and came away'. Jonathan Strong left the Mansion House a free man, 'no one daring to touch him'.

If that morning on Mincing Lane in 1765 had been the moment Granville Sharp had come to understand the brutality that marred the lives of the black slaves whom he had grown used to seeing around him in London, it was now, two weeks later at the Mansion House, that he began to comprehend just how desperate their legal predicament was. The laws on slavery in Britain were a jumble of contradictions, uncertainties and ancient case law. For Granville

Sharp this labyrinth of legal confusion and dispute became a rather personal issue because 'A few days after this transaction' at the Mansion House, he 'was charged, by a writ, with having robbed the original master, David Lisle, the lawyer, of a Negro slave'. Two weeks after that the situation escalated further. Sharp's diary contains the following entry for 1 October 1767. 'David Lisle, Esq. (a man of the law) called on me in Mincing Lane, to demand gentlemanlike satisfaction, because I had procured the liberty of his slave, Jonathan Strong. I told him, that, "as he had studied the law so many years, he should want no satisfaction that the law could give him." '[6] Granville Sharp was not a man to fight a duel, which is what Lisle had meant by his ridiculous demand for 'gentlemanlike satisfaction', but Sharp was a fighter, as Lisle was to discover.

In order to establish slave societies in North America and the West Indies two separate legal systems had evolved within the British Empire. The laws drafted by local legislatures in the New World colonies governed affairs there, while the people of England lived, as they had always done, under the common law, with its mosaic of precedents, determinations and case law. These two systems functioned well enough within their own jurisdictions but problems and uncertainties arose when enslaved black people were brought into Britain by planters returning from the colonies, or by slave captains selling 'privilege negroes' in British port towns. No one was clear as to what the exact status of those 'slaves' was within English law.

Laws in Virginia, Barbados and the other colonies had been drafted specifically in order to protect the slave system, and defend the rights of the men and women who profited from it. Laws there unambiguously defined Africans as chattel and established legal distinctions between white 'servants' and black 'slaves' and closed the loopholes that had enabled some black people to cast off their chains. But were any of these laws portable? Could Africans legally defined as slaves in the colonies be regarded and treated as such in 'free' England, or upon entering the kingdom did black slaves from the colonies automatically come under the protection of the common law, like everybody else? Should judges and juries treat them as men or as items of property under English law?

To the frustration and alarm of the planters and merchants there were no laws on the statute books of England recognizing or sanctioning slavery. The last laws to recognize any form of bondage in England had been those which had codified feudal villeinage, but that practice, a form of serfdom, had died out by the seventeenth century. If there were no positive laws legitimizing slavery then perhaps sanction for the practice might be found within case law and precedent? But here the legal history was contradictory and muddled. Hacking their way through a thicket of past judgements, judges and barristers uncovered cases going back to the sixteenth century. In 1569 a man named Cartwright had been seen beating another man. When questioned Cartwright defended his actions by claiming that his victim was a slave whom he had brought into the country from Russia. The ruling in this case – cited in a Star Chamber trial of 1637 – was that 'England was too pure an Air for Slaves to breathe in.' But what did that really mean; that slaves could not be beaten by their masters in England or that no one could be a slave in England? Despite the ambiguity of that antiquated judgement this lyrical phrase was to be quoted, misquoted, adapted and paraphrased for the next three centuries.

Forty years after the Star Chamber trial a case known as *Butts v. Penny* appeared to contradict that judgement. This case involved a claim for 'trover', damages resulting from the unlawful loss of private property. The property in question was ten black slaves. The Court of King's Bench ruled that these ten Africans were indeed property as it was the custom for black people to be traded as 'merchandise', which by 1677 they were. But the Attorney-General intervened to prevent a final judgement in the case, so the significance of the ruling was in doubt. A series of late-seventeenth-century cases seemed to suggest that religion might hold the key to the conundrum. In 1694 a judge concluded that a 'Negro boy' could be regarded as merchandise because black people were 'heathens, and therefore a man may have property in them'.[7] But rather than offer a definitive answer to the problem this judgement merely raised new questions. If black people could be enslaved because they were 'heathens' that suggested they would have to be freed if they were baptized. The belief that conversion to the Christian faith bestowed freedom upon a slave was widely held among black people and slave owners in the colonies, right up to the formal end of British slavery in the 1830s. Runaway slaves in the West Indies were known to seek out clergymen and demand to be baptized. There were reports of baptismal ceremonies being interrupted by irate slave owners, bursting in and dragging enslaved people away from the font, to the horror of the officiating ministers. In the West Indies, the planters dominated the local legislatures and were able to pass their own laws clearly stipulating that baptism did not confer freedom, but in Britain the slave owners were never able to quash the belief. Jonathan Strong had himself been baptized after his escape from David Lisle in 1765, and among the letters he wrote from his cell at the Poultry Compter were notes to his two god-fathers, both white.[8] There was also a shocking case in London. In 1760 a nine-year-old black girl who was being held as a slave by an abusive mistress escaped and rushed to a church, where she begged to be baptized. The ceremony had begun when the mistress burst in and 'violently forced her down the church and dragged her along the streets like a dog without pity or remorse regardless of her cries and tears, telling the people about her that the girl was a slave and she would use her as she pleased'.[9]

In 1696 the status of black people brought to Britain as slaves was thrown into even greater confusion when the issue came before John Holt, Lord Chief Justice of England. Holt was the judge who famously helped bring to an end the prosecution of women accused of witchcraft. In the case of *Chamberlain v. Harvey*, a black man who had been brought from Barbados to England and 'baptised without the knowledge of [his mistress] while there', argued that he was not a slave as that condition did not exist in England.[10] He claimed his freedom specifically on the grounds that, 'being baptised according to the rite of the Church' he had been 'thereby made Christian, and Christianity is inconsistent with slavery'.[11] The slave owner in the case argued against the notion that conversion changed the status of the enslaved. Chief Justice Holt, in his judgement, contradicted earlier rulings and concluded that black people could not be defined as merchandise since English law did not recognize them as being any different to other people, Christian or not. However, Holt judged that while black people could not be recognized by the law as slaves, they could be regarded as 'slavish servants', occupying a station not dissimilar to that of an apprentice – a person who had sold their labour to a master for an agreed number of years and was bound to him for the duration. This meant that a master potentially had the right to regard their service as his property but not their persons. A fine but critical distinction.

As the battle of case law and precedent rumbled on the stakes increased. When the royal monopoly was pushed aside and English and Scottish slave-traders enormously expanded the scale of the trade, legal decisions over the status of black Africans made by judges in England were no longer mere points of law, but judgements that could potentially have an impact upon the national economy. As the planter in the *Chamberlain v. Harvey* case asked, 'Who would squeeze the sugar from the cane once all slaves had been sprinkled with holy water?'[12]

In 1701, Lord Chief Justice Holt spoke again on the matter. In the case of *Smith v. Brown and Cooper*, the former sued the latter when they refused to pay him for a slave bought in London. Holt threw the case out with the emphatic statement, 'As soon as a negro comes into England, he becomes free. One may be a villein in England but not a slave.'[13] An African who was legally a slave in the colonies could not be held in that condition in England. Another judge, Mr Justice Powell, stated that 'the law takes no notice of a negro', and that 'a black was to be treated as an Englishman'.[14]

Holt's judgements horrified the planters, who felt their property rights were being dangerously undermined. So uncertain of their position were they that some were known to keep enslaved Africans on board ship when their vessels called at British ports, to prevent them from taking that first momentous step onto British soil, which their owners feared might be used, by some sympathetic magistrate, as a pretext to award them their freedom. Before he purchased his own freedom Olaudah Equiano was told by English lawyers that he could potentially be freed if he were to make his appeal on British soil.

In 1729 a group of 'many merchants and British Planters' petitioned the Attorney-General, Sir Philip Yorke, and the Solicitor-General, Charles Talbot – both of them future Lord Chancellors – for an opinion. The two lawmakers were received at a dinner in Lincoln's Inn after which they delivered to the gathered planters their learned opinion on the legality of slavery in Britain. The Yorke–Talbot opinion gave the planters everything they wanted. It stated that 'a slave coming from the West-Indies to Great-Britain or Ireland, with or without his master, doth not become free, and that his master's property or right in him' remained unchanged. They also opined that for a slave in Britain, 'baptism doth not bestow freedom on him, or make any alteration in his temporal condition in these kingdoms.' Just as importantly Yorke and Talbot stated, 'We are also of opinion, that his master may legally compel him to return again to the plantations.'[15] This after-dinner opinion appeared to put slavery on a far stronger legal footing. But within two decades two other cases – those of *Galway v. Cadee* in 1750 and *Shanley v. Harvey* in 1762 – appeared to confirm Holt's earlier judgements, that a slave became free upon setting foot on English soil.

This was the maze of case law, precedent, contradiction and vested interest into which Granville Sharp suddenly found himself thrust in 1765.

Granville Sharp was one of the least likely civil rights campaigners in all of history. The Sharp family came from Durham. Their grandfather had been the Archbishop of York, their father Archdeacon of Northumberland. Granville was one of five children who grew up in a comfortable and, of course, deeply Christian household. The Sharp brothers moved to London and excelled, William Sharp opening his doctor's surgery on Mincing Lane, James becoming an engineer manufacturing iron goods. Due to a deterioration in family finances the young Granville had not been given the educational advantages his older brothers had enjoyed. He worked in the linen trade and later became a clerk in the Ordnance Office. These somewhat mundane occupations allowed him time to indulge in what was his and his family's real passion, music. The Sharps were amateur musicians, but of a very high calibre. They gave regular Sunday concerts as a family ensemble. David Garrick came to see them play and on one occasion they performed for King George III, whose appetite for music was insatiable. Some years they performed on a barge on the Thames, and a rather stunning portrait of the whole family was painted by Johann Zoffany, some time around 1790.

Content in the bosom of his large and loving family, Granville Sharp's existence was given rhythm and meaning by his love of life and music and by his deep and earnest faith. When David Lisle, a tough colonial lawyer, learnt who his opponent was in the dispute over Jonathan Strong he might have grown more confident of the chances of regaining his 'property'.

From the portraits we have of him it seems there is little evidence of his personal contentment and familial serenity in the countenance of Granville Sharp. Thin-faced and punctilious, he was a descendant of Yorkshire Puritans and he looked the part. But this bookish, pious civil servant, who spent his spare time playing the flute, was the man who was to take on the slave owners of the so-called West India Interest and force the reluctant lawmakers of England to make a final and begrudged determination on the legality of slavery in Britain. He was to influence the lives of more people than he could possibly have imagined.

After being forced to make an undignified retreat under the gaze of the Lord Mayor, James Kerr, the man to whom Lisle had sold Jonathan Strong, focused his wrath upon Granville Sharp. Along with another of his brothers, James, Granville was accused of having denied Kerr the property he alleged to hold in Strong. In the ensuing legal row Jonathan Strong himself was not a party but merely the disputed item of property.

When Sharp sought legal representation to defend him against Kerr, the lawyers he approached advised him that his case was hopeless. Sir James Eyre, the Recorder of London, having spoken to the Lord Chief Justice, Lord Mansfield, advised Sharp that the Yorke–Talbot opinion of 1729 was decisive. Undeterred and despite having no prior knowledge of the law or legal training, Granville Sharp rejected this advice and set about researching the law himself. For a year Sharp spent his days working at the Ordnance Office, his spare time playing music with his family and friends, but devoting other waking hours to his meticulous study of the law. He met a number of leading lawyers and had conversations with the Solicitor-General. Trawling through the labyrinth of case law he read Holt's judgements and discovered that Yorke–Talbot, far from being a

1. Among the grave goods of the 'Ivory Bangle Lady' were two bangles, one made of English jet and another of African ivory. She was of mixed African heritage and lived in Roman York in the second half of the fourth century AD.

2. A forensic craniofacial reconstruction of the 'Beachy Head Woman', a third-century Afro-Roman who grew up and died in East Sussex.

3. The Hereford Mappa Mundi of 1280 shows the three known continents: Europe, Asia and Africa.

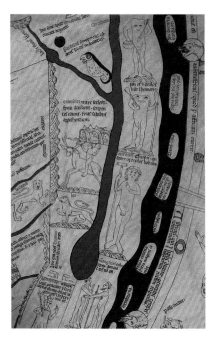

4. Detail showing the outer fringes of Africa on the Hereford Mappa Mundi. Here, in the medieval imagination, dwelt monstrous races such as the Blemmyes, a people whose faces were in their chests.

5. John Blanke (centre). The royal trumpeter is depicted on the Westminster Tournament Scroll, 1511.

6. A bronze plaque that once decorated the palace of the Obas of Benin, modern-day Nigeria. The first British visitors to Benin arrived in the middle of the sixteenth century. The palace was sacked by British forces in the 1890s.

7. Freedom was not merely given to the enslaved of the British West Indies, it was fought for. This sketch is of a flag taken from slaves who rebelled in Barbados.

8. Black enslaved child servants were very much in vogue for the European aristocratic classes in the seventeenth and eighteenth century. Elizabeth Murray, Lady Tollemache, later Countess of Dysart and Duchess of Lauderdale, is shown in a 1651 portrait. Her servant wears a silk shirt and a pearl earring, and stares attentively at the Countess.

9. This 1682 portrait of Louise de Kérouaille, Duchess of Portsmouth and mistress to King Charles II, shows the Duchess with an enslaved child servant.

10. Portraits of aristocratic men tended to celebrate manly pursuits. Here the third Duke of Richmond is depicted out on a shoot with a black boy in fine livery, c. 1765.

11. 'Be not amaz'd Dear Mother – It is indeed your Daughter Anne', reads the caption from this 1774 satirical engraving. The subject is a 'Town Miss', one of the infamous courtesans of Georgian London, for whom an enslaved black pageboy dressed in livery and turban (far left) was an essential fashion accessory.

Be not amaz'd Dear MOTHER – It is indeed your DAUGHTER ANNE.

12. This portrait, believed to be by Sir Joshua Reynolds, was for many years thought to be a likeness of Francis Barber, Dr Johnson's servant and surrogate son.

A STRIKING VIEW of RICHMOND.

13. Born into American slavery, Bill Richmond escaped the American Revolutionary War and became a cabinetmaker in England. Although of small stature and already in his early forties, he made the rather radical decision to enter into the world of Georgian bare-knuckle boxing, where he became known as the 'Black Terror', winning seventeen of his nineteen professional fights and becoming Britain's first black sports star.

14. The black trumpeter entertaining the crowds in the foreground of William Hogarth's Southwark Fair of 1733 is one of a number of black figures who appear in the artist's depictions of Georgian street life.

15. A satirical cartoon from the late eighteenth century shows Julius Soubise, the former slave turned Georgian rake, fencing with his patron Catherine Hyde, the Duchess of Queensbury.

16. An 1807 watercolour of the slave fortress on Bunce Island in the Sierra Leone River, from which tens of thousands of Africans were shipped to slavery in the Americas. The ruins of the fortress have been described as the Pompeii of the Atlantic slave trade.

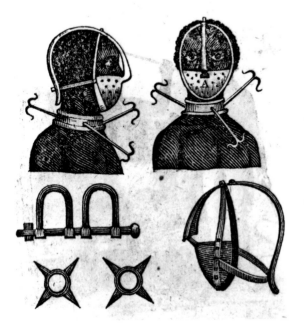

17. The implements of plantation slavery. This mid-eighteenth century engraving shows a punishment collar, an iron mask and leg shackles. These grim contraptions were often used to punish slaves who had escaped.

decision of case law, as many people had come to presume, was merely an opinion offered up after a cosy dinner with London's planters. In 1767 Sharp condensed his research into book form. He then distributed copies of his manuscript to a number of lawyers, before its publication. It was read by William Blackstone, the first Vinerian Professor of English Law, whose famous *Commentaries on the Laws of England* had recently been published. The legal argument this amateur had presented across 167 pages was detailed and compelling enough to convince James Kerr to drop his action. A second action brought by Kerr was similarly abandoned and David Lisle eventually gave up his favoured tactic of sending Sharp letters demanding the return of Jonathan Strong. Sharp had responded to these approaches by reminding Lisle that Strong was not an item of property that he had taken from him, but a free man over whom neither of them had any legal property rights.

With the collapse of Kerr's action Granville Sharp was no longer a defendant and Jonathan Strong was no longer at risk of being re-enslaved by Kerr or David Lisle. At this point Sharp could have ended his legal studies and returned to his flute and his monotonous job at the Ordnance Office. But he did not. In 1769, he published his book, *A Representation of the Injustice and Dangerous Tendency of Tolerating Slavery, or of Admitting the Least Claim of Private Property in the Persons of Men, in England.* Arranged across four parts it weaved together case law with notions of natural law and Sharp's deeply held Christian morality. In it he argued passionately against what he called the toleration of slavery, warning that, 'If such a toleration would ever be generally admitted in England, (which God forbid!) we shall no longer deserve to be esteemed a civilized people'.[16] Sharp predicted that any toleration of slavery in Britain would allow the cancer of unfreedom to spread and undermine the liberties of other groups, 'when any part of the community, under the pretence of private property, is deprived of this common privilege [rights under the law], 'tis a violation of civil liberty, which is entirely inconsistent with the social principles of a free state. True liberty protects the labourer as well as his lord'.[17] These were fine words, but they are not why Granville Sharp is remembered. What made him famous at the time, and what makes him deserving of continued recognition, was his legal crusade on behalf of the enslaved.

From 1765 to 1772 Sharp searched for *the* case, that might be brought to trial and that would force the judges to make a final determination on the legality of slavery in Britain. He was worldly enough to understand that taking on the institution of slavery in the colonies was, in the 1760s and 1770s, a futile task. In those decades the British slave trade and the plantation system were hurtling towards the zenith of profitability. Islands like Jamaica were among the most productive territories in the world and the planters and merchants of the West Indies a powerful political force. For now Sharp contented himself with seeking to prevent what he termed the 'toleration' of slavery in Britain, though his views on the slave trade were clear.

In the aftermath of his victory over Lisle and Kerr, Sharp began taking up cases that were brought to him by black people whose rights had been breached. The case of John Hylas, mentioned in the previous chapter, in which his wife Mary had been abducted and sold as a slave, was the first Sharp championed and took to court. The judgement reunited John and Mary Hylas and was the first in a string of legal victories, but no definitive determination on the status of slaves in Britain was drawn from it. By now the obsessive and combative aspects of Sharp's personality were in the ascendancy. In addition to taking on legal cases he scanned the press looking for causes to fight and potential allies whom he might convert to the cause. In 1769 the following advert appeared in the *Public Advertiser*.

> To be sold, a Black Girl, the property of J. B——, eleven years of age, who is extremely handy, works at her needle tolerably, and speaks English perfectly well; is of an excellent temper, and willing disposition. Inquire of Mr. Owen, at the Angel Inn, behind St. Clement's church, in the Strand.[18]

Sharp was so outraged that he wrote the same day to Lord Camden, the Lord High Chancellor of England, complaining about 'the frequency of such publications', which he felt 'must tend very much to extinguish those benevolent and humane principles which ought to adorn a Christian nation'. Sharp requested his Lordship 'take such notice of this notorious breach of the laws of nature, humanity, and equity, and also of the established law, custom, and constitution of England'.[19] Sharp enclosed a copy of his book. His monitoring of the London press also brought to his attention advertisements for the implements of slavery. Slave collars and an iron punishment muzzle particularly appalled him. Sharp copied these advertisements and included them as an appendix to the letters he sent to the powerful and the influential.

The legal case that seemed to offer the promise of advancing his cause arrived in July 1770. It concerned the abduction and attempted deportation of Thomas Lewis, a black man who was regarded as a slave by a retired ship's captain named Robert Stapylton. Seemingly in need of money, perhaps because of his advancing age, Stapylton had hired two Thames watermen, John Malony and Edward Armstrong, to seize Lewis. Compared to the abduction of Jonathan Strong by David Lisle and his hirelings four years earlier, this was a botched job, despite having been meticulously planned. Stapylton's thugs pounced on Lewis on the night of 2 July, having lured him to a spot by the Thames in Chelsea. They overpowered and tied Lewis up with cord, but as the site chosen for the abduction was directly in front of a row of riverside mansions, when Lewis screamed for help a number of witnesses arrived on the scene, among them the servants from one of the nearby mansions, some of whom even knew Lewis. They rushed out and confronted his attackers. All that prevented them from rescuing him was that one of the watermen produced an official-looking document and, 'pretended to have a warrant from the Lord Mayor for his apprehension'. Fearing arrest themselves the servants retreated. To silence Lewis, Malony and Armstrong gagged him 'by thrusting a stick into his mouth'. They then bundled the poor man into a boat and ferried him down the Thames to the *Captain Seward*, a ship moored in the river, on which he was chained, ready to be transported to Jamaica and sold.[20]

The mansion beside which the abduction of Thomas Lewis had taken place, and from where the servants had come in the hope of rescuing him, was owned by one Mrs Banks, and she too had heard Lewis's desperate screams and cries for help. Mrs Banks happened to be the mother of Joseph Banks, the celebrated botanist and one of the founders of the Royal Academy who, in the summer of 1770, was with Captain James Cook in Australia on his famous first voyage. It was Mrs Banks who contacted Granville Sharp about the case,

Sharp's reputation as the defender of black people having already spread through the city.[21] Mrs Banks even bore the costs of bringing the action against the men who attempted to kidnap Thomas Lewis, and Sharp's initial reservations about the case were founded upon his concerns over the costs Mrs Banks might have to incur. Nonetheless Sharp rushed into action. First he sought an injunction to have Lewis returned from Gravesend, but the servant dispatched there discovered that the ship had already departed. But bad winds momentarily kept the vessel off the Kent coast giving Sharp more time. As Sharp's memoirs tell us, 'a writ of Habeas Corpus was procured [and] sent down to Spithead, and served on board the ship, still lying in the Downs'.[22] According to one account, the officer who served the writ to the captain of the *Snow* came on board to find Lewis, 'chained to the mainmast, bathed in tears, and casting a last mournful look on the land of freedom, which was fast receding from his sight. The captain, on receiving the writ, became outrageous; but, knowing the serious consequences of resisting the law of the land, he gave up his prisoner, whom the officer carried safe, but now crying for joy, to the shore.'[23] Lewis had escaped slavery in Jamaica by the slimmest of margins. With the man in question now returned to London, Granville Sharp and Mrs Banks brought a private prosecution, 'against the author of the outrage!'. Robert Stapylton and the two watermen were charged with assault.[24]

The case came before William Murray, Earl of Mansfield, the Lord Chief Justice of England. Mansfield, whose name is for ever linked to that of Sharp, was a judge who on repeated occasions had granted writs of habeas corpus that returned slaves to their owners, and his prime objective in relation to the slavery question was to avoid making a judgement on the matter, for fear that such ruling would have far-reaching consequences.[25] In the Thomas Lewis case Robert Stapylton's defence was simply, 'Lewis belonged to him as his slave.' Appearing for the prosecution was John Dunning, the lawyer retained by Sharp and Mrs Banks and to whom Sharp had supplied a copy of his book. This Dunning used almost as a prop throughout the trial, brandishing it and quoting from it repeatedly. At one point, 'Mr. Dunning . . . held up Mr. Sharp's Tract in his hand, and declared, before Lord Mansfield and the Court, that he was prepared to maintain, in any of the courts in Great Britain, that no man can be legally detained as a Slave in this country'.[26] But Mansfield adamantly refused to judge the case on this larger question and restricted the jury to consider only the status of Thomas Lewis – was he a slave or not? As Stapylton could not prove his claim to ownership his case fell apart. In his summing up Mansfield noted that, 'whether they [slave owners] have this kind of property or not in England has never been solemnly determined', but as Stapylton was unable to prove ownership of Lewis the judge was able to avoid making that determination. 'We don't find he was the defendant's property', was the verdict of the jury, which solicited chants of 'No Property, No Property' from the supporters of Lewis and Sharp in the public galleries. Thomas Lewis, who had given evidence on his own behalf during the trial, left court a free man but the legality of slavery in England remained uncertain and undecided, as Mansfield had hoped it would. 'I don't know what the consequences may be', he stated, 'if the masters were to lose their property by accidentally bringing their slaves to England. I hope it never will be finally discussed; for I would have all masters think them free, and all negroes think they were not, because then they would both behave better.'[27] Sharp was bitterly disappointed that Mansfield had gone so far out of his way to avoid making a judgement on the legality of slavery in Britain.

The case that Granville Sharp had been waiting for ever since 1766 came knocking at the door of his lodgings in Old Jewry in the City of London. It arrived just six months after the Lewis case had concluded, not that Sharp could see its potential straight away. In his diary Sharp wrote that on 12 January 1772, 'James Somerset, a Negro from Virginia, called on me this morning . . . to complain of Mr. Charles Stewart. I gave him the best advice that I could.'[28]

Little is known of the life of James Somerset. We learn something of him from Sharp's diary and pick up the basic details of his life from the discussions in court and in various affidavits, though he himself was never to take the stand in the case that was to determine his own freedom. Like too many of the black people in our story he appears in the records more spoken about than speaking, the subject of events rather than an actor in them. What we do know is that he was a domestic slave from Virginia. Charles Stewart, a former Boston customs officer of Scottish origins, regarded Somerset as his property, and had done for twenty years. Under the laws of Virginia or Massachusetts, Stewart's ownership of Somerset was not in question but in November 1769 Stewart brought Somerset with him to London. Perhaps on the streets of the English capital, Somerset began to notice the numbers of free black people, and started to imagine that he might be able to simply slip among them, and find some degree of anonymity within the chaotic bustle of the multi-racial metropolis. There he could bide his time in the hope that Charles Stewart would give up looking for him and return to Virginia. Or perhaps, during his time in London, Somerset came to understand that the only chance of freedom that was ever likely to present itself required him to ensure that when his owner returned to Virginia he was not on board that ship with him. Somerset might also have come to question his status as a slave on spiritual grounds, as we know that on 12 February 1771 he was baptized at St Andrew's in Holborn. There he was welcomed into the Church and received by three white godparents. Whatever his reasons, after two years in London and two decades serving Stewart, on 26 November 1771 James Somerset escaped.

Like Mary Hylas, Thomas Lewis and an unknown number of black men and women in the seventeenth and eighteenth centuries the hired slave-hunters were unleashed against James Somerset. He was stalked on the streets of London. He was cornered and captured near Covent Garden, after having known just two months of the freedom he craved. From Covent Garden he was taken to the *Ann and Mary*, a ship in the Thames, and there put in chains, out of sight in the gloom of a lower deck. James Somerset was, however, not to be returned to his empty life as a domestic slave in Massachusetts but to be cast into the hellish existence of a Jamaican plantation slave. He was, it appeared, doomed.

Somerset reached out to his godparents from the church in which he had been baptized, and they came to his defence. Elizabeth Cade, Thomas Walkin, and John Marlow, all of them moral enemies of slavery, together secured a writ of habeas corpus on Somerset's behalf, which was granted, again by Lord Mansfield.[29] This compelled Captain John Knowles of the *Ann and Mary* to surrender Somerset to the court. Mrs Cade appears to have taken the lead. Yet although Lord Mansfield granted the writ and demanded that Somerset be presented to the court, Stewart and Knowles, the men who between them had arranged for the kidnapping and deportation, were initially regarded by Mansfield as the injured party in the affair. It was Somerset the plaintiff rather than Stewart and Knowles the defendants who was bound over to appear in court. Knowles brazenly complained in his affidavit that Somerset having 'departed and absented himself' from the service of Stewart had thereby deprived him of his property.

Despite knowing so little about the man, what we can say about James Somerset is that he was clearly determined to fight for his freedom and adamant that he would not return to Stewart, or be sold into Jamaican slavery at the hands of Captain Knowles. To fight his case he went to see Granville Sharp, whose fame and reputation had increased with each victory in court. The injustices of Somerset's plight appear, after a delay, to have fired Sharp's indignant temper. Two weeks later he agreed to take the case on and the usual flurry of frenetic activity began. On 29 January he records in his diary the payment to the relevant clerk of six guineas, 'to retain two counsel in the case of Somerset.' The legal team Sharp assembled quickly expanded. As well as the experienced and pugnacious William 'Bull' Davy and John Glyn, sergeants at law, Sharp accepted an offer of service from Francis Hargrave, a young barrister who was so passionately anti-slavery that he had researched the legal issues and the case-law history much in the way Sharp himself had done. The two swapped notes. Also on the team was the sergeant at law John Alleyne and the barrister James Mansfield, who was not related to the Lord Chief Justice. Both Hargrave and Alleyne worked pro bono on what promised to be a landmark case that might lift their professional reputations.

Against this impressive array of legal minds there appeared for the defence a figure who was familiar to Granville Sharp. The barrister whose services were retained by Charles Stewart and Captain Knowles was John Dunning, who only the previous year had defended Thomas Lewis. In that case he had declared, in public session and in front of Lord Mansfield, that England's 'Laws admit of no such property'. Throughout that case Dunning had brandished a copy of Granville Sharp's book. By appearing in the defence of Stewart, in support of his right to own property in Somerset, Dunning put himself in a ridiculous position and the whiff of hypocrisy undermined his case and his performance in court from the start.

When the case finally began in January 1772 the argument that Dunning struggled to present, to an often hostile courtroom, was one in which he attempted to sidestep the morality of slavery and instead lay out a commercial case. Dunning argued that to refuse to recognize the property rights of slave owners who had brought slaves into England would be to the detriment of British commerce. Another of Stewart's barristers, William Wallace, argued that it would be a grave injustice if Stewart lost his property merely because he had travelled to England to conduct legal business. Wallace also contended that any judgement that disavowed the slave owners' right to their 'property' would, in effect, liberate from bondage thousands of black people already resident in Britain. It was during the Somerset trial that the black population of the country was estimated at around fourteen to fifteen thousand. This dubious figure was arrived at, in part, to allow the defence counsel to make another equally dubious calculation of the potential economic costs of their mass liberation. By Dunning's reckoning the cost of freeing all the black slaves currently in England would exceed £800,000. Mansfield himself, at one point in the trial, remarked that 'setting 14,000 or 15,000 men at once loose by a solemn opinion, is very disagreeable in the effects it threatens.'[30] Another pertinent financial issue emerged during exchanges between William Wallace and Lord Mansfield when the court learnt that Charles Stewart's costs and expenses were being paid by the West Indian merchants.[31] To some extent the Somerset case became a proxy war between the West India Interest on the one hand and humanitarians like Sharp and his supporters on the other, as money was donated to pay the counsel on both sides.

Lord Mansfield, who was one of the architects of English commercial law, was innately sympathetic towards aspects of the arguments that were put forward by John Dunning, but as in previous cases he hoped to find a way to avoid making a definitive judgement. In an effort to prevent the case coming to trial Mansfield endeavoured to persuade Somerset, Stewart, and Captain Knowles to negotiate through their attorneys and reach a settlement outside of court. In court, during one of the many adjournments, he informed counsel that 'In five or six cases of this nature, I have known it to be accommodated by agreement between the parties: on its first coming before me, I strongly recommended it here'. On two separate occasions Mansfield suggested that Stewart could at a stroke 'end the question, by discharging or giving freedom to the negro'. On another he proposed that Elizabeth Cade, one of Somerset's godparents who had helped secure the writ of habeas corpus, should herself purchase him from Charles Stewart and then set him free. Elizabeth Cade, a poor widow opposed to slavery on religious principle, adamantly refused to even consider Lord Mansfield's suggestion as to do so 'would be an acknowledgement that the Plaintiff had a right to Assault and imprison a poor innocent man in this Kingdom, and that she would never be guilty of setting so bad an Example'.[32] What James Somerset thought of these various schemes for his manumission is not recorded.

Mansfield's other tactic was to repeatedly adjourn the case and delay proceedings. Between the writ of habeas corpus being granted in December 1771 and the final decision in late June 1772, there were eight separate hearings of the case; each of them, except the last, ended by an adjournment. This tactic backfired spectacularly on Mansfield, as it provided the legal team that Granville Sharp had assembled to expand the scope of their case, making it ever more difficult for him to offer a limited judgement, specific only to the case of James Somerset. The chain of adjournments also gave journalists on the London and provincial newspapers more time to report the case, which in turn increased public interest.[33] The later adjournments were reported almost as cliff-hanger endings in a long-running drama, one in which the great questions of freedom, slavery and property rights might be decided.

The case that Davy and Glyn presented on Somerset's behalf centred on the canon of legal arguments developed by Sharp during his studies in 1766. These arguments had been refined and practised by the barristers Sharp had worked with during the previous cases, including John Dunning. At the core of the case for the prosecution of Stewart and Knowles was the proposition 'that no man at this day is, or can be a slave in England'.[34] Therefore if Somerset was indeed a man, and Mansfield himself 'concluded him one' then 'it was impossible he could be a slave in England unless by the introduction of some species of property unknown to our constitution'.[35] Davy and Glyn argued that not only did English law not sanction slavery, the protections it offered applied to all people who entered into England, irrespective of race or even religion. The only laws or statutes that had ever sanctioned any form on bondage in England were the ancient laws pertaining to villeinage, which were clearly defunct. Only colonial laws sanctioned slavery and they were not applicable in England. If the slave laws of Virginia and Jamaica were accepted in England, they argued, then why not all colonial laws and statutes? Referring to the Cartwright case of 1569, which had famously resolved 'That England was too pure an Air for Slaves to breathe in', Davy, addressing Mansfield, commented that, 'I hope, my Lord, the air does not blow worse since. But, unless there is a change of air, I hope they will never breathe here; for that is my assertion,—the moment they put their foot on English ground, that moment they become free. They are subject to the laws, and they are entitled to the protection of the laws of this country, and so are their masters, thank God!'[36]

It was Francis Hargrave, the novice, who had offered his services free, whose speech most doggedly sought to expand the scope of the case beyond just the facts pertaining to James Somerset. Hargrave wanted to explore general principles and he did so brilliantly. 'The questions arising on this case do not merely conserve the unfortunate person who is the subject of it,' he said. 'The right claimed by Mr. Stewart to the detention of the negro, is founded on the condition of slavery in which he was before his master brought him into England; and if that right is not recognized, domestic slavery, with its horrid train of evils, may be imported into this country.'[37] This potent spectre of slavery imported into England, and 'tolerated' as Sharp had described it, was powerfully fleshed out by Hargrave in a barnstorming speech that demonstrated the extent to which slavery was out of step with English traditions and lacking a sound basis in English law – facts that Lord Mansfield despite himself fully understood. Hargrave's speeches were as much history lessons as legal arguments and Lord Mansfield's failure to prevent him and other counsel from expanding the scope of the case made it increasingly difficult for him, the further proceedings dragged on, to offer a narrow and limited judgement. For all his legal brilliance in the case of James Somerset, Lord Mansfield, to some extent, lost control of proceedings.

On 21 May 1772 Lord Mansfield adjourned the case for the last time, but not before making one final plea to Stewart for him to 'end the question, by discharging or giving freedom to the negro'.[38] With the money of the West India planters behind him Stewart had nothing to lose and no incentive to settle and had promised his paymasters that he would see the case through to judgement.[39] 'If the parties will have it decided', Lord Mansfield said, 'we must give our opinion. Compassion will not, on the one hand, nor inconvenience on the other, be to decide'.[40]

So Lord Mansfield retired to deliberate, fearful of the potential consequences that might flow from the judgement that was now expected of him. To find in favour of Somerset carried the risk of undermining the property rights of the slave owners and such a decision could, potentially, lead to the emancipation of the thousands of black servants and slaves in Britain. Whereas should he rule that the slave laws of Virginia protected Stewart's property rights in James Somerset while in England, 'to the extent it has been argued', carried what Lord Mansfield described as 'consequences altogether foreign to the object of our present enquiry'. These considerations were what he described as the 'obstructions that militate against an immediate decision'.[41] But he concluded in court that, 'If the parties will have judgment, "fiat justitia, ruat cœlum;" let justice be done whatever be the consequence. 50*l*. a-head may not be a high price; then a loss follows to the proprietors of above 700,000*l*. sterling. How would the law stand with respect to their [the slaves] settlement; their wages? How many actions for any slight coercion by the master? We cannot in any of these points direct the law; the law must rule us.'[42]

The Lord Chief Justice took over a month to make his judgement. During that time he returned to his mansion, Kenwood House in Hampstead. There, within his home, was his extensive law library and his bust of Homer, and also his family which — to say the least

– was not entirely conventional. Lord Mansfield's nephew, Captain Sir John Lindsay of the Royal Navy, had a daughter who was the product of an affair between Lindsay and an enslaved African woman named Maria. She had been named Dido Elizabeth Belle and in 1765, the year Jonathan Strong stumbled into Mincing Lane and Granville Sharp began his legal studies, Captain Lindsay brought her to England. When Lindsay returned to sea he entrusted his daughter to the care of Lord Mansfield and his wife Elizabeth Murray; they a wealthy childless couple, she a mixed-race girl of just four years old. Although technically Dido was merely Mansfield's illegitimate grand-niece she was brought up at Kenwood House, alongside the couple's orphaned niece Elizabeth. Her exact status within Mansfield's household is not entirely known, though it seems she might at times have been treated affectionately but not as a full equal, in much the way the poorer relations to wealthy families were regarded. Dido also performed some acts of service to the young Miss Murray and managed the dairy at Kenwood. But the extent to which Dido's status within the family was determined by her race, as opposed to her illegitimacy, is impossible to disentangle. Later Mansfield was to leave Dido an annuity in his will and use his legal skills to ensure that she was unambiguously recognized as a free person. Today Dido Belle is well known. The portrait, by Zoffany, of her and the young Elizabeth Murray is one of the best-known images of any black Georgian, but her existence was not widely known in 1772. At a time when the black population of London probably numbered fewer than ten thousand it is truly remarkable that the man who was to make a legal determination on the issue of slavery in England had a mixed-race niece, to whom he was evidently devoted, yet this was the case and Dido must, at times, have been in Mansfield's mind over the weeks during which he agonized over his judgement.

From the very start the Somerset case had attracted the attention of the public. The earliest hearings had been held before busy court-rooms, packed with interested spectators and supporters of Granville Sharp's campaign. By the summer of 1772, after more than six months of speeches, repeated adjournments and fresh hearings, all of it reported by the press, the case had become a national sensation and the topic of endless debate. Newspaper coverage was constant throughout the case but peaked between May and June. The powerful speech given by Francis Hargrave in the May hearings that stunned the court had been widely reported. Rather as Hargrave had done in court, journalists and correspondents to the newspapers endeavoured in print to link the case to wider issues and principles. Long before the case was anywhere near resolution, newspapers in London and the provinces had already painted a wholly distorted picture of the issues on which a judgement was, eventually, to be made. A Bristol periodical suggested that the point of the case was to determine 'how far a Negro or Black, is a slave in England'.[43] The picture was made more confusing still by reports of statements supposedly made by Lord Mansfield. Some newspapers widened the scope of the case even further; the future of British commerce and the security of the West Indian colonies were both said to rest on Mansfield's judgement. Other correspondents made dire predictions of the fate that would befall the nation if Mansfield ruled in favour of Somerset, while equally apocalyptical visions of the future were fleshed out by correspondents who imagined a bleak future in which slavery was tolerated in England and the violence of the plantation system imported into the mother country.

The scale of public interest was not accidental. Behind the scenes Granville Sharp had been busy raising awareness and building support. He had employed a shorthand writer to record the speeches given in court; these were then printed and disseminated across the country. Sharp sent copies, along with his personal letters, to influential figures in politics and the church. To reinforce the fact that the fates of real, flesh-and-blood human beings were at stake, Sharp, rather brilliantly, had James Somerset hand-deliver documents to these notables. Somerset even delivered a package of documents from Sharp to Lord Mansfield himself.[44]

Granville Sharp's campaign harnessed an interest in the issue of slavery that already existed and that was building within sections of the public. Here was an institution that raised difficult questions about the limits of the freedoms that Englishmen increasingly valued. Slavery was built on violence; it ripped families apart, separated husbands from wives and children from their mothers. All of this played on late Georgian notions of sentiment and tragedy. Much of this sentimentalism was paternalistic, and fixed the black African very much as a passive victim, but the emotions it elicited were real and powerful. The slow rise of a new Christian philanthropy, the same spirit that had provided both Jonathan Strong and James Somerset with white godparents from the churches in which they had been baptized, inspired a moral and religious fervour in people who, in later years, would be called abolitionists. To them the potential of the Somerset case was clear and unambiguous.

After so long a wait, and following so much fevered speculation and dubious misreporting, it was inevitable that when Lord Mansfield came to deliver his judgement on Monday 22 June 1772 he found Westminster Hall overflowing with members of the public, representatives of the interested parties and reporters from the newspapers. Among those present were the anxious agents of the West India Interest, who feared that Lord Mansfield was about to deliver a judgement far less favourable than the opinion the planters of the late 1720s had solicited from the obliging Lords Yorke and Talbot. Press reports speculating that the case was more likely to go in favour of Somerset than against him served to increase the alarm of the West India merchants and their supporters. Also in attendance were people who had more resting on the case than property rights. As the newspapers tell us there were a number of black people in Westminster Hall awaiting the judgement. Beyond the courtroom the case was being eagerly followed by Britain's black population, some of whom had reason to fear for their own legal status should Mansfield rule against James Somerset.

The mood of the crowd in Westminster Hall was made more febrile and expectant by news from the markets. As Mansfield prepared to read his judgement the nation appeared to be teetering on the brink of economic chaos. The collapse of a leading credit house, and the flight to France of the banker Alexander Fordyce who was unable to pay his debts, had sparked an eighteenth-century credit crunch. There had been a run on the banks and around twenty institutions had collapsed. On the day that Mansfield was giving his judgement, Horace Walpole complained, with some incredulity, that 'One rascally and extravagant banker has brought Britannia, Queen of the Indies, to the precipice of bankruptcy! . . . He has broken half the bankers.'[45] James Boswell writing in the *Scots Magazine* painted a vivid picture of the tense atmosphere that had pervaded the city that day: 'Words cannot describe the general consternation of the metropolis . . . A universal bankruptcy was expected, and the stoppage of every banker looked for. The whole city was in uproar, and many of the first families in tears. Every countenance appeared clouded, occasioned either by real distress, or by what they feared for their friends'.[46] It is against this backdrop of heightened tension that Mansfield prepared to give his judgement on slavery and the rights of slave owners, with all its potential implications for the national economy.

When Lord Mansfield appeared at Westminster Hall he began by reminding the court how, over a year earlier, James Somerset had been kidnapped and chained aboard the ship the *Ann and Mary* in which he was to be transported to slavery in Jamaica. The right that Somerset's owner Charles Stewart had presumed when he had kidnapped Somerset and attempted to deport him from England constituted, in Mansfield's view, 'so high an act of dominion', that it could only be permitted if such a right were 'recognized by the law of the country where it is used'.[47] He went on, 'The power of a master over his slave has been extremely different, in different countries. The state of slavery is of such a nature, that it is incapable of being introduced on any reasons, moral or political, but only by positive law, which preserves its force long after the reasons, occasion, and time itself from whence it was created, is erased from memory. It is so odious, that nothing can be suffered to support it, but positive law. Whatever inconveniences, therefore, may follow from the decision, I cannot say this case is allowed or approved by the law of England; and therefore the black must be discharged.'[48]

It was reported in the newspapers that on hearing those last words the black people within the crowd 'bowed with profound respect to the Judges, and shaking each other by the hand, congratulated themselves upon their recovery of the rights of human nature, and their happy lot that permitted them to breathe the free air of England.—No sight upon earth could be more pleasingly affecting to the feeling mind, than the joy which shone at that instant in these poor men's sable countenances.'[49]

To those who heard it, and to those who were to read about it later, the judgement appeared to grant freedom not just to James

Somerset but to all black people in Britain. This is not what Mansfield said, but it is what most people took his judgement to mean. The exact meaning of Lord Mansfield's judgement was debated at the time and has been the subject of more than two centuries of argument among both legal experts and historians. The fact that we do not have a precise written transcription of the judgement significantly clouds the waters, and expands the scope for interpretation and misinterpretation. Court reporting was haphazardly done in the eighteenth century and Mansfield's own copy of the judgement was destroyed, along with his other papers, when his house was targeted during the Gordon Riots of 1780. All that survives are the newspapers' accounts of what Mansfield said in court and law reports compiled some years later.[50] One of those reports puts into the mouth of Lord Mansfield words that were in fact said by Francis Hargrave, Somerset's counsel and perhaps the most ideologically anti-slavery member of his legal team. Through this haze of misreporting, the judgement was widely interpreted as a final determination by Lord Mansfield that slavery did not exist as a recognized institution within the laws of England, having never been introduced by any positive law or Act of Parliament. However, a more narrow interpretation of the judgement suggests that all Lord Mansfield ruled upon was whether a slave owner had the right to forcibly remove a slave from the country. A later ruling by Lord Mansfield in a case of 1785 relating to the enslaved black woman Charlotte Howe supports the view that what he had made in 1772 was a narrow ruling on the deportation of slaves out of England. But Lord Mansfield was never able to rein in the misinterpretation of the judgement for which he is best remembered today. Yet whatever the scope of the judgement the startling fact was that James Somerset was no longer a slave. Lord Mansfield had concluded that Charles Stewart did not have the right under English law to seize James Somerset on English soil and deport him to the colonies. He could arguably have thus returned him to Charles Stewart, still in a state of slavery. But he had concluded his ruling by saying that 'therefore the black must be discharged'. The judgement had made Somerset free and he, by the act of resisting deportation and taking the case to law, had manumitted himself. Lord Mansfield's later claims that his judgement was narrow and limited are to some extent undermined by the fact of Somerset's freedom.[51]

Ultimately the exact terms of his judgement and intentions became less significant than the popular understanding, or misunderstanding, of it. This popular interpretation overpowered and overwhelmed the dry letter of the law. Black people in Britain and their supporters were determined to take the decision as monumental and to regard its impact as wide and far reaching, despite the technical narrowness of what Mansfield had actually ruled. Just five days after the judgement, the *Public Advertiser* reported that 'On Monday near two hundred blacks with their ladies had an entertainment at a public-house in Westminster, to celebrate the triumph which their brother Somerset had obtained over Mr. Stuart, his master. Lord Mansfield's health was echoed around the room; and the evening was concluded with a ball.'[52] The *Public Advertiser* of 25 June noted that 'A Subscription is now raising among the great Number of Negroes, in and about this Metropolis, for the purpose of presenting Somerset with a handsome Gratuity, for having so nobly stood up in Defence of the natural Rights of the sable Part of the human Creation.'[53] The slave owners were unsure as to the scope of the judgement, but feared that when Mansfield had warned of 'inconveniences' that 'may follow from the decision', he had them and their Property rights in mind. In May 1772 the slave owners had asked Parliament to pass an act to end all uncertainty and legalize the holding of slaves in England. When Parliament refused, the slave owners took that decision as an indication that the anti-slavery mood in Britain was beginning to gain traction.

Granville Sharp himself had been unclear about what the judgement had achieved. He had not been in court to hear Lord Mansfield's judgement and had not appeared at any of the hearings. Having attended the earlier cases he had championed, Sharp had concluded that his presence in court risked annoying Lord Mansfield, and he stayed away. Furthermore he had his work in the Ordnance Office to occupy him. For Sharp the case ended as it had begun, with James Somerset calling upon him at the lodgings he shared with his brother in Old Jewry. On 22 June 1772 Sharp's diary reads, 'This day, James Somerset came to tell me that judgement was to-day given in his favour.'[54] From a number of later statements it is clear that Sharp was not convinced that the ruling had ended slavery in England.

Beyond 22 June 1772, when we can pinpoint him in Old Jewry delivering the news to Granville Sharp, James Somerset, the man whose personal freedom had become the subject of this epic trial, disappears from written records, his later life lost to us. His name, of course, linked for ever to those of Lord Mansfield and Granville Sharp, lived on, but the Somerset judgement for which he is remembered was not what most people at the time understood it to be and not what many historians subsequently reported.

Interpretation and misinterpretation aside, the judgement meant that slave owners no longer had the power to enforce their claims over enslaved people in England. The threat of deportation, the most powerful of the tools used to compel obedience on slaves in England – the ship as opposed to the whip, as one historian put it – had been taken from them. After Mansfield slaves in England could, in effect, free themselves by running away, and the slave owners knew it. The pro-slavery propagandist Edward Long saw the ruling in this light and regarded the loss of the right to imprison or transport slaves in Britain as virtually the same as granting him or her freedom. And there were black people who similarly interpreted the ruling and promptly left their owners to claim the freedoms they believed the Lord Chief Justice had granted them. In July 1772, less than a month after the judgement, one John Riddell of Bristol Wells wrote to Charles Stewart to report his slave Dublin had left him. 'I am disappointed by Mr. Dublin who has run away', Riddell wrote. 'He told the servants that he had rec'd a letter from his Uncle Sommerset [sic] acquainting him that Lord Mansfield had given them their freedom & he was determined to leave me as soon as I returned from London which he did without even speaking to me . . . I believe that I shall not give myself any trouble to look after [for] this ungrateful villain'.[55] In 1769 Joseph Knight, a Jamaican slave who had been taken to Scotland by his owner John Wedderburn, read of the Somerset judgement in the *Edinburgh Advertiser* and decided that Mansfield's decision applied to him, despite Scotland having her own separate laws and legal system. Knight emancipated himself and later got married, but was then arrested by John Wedderburn. Knight appealed and in 1778 the sheriff of Perthshire concluded, 'that the state of slavery is not recognized by the laws of this kingdom'.[56] At appeal before the Court of Sessions the Somerset case was cited repeatedly. At this higher court it was decided that Joseph Knight was a free man as the laws of Jamaica, where Wedderburn had purchased Knight, carried no more weight in Scotland than the laws of Virginia did in England. Yet these were isolated cases. After the Mansfield judgement there was not a large-scale dash for freedom among enslaved black Britons. The economic considerations that convinced black people to stay with their masters, whether as slaves or as servants, were unchanged by rulings from the King's Bench. Life among the black poor on the streets of London and elsewhere remained as precarious and harsh as ever and black slaves lacking family networks or marketable skills were barred by poverty from seizing the freedoms that the law appeared to have conceded.

But while black people and their supporters, along with a number of slave owners, believed that the Mansfield judgement had ended slavery in England, some masters understood that the judgement had been far less definitive and attempted to hold on to their slaves, while others chose to simply ignore the case. Long after 1772 advertisements for the sale of slaves were still appearing in British newspapers, as were notices offering rewards for the return of runaways. Furthermore, even for Mansfield's narrow judgement to take effect, and for kidnapped slaves to be saved from deportation to the plantations, their abductions had to be prevented and they themselves had to be liberated from the ships in which they were imprisoned. As the cases of Jonathan Strong, Mary Hylas, Thomas Lewis and James Somerset had all demonstrated, it took a combination of various factors – luck, literacy and determination on the part of the enslaved, botched abductions or the active involvement of outraged witnesses like Mrs Banks to alert the courts and bring cases of abduction to law. How many black Georgians were more discreetly abducted and covertly deported, both before and after the Mansfield judgement, will never be known. There are reports of black men and women being forced aboard West India-bound ships long after 1772. The tragic story, mentioned in the previous chapter, of the black man who, having been abducted, committed suicide while on the Thames, and became the inspiration for Thomas

Day and John Bicknall's poem *The Dying Negro*, took place in 1773. Even in 1823, sixteen years after the abolition of the slave trade, it was reported that a black woman named Grace Jones was forcibly transported by her mistress to slavery on the island of Antigua.

On 17 April 1773, as the repercussions of the Mansfield judgement reverberated around Britain and radiated across the empire, Granville Sharp, still in his lodgings in Old Jewry, recorded in his diary that 'Poor Jonathan Strong, the first Negro whose freedom I had procured in 1767, died this morning.' Jonathan Strong was only around twenty-five years old. He had never fully recovered from the vicious beating he had suffered at the hands of David Lisle in 1765.

FIVE

'Province of Freedom'

Despite his repeated attempts to limit the legal scope of the Somerset case, Lord Mansfield's begrudgingly delivered judgement had repercussions that were broader and more divisive than even he had feared. News travelled rapidly across the Atlantic. Twenty-one American newspapers published forty-three reports between them on the case and Mansfield's decision. The interpretations of the judgement and the accounts of what was said in court carried by the American papers were just as inaccurate as those that appeared in the British press. In the American colonies, as in Britain, the Somerset judgement came to be widely understood as having effectively outlawed slavery in England. News of the decision emboldened America's abolitionists and enraged the slave owners, some of whom saw it as another English attack on colonial property rights. Benjamin Rush, the American abolitionist and friend of Granville Sharp, published a pamphlet in Philadelphia celebrating the Somerset case as a first blow struck against slavery, while a letter from a correspondent to a British newspaper, repeatedly reprinted in colonial newspapers, warned that Mansfield's judgement appeared 'pregnant with consequences extremely detrimental to those Gentlemen, whose estates chiefly consist in slaves'.[1]

One of Lord Mansfield's stated objectives in the case was to avoid interfering in the legal systems of the North American and West Indian colonies. Before issuing his judgement he had even endeavoured to calm the nerves of the West Indian merchants by issuing a statement promising them that the case would have no implications for the trade in slaves. Under the laws of Virginia and Jamaica,

Mansfield reassured them, Africans, 'are goods and chattels, and, as such, saleable and sold'.[2] Mansfield had feared that any judgement made on the case of James Somerset risked becoming a precedent that might be used to free all the slaves in England – fifteen thousand of them, according to the lawyers defending Somerset's owner Charles Stewart.

Almost from the moment news of the judgement reached their shores, colonial slave owners feared that Mansfield's decision might have a direct impact upon them. Could the decision be limited to England alone? No one seemed sure. The Rhode Island attorney Henry Marchant, in London in 1771, had attended the first hearing in the Somerset case and concluded that the legal team Granville Sharp had assembled to fight for James Somerset's freedom had developed a legal case so compelling and so rooted in English legal tradition that it could potentially be deployed by lawyers representing slaves in the colonies. He warned his fellow colonists that the case was a 'plausible pretense' that might 'cheat an honest American of his slave'.[3] That fear was reinforced in 1774 when an attorney representing a Massachusetts slave who was suing to attain his freedom did indeed cite the Somerset case. The argument he put forward was that in Massachusetts, just as in England, no positive law had been enacted to make slavery legal. In the mid-1770s the colonists increasingly became the authors of their own difficulties on this matter. As they expressed, ever more vocally and stridently, their demands for full English rights they exposed themselves further to English law, and weakened the notion that the law within the empire was effectively federal, with different laws operating in different jurisdictions.

If the Somerset judgement was found to be limited to England the institution of colonial slavery might be safe but even then the slave owners had still lost an important liberty. Even under the most narrow and circumscribed interpretation of the Mansfield judgement it was clear that colonial slave owners could no longer bring their slaves with them when they returned to the 'mother country', in many cases the country of their birth. Those who might have planned to settle in England, or, more commonly, reside there while they conducted their business affairs, now understood that their personal and domestic slaves could abscond and, having done so, seek protection from the English courts. Otherwise they might demand wages

as recompense for their services, an idea the owners found uncon-
scionable. No matter how they looked at it, the Mansfield judgement
represented a loss of liberty. That loss might have been more tolerable had it not been one among a long litany of curtailed liberties
and perceived injustices that offended the American colonists by the
1770s. In that atmosphere the Somerset case had political implications far beyond any debates around case law, jurisdiction and
precedent. There was no question that the case posed a legal conundrum, but to the planters it was also a political betrayal, regarded
by some as a direct attack on the slave system.

For the half a million slaves of the American colonies – who made
up around one-fifth of the entire population, and two-fifths of all
the black people in the empire – the Mansfield judgement was
electrifying news. Rumours and reports swept across the plantations
as fast as they had raced across the ocean. The news was transmitted
across networks of communication that the whites could neither
explain nor control. Some American slaves heard of the judgement
from their owners. Like enslaved people across the New World,
domestic slaves in the American colonies listened while attending
tables and overheard conversations and arguments while going about
their work. Although America's slave owners had done their very
best to prevent the spread of literacy among the enslaved, a small
minority were able to read the reports; newspapers in the late
eighteenth century passed from hand to hand, a single copy being
read by numerous people. Some American slaves drew the same
conclusions about the case that Mr Dublin of Bristol had; that 'Lord
Mansfield had given them their freedom'. A few decided to risk
punishment and retribution and claim that liberty. At the end of
September 1773 a slave owner named John Austin Finnie placed an
advertisement in the *Virginia Gazette* reporting the loss of two of his
slaves: 'a Wench, named AMY, of a very black Complexion, about
27 Years old', and 'a Fellow, African born, named BACCHUS, about
19 Years of Age [he] speaks somewhat broken [English]'. Finnie
claimed to have 'some Reason to believe they will endeavour to get
out of the Colony, particularly to Britain, where they imagine they
will be free (a Notion now too prevalent among the Negroes, greatly

to the vexation and Prejudice of their Masters)'.[4] The following year Gabriel Jones, who owned land and slaves near Augusta, Georgia, placed a similar advertisement in his local newspaper. Jones offered a reward of five pounds for the return of a runaway slave, also named Bacchus. Jones was particularly anxious to see him captured as Bacchus had taken a purse of money and because Jones feared he would 'attempt to get on board some vessel for Great Britain, from the knowledge he has of the late Determination of Somerset's Case'.[5] It was against this backdrop that the early stirrings of what was to develop into the American Revolutionary Wars began.

There were two revolutions in the American colonies during the 1770s and 1780s.[6] In the first, the white colonists rose up against British rule and fought to realize their independence. Without any embarrassment the rebels and patriots of that revolution used the term 'freedom' to allude to their political aspirations, and the word 'slavery' to describe their exposure to British taxation. Even before the American patriots had issued a Declaration of Independence that professed 'all men equal', their hypocrisy had been noted and ridiculed. In 1775 Samuel Johnson, writing from the London town house he shared with Francis Barber, asked, 'how is it we hear the loudest yelps for liberty among the drivers of Negroes?'[7] Granville Sharp, still fearful of the dangers of 'toleration', warned that 'American liberty cannot be firmly established without some scheme of general Enfranchisement', as, 'The toleration of domestic slavery in the colonies greatly weakens the claim or natural right of our American brethren to Liberty. Let them put away the accursed thing (that horrid Oppression) from among them, before they presume to implore the interposition of divine Justice.'[8]

American hypocrisy was taken to unparalleled levels by Richard Henry Lee, the Virginian politician who moved the resolution in the Second Continental Congress calling for American independence. In a public parade against the imposition of the Stamp Tax, Lee had a number of banners unveiled which denounced how that most hated of taxes had placed 'chains of slavery' around the necks of white American colonists. Lee felt no embarrassment in having his banners carried on the parade by his own slaves and there are no reports to indicate that any of Lee's fellow Virginians felt any discomfort at the spectacle.[9]

In the second of America's eighteenth-century revolutions thousands of enslaved Africans revolted against a form of slavery that was real rather than metaphorical, one enforced with chains that cut into flesh rather than curtailed economic freedoms. The history of the first of these two revolutions has been extensively described and analysed elsewhere, most notably by historians from the nation it spawned. For our purposes it is the second revolution that is of most interest. That parallel revolution was launched by another declaration. It was issued in late 1775, over a year before the Declaration of Independence. The author was John Murray, fourth Earl of Dunmore and the Royal Governor of the colony of Virginia, the largest of the thirteen American colonies, and home to a hundred and eighty thousand enslaved Africans who toiled and suffered on hundreds of tobacco plantations.

In April 1775 a rebellion broke out in Virginia and began to spread across the territory. Lord Dunmore's strategy was to put down the uprising as fast as possible through ruthless and decisive action. After removing the gunpowder from Williamsburg, the colonial capital, he based himself and his forces on a flotilla of ships on the James River. In May he wrote to his superiors informing them of his next decisive step. He intended to 'arm my own negroes & receive all others that come to me who I shall declare free'. In November 1775, in a public proclamation that was printed and distributed, Dunmore declared that 'all indentured Servants, Negroes, or others, (appertaining to Rebels,)' were to be freed if they were 'able and willing to bear Arms'. To claim their freedom slaves had to join 'His MAJESTY'S Troops as soon as may be, for the more speedily reducing this Colony to a proper Sense of their Duty to His *MAJESTY'S* Crown and *Dignity*'.[10] Within two weeks around three hundred slaves had left their masters and made their way to Dunmore's forces, who were still concentrated on around one hundred ships on the James River. Some managed to reach the British ships in small boats, others waded through the swamps and literally swam to freedom. On board the British ships, they were formed into a new unit: Lord Dunmore's Royal Ethiopian Regiment. On their shoulders were placed British muskets and onto their new uniforms was sewn a badge bearing a slogan that was extraordinarily and intentionally provocative to the tobacco planters of Virginia – 'Liberty to Slaves'.

Dunmore calculated that freeing and arming slaves might so shock the rebels that they would back down and submit to the Crown. His actions had the opposite effect. Even before 1775 Dunmore had a reputation for being insensitive and autocratic. Now he was bitterly condemned by the colonists for 'exciting an insurrection of our slaves'. In a society that had known slave rebellions, placing guns in the hands of black men was transgressing the ultimate taboo. In the minds of some Southern planters Dunmore had turned the rebellion into a fight over the right to hold slaves. The *Virginia Gazette* was so outraged by the proclamation that it reprinted it in full, with an appended editorial in which the author – probably the patriot John Page – directly threatened the slaves with violent retribution if they dared to abandon their masters and go over to the British.[11] 'Should there be any amongst the Negroes weak enough to believe that Dunmore intends to do them a kindness, and wicked enough to provoke the fury of the Americans against their defenceless fathers and mothers, their wives, their women and children, let them only consider the difficulty of effecting their escape, and what they must expect to suffer if they fall into the hands of the Americans.' It concluded, 'Be not then, ye Negroes, tempted by this proclamation to ruin yourselves . . . I have considered your welfare, as well as that of the country. Whether you will profit by my advice I cannot tell; but this I know, that whether we suffer or not, if you desert us, you most certainly will.'[12]

To make real on this threat slave patrols were increased in Virginia and the 'fury of the Americans' was brutally exacted upon those unfortunate few who were caught attempting to escape. To further intimidate any slaves who might be considering joining the British, the slave owners spread the false rumour that the British intended to sell all those who joined them to the sugar planters of the West Indian islands, where death rates far exceeded birth rates and tropical diseases and the industrial nature of sugar production meant that the life expectancy among the enslaved was disturbingly low.

For all the bloodthirsty vitriol of its editorial, the *Virginia Gazette* was entirely correct in its assessment of Dunmore's proclamation. His offer of freedom to the slaves was a selective and self-interested tactic, motivated by military strategy not moral principle. Freedom was on offer only to slaves whose legal owners had joined the rebels, and only to those slaves who were 'able and willing to bear Arms', which excluded women and children. The slaves of colonists who stayed loyal to the Crown, who became known as the loyalists, were to remain in chains, and the future of colonial slavery was not to be threatened. The authorities stayed true to this commitment right up until the very end of British rule, when thousands of white loyalists lost their homes but kept their slaves.

Despite the grave threats published in the American newspapers, the enslaved were electrified by the news of Dunmore's proclamation. An officially sanctioned offer of freedom, issued by a representative of His Majesty's government just three years after the Somerset judgement, it inevitably generated an unparalleled exodus among the enslaved. The networks of communication that had broadcast news of Somerset's freedom now carried Dunmore's words across the Southern plantations; everywhere slaves drew up plans of escape, stole and stockpiled provisions and waited for the right moment to take flight. They gathered in the woods to discuss their options and strategize, black preachers held secret assemblies and everywhere the talk was of Dunmore, freedom and King George. On occasions whole communities – men, women and children – fled from bondage together. One South Carolina planter lost seventy-five slaves who, as well as 'stealing' themselves, took their master's horses. Across Virginia, Georgia and the Carolinas as news of the proclamation spread the scale of the first great migration increased.

By the end of 1775 there were three hundred black men in the Ethiopian Regiment. In 1776 enough former slaves had taken up British arms that a second regiment, the Black Pioneers, was formed. From November 1775 to the crushing British defeats of 1781 former slaves fought for their liberty and Britain's empire. They were there under Dunmore in the early clashes at Kemp's Landing and Great Bridge, fought just weeks after the formation of the Royal Ethiopian Regiment. Their initial impact upon events might have been far greater had not so many of them been struck down by a great epidemic of smallpox that ripped through the ranks of rebels and loyalists of both races, as those born in the colonies lacked immunity to the disease that was spread by the European soldiers who flooded into the country. A feared unit of former slaves known as the Black Brigade fought at the Battle of Monmouth and conducted a guerrilla war in 1778. They were led by the infamous Colonel Tye, Titus Cornelius, an escaped slave reputed to have been a grizzled early veteran of the Ethiopian Regiment, by then disbanded. At the most bitterly contested battles there were black American men in British red coats fighting, suffering and dying. They fought under the Union flag both in the infantry and the cavalry. Some were deployed as shock troops, infantry who assaulted enemy positions. Many knew the terrain and were therefore invaluable as scouts and guides to the soldiers shipped in from Britain and the mercenaries drafted from the German provinces. In a war that was fought as much on water as on land others served as sailors and as pilots on the ships that patrolled the rivers and supplied the armies. Some became spies behind enemy lines, but it was behind British lines that most worked, as general labourers, blacksmiths, wood-cutters, tailors, nurses and officers' servants. They dug trenches and prepared defences, they built the camps in which the armies were billeted and were constantly engaged in the task of supplying a force whose supply lines stretched across the Atlantic and over the empire. For all their talk of 'Liberty to Slaves', the British forces were largely racially segregated and some of the punishments to which black recruits were subjected, even for petty offences, were at times extreme and excessive. They had escaped slavery but not necessarily the whip.

It should not be forgotten that there were black men on both sides of the Revolutionary War. Those who fought for the patriots must have hoped that the ideals of the Declaration of Independence would, some day, apply to them, but more American slaves concluded that King George was likely to confirm their freedom than George Washington. Yet while George Washington was a slave owner, King George was monarch of a nation that in the 1770s and 1780s was the most prolific slave-trading power in the North Atlantic. That Britain, with her fleets of slave ships and her sugar islands carpeted with plantations, was regarded as the best friend of the slave shows how desperately short of friends Africans in the New World were.

In 1779, General Sir Henry Clinton, the commander-in-chief of the British forces in North America, issued a second proclamation that encouraged thousands more slaves to risk all and flee to the

British lines. Clinton's offer was broader and more comprehensive than that made by Lord Dunmore four years earlier. In order to claim their freedom the slaves had merely to abandon their rebellious masters and cross into British territory. They were not required to bear arms for the British. Over the course of the war, fifty thousand slaves escaped and defected to the British. It was the first mass emancipation in the history of the North American colonies. Yet Clinton's declaration, like that of Dunmore, was again an act of self-interest rather than moral purpose. Clinton's aim was not primarily to create new legions of black soldiers; by then an influx into the colonies of thirty thousand Hessian mercenaries had swelled the British ranks. The proclamation of 1779 was an act of economic warfare designed to strip the rebels of their property and destabilize their economy. It was a sign of military frustration.

The rebels and their leaders were appalled by the cynicism of the British tactics and personally aggrieved by their own losses. Slaves belonging to George Washington and James Madison escaped to join the ranks of their enemy, as later did black men and women owned by Thomas Jefferson, the author of the Declaration of Independence. Patrick Henry, famous for his great patriotic call to arms, 'Give me liberty or give me death', was horrified to discover that several slaves had escaped from his Leatherwood plantation, seizing their own liberty and rejecting the 'living death' that was the existence of a plantation slave.[13] Many factors motivated the rebellion of the white American colonists but Patrick Henry was not alone in considering Dunmore's proclamation of 1775 as one of the grievances that justified disloyalty. By 'encouraging insurrection among our slaves, many of whom are now actually in arms against us,' Henry ranted, the King had demonstrated himself to be a 'tyrant instead of the protector of his people'.[14] As thousands of slaves fled through the tobacco fields, hid in the forests or slipped along the nocturnal river valleys seeking out the British, there were white colonists so outraged at British actions, and so resentful of Dunmore's actions, that they rejected their King and took up arms against the Crown. Fear of losing enslaved property and livelihoods built on the foundations of forced labour motivated some loyalists to turn patriot.

*

Six years after Dunmore's proclamation British forces were trapped in a ramshackle, makeshift camp at Yorktown. Their position was defended by trenches and redoubts but surrounded by George Washington's Continental Army and their French allies. Within the British camp were more than a thousand slaves serving with the British forces, both labourers and soldiers, and an unknown number of others were attached to the camp unofficially, working as auxiliaries or merely concentrated around Yorktown having fled to take the British up on their promises of freedom. Yorktown was the Stalingrad of the Revolutionary Wars, a desperate siege that became the critical battle of the conflict. It was a battle fought by black men on both sides. The American army that besieged the British contained around fifteen hundred black soldiers, around a quarter of the entire force.

With the British garrison in Yorktown beginning to starve, and in the face of a concerted artillery bombardment, the British commander Cornwallis, in mid-October, gave the orders that amounted to the biggest betrayal of the black loyalists during the Revolutionary War. After the horses had been slaughtered to prevent their starvation, the unwanted blacks, auxiliaries and camp followers were forcibly driven from Yorktown. To the horror of a number of their white officers they were delivered into the hands of the rebels and their former slave masters, or left trapped in the killing zone between the two armies, where they faced enemy fire or simply starved. John Ewald, a Danish Hessian mercenary fighting for the British, witnessed their plight and described in his diary how under orders he and his comrades 'drove back to the enemy all of our black friends . . . We had used them to good advantage and set them free, and now, with fear and trembling they had to face the reward of their cruel masters.'[15] Later, while on patrol, Ewald came across a group of the abandoned black loyalists. Consoling himself with the thought that the 'scarcity of provisions' made 'this harsh act' justifiable as a military expedient, he admitted to his diary that 'we should have thought more about their deliverance at this time.'[16]

The war did not end at Yorktown but hopes of British victory did. When he received news of the defeat, the Prime Minister, Lord North, was said to have been overwhelmed, as if struck by musket ball in the chest. 'Oh God, it's all over,' he was reputed to have declared. The process, after the fall of Yorktown in October 1781, of bringing the war to an end, agreeing peace terms and evacuating the British forces and the loyalist sections of the colonial population, took two years. It would end in late November 1783, twenty-five months after Yorktown, when George Washington marched down Manhattan while from that island's southern tip the last British troops stepped into launches and cast off for the armada of British ships in New York Harbor.

For the white loyalists of North America the question after Yorktown was should they stay and take their chances in a new nation, one which they and the British had attempted to smother at birth, or should they leave and seek a new future in another of the King's dominions? For the black loyalists the choice was far more stark – evacuation or slavery? While founders of the United States discussed their future freedoms and liberties, the British concerned themselves not just with evacuating the white loyalists but also – and perhaps incredibly after Yorktown – with honouring the freedoms they had promised to the black men and women who had rallied to the colours during the war. A number of key British officers set themselves firmly against any repetition of Cornwallis' betrayal of the black loyalists.

Evacuations of white and black loyalists were arranged from the ports of Savannah in Georgia and Charleston in South Carolina, and land was allocated for them in Canada. White loyalists were evacuated with their slaves who, as their masters had remained loyal to the Crown, had been ineligible to claim freedom under the proclamations of either Dunmore or Clinton. The favoured destination of these Southern loyalist slave owners was East Florida, a territory that had remained loyal to Britain. There they hoped to establish new plantations on virgin pasture and recreate their colonial lifestyles in a conducive climate that was not dissimilar to that of their former homes in Virginia, Georgia and the Carolinas. Other loyalists attempted to do much the same thing by relocating to Jamaica, where there was less unoccupied land available but huge profits to be made from sugar cultivation. The options available to loyalist slave owners had of course been conspicuously narrowed as after the Somerset case even those who owned only a few domestic slaves dared not transport them to Britain even temporarily.

Some of the ships that left Savannah for East Florida in 1782

were in effect slave ships – though mercifully without the full
horrors of the slave deck – as the majority of those on board were
the property of the white loyalists. Five thousand whites were
evacuated from Savannah and ten thousand of their slaves. In many
of the ships that carried loyalists from Charleston the pattern was
repeated, with slaves easily outnumbering their owners. Whole
plantation communities were thereby transplanted from one colony
to another. In Charleston, slaves who had been the property of
rebels, but who had been seized by the British authorities during
the war, were left to be reclaimed by former masters, whom the
British regarded as their legal owners. However, those whom the
British defined as having 'rendered themselves particularly obnox-
ious on account of their attachment and services to the British
troops, and such as have had specific Promises of Freedom' were
to be evacuated.[17] A team of British inspectors was established to
identify former slaves who had come over to the British on the
direct promise of freedom and assertions to that effect were tested
and challenged. In all, around fifteen hundred black loyalists were
evacuated from Charleston. Around a third of them were settled
in Nova Scotia in British-ruled Canada.

The last great concentration of loyalists – black and white – was
in New York. Ultimately around three thousand former slaves gathered in that city, safe for now under British occupation. It was at
this moment that the slave fortress at Bunce Island on the Sierra
Leone River re-enters our story. The peace negotiations between
Britain and the United States were conducted in Paris towards the
end of 1782. The chief British negotiator was Richard Oswald who,
since the 1750s, had been the principal owner of Bunce Island.
Oswald had generated much of his personal wealth through the sale
of slaves imprisoned in the fortress before being shipped to South
Carolina. In the American colonies his business affairs were conducted
by his close friend Henry Laurens, one of the foremost figures among
the rice planters of South Carolina. Slaves from Laurens' estate were
among those who escaped to the British lines following the declarations of Lord Dunmore and then Sir Henry Clinton. Richard
Oswald's employees on Bunce Island marched shiploads of Africans
along the stone jetty and onto ships that were received on the other
side of the Atlantic by Laurens, who organized their auction in the

slave market in Charleston, South Carolina. Each sale of a Bunce Island slave yielded Henry Laurens a 10 per cent commission; the rest of the profits were siphoned back to Oswald. This transatlantic relationship had been plunged into crisis by the rebellion when these two friends and long-term business partners found themselves, suddenly, on opposing sides of the conflict. Their friendship had been placed under even greater pressure when in 1780 Henry Laurens, by then American Minister to the Netherlands, travelled to Europe on a diplomatic mission. His ship was intercepted by a British vessel, and when the draft of a proposed US–Dutch treaty was discovered, Laurens was arrested. Brought to England he was imprisoned in the Tower of London for fifteen months, during which time he received visits from Richard Oswald. Despite the fact that his friend was charged with the rather serious offence of treason, Oswald was eventually able to negotiate his release, obtaining a writ of habeas corpus which was granted on account of Laurens' alleged ill-health. Oswald then took Laurens before the King's Bench to arrange bail. The sum of £2,000 was agreed and duly paid by Oswald on Laurens' behalf. The judge who granted bail happened to be Chief Justice Lord Mansfield.*

In November 1782, when the provisional peace treaty was being negotiated, Laurens was called to Paris to assist Benjamin Franklin, who was leading the United States' negotiating team. Arriving after negotiations had begun Laurens was too late to influence the primary articles of the treaty. All that remained to be settled, he later noted, were 'a few points respecting the Fishery and the Loyalists'.[18] But Laurens was to have an influence on the peace agreement as he was able to push through a late amendment, which was accepted by the chief British negotiator, who happened to be Laurens' business partner Richard Oswald. This amendment to Article VII of the agreement, agreed by two close friends and partners in the Atlantic slave trade, concerned the fate of the black loyalists. Inserted literally into the margins, this late amendment prohibited the evacuating

---

* Laurens was part of a prisoner exchange and was swapped for the British general Lord Cornwallis.

British forces from 'carrying away any Negroes or other property of the American Inhabitants'.[19]

The terms of the preliminary peace treaty were published in March 1783. The thirty-five thousand white loyalists trapped in New York examined the feeble assurances the British negotiators had managed to wrench from the Americans and with good reason feared for their property and their welfare. The three thousand black loyalists trapped in the city alongside them feared chains and whips. They had survived their flight from slavery, evaded the slave patrols of the Southern states, fought for their liberty in epic battles and now faced the prospect of re-enslavement. They were left despondent and terrified. One, Boston King from South Carolina, described his horror of the terrible prospect of 'our old masters coming from Virginia, North-Carolina, and other parts, and seizing upon their slaves in the streets of New-York, or even dragging them out of their beds'.[20] When the first slaves had fled from the plantations of Virginia eight years earlier they had joined the British lines in the hope and expectation that Britain would put down the rebellion and win the war. Emboldened by their victory, patriot slave owners crossed through the British lines and came to New York to reclaim their slaves. There were reports of kidnappings and abductions. Black men and women were seized on the streets, bound and gagged and dragged onto waiting ships, as James Somerset and Thomas Lewis had been in London a decade earlier.

While former slaves like Boston King contemplated a life in chains and fended off nightmares of punishment and retribution, George Washington forwarded to his representatives in New York a list of escaped slaves who were believed to be in the city, in anticipation and expectation of their recapture. He added, 'Some of my own slaves, . . . may probably be in N York . . . I will be much obliged by your securing them, so that I may obtain them again'.[21] Washington was right. Hiding in New York were at least three of his former slaves, who had escaped from his Mount Vernon plantation. Among them was Harry Washington, who had served in the Black Pioneers. By 1783 George Washington had already succeeded in recapturing several of his former slaves, some in Philadelphia and others during the grim aftermath of the Battle of Yorktown. The fate of the black loyalists in New York, including those once owned by the future president, was in the end not to be decided by George Washington but by the British commander, Sir Guy Carleton. Carleton did not surrender the black loyalists but followed a procedure similar to that which had been established in Charleston. He set up a system by which they were assessed and registered by a special committee of inquiry. From April to November 1783, four British officials and three American representatives gathered each Wednesday at Fraunces Tavern at 54 Pearl Street, in a building that still stands. There they heard the testimonies of the black loyalists, who recounted their escapes from slavery or their service for the British forces. Those whose testimonies were accepted and authenticated were given a certificate of freedom and their name was recorded in a register known as the 'Book of Negroes'. The two original versions of this document, one recorded by the British officials in New York and another by the Americans, have survived the centuries. Appropriately one resides in London, the other in Washington DC. In them are the names of the three thousand black loyalists of New York to whom the British had promised freedom and refused to hand over to George Washington. In May 1783, when Carleton met Washington, the evacuation of black loyalists to Nova Scotia in British Canada had begun and news had reached the American commander. What Washington did not know was that on the first evacuation fleet from New York were some of his own slaves. At their meeting, the first between the two, Washington accused Carleton of having reneged on the amendment to the Paris Peace Treaty that had been inserted by Henry Laurens and agreed by Richard Oswald the previous year. Carleton's counter-argument was that as the black loyalists had been freed by the Crown they no longer counted as items of property to be returned or reclaimed. Further, Carleton retorted that 'delivering up Negroes to their former masters . . . would be a dishonourable violation of the public faith'.[22]

On 25 November 1783 George Washington, mounted on a grey horse, marched the Continental Army down the length of Manhattan. At 1 pm a cannon was fired to signal the departure of the last British soldiers. Among the very last to leave were the black auxiliaries of the Royal Artillery and the Wagon Master General's Department. General Washington did not find his slave Harry Washington in liberated New York; he was among the three thousand who had sailed for Nova Scotia. Of the twenty thousand black loyalists who escaped, most were sent there, and Birchtown became, for a while, the largest free black settlement in the Americas. Some of the loyalists who settled there eventually moved again to a settlement just a few miles from Bunce Island; others were sent to the West Indies – Jamaica, Nassau and St Lucia. A few hundred who had mainly been evacuated from New York crossed the Atlantic to Britain.

Most of the black loyalists who left New York did so with nothing more than the clothes on their backs and pitiful bundles of personal possessions. They rightly regarded themselves as fortunate to have survived an eight-year war and, at its messy conclusion, be among those evacuated. That fortune did not, however, alter the fact that they were penniless, without prospects and heading to a nation of which they knew little. They arrived in an England that had a black population that was almost certainly far smaller than the figure of fourteen to fifteen thousand blithely bandied around during the Somerset case. Whatever its size, Britain's black population had built up over decades; in that context the sudden arrival of the black loyalists constituted a mass migration. It is not clear what the balance was, before this influx, between those in the black population who were slaves or servants and had somewhere to sleep and food to eat, and those who were free but destitute. The arrival of black loyalists clearly shifted the balance in favour of the latter, though perhaps more so in terms of public perception than raw numbers. James Tobin, a slave owner and pro-slavery propagandist, noted that of the black people he saw in the London of 1785, 'those who are not in livery are in rags'.[23]

For a small proportion of the black loyalists arriving in Britain there was some hope of official support. In 1783 the British government established the Loyalist Claims Commission, which was charged with recompensing loyalists from the American colonies who had lost their land and property. Both black and white colonists applied but there are conspicuously few black people listed among the successful claimants. Those who had been free men before the revolution had the best hope, although many had their claims rejected as they lacked documentary evidence. Among those who were successful was a former slave from Virginia named Shadrack Furman, who was awarded a pension of £18 a year. The commission heard how he had worked providing provisions for the British forces. Captured by American patriot troops, Furman had been questioned about British troop movements, tortured for information and sentenced to five hundred lashes. During his ordeal he had also been struck about the head with an axe. As Furman said in his own petition, written in the third person, this ordeal had 'left him almost dead in the Field'. Although, somehow, he had survived, Furman explained that he had, 'lost his Eye Sight, and the use of one of his Legs by a stroke of an axe they gave him, and his Health is otherwise so much impaired from the wounds in his Head received from them.' Furman concluded his petition asking the commissioners to take his 'Case into Consideration and as your Petitioner and wife are from a comfortable Situation in Life reduced to the lowest Ebb of poverty and Distress on account of his Loyalty and attachmt. to His Majesty.' By the time, in 1788, Shadrack Furman was awarded a pension he had already spent four years living on the street begging and playing the violin.[24] Although his £18 a year will have saved him from destitution, it was a small amount compared to many of the pensions awarded to white loyalists, who were rarely awarded less than £25; many received much more.

Also among the black loyalists who landed in London in the 1780s was Benjamin Whitecuffe of New York, who had volunteered to spy for the British during the revolution. Captured by American patriot troops he was strung up from the gallows and was slowly asphyxiating when he was miraculously cut down and saved by passing British soldiers. By a convoluted route, which included being captured by privateers and serving in the navy in Gibraltar, Whitecuffe reached London. He had a white English wife and together they were just about managing to survive financially. Another loyalist who had fought in the Black Pioneers was Peter Anderson. Before the war he had made a living as a sawyer but had been press-ganged into Dunmore's Ethiopian Regiment. Anderson had seen the very worst of the Revolutionary War and was a survivor of the siege of Yorktown. He had subsequently been captured by the patriot forces, from whom he had escaped to re-join the British. He had made it all the way to London, only to be left on the streets to starve. Anderson told the commissioners, 'I endeavour'd to get Work but cannot get Any I am Thirty Nine Years of Age & am ready & Willing to serve His Britanack Majesty While I am Able But I am realy starvin about the streets, Having Nobody to give me A Morsal of Bread & dare not go home to my Own Country again'.[25] The commissioners were on the brink of dismissing Anderson's account of his war service as far-fetched and unbelievable, and for that reason rejecting this claim, when Lord Dunmore himself intervened and vouched for everything Anderson had said. He was awarded £10. John Provey had been enslaved to a lawyer in North Carolina and had fought with the Black Pioneers. In his petition to the commission he described himself as 'an entire Stranger in this Country *illeterate* and unacquainted with the Laws Thereof'. Rather than compensate him for his military service the commissioners suggested that Provey should feel fortunate to have come to 'a much better Country where he may with Industry get his Bread & where he can never more be a slave'. John Provey's supposed fortune did not change the fact that he and his white English wife Ann and their mixed-race daughter were destitute and desperate.[26]

Half of all the black claimants were rejected. Furman and others were successful in part because they had certificates of loyalty signed by their former employers. Others were awarded pensions or payments largely because British officers were able to vouch for their military service, but many lacked any form of documentation relating to the property they had lost as a result of the rebellion or the services they had performed for the Crown. The deeper problem, however, was that most of the black loyalists had been slaves before the revolution. They had not lost items of property but had been items of property. They had gained their liberty through the service they had provided to the nation; that they were now destitute and hungry was regarded as an unfortunate reality, but one that it was felt fell beyond the scope of the commission. With nowhere else to turn for assistance and little chance of finding work, these former soldiers and self-emancipated slaves, who had crossed an ocean to reach the mother country, now swelled the ranks of London's black poor. As well as those who had fought under British colours came former servants and slaves from the lost colonies who had been released from service amidst the ruptures of the revolution. There

were also free black men and women who had left the colonies to
escape the violence and uncertainty of the war. In London, which
is where almost all of them clustered, they mingled with former
domestic slaves of long residence in Britain, some of whom had
followed James Somerset's example and abandoned their masters.
With them on the streets were a handful of well-known black street
entertainers, celebrated charismatic beggars, 'characters of the
street' as they were later to be called. Alongside them were an
unknown number of black sailors and a small number of lascars –
Indian or Asian sailors who like their African shipmates were waiting
for employment on a ship that might take them home, or at least
to the next port. They were, together, the flotsam and jetsam of the
Atlantic world, refugees from the first of the two empires that
Britain was to build then lose between the seventeenth and twentieth
centuries. Huddled around the base of the slender, seven-faced
sundial at Covent Garden in St Giles', or seeking out shelter in the
docks or in the slums around Mile End, they fought their battles
now against hunger rather than the American rebels.

The scale of the new influx was small, perhaps between one and
two thousand – some sources suggest fewer than one thousand –
arriving in a city of more than six hundred thousand people. But the
black poor were a highly visible minority, marked out by their race
and their poverty. With no home parish in which to seek Poor Law
relief and with no families to offer them shelter, they were in deep
distress, begging on the street. Both alien and burdensome, their
public suffering was a reminder of Britain's recent and humiliating
defeat and an extremely uncomfortable demonstration of the nation's
disloyalty to men who had flocked to the flag and risked their lives
for the idea of British freedom. They were, for these reasons, not
just an inconvenience but, to some extent, also an embarrassment.

The winter of 1785–86 was unusually cold in the capital. The black
loyalists, their clothes turned to rags, were increasingly emaciated
and now struggled to keep warm; there are reports of some deaths.
That January the *Public Advertiser* complained of the terrible betrayal
of men who had 'served Britain' and 'fought under her colours',
but who 'are now left to perish by famine and cold, in the sight of

that people for whom they have hazarded their lives, and even (many of them) spilt their blood . . . And shall these poor humble assertors of [Britain's] rights be left to the agonies of want and despair, because they are unfriended and unknown?'[27] Around the same time this community, now defined and almost officially categorized as 'the black poor', became the belated focus of a flurry of energized compassion. A committee made up of wealthy businessmen was established to address the problem. At its head was Jonas Hanway, a prosperous if somewhat eccentric veteran of a number of philanthropic endeavours. A fervent opponent of the drinking of tea and an enthusiastic proponent of the carrying of umbrellas, Hanway had recently focused his charitable attention upon the plight of fallen women, the care of foundling children and the health of young chimney sweeps. He, like Granville Sharp, was an early prototype of the moralizing philanthropists who were to tackle many of Britain's most pressing social issues and moral causes in the coming century. This being late-eighteenth-century London, the Committee for the Relief of the Black Poor inevitably assembled, for their first meetings, in a coffee shop, Batson's in the City of London, opposite the Royal Exchange. The men of charity who joined Hanway made their own donations and then set about fundraising. By the end of January they were in a position to begin to distribute food to the black poor. Among those who donated to the appeal was Samuel Hoare, the Quaker abolitionist whose son Prince was to write the biography of Granville Sharp. But also contributing his time and money was John Julius Angerstein, a slave owner who saw no contradiction between donating money for the benefit of the black poor and keeping other Africans in chains on the plantations. Another contributor was Thomas Boddington, again a slave owner. The Prime Minister, William Pitt, contributed as did the Duchess of Devonshire. Also involved at this early stage, though not a member of the committee, was Granville Sharp himself. The bulk of the money that was used to assist the black poor, however, came from the government.

By February there were two hundred and ten people seeking relief from the committee. Food was provided from a baker's on Wigmore Street and at two London public houses, the Yorkshire Stingo in Marylebone, which has long been associated with London's black population, and the White Raven at Mile End to the east. At both establishments the black poor were provided with broth as well as bread. Those who had succumbed to the cold and fallen sick were sent to hospital; some were dispatched to St Bartholomew's, where Jonathan Strong had recovered his health in the 1760s. A few of the sailors were found berths on ships, and thereby taken off the streets. In the cold of a London winter, clothing was needed as urgently as food, and clothes along with shoes were gathered and distributed. By April 1786 the number reliant on the relief from the committee had reached four hundred and sixty. Small payments of sixpence a day were being distributed in addition to food. How many of the recipients were former American loyalists it is impossible to tell, but a proportion of them were certainly members of the pre-existing, marginalized black underclass into which the veterans had been absorbed.

While the immediate sufferings of the black poor were to some extent alleviated by the distribution of food, clothes and charity there was no obvious long-term solution. Britain in the 1780s was in deep recession. Unemployment was shockingly high and the land enclosure in the countryside brought increasing numbers of poor and uprooted rural people to London, where they too were struggling to find work and sustenance. The black poor, as both aliens and newcomers, were firmly at the end of the queue for the little work available in the capital. They were also in competition for employment with hundreds of thousands of British sailors and soldiers who had been demobilized at the end of the American Revolutionary War. Of the forty-five claimants who presented their cases before the Loyalist Claims Commission only a handful suggested that they had had any paid employment while in England, and they probably represented the better educated and more highly skilled portion of the black loyalist population.[28] When set against that economic backdrop it was clear that there was little prospect of the black poor finding jobs and security. They were likely to remain a visible and persistent social problem and an unwelcome reminder of military defeat and apparent national ingratitude.

There were those in London, including some figures on the committee, who just wanted them gone, and cared little about their long-term prospects. By the 1780s the defenders of slavery had begun a campaign of racist propagandizing that lasted until the 1830s. By the time the committee was formed, Edward Long's influential *History of Jamaica*, with its hysterical warnings about the dangers of racial mixing, had been in print for twelve years. The view that the presence of black men in Britain would lead to a form of racial pollution was gaining currency. As the idea took hold, fuelled by pro-slavery pamphlets and satirical cartoons that lampooned black people, it was not just the sight of black men reduced to vagrancy that disturbed many wealthy Londoners, but the sight of black men with white wives and mixed-race children that stuck in their throats. Unlike the slaves dressed in livery who opened the doors of fashionable West London homes, or the little black pageboys in feathered Ottoman turbans making tea for their mistresses, the black poor were regarded as a threat rather than a novelty.

If British society in the 1780s could find no work and no place for the black poor then other solutions had to be identified. Resettlement was one option. Hanway suggested it as early as March 1786.[29] But there were those among the black poor who wanted the government to transport them to another country, where they might find work, or be given access to land that offered a chance of self-sufficiency. Some proposed returning to the former American colonies as free men. Others wanted to settle in the West Indies or Nova Scotia, where they would join the three thousand black loyalists already there who, unbeknownst to the black poor of London, were suffering from lack of opportunity and economic exploitation by white settlers. Even as the worst of the winter weather abated, the black poor remained fully aware how bleak their immediate prospects in Britain were and that the relief from the committee upon which they had come to rely would be only temporary. Once again the only alternative to slavery offered to black people in Britain was starvation. If so, some form of transportation and resettlement seemed a better option.

The man with the plan was one Henry Smeathman: adventurer, botanist, amateur entomologist and – tragically for the black poor – amoral con artist. Smeathman's links to Africa began a decade and a half earlier when he was dispatched to coastal Sierra Leone by

Joseph Banks of the Royal Society. It was 1771, the year Banks's mother was working with Granville Sharp to defend the abducted slave Thomas Lewis. Smeathman had been asked by Banks to collect plant specimens for the fast-expanding collection at Kew. He spent much of his time and did most his work on the Banana Islands, off Sierra Leone, and there he diversified, studying the insects of the region as well as its flora. Among the places Smeathman frequented during his time in Africa was the slave fortress on Bunce Island, where he was entertained by the slave-traders. He returned to England, gave some lectures and then moved to Paris and wrote a book, *Some account of the termites, which are found in hot Climates*, which, unsurprisingly, was not one of the bestsellers of the age. Smeathman's hard labours in those hot climates, and his concerted efforts to insert himself into London's scientific elite, had earned him the nickname 'Mr Termite', but not much else. By 1786 he was short of options. He was forty-four years old, his health had been severely damaged by long-term exposure to tropical diseases and his creditors were closing in. But the plight of the black poor, and the sudden and pressing need to identify a land upon which they might be resettled, allowed Smeathman to place himself at the centre of significant events, win the confidence of the great and the good and make some money.

In February 1786 he wrote to the Committee for the Black Poor, outlining what he called his 'Plan of a Settlement to be made near Sierra Leona'. In this short pamphlet he proposed a scheme by which he personally would undertake to 'remove the burthen of the Blacks from the public for ever', by transporting London's 'troublesome Blacks back to Africa'. To win over the men of the committee Smeathman presented to them an almost entirely fictitious version of Sierra Leone. This imaginary land bore little resemblance to the country he had lived in and travelled across in the early 1770s. Smeathman described the deadly and storm-prone coastline as 'one of the most pleasant and feasible countries in the known world', a land so benign and welcoming the settlers could be housed all year round in simple huts, which would offer ample shelter. In this most benevolent of climates they would live comfortably and eat well, as the natural fecundity of the region was such that livestock bred 'with a rapidity unknown in these colder climates'. 'Such are the mildness and fertility of the climate and country', Smeathman brazenly assured the committee, 'that a man possessed of a change of cloathing, a wood axe, a hoe, and a pocket knife, may soon place himself in an easy and comfortable situation . . . it is not necessary to turn up the earth more, than from the depth of two or three inches, with a slight hoe, in order to cultivate any kind of grain.'[30] These bumper crops would be supplemented by the unlimited numbers of wild game that supposedly wandered through the nearby forests and the incalculable stocks of fish in the rivers of the region.

There were, in the 1780s, a handful of written sources that offered more cautious and balanced assessments of the soil, landscape and climate of Sierra Leone but these were brushed aside as Smeathman won over his audience with a ceaselessly upbeat assessment of his scheme and its chances of success. As this intoxicating vision was unfolded, the fact that it came from a man who had lived in the region gave his words credibility and substance they did not deserve. To further entice the committee, he spun them the fiction that his proposed settlement of former slaves would, almost instantly, become a going economic concern. As the settlement was to be established on such fertile soil, cash crops produced by the settlers could repay potential future investors in the region and turn the settlers themselves into a happy and well-off peasantry. Furthermore this new outpost of British philanthropic colonialism would become a bridgehead from which the Grain Coast of Africa could be opened up to British commerce. Smeathman's pitch had everything. It fused philanthropy with commerce and he sweetened the deal with some vague mumblings about Christianity. It also promised to spare well-to-do Londoners from the embarrassing inconvenience of having to walk past black veterans who had fought for their country only to be reduced to freezing beggars, sitting in rags on the street and slowly dying. The way Smeathman put it, there was nothing not to like. In a final flourish he sealed the deal and silenced any lingering doubts by offering to lead the expedition and settle on the coast of Sierra Leone himself, with the black poor. It was a masterful piece of salesmanship and a reprehensible act of deception.

Henry Smeathman knew exactly what the real dangers of Sierra Leone were. He had watched his own assistant, the Swedish botanist

Anders Berlin, succumb to a tropical fever – probably malaria – and die within just a few months of arrival. He himself had been repeatedly struck down by tropical maladies and had never fully recovered. He knew of the terrible storms that raked the coastline, of the inundations that came during the rainy season, and of floods that poured off the mountains and which were capable of stripping away topsoil and devastating crops. Most damningly of all, he had, just one year earlier, offered a full and frank assessment of the dangers of Sierra Leone when speaking to another committee.

Here the history of Britain's black population and her criminal underclass momentarily come together. In May 1785 a House of Commons committee had been gathering evidence to determine the best site on which to establish new penal colonies. The loss of the American colonies, as well as being an acute national embarrassment, had created an immediate and practical problem. It was to those now lost colonies that Britain had exported her convicts. Almost everyone who mattered agreed that penal servitude in distant colonies was a preferable (and cheaper) option than building more prisons, and it had long been thought that the sight of chain gangs in British fields would be an unacceptable insult to the natural freedoms which Englishmen regarded as their birth right. The chain gang was regarded as a feature of French Catholic tyranny that was entirely alien and repellent to British sensibilities; unless of course the men in chains were black slaves in the West Indies. In the 1780s, therefore, the search was on for a new location in which Britain could establish her penal colonies and to which she could disgorge her criminals. Most eyes turned to Africa, which in the 1780s was regarded as a continent of great promise and untapped potential. All sorts of schemes for African settlement, many of them utopian and impractical in nature, were proposed.[31] One of the suggested sites for a convict settlement was an island off the coast of the Gambia, not far from Sierra Leone, and Henry Smeathman was brought before the committee as an expert witness. To this committee Smeathman described Sierra Leone not as some earthly paradise but as a death trap. If convicts were settled there, he told them, 'not one in a Hundred would be left alive in Six Months'.[32] Smeathman's testimony helped spare the convicts miserable deaths on the coast of West Africa, and another scheme to settle them on the equally fatal shore of Namibia – later dubbed the Skeleton Coast – was abandoned when the Royal Navy's HMS *Nautilus* returned from a fact-finding mission.[33] Eventually all African options were discounted and the convicts of Georgian Britain were loaded aboard the First Fleet and dispatched to Botany Bay, making the colonization of Australia a bizarre and unintended consequence of the loss of America, and the unsuitability of Africa.

In 1786 nobody on the Committee for the Black Poor thought to dig out Smeathman's earlier testimony, nor investigate why the House of Commons committee had rejected the Gambia as a possible site for a penal colony. When Smeathman was questioned by the Committee for the Black Poor about earlier attempts to settle on the West African coast, all of which had been derailed by tropical fevers, he brushed aside these concerns by claiming that settlers of those previous ventures had succumbed to tropical sickness because of their own 'intemperance' and their failure to follow proper medical procedures.

The illusory Eden that Smeathman presented to the committee in 1786 was strictly for their consumption. He knew where he was going and planned – while there – to get rich. During his time in Sierra Leone in the 1770s Smeathman – when not sick with fever – had looked upon the region not just as a field of entomological study but as virgin pasture on which he might, one day, establish his own plantations. It was commercial opportunity rather than scientific investigation, or any genuine desire to assist the black poor of London, that inspired him to return. He imagined himself growing wealthy from sugar or cotton, planted in African soil and tended by African hands. These were the crops that had made so many of his countrymen rich and on his return to London, in the hope of luring in an investor or two, he had proposed such schemes to anyone who would listen. In one of those proposed schemes he had suggested that a new form of labour might be pioneered in Sierra Leone, in which captives bought direct from slave ships on the West African coast would be set 'free' on the their own continent. However, in order to pay back the cost of their purchase, these supposedly free men and women would be forced to work on British plantations. Smeathman called it 'Redemption'. It looked suspiciously like a form of temporary slavery, or of indentured labour.[34] Smeathman had completely failed to find financial backers for any of his schemes, but had never stopped nursing dreams of returning to West Africa as a planter. The 'Plan of a Settlement to be made near Sierra Leona' that he presented in 1786 was in fact a reworking of one of those earlier commercial schemes. Unexpectedly, and for him fortunately, the crisis of the black poor had suddenly put him in a position to revive those ambitions. He now had the ear of the great, the good and the very rich and he finally persuaded two London merchants to invest in his side project, a scheme to cultivate cotton in Sierra Leone. This was the man into whose care the black poor were to be delivered.

By spring 1786 Smeathman had addressed all problems and allayed all fears. The committee was sold and on 17 May a proposal outlining the scheme was submitted to the Treasury. The cautious civil servants were not overly enthusiastic about Sierra Leone as a site of settlement, but they deferred to the judgement of the committee. The plan then went to the Commissioners of the Navy, who approved it the same day. The Treasury then agreed to find the funds and Henry Smeathman's 'Plan of a Settlement', with all its fatal overconfidence and bluster, was given state sanction and state funding. The Treasury was to bear the costs of the scheme, paying £14 for each person settled and providing them with three months' worth of food, as well as tools, clothes, medicines and some building materials. After three months it was hoped the settlers would have completed their huts and be on the verge of harvesting their first crops.

With the Treasury on board the pace of events increased rapidly. Smeathman was appointed 'Agent for the Settlement', and offices were established at 14 Cannon Street in London. Over the spring and into the summer of 1786 preparations moved at an incredible pace. Ships to carry the settlers were promised by the Navy Board. The Treasury proved to be more generous than expected and additional funds were given to pay for tools and equipment. Private donations were also gathered. Granville Sharp offered twenty-five guineas of his own money to buy gifts that might appease the local African kings.[35] The plan was for the ships to sail in the autumn. This would spare the black poor another winter in London and ensure that they were settled before the arrival of Sierra Leone's rainy season in May, one of the few climactic realities of the region the existence of which Smeathman had admitted.

In the meantime there were numerous issues to address. Firstly the black poor, refugees from one continent who had become destitute on another, needed certain reassurances before they were willing to travel to a third continent, and there forge an entirely new society. For one thing they were aware that Sierra Leone lay at the centre of the slave trade. To convince them of the wisdom of settling on a coastline patrolled by the slave ships of numerous nations, it was agreed that each settler would be provided with a parchment certificate confirming them as a free citizen of the 'Colony of Sierra Leone'. How much protection these parchments might be was debatable but they kept the scheme on track for now.

To persuade more of the black poor to sign up, Jonas Hanway selected eight leaders whom he dubbed 'corporals' but who worked more like recruiting sergeants, convincing others to sign on for resettlement. We know a little more about the black poor through them. All the corporals were in their twenties, thirties or early forties. The youngest, John William Ramsey, was a seaman born in New York and only twenty-four. The oldest men, both forty, were John Cambridge and William Green; they were former servants. One, John Lemon, was a lascar from Bengal and two others had been born in Africa. The rest were American or from the West Indies.[36]

In early July, with preparations racing ahead, Henry Smeathman suddenly died. Appropriately enough, given his blasé dismissal of the tropical diseases of Sierra Leone, he may well have succumbed to the long-term effects of a fever he had caught there. His death was put down to what was called a 'putrid fever', which probably meant malaria.[37] Smeathman's demise was a belated opportunity to forestall disaster. With Mr Termite no longer around to spin fantasies his motives and his financial probity were called into question; Smeathman, it appeared, had been less than punctilious in his distribution of payments to the black poor. In the light of this, his rosy assessment of Sierra Leone was momentarily questioned. Alternative locations for the black colony in the Americas that had been discounted were now reconsidered by Hanway and others. A month before Smeathman's death the second chairman of the committee, Benjamin Johnson, fell so ill that he fled London for his country home and two months after Smeathman's demise the elderly Jonas Hanway passed away.[38] Had anyone been on the lookout for bad portents they were not in short supply, but instead a replacement for Smeathman, Joseph Irwin, was appointed and the scheme limped on.

Among the voices that were raised in defence of Sierra Leone, in the absence of Smeathman, were those of the black poor themselves. Some of the corporals selected to lead them had, as much as anyone on the committee, been inspired by Smeathman's vision of an African Eden. Some may have been romantically attracted to the idea of returning to the continent of their ancestors.[39] Delegations of the black poor now approached Granville Sharp to get his support for Sierra Leone, and the post-Smeathman panic subsided. Even some of the Indian lascars seem to have been committed to Sierra Leone as their final destination. It was at this point that Sharp became more actively involved in the settlement scheme. Despite the Somerset judgement, slave owners did still attempt to seize and transport black men and women to the West Indies to be sold as slaves and Sharp was still from time to time called upon to extract writs of habeas corpus from the judges and rush to the assistance of imprisoned Africans. In the summer of 1786 he saved a man named Henry Demane, plucking him from the ship in which he was being held captive at the very last minute. Having rescued him, Sharp persuaded him to become one of the prospective settlers.

The Sierra Leone scheme survived Smeathman's death because it was broad enough and vague enough for men of widely opposing views to find comfort in it, and it was sponsored and supported by a wide spectrum of opinion. To Granville Sharp and others of an anti-slavery bent, it was a unique opportunity to build a new society dedicated to ancient English principles and freedoms. Sharp believed that a black settlement founded on free labour, self-reliance and Christianity would become a practical demonstration of an alternative system of trade with Africa that was economically as well as morally superior to the slave trade and slavery. For those who simply did not like the presence of poor black people on the streets of the capital, it was a means of removing at least some of the unwanted black people who offended them, and thereby also reduce levels of racial mixing, which they found especially troubling.

In October three ships were assigned to the mission, the *Belisarius*, the *Atlantic* and the *Vernon*. They anchored off Deptford in the Thames and awaited their passengers. It was now that the enthusiasm of some of the would-be colonists began to wane. Very few had been born in Africa; like the corporals selected to represent them, most were North American or West Indian, yet the committee was convinced that their best chances of a successful future were to be found on an entirely unfamiliar 'home' continent. Some of the black poor made it clear that if they were to leave England they would prefer to go to Nova Scotia or the West Indies. To encourage them to go and to accept Sierra Leone as the only viable destination, the committee, during the summer of 1786, attempted to make the weekly allowances they had been paying since February dependent upon their agreeing to resettlement. In June some rejected the payment rather than sign on for resettlement and there was much disagreement and changing of minds. The committee and the government together made various moves to pressure them. The committee asked members of the public to stop giving charity to black beggars and the vagrancy laws were deployed to make their lives on the streets even more difficult. The question of how voluntary the scheme was is a controversial one, long debated by historians. While there was certainly some attempt at coercion there was also, at certain times, palpable enthusiasm for the project among members of the black poor, an increasingly organized and vocal community. Some were literate, and they did not simply submit to the committee's plan; they negotiated terms and sought reassurances. Interest in the scheme had even begun to spread beyond the black loyalists. Some of those who wanted to leave for Sierra Leone were former domestic slaves who had been brought to Britain before the 1780s, but who could see no future for themselves in London and were inspired by the vision of an African settlement. Sections of the black poor may have been reconciled to the scheme by the growing prominence of Granville Sharp. If so they will have been further comforted when they learnt that the man appointed to the role of commissary, in charge of the mission's supplies and stores, was the former slave Olaudah Equiano. A former sailor himself and an educated and respected figure, he was perfect for the role. This was the highest-ranking position to which a black Briton had ever been assigned by the British state.[40]

The doubts of the black poor and the organizational paralysis that followed the deaths of Smeathman and Hanway meant that the scheme, which had progressed so rapidly in the spring and early summer, suffered a series of crippling delays. This ensured that the original timetable which had been agreed between the committee and the navy collapsed. By September 1786, almost a thousand people were in receipt of charity from the committee. The government was meeting most of the cost in the hope that the majority of them would agree to resettlement in Sierra Leone. Nearly seven hundred had signed on, but by November, a month after the scheduled departure, only two hundred and fifty-nine were on board the transport ships. While they waited in the Thames, the committee was making final arrangements and attempting to cajole and convince others to join them. One factor that made this more difficult was that in the same months another armada was being assembled on the southern coast of England. At Portsmouth the ships of the First Fleet were making their preparations to carry the first convict colonists to Botany Bay. Rather unhelpfully there were those in the press who compared the two schemes, and a rumour spread that the black poor were to be sent not to Africa but to Botany Bay, along with the criminals. There was some logistical crossover between the schemes – surplus clothes gathered for the black poor were sent to the convicts – and the belief grew that the plan for an African settlement and the creation of the Australian penal colony were connected. The general public was fascinated by both projects and press reports linking and comparing the two schemes had an unfortunate and destabilizing effect on members of the black poor, many of whom were already having second thoughts about resettlement. They were even warned against the scheme by Lord George Gordon, the infamous rabble-rouser and hero of the London mob who instigated the Gordon Riots of 1780.[41]

To make matters worse, those who had signed up and were on board the ships at Deptford were living in terrible conditions, subsisting on inadequate naval rations of salted food. Conditions in the ships were comparable to those in the hulks, the dreaded floating prisons, which did little to quell rumours that they were bound for a convict station. As the winter of 1786–87 came on, the situation at Deptford became even more desperate. Although it was not an exceptionally cold winter, temperatures started to drop in September and November was one of the coldest on record. Sickness cut a swathe through the people on board. Even at this late stage the black poor appear to have still been lacking warm clothes and perhaps as many as fifty of them died while the ships lay at anchor. Others abandoned them, preferring to take their chances on the streets. Among those who succumbed to fevers on board was John Provey, who had served in America with the Black Pioneers, only to have his petition to the Loyalist Claims Commission rejected. With no pension or prospects, Provey, his white English wife Ann and their daughter Louisa had agreed to be resettled in Sierra Leone and signed an agreement to that effect.[42] But both John and Louisa died, leaving Ann to travel to Africa widowed and bereaved.

The conditions on board the ships were inexcusably bad. There was a lack of beds and bedding; wood for stoves seemed always to be in short supply, as did drinking water and candles. Olaudah Equiano became suspicious that Joseph Irwin, Smeathman's replacement, was siphoning off money intended for the care of the black poor and he resented the high-handed treatment meted out to them by both Irwin and the Reverend Patrick Fraser, whom Granville Sharp had appointed as missionary for the Sierra Leone settlement, after having categorically refused to accept the appointment of preachers from any of the Nonconformist denominations. Equiano wrote to Otobah Cugoano, another famous and literary black Londoner, detailing the misuse of funds and mistreatment of the settlers. When Equiano's letter made its way into the press there was a bitter dispute between him and Irwin. Captain Thomas Boulden Thompson of HMS *Nautilus*, which was to accompany the black poor to Africa, believed that Irwin was incompetent but in a row between a black man and a white man, Equiano was almost bound to lose. It was decided that Equiano was a disruptive influence who had poisoned the minds of the black poor, who had become 'troublesome and discontented' as a result of his intrigues. He was dismissed and put ashore at Plymouth. Later he was awarded £50 in compensation by the Admiralty.

By 22 January the last of the settlers had been assembled and once again the records speak, giving us a glimpse of who the black poor were. On board the three ships were four hundred and eighteen passengers. By Equiano's reckoning there were two hundred and ninety black men, forty-one black women, seventy white women, six white children and eleven black children, some of whom, like Louisa Provey, were the mixed-race offspring of inter-racial couples. Accompanying them were thirty-eight white men in various roles – supervisors, doctors, missionaries and craftsmen. There was also one courageous private passenger. The lists for the three ships were drawn up, with each person listed under one of various headings. The category that has most surprised historians is 'White Women married to Black Men'. It used to be believed that these women were prostitutes who had been gathered up at Wapping and forced to marry the black men on the ships. As unwanted and reviled as the black poor they too, it was said, had been transported to Sierra Leone. The original source of this interpretation is an account by Anna Maria Falconbridge, the wife of the abolitionist campaigner Alexander Falconbridge, who visited Sierra Leone in 1791. We shall hear more of Mrs Falconbridge later. In her letters, which were later published as a travel account, she described coming across 'seven of our country women, decrepid with disease, and so disguised with filth and dirt, that I should never have supposed they were born white'. Falconbridge then recounted a conversation she claimed to have had with one of the women in which she was told that 'the women were mostly of that description of persons who walk the streets of London, and support themselves by the earnings of prostitution; that men were employed to collect and conduct them to Wapping, where they were intoxicated with liquor, then inveigled on board of a ship, and married to Black men, whom they had never seen before; that the morning after she was married, she really did not remember a syllable of what had happened over night, and when informed, was obliged to inquire who was her husband . . . "to the disgrace of my mother country, upwards of one hundred unfortunate women, were seduced from England to practice their iniquities more brutishly in this horrid country".[43]

Falconbridge's assertion that the women who had travelled to Sierra Leone as the wives of the black settlers had effectively been press-ganged went unquestioned for many years. Yet it is extremely doubtful when considered in context. As Simon Schama has pointed out it is hardly credible that a man as pious and principled as

Granville Sharp, who had overseen every tiny detail of the Sierra Leone mission, would, at the last minute, have agreed to the transportation to his Province of Freedom of sixty to seventy London street prostitutes,[44] while the historian Norma Myers points out that as the ships carrying the black poor were delayed by several months there was surely ample time for any press-ganged prostitutes to effect their escape. Another practical problem with Falconbridge's account is that the ships carrying the black poor were never anchored at Wapping, and given the vast scale of Georgian London's sex industry it would have taken a far larger armada of ships to have even begun to clear the city of its sex workers; the numbers transported to Sierra Leone, even if they all had been prostitutes, would have hardly scratched the surface.

Falconbridge's account perhaps speaks of a mindset in which prostitution was the only conceivable, or at least the only palatable, explanation as to why white women might enter into relationships with black men. The more obvious, more domestic and mundane reality, that Anna Maria Falconbridge found inconceivable, is that these poor white women had married these equally poor black men and together, despite their poverty, they were attempting to build families and secure a livelihood. The black poor had after all been in London for three years, and were for the most part men in their twenties and thirties. As the parish registers of many London churches testify and as the prints of Hogarth graphically illustrate, the Georgian poor did not allow poverty to stand in the way of romance or pour cold water on the fires of lust.

By cross-checking the columns of names on the passenger lists for the ships, *Belisarius*, *Atlantic* and *Vernon*, the inter-racial couples are revealed. There are forty-four in total.[45] Eliza Benn was likely the wife of Isaac Benn, Jane Working the wife of William Working, Sarah Needham the wife of John Needham. Elizabeth and Peter Ornfield are recorded as leaving England with their son William Ornfield, who like other mixed-race children was categorized in the passenger list under the heading 'Black Children'. It seems equally likely that Sarah Cambridge was the wife of John Cambridge, one of the appointed 'corporals', and another of the 'corporals', John Lemon, the lascar from Bengal, is listed as travelling to Africa with his white wife Elizabeth, neither of them having any obvious connection to the continent on which they hoped to make their new home. What the passenger lists demonstrate is that this London community of the late eighteenth century, although categorized by the rich and influential as the 'black poor', was in reality inter-racial, made up of recent immigrants and those born and bred in Britain, their mixed-race children what we today incongruously call second-generation immigrants. Their ragged clothes and sunken cheeks aside, these multi-racial, multi-ethnic London families – African, West Indian, North American, Asian, mixed-race and white – will have looked very much like thousands of families who have made their homes in the London of the early twenty-first century.

The *Belisarius*, *Atlantic* and *Vernon* finally sailed out of the Thames in January 1787, a full four months behind schedule. The first stop was Portsmouth, where they rendezvoused with their escort, HMS *Nautilus*. After a further outbreak of fever and a terrifying encounter with a winter storm in the Channel that forced them to regroup in Plymouth, they finally set sail for Africa in early April, by which time 411 of the original 456 remained. On 10 March, after a difficult month at sea, the little flotilla slipped into Africa's greatest natural harbour, at the mouth of the Sierra Leone River. Ahead of them, in the far distance, they saw the hazy peaks of the Sierra Leone mountains, named by Portuguese sailors in the fifteenth century. The coastline was green and verdant, fringed with white sand beaches that remain some of the loveliest in Africa. In a century during which around seven million people had been shipped from Africa in chains and shackles, the three ships carrying the black poor of London were uniquely heading in the opposite direction, taking former New World slaves, along with their white wives and mixed-race children, back to Africa. This strange, hopeful community of free peoples had arrived to establish a settlement that Granville Sharp had grandly dubbed the *Province of Freedom*.

They landed in the sheltered harbour of the peninsula that sits near the mouth of the Sierra Leone River. The landing site was called Frenchman's Bay. This was immediately remedied and Frenchman's Bay became St George's Bay. Almost as rapidly, a treaty was agreed with King Tom of the Koya Temne people, who, after a

thirteen-gun salute from HMS *Nautilus* and a short period of negotiation, 'sold' the settlers a twenty-square-mile block of territory
upon which they built their settlement. King Tom, a coastal king
and subsidiary ruler with limited power, happily agreed to the
transaction, partly because he disavowed the European notion of
land-ownership. With long experience of trading with Europeans,
and fluent in the pidgin Portuguese of the Grain Coast, King Tom
was not some befuddled innocent, but a player in the Atlantic world
economy. In his mind what he sold the colonists was merely permission to settle. In return he received the usual jumble of goods, some
functional, others impractical luxuries. King Tom's haul on this
occasion included 130 gallons of rum, some clothes and hats. Sharp,
in a later letter, derided the payment as 'a trifling expense'.[46]

In the weeks that followed, parcels of land were cleared of trees
and scrub, huts built and a Union flag raised. The pioneers called
their little settlement Granville Town in honour of Sharp. HMS
Nautilus remained at anchor to offer the settlers some protection.
When, some months later, Granville Sharp received the first reports
of their arrival and early progress he enthusiastically informed his
supporters of their purchase of 'twenty miles square of the finest
and most beautiful country (they all allow) that was ever seen! The
hills are not steeper than Shooter's Hill [in London]; and fine streams
of fresh water run down the hill on each side of the new township;
and in the front is a noble bay, where the river is about three leagues
wide: the woods and groves are beautiful beyond description, and
the soil very fine. So that a little good management may, with God's
blessing, still produce a thriving settlement.'[47]

What Sharp wanted to create in Sierra Leone was not merely a
refuge for those unfortunates among the poor of London who
happened to be both destitute and black. In a letter written in 1789
he described the establishment of his Province of Freedom as the
culmination of his life's work, the climax of a providentially ordained
personal mission that had begun two decades earlier, on the day in
1765 when he had happened upon Jonathan Strong, sitting beaten
and bloodied, outside his brother's surgery in Mincing Lane. Sharp
wrote of how his mission had demanded that he had, 'with indefat-
igable labour, for above twenty-two years, and at a great expense,
asserted and maintained the glorious principles and foundations of

the English Law (and having thereby, through the blessing and providence of God, prevented slavery from taking root in England)'.
After winning that sacred struggle he had now 'obtained from
Government a tacit permission to plant the same noble privileges
even in Africa itself, that the new settlement might be truly deemed
a Province of Freedom'.[48]

To ensure the settlement was the true realization of this sacred
mission, Sharp had provided the settlers with a book, which he
had entitled *A Short Sketch of Temporary Regulations (until better shall
be proposed) for the Intended Settlement on the Grain Coast of Africa, near
Sierra Leona*. At 226 pages it was a pretty long short sketch. It was
in effect his blueprint for the new form of government that the
black settlers were to establish. After a long preface, heavy with
biblical quotations, the *Short Sketch* described this new society. It
was to be steeped in the traditions of English common law, in which,
after his victory in the Somerset case, Granville Sharp had fathom-
less conviction. The social structure that he proposed for the black
settlers was based upon his own interpretation of 'Frankpledge', an
Anglo-Saxon communal social structure that had existed in England
and Denmark in the early Middle Ages. The Province of Freedom
was to be a society in which households were responsible collectively
for order and justice. Citizens were organized into groups of households, each ten persons strong, and were bound to one another and
obliged to 'the protection and preservation of their common
freedom.'[49] There was to be a 'publick Exchequer', which was to
administer the economy of the settlement, and all unoccupied land
was to be common land. Overlaid onto this archaic social structure
was a regime of ceaseless prayer and Christian worship. Sharp's *Short
Sketch* contained a chapter on regulations for the collection and
expenditure of public revenue, and another on agrarian law. There
was also an appendix listing numerous 'Short Forms of Prayer for
various Occasions, with Previous Exhortations'. There was even
guidance on diet, which repeatedly stressed the importance of
temperance. Among the early chapters was one outlining the system
of free labour that the settlers were to adhere to. 'Human Labour
is more essential and valuable than any other article in new settlements', Sharp wrote, and to sanctify it further he ordained that
work was to become a medium of exchange as well as a means of

personal betterment. Sharp had a form of currency printed; each note came replete with verses from the Bible and was, in theory, redeemable for a certain number of days' work. There were also to be limitations on indentured servitude and a demand that fugitive slaves who fled to the settlement be 'protected and allowed to purchase Land,' through their own labour.[50] Sharp's fervent religiously inspired detestation of slavery burns through numerous pages. In his section on Redemption from Slavery, Sharp insists that 'no person can retain, or sell or employ, a slave within the bounds of the settlement.'[51]

There was much in Sharp's *Temporary Regulations* that was commendable; this, after all, was a blueprint for self-rule and equality drafted at a time when millions of Africans in the New World occupied a chattel status akin to that of livestock. However, that settlement had been established, on the advice of the late Henry Smeathman, just twenty miles from the slave fortress at Bunce Island. The colonists were able to stand on their allotted plots within the Province of Freedom and watch slave ships slip up and down the Sierra Leone River, carrying trade goods to the chiefs and traders inland, and returning with hundreds of fellow Africans, chained and terrified, on their lower decks. The British slave ships that cruised along the shore travelled, as the settlers themselves had done, under the protection of the warships of the Royal Navy. Not only had they set themselves up within one of the centres of the Atlantic slave trade, they had done so in one of the boom decades of that trade. There was so much slave-trading activity on the Sierra Leone River in the late 1780s partly because the end of the American Revolutionary War, in which so many of the settlers had fought, allowed Europe's slave-traders to focus on business rather than worry about enemy vessels. Around eighty thousand Africans were carried across the Atlantic to lives of slavery each year during the peak decade of the 1780s. Had they not been so heavily burdened by the tasks of building homes, planting crops and trying to survive, the settlers of the Province of Freedom might have had time to contemplate the mountain of contradictions upon which the whole scheme teetered. On a peninsula protruding into one of the great highways of the Atlantic slave trade, a few hundred refugees from British slavery in North America were attempting to recreate the social structures of Northern Europe in the Middle Ages. Yet while they in their little clearing debated the complexities of Danelaw, just twenty miles away the traders of Bunce Island lived an existence that was no less surreal.

The ruins of the fortress belie its former luxury: this was also a mansion. By 1787 Bunce Island was owned and run by the firm of John and Alexander Anderson. They were the nephews of Richard Oswald, the British slave-trader and diplomat who, just five years earlier, had negotiated the terms of the Paris Peace Treaty, ending the Revolutionary War. The traders who worked for the Anderson brothers lived on the upper floors of the agents' house at the centre of the fortress. There they sat drinking their rum and wine on a broad, shaded wooden veranda that offered them great sweeping views across the river. In the afternoons they played golf on their own two-hole golf course on the southern side of the island. At night they slept in rooms on the upper floors of the agents' house, entertained by concubines selected from the enslaved women ferried to the island by the local African and Afro-European traders. Below them, behind the stone walls of the open air slave yards, hundreds of captives, men, women and children, sat in the darkness, bewildered and terrified. Compared to the dismal realities of Bunce Island, Granville Sharp's naive utopianism seems harmless. Sadly for the settlers it was anything but, as in the climate of Sierra Leone, Sharp's pious naivety, combined with the cynical dishonesty of the late Henry Smeathman, proved deadly.

The four months the expedition had wasted lying in the Thames had not only exposed the settlers to another English winter, it had ensured that they had arrived in Sierra Leone at the worst possible time of year. The rainy season started within two weeks of their arrival. Much of what they had planted in their newly marked-out fields was washed away, along with much of the topsoil, which had been left vulnerable to erosion by clearing away the natural vegetation.[52] Large areas of the peninsula quickly became waterlogged. The crops that were not drowned by the rains were consumed by pests and moulds. The heat was debilitating, especially to men and women most of whom had known only the temperate climates of the North American colonies. The forests in which Henry Smeathman had suggested the settlers might effortlessly hunt local game turned out to be impenetrable jungles, dark thickets of tangled vines. The settlers thought they had seen the worst of it when, in June, the skies turned an angry grey, the temperatures dropped and a series of tropical storms and gales hammered into the coastline, one after another. Water cascaded down the mountains that had appeared so benign on their arrival and dirty rivulets spread their tendrils across the settlement. The miserable huts the settlers had begun to build were saturated by constant rain and then ripped apart by the high winds. The tents with which they had been supplied were similarly obliterated, and when they made improvised tents from old sails they too were overwhelmed and offered little protection. But the land was not just hostile; it was pestilential. Soon after their arrival the residents of Granville Town began to fall ill. The tropical diseases that just one year earlier Henry Smeathman had claimed were easily preventable started to take their toll. Millions of mosquito larvae swarmed and multiplied in the pools of water left by the rains and swarms of insects emerged. Many of those afflicted with tropical conditions like malaria were further fatally weakened by an outbreak of dysentery, and the death toll rose. In the middle of September HMS *Nautilus* returned to Britain, as had always been planned. By the time she weighed anchor, one hundred and twenty-two of the settlers who had stepped ashore in May were dead.

Men who had survived the smallpox outbreaks that had decimated the black regiments of the Revolutionary War, or lived through the epic bombardments and unpardonable betrayal of Yorktown six years later, died of fevered dehydration in half-completed, mildewed huts, in a pitiful clearing by the Sierra Leone River. The late Mr Smeathman's betrayal of the black loyalists, delivered albeit from the grave, compared even to that of Cornwallis at Yorktown.

Rather than attempt to build the utopia outlined in Sharp's *Short Sketch of Temporary Regulations*, the settlers threw themselves desperately into the trading economy of the Grain Coast. They gathered the tools with which the Committee for the Black Poor had imagined they would build this New Jerusalem and bartered them for food with the local Temne people and with the slave-traders of Bunce Island. The white supervisors who had control over the settlement's supplies did best out of these sales.

The letters that Granville Sharp wrote from London and the

correspondence he received from the settlers plot the decline of the scheme and the well-being of the settlers. As letters from the colonists reached him in London, Sharp dashed off a string of correspondence to his supporters and financial backers that reveal the alarming intelligence he was receiving and his own desperate misery about the fate of the settlers.[53] By October 1787, six months after the settlers had arrived, Sharp was complaining of being in receipt of 'melancholy accounts of my poor little ill-thriven swarthy daughter, the unfortunate colony of Sierra Leone'. But at this stage he was still able to convince himself that the scheme had a chance of success. In July 1787 Abraham Elliott Griffith, one of the black poor who had survived the epidemics and pestilence, wrote to Sharp. 'I am sorry, and very sorry indeed, to inform you, dear Sir,' he began, 'that this country does not agree with us at all and without a very sudden change, I do not think there will be one of us left at the end of a twelvemonth. Neither can the people be brought to any rule or regulation, they are so very obstinate in their tempers. It was really a very great pity ever we came to this country, after the death of Mr. Smeathman; for we are settled upon the very worst part. There is not a thing, which is put into the ground, will grow more than a foot out of it . . . quite a plague seems to reign here among us. I have been dangerously ill myself, but it pleased the Almighty to restore me to health again and the first opportunity I have, I shall embark for the West Indies.'[54]

When the news from Sierra Leone became even more bleak, Sharp, in one of his least admirable moments, blamed the failure of the settlement not on the many impracticalities of the scheme, but on the easy target of alcohol, thereby falling back on the same excuse Henry Smeathman had deployed when explaining away the failure of every previous scheme to settle the region. Writing in January 1788, Sharp acknowledged that the four-month delay in leaving England had 'fatally postponed their arrival on the coast till the rainy season commenced', which he accepted had allowed 'dreadful fevers and a great mortality' to cut a swathe through the settlers. So calamitous had been their arrival, Sharp conceded, that the settlers had not even had 'time to prepare sufficient shelter and accommodation for themselves at their landing'. But he convinced himself that while all that was true, 'the greatest blame of all is to be charged on the intemperance of the people themselves; for the most of them (both Whites and Blacks) became so besotted during the voyage, that they were totally unfit for business when they landed, and could hardly be prevailed on to assist in erecting their own huts. Besides, the distempers occasioned by their intemperance carried off a large proportion of them before they reached the coast; so that the climate of Africa is by no means chargeable with the mortality'.[55] Sharp maintained that the land would yield crops with 'very little labour'. Even in the wake of so much bad news and evidence to the contrary he remained dedicated to the fanciful (and in the circumstances self-indulgent) belief that if the settlers would only commit to following his regulations 'they would become the freest and the happiest people on earth'.[56] The puritanical, fanatical aspects of Sharp's nature that had made him such an effective and belligerent campaigner against slavery in England in the 1760s and 1770s now blinded him to the deadly calamity that was being played out three thousand miles away in a doomed settlement named in his honour.

By September 1788 only a hundred and thirty of the original settlers were left alive. Sharp was aggrieved by the loss of life but what shocked him most profoundly was that some of the desperate settlers, and a number of the white functionaries sent out to help them build their Province of Freedom, had fled to Bunce Island and there sought safety and employment among the slave-traders. A few became slave-traders of sorts themselves, or at least handmaidens to the process – working as clerks in the fortress or on the repair of ships in Bunce Island's own dockyard. Among those who found refuge were Charles Tacitus, Henry Estwick and Richard Collins, three white men who had been dispatched to Sierra Leone to perform various functions. In November 1789 Sharp wrote from London, 'It gives me great concern to find, by these letters, that Mr. Tacitus, Captain Estwick, and Mr. Collins, have deserted the Province of Freedom, in order to enter into the Slave Trade. By the laws of the settlement, they have forfeited, of course, every right and claim they had to any share in it; and I hope you will be careful that none of them be ever permitted to return'.[57] Another 'deserter' was Patrick Fraser, the white chaplain. As Sharp had received reports of Fraser's extreme ill-health he was more understanding in his case. Safe and fed behind the walls of the slave fortress, Fraser recovered from tubercular fever and began to offer his ministries to the slave-traders. They were more interested in women and rum, so he attempted also to minister to the slaves. The defection that clearly most shocked and hurt Sharp was of Henry Demane, the former slave whom he had saved from being transported to the West Indies in the summer of 1765. The news that a man he had released from chains was now fixing collars and shackles onto the necks and legs of others brought out all of his fiery religiosity. In a furious letter of late 1789 he demanded that Demane, 'who, I am informed, is now a great man on the Bulam shore, and a dealer in Slaves', be reminded 'of the joy he felt when he saw two men, sent with a writ of Habeas Corpus, so exactly in time (most providentially) to rescue him . . . Remind Mr. Henry Demane of his own feelings under the horrors of slavery, when he turned his face to the mast of the ship (into which he was trepanned by his wicked master), and formed a resolution, as he afterwards confessed, to jump overboard that very night, rather than submit to a temporary slavery for life; but he is now in danger of eternal slavery!'[58]

What finally ended the social experiment and destroyed the Province of Freedom was not malaria nor the lure of an easier life as a slave agent on Bunce Island but an accident. When a stray shot was fired by a young marine from the crew of the visiting HMS *Pomona*, the thatched roof of a hut in a nearby Temne village caught fire, and the whole settlement was razed. Fighting then broke out between the British forces and the Temne, which lasted several days. After the confrontation had abated, King Jimmy, the successor to King Tom who had agreed to the settlement back in early 1787, sent his men to burn to the ground what little was left of Granville Town and drive out the last surviving settlers. It was December 1788 and the people were given three days to evacuate. To make their failure complete the canoes that came to rescue them were those of the slave-traders of Bunce Island. After this calamity Sharp wrote to William Pitt, then Chancellor of the Exchequer, who had supported the scheme from the outset, to admit that only around seventy of the settlers remained alive and that about ten of them were making their living working for the slave-traders. The rest attempted to build a new settlement upstream from the slave fortress. 'If they are neglected much longer', Sharp warned, 'they must perish and fall into the snares of their enemies, the neighbouring slave-dealers, by whose machinations their misfortunes have been occasioned, and the advantage of opening a free and honest trade with the internal parts of Africa . . . will be irrecoverably lost'.[59]

To those Londoners who, unlike Granville Sharp, cared little about opening free and honest trade in Africa, and had merely wanted the black poor brushed off the streets, the Sierra Leone scheme had been a limited success. Once the three transport ships had set sail for Africa, the Committee for the Black Poor had dissolved itself and its members had moved on to the next philanthropic cause. Granville Sharp had sunk over £1,700 of his own money into the scheme and remained resolutely convinced that on the Grain Coast of Africa – a land upon which he never had and never would set foot – a model community might yet be created that could demonstrate that there was an economically viable alternative to the vast, hyper-profitable slave economy of the Atlantic world.

Perhaps the most extraordinary feature of any of the improbable settlements that were established by Britain on various continents in the last years of the eighteenth century is that anything came of any of them. That so many of the convicts of the First Fleet survived their journey and their first years in Australia, and that Britain was able to establish working penal colonies, and then a viable settler society, on a largely uncharted continent ten thousand miles away is entirely remarkable. Almost as incredible is the fact that the site on which the black poor of late Georgian London attempted to forge their Province of Freedom is not today some anonymous patch of coastal forest but lies instead beneath the sprawling concrete and corrugated-iron metropolis of modern Freetown, the capital of Sierra Leone. Perhaps this stunning peninsula, jutting out into a near-perfect natural harbour, was always destined to become the site of a city but the process that created modern Freetown had its roots in the failure of the Province of Freedom.

Even before King Jimmy had driven the last of the settlers out of Granville Town, the man in whose honour that little settlement had been named had been industriously planning further waves of settlement and organizing missions of resupply. Unable to draw further on the Sharp family's own wealth, he came together with others to create the St George's Bay Company in 1790, quickly reorganized into the financially more robust Sierra Leone Company, a joint-stock company – one of the great innovations of the age. Among its investors were some of the men with whom Sharp had already established the Society for the Abolition of the Slave Trade – William Wilberforce, Thomas Clarkson, and James Phillips. The company promised to develop future settlements on the Grain Coast and to provide financial returns to its investors from the settlers' crops. Article 2 in the founding documents of the company read, 'The Object for which Sierra Leone Company is instituted is the establishment of a trade with Africa on the true principles of Commerce, carrying British manufacturers and other articles of traffick and bringing back African produce in exchange'.[60]

Again sugar and cotton, the two great slave-produced, monoculture crops of the age, were notionally favoured. Sharp and his abolitionist colleagues hoped that sugar grown by free black settlers in Sierra Leone would do more than merely generate profits. They imagined that it might play a part in the boycott of slave-produced sugar that was proposed by Thomas Clarkson, an ethical alternative to the millions of tons of sugar that streamed incessantly off the ships of the triangular trade. Future settlers might trade with the inland peoples up the rivers of the region, offering British products in return for the legitimate produce and raw materials of Africa – dyewoods, ivory and other commodities. This exchange was also envisaged as a means by which the dominance of the trade in human beings could be undone. More and more schemes for settlement in Sierra Leone were beginning to resemble aspects of Henry Smeathman's plan for commercial colonization. Sharp was willing to accept this new commercialism so long as the principles of liberty remained central to the administration of the settlement and the lives of any future settlers. Article 3 of the company's founding document read: 'The Proprietors of the present company are fully persuaded that if proper means are taken and prosecuted with diligence and perseverance, the Continent of Africa will furnish commodities for the support of an extensive and increasing Commerce, without resorting to the miserable expedient of selling the inhabitants as slaves in order to furnish a return . . .'[61]

In 1791 the company sent a commercial agent to Sierra Leone to negotiate with the Temne king and persuade the survivors of Granville Town to return to their plots and begin planting crops. The man chosen was Alexander Falconbridge, who had worked as a surgeon on slave ships but after a profound crisis of conscience had renounced the slave trade. In 1788 he had published his damning and graphic *Account of the Slave Trade on the Coast of Africa*, one of the early and most harrowing of the anti-slavery tracts that Britain's abolitionists published in the last decades of the eighteenth century. Falconbridge travelled to Africa with his wife Anna Maria and his brother William on a ship that was bound ultimately for Bunce Island and was owned by the Anderson brothers, the proprietors of the fortress. With inexcusable haste William Falconbridge, shortly after arriving in Sierra Leone, betrayed his brother, abandoned their philanthropic mission and joined the slave-traders on Bunce Island.[62]

From his desk in London, Granville Sharp received only inter-mittent letters and reports from Sierra Leone. From these flickering snapshots he struggled to comprehend exactly what had become of the settlers. How many had survived, and of those who had been spared the attentions of the mosquito and the rage of King Jimmy, how many might yet become reliable, Christian settlers in a newly constituted Province of Freedom? But with so few of the original emigrants reportedly alive – between seventy and eighty, Sharp was informed – new blood was needed.

The settlers who risked their lives in the second attempt to create a Province of Freedom in Africa were, like their unfortunate prede-cessors, black loyalists, men and women who had escaped from New York, Charleston and Savannah in the early 1780s. The bulk of those who had been evacuated in the dying months of the Revolu-tionary War had found themselves not on the streets of London but settled on the cold, empty plains of Nova Scotia, in British North America. There three thousand of them had settled. In 1783 they had been promised not just freedom but also land but in the majority of cases that solemn promise had been broken. The best land in Nova Scotia was distributed to the white settlers, while many of the plots that were awarded to black loyalists were on marginal farmland, difficult to cultivate and impossible to cultivate profitably. They struggled to farm on these bleak, stone-strewn fields, often without the necessary agricultural tools and equipment, which were in short supply. Some were forced to abandon their unprofitable plots and become indentured servants to white settlers, selling their labour and to some extent their liberty, for an agreed number of years. It was an existence that was uncomfortably redolent of the slavery they had done so much to escape. Black Nova Scotians were also subject to taxation while being denied representation. They were the victims of routine prejudice and lived uneasily in a territory into which the white settlers had brought over a thousand black slaves. Slavery remained legal in British colonial territories right up until the 1830s. Like free black people in the North of the United States, the black Nova Scotians also lived in fear of the kidnapping gangs who seized the unwary, bundled them onto ships and trafficked them to the plantations of the Southern United States and the West Indian islands.

Towards the end of 1790 one of their number, Thomas Peters, a former slave from North Carolina and a veteran of the Revolutionary War, persuaded two hundred black loyalist families to award him power of attorney. Peters, who had risen to the rank of sergeant during the war, travelled to London carrying with him a list of complaints and a petition from the black loyalists demanding the land that had been promised to them. Peters' plan was to present the petition to William Grenville, the Home Secretary. To gain access to these exalted circles Peters hunted down his former commander-in-chief, Sir Henry Clinton, the author of the second proclamation offering freedom to slaves. It was through Clinton, it seems, that Peters was introduced to several members of Parliament and, eventually, to Granville Sharp. At some point during Peters' time in London – and here the records are frustratingly vague – it was decided that the misfortunes and unhappiness of the black Nova Scotians might be ameliorated if they agreed to form the second wave of settlers to Sierra Leone.

Every black loyalist willing to travel to Sierra Leone was promised twenty acres of land and free transportation. The new settlement was to be built upon the ruins – both physical and conceptual – of the Province of Freedom and Sharp remained determined that the new society was to be committed to his original principles, as much as its new commercial system would allow. Living as they were through an age in which innate freedoms and natural rights were being enshrined in proclamations, declarations and constitutions, in both Europe and the Americas, Sharp and his abolitionist allies were carried along by the passions of their times. In this, their second draft of a black settler society, women householders were to vote alongside men in the election of public officials, racial prejudice in the selection of public servants was to be legislated against and all children were to attend school; this in a time when universal education and suffrage were a distant aspiration among social reformers in Britain.[63] Yet for all this the settlers were to be ruled over by a white governor who was himself to be answerable to a board of directors in London, all of them white.

To lead the recruitment of the Nova Scotians, and to ensure that the new colony lived up to its creed, the company appointed a 'Conductor'. The man chosen was twenty-seven-year-old John Clarkson. Another veteran of the American Revolutionary War, he was a member of the recently formed Society for the Abolition of the Slave Trade and the younger brother of Thomas Clarkson, the moral leader of the British abolitionist movement and a man about whom we shall hear more later. The company appear not to have considered offering this post to Thomas Peters, despite the fact that he had the confidence of hundreds of his fellow black loyalists, had won the support of British parliamentarians and the abolitionist elite and had been the spark that had ignited the whole scheme.[64]

In 1791 John Clarkson left his fiancée Susan Lee behind in England and travelled to Nova Scotia with Thomas Peters. Together they began a tour of all the regions in which the black loyalists had been settled. Speaking from the stages of meeting houses, from the pulpits of the black churches and while seated around the tables of poor black men and women in their own simple homes they promoted the new Sierra Leone scheme. Thomas Peters' reputation for integrity and John Clarkson's much commented upon personal charm rapidly began to win over the loyalists; William Wilberforce had advised Clarkson to refer to them as 'Africans', as it was more respectful than 'blacks' or 'negroes'. Peters and Clarkson were able to promise that every man who emigrated would be awarded twenty acres of land, every woman ten and five for each child. They assured the black Nova Scotians that in Sierra Leone they would be free from the racial prejudice that disfigured their life chances in British North America. In a little over three months they convinced 1,196 black men, women and children to commit to their second migration in a decade. This was around eight times the number the company had imagined might be induced to migrate.

That so many were willing to abandon their lives in Nova Scotia for an uncertain future in Sierra Leone reveals how little faith they had that their treatment in British North America was likely to improve. Not only were they were prepared to cross the ocean in search of a better life, they were, in some cases, willing to abandon the freeholds they held on land granted to them in Nova Scotia. Among this more fortunate section of the black loyalists was Harry Washington, one-time slave of George Washington, by then President of the United States. Harry Washington had been listed in the Book of Negroes and was one of the 405 former slaves who had been evacuated from New York on board the *L'Abondance* in July 1783. In 1791 his name was listed in another register which recorded the names of the settlers leaving Birchtown for Sierra Leone, along with his wife Jenny. Between them they were abandoning two lots of land in Birchtown, their house and forty acres of farmland. The couple carried with them to their new lives their portable possessions – an axe, a saw, a pickaxe, three hoes and two muskets – and a little of their furniture. Having been born in Africa and sold into American slavery, this last journey represented a form of return for Harry Washington, the third great migration of his life. The same was true for around one-third of the new settlers.

The fleet that sailed from Halifax, Nova Scotia, on 15 January 1792 was five times the size of the armada which had carried the black poor of London to Sierra Leone. On board the fifteen ships were whole families as well as lone individuals. Seven weeks later, and after a terrible storm-tossed crossing, they landed in St George's Bay, as the black 'Londoners' had done four years earlier. On their way into the mouth of the Sierra Leone River they had passed a slave ship out of Bristol heading inland to collect its cargo, a harsh reminder that they were travelling up one of the superhighways of the Atlantic slave trade.[65]

Over the course of several days the ships carrying the new settlers appeared one by one on the horizon and slipped into the Sierra

Leone River. The settlers came ashore, landed their supplies and began to explore what remained of the original Granville Town. The settlement was overgrown and partially reclaimed by the bush. The settlers had been promised that a team of white administrators under Alexander Falconbridge would have prepared the site for their arrival and they were appalled to discover that almost nothing had been done. So they set about the enormous task of building their new settlement almost from scratch. This was not to be a wholesale resurrection of the old Granville Town. The new settlement was to be larger and more extensive. It was named Freetown – literally free town; a settlement in which former slaves could forge a free existence. On arrival John Clarkson discovered his own freedoms had been somewhat curtailed. Correspondence from England informed him that he had been appointed superintendent to the settlement and would therefore not be returning to England to marry his fiancée.

The birth of Freetown was as difficult and arduous as the attempt to create Granville Town had been. The new settlers struggled to disinter the site of the great entanglements of elephant grass that had colonized the old clearings. As they did, the plots slowly emerged and black loyalists who had been evacuated from Charleston, Savannah and New York Harbor a decade earlier finally received the land that had been promised to them by the British Crown; seven years late and on a different continent. Thomas Peters, the spokesman of the landless and dissatisfied loyalists, received a plot of nine acres. He had had to cross the Atlantic three times in order to secure it. As they settled down to work they forged a community through regular communal meetings, or palavers. They assembled together, sitting on the hard, dark brown earth under the shade of a huge cotton silk tree. That cotton tree is not the one that stands in the centre of modern Freetown, spreading its branches across an intersection of five converging roads – that is believed to have been closer to the harbour. The present tree, however, ancient and imposing, has become the spiritual as well as the physical centre of Freetown and the symbol of Sierra Leone. It appears on the 10,000 leone banknote and Sierra Leoneans gather there to mark significant national events.

The appointment of Clarkson as superintendent to the settlement meant the marginalization of Thomas Peters, who was given no official role despite having been the instigator of the whole project. Tensions between the two men culminated in a dramatic and very public confrontation in April 1792. At a tense public meeting under the cotton tree, Clarkson prophesied, rather melodramatically, that 'one or other of us would be hanged on that tree' before the dispute between them was settled.[66] We only have Clarkson's account of what happened but it appears that to prevent Peters from forming what would have amounted to a parallel administration, Clarkson persuaded the settlers en masse to side with him, by casting Peters as the agent of discord and division, forces that he warned would be the undoing of the settlement. The outcome of this clash was that Thomas Peters was even further sidelined. Just three months later he died feeling that he had been as mistreated and betrayed in Sierra Leone as he had been in Nova Scotia.

The existence of modern Freetown is proof that ultimately the Nova Scotians were able to establish a lasting settlement, but they suffered the same trials and losses that had overwhelmed the black poor of London. High summer temperatures, heavy rains in the long and cold rainy season and tropical diseases all wrought death and devastation upon them. Two hundred died from disease in the first year and the rainy season in 1792 was said to be worse than that of 1787, which had been the death of so many of the black 'Londoners'. One night a leopard found its way into one of their tents and had to be driven off and on another occasion a baboon attempted to seize one of the children. These losses were partially compensated by the incorporation into the new settlement of the survivors of Granville Town and made easier to bear as their initial numbers were greater.

A few of the Nova Scotians who signed up to settle on the banks of the Sierra Leone River did so despite the fact that it was from that river that they had been sold into slavery. One of them, John Gordon, who had been held captive in Bunce Island, after several years settled in Freetown accidentally encountered the man who had kidnapped and sold him. Having become a Methodist preacher in North America, Gordon forgave the slave-trader as he had come to regard his own enslavement as a necessary part of a divine plan that had led to both his conversion and his return to his motherland.

Other former slaves encountered their lost relatives; one woman, Martha Webb, saw her mother among a group of slaves being led away in chains and frantically arranged to pay to have her released.[67] Africans who were being pursued by the kidnappers and slave-traders sometimes sought refuge in the new Freetown, as did sailors from British ships, who had themselves often been press-ganged, and were desperate to escape. From time to time enraged ship's captains came into the town looking for deserters. The slave-traders of Bunce Island looked upon the settlers of Freetown with the same distrust with which they had regarded the population of the Province of Freedom. John Clarkson declined offers to drink and dine at the grand agents' house on Bunce Island.

After eighteen months Clarkson finally left the colony. He named the harbour from which he departed Susan Bay after the fiancée to whom he was returning. It still carries the name but has sadly degenerated into one of Freetown's most desperate slums, home to migrants pushed out of the inland provinces by the disastrous civil war of the 1990s. Clarkson's replacement as governor, William Dawes, had, rather inauspiciously, been an official in the convict station at Botany Bay; the two settlement projects, one in Africa the other in Australia, were it seems destined to be further intertwined. With the departure of Clarkson and the appointment of Dawes tensions between the settlers and the company director in London reached new heights. The settlers drafted a petition to protest against the rule of Mr Dawes, who they claimed 'seems to wish to ruin us just as bad as if we were all Slaves'. The grievance that ran deepest among the Nova Scotians was the company's insistence that they pay quit-rents on the land allocated to them; this company policy was in direct contravention of the assurances that had been given to the black loyalists by Clarkson and Peters in 1791. The new rents in effect made the people of Freetown sharecroppers, forced to perpetually service a debt they would never pay off and to rent land that would never be theirs in freehold. The move was bitterly resented and resolutely resisted. Tensions ran so high that there was effectively a rebellion. A group of black loyalist men who had already rebelled against slavery in North America, and fought with arms for their rights to freedom in the Revolutionary War, marched out of Freetown and took up positions on a bridge on the outskirts of the settlement. They had, so they believed, the support of the local Temne people and they aimed to overthrow company rule and challenge imperial authority. The rebellion divided the people of Freetown; half supported it, half did not. Events were decided in an armed confrontation at the bridge. The leaders of the rebellion were killed in action, others were captured and in a few cases hanged. Others, who had supported the rebellion, were banished from the colony and had no choice but to clear new plots on isolated shore regions of the Freetown peninsula. Among the exiles was Harry Washington. It was twenty years since he had escaped from the Mount Vernon plantation. After his banishment there is no further record of him.

The grave of Harry Washington, like those of Thomas Peters and their fellow settlers, lie somewhere beneath modern Freetown. No graves and no structures built during those early waves of settlement have survived the passage of two centuries and even the exact sites and dimensions of the Province of Freedom and of the Nova Scotian settlement are unclear. The memory of those years are preserved only in the documents held in the National Archives and through the names that appear on the map of modern Freetown. The narrow bay to the north of the ancient cotton tree in the centre of the city is known as Susan's Bay, named for John Clarkson's long-suffering fiancée. The promontory that defines the eastern limits of Susan's Bay is called Falconbridge Point, dedicated to the memory of Alexander Falconbridge, the committed abolitionist but hapless company administrator who died while in Sierra Leone having drunk himself to oblivion. The names of the black settlers are not commemorated on street signs but are recalled in another way. The Nova Scotian settlers who survived the establishment of the settlement built themselves homes in a style reminiscent of the colonial architecture of North America. These large, wooden, two-storey houses stood on substantial stone foundations and rapidly became a feature of the city of Freetown. The last of them still exist along the narrow streets of central Freetown. Many are patched up with corrugated iron, their outwards-facing boards coated in bright but blistered paint. As the city has expanded and the population increased more of these old board houses have been sold and demolished to make way for grander concrete buildings of three or four storeys, better able to accommodate large families. As the forests have been cut back on the Freetown peninsula the economic rationale for building in hardwood has evaporated. Wood that has to be transported from the interior is more expensive than concrete, and in difficult economic times the cost of maintaining these old homes, with their links back to the founders of the city, has proved too much for many families.

Another echo from those formative years is the St John's Maroon Church, which stands on one of the city's main roads. It was founded by yet another influx of settlers. In 1800 the Nova Scotians and perhaps the last few of the London black poor were joined on their peninsula by around five hundred Maroons, former slaves from Jamaica. The Maroons were a people of Ashanti heritage who had escaped from slavery, established their own settlements up in the mountains and fought two wars against British forces. After the Second Maroon War the defeated Maroons of the town of Trelawny were transported to Nova Scotia and from there they too were shipped across the Atlantic and drawn into the experiment being played out on the coast of Africa. Their little whitewashed church stands not far from the waterfront in Freetown and their descendants still live in the city, part of a so-called Krio population made up of people of various heritage. Respectable, pious and passionately dedicated to education and self-improvement they seem too gentle a people to be the descendants of the slave rebels whose guerrilla warfare against the British forces remains legendary in Jamaica. The younger generations of Freetown Maroons have themselves become settlers, they are part of a Krio diaspora that has clusters across Britain and the United States.

Freetown today is largely a product of subsequent waves of settlement, of which we shall hear more later, and there is perhaps nowhere in Africa upon which the energy and optimism of the British abolitionist impulse has been so deeply inscribed into the local geography and demography. To reach Susan's Bay the visitor passes along the broad thoroughfare upon which the Maroon church stands, passing smaller side streets whose names read like a who's-who of nineteenth-century British politics. Each is named in honour of a prime minister, abolitionist or politician – Percival Street, Walpole Street, Bathurst Street, Wellington Street and

Liverpool Street, after the Prime Minister Lord Liverpool. One of the last streets before Susan's Bay is Wilberforce Street.

Freetown was never a dumping ground for unwanted black people. Although the establishment of the Province of Freedom went disastrously wrong and although the treatment of the Nova Scotian settlers was never free from racial bias these schemes of settlement were relatively well funded and for the most part well meaning – in the mind of Granville Sharp they were intended to be almost utopian. The descendants of those early settlers, who form portions of the Krio population, are a people whose identities have been profoundly shaped by British slavery and by popular British opposition to slavery, a political and moral impulse that became one of the defining issues of the late eighteenth and early nineteenth centuries. Living in their colonial-style wooden homes, imported from another lost British colony or gathered in the Maroon church they are a people who are as much a part of what we term 'black British history' as any community in Brixton, Toxteth or St Paul's.

SIX

'The Monster is Dead'

In 1618 the English explorer Captain Richard Jobson was in Sene-gambia, in West Africa, in search of gold. By the banks of the Gambia River, Jobson encountered the African slave-trader Buckor Sano, who presented him with a group of 'certaine young blacke women, who were standing by themselves, and had white strings crosse their bodies, which hee told me were slaves, brought for me to buy'. Indignantly he refused the transaction, telling his would-be trading-partner that the English 'were a people, who did not deale in any such commod-ities, neither did wee buy or sell one another, or any that had our owne shapes'. When Buckor Sano asked why it was that the English refused to trade in slaves when other 'white men . . . earnestly desired them, especially such young women', Jobson replied that the other Europeans 'were another kinde of people different from us'.[1]

Between that moment in 1618, when Richard Jobson recoiled at the mere suggestion that he or any Englishman would engage in the buying and selling of other human beings, and the passing, in 1807, of the Act for the Abolition of the Slave Trade, Britain became the dominant slave-trading nation in the North Atlantic. Half of all the Africans who were carried into slavery over the course of the eighteenth century were transported in the holds of British ships. Some estimates put the total shipped by the British at around three and a half million. It took around eleven thousand separate slave-trading expeditions to complete such a vast forced migration, a movement of people that remained without precedent until the twentieth century. The wealth generated through the slave trade and the sale of the tropical goods that their labour produced transformed cities like Bristol, Liverpool and Glasgow into boom towns; frenetic centres of global commerce, investment, conspicuous consumption and philanthropic endeavour.

How did all this come about? How did the English overcome the revulsion that Richard Jobson expressed and why, in the last quarter of the eighteenth century, did that revulsion seemingly return, motivating millions of Britons to turn their backs on an institution and a trade that had so enormously enriched their nation? Why did the British come to care so greatly about the fates and lives of the slaves who laboured thousands of miles away, when they had been largely uninterested in them during the preceding decades? How could those opposed to slavery draw public attention to the suffering of the enslaved and the horrors of the slave trade when other issues – war with France, revolution, ideological discord, failed harvests and mass distress – were all seemingly more pressing and closer to home?

The forces that led Britain to become a slave-trading and slave-owning nation in the seventeenth century have been discussed earlier, and are relatively straightforward. The nation was drawn into the trade for the same reason that English traders like John Lok and Thomas Wyndham broke Portugal's monopoly of the African gold trade in the sixteenth century and English planters on Barbados moved into sugar cultivation a century later. Simply put, the English (later the British) saw the profits being made by their Portuguese, Spanish and then Dutch competitors and wanted a slice of the action. By contrast the forces that led to the abolition of the slave trade in 1807, and then of slavery itself in 1833, are far more complicated, opaque and contested. What we do know is that the view that the trade in slaves was a national sin emerged in the 1770s and then spread rapidly, growing to become an intellectual and ethical current that ran through society and carried the abolition movement forward. Once it emerged, British abolitionism forced the issue of slavery and the contested humanity of black people into the centre of British politics, where it remained long after the slave trade and slavery had been abolished. Abolitionism, and the developing sense that slavery belonged to the past rather than the future, was one of the forces that shaped and influenced Britain's relationship with Africa and people of African descent on three continents until at least the end of the nineteenth century.

To fully understand how remarkable the rise of British

abolitionism was, both as a political movement and as a popular sentiment, it is important to remember how few voices were raised against
slavery in Britain until the last quarter of the eighteenth century. The
Church of England was largely silent on the issue as were most of the
politicians. To most people in Britain, until the 1770s and 1780s, there
seemed to be no way out. Britain was addicted to slave-produced
products and therefore addicted to slavery. Too much money, too many
livelihoods and too much political power were invested; millions of
British people lived lives that were intimately connected to the
economics of slavery and the sugar business. Edward Long, the
pro-slavery propagandist and one of the original authors of English
racism, was not wrong when he wrote in 1774:

> If, upon the whole, we revolve in our minds, what an amazing
> variety of trades receive their daily support, as many of them did
> originally their being, from the calls of the African and West India
> markets; if we reflect on the numerous families of those mechanics
> and artisans which are thus maintained, and contemplate that ease
> and plenty, which is the constant as well as just reward of their
> incessant labours; if we combine with these the several tribes of
> active and busy people, who are continually employed in the
> building, repairing, rigging, victualling, and equipping the multitudes
> of seamen who earn their wages by navigating, and the prodigious
> crowds who likewise obtain their bread by loading [the] ships . . .
> we may from thence form a competent idea of the prodigious value
> of our sugar colonies, and a just conception of their immense
> importance to the grandeur and prosperity of their mother country.[2]

These economic arguments were widely accepted and were
buttressed by a set of theories about race and the supposed inferiority of the Africans that had been developing and mutating for
centuries. Notions about the innate savagery and sexual immorality
of Africans that had been expressed on the pages of Mandeville's
Travels in the fourteenth century and in Richard Hakluyt's collated
travel accounts of the sixteenth century were still in circulation.
Likewise the idea that the people of Africa were the descendants of
Ham, the cursed son of Noah, was still deployed from time to time
to legitimize slavery, and other passages from the Bible which

appeared to sanction it had also been identified. Africans were presumed to be inferior, and that inferiority was regarded as a warrant for their enslavement and exploitation. Yet as the abolitionists discovered, there were many people who tolerated slavery not because they believed it was ordained by God or sanctioned by racial difference but simply because they knew very little about it. Although there were thousands of black people living in Britain in the eighteenth century the plantations of the West Indies, the crucible of their suffering, were an ocean away and the nauseating conditions that prevailed on the lower decks of slave ships were a guilty secret, hidden from public view. For these reasons the abolition movement was as focused on the task of educating the public about the realities of slavery and the trade as it was on campaigning for their abolition.

Various theories have been put forward to explain why and how the abolition of the British slave trade came about in 1807. In the middle of the last century the Trinidadian historian Eric Williams passionately argued that the slave trade and slavery were abandoned primarily because they were in economic decline and becoming increasingly marginal to the economy of a nation undergoing rapid industrialization. While much of Williams's work has withstood rigorous analysis by later scholars, his theory that slavery was economically spent at the moment of its abolition has been largely demolished by modern historians, most notably Seymour Drescher. They have shown that in the 1780s, the decade in which the abolitionist movement found its voice, British ships transported around a third of the one million Africans who were shipped across the Atlantic to the plantations of the New World. Historians have also demonstrated that while over-planting had exhausted the soil in parts of Jamaica which, Williams argued. reduced the profitability of the plantations, in the 1830s, the decade in which Britain abolished slavery, new estates in Trinidad and Guyana were in full production and were proving to be extraordinarily profitable. As Drescher wrote, 'In terms of both capital value and of overseas trade, the slave system was expanding, not declining, at the turn of the nineteenth century.'[3] Slave-traders, ship owners, plantation owners, insurers, shipbuilders, sugar merchants and investors of all types were looking to the future and making plans for consolidation or expansion.

If declining profitability cannot explain abolition – and few historians today feel that it can – perhaps it was down to the ferocity of the slave rebellions that broke out across the West Indies during the late eighteenth and early nineteenth centuries? The determination of the enslaved to resist and rebel undoubtedly played a far larger role than historians were once willing to acknowledge, but even this does not, by itself, explain why Britain ended the slave trade, banned her citizens from taking part in it and in 1838 set 800,000 people free from bondage. If explanations for the success of the abolitionist campaign and the enormous levels of support it generated are difficult to come by, historians do at least have a good understanding of how the movement catalysed and evolved.

The campaign against slavery that was to invade the consciousness of millions of people began as a mere rumbling of discontent among minority religious groups in the 1770s and 1780s. From those unpromising beginnings it became a vast national movement. Within the span of a single lifetime it encouraged the people of Britain to reject and repudiate a trade which their own countrymen had perfected and a plantation system that provided products upon which almost everyone relied upon to some extent. The story of that great transition cannot be told without reference to a man we have already met, Granville Sharp. This is because one of the first milestones in the emergence of the abolitionist movement was the Somerset case. Although Lord Mansfield's judgement was, as we have seen, limited to a very specific point of law and applied only within England, the publicity it generated was a coup for the opponents of slavery and a disturbing blow to the West India planters. To foreign observers the sudden squeamishness of the British about the fate of former slaves on the streets of London reeked of hypocrisy. Responding to the Somerset case, Benjamin Franklin railed in the *London Chronicle* against what he saw as English duplicity. Freeing James Somerset surely meant little so long as Britain held vast numbers of black men, women and children in chains. 'Pharisaical Britain!', he snorted, 'to pride thyself in setting free a single Slave that happens to land on thy coasts, while thy Merchants in all thy ports are encouraged by thy laws to continue a commerce whereby so many hundreds of thousands are dragged into a slavery that can scarce be said to end with their lives, since it is entailed on their posterity!'[4] In another part of the article, which Franklin wrote anonymously, he laid out the scale of the challenge facing the opponents of slavery and the moral case for abolition.

> By a late computation made in America, it appears that there are now eight hundred and fifty thousand Negroes in the English Islands and Colonies; and that the yearly importation is about one hundred thousand, of which number about one third perish by the gaol distemper on the passage, and in the sickness called the seasoning before they are set to labour. The remnant makes up the deficiencies continually occurring among the main body of those unhappy people, through the distempers occasioned by excessive labour, bad nourishment, uncomfortable accommodation, and broken spirits. Can sweetening our tea, &c. with sugar, be a circumstance of such absolute necessity? Can the petty pleasure thence arising to the taste, compensate for so much misery produced among our fellow creatures, and such a constant butchery of the human species by this pestilential detestable traffic in the bodies and souls of men?[5]

The traffic in enslaved Africans was never more detestable than in 1783 when the details of what took place on board the *Zong* became known in Britain. The basic facts are simple and shocking. In September 1781 the *Zong*, a Liverpool-registered slave ship, sailed from Accra in Ghana with four hundred and forty-two slaves on board, around twice the number a ship of that size could reasonably expect to transport without catastrophic loss of life. By early December, after a series of amateurish and baffling navigational errors, the ship was running out of fresh water and disease had broken out on the slave decks and among the crew. To preserve supplies and protect their profits by ensuring that at least some of the slaves reached market in Jamaica alive, the crew of the *Zong* cast a hundred and thirty-three of the most sickly slaves overboard. This was not done in a single moment of murderous haste but gradually and systematically, over the course of three days. The victims were selected from the decks below by the captain, Luke Collingwood. It was a clinical massacre of innocents but it had stemmed from a strange mixture of callous self-interest and professional incompetence, for when the *Zong* arrived in Jamaica just three weeks later there were still 420 gallons of water on board. Just two hundred and eight of the four hundred and forty-two Africans who had been packed into the *Zong* in Accra were still alive.

This terrible incident was brought to wider national attention only when the owners of the *Zong* filed an insurance claim against the loss of 'cargo', demanding £30 for each slave cast overboard. Their insurance underwriters disagreed and refused to pay.[6] The first anonymous reports of the case were spotted in the English newspapers by the watchful eye of Olaudah Equiano. When the insurance case came to court in 1783 the cold, financial reasoning behind the massacre appalled all those who heard it. It was explained in court that the 'master of the ship called together a few of the officers, and told them to the following effect : – that, if the slaves died a natural death, it would be the loss of the owners of the ship; but if they were thrown alive into the sea, it would be the loss of the underwriters'.[7] After hearing such evidence even the redoubtable Lord Chief Justice, Mansfield, before whom the case was heard, privately admitted that the case 'shocks one very much'. Mansfield found against the ship owners. The popular outrage that reverberated from the *Zong* affair made it the next milestone in the development of the abolitionist cause. Among those who attended court throughout much of the *Zong* case was Granville Sharp. As he had done during the trial of James Somerset a decade earlier Sharp employed a shorthand writer to attend court and record the speeches and testimonies given. These transcriptions were then published, adding to the moral case against the slave trade that was slowly building in the public's consciousness. Sharp also sought unsuccessfully to bring criminal charges against the crew of the *Zong*, although the main culprit, Captain Collingwood, was by this time dead. In this he was unsuccessful and no one ever faced trial for the massacre. Yet the fact that the case had garnered so much publicity and shocked so many millions was significant in itself. The murder of the sick or the disruptive on board slave ships was a routine practice. Never before had the details of so terrible a case been brought to the attention of so many. A light had been shone upon some of the darkest secrets of the slave trade.

In 1787, four years after the *Zong* affair and the year in which the black poor of London departed for the new colony of Sierra Leone, the abolitionist movement was formally born. Its place of birth was a printing shop at 2 George Yard, London, a building long ago demolished. There, on 22 May, twelve men gathered together. The minutes taken of this little assembly recorded that, 'At a Meeting held for the Purpose of taking the Slave Trade into consideration, it was resolved that the said Trade was both impolitick and unjust.' This group of twelve – nine Quakers and the rest Evangelical Anglicans – formed themselves into the Society for Effecting the Abolition of the Slave Trade. They included the Staffordshire pottery entrepreneur Josiah Wedgwood, the Quaker banker and philanthropist Samuel Hoare and Granville Sharp. But perhaps its most significant member was Thomas Clarkson. His conversion to the cause had begun one year earlier as an academic exercise. As a graduate deacon at St John's College, Cambridge, Clarkson entered a Latin essay into a competition. Entrants were asked to adopt a position either for or against slavery and put forward their most compelling case. Clarkson's submission was entitled 'Essay on the slavery and commerce of the human species'. It was eloquent enough to win the prize and compelling enough to win over the man who became the other great champion of the abolitionists' cause, William Wilberforce MP. For the next two decades Wilberforce, a fellow Cambridge graduate, worked alongside Clarkson – the former in Parliament and the latter at the hustings and in the lecture hall.[8] Their partnership epitomizes the movement's twin-track approach of popular agitation and parliamentary strategizing.

The men who gathered together in George Yard in 1787 and committed themselves to fighting against the slave trade were disproportionately Nonconformists, and their hostility towards slavery and the trade stemmed from their moral and religious views. Yet secular philosophy and even economics had drawn similar conclusions at around the same time. A number of Enlightenment thinkers, especially those from Scotland and France, had condemned slavery. The Scottish Enlightenment thinker Francis Hutcheson condemned slavery as it violated the 'original rights' with which he believed all human beings were born. The English philosopher and MP Edmund Burke opposed slavery and favoured a scheme of gradual emancipation in order to spread liberty, which he and many others increasingly regarded as an automatic good. Other philosophical voices spoke against slavery from across the English Channel: Voltaire, Rousseau, Montesquieu and Abbé Reynal. One recurring theme repeated and developed by many of those who disapproved of slavery was that it was outdated; that while it might be profitable in the short term its continuation risked impeding human development. Slavery, its opponents argued, was not just immoral but also very much inferior to free labour, free enterprise and free trade. The enemies of American slavery were making the same arguments right up until the US Civil War in the 1860s.

To modern sensibilities, one of the central strategies adopted by the men who formed the Society for Effecting the Abolition of the Slave Trade is difficult to comprehend. The early abolitionists focused upon the slave trade, rather than slavery. This distinction is often lost on us in the twenty-first century, as we tend to see them as the twin branches of a single reprehensible industry. The abolitionists saw things differently, in a strange mixture of worldly pragmatism and naive over-optimism. They concluded that the Middle Passage of the slave trade was the most deadly and inhumane aspect of slavery. At no other point in his or her life was the individual slave to suffer so greatly or face a greater risk of death. All this was true but the members of the society also understood that the abolition of plantation slavery was a more daunting challenge. Under colonial law slaves were property – which had not been altered by the Somerset case. An attack on slavery was therefore, by its nature, an assault on property rights which were a near-sacred concept in the late eighteenth century, when voting rights and political power were dependent upon the ownership of property.

Many abolitionists reconciled themselves to this political reality because they were convinced that the cessation of the trade was the key to ending slavery: if the trade was ended and the supply of slaves cut off then the whole system would 'wither on the vine'. If the slave owners understood that their human property could not be replaced, they would treat the slaves better. Impelled by enlightened self-interest they would be less likely to force enslaved women to work long into their pregnancies, and would improve the diets, housing and health of their valuable human assets. With conditions improved, death rates would fall, infant mortality would decrease and life expectancy would rise. In the long run, it was hoped, some form of freedom would emerge on the plantations to supplant chattel slavery. The hypothesis that plantation slavery could be reformed and that abolition of the slave trade would automatically bring this reform about was believed by supporters and enemies of slavery in both Britain and the West Indies. There were those who were unconvinced, though, including Granville Sharp, who accepted the strategy put forward by his colleagues but remained personally committed to the ending of slavery as well as the trade.

To achieve even their limited aim the early abolitionists embarked upon a campaign of public education, popular persuasion and political lobbying that was unprecedented in scale and revolutionary in nature. They wrote and published thousands of tracts and pamphlets and pioneered the use of the mass petition as a campaigning tool. They harvested millions of individual signatures from the British public and delivered to Parliament hundreds of petitions. Historians have calculated that between 1787 and 1792, 1.5 million people in Britain signed petitions against the slave trade, when the national population was just 12 million.[9] The first anti-slave-trade petitions had been presented to Parliament even before the formal establishment of the anti-slavery movement in 1787. The abolition movement also deployed the boycott as a political weapon. Abolitionists were encouraged to eschew the use of rum and cane sugar produced by slaves and instead use sugar produced in India by free labour, or else add lemon to their tea. In his *Address to the People of Great Britain* of 1791, the abolitionist William Fox wrote, 'If we purchase the commodity we participate in the crime. The slave-dealer, the slave-holder, and the slave-driver, are virtually the agents of the consumer, and may be considered as employed and hired by him to procure the commodity . . . In every pound of sugar used . . . we may be considered as consuming two ounces of human flesh'.[10] Two hundred thousand copies of William Fox's *Address* were printed, and they circulated around Britain and America.

From the original twelve founders of the Society for Effecting the Abolition of the Slave Trade, abolitionism expanded to become a mass membership movement; an enormous and enormously complicated network of local societies, committees and energetic campaigning individuals. Abolitionism mobilized the Quaker and Evangelical communities of Britain, whose churches and meeting halls became the physical infrastructure of the movement. The Quakers were able to call upon their brothers from America. Among the works Clarkson consulted while writing his prize-winning Cambridge essay was *Some Historical Account of Guinea* by Anthony Benezet, the famous American Quaker abolitionist. Dynamic, committed and innovative, Benezet was a friend of Granville Sharp and a powerful anti-slavery voice. Alongside Clarkson he was one of the great educators of the movement as he was convinced that slavery could only be challenged if the public were confronted with the reality of the institution and made to understand just how miserable the conditions were in which the enslaved toiled and suffered. To remind the public that slavery existed in temperate as well as tropical zones Benezet once stood barefoot in the snow outside a public meeting, in order to bring home the point that the enslaved were given no shoes and suffered in the cold as much as any white person.[11] Alongside the Quakers other denominations underwent their own conversions to the anti-slavery cause. John Wesley, the founder of what became Methodism, had seen slavery for himself in Georgia in the 1730s and was appalled both by the brutality and by the slave owners' determination to withhold the Christian Gospel from the enslaved. The Wesleyans spoke against slavery and in 1774 John Wesley published *Thoughts upon Slavery*, a fiery tract that denounced the owners and traffickers of enslaved people as murderers and thieves. For Wesley, as much as any of the French philosophers, slavery was a crime because it denied human beings the inalienable rights that were theirs according to 'the law of nature'.

The religious fervour and moral philosophy behind abolitionism were broadcast and disseminated through the great shared spectacle of the movement – the public meeting, of which thousands were held across the country. Abolitionist meetings and lectures stoked the fires of indignant opposition that burned in the breasts of the converted and convinced those who attended out of interest or curiosity to dedicate themselves to the great moral crusade. At some gatherings a single speaker was invited to the lectern; on other occasions there were multiple speakers. Abolitionist meetings were never brief affairs. Speeches often went on for hours and speakers were known and celebrated for the duration of their orations. Most of the key anti-slavery speakers – men like Clarkson, Newton and Falconbridge – became renowned for their oratory skills and passion. The most successful of the abolitionist gatherings became enormous events, attracting crowds tens of thousands strong, and at the end of the speeches there were always opportunities to sign petitions and to purchase abolitionist tracts, pamphlets and, increasingly, books as abolitionism spawned a new literary genre.

There was a ready and appreciative market for abolitionist books. Evangelical Christianity placed enormous importance on reading and studying; John Wesley asked his followers to read for five hours each day. However, the most remarkable and compelling abolitionist books were the autobiographies of men and women who had themselves been enslaved. Two of the most important were written by two of the most active black abolitionists, Olaudah Equiano and Ottobah Cugoano who were friends as well as collaborators. Cugoano's *Thoughts and Sentiments on the Evil of Slavery and Commerce of the Human Species* was published in 1787, the year the Society for Effecting the Abolition of the Slave Trade was formed. He was born in the late 1750s on the Gold Coast, in what is today Ghana, and kidnapped by slave-traders at around the age of thirteen – 'snatched away from my native country' as he described it. He was enslaved on the island of Grenada and forced to work on the island's sugar plantations until he was sold to a new owner who brought him to England. It was in 1772, the year of the Somerset case. Cugoano claimed his freedom and in August 1773 was baptized in London, taking the name John Stuart. No longer bound to his former owner he entered the paid service of Richard Cosway, a well-known painter of miniatures. Learning to read and write, Cugoano became active among the black population of Georgian London and, with the help and guidance of his friend Olaudah Equiano, wrote his autobiography. The literary influence of Equiano is evident in several passages across the book and he may well have edited and helped revise his friend's manuscript. In a strident and damning work, Cugoano demanded an immediate end to both the slave trade and slavery and used his own life story to build his case. He offered his readers graphic insights into the lives of the men and women who produced the sugar that sweetened their tea, recounting the 'dreadful scenes of misery and cruelty' he had encountered on a daily basis while a slave on Grenada. He also detailed the terrible punishments that were inflicted upon black bodies, describing how, for merely eating a piece of sugar cane, 'some were cruelly lashed, or struck over the face, to knock their teeth out . . . Some told me they had their teeth pulled out to deter others, and to prevent them from eating any cane in future.'[12] Cugoano's shocking book was distributed among the great and the good; even George III was reportedly given a copy. Cugoano is another of the many notable black Britons who left us their words and experiences only to later disappear from the historical record. It's believed he married an English woman and laid plans to open a school but nothing certain is known. If he has descendants they carry his blood line unknowingly.

Cugoano's friend and collaborator Olaudah Equiano's commentary on slavery came in the form of his bestselling *Interesting Narrative of the Life of Olaudah Equiano*. Running into nine editions, it became one of the literary sensations of the late eighteenth century, though some historians today debate the veracity of certain aspects of his account. Believed to have been born around 1745 in what is now Nigeria, he was captured by African slave-traders around the age of eleven, and trafficked to Barbados and then Virginia. Equiano's life story stands out from that of most of the other former slaves who wrote narratives of their lives in that he was not put to work on the plantations. Instead he worked on board the ships that linked the whole system of colonial slavery together. Equiano's bizarre life reads almost like an ugly parody of modern globalization. Torn from his African childhood and identity by slave-traders he was forcibly made into an American slave and was later purchased by a British naval officer with a French name (Michael Pascal) who decided to rename him Gustavus Vassa after a sixteenth-century Swedish king. This was one of a succession of names that were foisted upon Equiano as he passed from owner to owner. The only constant in this phase of his life was that, although he was sold three times and owned by three different men, he remained employed on ships and for twenty years he travelled across the West Indies, North America and Central America all the while the property of other men. Other trips took him to Europe and Turkey. Later, as a free man, he even sailed to the Arctic. Through his own industriousness and a degree of luck Equiano was ultimately able to purchase his freedom and make his way to Britain. By the 1780s he was a free man in London, although he continued to travel, and by 1783 he was involved in the early abolitionist movement and in contact with Granville Sharp, whom he approached for assistance whenever he became aware of cases in which black people had been abducted by their former masters. His *Interesting Narrative* made Olaudah Equiano famous. Demand for the book was so great that it went through eight editions in England. It was also rapidly translated into German, Russian and Dutch and an American version appeared. John Wesley read the *Interesting Narrative* on his death-bed and it was reviewed by Mary Wollstonecraft. In his forties when his narrative was published, and by then a forceful speaker and passionate campaigner, Equiano used his fame and his extraordinary life story to establish himself as a critical figure on the abolitionist circuit.

With a group of other eighteenth-century black Britons, Olaudah Equiano and Ottobah Cugoano formed the Sons of Africa, a group of men who had known slavery themselves or who were descended from enslaved parents, and who met to fight against that institution. They included Boughwa Gegansmel, Jasper Goree, Cojoh Ammere, George Robert Mandeville, Thomas Jones, William Stevens, Joseph Almze, John Christopher, James Bailey, Thomas Oxford and George Wallace. The Sons of Africa were just as energetic as the white aboli-tionists, writing letters and making speeches, although the records of their activities are far from complete and much about them remains unknown. One document that did survive was a petition written by the Sons of Africa in thanks and recognition of their greatest ally, Granville Sharp. It was drafted in December 1787, twenty-two years after Sharp had stumbled upon the broken figure of Jonathan Strong outside his brother's surgery on Mincing Lane. It read,

> And we must say, that we, who are a part, or descendants, of the much-wronged people of Africa, are peculiarly and greatly indebted to you, for the many good and friendly services that you have done towards us, and which are now even out of our power to enumerate. Nevertheless, we are truly sensible of your great kindness and humanity; and we cannot do otherwise but endeavour, with the utmost sincerity and thankfulness, to acknowledge our great obli-gations to you, and, with the most feeling sense of our hearts, on all occasions to express and manifest our gratitude and love for your long, valuable, and indefatigable labours and benevolence towards using every means to rescue our suffering brethren in slavery.[13]

The Sons of Africa whose words – both spoken and written – were broadcast across their society were able to present themselves to the British public as living proof of black humanity, in an age when that self-evident fact was still called into question by some.

Alongside Olaudah Equiano, Ottobah Cugoano and their colleagues other black Britons took part in the struggles against the trade and slavery. Phillis Wheatley, James Gronniosaw, Ignatius Sancho and later Mary Prince through their letters, poems, memoirs, speeches, journalism and very living presence in Britain acted as a counter to the propaganda of the growing pro-slavery lobby that emerged.

The talents and life stories of black people who had personal experiences of slavery enabled the abolitionist movement to fine-tune its message, but it was also able to administer its various campaigns and expand its reach across society because it was willing to free the enormous amount of wasted intellect and energy that in the eighteenth and nineteenth centuries was bottled up within the women of Britain. Denied the vote or any meaningful role in politics – which was regarded as being an entirely male preserve – women were, to some extent and in some quarters, permitted to become active participants in individual causes. Significantly, it had long been deemed socially acceptable for women to raise petitions, which were then delivered to Parliament – an assembly which, of course, was then entirely male. Propriety set limits on how active and how vocal women were able to become in their chosen cause but the humanitarian nature of the abolitionist crusade, with its emphasis on mercy, compassion and the preservation of the family, was deemed fittingly feminine. The energies and compassion of women were thus given an outlet and female abolitionists formed their own organizations and committees. They held abolitionist events, wrote pamphlets, tracts and poems, gathered signatures for the petitions and raised campaign money. At certain times and in certain places they were the engine room of the movement. Traditionally confined to the domestic sphere, women brought anti-slavery politics into the home via the sugar boycott. It was women who did the most to promote and propagate that campaign which drew the mocking scorn of journalists and the engravers of satirical cartoons. The abolitionist movement, especially in its campaigns of the 1820s and 1830s, could not possibly have achieved what it did without their involvement.

The abolitionists were as much educators as activists and abolition meetings were as much tutorials as they were rallies. To demonstrate the most brutal aspects of the slave trade the abolitionists acquired its tools – manacles, shackles, metal punishment collars and whips.

With these vile props they confronted their audiences with physical evidence of the violence always underwriting slavery and the trade. In that spirit Wilberforce acquired a set of shackles and thumbscrews and Thomas Clarkson, one of the greatest political educators of his age, had two models of the slave ship *Brooks* – sometimes called *Brookes* – built by a carpenter. The upper deck could be removed to reveal the slave decks below, upon which had been painted an image of the slaves, four hundred and eighty-two of them, shackled tightly together to the deck. The *Brooks* was built in Liverpool and fitted out to carry four hundred and fifty-one captives. Three times the size of the *Zong*, the *Brooks* was selected by Clarkson as she was typical of the vessels engaged in the trade at that time and so there could be no accusations of exaggerating her size. Her dimensions were made available to Clarkson by one Captain Perry of the Royal Navy, who had overseen an inspection of the ship in dock at Liverpool for the 1788 Privy Council committee of inquiry into the slave trade. The *Brooks* was one of nine slave ships that had been carefully measured by investigators working for the committee. Clarkson took one of his model ships with him on his speaking tours and gave the other to William Wilberforce, who showed it to his fellow MPs in the House of Commons. Wilberforce's model can still be seen in a museum in his home town of Hull. Posters of the slave decks of the *Brooks* were also produced. They were distributed across the country and reproduced on the Continent and in the United States. Yet even this shocking and extremely famous image might have understated the horrors of the Middle Passage, as it is known that in 1783 the *Brooks* had set sail with six hundred and nine enslaved Africans on board, one hundred and fifty-eight more than she had been fitted out to accommodate.[14]

The abolitionist message was often at its most persuasive when it came from the mouths of men who had personally been involved in the slave trade. The voices of former slaves like Olaudah Equiano and Ottobah Cugoano had a uniquely powerful impact but almost as potent were those of repentant former slave-traders. John Newton worked on ships and eventually became captain of one, regarding the trade as 'an easy and creditable way of life'. After a conversion to Christianity he had – some years later – an epiphany and wrote a powerful anti-slavery tract, *Thoughts upon the African slave trade*. In 1797 he concluded that Britain's 'African trade is a national sin, for the enormities which accompany it are now generally known; and though perhaps the greater part of the nation would be pleased if it were suppressed, yet as it does not immediately affect their own interest, they are passive.' [15] Newton was also the author of the hymn 'Amazing Grace'. As the words of that famous hymn hint, his conversion from slave-trader to abolitionist came about after his moral epiphany – 'I once was lost, but now am found, Was blind, but now I see'.

Another convert was Alexander Falconbridge, whom we met on the banks of the Sierra Leone River. Before being recruited by Granville Sharp and dispatched to the Province of Freedom, Falconbridge gained experience of Sierra Leone. For seven years he was a doctor on board the slave ships that patrolled the coast of West Africa and he spent much time in Sierra Leone. Horrified and apparently traumatized by the scenes he witnessed on slave decks during the Middle Passage, Falconbridge returned to England in 1787 and after meeting Thomas Clarkson and Granville Sharp joined the abolitionist cause, as an authority on the slave trade, in effect an expert witness. In 1788 he published his vivid and harrowing memoir *Account of the slave trade*. The passions and disagreements that were whipped up by the abolitionist crusade often spilled over into violence. Indeed, one of the roles that Alexander Falconbridge performed for the movement was to act as a bodyguard for Thomas Clarkson. But it was as a writer, and as a man who had come over from the other side, as it were, that Alexander Falconbridge flourished. His impassioned writings include this classic description of the Middle Passage:

> The hardships and inconveniences suffered by the Negroes during the passage are scarcely to be enumerated or conceived. They are far more violently affected by seasickness than Europeans. It frequently terminates in death, especially among the women. But the exclusion of fresh air is among the most intolerable. For the purpose of admitting this needful refreshment, most of the ships in the slave trade are provided, between the decks, with five or six air-ports on each side of the ship of about five inches in length and four in breadth. In addition, some ships, but not one in twenty, have what they denominate wind-sails. But whenever the sea is rough and the rain heavy it becomes necessary to shut these and every other conveyance by which the air is admitted. The fresh air

being thus excluded, the Negroes' rooms soon grow intolerable hot. The confined air, rendered noxious by the effluvia exhaled from their bodies and being repeatedly breathed, soon produces fevers and fluxes which generally carries off great numbers of them.[16]

The man who wrote that account, who acted as bodyguard to Thomas Clarkson and withstood four whole days of probing questions from a Parliamentary Privy Council Committee in the House of Commons on the matter of the slave trade, was a very different man to the Alexander Falconbridge who drank himself to death in Freetown in 1792, to the indifference of his wife Anna Maria.

The progress of the abolitionist movement was repeatedly delayed and enormously complicated by the turmoil of the age. The French Revolution drastically transformed the political and philosophical landscape over which the campaign traversed. By 1792 the revolution had begun to devour its children and in the terrible year of 1793 King Louis XVI was executed, Maximilien Robespierre's 'Terror' began and Britain went to war with Revolutionary France. The following year was marred by a ferocious winter that presaged a terrible harvest. There was hunger in England, deserters from the army were hunted down in the streets, Tom Paine's book *The Rights of Man* was banned and a radical, fractious mood hung in the air. The British propertied classes, the more radical and idealistic of whom had cautiously welcomed the fall of the French Ancien Régime, recoiled in horror at the bloodletting and destruction on the streets of Paris. The 'men of property' who controlled Parliament became increasingly conservative and looked upon all proposals for radical change or reform with deep suspicion. The rich and their representatives craved political and economic stability above anything else and the fates of the enslaved Africans, far away on the sugar islands of the West Indies, slipped precipitously down the political agenda. Even more dishearteningly events in France and within the French empire enabled the defenders of slavery to portray abolitionism as a threat to stability. The only good news came from Copenhagen. In March 1792 the Danish government abolished the importation of enslaved Africans into the Danish colonies. Denmark was only a minor player in the Atlantic slave trade but she was the first to abandon it, a little-remembered historical detail about which the Danes remain rightly proud.

The rallying calls of freedom, equality and brotherhood that erupted on the streets of Paris in 1789 and the publication of the *Declaration of the Rights of Man* resonated across the world, reaching France's slave colonies in the West Indies. In 1791 the half a million people of African descent who toiled in chains on the island of St Domingue – modern Haiti – rose up to seize their freedom. The revolution of the 'Black Jacobins' lasted until 1804 and was one of the most profound events in the history of Atlantic slavery. It was the largest slave rebellion in history and the only one that was successful. The Haitian Revolution ended slavery on that island and led, eventually, to the creation of the first sovereign black state in the Western hemisphere. The causes and consequences of the Haitian Revolution are too many and too complex to discuss in detail here but to the gentlemen of property in Britain it was a deeply troubling event, mixing as it did French revolutionary ideology with potent and ancient fears of supposed black savagery.

There is no question that the Haitian Revolution was one of the most violent and dreadful conflicts of the age. The cane fields of St Domingue, which produced around 30 per cent of all the world's sugar, were put to the torch and the acrid black smoke that rose from those thousands of acres blotted out the sun and provided a hellish backdrop for the terrible battles fought between the rebel armies and the French garrison. The rebels targeted their former masters and there was a wave of bloodletting in both the white and mulatto populations, which inspired dreadful acts of vengeance and retribution. To British defenders of slavery and an increasingly conservative ruling class the carnage in St Domingue was viewed as evidence that slavery, for all its inherent evils, was capable of restraining the supposedly innate violence of the black race. For this reason it was argued it should be tolerated and all talk of abolition ended. 'It is to be hoped, for heaven's sake, we shall hear no more of abolishing the slave trade,' wrote a correspondent to the *Gentleman's Magazine* who believed the rebellion in St Domingue was incontrovertible proof that 'the Negro race are but a set of wild beasts'.[17] This viewpoint attracted further subscribers in 1793 when British forces invaded. Like the French before them they were decimated by tropical disease and unsuccessful on the battlefield, having enormously underestimated the tactical brilliance of the rebel general, former slave Toussaint L'Ouverture. When the army finally withdrew in 1798 they left behind them, buried in the soil of Haiti, the bones of forty-five thousand British soldiers. So potent was the memory of the violence of the Haitian Revolution that it lingered in the British imagination right up until the Morant Bay rebellion in Jamaica in the mid-1860s.

Before the French Revolution the island of St Domingue was the most profitable in the West Indies. Over the course of the revolution and through the successive waves of invasion and counter-invasion the sugar industry of the island was devastated. The opening act of the rebellion was the burning of the cane fields and the boiling houses and sugar factories, the wholesale annihilation of the industry which the rebels rightly regarded as the mechanism of and the reason for their exploitation. Over a thousand plantations were destroyed and the economy that had produced more sugar than all of Britain's West Indian colonies combined was largely eviscerated by the sudden release of pent-up anger. However, this enabled the defenders of slavery in the British Empire to suggest that any challenge to the slave system would lead not merely to black violence but also economic chaos and national impoverishment. This economic argument was repeatedly and energetically made by a group of plantation owners and their supporters who had come together to counter the arguments of the abolitionists and defend slavery.

The West India Interest was the name for a shadowy and sinister grouping. It was, in effect, the lobbying organization of the slave owners and slave-traders and was led by a man who was heavily involved in both of those activities, the Jamaican planter George Hibbert. As well as owning slaves, plantations and slave ships, Hibbert was the chairman of the cabal of West India merchants who financed and built the West India Docks in east London, a vast system of docks that were opened in 1800 and into which the slave-produced sugar of the West Indies was landed. Although parts of it still exist today, the name 'West India Docks' has almost disappeared from the map of London, surviving only as the name of a street and a railway station. The area is today known as Canary Wharf. In the same way that the link between Canary Wharf and slavery has been buried, George Hibbert too has been forgotten. Yet it can be argued that the story of abolition cannot be properly told without him, as Hibbert is the villain of the piece. He

18. A model of the slave ship *Brooks* that was commissioned by abolitionist Thomas Clarkson to demonstrate how the captives were 'crammed together like herrings in a barrel'. This model was given to William Wilberforce, who used it in parliament to demonstrate the horrors of the middle passage to his fellow MPs.

19. This famous poster of the *Brooks* was distributed across the world as part of the abolitionist campaign. The diagram shows 451 Africans packed into the slave decks yet in 1783 the ship had sailed with 609 slaves on board.

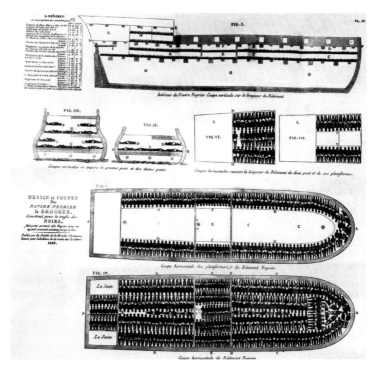

20. Ignatius Sancho. Born on a slave ship he later, with the help of the Duke and Duchess of Montagu, set out to educate himself, eventually befriending a number of eminent Georgians and settling down as a shopkeeper.

21. Saartjie Baartman, a woman of the Khoikhoi people of southern Africa, suffered a great many torments and was put on public display in Britain and France in the early nineteenth century. She was described as the Hottentot Venus.

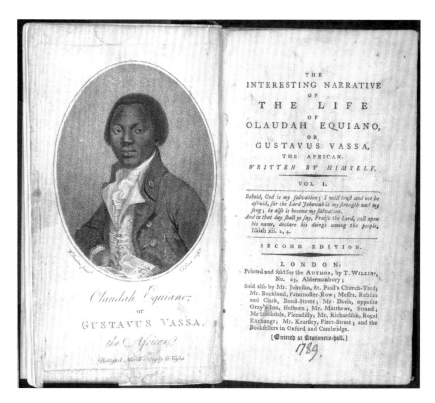

22. Olaudah Equiano, also known as Gustavus Vassa, was one of the most remarkable of the black Georgians. He published his autobiography, *The Interesting Narrative of the Life of Olaudah Equiano*, in 1789.

23. Granville Sharp, who, after meeting the enslaved boy Jonathan Strong on the streets of London in 1765, dedicated fifty years of his life to campaigning against slavery.

AM I NOT A MAN AND A BROTHER?

OUR COUNTRYMEN IN CHAINS!

By J.G. WHITTIER.

24. 'Am I not a man and a brother?' The great campaigning slogan and iconic image of the abolitionist movement appears above John Greenleaf Whittier's 1837 anti-slavery poem, 'Our Countrymen in Chains!'.

25. William Wilberforce,
abolitionist and MP,
aged twenty-nine.

26. William Knibb,
the missionary and abolitionist
who watched the 'monster'
of slavery die in Jamaica
in 1838.

27. Thomas Clarkson, the moral leader of British abolitionism, calls for the country to lead a global moral crusade against slavery in Benjamin Robert Haydon's painting of the World Anti-Slavery Convention of 1840.

28. A young Frederick Douglass, the great African American abolitionist. This photograph was taken in 1848, not long after Douglas's first lecture tour of Britain.

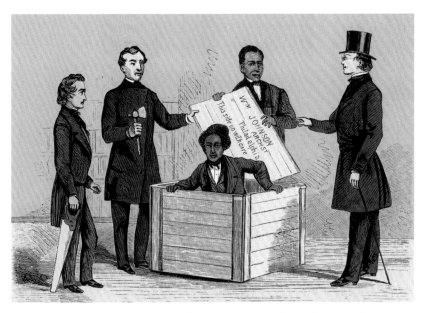

29. Henry 'Box' Brown escaped from slavery in 1849 by mailing himself in a wooden box from Virginia to the free state of Pennsylvania. He later re-enacted his escape on the anti-slavery circuit in Britain.

30. 'Ethiopian Serenaders' on King Street, Greenwich, London in 1884. 'Blackface minstrelsy' first came to Britain in the 1830s and remained part of British stage culture up to the 1980s.

CAPTURE OF A LARGE SLAVE-SHIP BY H.M.S. "PLUTO."—SEE NEXT PAGE.

31. The *Illustrated London News* reports the capture of a slave ship by HMS *Pluto* (right) in April 1860. This 365-ton, heavily-armed paddle steamer patrolled the coast of Africa intercepting slave ships as part of the British West Africa Squadron.

32. King Ghezo of Dahomey. Alongside his business partner, the infamous Brazilian slave-trader Francisco Félix de Sousa, Ghezo ensured that Dahomey became one of the most prolific slave-trading states in West Africa.

can be thought of as the 'anti-Wilberforce', the passionate, committed and defiant figure who fought a restless battle for what he believed which, in Hibbert's case, was to ensure that Africans remained items of chattel that could be bought and sold, beaten and whipped. An accomplished political tactician and a Member of Parliament, Hibbert took on Wilberforce and his supporters directly from the benches of the House of Commons. While outside the chamber he used his prodigious skills as a propagandist to wage a war of ideas, pamphlets and satirical cartoons that was intended to neutralize and defeat the efforts of Thomas Clarkson and Granville Sharp. In this endeavour he largely failed. With funds collected from the slave owners, traders and others who had financial interests in the continuation of slavery, Hibbert built a war-chest with which he funded his activities. In our traditional telling of the history of slavery, which is so heavily focused on the abolitionists and their struggles, the men against whom the abolitionists struggled have, bizarrely, been written out of the story. With our national gaze fixed firmly on the saintly figure of William Wilberforce, George Hibbert remains a forgotten figure. Yet his association with Wilberforce runs deep, and without him this history is incomplete.

Both Wilberforce and Hibbert lived in homes overlooking Clapham Common and both men worshipped at Holy Trinity, an elegant Georgian church that stands under the shade of some broad trees in one corner of the Common. Wilberforce and his supporters – the pious men of what was called the Clapham Sect and sometimes the Clapham Saints – shared the pews of their little church with their greatest and most effective enemy. There are no records of services being disrupted of passions spilling over. While the names of the Clapham Saints are engraved into a stone plaque fixed into the walls of Holy Trinity, George Hibbert is notably absent. Whereas the home that Wilberforce shared with his cousin Henry Thornton is proudly and rightly stamped with a blue heritage plaque, the elegant town house that once belonged to George Hibbert is unmarked and anonymous.

Although it was the most volcanic and the largest, the revolution in Haiti was just one in a series of uprisings by the enslaved people of the West Indies that punctuated the late eighteenth and early nineteenth centuries. There were slave risings in Jamaica, St Vincent,

Demerara (Guyana), Grenada and at St Lucia. The determination of the enslaved to resist their oppression weakened the slave system but simultaneously had the effect of alarming an already nervous British public and, periodically, wrong-footing the abolitionist movement.

The icon of the abolition movement was the famous image of the enslaved man kneeling with his hands in chains, asking plaintively 'Am I Not A Man And A Brother?' Designed by the Quaker abolitionist Josiah Wedgwood it was one of the most compelling and brilliant pieces of political marketing ever devised. By depicting the enslaved man as a fellow human being, but helpless, it emphasized the idea that abolition was an act of Christian charity and humanitarian compassion. Abolition was portrayed as something that was to be given to the enslaved by the British people rather than seized by them. Yet when the enslaved rose up against their brutalization and commoditization, whether on a plantation or a slave ship of the Middle Passage, and demanded freedom through physical force there were many in Britain who found this alternative picture of the African profoundly disturbing. This discomfort about black agency was repeatedly seized upon by the growing pro-slavery lobby and channelled into propaganda that played upon the well-established racial caricature of Africans as savage people whose innate capacity for violence necessitated brutal suppression and justified slavery. This is not to say that everyone considered slave rebellions a reason to oppose abolition or support slavery. Despite being conservative on many domestic issues the great Samuel Johnson shocked his fellow diners at Oxford when he proposed a toast to 'the next insurrection of the Negroes in the West Indies'.[18]

The first significant parliamentary breakthrough in the abolitionist struggle was the Dolben Act of 1788, named after Sir William Dolben, the Oxford MP who proposed it as a private member's bill. Dolben was a friend of Wilberforce and was in a party of MPs that travelled up the Thames to undertake an official examination of a slave ship being fitted out. Even without a cargo the slave decks were a horrifying sight. The cramped conditions and the stores of chains and shackles that Dolben saw on board were ample evidence of how slaves in the Middle Passage were 'crammed together like herrings in a barrel', as he memorably put it.[19] It was clear that there was not enough support in Parliament to bring about the abolition of the slave trade but Dolben concluded that it might be regulated. The

Dolben Act set limits for the number of slaves that could be carried on a ship, at five slaves per three tons, although there were various exemptions and qualifications added to the bill during its passage through the House of Lords. The act also imposed a legal requirement that every slave ship sailed with a doctor on board and that a log be kept detailing illnesses and mortality rates among the captives. Historians disagree as to the effectiveness of the Dolben Act but it was at least a form of governmental oversight imposed upon a trade that had been an unregulated free-for-all ever since the Royal African Company had lost its monopoly in the early eighteenth century.

Some abolitionists feared the Dolben Act might confer the legitimacy of legal oversight upon the slave trade, and thereby weaken the case for outright abolition, but the Sons of Africa disagreed. They regarded it as a first step forward. Writing to Dolben they thanked him for his 'benevolent law . . . by which the miseries of our unhappy brethren, on the coast of Africa, may be alleviated'. The letter, which was signed by Olaudah Equiano, Ottobah Cugoano and four of their comrades, also expressed their collective hope that the Africans who were now being transported to slavery in somewhat better conditions thanks to Dolben's Act 'may be preserved, as we hope, for future and for greater mercies.'[20]

William Wilberforce began his struggle to bring about those 'greater mercies' in May 1789. Leader of the parliamentary side of the abolitionist campaign, he delivered his first speech against the slave trade to the House of Commons that year. It was a brilliant and conciliatory speech – three and a half hours long – in which he avoided openly criticizing the slave-traders and spoke instead of collective national guilt. He was able to support his critique of the trade by bringing to the attention of his fellow MPs the enormous body of damning evidence that had been compiled by Thomas Clarkson. The first bill to bring about the abolition of the trade was introduced to the House of Commons by Wilberforce in 1791. With Clarkson viewing from the public gallery it was easily defeated, 163 votes to 88, in a Parliament rendered more cautious and conservative than ever by the recent outbreak of the French Revolution. Wilberforce introduced a second bill the following year which was supported by over five hundred petitions against slavery and the slave trade that between them contained the signatures of four hundred thousand people, 0.3 per cent of the population. Even this conspicuous display of public animosity to the trade did not persuade Members of Parliament to support the bill. Wilberforce went on to introduce bills for the general abolition of the slave trade every year between 1794 and 1799. They were all voted down. Despite huge public agitation and the continuing growth of the abolitionist movement the issue of slavery rarely dominated the attention of parliamentarians. The wars with France, poor harvests, widespread distress among the poor and a rebellion in Ireland made it increasingly difficult for Clarkson, Wilberforce and their allies to keep the abuses of the slave-traders at the forefront of MPs' minds – despite the constant barrage of new abolitionist pamphlets and the constant drumbeat of mass public meetings and fiery speeches. Yet the bill of 1796 failed by only four votes after one group of pro-abolition MPs went to the opera and missed the vote. There were rumours that the performance of the comic opera *The Two Hunchbacks* that had drawn the lawmakers away from the chamber had been arranged by the supporters of the slave trade.

By 1804 Wilberforce had come to fear that the momentum that had been built up behind the movement in the 1790s had been lost. Nevertheless he introduced yet another abolition bill to Parliament which this time passed through the House of Commons only to be rejected by the House of Lords. In 1805 yet another bill was defeated in the Commons by a narrow margin but that year the political mood began to shift. Decisive victory over the French at Trafalgar strengthened Britain's military and economic position in the world. Parliament had changed too. Many of the pro-slavery members who had thwarted attempts to prohibit the trade had retired or passed away and the election of 1806 changed the complexion of Parliament. A new, younger generation of parliamentarians took up their places on the benches of the House of Commons and Wilberforce, with the encouragement of the Prime Minister, Lord Grenville, seized the opportunity. After so many parliamentary failures and after years of opposition from the Lords, Wilberforce's final abolition bill was presented before a Parliament far more sympathetic to his ambitions than any that had been called previously. The bill passed through both houses, receiving the Royal Assent from George III on 25 March 1807, and came into force on 1 January 1808. The British slave trade, begun in the 1660s under King Charles II, had, by this act, been 'utterly abolished, prohibited and declared to be unlawful'.[21] It has been estimated that between 1789 and 1807, the two decades in which the political battle to end the slave trade was fought, 767,000 Africans were transported to slavery in British ships.[22]

In the aftermath of the historic victory of 1807 the next target was obvious, yet for over a decade very little happened. On the islands of the West Indies hundreds of thousands of black people remained subject to the manifold horrors of plantation slavery and in Britain there was no great rallying call for a new abolitionist campaign. Abolitionism went into hibernation. During their long campaign against the slave trade the abolitionists had repeatedly reassured the slave owners and the pro-slavery West India lobby that once the trade was ended they did not propose to seek the abolition of slavery. Immediate emancipation of the slaves, they argued, would be a disaster for both the slaves and the slave owners. Publicly and privately William Wilberforce, Thomas Clarkson and almost all of the more vocal of the abolitionists were committed to the principle of 'gradualism'. This view was predicated upon the belief that the slaves were unready and ill-equipped for freedom and any sudden transition might lead to violence and chaos. It was suggested that the enslaved people might be prepared for their liberty – through a vaguely delineated programme of education and Christian missionary work – but that this process would take many years to complete. To this end many of those who had campaigned for abolition channelled their energies into supporting missionary work among the slaves of the West Indies. The institution of West India slavery, if it was to eventually come to an end, was to be slowly dismantled. Freedom would be delivered incrementally, in carefully spaced stages with white men judging and assessing the capacities of black people to manage their own affairs and adhere to European norms. The faith in gradualism said much about the racial ideas that prevailed among the abolitionists and most people in nineteenth-century Britain. It said nothing about the capacities and inner nature of African people.

This commitment of the abolitionists to gradualism when it came to slavery was in contrast to their fiery determination to enforce and extend the prohibition of the slave trade in the years after 1808. As we shall see in a later chapter, the British were to take other practical steps to suppress the slave trade of other European states. Peace with France in 1814 raised the possibility of a revival of the French slave trade. This British public opinion would not countenance. A mass meeting was called in London's Freemasons' Hall and the whole apparatus of the national abolitionist movement was wound back into action, with Wilberforce and Clarkson again taking the lead. In order to influence the British negotiators dispatched to the Congress of Vienna that would draw the borders of the new Europe, a massive petition was organized. One and a half million British people signed it, registering their opposition to any restoration of the slave trade. The French negotiators complained of English 'fanaticism' on the issue.

With the trade prohibited and the principle of gradualism widely accepted, the old abolitionist theory that an end to the slave trade would lead to the reform of slavery could now be put to the test. The plantations of the British West Indies became, in one sense, an enormous field experiment; a laboratory. Wilberforce remained confident abolition represented the 'deathblow' of plantation slavery and that the literal irreplaceability of the slaves would have transformative effects. Thomas Clarkson likewise believed that the abolition of the trade was the seed from which black freedom would flower. But their faith required evidence. During the campaign against the slave trade the abolitionists (most notably Thomas Clarkson) had been energetic and persistent gatherers of data. Clarkson had crisscrossed the country conducting interviews with those involved in the trade and, where he could, with its victims. That tradition of measurement, investigation and statistical analysis was now applied to the plantations. Both the abolitionists and the government set about gathering statistics about West Indian slavery. An act, passed in 1819, required all slaves to be registered. This permitted the creation of a census of the slave population, which in turn provided the government and the abolitionists with the population data that could be used to identify any changes in slave mortality, life-expectancy and infant mortality.

This injection of raw data into the debate was one of the factors that eventually led to a revival of the old abolitionist spirit as, by the 1820s, the data coming back from the West Indies had begun to show not a slow amelioration of slavery but the opposite. Unable to buy new slaves but determined to maintain their profits the slave owners had increased the burdens they placed upon their human property. To maximize the available labour force slaves were moved around, from plantation to plantation, and put to work wherever their labour was required. This led to the break-up of families and disrupted the growing of subsistence crops that had allowed slave communities to supplement their diet with vegetables. Life became more physically and more emotionally demanding. Rather than being regarded as valuable assets, women and children were compelled to work harder, many in roles that demanded greater physical exertion. More women were forced to work in the fields and women and men who had grown accustomed to the lighter work of the domestic slave were marched to the fields to make up the numbers. The conditions under which the slaves lived and laboured had not – in the language of the time – been ameliorated by the abolition of the slave trade. The experiment had failed.

In the same decades another experiment was under way in the British West Indies. For the first time the slaves had allies in their midst. They were the Nonconformist preachers – Methodists, Moravians and most significantly Baptists – who arrived in the West Indies offering the slaves a radical message of redemption and hope. They had been instructed by their superiors in Britain that their mission was to spread the Gospel, not oppose slavery. They were ordered to avoid entanglements within the colonial authorities and be cautious in their dealings with the slave owners. But the Christian message itself, when introduced into societies in which the majority of human beings were the property of others, was radical enough to prove profoundly destabilizing. The concept of the soul and the belief that all souls were equal before the eyes of God did not sit comfortably with the practice of chattel slavery or the maintenance of racial hierarchies. The biblical stories of redemption, of a Promised Land and salvation seemed to speak directly to the slaves, and offer them the hope that their plight might be ended. For the most committed of the slave converts the churches offered education, literacy, a new sense of community. For all those who attended the makeshift chapels or who joined services that were held under the shade of trees, the mesmeric communal euphoria of the prayer meeting, with its hymns and sermons, was a profound experience. The Christian Gospel was powerful enough when delivered by Baptist and Methodist preachers sent out from Britain; it was doubly potent when the words of scripture and catechism sprang from the mouths of black lay-preachers who were themselves slaves. To those black deacons the chapels offered the gift of literacy and the enthralling possibility that they might attain a position of status and significance within their community, an incredible prospect to men who lived in bondage.

The missionaries who proselytized among the slaves of the British West Indies encountered a people more welcoming and eager to imbibe the Christian message than any they had known. In the slave owners, however, they found a resentful and brooding enemy. The planters regarded the preachers as a dangerous intrusion into their world. They feared the impact that the Christian message might have upon the slaves and warned that such proselytizing would lead to rebellion and ruin. The slave owners regarded the missionaries, and particularly the Baptists, as a bridgehead through which the abolition movement could penetrate plantation society, and to some extent they were correct. The impact of the preachers and the growing literacy of an expanding number of black deacons meant that the slaves increasingly understood that a great battle of ideas was being fought over slavery. They knew that the system that held them in chains was in question, if not yet in crisis. Collectively they were able to deduce that differences existed between the government and populace of far-away Britain and the slave owners in the colonies. This new knowledge informed their strategies of resistance.

In 1823 a new generation of abolitionists, along with a smattering of the old guard, launched a second crusade. Their first meeting was held in a London pub, the King's Head Tavern in the Poultry, which stood close to the old Poultry Compter, the city centre gaol in which Jonathan Strong had been temporarily imprisoned back in 1765. Wilberforce was not among them. Elderly and frail, he had largely bowed out of active campaigning. Also absent was Granville Sharp, who had died in 1813 aged seventy-eight, having spent almost fifty years fighting against slavery. The new movement was the London Society for Mitigating and Gradually Abolishing the State of Slavery. Its name was indicative of the cautious and tentative nature of the new campaign, committed as it was to the principle of gradualism.

Yet even this timorous battle cry was enough to draw thousands to the colours. By the following year there were two hundred and thirty branches of the new movement. The rapid proliferation of the society was partly down to Thomas Clarkson. Still active and energetic at sixty-three he embarked upon another epic journey around the country, gathering information, mobilizing the faithful. But in the 1820s the faithful were increasingly more radical than their leaders. Clarkson reported that everywhere he went the demand for immediate abolition was growing and faith in gradualism fading. The most eloquent and compelling of the advocates of 'immediatism' were women and the most dynamic of them was Elizabeth Heyrick, a Quaker schoolteacher from Leicester. In 1824 she wrote a pamphlet entitled *Immediate, not Gradual Abolition*. Heyrick was almost as critical of the abolitionist establishment as she was of the West India planters, rounding upon the abolitionist establishment for its lack of moral fervour. In one passage she savaged proposals that had been put to Parliament 'that our colonial slavery should be suffered – "to expire of itself, – to die a natural death." ' She had other ideas.

> It must be crushed at once, or not at all. While the abolitionists are endeavouring gradually to enfeeble and kill it by inches, it will gradually discover the means of reinforcing its strength, and will soon defy all the puny attacks of its assailants. In the mean time, let the abolitionists remember, – while they are reasoning and declaiming and petitioning Parliament for gradual emancipation, – let them remember that the miseries they deplore remain unmitigated, – the crimes they execrate are still perpetuated; – still the tyrant frowns – and the slave trembles; the cart-whip still plies at the will of the inhuman driver – and the hopeless victim still writhes under its lash.[23]

Like Samuel Johnson before her, Elizabeth Heyrick was radical enough to be openly sympathetic towards slave rebellions, seeing them as legitimate rejections of tyrannical rule. Heyrick was a product of the second wave of female abolitionism that was concentrated in women's abolitionist committees and societies across the country. Again women became the proselytizers of the sugar boycott and the organizers of abolitionist meetings and petitions. But in the 1820s female abolitionists appeared more radical than their male counterparts. In the city of Sheffield there was something approaching a schism, with the women's abolitionist society demanding immediate abolition and the men's committee advocating gradualism. [24]

The final years of the abolitionists' campaign were set against the backdrop of political crisis. A split in the Tory party opened the way for the long-delayed reform of Parliament. The gradualist caution of the 1820s was superseded by a new mood led by the Agency Committee, made up of younger radical abolitionists: Joseph Sturge, James Stephen and James Cropper. With Wilberforce still committed to gradualism there was effectively a split within abolitionism. Now the meetings got bigger, the petitions larger and more frequent. The Agency Committee and the female abolitionists hired professional, paid anti-slavery speakers who were fanned out across the country. With all the fire and fury of revivalist preachers these paid propagandists railed against slavery. Once again chains and shackles were waved and rattled before outraged and horrified audiences. The ensuing public clamour for the abolition of slavery was maintained at a fever pitch in the first three years of the 1830s.

At Christmas 1831 events in the West Indies gave the issue of slavery a new and deadly urgency. A rebellion broke out in the west of Jamaica. It was led by Sam Sharpe, a slave who was both literate and a Baptist deacon. What Sharpe had in mind was a form of strike. The rather modest demand he and his followers made was that they should be paid for their labour and they pledged to refuse to work after Christmas unless they were offered wages. So the most deadly slave rebellion in Jamaican history began as a sit-down strike in the cane fields, an almost Gandhian act of non-violent civil disobedience. The planters were already on edge and had been expecting some form of disturbance and they met the appeals of the strikers with bullets and bayonets. When the militia were unleashed and black lives taken the strikers became rebels. At least twenty thousand slaves rose up – some reports suggested the final figure was fifty or even sixty thousand – and the cane fields were set ablaze and the great houses of the planters put to the torch, each one acting as a fiery beacon that heralded the outbreak of rebellion spreading the violence to adjoining plantations. The rebellion lasted two weeks and it took the local garrison, the white militia and regiments of black conscripts three months to completely pacify the island, a grim task that was accomplished with ferocious violence. More than three hundred rebels were killed and at least three hundred and forty more, including Sam Sharpe, were executed. A further one hundred and forty were shipped off as convicts to New South Wales.[25] Over a million pounds' worth of damage had been done and the planters and the Jamaican Assembly blamed the white Baptist preachers for inciting the rebellion. Nonconformist chapels were attacked across the island, the Baptist missionary William Knibb was arrested and his fellow Baptist Henry Bleby was beaten and covered in hot tar. Bleby was saved from death at the hands of a white lynch mob only by the arrival of members of his black congregation. The rebellion – which came also to be known as the Baptist War – was arguably the final factor that tipped the scales in favour of abolition. The savagery with which the local garrison and the militia had hunted down the rebels, long after the real danger had passed, and the scale of the mass executions that had followed the insurrection played into the hands of the Agency Committee. William Knibb travelled to Britain to speak at abolitionists' meetings, presenting a first-hand account of the unameliorated horrors of Jamaican slavery and the orgy of violence that had been deployed to defend it. He also lectured at Nonconformist gatherings cataloguing all the ruses, tricks and abuses the planters used to prevent their slaves from receiving the holy Gospel.

In the same year, 1832, it became clear that if the slaves were not emancipated there would inevitably be a second and even greater rebellion in Jamaica, one that might well result in the large-scale loss of white life. The government was concerned that the cost of putting down any future uprising would be colossal, and MPs were assured by experts recently returned from the island that all that was preventing the outbreak of the expected rebellion was the belief among the slaves that they were, at any moment, to be emancipated by the King. As literacy had spread among their ranks it was no longer possible to withhold from them news of the campaign for abolition. Even before the outbreak of the Baptist War the Governor of Jamaica had felt it necessary to issue a special proclamation specifically denying rumours that the King had freed the slaves and that the planters had withheld the news. Tensions on the island continued to simmer through 1832 and Lord Howick, the Prime Minister's son, the parliamentary undersecretary of the Colonial

Office, admitted to his diary, 'I would not be surprised any time to hear that Jamaica is in the possession of the Negroes'.[26]

During the election of 1832 the activities of the abolitionists reached a crescendo. Reports from Jamaica of the persecution of the black rebels and Baptist preachers were relentlessly publicized. As the day of the poll approached the position of all prospective parliamentary candidates on the issue of slavery was investigated by the abolitionists. Those known to favour emancipation were recommended to the voters. In response a number of hopeful candidates and several sitting MPs made public declarations of their support for immediate emancipation. When the new Parliament met the balance in the House favoured emancipation and the debates got under way. Outside the House the popular pressure of the abolitionist movement did not abate. The drum beat of abolitionist newspapers demanding immediate abolition was maintained and there was a ceaseless programme of public meetings. In May 1832 the newly elected Whig government finally introduced a Slavery Abolition Bill into a Parliament in which the majority of members favoured abolition and emancipation.

Perhaps inevitably when the great moral issue of the late Georgian age was finally decided it was through an unromantic process of technocratic political negotiation and pragmatic compromise. All three sides involved in the debate made concessions that enabled the bill to pass through Parliament in the summer of 1833. The slave owners and the West India lobby accepted that slavery was doomed. The abolitionists acknowledged that the slave owners would be compensated for their loss of property, something the planters had been lobbying to achieve for decades. The government recognized that it would have to foot the bill: twenty million pounds was raised and set aside to compensate the forty-six thousand slave owners. That sum represented 40 per cent of all government spending for the year 1833 and is the equivalent of around seventeen billion pounds today, making it then the largest pay-out in British history. The eight hundred thousand slaves were to be freed, but not immediately. They were to be compelled to pay some of the cost of their own manumission. All slaves who worked the fields were to continue their labours for an additional six years, unpaid and for the same masters. Domestic slaves were to work for a further four years. This system was euphemistically called 'apprenticeship', as it was envisaged as a period in which the enslaved would learn the skills required for full freedom. In the last great outpouring of abolitionist energy investigators were dispatched to the West Indies, and reports were drafted which exposed this apprenticeship as a system rife with abuse and exploitation. There were protests, strikes and acts of resistance among the now former slaves, who struggled to see any significant change in their conditions and treatment. In Britain yet another mass petition was organized and more than one and a half million people added their signatures to it. The government once again bowed to popular abolitionist pressure and the date of emancipation was brought forward to 1 August 1838.

The most vivid account of that moment comes from the memoirs of the Baptist preacher William Knibb. On his arrival in Jamaica in 1824 he found slavery unameliorated and barbaric. Writing home he reported that 'The cursed blast of slavery has, like a pestilence, withered almost every moral bloom. I know not how any person can feel a union with such a monster, such a child of hell. I feel a burning hatred against it and look upon it as one of the most odious monsters that ever disgraced the earth . . . the iron hand of oppression daily endeavors to keep the slaves in the ignorance to which it has reduced them.'[27] Fourteen years later Knibb welcomed his black congregation into their little chapel in the port town of Falmouth, in the northwest of Jamaica. It was the evening of 31 July 1838 and over the entrance to the chapel yard a banner had been placed carrying the single word – 'FREEDOM'. As the day of emancipation approached, Knibb theatrically pointed to the clock on the chapel wall and spoke. 'The hour is at hand, the monster is dying.' As the bell struck the first chime of midnight he continued, 'The clock is striking. The monster is dead: the negro is free.'[28] In the early morning of the Emancipation Day one of the most unusual funerals in British history took place. In the grounds of a nearby school a grave had been dug. A coffin was then brought forward into which were placed the instruments of slavery; a pair of shackles, a chain, a whip and an iron collar. A crowd assembled and in the dawn light the coffin was lowered into the earth, Jamaican soil into which the bodies of around a million slaves had been interred over the previous three centuries. The congregation sang their hymns and gave their cheers and the flag of freedom, with the Union flag set into its corner. A headstone placed above the grave read, 'Colonial Slavery died 31 July 1838, Age 276 years'.[29]

When William Knibb and his congregation of newly emancipated slaves symbolically buried the chains of slavery at Falmouth in 1838 they did so in the hope that three centuries of British slavery would not be forgotten. There is some irony therefore in the fact that what largely obscures our national memory of slavery is the history of abolition, and a very specific reading of it. The first historian of the abolition movement was Thomas Clarkson who, in 1807, rushed out an account of the triumphant campaign to end the slave trade. That book was completed and in print by 1808. Clarkson understood the importance of seizing the historical narrative and wanted to use the movement's history to further its continuing ambitions. But after 1833 he himself became a victim of a new history that was centred around the figure of William Wilberforce. This narrative was masterminded by William Wilberforce's two sons, who, in their five-volume biography of their father, demoted Thomas Clarkson. In their account Clarkson was not the movement's inspirational moral leader but merely a hired functionary. The two younger Wilberforces also committed one of the most outrageous acts of historical vandalism when they convinced Clarkson to send them much of his correspondence with their father. These letters were not returned and have never been found. They are presumed destroyed. But Clarkson was just one among a long list of historical casualties. The contributions of the black abolitionists, Olaudah Equiano, Mary Prince, Ottobah Cuguano, the Sons of Africa and others were also redacted, and a similar fate befell the female abolitionists, like Elizabeth Heyrick and Hannah More. The pro-slavery men of the West India Interest are rarely discussed and nor is their leader George Hibbert. The slave rebellions that had nudged the nation towards final abolition were likewise forgotten; the black men and women who had led those uprisings, perished in them or who had been executed in the retribution that followed were reduced to footnotes or expunged entirely. The notion that the enslaved people had played a role in their own emancipation, that liberty had been demanded and fought for, rather than simply given, was for the most part forgotten. This version of the history of slavery and abolition, that first took form in the latter half of the nineteenth century, remains dominant even in the twenty-first century, despite half a century of challenge and reassessment by generations of Caribbean and British historians.

SEVEN

Moral Mission

In the Victorian Galleries of the National Portrait Gallery in London hangs one of the larger paintings of the collection. At almost three metres by four and containing more than a hundred identifiable figures it is too vast and over-populated to be considered a mere group portrait. The painting, Benjamin Robert Haydon's depiction of the World Anti-Slavery Convention of 1840, belongs to the genre of art known as history painting, great panoramas that capture decisive moments in human affairs. Almost extinct in the twenty-first century, it was in the nineteenth century one of the dominant genres. History paintings were visual narratives through which the story and the significance of an event could be read and understood, and as all the significant actors were depicted with portrait likeness, the viewer was able to pick out the faces of the famous and the celebrated from amidst the dramatic action. Jacques-Louis David's *The Tennis Court Oath*, a depiction of a critical moment in the French Revolution, is – despite never being completed – among the most renowned examples of the genre. Haydon's painting, however, must rank among the least successful. It is static despite trying to be dynamic, almost completely lacking in genuine drama and suffocatingly overcrowded. It was a critical failure and a flop with the public, all the more lamentable given that the event Haydon was attempting to capture on canvas was anything but dull.

The World Anti-Slavery Convention was held in the Freemasons' Hall, Great Queen Street, London between 12 and 23 June 1840. It had been called by the recently formed British and Foreign Anti-Slavery Society, an organization born out of a schism in British abolitionism that outlasted all of its contemporaries. It still exists today, as the NGO Anti-Slavery International. The Convention of 1840 was attended by over four hundred leading anti-slavery activists. Most came from Britain, many travelling to the capital from the important provincial outposts of the broader abolitionist movement. There were delegates from Canada, France, Haiti and Mauritius, but critically there was a delegation of fifty-three Americans. From the British Caribbean came a group of black and white abolitionists that included William Knibb, who less than two years earlier had watched 'the monster' die in Jamaica.[1] Knibb's companions were Edward Barrett and Henry Beckford, two black abolitionist campaigners who were described in the notes that accompany Haydon's painting only as 'liberated slaves', and were not named as individuals.[2] In all, the gathered delegates represented thirty-nine nations.[3]

Over the ten days of the Convention many of the tensions and divisions that existed within the abolitionist movement were exposed. Within the profoundly religious culture of abolitionism, sectarian disputes surfaced and had to be papered over, while the pacifism of many of the Quaker and Evangelical abolitionists led to disquiet when military methods of suppressing the slave trade were discussed. The most significant and damaging dispute broke out over the position of women in the anti-slavery struggle. The Convention had been conceived as an all-male affair. Britain's female abolitionists, despite their critical importance to the workings and funding of the movement were refused permission to speak. The women abolitionists who had arrived as part of the American delegation and who were followers of William Lloyd Garrison, the most uncompromising, outspoken and passionate of the American abolitionists, were not permitted to attend as delegates. Refused entry to the main hall, they watched in silence from the public galleries. They can be seen as tiny details in Haydon's painting, a semicircle of respectable Victorian women in their shawls and bonnets.* Garrison, who arrived halfway through the Convention, elected to join the

---

* Ultimately some of the more significant female abolitionists were included in the main body of figures in Haydon's painting.

women in an act of solidarity, but he was vocal in his condemnation of this aspect of British political culture.

That Haydon, a creator of history paintings, was commissioned to record the Convention reveals that the organizers imagined the event as a significant moment worthy of memorialization.[4] Haydon attended the event and was deeply moved by a number of the speeches and debates. He chose to depict what most people believed was the most powerful moment, the opening speech by the moral godfather of British abolitionism, Thomas Clarkson. Haydon has Clarkson frozen in full oratorical flourish. His left hand is raised over his head, forefinger pointing to the heavens, as he denounces the evils of slavery. Every head is tilted in his direction, every eye focused upon his face. In reality Clarkson, who by 1840 was a frail octogenarian, spoke briefly and in what was described as a 'tender feeble voice'. His health was so precarious that he was accompanied into the hall on the supportive arm of Joseph Sturge, the driving force behind the British and Foreign Anti-Slavery Society. In order to protect the old man's nerves the organizers had also 'begged no tumultuous applause . . . greet his entrance, as his infirmities were great, and he was too nervous to bear [them] without risk of injury to his health.'[5] The men of the British and Foreign Anti-Slavery Society had similarly ensured that Clarkson's speech would be greeted not with thunderous applause but with a quiet, respectful 'Amen', which was, in the event, accompanied by an unprompted wave of tearful emotion. Haydon, in his published description of his painting, admitted to being incapable of conveying in words – as he was later to be in paint – 'the effect on the imagination . . . of such deep sincerity. Never did I witness', he went on, 'in life or in the drama, so deep, so touching, so pathetic an effect'.[6]

Although the Anti-Slavery Convention of 1840 provided powerful speeches and passionate orations, what was perhaps most genuinely dramatic about the event was something that Haydon, or any artist, would struggle to capture on canvas – the declared mission of the delegates to end slavery across the world. Some of the fervour and passion with which the abolitionists embarked upon that crusade survives in the Official Proceedings of the Convention. The preface to that work of over six hundred pages contained what was described as 'a brief statement of facts', an overview of the task that confronted the movement.

> In the United States of America, the slave population is estimated to be 2,750,000; in the Brazils, 2,500,000; in the Spanish Colonies, 600,000; in the French Colonies, 265,000; in the Dutch Colonies, 70,000; in the Danish and Swedish Colonies, 30,000; and in Texas, 25,000; besides those held in bondage by Great Britain, in the East Indies, and the British settlements of Ceylon, Malacca, and Penang, and by France, Holland, and Portugal, in various parts of Asia and Africa, amounting in all to several millions more; and exclusive also of those held in bondage by the native powers of the East, and other parts of the world, of whose number it is impossible to form a correct estimate. To supply the slave-markets of the Western world, 120,000 native Africans are, on the most moderate calculation, annually required; whilst the slave-markets of the East require 50,000 more. In procuring these victims of a guilty traffic to be devoted to the rigors of perpetual slavery, it is computed that 280,000 perish in addition, and under circumstances the most revolting and afflicting . . . These facts exhibit also the magnitude of the responsibility which devolves upon Abolitionists.[7]

The 1840 Convention was an event conceived and organized from within the traditions and culture of British abolitionism. The organizers prepared and disseminated an array of statistical data, and assembled a four-man press team to secure newspaper coverage, thereby demonstrating that the movement had lost little of its genius for public presentation.

The proceedings were open to all and each day around a thousand members of the public filled the visitors' gallery. Over the ten days there were presentations of papers and discussion sessions, in which plans of action were debated and committees appointed to look into various aspects of global slavery. In their papers the delegates presented a vast panorama of unfreedom. Some delegates had been on fact-finding tours: they discussed the significance of slavery to the Ottoman Empire and the role of Islamic slave-traders in the plight of the African peoples. There were discussions of the various forms of slavery, many of them quite distinct from the chattel slavery of the Atlantic world. The slavery that held many millions of India's people in bondage was outlined and condemned. Likewise a presentation of the serfdom that condemned so many of Russia's millions to lives of unfreedom, prepared by 'a gentleman long resident in Russia', listed the 'atrocities and horrors' of a system of bondage that had been 'carefully hidden from the enlightened eye of Europe'.[8] In the highly religious atmosphere of the Convention there were calls from the American delegates for all Christian sects to publicly denounce slavery and a controversial demand that churches be called upon to expel members who continued to hold slaves. Clarkson wrote an open letter in support of this proposal. Most provocatively, open letters addressed to the monarchs and heads of state who led nations still involved in slavery were drafted, despite there being no known precedent for such actions. When the legality and propriety of such letters was questioned, one delegate brushed all concerns aside declaring, 'This Convention occupies a moral elevation from which it may look down on any throne on the face of the earth . . .'[9]

From the viewpoint of the early twenty-first century what is striking about the speeches delivered and the resolutions passed at the World Anti-Slavery Convention is the revolutionary confidence that infused the event and energized the delegates. By the 1840s British abolitionism was in its sixth decade and the new struggle represented its third wave of activism. Despite divisions and disagreements the British abolitionists were infused with that rare sort of confidence that flows through a movement that has recently realized an objective that most commentators had concluded was impossible. One of the early speakers took a moment to access the magnitude of their achievement. 'Under the British flag, with the exception of the East Indies, slavery no longer exists . . . It would be quite impossible', he suggested, 'to exaggerate what had been done. You have struck off the fetters from 800,000 human beings'.[10] In another moment of true poignant drama, Joseph Sturge introduced Henry Beckford to the Convention, describing him as a man who 'three years ago was himself a slave'. Beckford, a skilled orator, asked 'God to look down in mercy upon the labours of this Society, which has been formed in this country to deliver us from bondage. I rejoice', he said, 'to see the kind gentlemen who, as the root of this Society, relieved my body from suffering.' But his expression of gratitude was immediately followed with a call to action. 'I was a slave for twenty-eight years, but look at me and work on. There are other parts of the world where slavery now exists, but I trust the negroes there will soon become freemen as I am to-day.'[11]

In the 1840s, as there still is now, there was a degree of exaggeration about the causes and the significance of British abolition. The abolition movement was just one of the forces that had led to abolition and then emancipation. Furthermore, Britain had not been the first nation to end the slave trade, and she had not been the first emancipator; the black people of Haiti had emancipated themselves with the sword and the musket during their revolution which had begun in 1791. Yet none of that changed the fact that the speakers in the Freemasons' Hall were right; what Britain had done was remarkable.

Britain had not only ended her slave trade and then slavery itself, she had done so by paying compensation to the slave owners, which had its own significance. That was blood money in the minds of some, but regarded by others as having absolved the nation of some of the guilt accrued during her two centuries of slave-trading and slave-owning. Anthony Trollope, the novelist, spoke years later of slavery as the sin from which 'we have cleansed ourselves', while Darwin, writing around the same time, believed that Britain had 'made a greater sacrifice, than ever made by any nation, to expiate our sin, of slavery'.[12] The men and women gathered in the Freemasons' Hall saw themselves as having been the driving force for that great act of moral purging; Britain's clear and righteous mission was therefore to help other nations undergo the same process. The nation's often repeated boast of being a land uniquely dedicated to principles of freedom and personal liberty – the claims the independent slave-traders had deployed against the Royal Africa Company a century earlier – were now repeated, but this time founded upon the reality of abolition.

Exhilarated by their historical triumphs and reinvigorated, more latterly, by the successful campaign against the hated apprenticeship system, the speakers of 1840 declared their firm belief in the notion that abolition placed Britain in a position of global moral leadership,

a view that was reinforced on several occasions by the foreign delegates, who vied with one another to praise Britain.

The delegates at the Freemasons' Hall were not alone in looking to
Britain for moral leadership. The significance of what had taken place
in the West Indian islands in August 1838 was grasped not just in
the meeting halls of London but in the slave huts of Mississippi and
South Carolina. If the idea of Britain as the light of the world and
champion of the anti-slavery cause was believed anywhere it was
among the slave states of the American South. Before the 1830s the
West Indies, in the minds of American slaves, was a place to fear.
Those islands were where troublesome slaves, repeat escapers and
the disruptive were sent to break their spirits and quell their rebellious tendencies. But in 1838 those fearful colonies were erased
from the map of world slavery. If slavery could end on Jamaica, on
an island that had consumed the lives of three-quarters of the 1.3
million slaves transported there, it could be ended anywhere. So
strong was the link between the example of Britain and the hopes
for emancipation in America that in the 1840s and 1850s Britain's
Emancipation Day, 1 August, was celebrated by free black people
in the Northern states on behalf of their unemancipated brothers
and sisters south of the Mason–Dixon line.[13] Black abolitionists and
the congregations from which they emerged dismissed America's
4 July holiday as a hypocrisy that was irrelevant to a people who
were held in bondage in the South and humiliated by segregation
in the North. Among free black communities, 1 August was a day
to fill the churches and meeting halls and sing the praises of Britain
and her abolitionists. In other speeches there were condemnations
of the United States, a nation that had disastrously failed to live up
to her founding principles when it came to her black population.
So confident were free African Americans of Britain's commitment
to abolitionism that all British visitors to the US were presumed to
be opposed to slavery and warmly embraced by delegations of black
Americans, whether they deserved such plaudits or not.[14]

In 1841, one hundred and twenty-eight slaves on board an American brig expressed their faith in the notion of British freedom more
directly. The *Creole* was carrying them from the declining tobacco

fields of Virginia to the booming cotton plantations of Louisiana, where they would be more valuable and their labour more profitable, but they seized control and changed course for Nassau in the British Bahamas. There they were deemed to be rendered free by setting foot on British territory. When the nineteen leaders were tried for piracy, the court ruled that they had been illegally held in slavery and their use of force to effect their freedom was justified. It was a judgement greeted with fury by the owners and it rumbled on for years, to the detriment of Anglo-American relations. The seizure of the *Creole* was the largest successful slave rebellion in American history, but it is largely absent from the black history of Britain. Twelve years later two slaves on board the *Paraguay* achieved their freedom when they landed in Kingston, Jamaica. Two years after that a black man who was held on board a ship newly arrived in the west Jamaican port of Savanna-la-Mar from Baltimore, and who was believed by local people to be a slave, was freed by a crowd several hundred strong, who had gathered at the wharf. His freedom was confirmed by the judge of a local Court of Petty Sessions.

The concept of 'British freedom', so abused and contorted for so many years, once again resonated among those in American bondage, as it had during the American Revolution. Likewise, the belief that by reaching British territory a slave was freed, the concept that had been tested in the courts by Granville Sharp, Jonathan Strong, James Somerset and Lord Mansfield, was revived in the imaginations of African Americans, both free and in chains.[15]

In his opening speech to the Anti-Slavery Convention, Thomas Clarkson was unequivocal about whom he regarded as the great enemy of abolition. 'Your opponents who appear the most formidable,' he told the Convention, 'are the cotton and other planters of the southern parts of the United States; who, I am grieved to say, hold more than two *millions* of their fellow-creatures in the most cruel bondage.'[16] Similar condemnations of the planters of the American South were repeated by speakers both British and American. Daniel O'Connell, the architect of Catholic Emancipation, who spoke on the first day of the conference, was careful to draw a distinction between American slaveholders and 'the honest citizens of America'. O'Connell thundered that there was nothing 'more glorious to America than the number of anti-slavery societies already established in that country', with whom he urged British abolitionists to establish a 'perfect brotherhood of affection'. But, he warned, 'I can never speak but with indignation of the monsters who claim liberty to themselves, and yet inflict on the backs of the slaves the vilest marks of their *tyranny*.'[17]

This refrain was refined and repeated for the next two and a half decades, by waves of British abolitionists and African American campaigners who joined their ranks, as all jostled to remind Americans that while they held millions of their fellow countrymen in bondage their declarations of rights and equalities rang hollow. In many of these denunciations sympathy for enslaved Africans was tainted by a degree of triumphalist patriotism. Americans were prone to respond by condemning the motives behind British abolitionism, attacking her growing imperialism, and decrying the nation's devotion to the 'tyranny' of monarchs. The two countries were, in this respect, bound together. Each believed in its own exceptionalism and each considered itself a realm in which the people, their rulers and laws were uniquely devoted to the principles of liberty, which were defended as inalienable rights and natural freedoms. Britain had abolished slavery while America had not. But Britain had also been the originator of American slavery and after its own abolition was still the purchaser of the cotton the American slaves produced.

As Britain's position as the supposed arbiter of global morals was based on her own virtue, British abolitionists sought to preserve their own moral purity. The delegates of 1840 denounced everything but schemes for immediate abolition and attacked the American colonization movement, which wanted to end slavery but transport the former slaves to colonies in Africa, rather as Granville Sharp had done for the black poor of London and the Sierra Leone Company had done to the Nova Scotians half a century earlier, although those schemes had been minuscule compared to the American colonization movement's proposals. The delegates of 1840 also dismissed any suggestion that slavery should be ended in America through any scheme of compensation. Papering over historical divisions, they were quick to remind the fifty-three American delegates that compensating Britain's slave owners was a pragmatic measure forced upon them by the slave owners and the government, and had never been their chosen tactic.

Having identified the planters of the South as the greatest foe, the pious Thomas Clarkson warned that as such men lived 'in the daily habits of injustice, cruelty and oppression [they] have no true fear of God'. So how then, he asked, were the abolitionists of Britain and their comrades in the US 'to get at them so as to influence their conduct?'[18] One clear strategy when confronting those who were amoral, Clarkson suggested was, 'to make them feel their guilt in its consequences. . . You must endeavour, among other things, to affect their temporal interests.' American slavery was to be undermined economically by being undercut by cheaper goods from India and elsewhere that were produced by free labour, in what at the time was described as the 'mighty Experiment'. The other strategy was to isolate the United States behind what the great American abolitionist Frederick Douglass later described as a 'cordon of anti-slavery feeling' built around the American slaveholder, 'so that he may see the condemnation of himself and his system glaring down in letters of light.'[19] This barrier was to be erected by an international alliance of abolitionists, inevitably led by Britain. A resolution was proposed and approved that called for Britain to become the base from which an anti-slavery propaganda mission should be launched directly and specifically against the slaveholders of the United States. The promoter of the motion was Henry B. Stanton, who appears in Benjamin Haydon's painting. Stanton's journey to attend the Convention with his new wife, the feminist and equally committed abolitionist Elizabeth Cady Stanton, was taken in lieu of a honeymoon. From the podium Stanton stated that 'the literature of Great Britain exercises so vast an influence over the public opinion of America, British abolitionist periodicals must spread before the American public evidence of the deep indignation of the civilized world against the slaveholding republic.'[20] In other words, Britain should shame America towards abolition, isolating her from what we would today call the international community. This strategy, as the historian Richard Huzzey has pointed out, involved the exercise of what twenty-first-century politicians call 'soft power'.[21]

It was, ironically, the closeness of America's relationship with Britain that made the abolitionist strategy of moral isolation theoretically feasible. John Bull and his American equivalent Brother Jonathan – a figure long since supplanted by Uncle Sam – had a relationship, in the mid-nineteenth century, that was in different ways as 'special' as that of the mid-twentieth. There were strong economic and trading links, close ties within various religious sects and innumerable familial connections. America in the middle of the century was not the economic and cultural giant she was to become. In this relationship Queen Victoria's Britain was the imperial super-power and America the young republic. With a common language, Britain's cultural reach into America mirrored her economic power and British books, novels and works of science and ideas were published in huge numbers in America. The enormous popularity of Charles Dickens there reinforced the dominance of Britain in literary matters.* However, ideas, debates and individuals flowed back and forth across the Atlantic, assisted by ever-faster ocean cross-ings. These communications and other factors meant that, ultimately, it was to be the words of American abolitionists – spoken by them in person, in British town halls directly to British audiences – along with the publication of American books and pamphlets that would stoke the engines of the transatlantic campaign against American slavery, and do so more effectively than any 'British abolitionist periodicals'.

Between the 1830s and the American Civil War most of the prom-inent African American abolitionists, who had escaped to or risen to prominence within the free states of the North, came to Britain to campaign against slavery. Together with their supporters in Britain, they embarked upon speaking tours that were one of the most dynamic and energizing features of the transatlantic anti-slavery

* America in the middle of the nineteenth century was a nation cursed by something comparable to the cultural cringe of post-war Australia, a literary and cultural inferiority complex, one that was fed by a sense that British writers looked down upon the efforts of Americans and that the nation lacked a literary tradition or much sign of literary talent. The desire to escape from the literary shadow of Britain and create authentic American literary forms motivated many American writers in the latter half of the nineteenth century.

culture. Most were former slaves. Some, at the time they came to Britain, were fugitives from slavery who presented themselves to appalled British audiences as the legal property of other men. They had known slavery, seen it from the inside, recorded its most dreadful details, and from the podiums of British meeting rooms and church halls were able to recount its dreadful impact upon their own lives – the beatings, the whippings, the sale of wives, husbands and children and the sexual abuse of women. They brought to Britain what were in effect dispatches from the front lines of the global abolition battle. In an age when British abolitionists were occasionally dismissed by their opponents as mere 'drawing-room philanthropists', African Americans brought a raw authenticity to the campaign and became some of its most successful recruiting sergeants. Their anti-slavery campaigns were every bit as slick and effective as the far better-known campaigns that the British abolitionists had masterminded during their struggles against British slavery and the trade in slaves.

Between 1840 and the 1860s the majority of small towns and major cities of the United Kingdom were visited by one or other of the African American abolitionists. There developed what amounted to a circuit, a network of town halls, church halls and assembly rooms in which anti-slavery speakers could gather an audience. Some travelled to small village halls, taking their stories of plantation slavery in rural America into the British countryside. Scotland was a critical part of the anti-slavery circuit, Wales much less so. Ireland was visited on numerous occasions by most of the more prominent speakers. Like travelling musicians they passed one another on the roads and lodged in the homes of the same sympathetic supporters.

Among the first to arrive was Moses Roper.* He was born into slavery in North Carolina. His mother was an enslaved woman, his father was her white owner. Because there was a strong resemblance between father and son, Moses was sold to another plantation as a young boy. In all he was bought and sold seventeen times before escaping bondage in 1834. He came to Britain the year after and

---

* The very first was James McCune Smith in 1831.

there received support and an education from British abolitionists, before heading out on tour, speaking on the evils of slavery. Roper's tours were popular not just because of his power as a speaker but because at six feet five inches tall his physical frame and countenance were as impressive as his speaking style; he used both to add theatrical drama to his shocking personal story.

Another powerful performer and firm favourite among British audiences was Henry 'Box' Brown. A slave from Virginia, Brown saw his three children and their mother, then pregnant with a fourth, sold to an owner in North Carolina, slave marriages having no basis in law. The loss of his family inspired a determination to escape. His ingenious plan, which was devised and executed with the assistance of two free accomplices, one white, the other black, was for Brown to hide in a wooden mail crate and have himself literally mailed from Richmond to Philadelphia in the free state of Pennsylvania. The box was just three feet long and two feet wide, and marked as 'dry goods'. In March 1849, twenty-seven hours after entering the box, and having narrowly escaped suffocation, he arrived in Philadelphia, at the home of a sympathetic Quaker abolitionist. 'I had risen as it were from the dead', Brown later wrote. He came to Britain in October 1850 and went on tour. A year later he published an English edition of his *Narrative of the Life of Henry Box Brown,Written by Himself*. Brown and others presented his astonishing escape as proof of the desperate desire for freedom among the slaves, who Southern propagandists often claimed were content to live in a state of bondage. Brown repeated the feat by having himself successfully posted from Leeds to Bradford in the same box.[22] He toured the country with his 'unrivaled Panorama of African and American Slavery', which one provincial English newspaper described as being 'painted on 50,000 feet of canvas' and as having 'been exhibited to three hundred and sixty-five thousand persons since its arrival in this country!'[23] During the 1850s Henry 'Box' Brown honed his performing skills on the anti-slavery circuit. In addition to exhibiting his panorama he appeared from his box in front of audiences. He became such a confident performer that he eventually became a stage mesmerist and conjuror. A quarter of a century after his arrival in Britain he finally returned to America to tour as the magician Professor H. Box Brown.[24]

An American abolitionist who, despite being born free, was powerfully able to convey the realities of slavery to her audience was Sarah Parker Remond. She came from a free black family with strong links to many of America's leading abolitionists, including William Lloyd Garrison and Henry Stanton. Her older brother, Charles Lenox Remond, became the first black anti-slavery lecturer within the American Anti-Slavery Society and was one of the fifty-three American delegates at the 1840 Anti-Slavery Convention in London. Sarah Parker Remond combined powerful and emotive descriptions of the realities of slavery with carefully worded exposés of hidden aspects of the system. She horrified British audiences by revealing how the rape of enslaved women had created generations of mixed-race female slaves who, in turn, had themselves come to be regarded as a specialized commodity within the larger slave market. The African Americans were drawn to Britain by what the historian Richard Blackett called the nation's 'moral prestige',[25] and came to regard the country as a pulpit, a sanctuary from which they could preach against the sins of American slavery and a place where their message would be warmly received and they themselves would be safe, and for thirty years Britain performed exactly that function. Some spent months touring the UK; others were resident for years.

Public speaking in the middle of the nineteenth century was a form of mass media, a well-recognized and appreciated art and a species of public entertainment. A good speaker, who could take an audience with him or her on an emotional as well as an intellectual journey, was able to generate significant press coverage and build a nationwide reputation as an orator, fame that would itself generate audiences. Newspaper reports from the day repeatedly refer to the 'eloquence' of public speakers, describing in detail the cadence of their voice, their appearance and dress, as well as the content of their message. During the 1840s and 1850s audiences of over a thousand were relatively common, and for the more famous speakers at the larger auditoriums, attendances of two or even three thousand were not unknown. The tours of the African American abolitionists became one of the spectacles of the era. Not only were they speaking on one of the most emotive issues of the day, they were in most cases formidable communicators; some were skilled showmen. Furthermore they were foreigners who came from a nation that increasingly fascinated the British public. They were also exotic visitors arriving at a time when the British black population was declining, as the end of the British slave trade dramatically reduced the numbers of black people coming into the country.

As the reports of their lectures reveal, abolitionists' talks were evening-long affairs, with individual speeches of over two or even three hours not uncommon. Some speakers added further drama to their talks by brandishing implements of slavery – neck collars and chains – some of which were manufactured in Britain even after British abolition, an uncomfortable fact which they made abundantly clear. Each of the African American abolitionists had their own speaking style, although many shared certain devices or structures. Some introduced themselves with an apology for their lack of education and learning, a consequence of slavery. After lowering expectations they then confounded their audience with eloquent phrases and cleverly structured arguments, in lectures that overflowed with clear evidence of learning and educational attainment. They also had their own personal narratives, stories of suffering and family break-up that gave their accounts of slavery an emotive impact that was beyond the reach of their white brethren in the abolitionist movement. This authenticity added to their appeal as very few Victorians had any first-hand experiences of slavery as it had existed in the British Empire. The African American speakers were also able to stir indignation and flatter their audiences by tapping into the national rivalries that existed between Britain and America. Stripped of American citizenship, and routinely denied passports, even when legally free, the black men and women who stood on the stages of British meeting rooms were living refutations of America's claims to be a 'land of the free'. But some of them were also known to play upon British sensitivities, by reminding audiences that it had been Britain that had introduced slavery into America. This historical fact, they argued, gave her a special responsibility to fight for its abolition in her former colony. Most powerfully of all, the black anti-slavery speakers who toured Britain stood before the hundreds of thousands of people who came to see them speak as living proof of the intelligence, humanity and Christianity of Africans. In this way they profoundly challenged the racism upon which slavery had been built and upon which slave societies depended.

There is debate as to how widely across the social spectrum of Victorian Britain their message was transmitted, but there is much anecdotal evidence from the diaries and journals of the African American abolitionists and from the pages of the provincial newspapers to suggest that the working classes as well as the wealthy and well-to-do attended anti-slavery events and lectures and were drawn to the famous African Americans who appeared in their towns and cities.

In 1850 the numbers travelling to Britain increased when in that summer the US Congress passed the Fugitive Slave Act. Patching up the holes in earlier laws it compelled American citizens and officials, in the free as well as the slave states, to cooperate in the return of escaped slaves to their legal owners, and mandated serious fines and prison sentences for those who refused to cooperate or who harboured escapees. One result was that around thirty thousand African Americans fled to British Canada in the two years after 1850 to escape the dangers of recapture.* Others elected to put an ocean between them and the armies of slave-catchers, kidnappers and bounty hunters who were unleashed upon people of colour by the 1850 law. African American abolitionists who might have come to Britain in the hope of receiving support for their cause now had an additional reason to set sail for Liverpool or London. Henry 'Box' Brown, one of the most famous escapees, came to Britain within three months of the passing of the Fugitive Slave Act. William Wells Brown had to make the calculation in reverse. He was in Britain on an anti-slavery lecture tour with his two daughters when it was passed. Wisely he decided not to return to the US, remaining in Britain and going on to speak against slavery at over a thousand talks and lectures. He only left Britain after his freedom had been purchased on his behalf by Ellen, Anna and Henry Richardson, a remarkable family of Quakers from Newcastle upon Tyne, of whom we will hear more later.

*

---

* Even before the 1850 Act free black people in the United States were at risk of kidnap. Solomon Northup, the author of *Twelve Years a Slave*, was kidnapped from Washington DC in 1841. Although Northup did not join his fellow authors and tour Britain, *Twelve Years a Slave* sold thousands of copies there. Twenty-seven thousand were bought in Britain and America within two years of publication.

Not every African American who landed in Britain in the middle of the nineteenth century was an anti-slavery speaker. Some were free people of colour who came as students or entertainers; others, after 1850, were fugitives who had come not to fight for abolition but simply to find refuge. We will never know how many came and what happened to them but it does seem clear that most were men. Those who arrived with skills or were simply lucky found work and became black Victorians, mostly marrying white British women, their descendants disappearing into the background population after a couple of generations, as had the children and grandchildren of the black Georgians. The less fortunate slipped into the world of the Victorian streets. Henry Mayhew, the great social explorer and journalist, encountered a handful of men who claimed to be fugitive slaves on London's streets while researching his epic book *London Labour and the London Poor*. The fourth volume of that work, subtitled *Cyclopedia of the Condition and Earnings of Those that Will Not Work*, published in 1862, contained a section on encounters with 'Negro Beggars'. 'The negro mendicant,' Mayhew informs us, 'who is usually an American negro, never studies the picturesque in his attire. He relies on the abject misery and down-trodden despair of his appearance and generally represents himself as a fugitive slave.'[26] In a separate encounter in the same volume Mayhew recorded another tragic tale, that of a man who had stowed away on a ship bound for Britain in the hope that there he might escape unemployment and poverty. His account reveals how British racism could force black immigrants into marginal and temporary work in entertainment and manual labour.

My father was a slave, so was my mother . . . I am the eldest son. I had only one brother. Three years after his birth my mother died. My father was a shoe-black in New York. He very often had not enough to eat. My brother got a place as a servant, but I went out in the streets to do what I could. About the same time that my father, who was an old man, died, my brother lost his place. We agreed to come to England together. My brother had been living with some Britishers, and he had heard them say that over here niggers were as good as whites; and that the whites did not look down on them and illtreat them, as they do in New York. We went about and got odd jobs on the quay, and at last we hid ourselves in the hold of a vessel, bound for Liverpool. I do not know how long we were hid, but I remember we were terribly frightened lest we should be found out before the ship got under weigh. At last hunger forced us out, and we rapped at the hatches; at first we were not heard, but when we shouted out, they opened the hatches, and took us on deck. They flogged us very severely, and treated us shamefully all the voyage. When we got to Liverpool, we begged and got odd jobs. At last we got engaged in a travelling circus, where we were servants, and used to ride about with the band in beautiful dresses, but the grooms treated us so cruelly that we were forced to run away from that. I forget the name of the place that we were performing at, but it was not a day's walk from London. We begged about for some time. At last, my brother – his name is Aaron – got to clean the knives and forks at a slap-bang (an eating-house) in the city. He was very fortunate, and used to save some bits for me. He never takes any notice of me now. He is doing very well. He lives with a great gentleman in Harewood-square, and has a coat with silver buttons, and a gold-laced hat. He is very proud, and I do not think would speak to me if he saw me. I don't know how I live, or how much I get a week. I do porter's work mostly, but I do anything I can get. I beg more than half the year. I have no regular lodging. I sleep where I can. When I am in luck, I have a bed. It costs me threepence. At some places they don't care to take a man of colour in. I sometimes get work in Newgate-market, carrying meat, but not often. Ladies give me halfpence oftener than men. The butchers call me 'Othello,' and ask me why I killed my wife.[27]

In his 1852 travelogue *Three Years in Europe: or, Places I have Seen and People I have Met*, William Wells Brown describes seeing black people on the streets of London as an everyday experience. Many of those he met were students from Africa and the Caribbean, but he also left us an account of a meeting with one of his fellow countrymen.

I observed . . . a coloured man, and from his general appearance I was satisfied that he was an American. He eyed me attentively as I passed him, and seemed anxious to speak. When I had got some distance from him I looked back, and his eyes were still upon me. No longer able to resist the temptation to speak with him, I returned, and commencing conversation with him, learned a little of his history . . . He had, he said, escaped from slavery in Maryland, and reached New York; but not feeling himself secure there, he had, through the kindness of the captain of an English ship, made his way to Liverpool; and not being able to get employment there, he had come up to London. Here he had met with no better success, and having been employed in the growing of tobacco, and being unaccustomed to any other work he could not get labor in England. I told him he had better try to get to the West Indies; but he informed me that he had not a single penny, and that he had nothing to eat that day . . . I took from my purse my last shilling, changed it, and gave this poor brother fugitive one-half. The poor man burst into tears as I placed the sixpence in his hand, and said – 'You are the first friend I have met in London.' [28]

It was not necessary for Victorian Britons to attend anti-slavery lectures or happen upon a fugitive slave on the city streets in order to learn of the many horrors of American slavery. In an age of increasing literacy there was a rapid expansion in newspaper circulation and reports from the slave states of the US were a regular feature. The papers were especially fond of contrasting British attitudes towards slavery, and sometimes towards the rights of all black people, with the racism of America, North and South. General accounts of life in America rarely failed to dedicate a few passages to the brutality of slavery and the crimes of American slaveholding classes. The same papers and the booming local press relished in reporting the speeches of the African American abolitionists, especially when they poured praise on Britain and scorn on their homeland. British newspapers liked to draw particular attention to the warmth with which black abolitionists were greeted by British audiences in contrast to the abuses they had suffered at the hands of Southern planters.

The other great literary expression of the transatlantic abolitionists' campaign was the huge popularity of slave narratives, biographies of African Americans who had escaped slavery. Just as *The Interesting Narrative of Olaudah Equiano* had been a powerful propaganda tool for the British abolitionists, the life stories of escaped American slaves became Victorian bestsellers and works that helped spread the abolitionist message. The popularity of slave narratives peaked in the 1840s and 1850s. Moses Roper's *A Narrative of the Adventures and Escape of Moses Roper from American Slavery*, published in 1837, was said to have sold twenty-five thousand copies in England and another five thousand in Welsh translation. *The Narrative of the Life of Henry Box Brown, Written by Himself,* the second of Brown's autobiographies, was written in the UK, published in Manchester in 1851 and sold by the author during his lecture tour. William Wells Brown sold twelve thousand copies of his narrative while in Britain but being a more versatile and energetic writer than many other anti-slavery speakers, went on to write novels as well as works of history and travel writing.

Most slave narratives tended to follow a similar trajectory, a journey from suffering, oppression and violence to escape and finally freedom. There was a strong tendency towards sentimentality but most were, in truth, much more than narrative biographies. They were powerful exposés of the slave system in America, an unveiling of its bleak inner workings. What gripped British readers were the emotive accounts of punishments and the cruel break-up of slave families, something that spoke loudly to the Victorian cult of the family as the basic unit of a functioning and decent society. Some narratives also described, in carefully calibrated detail, how female slaves were made the sexual prey of male owners and overseers, a notion highly offensive to Victorian beliefs in female vulnerability and inviolability. These shocking details and dramatic passages were punctuated with descriptions of more mundane details: how slaves lived, their huts, their food and the hours and conditions of their work, which varied enormously from plantation to plantation, season to season and owner to owner. These nuanced, granular details remain useful for historians of slavery today. Other passages explained the laws that underpinned the slave system and the economics of cotton cultivation.

Slave narratives were in wide circulation; many were sold directly to the public during the speaking tours. Book sales, combined with donations offered by admirers and members of the audience, became a means of keeping the abolitionist tours out there on the circuit.

To some extent the tours became self-funding and self-perpetuating, so long as British people were willing to pack church and town halls to hear of the horrors being perpetrated an ocean away, and right up to the Civil War, with peaks and troughs, the audiences kept coming.

The most celebrated and most eloquent of the African American abolitionists who spent time in Britain was the author of the best selling of the slave narratives, Frederick Douglass. After escaping from slavery in 1838 with his wife Anna Murray, a free black woman, Douglass became a preacher and anti-slavery speaker in Massachusetts. He was allied to William Lloyd Garrison, and rapidly developed into one of the most effective and persuasive abolitionist speakers on either side of the Atlantic. In 1845 he published the *Narrative of the Life of Frederick Douglass, an American Slave*, in which he revealed details of how he escaped, and named his legal owner – one Thomas Auld. The book made Douglass famous, an extremely dangerous condition for a man who was the legal property of another. In large part because he feared Auld would attempt to have him kidnapped, in August 1845 he boarded a ship bound for Britain.

During the nineteen months from his arrival in 1845 to his departure in April 1847, Frederick Douglass, by his own estimation, lectured on slavery on three hundred occasions, meaning that he spoke publicly against slavery on more days than he was silent. In some ways he completed his development in Britain. Freed from the daily fear of re-enslavement, and able to live a more expansive existence in an unsegregated society, he had the emotional space to evolve intellectually. In January 1846, in a speech in Belfast, he described how he had been 'persecuted, hunted, outraged in America, I have come to England, and behold the change! A chattel becomes a man. I breathe. I am free.'[29]

In Britain, Douglass was also free from the schisms and disputes within American abolitionism and became more of his own man, determined to forge his own alliances. It was during his eighteen months in Britain that he gathered the funds to set up his abolitionist newspaper, the *Northern Star*. They came again from British supporters. His fundraising efforts were assisted by Jonathan D.

Carr, the proprietor of Carr's of Carlisle, a firm which still exists as the makers of Carr's Water Biscuits, who acted as the treasurer of the Douglass Testimonial. By 1847 Douglass' admirers had raised over $2,000, which he used to found the paper, which was later renamed the *Frederick Douglass Newspaper*, a testimony to his fame. In this respect and in other ways Britain played a significant part in the making of Frederick Douglass.[30]

Douglass' impact on Britain was just as profound. Partly through his incredible energy and endless touring, he became a national sensation and revitalized the anti-slavery issue as no other speaker had managed. He was able to build on the idea that the abolition of British slavery in 1838 was not the closing of the account, and that the global mission that had been launched at the Convention of 1840 was Britain's destiny and perhaps her duty. Speaking in Leeds in 1846 he argued that 'of all of the nations of the earth England should be foremost in advancing the great cause of emancipation'.[31] Douglass excelled at putting forward one of the key arguments in the abolitionist arsenal that slavery was a moral rather than a political issue. As such it could not be contained by political borders and should never be considered only a domestic issue of any sovereign state. Slavery anywhere was a challenge to moral people everywhere, he argued. Humanity was an indivisible brotherhood and 'when any part of that brotherhood is trampled into dust,' he proclaimed, 'all should spring at once to the rescue, and for their instant deliverance'.[32] It was an argument designed to further internationalize the slavery issue and nullify American arguments that abolitionists in Britain had no right to interfere in American affairs.

Throughout all of this he remained legally a slave. Then in 1846, while on his anti-slavery tour, he met Ellen, Anna and Henry Richardson, a family of Quakers from Newcastle upon Tyne. The Richardsons had long been involved in anti-slavery work. They were highly independent, self-organizing and most importantly their strand of abolitionism eschewed ideology for pragmatism. To Ellen and her sister-in-law Anna, Douglass' legal status and the predicament in which he lived were intolerable. On 29 October the two women arranged a meeting of abolitionists in Edinburgh, at which they began a campaign to purchase his freedom. Tapping into both religious and abolitionist networks they raised the money within weeks. Meanwhile Anna Richardson wrote directly to Thomas Auld to negotiate. For £150 Auld agreed to make Douglass a free man and with the help of a team of abolitionist lawyers in Boston the transaction was completed on 5 December.

What Ellen and Anna Richardson had done was immediately criticized. They had made the same compromise that the British abolitionist movement had been forced to accept during their negotiations with the planters and the government over the Abolition of Slavery Act in 1833 and, in the name of pragmatism, suspended their moral objection to the principle of 'property in man'. In a flurry of transatlantic correspondence between Douglass and leading members of the American abolitionist movement, he too was condemned for having acquiesced with the Richardsons. The abolitionist and journalist Henry Clarke Wright wrote to him denouncing 'That certificate of your freedom, that "Bill of Sale", of your body and soul, from that villain, Auld, who dared to claim you as a chattel . . . you are free, you always were free, and the man is a villain who claims you as a slave, and should be treated as such.'[33] Douglass, writing from Manchester, replied ten days later and, in terms that are as stark as they are eloquent, reminded Wright of the realities of his legal status. 'I am legally the property of Thomas Auld, and if I go to the United States . . . Thomas Auld, aided by the American Government, can seize, bind and fetter, and drag me from my family, feed his cruel revenge upon me, and doom me to unending slavery . . . it was not to compensate the slave-holder, but to release me from his power; not to establish my natural right to freedom, but to release me from all legal liabilities, to slavery.'[34]

That two Americans were in disagreement over the philanthropic actions of a family of abolitionists who lived by the banks of the River Tyne, thousands of miles away from the cotton fields of the Southern states, testifies to how closely entwined and transatlantic the abolitionist and anti-slavery struggles had become by the 1840s. When Douglass returned to America he was not just a free man, he was an international celebrity, famous in London as well as in New York.

*

In his 'Farewell to the British People', a speech he delivered to a London audience in March 1847, Frederick Douglass contrasted his treatment in Britain over the previous eighteen months to the life he had known in the United States in the years after his escape from slavery.

> I came to this city accustomed to be excluded from athenaeums, literary institutions, scientific institutions, popular meetings, from the colosseum – if there were any such in the United States – and every place of public amusement or instruction. Being in London, I of course felt desirous of seizing upon every opportunity of testing the custom at all such places here, by going and presenting myself for admission as a man. From none of them was I ever ejected. I passed through them all; your colosseums, museums, galleries of painting, even into your House of Commons . . . In none of these places did I receive one word of opposition against my entrance . . . however much the Americans despise and affect to scorn the negroes, that Englishmen – the most intelligent, the noblest and best of Englishmen – do not hesitate to give the right hand of fellowship, of manly fellowship, to a negro such as I am, I will tell them this, and endeavour to impress upon their minds these facts, and shame them into a sense of decency on this subject.[35]

Douglass was, of course, doing his best to flatter his audience and embarrass his homeland but his experiences and his conviction that Britain was largely free from racial prejudice are broadly representative of those of the other African Americans who toured the country in this period. Harriet Jacobs wrote that being in Britain felt like 'a great millstone had been lifted from my breast', as 'for the first time in my life I was in a place where I was treated according to my deportment, without reference to my complexion'.[36] This might be because British racism was mild in comparison to the strains they had known in the United States, and was therefore deemed to be not worth reporting. But as a key strategy of the abolitionists was to lionize Britain and repudiate America, they also had a clear motivation for under-reporting the racism that was a feature of British culture. In *The Heroic Slave*, his novella of 1853, Douglass had his central character explain that to be an American slave in Britain was to nestle 'in the mane of the British lion, protected by his mighty paw from the talons and the beak of the American eagle'.[37] The character into whose mouth Douglass placed those words was a slave on board the *Creole*, the American ship seized by the slaves on board and diverted to the Bahamas in 1841, in order to find their own safety.

Despite the positive experiences of Douglass and others, Britain was a land that was far from being free from racism. In 1852 Henry Box Brown was the victim of an incredibly vicious and racialized attack by the *Wolverhampton and Staffordshire Herald*, which dismissed his audiences as the 'shoeless daughters of the slums and alleys' and him as a 'bejewelled and oily negro'. Brown sued the editor and won £100 in damages.[38] Historians have suggested that the African Americans might well have chosen not to report incidents or remarks out of politeness to their hosts and in order to shore up their strategy of contrasting post-abolition Britain favourably against the slave-holding United States. They might also have not been subjected to British racism because of their novelty and exoticism; as royal African visitors to Britain discovered later in the century, celebrities with black skin, who moved in exalted circles at the top of British society, were to some extent exempt from the mundane, daily racism of the Victorian street. But even within the exalted and sympathetic circles of the British abolitionist movement into whose embrace the African American abolitionists were welcomed, ideas of the racial inferiority of black people were not unknown, as was revealed by an incident that took place during the creation of Benjamin Haydon's painting of the Anti-Slavery Convention in 1840.

In order to make his preparatory sketches, which were executed with great speed, Haydon attended the conference. Over five days he produced fifty-two portrait studies but even working at that pace he was unable to sketch all the delegates whose portraits were to appear in the finished painting. Haydon had to complete his preparatory work over the following months, by inviting the delegates he had been unable to sketch to attend his studios or by visiting them in their homes. Some of these additional studies were necessary because the London Committee of the British and Foreign Anti-Slavery Society, which had commissioned the painting, asked for additional figures to be included. Haydon was well aware that the result of all these extra faces being squeezed into the finite space of his canvas would result in precisely the sort of compositional mess for which his painting has long been criticized. Among the delegates depicted by Haydon was Henry Beckford, the black abolitionist who had travelled from Jamaica with William Knibb. Beckford, who was a powerful anti-slavery speaker, was placed in the very centre of the foreground, beside the eminent Secretary of the British and Foreign Anti-Slavery Society, John Scoble.[39] As Scoble sat for his portrait Haydon informed him of the compositional arrangement, and of his proximity to Beckford, presuming, as he said in his journal, that as 'an abolitionist on thorough principle [he] would have gloried in being so placed'.[40] Haydon noted however that Scoble was resistant to the composition and his proximity to a former slave, suggesting that there was, in Haydon's words, a 'greater propriety of placing the Negro in the distance, as it would have much greater effect'. Scoble was passionately committed to stand up for black people but, so it seems, not to stand beside one. Haydon asked other abolitionists who came to sit for their portraits later if they would be willing to be placed next to a black man, and recorded a tally of those who objected and those who, like the radical moralist William Lloyd Garrison, declared themselves happy to be painted shoulder to shoulder with Beckford. Irrespective of Scoble's obfuscations he was placed next to Henry Beckford in Haydon's completed painting.

It is our modern supposition that those who were opposed to slavery and felt genuine compassion and empathy for the enslaved were disposed to regard all men as equals and oppose racism. We similarly imagine that they would have adopted other humanitarian, liberal, feminist or anti-colonial stances. But the reality is that among abolitionists in both Britain and America an anti-slavery position, even one that was passionately held and courageously campaigned for, did not necessarily go hand in hand with a belief in racial equality. As the historian Catherine Hall and other scholars have pointed out, the abolitionists, while opposing the racial ideas generated by the pro-slavery lobbies on both sides of the Atlantic, were still as liable as their opponents to see black people as stereotypes. Rather than rejecting the principle of racial stereotyping, they generated an alternative stereotype of their own that was designed to 'counter that of the planters, which represented "*Quashee*" [a black person] as lazy, mendacious, incapable of working without the whip, mentally inferior and sexually depraved.' The abolitionist stereotype of the African was of 'new black Christian subjects – meek victims of white oppression, grateful to their saviours, ready to be improved and transformed.'[41]

That Victorian capacity for being passionately committed to anti-slavery as both a moral principle and an article of British national identity while at the same time holding old racial ideas and dabbling in new ones can be seen in the writings of one of the most famous men of the age, Charles Dickens. He was born in 1812 and died in 1870 – thereby missing the last thirty-one years of the Victorian era of which he is regarded as the narrator – and so, like most of his generation of Britons, did not see British slavery in operation. In 1842 he made the first of his two trips to the United States. He was already a successful writer although his greatest work lay ahead of him. While there he expressed a desire to visit the South and see the peculiar institution of slavery in the flesh. He travelled to Richmond, Virginia, the city that became the capital of the Confederate South, and there saw William Knibb's 'monster' alive and well.

Dickens was appalled by the violence of slavery, the results of which he saw manifested in the wounds, scars and disfigurements on the bodies of the slaves. He was also disturbed by his exposure to the full force of Southern racism, and the dismissive swagger with which Southerners defended the slave system and their power over black people. Descriptions of his encounters with slavery were included in *American Notes for General Circulation*, Dickens' journalistic account of his time in America. But even before his immersion in the antebellum South, Dickens reported feeling uncomfortable during a dinner in Baltimore by the fact that the waiting staff were enslaved Africans. He felt overwhelmed, he tells us, by 'a sense of shame and reproach' for being in the presence of 'human creatures who are bought and sold' and passionately condemned the 'upholders of slavery in America' and the 'horrors of the system'. He dedicated four pages to reprinting a total of forty-four shocking notices and advertisements from American newspapers concerning runaway slaves, which listed the various injuries and scars by which they might be identified and offered rewards for recapture. We don't know if Dickens was aware that similar advertisements had appeared in the pages of British news-papers only a few decades earlier.

However, Dickens' vivid heartfelt denunciation of American slavery exists on the same pages as his highly derogatory racialized descriptions of the black people he encountered. His description of a black coachman he met at Potomac Creek contains many of the well-worn racial stereotypes that had emerged over the previous century and a half. The black coachman is described as 'rolling his eyes' and 'grinning ear to ear'. Dickens castigates him for performing what he labels an 'insane imitation of an English coachman'. Throughout this passage and others, Dickens fixates on the darkness of black people's skin.[42] There is no question that Dickens' revulsion at slavery was real and that it stayed with him in later life, but so did his dislike of black people and their physical appearance. Six years after his tour of America, Dickens sent a copy of *The Narrative of the Life of Frederick Douglass* to his friend the actor William Charles Macready, who was himself about to embark for the United States. In his accompanying letter Dickens informed his friend that, 'There was such a hideous and abominable portrait of him [Douglass] in the book that I have torn it out, fearing it might set you, by antic-ipation, against the narrative'.[43] Dickens, who we know admired Douglass' writing and was able to empathize with the sufferings he had endured as a slave, still felt compelled to remove his portrait from a copy of his biography he was sending to a friend. No matter how difficult it is for us to understand, the fact remains that many millions of Victorians who, like their most famous author, passion-ately opposed slavery saw no contradiction between that opposition and an unshakable belief in black inferiority.

On 20 March 1852 a book was dispatched to Windsor Castle, from the town of Brunswick, in the American state of Maine. The accom-panying letter, written by the book's author, was addressed to 'His Royal Highness Prince Albert', Queen Victoria's consort and, by then, her husband of twelve years. After some initial niceties the author confessed that she had sent her novel to the prince in the hope that 'He who is nearest to her' might present the Queen with 'this simple story', believing that it might 'win from her compassionate nature, pitying thoughts for those multitudes of poor outcasts who have fled for shelter to the shadow of her throne', by which she meant the fugitive American slaves who, she wrote, are 'by thousands . . . crouding [sic] British shores'. The enclosed novel, she went on, was, 'an honest attempt to enlist the sympathies both of England & America in the sufferings of an oppressed race, to whom in less enlightened days both England & America were unjust'. The book was *Uncle Tom's Cabin*, and the author, the American abolitionist Harriet Beecher Stowe. Her letter to Prince Albert, despite the overdose of meek humility, was arguably as brilliant a work of emotional manipulation as the novel it accompanied. At one point Stowe appealed woman to woman to the Queen, writing that she was 'encouraged by the thought that beneath the royal insignia of England throbs that woman's & mother's heart'.

On the day Stowe dispatched her appeal to Windsor Castle, some of the more vocal of the 'poor outcasts' who had fled to Britain were in the energetic vanguard of the transatlantic campaign against slavery. That very evening the fugitive slave Henry 'Box' Brown was at the Corn Exchange in Wolverhampton presenting his famous *Panorama of African and American Slavery*, the last performance in a run of five that the local newspaper informs us had been organized 'on behalf of the three and a half million of his race in a state of degradation and slavery in America'.[44] 1852 also saw William Wells Brown tour across Britain promoting his newly published travel narrative, *Three Years in Europe*. But within a year of the arrival of that first copy of *Uncle Tom's Cabin* at Windsor Castle, this one work of fiction had begun to have a more powerful influence on how Queen Victoria's twenty million subjects regarded and envisaged slavery and black people than any anti-slavery speech or slave narrative.

It would be a blithe understatement to describe *Uncle Tom's Cabin* as a publishing success. It was a book that redefined what success in publishing looked like and that altered perceptions of what literature could achieve. Between its publication in March 1852 and the close of the following year, it sold a third of a million copies in the United States. More remarkably over the same period an unprecedented one and a half million copies were sold in Britain and her empire. In Britain alone eighteen different publishing houses issued forty different editions between them, many of them unofficial pirated editions from which the author gained no royalties; this allowed British publishers to offer the book to the public for as little as one shilling, which in turn increased sales.* In part because it was written by an American and set in the United States, *Uncle Tom's Cabin* is not usually thought of today as a Victorian novel, and its impact upon Britain and British culture has largely been forgotten, yet after the Bible it was the best-selling book in Britain during the entire nineteenth century. It went on to become the best-selling book of the century across the world.

The subtitle, *Life Among the Lowly* – rarely mentioned today – is a reminder of how unlikely its success was. This was a book that managed to take black characters, people who occupied the very lowest strata of another society, and place them in the minds and the hearts of millions of British people. For at least two generations Stowe's enslaved black characters – Topsy, George Harris, Eliza, Harry and Uncle Tom himself – were as familiar to British readers, both adults and children, as Oliver Twist, Scrooge, Miss Havisham, David Copperfield, or any of the other creations of Charles Dickens. Even in the 1940s, ninety years after publication, it was recorded that *Uncle Tom's Cabin* was still among the most commonly read books by working-class schoolgirls in Britain.[45] On the shelves of hundreds of antiquarian bookshops in Britain today can be found thousands of Victorian and Edwardian copies, many with the carefully inscribed signatures of the British children who had won them as prizes in schools and Sunday schools. For well over a century *Uncle Tom's Cabin* was ubiquitous, carried by every library and passed down through millions of British families. But its impact spilled over far beyond the Sunday school or the family bookshelf. Within its first few years in circulation the novel exploded into Victorian popular culture. It broke free from its literary form and invaded the theatres and the music halls. It inspired comic sketches and satirical cartoons; there were versions that both celebrated and mocked the book, its

---

* These were extremely cheap as there were no reciprocal copyright arrangements between Britain and America, which meant that publishers in Britain were able to print and sell books by American authors without paying the writers any royalties. American publishers returned the favour, to the fury of Charles Dickens in particular.

characters and the issues around slavery and abolition that it raised. *Uncle Tom's Cabin* infiltrated the English language and was refracted through British popular music and collided with another lost feature of Victorian popular culture, the enormous popularity of blackface minstrel acts.

In the vaults of museums and in private collections are the physical relics of Britain's fascination with *Uncle Tom's Cabin*. The book spawned a vast array of what we would today call tie-in merchandise. Uncle Tom figurines poured out of the Staffordshire potteries and bronze statuettes were cast in their thousands. Playing cards and jigsaws appeared, as did tableware – crockery and cutlery.[46] One manufacturer even produced *Uncle Tom* wallpaper that depicted the key scenes from the book, while a London bookshop let it be known that it stocked 'Uncle Tom's New and Second Hand clothing'.[47] Toy makers manufactured thousands of dolls of the main characters and *Uncle Tom* board games were hastily devised. One of them, entitled Justice, allowed each player to take on the role of a central character.[48] Parlour songs were composed based on Uncle Tom storylines, and popular ballads were cheaply printed, often illustrated with scenes from the book, and sold in large numbers. Sermons were delivered from the pulpit and poems were composed in praise of the book and its humanitarian, Christian themes.

Even a hundred and sixty years later the unprecedented popularity of this one book is not fully explainable. Some of its extraordinary success must rest upon the foundations of sympathy and engagement with the issue of slavery that had been laid down during the previous seventy years of abolitionist activity in Britain. There is also the possibility that the popularity of the many slave narratives published in Britain over the preceding two decades had to some extent cleared the way, though it has to be said that in 1852 no slave narrative had sold even fifty thousand copies, never mind one and a half million.

Today *Uncle Tom's Cabin* is one of those books that almost everyone has heard of but few people have read, and to us it is a difficult read – clumsily proselytizing at times, melodramatic in places while slow-moving and overly wordy in others. In the least successful passages, Stowe's characters become ciphers for her own anti-slavery convictions and at times for her other moral views. Her passionate belief in temperance is particularly poorly camouflaged. But at its most persuasive and in its most humane passages *Uncle Tom's Cabin* still has the capacity to stir emotions and elicit genuine sympathy. In those passages, particularly those that explore broken family bonds and parents' love for their children, the raw emotional power of the book is little dimmed by the passing of the decades.

At its heart *Uncle Tom's Cabin* is the story of the break-up of two enslaved families, but like the narratives penned by fugitive slaves it explores other aspects of American slavery. Uncle Tom himself, a man in late middle age, is literally 'sold down the river', eventually to Simon Legree, who becomes the personification of the vindictive Southern slave owner, and who was probably based on a number of infamous Southern planters whom Stowe had read about or heard reports of. While Uncle Tom is abandoned to the cruelties of his new owner, another group of slaves, George Harris with his wife Eliza and child Harry, make a long and perilous progress across America, finally escaping to freedom by reaching British Canada, a significant detail that was not lost on British readers. In the scene in which they land in Amherstburg, Stowe describes the British territory as an almost mystical realm of natural freedoms: 'clear and full rose the English shores; shores charmed by a mighty spell, – with one touch to dissolve every incantation of slavery no matter in what language pronounced or by what national power confirmed'.[49] The Virginian slaves who followed Dunmore's Proclamation of 1775 and the slave mutineers who sailed the *Creole* to the Bahamas prob-ably envisaged British territory in similarly idealized terms. The chapters describing the escapes of the enslaved characters and their pursuit by slave-catchers were a pointed and timely attack on the Fugitive Slave Act, passed two years before publication. Stowe herself had harboured a fugitive slave in her own home and appreciated the vindictiveness of the new ordinance. The climax of the book is the murder of Uncle Tom by Simon Legree. In his determination to crush the honest spirit of the old man, and, significantly for Stowe, to break his faith in God, Legree whips Tom to death in an uncon-trollable explosion of animal rage. Yet even at the moment of his death Tom forgives his murderer.

Uncle Tom's Cabin remains largely unread in the twenty-first century not simply because its melodramatic style has fallen from literary favour but also because it is highly contentious. In the second half of the twentieth century it was largely disowned by African Americans, who recoiled at the meek passivity of the central character, whose name has become a pejorative shorthand for a black person unable to stand up for his own life and in thrall to white power. Tom is the simplistic and saintly figure that Stowe intended him to be, but also the embodiment of the stereotype of Africans that had emerged from within transatlantic abolitionism; honest, childlike, uncomplicated and deeply imbued in the Christian message. Other characters can also appear to be personifications of various stereotypes, or at least to display traits that accord with the racial paternalism of the abolitionist movement. As these characters were some of the best known ever generated by any work of fiction, the significance of these failings and limitations is enormously magnified. Yet there are other characters who demonstrate autonomy, resistance, pride and devotion to family, most notably George Harris, who bravely leads his family to liberty in Canada.* Even Uncle Tom, who refuses to whip another slave and is punished for his disobedience, does not fall neatly into the stereotype.

Whatever our modern difficulties with the novel and its characters, for the millions of British people who encountered the book in the 1850s the experience of reading *Uncle Tom's Cabin* could be revelatory and visceral as they encountered Stowe's characters and bore witness to their sufferings in the sobering knowledge that as they sat reading, almost four million black people were living in similar conditions across the ocean, quaking under the private tyrannies of slaveholders like Simon Legree.

The book's raw intensity came from its portrayal of the slave family as a network of emotional bonds and shared kinship that was wrought apart by slavery. This was something that British readers appreciated from the outset. Through the sufferings of its central characters, who were scattered across America, the novel cast the slave system as the enemy of what we today call the nuclear family. Its thunderous central message was that to be pro-slavery was to be anti-family, a notion repugnant to Victorian religious and moral

---

* Significantly, George and Eliza Harris were mixed-race, and in some visual depictions of the novel appear almost as a white couple.

sensibilities. The brutal punishments suffered by the black characters, their desperate escapes from both slavery and the white slave-catchers, combined with their emotional and familial loyalties to one another could have the effect of re-humanizing, in the British popular imagination, a people who had been systematically de-humanized by the slave system.

The intensity of this moral message was known to incite a phys-ical and visceral reaction. Readers were reported weeping and shuddering at the most violent or emotionally resonant passages. The brutality of the punishment scenes was seen as so shocking that Stowe was repeatedly accused of exaggeration. In 1853 she responded by publishing *A Key to Uncle Tom's Cabin*, a 270-page, point-by-point defence of the novel's characters and plot. In this second work, Stowe openly acknowledged that *Uncle Tom's Cabin* was an 'inadequate representation of slavery', but only because 'slavery, in some of its workings, is too dreadful for the purposes of art. A work which should represent it strictly as it is, would be a work which could not be read'.[50] Inadequate or not as a description of slavery, the emotional journey that Victorian readers were taken on by the novel could be overwhelming. A stage performance put on in a north Welsh mining village, graphically demonstrated how it permitted white Britons, both men and women, to immerse themselves in and even publicly express their powerful feelings of empathy for the enslaved.

> *Uncle Tom's Cabin* played absolute hell with our emotions. We felt every stroke of the lash of the whip. It cut us to the quick, heart and soul. In the audience some people wept unashamedly, like the Greeks of old who considered it manly to give vent to their feel-ings when moved. Others with obvious efforts restrained themselves by the exercise of great control from rushing on the stage, taking the whip out of the hand of the cruel task master and giving him a taste of his own medicine.

One member of the audience, a Mrs Whalley, was 'loudly sobbing, looking up and calling out, "Oh, oh" as each lash discordantly cut the air and Tom's poor body. At one juncture her grief was awful to behold and she was sympathetically escorted out to the back . . . she was still sobbing and crying and would not be comforted.'[51]

Yet it was not just empathy that allowed the book to achieve its unprecedented sales figures, and what made *Uncle Tom's Cabin* genuinely loved in its day was the way it mixed tragedy with comedy. Reading it was not an act of dutiful solemnity. Both British and American reviewers noted how the book was able to shift the reader between the extremes of tears and laughter. *Putnam's Monthly*, a New York magazine, recounted the story of a man who, while spending the night in a strange house, became 'annoyed by hearing someone in the adjoining chamber alternatively groaning and laughing'. Eventually, 'he knocked upon the wall and said, "Hallo, there! What's the matter? Are you sick, or reading *Uncle Tom's Cabin*?"'[52]

Historians have debated the extent to which Britain's anti-slavery culture of meetings, pamphlets and speaking tours reached down into the lives and experiences of working-class people. We know that the poor as well as the well-off attended anti-slavery lectures and talks, and were especially drawn to listen to figures like Frederick Douglass, as his celebrity radiated out beyond traditional abolitionist and Nonconformist circles. But there is no doubt that Uncle Tom helped spread the anti-slavery message into regions of the country and sections of society that had been less interested and less engaged. The novel won converts to the anti-slavery mission, inspired some of its readers to become involved in the crusade against American slavery and generated a new wave of activity that helped British anti-slavery campaigners transmit to this broader audience one of their most persuasive arguments – that slavery was a moral sin, no matter where it took place. Within a few years of publication, the book had become what the scholar Sarah Meer describes as 'the frame for the majority of British discussions of slavery.'[53] *Uncle Tom* did more to damage the reputation of America abroad and shine a light on Southern slavery than any other feature of the transatlantic abolitionist campaign. Its runaway success in Britain and popularity in the free states of the North also helped reaffirm the links between the anti-slavery movements on both sides of the Atlantic.

The sensational impact of the novel inevitably made the author internationally famous and in 1853 Stowe travelled to Britain, along with her husband Calvin. They came to promote *Uncle Tom's Cabin*, revel in its success and support the anti-slavery cause. Stowe's arrival added fresh fuel to the Uncle Tom bonfire. She attended several anti-slavery gatherings, but hid behind the veil of Victorian propriety and had her husband speak on her behalf. Also on her behalf, a petition was initiated by the Earl of Shaftesbury, guided by the offices of the Queen's close companion the Duchess of Sutherland. It was entitled 'An affectionate and Christian address of many thousands of women of Great Britain and Ireland, to their sisters, the women of the United States of America' and generated over half a million signatures from British women. This was deemed to be a socially acceptable way for respectable British women to express their support for Stowe and their opposition to American slavery without being seen to have strayed too far into the male realm of politics and international relations. It was envisaged as a direct appeal to the women of America to reflect on slavery in their nation, a force that broke up families and that was simply 'an Affliction and disgrace' that had to be removed 'from the Christian world.'[54] To make the address more palatable in the United States, it did admit that Britain had 'introduced' slavery into her former colonies. Among the ladies who added their names to the address and helped organize it was Catherine Dickens, who had accompanied her husband on his American tour and who shared his opposition to slavery. Gathered together into twenty-six bound and heavy volumes, the petition was presented to Stowe, reinforcing British womanhood's commitment to the anti-slavery cause and the personal celebrity of the author of *Uncle Tom's Cabin*.

As *Uncle Tom's Cabin* changed the landscape of anti-slavery sentiments in Britain, all those involved had to adapt. African American abolitionists on lecture tours increasingly encountered audiences who viewed American slavery through their own reading. To tap into this new interest anti-slavery speakers began to refract their own personal experiences and readings from their own slave narratives through references to famous passages in *Uncle Tom's Cabin*. They were also able to use their own authority as former slaves to confirm that the terrible abuses and outrageous violations Stowe had described accorded with their own real experiences of American slavery. In these ways they tailored their message to the new mood, and largely welcomed the novel as a new and powerful feature of the struggle against slavery, one that had created a welcome wave of new interest and enthusiasm. The popularity of *Uncle Tom's Cabin* with British readers also became a fundraising opportunity. The anti-slavery societies began to organize Uncle Tom Penny Offerings, a campaign which gathered significant funds to support American abolitionist activities. As was the case with the phenomenal success of Frederick Douglass' tour in the 1840s, a great deal of the activity was directed and organized by women. That the author of *Uncle Tom's Cabin* was herself a woman naturally feminized the immediate response to its runaway success in Britain.

But *Uncle Tom's Cabin* and its slave characters did not remain fixed in Britain. The book was adapted to fit British tastes and agendas, and was used and misused in various forms. On the stage it mutated through hundreds of productions and innumerable versions, rewrites and reimaginings. By the end of 1852 eleven British theatres had produced *Uncle Tom* plays.[55] These variants and plays become almost a sub-genre of British theatre, and Uncle Tom-themed plays were among the most performed during the second half of the century. White actors blacked up to play the roles of the enslaved, and later in the century African American theatrical troupes or individual performers travelled to Britain to take Uncle Tom on tour. Playwrights simply cannibalized the original, selecting from its key scenes, reordering where necessary, rewording when they saw fit, dropping other parts of the book to highlight their chosen themes. As a consequence the play could be put on almost anywhere, from the rough theatres of the East End, where the audiences were male and predominantly working class, to the refined theatres of the city centre and the West End. Some Tom plays took the key characters and placed them in scenarios that were not in Stowe's novel. Others invented new characters and threw them onto the stage to mingle among Stowe's originals. Some playwrights recoiled at the prospect of dramatizing the brutal murder of Uncle Tom by Simon Legree before refined, middle-class audiences; in one British version Tom's saintly kindness overcomes Legree's inner demons and he is freed, escaping to Canada. In another version Legree is shot by his enslaved concubine Cassy. Other Tom plays even depicted slave revolts and the burning of Legree's plantation, to the shock and horror of American visitors to London, who the British Army *Despatch* noted were 'disgusted with the Uncle Tom Mania here'.[56] Other American theatregoers of the 1850s were disturbed more by the appearance on stage of Uncle Toms who delivered their lines with strong cockney accents. Perhaps the most interesting reworking was *The Tyrant*, which interjected into Stowe's story a British sailor, a Jack tar, who acted as a device to link the anti-slavery theme of the novel to British patriotism. Other plays made much of George Harris' escape with his family to British Canada, thereby providing an excuse for a burst of British pride and moral self-satisfaction, served up, at times, to the strains of 'Rule, Britannia'.

From the very start readers and reviewers of *Uncle Tom's Cabin* compared and contrasted the characters in Stowe's novel to the caricatures of black people that could be found within another cultural phenomenon that had firmly taken root in Britain. No precise date can be given for its entry into British popular culture but one critical moment came in September 1836 when a new musical play, *The Black God of Love*, was performed at London's Surrey Theatre. *The Times* carried a review of the play which commented upon the extraordinary effect that its star performer, 'Mr. Rice, the American comedian', had exerted upon his mainly male and working-class audience. The review noted that

> though his audience did not at first appear to understand his drift, it was not many minutes before he completely secured their attention and gained their applause. At the conclusion of the 'extravaganza,' . . . the curtain fell amidst an uproar of applause from every part of the house. The audience were, however, resolved to have a farther treat, and an unanimous call for 'Jim Crowe' [sic] succeeded. The curtain again rose, and Mr. Rice, in the character of Jim Crowe, immediately came forward and sung the song, which was encored four times![57]

In 1836 Jim Crowe was the comic persona and dance routine of Thomas Dartmouth Rice, a white New Yorker who had emerged as an actor and comedian in the 1820s. It was later in the nineteenth century that the name Jim Crow was appropriated as shorthand for the system of segregation and violent repression that condemned

African Americans to spend a century in the wilderness, between the Civil War of the 1860s and civil rights campaigns of the 1960s.

At some point in the 1830s, Rice began to appropriate aspects of the musical and dance traditions that had developed among the enslaved people of the Southern states. He had assembled these cultural fragments and added his own distortions to black speech patterns and exaggerations of black dancing, and created the stage character Jim Crow, an enslaved man dressed in rags and faded finery who sang songs, danced and told jokes. To complete the persona, Rice blackened his face and hands, as earlier minstrel performers had done. In 1836, at the height of British abolitionism, three years after the passage of the Emancipation Act and four years before the World Anti-Slavery Convention, Jim Crow came to Britain.

The arrival of Jim Crowe, and his dance 'Jumpin Jim Crowe', was not something entirely new to Britain. In the 1820s the stage performer Charles Mathews had brought to Britain his own adaptation of early American minstrelsy routines that pre-dated Thomas Rice, which he had seen on a trip to the United States.[58] Britain also had her own traditions of blackface and British audiences had, after all, been watching white actors in black make-up play Othello for two and a half centuries. The new forms of blackface minstrelsy that emerged in the 1830s and 1840s, rather like abolitionism, were transatlantic phenomena, in that ideas, people and innovations moved in both directions. It cannot be simply thought of as an American import. Although blackface minstrelsy, its popular songs, slang phrases and comic routines, has been largely airbrushed out of our standard, Dickensian image of Britain in the Victorian age, it was enormously popular right through into the twentieth century. There were times during which minstrels acts were at least as widespread in Britain as in the United States, and one British blackface performer of the late nineteenth and early twentieth centuries was adamant that minstrelsy had reached its most heightened stages of perfection in Britain rather than the US.[59] By the 1850s minstrel songs had usurped many of the ballads that had been popular earlier in the century to become some of the best-known tunes in Britain. The near ubiquity of minstrel shows and minstrel imagery made it one of the cultural forces that helped shape how black people were imagined and how slavery was envisaged in Victorian Britain.

Minstrelsy was in essence a form of musical clownery, but one that is so racially toxic to the twenty-first-century observer that it is almost impossible to regard it as anything other than a racist attack on black people. The racial stereotyping, the exaggerated gestures, the faux African American dialects and above all the blackening of white faces with burnt cork in a grotesque act of racial imperson-ation – everything about blackface is profoundly unpalatable today. Yet, difficult though it is to grasp, minstrel shows were not initially and not always the enemy of the anti-slavery position. Broadly speaking, in the period between British abolition in 1833 and the early 1850s, minstrelsy was not as racist as it was to become later in the century. As the historian Robert Nowatzki has pointed out, minstrel shows were capable of 'appropriating abolitionism's melo-dramatic depiction of the separation of slave families and other sorrows caused by slavery'.[60] On occasions the most benign of the minstrel songs and sketches presented the anti-slavery cause as a form of anti-slavery entertainment, one that condemned American slavery while at the same time lampooning and stereotyping black people. From the 1830s to the 1850s white men in blackface delivered anti-slavery speeches from the stages of British theatres and music halls, in the same acts in which they rolled their eyes and crudely imitated black dancing, during their high-speed comic routines. Thomas Rice's first performances as Jim Crowe in the Surrey Theatre were a mixture of singing and dancing, racial lampooning but also anti-slavery statements.

In the mid-1840s, the Ethiopian Serenaders, the first of many extremely popular American minstrel troupes, toured Britain. They arrived in the country around the same time as Frederick Douglass, coming in 1846 and staying until 1847. Their tour, like that of the great abolitionist, took them across the provinces and brought them both rave reviews and national fame. Their progress around the country was even more arduous than that of Douglass; they played on over four hundred occasions in their eighteen months in Britain, in many of the towns and cities that welcomed and embraced Douglass and the other black abolitionists. How was it that audiences who attended anti-slavery lectures and who heard fugitive slaves recount their highly personal experiences of suffering and family break-up apparently felt no discomfort in attending the minstrel shows? Not only did British audiences attend both anti-slavery lectures and minstrel performances, they were, on occasions, encouraged to do so. In 1846 the people of Exeter, not long after they had welcomed Frederick Douglass to their city, were informed by the *Western Times,* their local newspaper, that a troupe of minstrels had arrived in town. The newspaper that had praised, in solemn tones, the words and the gravitas of Douglass gushed enthusiastically about the delights of the blackface performers and suggested that its readers would appreciate their performance, since 'The negroes of America, a light-hearted and joyous race, whenever they are treated with the least kindness, have a great love of music'. This music, the report explained, was 'unsophisticated and their instruments simple and crude', yet 'Some of them have fine voices'.[61] The minstrel acts, even when anti-slavery in sentiment, presented black people as childlike and unsophisticated. This was in striking contrast to how contemporary audiences reported their encounters with Frederick Douglass. Many accounts noted his obvious intelligence and evident learning, attributes which were cited on occasion as proof that when freed from slavery and given the gifts of education and moral instruction black people were able to demonstrate their intellectual capacities and potential for refinement. Douglass played on the gulf between his intellectual abilities and the expectations some of his audience might have had of him within the strictures of some of his lectures.

There is no single explanation as to why blackface minstrel acts caught hold of the British popular culture so profoundly in the Victorian age. This incongruity, along with minstrelsy's American origins, might partly explain why minstrelsy has been airbrushed out of our historical memory of Victorian theatre and music hall. One suggestion for its success at the time is that minstrelsy in Britain may have tapped into a reservoir of implicit sympathy for black people built up over decades of anti-slavery campaigning. Some historians have argued that blackface characters, performing the role of slaves who were often persecuted and exploited by figures of authority, enabled a play of words and meanings around issues of class and exploitation that working-class British audiences could easily relate to. When minstrel characters mocked and ridiculed their oppressors was it that difficult for the white working-class audiences to draw parallels and even choose sides? After all both the emerging trades unions and some Victorian social reformers had used terms like 'white slavery' and 'wage slavery' to compare the privations of industrial and agricultural workers to the conditions and sufferings of the more pitied slave.* It seems likely that there were occasions when white working-class audiences were able to see through the burnt cork and to some extent identify with the hard labour, endless poverty and abject powerlessness of the 'slave' characters. The historian Robert Nowatzki speculates as to whether blackface minstrelsy, for all its racism, 'may have done more to stir up anti-slavery sentiment among the British working classes than formal anti-slavery campaigning was able to do'.[62] The almost unfathomable strangeness of minstrelsy was that it was capable of drawing its emotional power from these sorts of identifications and from the reservoir of sentimental, anti-slavery feelings that were held by many British people while at the same time pandering to the stereotypes of black people that reduced them to childlike clowns who were endlessly imitative, often joyous, occasionally witty, always musical but never intellectual or reflective.

During their 1846–47 tour the Ethiopian Serenaders took their act not just across the country but also up the social scale. As well as East End theatres and provincial concert halls they played in West End theatres such as the St James. Two years later they were back in London, this time performing with William Lane, an African American dancer known as Master Juba who is believed to be the dancer Charles Dickens saw perform in the Five Points district of New York during his American tour, an encounter he described in *American Notes*, another 'Dickensian' scene of rolling eyes and flailing limbs in which he fixated on black physical difference. The Ethiopian Serenaders also popularized in Britain the song 'Lucy Neal', a slave lament of which there were innumerable different versions, different lyrics arranged around the same melody and chorus. Versions of

---

* Only later in the century did the phrase 'white slavery' come to denote the trafficking of women and girls for sex.

'Lucy Neal' ranged from sorrowful anti-slavery ballads to raucous versions that are both racially derogatory and sexually obscene. Its flexibility was both a reason for and evidence of its popularity; the song became one of the most common in Britain in the mid-nineteenth century, reaching far beyond the theatres and music halls. The huge success of the Ethiopian Serenaders not only increased the popularity of minstrel shows, it encouraged British performers to abandon their traditional acts and form minstrel troupes.

While the more successful and astute minstrel troupes followed the American acts and migrated towards the more respectable theatres, adapting their acts to meet the tastes of middle-class audiences, other minstrel performers took the music of the theatre shows out onto the streets. By the 1850s working-class white Britons, often men on the margins of society, were blackening their faces. They tended to play banjos and for rhythm and percussion the bones, the two classic African American instruments of the period. The street minstrels, who described themselves using the N-word, played at the newly popular Victorian seaside resorts, to the enormous crowds that flocked to the race tracks and were drawn to any fair, fete, market or public gathering that offered them a crowd to work with and at which they were tolerated. While exploring the streets of London in the summer of 1850, researching for his book *London Labour and the London Poor*, Henry Mayhew encountered a minstrel duo who were scraping a living as what he described as 'Ethiopian serenaders'. Although the two men were 'dressed like decent mechanics, with perfectly clean faces', Mayhew identified them as minstrels because 'a little of the professional black' remained 'at the root of the hair on the forehead.' They claimed, probably erroneously, to have been the city's first blackface street entertainers and Mayhew, who had his interviews recorded by assistants using a form of shorthand, left us this highly detailed account of these street minstrels, their trade and their repertoire of minstrel tunes they had mastered, many of them containing references to slavery.

'We are niggers,' said one man, 'as it's commonly called; that is, negro melodists. Nigger bands vary from four to seven, and have numbered as many as nine; our band is now six. We all share alike. I (said the same man) was the first who started the niggers in the

streets, about four years ago . . . Last year was the best year I've
known. We start generally about ten, and play till it's dark in fine
weather. We averaged 1*l*. a-week last year. The evenings are the
best time. Regent-street, and Oxford-street, and the greater part
of St. James's, are our best places. The gentry are our best
customers, but we get more from gentlemen than from ladies. The
City is good, I fancy, but they won't let us work it; it's only the
lower parts, Whitechapel and Smithfield ways, that we have a chance
in. Business and nigger-songs don't go well together . . . When
we started, the songs we knew was 'Old Mr. Coon,' 'Buffalo Gals,'
'Going ober de Mountain,' 'Dandy Jim of Carolina,' 'Rowly Boly
O,' and 'Old Johnny Booker.' We stuck to them a twelvemonth.
The 'Buffalo Gals' was best liked . . . Things are not so good as
they were. We can average 1*l*. a-piece now in the week, but it's
summer-time, and we can't make that in bad weather . . . there's
no demand for us now at the theatres, except the Pavilion.[63]

It is clear from Mayhew's evidence that London's street minstrels
often struggled to make enough money and were drawn from the
poorer sections of London society. The more vocal of the two men
Mayhew encountered in 1850 candidly admitted that 'we're more
of a poorer sort, if not to say a ragged sort, for some are without
shoes or stockings. The "niggers" that I know have been errand-
boys, street-singers, turf-cutters, coalheavers, chandlers, paviours,
mudlarks, tailors, shoemakers, tinmen, bricklayers' labourers, and
people who have had no line in particular but their wits.'[64] The
witness enlightened Mayhew as to the ethnic origins of the mid-
century street minstrels, and here the history of the portrayal of
black people in Britain and their presence in the country overlapped.
'Some niggers are Irish', he told the social explorer. 'There's Scotch
niggers too. I don't know a Welsh one, but one of the street nigger-
singers is a real black, an African.'[65]

Mayhew's impromptu interview with the two blackface musicians
took place around the same time as William Wells Brown's poignant
London encounter with a fugitive American slave. The city that
sustained numerous troupes of blackface minstrels was in the same
years home to black students and preachers, fugitive Americans and
black and mixed-race Britons, some from families of long standing

with roots in the eighteenth-century black communities. All lived their lives alongside these musical parodies of blackness. But not only did black people pass by blackface performance on the London streets, African American musicians themselves came to Britain to take advantage of the huge new interest in black American music that had been inspired by the minstrel craze. Black men now performed on stages alongside white men in blackface, they shared the bill with acts built on the racial lampooning of African American slaves.

Some black performers arrived in Britain as established stars of the American stage and were able to attract large audiences. Bill Kersands, a comedian and minstrel dancer of legendary athletic skill, toured Britain in the 1880s. Kersands performed his dance routines for Queen Victoria and was a hit on both sides of the ocean. His routines however struggled to escape the crude stereotyping of the blackface shows. Known for his large mouth, one feature of his act involved him putting billiard balls in his mouth, several at a time, and contorting his face to comic effect. To uproarious laughter he would attempt to regale his audience with comic anecdotes through a mouthful of billiard balls or even while holding a complete cup and saucer between his lips. When he met Queen Victoria, Kersands is reputed to have said, 'If God ever wanted my mouth any bigger, he would have to move my ears.'[66] Given that throughout the nineteenth century it was not unknown in both Britain and America for physically disabled people, or those with congenital birth defects, to be put on public display in travelling circuses, the contortions of Bill Kersands' large mouth might have seemed relatively harmless in comparison, were it not for the fact that his physical comedy was so in keeping with prevailing stereotypes of black people as a race that was marked out by outlandishly sized lips and mouths – as well as other features. Kersands' act was made more troubling by his regular renditions of minstrel songs with all their derogatory lyrics and his racial caricaturing. Just as popular although less controversial were the Bohee Brothers, James and George. They first arrived in London as part of the black minstrel troupe Haverly's Genuine Coloured Minstrels but saw a business opportunity and decided to stay on in England, forming their own act, The Bohee Operatic Minstrels. This consisted of them and around thirty other musicians, both black and white. Master showmen, the Bohee brothers announced their arrival in provincial towns with street parades, and they were known for their luxurious stage costumes. The Bohees' fame was built on the enormous popularity of the banjo, the central instrument of minstrelsy in all its forms, which, in its original but now antiquated form, was an authentic African American instrument. So renowned were the Bohees for their sophisticated finger-picking banjo style that they launched a profitable sideline manufacturing banjos in Britain, deploying their name and their fame as a guarantee of quality. The brothers played a part in sparking a banjo craze in the late nineteenth century that saw the instrument become a favourite among the rich and the aristocratic. It's believed that the Prince of Wales, the future Edward VII, took banjo lessons from James Bohee.[67] In a programme for a Bohee Brothers performance in London, the brothers explained the ethnic roots of their banjo music. Although from the Northern states, the Bohees offered their British audiences comforting and familiar eulogies to the simplicity of black life in the American South, painting a picture of their people as comic, naturally musical, home-orientated and essentially harmless. They wrote,

> The banjo is essentially a home instrument and among the Negroes of the South of the United States, that is to say amongst probably the most domesticity loving community in the world – the banjo is at once a solace and a joy. It is even more to the humble 'darky' than the pipe is to the British working man; for, not only does it keep him company when he is alone, but it is the national instrument of mirth and festivity.[68]

By far the most important of the black American musical troupes to tour Britain in our period were the legendary Fisk Jubilee Singers, who arrived in 1873. They came from Nashville, Tennessee, and were directly responsible for introducing British audiences to the world of Negro spirituals. Their impact upon British music tastes is too significant to be dealt with here, but more than any other troupe they changed British tastes, introducing into the national song book standards like 'Swing Low, Sweet Chariot', 'Nobody Knows the Trouble I See' and 'Deep River'; songs that became part of the lives of millions of Victorian churchgoers. The Fisk Jubilee Singers performed for Queen Victoria and symbolically they gave a concert at London's Exeter Hall, the historic headquarters of the British abolitionist movement. Two further tours followed, in 1875 and in 1884, during which their popularity remained undimmed. The Fisk Jubilee Singers, thanks to their ever-changing line-up, survived into the twentieth century and gramophone recordings of their singing exist. From these discs emerges music that is powerfully sombre and radically original when set aside the plodding music-hall routines and dated minstrel clichés that were popular throughout the era.

The cultural penetration of minstrel music, and later of genuine African American spiritual music, from which the minstrels had borrowed, was remarkable. Minstrel tunes were ubiquitous. Karl Marx, then resident in London, was said to have sung minstrel songs and taught them to his children. In addition to the flow of minstrel music into Victorian family life, terms and slang that were used in minstrel songs and in blackface stage acts infiltrated everyday speech, and not just that of the poor. Among the words that surface in the letters of even the highly respectable are 'Mammy' and the N-word. Charles Darwin, writing to his wife Emma in a letter of May 1848, signed off, 'Your old nigger—C.D'.[69] He deployed that word – so repugnant to us today – as a term of endearment, using it to playfully imply that his love for his wife was so great that he was her slave. Emma Darwin used the same term in her own letters, calling Darwin her 'nigger' and describing him as 'Chattel'.[70] In a letter to his sister in 1836 Charles Darwin told the story of how his brother Erasmus Alvey Darwin was being so overworked by his sweetheart, Miss Harriet Martineau, that he had begun to claim that his lot in life '(to use his own expression) . . . shall be not much better than her "nigger". – Imagine poor Erasmus a nigger to so philosophical & energetic a lady'. Darwin concluded, 'We must pray for our poor "nigger" '.[71] Unlike most of his contemporaries, Charles Darwin had actually seen slavery in operation and witnessed the trade in slaves while in South America during his travels on board HMS Beagle in the 1830s. These experiences had reinforced the strong anti-slavery sentiment with which he had been brought up, and throughout his life Darwin was a committed anti-slavery man. The use of the N-word in jest, whether imbibed from the culture of anti-slavery or the popular culture of minstrelsy or perhaps from

both, was, it seems, an accepted joke within a family whose abolitionist credentials were unquestioned.[72]

In 1859 Frederick Douglass returned to Britain and embarked upon
a second speaking tour. He came seeking sanctuary, once again
fearing for his liberty. Although a free man, he believed he was at
risk of extradition to Virginia to stand trial for his association with
the radical John Brown. In October 1859 Brown had launched a
doomed raid on a government munitions depot at Harpers Ferry,
Virginia in the hope of inciting a slave rebellion; the raid is regarded
as one of the stepping stones that led America towards civil war.

In Britain, Douglass reacquainted himself with old supporters,
some of whom had continued to raise funds for his anti-slavery
activities in the United States. In anti-slavery circles he was feted
and celebrated, as he had been in the 1840s. But he noted a change.
Britain of the late 1850s felt distinctly less welcoming than thirteen
years earlier. Anti-slavery, both as a movement and as a popular
tendency, had diminished, despite the enormous success of *Uncle
Tom's Cabin*. The fervour of the 1840s, which had convinced millions
of Britons that slavery was so dreadful a sin that it had to be ended
wherever it was found, was now challenged by a new belief in
non-intervention in the affairs of other nations and the United States
in particular. Despite this, Douglass still had considerable success
on the lecture circuit, in part due to his international fame, but he
was conscious that the British newspapers were less keen than they
had been in the 1840s to publish his words or contrast his treatment
in Britain with the racism he endured in America. Equally disturbing,
he sensed not just a decline in anti-slavery sentiment but a rise in
racism. A harsher, less sympathetic attitude towards black people
was in evidence.

On more than one occasion Douglass suggested that these changes
were the result of the infiltration into the country of what he
described as 'American prejudice'. He detected in the mood of
Britain in 1859 and 1860 the toxic influence of what he called
'pro-slavery ministers'. To counter this he included in his lectures
appeals for the rejection of these American influences. During a visit
to Newcastle upon Tyne in 1860, the city that was home to the

Richardson family who had purchased his freedom in 1847, Doug-lass identified another route by which American racism had seeped into Britain. He complained that 'Ethiopian minstrels', who he regarded as a 'pestiferous nuisance', had 'brought here [to Britain] the slang phrases, the contemptuous sneers all originating in the spirit of slavery'. Minstrelsy, Douglass warned, represented black people as being 'contented and happy as a slave, thoughtless of any higher life than a mere physical one'.[73] The increasing popularity of minstrel shows, and the increasingly derogatory nature of blackface performances and routines in British theatres – whether performed by visiting American troupes or home-grown bands – was more likely a symptom of hardening racial attitudes than a cause. Minstrel acts had themselves adapted to the new atmosphere, but were not directing it. Douglass was probably right that American racial atti-tudes had found favour in some parts and some sections of Britain, and there were figures who could qualify as 'pro-slavery ministers'. Britons resident in the United States had returned with their own views on America's 'peculiar institution' and a number of prominent Americans who had travelled through or settled in Britain had publicly suggested that slavery was not the inhuman system that the anti-slavery lobby claimed. Much like some of the minstrel shows, the defenders of American slavery peddled the familiar line that the slaves in the warm climes of the Southern states were happy in their current condition and aspired for no more complicated a life. In 1859 Douglass identified the economic and political influence of the Southern states most clearly in Liverpool, the key port in the cotton industry and home to a number of American cotton factors, Southern businesses and their British supporters, whose pro-slavery voice was heard loud in the city. However, much of the hardening of racial attitudes that Douglass was right to be troubled by was home-grown. What he was sensing was a generational shift in both people and ideas. The generation that had called the World Anti-Slavery Conven-tion twenty years earlier, many of whom had been veterans of the abolition campaigns of the 1820s and 1830s, were ageing and fading away. In the same years, the optimism of those earlier decades was being overwhelmed by newly emergent racial ideas. The capacities of black people, intellectual, spiritual and political, were increasingly being called into question by new supposedly scientific ideas about race and the capacities of the various branches of humanity. These new ideas fused and mingled with the older racisms. In this new atmosphere not only did increasing numbers of Britons believe that the nation had no business intervening in the issue of slavery in America, some suggested that even abolition in the West Indies, the great act of moral absolution on which so much of Britain's self-image and patriotic triumphalism rested, might have been a mistake.

EIGHT

'Liberated Africans'

In October 1807 the last four British ships that were ever to legally transport Africans into slavery set sail across the Atlantic.[1] In their holds were eleven hundred African men, women and children, chained to the decks. Some of these captives would die of dehydration, disease and general mistreatment during the journey, as, by 1807, had generations of Africans subjected to the horrors of the Middle Passage. Like the British slave ships that had gone before them, this last flotilla sailed under the protection of the Royal Navy, a sleek frigate shepherding the four slavers across the ocean. In 1808 the navy dispatched the 32-gun frigate HMS *Solebay* and HMS *Derwent*, a sloop of 18 guns, to the coast of West Africa. Their mission was not to escort British slave ships to the slave markets of the Caribbean but to intercept them at sea, arrest their captains and crews and liberate the captives. The arrival of the *Solebay* and the *Derwent* in the warm, blustery waters off the coast of Sierra Leone marked the beginning of a mission that lasted for the next sixty years. Three generations of sailors took part and seventeen thousand died of tropical diseases or in armed clashes with the increasingly ruthless slave-traders.

Britain's anti-slavery patrols were intended to stop British slave-trading, but their mission expanded rapidly. Through a series of bilateral treaties negotiated over the next half-century, the patrols targeted the slave ships of other trading powers. At times their mission was extended into the Caribbean and during the 1850s they loitered off Brazil, intercepting slave ships at sea and burning others that were caught at anchor. In the latter half of the nineteenth century Britain's crusade against the slave trade turned to the East, and British warships surged into the Indian Ocean, where they pursued the dhows of the Muslim slavers, who continued their ancient trade in human flesh long after the Atlantic trade was reduced to a trickle. They were not stopped until the twentieth century and even then not comprehensively.

It is one of the great questions of British history: why was it that the nation that had refined and perfected the slave trade, and become the dominant player in that global industry, turned her back on its profits, and committed herself to its suppression? That mission was fought by the crews and the commanders of British ships off tropical shores but also by British diplomats in embassies across the world and by beady-eyed civil servants writing dispatches at Whitehall desks. This deployment of Britain's military might and her diplomatic influence to suppress slave-trading activities by other sovereign nations, which although abhorrent were legal, antagonized her friends and foes alike. It stretched international law to breaking point and on various occasions it materially damaged her relations with Spain, France, Portugal, Brazil and the United States. With limited resources and confronting determined opposition, the Preventative Squadron of the Royal Navy, also known as the West Africa Squadron, was never able to intercept anything even approaching the majority of the ships that carried on the trade in human beings. They were hampered by poorly drafted treaties riddled with legalistic loopholes, some of which created perverse incentives and had unintended, even tragic consequences, and the bureaucratic oddities of the system of legal adjudication set up to determine the status of intercepted slave ships and their crews resulted in bizarre contradictions and procedural absurdities that led to the deaths of African captives. Slave ships intercepted by the Royal Navy and then judged to have been trading legally were released to carry their human cargo to the plantations, usually in Brazil or Cuba. The complexity of the system and resistance from the nations subjected to British pressure meant few slave-traders were punished for their crimes and many who evaded justice were repeat offenders. Yet for all its failings this enormous global undertaking cost Britain both blood and treasure. It was an early example of what we today would call a 'humanitarian intervention' but it remains a largely forgotten chapter in the long and troubled history of Britain's relationship with Africa and her peoples.

The Abolition Act that had finally made its way through the British Parliament in 1807 allowed for the confiscation of any British ship caught trading in slaves, and slave-traders faced fines of as much as £100 for each captive liberated. In 1811 the punishments for trading were made more draconian still. To further deter British subjects, the Slave Trade Felony Act decreed that those apprehended were henceforth to be 'transported beyond the Seas', as sentencing judges quaintly described exile to Australia. In 1824 the Slave Trade Consolidation Act made it illegal 'for any person to . . . fit out, man, navigate, equip, dispatch, use, employ . . . any ship, vessel or boat' engaged in the trading of slaves. British subjects were further banned from becoming officers or crew in foreign slave ships and British businessmen were no longer able to 'insure or to contract for the insuring of any slaves', or to 'lend or advance' money for slave-trading ventures.[2] Section 9 of the Consolidation Act also increased the penalty for slave-trading to 'death without the benefit of clergy, and loss of lands, good and chattel'. Eleven years later Britain's lawmakers thought again and reduced the punishment back to transportation.[3]

Such grave penalties, combined with a series of later legal measures, meant that most British ships and traders did withdraw from the trade, but there were British merchants who remained addicted to the business that had made them wealthy, and British money still funded the slave economy of the Atlantic. A proportion of the foreigners who rushed in to fill the gap left by Britain's departure were financed by British merchants, some of whom operated brazenly through these foreign proxies. British industrialists who specialized in manufacturing the 'trade goods' with which slaves were bought from Africans exported them to other Europeans who carried them to Africa. Long after the 1807 Act, guns, beads, cloth, clothes and cheap liquor made in the West Country and the Midlands were unloaded onto African beaches and stacked up alongside chained and bewildered captives. Other British manufacturers continued to supply the hardware and paraphernalia of the trade:

chains, manacles, leg-irons and the more specialized contraptions used to restrain and punish slaves. In addition there was a small number of British ships that were effectively re-badged as foreign slavers and sent back to the Slave Coast, and the most defiant and reckless captains refused outright to abandon the trade and continued to lead expeditions, sailing now in foreign ships under foreign flags.

But the efforts of British merchants to circumvent the Abolition Act were dwarfed by the flood of newcomers who built vast fortunes by catering for the insatiable demand for slaves on the plantations of Brazil, Cuba and North America. None of this was unexpected. The penalties for slave-trading under the 1807 Act applied only to British citizens and British ships, and the Atlantic slave trade was so highly developed and so incredibly profitable in the early years of the nineteenth century that no mere legal sanction could bring it to an end. While British rejection of the trade did encourage some other nations to do likewise, those few unworldly idealists who had hoped that its extinction was at hand were disappointed.

The stark realities of the Atlantic world, and the basic economic and demographic facts that had initially inspired the Atlantic slave system in the sixteenth century, remained largely unchanged. Labour existed but not on the continent on which it was needed and where it could be deployed to generate maximum profits. Land in the Americas that had been violently wrenched from the hands of its indigenous population centuries earlier produced highly desirable tropical products for the markets of Europe, but those millions of acres were most profitably brought into production using labour from Africa. That labour was readily available; some of it was already enslaved. Even in 1807, there were more enslaved people in Africa than in the Americas, although the institution of slavery existed in Africa in many varying forms of differing degrees of severity and not all of them were permanent. In parts of the continent new slave-trading states were on the rise and in many societies slavery – in its domestic, agricultural and even military forms – was so normalized as to be ubiquitous and largely unquestioned. Various African leaders puzzled, after 1807, as to why the British, formerly their most enthusiastic trading partners, had become so squeamish about the trade in human flesh, a commerce that they themselves had so recently dominated.

Britain's withdrawal from the Atlantic trade and the Royal Navy's initial efforts to suppress slave-trading by other European powers and the United States undoubtedly meant that tens of thousands of Africans who would have been transported to the Americas remained on their home continent. That sudden change temporarily destabilized the economies of some coastal African nations. But beyond that, little changed. The African traders of the interior quickly adapted to the new reality, as did the private European traders who had built their slave 'factories' on the coast – these were warehouses and barracoons in which the captives were stored and readied for the Middle Passage. After 1807 all of them embraced new trading partners from Portugal, Brazil and Spain, as Britain's former rivals expanded their fleets and increased the frequency of their expeditions. Within a year the Portuguese, with their long-established links to African kingdoms, reinforced by the existence of mixed-race, Portuguese-speaking coastal communities, declared their intention to maintain and if possible expand their trade. Spain regarded Britain's abandonment of slaving as no reason for her to reduce or halt the supply of Africans to her South American colonies. Elsewhere Britain's decision went largely unnoticed. Away from the coasts, in the forest belts and along the rivers of West Africa, the ancient slave trades that stretched up across the Sahara to the Mediterranean continued, as did the trade eastwards across the Indian Ocean into Arabia, the Ottoman lands and beyond.

The very first slave-trade-suppression mission, that of the *Solebay* and the *Derwent*, was a largely fruitless token gesture. The Abolition Act was passed two years after the Battle of Trafalgar. Britain was at war with Napoleonic France in a conflict that had, through its various bloody stages, already dragged on for fourteen years. While the war continued, the Admiralty was, perhaps understandably, reluctant to spare ships for suppression duties. In 1808, when HMS *Solebay* and HMS *Derwent* were ordered to Africa, the Royal Navy had 726 ships, which meant the navy had committed 0.28 per cent of its vessels to the task of suppressing the slave trade.[4] Not only were the first ships dispatched to Africa few in number, they were often aged and of dubious quality. The *Solebay*, launched in 1785, was a decrepit veteran of twenty-two years when she arrived off the coast of Sierra Leone, and that pattern was to be continued. In

1862, after almost half a century of anti-slavery activity, Prime Minister Lord Palmerston – twice Prime Minister, three times Foreign Minister and in office for most of the period in question – complained that if the Admiralty knew of any 'particularly old slow-going tub in the Navy she was sure to be sent to the coast of Africa to try and catch the fast sailing American clippers [of the slave-traders]'.[5] The anti-slavery patrols reinforced Britain's incredible transition from slave-trader to anti-slave-trade crusader and it demanded a significant cultural shift within the Royal Navy itself. While there had long been black sailors in British ships, the navy had also long acted as defender of the British slave trade. A number of officers were slave owners. Some brought their slaves on board as personal servants, a practice the Admiralty disapproved of. There were even officers who owned slave plantations in the Caribbean. These men and their comrades now found themselves in common cause with the pious men and women of the anti-slavery society, as Britain's opposition to slavery transitioned from a popular movement to national policy.

The wars with France and her allies gave the navy an excuse to withhold ships from African duties, but while the conflict raged it gave those first few anti-slavery patrols an early advantage. So long as Britain was at war, British warships were free to intercept slave-trading vessels flying the flags of enemy nations, and to search the ships of neutral powers which were suspected of carrying goods destined for enemy ports. This meant that during the war years the anti-slavery ships of the Royal Navy – which were soon increased in number – boarded, searched and seized French and Spanish slave ships, as prizes. Around the same time they began to intercept and search Danish and American ships. This they justified with a neat piece of casuistry: as both nations had prohibited the slave trade, intercepting ships from those nations was an act of international solidarity, which prevented Danes and Americans from breaking their own laws.

The final defeat of Napoleon in 1815 ushered in a new era in which Britain was the only global sea power. Confident and preeminent, the Admiralty was finally willing to release more ships for the anti-slavery patrols, yet even with her enemies vanquished the navy never dispatched anything like the number of ships required to seriously take on the slave-traders. By 1819 the Admiralty had still sent only six ships, which was, at least, enough to be usefully organized into the British West Africa Squadron, which was settled in a new African base. The anchorage chosen was, perhaps inevitably, Freetown in Sierra Leone, where London's black poor had struggled against the tropical rains thirty years earlier and where the Nova Scotians and the Maroons from Jamaica had later established a firmer toe-hold.

With the six ships, and with supplies from Ascension Island and Cape Town, the squadron was placed under the highly competent Commodore Sir George Collier. But the task facing it was formidable. Its six ships were to patrol three thousand miles of the West African coast, from the mouth of the Gambia River in the west to the Bight of Biafra in the east. At times the ships ranged north up to Senegal and as far south as Angola. In the first half of the nineteenth century most of the coastline of West Africa was poorly charted and little understood. It had few natural harbours and hundreds of miles of dangerous surf. There were the deltas and mouths of the great rivers and hundreds of small rivers and inlets. The coastlines of what are now the nations of Benin, Nigeria and Cameroon were made especially difficult to patrol due to offshore sandbanks and vast inshore labyrinths of meandering lagoons. In those still waters and narrow channels slave ships could loiter, load their cargoes and evade detection. The rivers of Calabar and Bonny in Nigeria proved particularly alluring to illicit slave-traders, as the trade progressively moved eastwards over the course of the century. Before the invention of steam-powered paddle ships, the task of suppressing the trade was further hampered by the difficulties of manoeuvring ocean-going sailing ships in the variable winds of these coastal waters. The difficulties of patrolling the inland waterways were eventually remedied by the addition to the squadron, in 1832, of HMS *Pluto*, a 365-ton paddle steamer. Although slower over open water than the brigs used by the slave-traders, HMS *Pluto* – shallow-draughted and self-propelled – crept up the rivers and inlets and caught slave ships at anchor or loading their cargo, when they were at their most vulnerable.

For much of its history the ships of the West Africa Squadron were repeatedly outpaced by slaving vessels that were faster, sleeker and increasingly better armed. The potential profits justified the investment in these state-of-the-art vessels, against which the Royal Navy was usually unwilling to dispatch comparably advanced ships. Many of the slave ships also had the advantage of being commanded by men who, through many years of activity in their appalling trade, had accumulated an intimate knowledge of the African coastline.

The suppression of the slave trade in the Atlantic Ocean was founded upon the military power of the Royal Navy but that power could only be exercised within the confines of international law. Throughout the first half of the nineteenth century British diplomats and politicians set about expanding the scope and the legality of the nation's slave-trade suppression by bilateral treaties and one-off agreements. These treaties gave the signatories the right of search over one another's shipping. But as Britain alone had the ships and the will to patrol the slave coasts of Africa, the treaties, in effect, gave her the right to intercept and search foreign ships suspected of slave-trading. Britain also entered into a series of treaties that obliged the signatories to use the most efficient means available to suppress their own slave trades and to prevent ships sailing under the protection of their flags from engaging in the trade. By 1830 twelve suppression treaties had been agreed, and between 1831 and 1841 a further eighteen. European nations that fell into line included Spain, Denmark, Sweden and Norway, as well as the German Hanse towns. Partly due to the enormous power of Britain's 'informal empire' of capital, trade and investment, other signatories included the South American states of Ecuador, Venezuela, Argentina, Chile, Bolivia and Uruguay, all of which were too entangled in the web of British finance to risk offending London. What should have been the most significant treaty was formalized in 1841 between Britain, Russia, France, Prussia and Austria. The Quintuple Treaty allowed ships from all signatory nations to search merchant ships if there were 'reasonable grounds' to suspect they were 'engaged in the traffic of Slaves'. The treaty also declared slave-trading to be a form of piracy. Although little remembered today the treaty was one of the most ambitious diplomatic undertakings of the century, but was undermined in its final stages by French opposition.[6]

Similar diplomatic pressure was applied to the leaders of the states of the Islamic world, and the activities of the West Africa

Squadron were mirrored by missions against the Barbary slave-traders of North Africa.[7] Here London tended to tread more carefully but was able to use the promise of good relationships with the British Empire as an inducement for formal denouncements of slave-trading. In 1847 the Ottoman Sultan acquiesced to British demands to suppress the long-established slave-trade routes of the Persian Gulf, and in the same year the slave market of Istanbul was quietly closed down, which meant that for a few years it was possible to publicly and legally purchase slaves in Washington DC but not in the Ottoman capital.[8]

The mission's great champion, and at times its defender, was Henry Temple, Lord Palmerston. His support for abolition and anti-slavery is often obscured by the far more vivid historical memory of his ruthless colonial policies, his penchant for gunboat diplomacy and his role in the Opium Wars, but he was the driving political force behind the sustained mission to suppress the slave trade. He repeatedly demonstrated his willingness to cajole and where necessary bully other states and worked energetically to keep the suppression policy in the minds and in the dispatches of the small staff who ran the mid-Victorian Foreign Office. In an 1844 speech to the House of Commons, he reminded his fellow members why he had committed the nation to the task, even in the face of constant griping and opposition. 'If all crimes which the human race has committed from creation down to the present day, were added together in one vast aggregate,' he told the House, 'they would scarcely equal the amount of guilt which has been incurred by mankind in connection with this diabolical slave trade'.[9]

The legality of the searches and seizures of foreign slave ships by the West Africa Squadron was dependent upon the terms of each individual treaty, and the exact rights and powers of British commanders in relation to the ships they pursued were often in doubt, until the moment the ship was boarded. The commanders were well aware that each action risked sparking a diplomatic incident that might damage Britain's international relations as well as their own career prospects. The complexity of the network of treaties under which the squadron operated and the dangers of exceeding the authority they granted, is evident in the *Instructions for the Guidance of Her Majesty's Naval Officers Employed in the Suppression of the Slave Trade*, an official document of 684 pages issued by the Admiralty in 1844. By that point the squadron had expanded to twenty-one ships and the number of interceptions had increased significantly. In order to determine whether they were acting within their rights, all captains and senior officers were instructed to make themselves 'thoroughly conversant with the Treaties, Conventions, and Laws, as well as with all the Instructions given to you relative to the Slave Trade'[10] and to ensure that junior officers under their command had access to copies of the treaties.

As British diplomats were constantly engaged in negotiating new treaties and seeking to extend, amend or ratify existing ones, commanders off the coast of Africa struggled to keep up to date. Even if a captain mastered the international law upon which his authority rested there was still some degree of interpretation. The latitude for error, and consequently the potential for diplomatic incident, was vast, especially as one trick of slave-traders was to operate under false flags. A favourite flag was that of the United States, with which Britain struggled to agree a lasting, enforceable and mutually acceptable anti-slave-trading treaty. Some slave ships were caught travelling with multiple flags ready to be hoisted in the hope that they would ward off the attentions of the Royal Navy cruisers. This disguise was completed by false documentation that pretended to demonstrate that the ship belonged to a nation with which Britain had no anti-slavery treaty.

Lieutenant Fitzgerald, the commander of HMS *Buzzard* of the squadron, was one of the speakers at the World Anti-Slavery Convention in London in 1840. He told the delegates about a recent incident in which the captain of an intercepted ship that was clearly equipped for slave-trading attempted to conceal her identity in order to avoid being sent to the Mixed Commission Court, which adjudicated over seized ships of other nations. In this case the court was in New York, where, in theory at least, he might have faced the death penalty. Fitzgerald explained that, 'In January last, I arrived off a port of the African coast in the ship I commanded, about two o'clock in the morning. I sent my boats to . . . the American brig [the] *Eagle* . . . I went on board, . . . and stated that I should send an increased force to convey her to America. The Captain then said that it was in vain to hold out longer; that she was a Spanish vessel; that he was an American; and that he had hoped to prevent her detention by British cruizers, by displaying the American flag . . . We took possession of the vessel, and the American Captain threatened to complain to his government, alleging that the capture of the vessel would lead to a war between the two countries'.[11]

False papers and false colours were two among an arsenal of ruses and evasions employed by the slave-traders. From the boom in slave-trading in the 1820s until its slow decline in the 1850s and 1860s deadly games of cat and mouse were played off the coast of Africa, as both sides sought to refine their tactics and find new ways to achieve their ends. Slave ships learnt to loiter in the blockaded rivers and lagoons around the Bights of Benin and Biafra until the ships of the West Africa Squadron were forced to return to Freetown for supplies; only then would they make for the open sea. Slave captains would wait for moonless nights, then race to the river mouths and silently slip past the British patrols in the inky darkness.

The consistently high prices paid for slaves, especially in Brazil and Cuba, encouraged slavers to invest in what amounted to a technological arms race, and slave ships became faster, sleeker and better gunned. Slave-ship captains also took greater risks when confronted. With so much at stake, slave captains fought with increasingly grim determination, willing to accept casualties among their own crews and prepared to inflict them on the British. Deaths among the helpless captives on the slave decks were regarded as collateral damage, the mere loss of valuable stock.

In the mid-1850s the British explorer William Baikie, on an expedition across parts of what is today Nigeria, saw this game of cat and mouse at close quarters and understood the motivations behind it. In the conclusion to his book describing his journey he warned that while the squadron was 'a very valuable agent', from what he had seen, 'its influence is only temporary and local. As long as we closely blockade the known slaving-ports, the traffic will be for the time knocked up in them; but as soon as the ships are withdrawn, slavers again appear . . . for such a lucrative trade other outlets are soon formed.'[12] Having witnessed the international slave trade at its most determined, Baikie believed that the profits were so high that the only way it could be suppressed would be for Britain to declare slave-traders to be pirates and therefore liable to more draconian punishments and subject to more vigorous military actions. Frederick Forbes, a highly successful commander with the West Africa Squadron, concluded that 'So long as there is a demand there will be slavers.'[13]

Beyond the difficulties of locating and intercepting the slave ships, the greatest limitation to the activities of the West Africa Squadron was its terms of engagement. The bilateral treaties under which it operated stipulated the ships could only be seized if they were caught, so to speak, red-handed, with slaves on board. This meant that intercepted ships loaded with chains, manacles and the general, grotesque paraphernalia of the trade, as well as ships that had been clearly fitted out to carry slaves, were immune, even though their intentions were obvious to all. This inspired a brutal logic. When West Africa Squadron ships were sighted the captives were landed on the nearest shore, but if the slavers were pursued the commanders threw the slaves overboard. If they were searched their slave decks would be empty, leaving the navy with no legal cause to arrest the crew or confiscate the ship, which was free to seek a new cargo. It was a calculation similar to that made by the crew of the *Zong* in 1781 when they threw 133 slaves overboard in the hope of claiming the insurance upon their loss. William Baikie believed 'there is no captain who has carried slaves, who has not been, either directly or indirectly, guilty of murder'.[14]

To eliminate this perverse incentive, Equipment Clauses began to be written into the treaties, allowing the West Africa Squadron to seize vessels fitted out for the trade even if there were no slaves on board. They were clearly drafted by men who knew their business and who had listened to the accounts of officers with direct experience of the tactics of the slave-traders. Material that rendered a ship liable for seizure included not just chains and 'handcuffs' but also 'extraordinary' quantities of rice, manioc or cassava, 'or any other article of food beyond the probable wants of the crew'. Modifications to a ship were also regarded as evidence of the intent to traffic slaves. These included the presence on board of 'a boiler, or other cooking apparatus, of an unusual size', 'divisions, or bulkheads, in the hold or on deck, in greater number than are necessary for vessels engaged in lawful trade' or additional planks that might be 'laid down as a second or slave deck'.[15] Slave ships seized by the squadron were known under maritime law as 'prizes', and they were sailed to the West Africa Squadron's base at Freetown and anchored in one of the many bays that surrounded the settlement. In 1819 the British established a Vice Admiralty Court there to try British subjects caught trading in slaves. Also in Freetown was the Mixed Commission Court, staffed by a British magistrate, a commissary judge and a commissioner of arbitration from each of the nations with which Britain had signed an anti-slavery treaty. There were at various times Anglo-Spanish, Anglo-Portuguese, Anglo-Brazilian and Anglo-Dutch judges in Freetown, the lists of judges and the nations they represented constantly changing as treaties were signed and lapsed. To administer what had become a global system of slave-trade suppression there were also Vice Admiralty Courts at St Helena and the Cape of Good Hope, and Mixed Commission Courts in Cape Town, New York, Rio de Janeiro, Paramaribo in Suriname and Kingston in Jamaica. Slave ships of no known nationality, described as being 'without colours or papers', were handed over to the Vice Admiralty Court in Freetown, but as in the case of the American brig *Eagle*, ships were occasionally sailed across the Atlantic, with the enslaved people still on board, to be legally confiscated by the appropriate court. Sierra Leone's deserved reputation for deadly tropical diseases meant that the list of lawyers and judges willing to consider an appointment to the Freetown courts was always short, and lack of qualified officials meant that its early years were marred by corruption and administrative chaos. When it was first established, it had to wait for two years for the appointed judge, Robert Thorpe from Canada, to arrive. Thorpe, who was a committed believer in abolition, went some way to improving the situation.

The court confiscated slave ships and slave-trading equipment and formally freed the captives, but were largely unable to impose punishments upon the crews or owners of foreign slave ships, as foreign powers resisted giving Britain these rights. They were technically subject to criminal charges by their own governments but this was rarely enforced. Consequently the inns and bars of Freetown were full of the crews of slave ships that had been confiscated but who evaded any personal punishment, and they were open to offers from slave-traders and captains who used Freetown almost as a recruiting office for future expeditions. The Florentine slave-trader Theophilus Conneau noted that Freetown abounded with 'prisoners from prizes [ships] and men of all nations', gloating that he was free to gather together crews for slave-trading expeditions from the bars and the back streets.[16] The authorities and governors of Freetown were well aware of the actions and attitudes of men like Conneau, but as the only means of closing this loophole was to renegotiate the bilateral treaties, they were powerless to intervene.

Although largely forgotten today, Britain's mission to suppress the slave trade was celebrated at the time. Ships that were particularly successful interceptors became momentarily famous, along with their captains. A handful, most notably the *Black Joke*, enjoyed longer fame. She gained her formidable reputation in early 1829 after a thirty-one-hour, night-and-day pursuit of the Spanish slave ship the *Almirante*. The *Black Joke*, a sleek Baltimore-built clipper, was a former slave ship. Under the flag of Brazil and the name *Henriqueta*, she transported over three thousand Africans to the New World plantations, but ran out of luck one day in 1827 when she was intercepted by HMS *Sybille*. Caught with five hundred and sixty-nine captives on board there was no need to resort to the Equipment Clauses and the *Henriqueta* was claimed as a prize, sold at auction in Freetown and purchased by the navy. Poacher was turned gamekeeper and she became the fastest ship in the squadron. In her action with the *Almirante*, *Black Joke* pounded the larger, more powerfully armed ship into submission, killing fifteen members of the crew and liberating 466 Africans from the hellish conditions of her fetid slave decks. That epic pursuit and victory against the odds, combined with the subsequent capture of three further slave ships and the liberation of over a thousand more Africans, made the *Black Joke* a legend, the subject of excited newspaper reports and admiring paintings. The *Black Joke* was as famous in Freetown as in London. In 1832 it was discovered that some of her timbers were rotten and the Admiralty ordered that she be destroyed. She was burnt in

Freetown on 3 May. A British writer who visited the city the following year claimed that, 'So efficient were her services, that many a negro who had been liberated by her is said to have wept on beholding the conflagration'. He claimed that there were 'feasts and rejoicings amongst the slave-merchants' of West Africa as they celebrated the 'destruction of their scourge.'[17]

In the cavernous storage facility in which the National Maritime Museum keeps its vast collection of naval art – one of the largest in Britain – are numerous paintings of the ships of the British West Africa Squadron. Contemporary artists tended to depict the squadron's ships in action rather than at anchor. They are shown, heroically pursuing or confronting the slave ships. William John Huggins' painting *The Capture of the Slaver 'Formidable' by HMS Buzzard, 17 December 1834* is one of the more dramatic.[18] It records the moment the Spanish slaver *El Formidable* surrendered to the British brigantine in the Bight of Benin. The chase lasted seven hours and the engagement between the two ships a further forty-five minutes. The *Buzzard*, which was at a considerable disadvantage with only ten guns to the eighteen of the *Formidable*, is largely concealed in the painting behind the smoke of her own gunfire. The Spanish ship lost seven of her crew and she is shown with her sails ripped by British shots. The painting contains other details that the informed viewer could pick out, such as the netting that festoons the slave ship's deck, which was deployed to prevent escape attempts by the enslaved. The *Formidable* is foregrounded in the painting, emphasizing the huge 'disparity of force' that existed between the two vessels, a disadvantage that, it implies, was overcome by British bravery. Huggins' painting was the product of a morally and militarily confident nation. Both paintings and press reports tended to pander to a British public that, during the long wars with France, had grown used to regular accounts of military engagements and now, in an age of relative peace, still hankered for tales of British military prowess. Viewers of British naval art and the readers of the increasingly popular newspapers and periodicals could feel doubly proud of these feats of arms that demonstrated the nation's power and her moral rectitude. What paintings of the West Africa Squadron tended to skirt over were the victims of the slave trade themselves.[19] There were seven hundred and seven Africans on board *El Formidable*, three hundred and seven of whom had 'perished from disease and misery'[20] by the time she had sailed to Freetown. Similarly absent from popular accounts and paintings of the squadron is the role that Africans played in the crews of the slavery suppression vessels. A number of ships, including the *Black Joke*, had sailors from the Kru people of Liberia, the state which neighbours Sierra Leone. The Kru, who traditionally worked as fishermen, possessed detailed knowledge of the West African coastline, and as pilots and regular seamen, they assisted the British commanders, who often struggled to compete with the more experienced slave-traders. Some Kru, along with Bassa peoples from Liberia, migrated over the border and settled in and around Freetown and elsewhere. There is a district of modern Freetown still known as Kru Bay, where the Kru immigrants settled in the nineteenth century. Today Kru Bay has sadly degenerated into one of the city's worst and the most polluted slums, the waters covered in a shifting tide of plastic bottles and sewage, the shoreline patrolled by herds of large black pigs. Later in the nineteenth century Kru communities slowly emerged in other British ports including Liverpool and London.[21]

With some justification, the efforts of the British West Africa Squadron and Britain's wider commitment to the suppression of the international slave trade have been criticized for being half-hearted or tokenistic. Critics at the time believed the task of halting the Atlantic trade was too vast an undertaking even for Britain, and went against her national interests, while more recently historians have pointed out how the mission to end slavery dovetailed with suspicious ease into British colonial expansion in Africa, allowing British power and trade to penetrate into the region in the second half of the nineteenth century. There is little doubt that the West Africa Squadron was never given the resources to comprehensively confront the slave-traders. From the start the ships were too few, and many of those later dispatched to increase its strength were too old and too slow to perform their task effectively. Lord Palmerston complained that too many of the squadron's ships were 'old tubs' and it is significant that the *Black Joke*, most successful and celebrated ship of the squadron, was a converted slaver and not dispatched from Britain by the Admiralty.[22] Yet Britain's crusade was supported by successive British governments of different political stripes, all of which found funds for it and defended it from its detractors. The mission was also given considerable bureaucratic backing and diplomatic assistance, and in 1841, a dedicated Slave Trade Department was created within the Foreign Office. This department had its own offices and staff, who administered the jumble of treaties, kept track of the global slave-trading networks,[23] and drafted diplomatic agreements between Britain and the states whose trades it was seeking to suppress.[24] British consuls and ambassadors monitored the movement of shipping, gathering intelligence and even paying bribes for information in support of the anti-slavery cause.[25] They fed their dispatches and reports into the Foreign Office, which collated a detailed global picture of the trade. All this activity was a significant item of national expenditure. The navy spent around a twentieth of its budget to man and provision the West Africa Squadron,[26] while over a million pounds was paid out in prize money to the officers and crews between 1807 and 1846.[27] The expense was a constant complaint for those opposed to the mission. In 1845 the Liberal MP William Hutt claimed that the cost to the nation of almost four decades of anti slave trade patrolling had reached a figure double the £20 million the government had paid to forty-six thousand British slave owners who had claimed compensation eleven years earlier.[28] Alongside the expense of manning and supplying the ships of the squadron there was also the not inconsiderable cost of administering and developing the colony of Sierra Leone. Expenditure there irked opponents, especially when it increased under Charles McCarthy, the most energetic and far-sighted of the colony's governors, who began a series of infrastructure projects in the 1820s, the remnants of which are scattered across the centre of modern Freetown.

Opponents and critics also suggested that Britain's attempts to quell the international trade had given rise to a number of unintended and unfortunate consequences, some of which were exacerbating rather than alleviating the suffering of Africans. They suggested that the threat of being caught by British cruisers encouraged slave-traders to transport their captives in conditions even more inhumane and injurious to health than those they might be persuaded to adopt if the trade were legal and regulated, and called for Britain to use her military power to police and regulate the international trade. Another unintended effect was the increase in the price of slaves in the Americas, which of course, in turn, increased the potential profits of slave-trading and encouraged more adventurers to enter into the trade. One of the most bizarre and counterproductive aspects of the system related to the slave ships at Freetown. The treaties demanded that impounded ships be auctioned off – their destruction was explicitly prohibited under some treaties. While this ensured the proceeds were divided between the two relevant states, the ships were sold to the highest bidder, and ships designed for slave-trading or adapted and fitted out for it inevitably attracted foreign slave-traders and their agents. Notorious slave-traders arranged for prize ships to be purchased in Freetown then redeployed on slave-trading expeditions under false flags and papers. The Spanish slave-trader Pedro Blanco, who was based at the Lomboko slave factory at the mouth of the Gallinas River in southern Sierra Leone, openly maintained an agent in Freetown who bought prize ships and transported them to his employer.[29] Similar purchases were made by the Florentine slave-trader Theophilus Conneau, who left us a detailed account of his dismal career. In *A Slaver's Log Book: Or 20 Years' Residence in Africa*, he bragged that 'At Sierra Leone in 1829, prize vessels were publicly sold and fitted out with very little trouble for the coast of Africa. Availing myself of the nonchalance of the Government officer, I fitted my schooner in perfect order to take a cargo of slaves immediately on my leaving port. My crew consisted of prisoners from prizes and men of all nations'.[30] Auctioning off seized slave ships eventually stopped: breaking-up clauses were inserted into the treaties and from the mid-1830s onwards they were taken to pieces or burnt. The site, on the northern edge of the Freetown peninsula, is still known as Destruction Bay. Lined with grim favelas, its beach is constantly lined with fishing boats that head out to their fishing grounds over the watery graveyard of the slave fleets of Brazil, Spain and Portugal. Another criticism was that the bounty paid to the captains, officers and crews allowed men to profit from what was generally portrayed, in Britain, as a purely moral and selfless crusade. The payment of bounties was a long naval tradition; as enshrined within the Act of 1807 it meant that money was paid for every captive liberated from a slave ship; the going rates were £40 for a man, £30 for a woman and £10 for a child under fourteen. There were changes to these rates over the years but the financial incentive remained part of the mission to the end, although a slow and opaque bureaucracy that siphoned much of the money off to various intermediaries meant that crews often received little of what was due to them on paper. A further attraction to service in the squadron was the potential for career advancement and there were men who regarded a commission to West Africa as a means of improving their prospects. The lure of prize money and opportunities to rise through the ranks that service in the West Africa Squadron offered were attractions that had to be weighed against a number of powerful disincentives. Service in the slavery suppression ships carried serious risks of disease and death. Crews were ravaged by malaria and yellow fever, which came on top of the long list of maladies to which nineteenth-century sailors were exposed whatever the nature of their duties and wherever they were deployed. Over its sixty-year history more than seventeen thousand British seamen died while serving in the West Africa Squadron, most from disease. Yet the real victims of this practice were of course the enslaved Africans. We know how British crews were expected to behave towards the captives they found on board slave ships. The 1844 *Instructions for the Guidance of Her Majesty's Naval Officers Employed in the Suppression of the Slave Trade* stipulated that 'Every effort' was to be made 'to alleviate their sufferings and improve their condition'. This was to be achieved in the immediate term 'by a careful attention to cleanliness and ventilation, by separating the sickly from those who are in good health, by encouraging the Slaves to feel confidence in Her Majesty's Officers and men, and promoting amongst them cheerfulness and exercise.'[31] The gulf between these earnest instructions and what sometimes occurred is demonstrated in the case of the Brazilian schooner the *Umbelina*. She was intercepted by HMS *Sybille* in mid-January 1829, two days out of Lagos with 377 slaves on board. A British officer from the *Sybille* was appointed prize-master, and he and a crew were sent on board the slaver to sail her to Freetown. But it was not until 13 March, two months later, that the *Umbelina* arrived in Sierra Leone, by which time, as the relevant

Parliamentary papers tell us, '194 of the unfortunate creatures' she had been attempting to liberate had perished. The death toll among the captives was so shocking that the prize-master issued an affidavit, 'accounting for the immense number of deaths that had occurred on the passage up; he deposed, that those deaths did not ensue through the neglect of himself, or any of his crew'.[32] As the centre of slave-trading activity moved further to the east towards the Bights of Benin and Biafra there were calls for the West Africa Squadron to abandon its base at Freetown and relocate on the island of Fernando Po. When that location proved to be every bit as malarial and sickly as Sierra Leone, the plans were abandoned.

Captives who survived their journey to Freetown were kept on board the prize ships until the courts adjudicated on their legality or illegality. As ship's captains and the agents of the slave-traders were prone to string proceedings out and argue for time, conditions worsened and death tolls increased. It was for this reason that the sufferings of the victims of the Brazilian schooner *Umbelina* did not end in March 1830, when the ship was anchored in Freetown harbour. They were kept on board awaiting the adjudication of the Mixed Commission Court, which took until 13 May to determine her 'good and lawful prize to Great Britain and Brazil, and as taken in the illicit traffick in slaves'. During those two months twenty of her captives died, and only after the verdict had been read out were the remaining 163 finally brought ashore.[33] In May 1833 a Spanish ship, *La Pantica*, which had sailed from Havana and been intercepted off the coast of what is now Nigeria, was brought into Freetown. As the ship 'glanced up the estuary', she was spotted by lookouts on the hills above the city and preparations for her arrival made. The English writer F. Harrison Rankin was permitted to go on board. He described the scene he encountered in his African memoir.

> We easily leaped on board, as she lay low in the water. The first hasty glance around caused a sudden sickness and faintness, followed by an indignation more intense than discreet. Before us, lying in a heap, huddled together at the foot of the foremast, on the bare and filthy deck, lay several human beings in the last stage of emaci- ation — dying. The ship fore and aft was thronged with men, women, and children, all entirely naked, and disgusting with

disease. The stench was nearly insupportable, cleanliness being impossible. I stepped to the hatchway; it was secured by iron bars and cross bars, and pressed against them were the heads of slaves below. It appeared that the crowd on deck formed one-third only of the cargo, two-thirds being stowed in a sitting posture below between-decks; the men forward, the women aft. Two hundred and seventy-four were at this moment in the little schooner. When captured, three hundred and fifteen had been found on board; forty had died during the voyage from the Old Calabar, where she had been captured by [the Royal Navy ship] H. M. Fair Rosamond, and one had drowned himself on arrival . . . It was not, however, until the second visit, on the following day, that the misery which reigns in a slave-ship was fully understood. The rainy season had commenced, and during the night rain had poured heavily down. Nearly a hundred slaves had been exposed to the weather on deck, and amongst them the heap of dying skeletons at the fore-mast. After making my way through the clustered mass of women on the quarter-deck, I discovered the slave-captain, who had also been part-owner, comfortably asleep in his cot, undisturbed by the horrors around him.[34]

On his second visit to the captured ship the author observed how, even while they were at anchor in harbour at Freetown, the sufferings of the enslaved did not come to an end. He described how, having been registered on board the *La Pantica*, the slaves were forced back into the slave deck, which was only twenty-two inches from floor to ceiling.

The captives were now counted; their numbers, sex, and age written down, for the information of the Court of Mixed Commission. The task was repulsive. As the hold had been divided for the separation of the men and the women, those on deck were first counted; they were then driven forward, crowded as much as possible, and the women were drawn up through the small hatchway from their hot, dark confinement. A black boatswain seized them one by one, dragging them before us for a moment, when the proper officer in a glance decided the age, whether above or under fourteen; and they were instantly swung again by the arm into their loathsome cell, where another negro boatswain, with a whip or stick, forced them to resume the bent and painful attitude necessary for the storage of so large a number. The unfortunate women and girls, in general, submitted with quiet resignation . . . A month had made their condition familiar to them. One or two were less philosophical, or suffered more acutely than the rest. Their shrieks rose faintly from the hidden prison, as violent compulsion alone squeezed them into their nook against the curve of the ship's side . . . The agony of the position of the crouching slaves maybe imagined, especially that of the men, whose heads and necks are bent down by the boarding above them. Once so fixed, relief by motion or change of posture is unattainable. The body frequently stiffens into a permanent curve; and in the streets of Freetown I have seen liberated slaves in every conceivable state of distortion . . . Many can never resume the upright posture.[35]

The most horrific account of the failure of the squadron to protect the lives of the Africans in its care comes from the Reverend Pascoe Hill, who was the chaplain on board HMS *Cleopatra*. In 1834 the *Cleopatra* captured a Spanish slave ship and Hill was witness to an incident that is shocking even by the bleak standards of the Atlantic slave trade. His description of what took place, which he published under the title *Fifty Days on Board a Slave-Vessel in the Mozambique Channel*, tells of how the four hundred and forty-seven captives liberated from the Spanish ship were brought out on deck to regain their strength. The suggestion that a hundred of them should be transferred to the *Cleopatra*, in order to reduce the overcrowding, was rejected as some of the enslaved were thought to have smallpox, but later, when the British sailors 'having to shorten sail suddenly . . . found the poor helpless creatures lying about the deck an obstruction to getting at the ropes and doing what was required', the calamitous decision was made 'to send them all below', into a slave hold that was just twelve yards in length and seven in breadth, and only three and a half feet high. The results were horrific yet predictable.

Being thrust back, and striving the more to get out, the after-hatch was forced down on them. Over the other hatchway, in the fore-part of the vessel, a wooden grating was fastened. To this, the sole inlet for the air, the suffocating heat of the hold, and, perhaps, panic from the strangeness of their situation, made them press; and thus great part of the space below was rendered useless. They crowded to the grating, and, clinging to it for air, completely barred its entrance. They strove to force their way through apertures, in length fourteen inches, and barely six inches in breadth, and, in some instances, succeeded. The cries, the heat, – I may say, without exaggeration, 'the smoke of their torment,' – which ascended, can be compared to nothing earthly. One of the Spaniards gave warning that the consequence would be 'many deaths.'[36]

The following day, Holy Thursday, the slave decks were opened.

The Spaniard's prediction of last night, this morning was fearfully verified. Fifty-four crushed and mangled corpses lifted up from the slave-deck have been brought to the gang-way and thrown overboard. Some were emaciated from disease; many, bruised and bloody . . . some were found strangled, their hands still grasping each other's throats, and tongues protruding from their mouths. The bowels of one were crushed out. They had been trampled to death for the most part, the weaker under the feet of the stronger, in the madness and torment of suffocation from crowd and heat. It was a horrid sight, as they passed one by one, – the stiff distorted limbs smeared with blood and filth, – to be cast into the sea. Some, still quivering, were laid on the deck to die; salt water thrown on them to revive them, and a little fresh water poured into their mouths.[37]

The high rates of death among the supposedly liberated slaves shocked the anti-slavery lobby in Britain and accounts like that of the Reverend Pascoe Hill were published in magazines and discussed at public meetings. To opponents of the West Africa Squadron it was the high mortality rates among British sailors rather than African captives that drew their ire. The high death rates of sailors in the squadron and the high costs of treating many who were sent for hospitalization in the healthier Royal Navy bases of St Helena and Ascension Island were seized upon by those who argued that the mission was too dangerous and expensive and who called for the withdrawal of the squadron and the abandonment of the mission.

Despite the dangers and despite disasters like the deaths on board the *Umbelina* there were officers and men of the squadron who were willing to take risks and endure hardships as they were personally committed to their nation's crusade against the slave trade. Some were abolitionists by conviction. A few had campaigned for the abolition of the slave trade or were the sons of notable abolitionists. Captain Edward Columbine, who in 1809 became Governor of Sierra Leone, was a personal friend of William Wilberforce. Captain Joseph Denman of HMS *Wanderer*, who commanded the northern division of the squadron between 1839 and 1841, was the son of the abolitionist Chief Justice Lord Denman and a diligent and tire-less pursuer of slave ships. In 1840 Denman took one of the most decisive and controversial actions in the entire history of the squadron. He was asked by the Governor of Sierra Leone to effect the rescue of Fry Norman, a Freetown washerwoman who, along with her baby, had been seized and taken to a cluster of islands in the Gallinas River. This region, south of Freetown on the border between Sierra Leone and Liberia, was a favoured point of departure for slave ships and it was presumed that mother and child, both British citizens, were at risk of being transported into slavery. Denman arrived at the Gallinas and found Spanish slavers in posses-sion of a large number of captives. He freed ninety of them, located Fry Norman and her child, and then over the next three days destroyed the Spanish slave stockades. Denman and his men then liberated hundreds of other captives and drove away the slave-traders. Exceeding his orders and acting extra-legally he also persuaded the local king, under the threat of military force, to sign a treaty denouncing the slave trade. Denman returned to Freetown with eight hundred and forty-one liberated Africans. He was soon after promoted, and congratulated by Lord Palmerston. However the Spanish slave-traders sued him for damages in the Court of the Exchequer. The case rumbled on for eight years. Eventually Denman was acquitted and all claims for damages brought by the slave-traders of the Gallinas were rejected.[38]

The greatest criticism of Britain's crusade against the Atlantic slave trade has to be that the vast majority of slave ships were not intercepted. When measured in raw statistical terms, the anti-slavery squadron was a failure. It has been estimated that around one in five of the approximately 7,750 slave ships that were engaged in the Atlantic trade between 1808 and 1867 were condemned by the courts; 85 per cent of those interceptions were the work of the Royal Navy.[39] In all, around a hundred and sixty thousand African captives were liberated. For those thousands of men, women and children, people whose shackles were broken off and who were guided out of the gloom of the slave decks and landed on King Jimmy's Wharf in Freetown, their personal liberation was miraculous. But they represented only around 6 per cent of the approximately 2.7 million Africans who were captured and put on slave ships bound for the Americas in the three decades after 1836.[40] In its first decades of operation not only did the squadron fail to have a significant impact on the scale of the Atlantic trade, it watched impotently as the trade increased markedly. By the 1820s it reached levels of intensity beyond even those of the 1780s, when the British trade was at its apex. Those statistics can be looked at another way. The frenetic intensity of early-nineteenth-century slave-trading, and the surging demand for enslaved Africans in Cuba and Brazil, could be read as further proof of how remarkable Britain's decision to abolish the slave trade in 1807 was. The historian of slavery Seymour Drescher has described British abolition as an act of 'econocide', a policy that ran counter to British economic interests. However, the decision to abandon the trade somewhere near the apex of its profitability made the task of suppression almost impossible in the 1820s and 1830s, as ruthless new players joined the trade. There were hopes that the coming of peace in 1815 would free ships for service off the African coast, but peace also meant that thousands of mariners who had served on warships and merchantmen during the long wars were suddenly diverted into the slave trade.

Despite its evident inability to turn the tide against the slave-traders, there is evidence to suggest that the efforts of the West Africa Squadron acted as a deterrent, reducing the numbers of ships and captains who were tempted to embark upon slave-trading expeditions and reducing the numbers of Africans carried into bondage.[41] Britain's slave-trade-suppression policy was at its most effective in the 1840s and 1850s, and was at its most impressive when confronting the trades of the states that most determinedly resisted British diplomatic and military pressures. In the 1830s Portugal was the most recalcitrant power, in part because of her own political chaos and the inability of weak governments in Lisbon to stand up to their own slave-traders. By the middle of the nineteenth century it was Brazil that had established herself as the greatest obstacle to ending the Atlantic trade, and it was to her harbours that the majority of the captives shipped from Africa were dispatched. In 1845, after failing repeatedly to secure a long-term and meaningful anti-slave-trading treaty with Brazil, an Act of Parliament unilaterally authorized British ships to intercept and search Brazilian ships on the high seas. This tactic provided the anti-slave-trading ships of the Royal Navy with powers that were normally exercised only against nations with which Britain was at war. Between 1846 and 1850 the majority of ships the squadron targeted were Brazilian or bound for Brazil. In 1850 Britain engaged in what amounted to a blockade of Brazil's slave ports. That year the West Africa Squadron, under Admiral Sir Barrington Reynolds, launched an attack on the Brazilian port Macaé, to the north of Rio de Janeiro. There they caught four Brazilian slavers at anchor. Two they burned, one was scuttled by her own crew and the fourth was sent back to Africa under escort to face the Mixed Commission Court. This abandonment of diplomatic persuasion in favour of military force represented a flagrant violation of international law and Brazilian sovereignty. But by the end of the 1850s this aggressive policy had paid off and Brazil's slave trade had been reduced to a trickle.

If the West Africa Squadron was a humanitarian intervention then Freetown in those decades became what today we would call a reception centre for the refugees of the Atlantic slave trade. The city and the peninsula behind it were transformed. Britain's mission to confront and stifle the Atlantic trade added new demographic strata onto the existing layers of settlement and, in doing so, largely created the unique arrangement of communities, ethnicities, faiths and languages that to some extent characterizes the modern city. The way was cleared for these new influxes in 1807. That year the Sierra Leone Company, having incurred mounting losses, handed its interest in the colony over to the government and Sierra Leone became a Crown Colony, still ruled from London but by civil servants rather than company directors. This transition, as the historian Robin Law has noted, marked the start of Britain's colonial empire in tropical Africa. Between 1808 and the 1860s around ninety thousand Africans from the intercepted slave ships were freed from slavery by the courts in Freetown.[42] They were known as the Liberated Africans or the 'Recaptives' – as they had been captured by slave-traders and then recaptured by the navy. They were concentrated in Sierra Leone as it was there that the squadron was based and there that the Mixed Commission and Vice Admiralty Courts sat. Most of the Recaptives were settled in and around Freetown because it had been decided in London that attempting to return them to their home regions across West and even Central Africa would be impossible, and would place newly liberated peoples at renewed risk of recapture and re-enslavement as their homelands remained within reach of the inland slave-traders and their business partners on the rivers and at the coast. The reception of the Recaptives in Freetown and their treatment by the British authorities varied somewhat from year to year and through the various stages during which the West Africa Squadron and the courts were operative, but in general Africans, newly liberated from the slave ships, first placed their feet back on African soil at King Jimmy's Wharf, named after the king who had destroyed Granville Sharp's Province of Freedom in 1789. The wharf was close to where the Nova Scotian settlers had established themselves in the 1790s and it is believed to have been near where the first Portuguese slave-traders had laid anchor centuries earlier. From the waterfront they were brought to a special compound known as the King's Yard. One of the two original gateways that led into the King's Yard has survived the passing of two centuries. It is made from a heavy local stone, which can be seen peeking out from beneath several coats of white and grey paint that have blistered and flaked away under the glare of the West African sun. Above the arched gateway is a small limestone slab on which is written an inscription dating from 1817: 'Royal Asylum and Hospital for Africans rescued from slavery by British Valour and Philanthropy Erected AD MDCCCXVII – H.E. Lt. Col. McCarthy'. This modest marker belies the significance of the King's Yard in African history. During the decades of the West Africa Squadron, the King's Yard was where the liberated Africans were assembled, counted and medically assessed. The sick were admitted to the rudimentary hospital that used to stand on part of the site. The connection between that portion of Freetown and medicine has been retained; there are still a number of medical centres clustered around the site and within what was the King's Yard is an eye hospital.

We have a first-hand account of the workings of the West Africa Squadron and the King's Yard from F. Harrison Rankin, who visited Freetown in the mid-1830s. He described his experiences and his observations in his book, *The White Man's Grave: A Visit to Sierra Leone*. Although Rankin's account repeatedly betrays his own racial thinking, he was an important witness to the processes by which the majority of the liberated Africans were – despite enormous logistical difficulties and despite numerous ethical lapses – registered, processed and set on the road to becoming free and independent settlers in the Freetown colony. Rankin described the King's Yard as a 'large species of prison, consisting of the central house, within a square yard, surrounded by open sheds; the whole encompassed by high walls, and secured by well-guarded gates'.[43] His most powerful account was written in the summer of 1833 when the Spanish slave ship *La Pantica* was brought into Freetown harbour. The ship sailed from Havana and was intercepted by the Royal Navy with 317 slaves on board off the Old Calabar River, in modern Nigeria. When the ship was transported to Freetown the case was brought before a British and a Spanish judge of the Mixed Commission Court and *La Pantica* was quickly adjudicated as having been engaged in 'illicit slave trading'.[44] Rankin was there when the 270 slaves who had survived the journey from Calabar to Freetown were landed.

> Fifty were conveyed in each canoe; one expired during the transit, and another, a few minutes after landing, died before my eyes . . . The men and children were first brought into the Liberated Yard; and, being ranged in a line, a piece of cotton was given each. Several had no idea of the purpose for which it was intended. Few of the children seemed to approve of the new uncomfortable fashion. Decency had suggested the distribution of the scanty checked chemises to the women, previous to their landing. When clothed, and again counted, the whole were marched across the

street, from the Liberated Yard to the King's Yard, to await their final distribution as soldiers, wives, apprentices, and country gentlemen . . .

The young children soon recovered from their sufferings, and their elastic spirits seemed little injured. The men next rallied; but several died in the shed devoted to the most sickly, chiefly from dysentery: they were wrapped in a coarse grass mat, carried away, and buried without ceremony. Of the women many were dispatched to the hospital at Kissey, victims to raging fever; others had become insane. I was informed that insanity is the frequent fate of the women captives . . . The women sustain their bodily sufferings with more silent fortitude than the men, and seldom destroy themselves; but they brood more over their misfortunes, until the sense of them is lost in madness.[45]

Rankin also revealed that in the mid-1830s unmarried liberated women in the King's Yard were 'made available to Recaptive men as wives'. In a rather judgemental passage he reported that, 'captive women are eagerly pounced upon' by Recaptive men as wives.[46] He believed that 'The arbitrary consignment of women to matrimonial discipline might have been an experiment; the practice was mentioned as of recent adoption', and summarizing his observations on the practice he concluded: 'Their lot is not, perhaps, an unhappy one to themselves; it seems to violate no custom, it secures the usual comforts of married life where marriage is never the result of sentiment, and a disposal of them in every respect consistent with philanthropy and their own tastes might be difficult to devise . . . On the whole', Rankin determined, 'this method is not without its merits', though he conceded that 'its introduction would scarcely be popular in England.'[47]

Another process that took place in the King's Yard, or at other times on the decks of slave ships in Freetown harbour, was the registration of the Recaptives, and that process has generated a remarkable series of documents. The Registers of Liberated Africans are today held in the Sierra Leone National Archives at the new Fourah Bay College, in the hills above Freetown. A series of heavy, red-leather-bound ledgers, they contain hundreds of yellowing pages on which are recorded, in long columns, the names and identities of thousands of Africans who were landed at Freetown. When a slave ship was condemned and the people brought ashore, attempts were made to determine their origins and ethnicities. Then the call went out for people from the same regions who knew the local languages to come to the King's Yard and act as translators. The Registers of Liberated Africans are the result of these efforts. They begin in 1808 and run through to 1848 and contain 84,307 names. The name of each Recaptive was spelled out, as best as could be managed, by the registrars, and each Recaptive was assigned a unique number. Across the many pages and multiple volumes a running total was maintained, a figure which plotted the gradual re-population and demographic reordering of Freetown. The very last name in the registers is a girl named Marloryar, who was freed from the slave ship *Bela Miquelon* on 5 August 1848.[48]

Alongside the lists of names, in separate columns of the specially pre-printed ledgers, are recorded the age, height and sex of each Recaptive. The most revealing and most telling of the columns is 'Description'. Here the registrars catalogued the tattoos, scars, tribal marks, old injuries and scarifications of the tens of thousands of men, women and children brought before them. Their entries described ornate lines of long, flowing body tattoos and the raised keloid scarifications, stretching across the chests and stomachs, that indicated ethnic belonging or the attainment of adulthood. When faced with particularly elaborate patterns some of the registrars penned tiny drawings, rather than attempt to fit a complex description into the small space available: crosses and circles, long runs of small lines, or flourishes of dots and dashes. They record arrow-like symbols and extended tattoos that reached from necks and tapered around torsos. Some Recaptives are recorded as having been marked on their faces, cheeks and forehead. Others had black spots – presumably tattoos – under their eyes. One man called Renga, Recaptive number 1,030, was recorded as being five feet two inches tall and distinguishable by a 'large round scar on back, d[itt]o below right breast'. Under his left armpit there was a mark that was sketched out by the registrar.[49] Other entries record the marks impressed upon the bodies of the Recaptives by disease rather than cultural practice. The marks of smallpox were, seemingly, the most common disfigurement. One entry described a young man with no distinguishing marks who was listed as being 'without name'. In the Description column this was explained; he was 'deaf and dumb'. Other entries recorded the type of injuries and scars that might be expected to be found on the bodies of people who had been recently captured by slave-traders, marched long distances to the coast and shackled on slave decks. There were open wounds and cuts and one man had a musket wound through his left thigh. Some of the liberated Africans had been branded before their liberation, and carried the permanent stigmata of slavery into their lives as free people in Freetown..

The Atlantic slave trade channelled its victims through a process of deliberate de-individualization. As chattels the enslaved were rendered anonymous – at least in the eyes of the traders and the slave owners. This notion of the victims of the Atlantic trade as a great mass of de-individualized black humanity is suddenly and strikingly overthrown by the Registers of Liberated Africans. They cast a sudden flash of light upon the identities of individual Africans, at the very moment they were liberated from the slave ships of the Atlantic trade. Having somewhat miraculously escaped transport to the plantations in Brazil and Cuba we find them in the registers still with their African names, cultures, personal identities and sometimes their familial connections all intact, not yet obscured, hidden or contaminated by new slave personae that, in the Americas, were imposed from above or adopted from below as part of complex survival strategies. The Registers of Liberated Africans, especially when cross-referenced with other sources and evidence about slave voyages and the activities of the West Africa Squadron, open up possibilities for historians who hope to use the names and descriptions to determine where on the continent they came from and perhaps build up new understandings of which peoples were being caught in the great dragnet of the Atlantic trade during the early and middle decades of the nineteenth century.

The registers contain entries for liberated men who have the letters 'R.A.C.' following their names. This indicates that they were recruited directly into the Royal African Corps in the King's Yard compound itself, going from slave to free man and finally to soldier in days or perhaps even hours. These men served in regiments that operated both in Africa and the West Indies and some of the

Recaptives recruited into these units had little choice in the matter. Of the fifty-six thousand male Recaptives landed at Freetown during the period of the West Africa Squadron, more than two thousand 'Entered his Majesty's land services as Soldiers', four hundred of them being enlisted in the Royal African Corps for military service within West Africa.[50] The remaining men recruited from the King's Yard in Freetown were incorporated into the West India Regiment, a force whose duties included suppressing slave revolts on the sugar islands of the Caribbean. For a period recruits to both regiments were trained and garrisoned in the former slave fortress on Bunce Island. There they displaced the last employees of the company Anderson & Anderson, who had stayed on despite the end of the slave trade, the fortress and the once grand agents' house rotting away under their feet. The army approved of Bunce Island as a barracks as it was almost impossible for reluctant 'recruits' to escape. Both the Royal African Corps and the British West India Regiment have long and troubling histories, too complex to be explored here. Other Recaptives were recruited into the navy; some served in the ships of the West Africa Squadron – former slaves becoming crewmen on ships that intercepted slave vessels. During the 1820s and later, soldiers of the regiments recruited from the King's Yard and trained on Bunce Island were occasionally ordered to fight alongside the ships and men of the West Africa Squadron, confronting the slave-traders and their African trading partners – attacking their slave factories and barracoons on the coast.[51]

The most shocking aspect of what took place in the King's Yard in Freetown during the era of the anti-slave-trade mission involved the fates of children. A system of so-called apprenticeship operated in the Freetown colony, with children under fourteen liable to serve terms of three to seven years working for a master without pay. It was a system similar to that imposed upon the slaves of the British West Indies in 1833 and was, from the start, open to serious abuse. F. Harrison Rankin watched the process by which the children were selected as apprentices while being processed in the King's Yard. He noted that 'any resident in the colony, of any colour, may enter the King's Yard, select a girl or boy, and thereupon tie a string or a piece of tape around the neck as a mark of appropriation. He then pays ten shillings; and the passive child becomes his property, under the name of apprentice, for three years'.[52] He also noted that while 'The whites call the child so purchased . . . an apprentice, the blacks uniformly term it a slave'. 'I cannot conceive', he wrote, 'a system better adapted to favour the slave-trade than that of apprenticeship at Sierra Leone'.[53] There is incontrovertible evidence that apprentices in Freetown were badly treated and more disturbingly still that some of these infants were sold back into slavery. Having paid only 10 shillings for each apprentice, unscrupulous masters were able to make huge profits by selling them to inland slave-traders. The ten-shilling fee itself was imposed in 1824; before that, child apprentices were distributed free of charge. The fee was introduced in the hope that it would encourage masters to care more for their apprentices.[54] As a result of the re-enslavement of apprentices an unknown number of the captives brought into Freetown on slave ships intercepted by the Royal Navy were being liberated for a second time, having been kidnapped and resold. In 1831 three men were hanged for slave-trading in the colony.[55] As well as being apprenticed in Freetown, children from the King's Yard were also sent to work on Ascension Island and some were dispatched to the West Indies, where they found themselves labouring on New World plantations, as their original captors had intended – but as apprentices rather than slaves. A Commission of Inquiry into the state of captured Negroes in the West Indies was established to examine their conditions. Despite these abuses there were many child apprentices in Freetown who were happily drawn into communities made up of people with whom they shared language and culture. Some learned trades from their masters and effectively became part of their extended families. When a group of Recaptives from the Ashanti tribe, from what is now Ghana, arrived in Freetown they were adopted by the Jamaican Maroons, whose ancestors had been Ashanti. The Maroons evidently still regarded themselves as part of that ethnic grouping, despite having crossed the Atlantic and back again as slaves and then as rebels, over several generations.[56] Records of home-building and land-ownership held in the Freetown archives demonstrate that some apprentices thrived, built stone houses and established themselves in business. From the King's Yard those who were not recruited as soldiers, wives or apprentices were resettled in Freetown itself or in one of the villages that were established

around the Freetown peninsula, some of them in the hills behind
the city. The Recaptives were given a few months' financial support
to enable them to build a home and plant some crops, and it was
hoped that from that point onwards they would become independent.[57] Rankin noted that in the mid-1830s each liberated African,
having just been released from a slave ship with no possessions or
clothes, 'receives an outfit of a piece of cotton; and Government
allows him an iron pot for boiling rice, a spoon, and a few additional
domestic implements of similar simplicity and usefulness. He rears
a hut, with assistance from his neighbours; it is a square shed,
supported on a frame-work resting on eight or ten poles . . . Its
construction occupies from a few days to a month . . . Round his
rude dwelling the newly naturalised British subject obtains a grant
of land . . . . Being now established, and having started into civilised
life under the same auspices and advantages as others enjoyed before
him, he is henceforth left to his own management.'[58]

There were said to be seventeen 'nations' among the Recaptives
and after only three years of anti-slave-trade activity one thousand
nine hundred and ninety-one Recaptives had been landed in Freetown. By 1811 the new arrivals outnumbered the survivors from
the earlier waves of settlement and their children. The combined
populations of the Nova Scotians, the Maroons and the descendants
of the London black poor of the 1780s, if any had survived until
the early years of the nineteenth century, became the minority. By
1850 one hundred different ethnic groups had been jumbled together
onto the Freetown peninsula. They came from all along the three
thousand miles of coastline patrolled by the squadron. This incredible inflow of tens of thousands of Africans from disparate cultures
and of differing religions made Victorian Freetown a unique place,
its population growth unpredictable, its demographics unprecedented. At night it was said that the sounds of horns, drums and
songs of numerous tribes calling people to feasts and rites resonated
through the air, furrowing the brows of the earnest men of the
Church Mission Society and their converts who struggled to sweep
the city of idols and traditional forms of worship.[59] Until Sierra
Leone's brutal civil war in the 1990s, the majority of Freetown's
population was probably descended from men and women who
arrived in the city in captured slave ships and passed through the

gates of the King's Yard. A new lingua franca developed, a hybrid, amalgam language known as Krio. It has become one of the national languages of modern Sierra Leone, a nation in which the Krio people – the descendants of the original settlers and liberated Africans – were for so long politically, economically and culturally dominant.

The new arrivals tended to form communities based on their shared languages and ethnicities, and this process of community formation can be read even now on the map of modern Freetown. One district of the city retains the name Congo Cross, as it was near there that a group of Recaptives from the Congo decided to settle. They found a space for their new homes on the waterfront, after having tried and failed to settle in an inland village that had been abandoned by the local Temne people. To the east of Congo Cross is Kissy and the Kissy Road, where it is thought a group of Recaptives from the Kise-Kise River to the north of Sierra Leone built their dwellings and founded a community. Another group of Recaptives from a Portuguese-speaking region of the continent were landed in Freetown; where they settled is the district of Portuguese Town. Other Recaptives who had been imprisoned together on slave ships formed, in some instances, what was known as a 'Big Company', a community built on shared experience rather than shared language or kinship. Slaves in Jamaica who had endured the horrors of the Middle Passage were known to express similar bonds, regarding themselves as 'shipmates'. Decades after Granville Sharp had dreamed of transplanting the Anglo-Saxon Frankpledge onto the Freetown peninsula, the urge for social experimentation lived on. Some of the villages were designed as model communities, the missionaries and the local administrators gripped by a utopian spirit. For once the biggest dreamer was the man with the most power. Governor Charles McCarthy was determined to form the Recaptive villages into idealized Christian settlements. He ordered clocks, weathercocks and brass bells from England and had them installed in newly built stone churches. The schools were equipped with prayer books, quill pens and various textbooks. The missionaries taught the children English and the Bible, and one missionary wife taught the Recaptive women how to sew and make their own clothes. All this was paid for with government money and Church Mission

Society donations. When the Foreign Office received the bills they ordered the governor to make savings.[60]

By the 1820s the majority of the Recaptives arriving in the King's Yard were people of the Yoruba tribe from what is today Nigeria. Their arrival in Freetown was a reflection of the warfare and anarchy that had consumed that part of Africa. As the Oyo empire collapsed and new nations emerged from its ruins, African kings and Brazilian slave-traders launched slave raids and enslaved prisoners of war. The Nigerian slave ports of Lagos and Badagry became the new centre of the Atlantic trade, competing with the King of Dahomey's key slave port at Ouidah. It was on those waters that the squadron focused much of its attention.

In Sierra Leone the new arrivals became known as the Aku, a corruption of the common Yoruba greetings – phrases such as ek'abo and ek'ale. The Aku were scattered across the numerous villages built around Freetown – Murray Town, Aberdeen, Campbell Town, Leicester. In their villages they appointed headmen, and in the larger settlements chose oba, minor kings. They maintained their languages and traditions, some of which still survive in Freetown today. In another part of the Freetown peninsula, men who had served their term in the Royal African Corps were settled. These veterans of Britain's colonial wars named their villages after British military victories and the heroes of the British army – settlements named Hastings, Waterloo and Wellington can all be found on the modern map of the region. The village of Waterloo was founded in 1819, after the Napoleonic Wars, and named after the battle that ended that conflict. One of the streets of Waterloo, where the veterans built their houses and farmed their little plots, gained the name Soja (soldier) street.

Freetown in the middle decades of the nineteenth century became an exceptional settlement, part naval base for the West Africa Squadron and part burgeoning colonial city with an ever-expanding and uniquely disparate African population. The old settlers from Nova Scotia and Jamaica built distinctive homes in North American and West Indian colonial architectural styles. These dwellings had sweeping wooden verandas and stood on firm stone foundations. Liberated Africans who made some money in the city tended to copy the style, which became a feature of the city. A handful of Krio houses survive today, most of them in desperate states of disrepair. The somewhat unreal military economy of the city and the construction of a long list of civic buildings by the dynamic Governor Charles McCarthy led to a property boom. Goods and local agricultural products flowed into the city and like other colonial settlements Freetown became a magnet for European drifters and chancers. Europeans arrived as tailors, hairdressers and cooks, all looking to set up little businesses. Hotels sprang up, a racecourse was constructed and a society was founded to promote the arts and sciences. Both old settlers and Recaptives were drawn to the city, and became traders of various sorts. The more far-sighted and business-savvy bought consignments of trade goods that had been confiscated from the slave ships by the courts, alcohol, tobacco and cotton being common commodities.[61] With slave ships condemned on a regular basis, old settlers and liberated Africans jostled for trade. Many struggled to compete with European traders who had the connections and the capital to get the best deals and buy in bulk, among them former officers of the Royal African Corps. Despite these disadvantages there were notable business successes among the Recaptives. A few made enough money to buy and refit former slave-trading vessels and become coastal traders. Other trades and industries flourished. Timber was felled and then worked by sawyers; others traded in valuable dyewoods. As the number of stone buildings increased, people learnt to gather and burn oyster shells for the lime, which was brought to the city and sold to make mortar. Newly liberated Africans raised their first crops and tried to sell the surplus, usually cassava, and from this gather a little capital to invest. Others found work out on the Sierra Leone River as fishermen – the river remains an enormous source of food and sustenance for the people of Freetown.

The greatest problem confronting early Victorian Freetown was the problem that had decimated earlier waves of settlement: disease. Tropical fevers still carried away the lives of large numbers of Recaptives and British officials. The loss of colonial officials and administrators was so common that surviving officials had to hold numerous posts at the same time, while they awaited new arrivals from Britain. Of all the British colonies to which a sailor or colonial administrator could be dispatched, Sierra Leone, in the 1820s, remained the one with the highest rate of death by disease.[62] Yellow fever, cholera and malaria – often called remittent fever due to its habit of recurring – were common, as were a whole range of conditions that the local doctors struggled to identify. It was commonly believed that the most dangerous period for Europeans was their first few weeks in the country. If they survived their first and inevitable bout of tropical illness, their chances of long-term survival were said to be good. Locals called this period the 'seasoning', the term for the process by which newly landed slaves were forced to adjust to the brutal realities of plantation life in the West Indian colonies. The problem of disease was so severe and intractable that the Church Mission Society reduced the term that its missionaries were expected to spend in the colony. Between 1804 and 1824 the society dispatched seventy Europeans to Freetown. Only thirty-two survived their posting, and seven who did make it home were ill on their return.[63] This encouraged the CMS and the other missionary groups to rapidly establish schools and other institutions where willing Recaptives could be trained as teachers and missionaries, and left to lead the education and conversion of their fellow Africans. The Anglican Church Mission Society had strong links to Charles McCarthy, Governor of Sierra Leone from 1814 to 1824, and working with the colonial administration it created nine of the villages that sprang up nearby. The colonial government helped the missionaries to build church schools and homes for the superintendents of each of the new parishes created. The very first stone building in the colony was the missionary church in the village of Regent. McCarthy dreamed of a Christian mission in every village and of Sierra Leone as the great centre of Anglican devotion on the West African coast. Although the CMS led the way, harvesting the souls of thousands of heathen Africans as they were disgorged from the slave ships, the Methodists too arrived in Freetown, initially to minister to the old settlers from Nova Scotia, and set up their own schools. The descendants of the Maroons built their little church in 1822, which still stands today and attracts a congregation.

As well as being a patchwork of African identities and ethnicities, Freetown was where new hybrid identities were created. Tens of thousands of people liberated from the holds of slave ships emerged into the light of Freetown disconnected from their indigenous cultures and religions. While many tribes – most successfully the Yoruba of Nigeria – maintained much of their culture, even in Freetown the Recaptives were uniquely susceptible to proselytizing. Dislocated and disorientated, the Recaptives were far more receptive to the Christian message than the tribes found inland. Sierra Leone appeared to offer a unique opportunity and the Church Mission Society, working hand-in-hand with Governor Charles McCarthy, made the colony the focus of its efforts. The new identities forged in Freetown involved the distribution of new names. The society, operating from its Christian Institution at Leicester Mount, offered to name Recaptive children after any Briton willing to donate five pounds towards the cost of their education. As a result the first generations of Sierra Leonean families named after society missionaries and donors and supporters were established. Today there are still families of Venns, Crowthers, Willoughbys, Pratts and Sibthorps in Freetown. Those surnames can be found in London, New York and in all the cities to which the Sierra Leonean diaspora has spread. While the society named children, Governor McCarthy named settlements. In recognition of the society's unique dedication to the colony, new villages were named after its members. From the society's schools emerged a new generation with a new hybrid identity. A handful of them lived such extraordinary lives that they are worth getting to know in depth.

The first was Samuel Ajayi Crowther, who like so many of the Africans who were landed on King Jimmy's Wharf in the 1820s came from the Yoruba tribe of southern Nigeria in the modern state of Benin. In 1821 he was captured by slavers from the Muslim Fulani people and then sold on to Portuguese slave-traders. The ship that was to carry him to life on the plantations in Brazil was intercepted by HMS *Myrmidon* of the West Africa Squadron. Aged just thirteen, he was liberated in Freetown and handed over to the care of the missionaries. They provided him with an education and his new name – given in honour of the London vicar and Church Mission Society pioneer Samuel Crowther. So sincere was his faith and so prodigious his talents, Crowther was sent to Britain to further his education, specializing in languages. He went on to be the first man to translate the Bible and the Book of Common Prayer into his native Yoruba. He was the first student at the CMS's Fourah Bay

College when it opened in 1827 and by the end of his studies he could speak English, Latin, Greek, Yoruba, Hausa, Ibo, Nupe and Temne. Later in life he came to regard his initial enslavement as a necessary step in the journey that led him to religious redemption and divine purpose. He wrote that 'the day of my capture was considered to me a blessed day'.[64] Another key figure who led an equally extraordinary life was James Pinson Labulo Davies. The son of Yoruba Recaptives, he was educated at the Church Mission Society's Sierra Leone Grammar School in Freetown and joined the Royal Navy, serving in the West Africa Squadron that had liberated his parents. We shall hear more of both of them later.

By 1851, Lord Palmerston, then Foreign Secretary, had concluded that after the destruction of the slave barracoons of the Gallinas River, which had been controversially achieved by Captain Joseph Denman of HMS *Wanderer* in 1840, Britain had 'nearly rooted out the Slave Trade from the coast north of the [Equator]'. The slave trade of the North Atlantic, he contended, was now dominated by the 'two persevering offenders the King of Dahomey and the Chief of Lagos'.[65] While Abomey, the capital city of Dahomey, where the infamous King Ghezo maintained his vast palace complex, was sixty-five miles inland, the city of Lagos had the distinct disadvantage of being a coastal settlement and therefore subject to British naval power. The motivations for Britain's eventual annexation of Lagos have been the subject of long disagreement among historians and are too complex to be discussed here. What is clear is that Britain wanted to stabilize the region, increase the flow of palm oil – which, as one of the key ingredients in soap, had joined cotton in the short list of cash crops that had the potential to change Africa's fortunes – and knock out one of the last great slave-trading ports, thereby reducing the numbers of Yoruba people caught up in the 'abominable traffic'.[66]

By the 1850s the Yoruba, known in Freetown as the Aku, were still flooding into the city in the ships intercepted by the West Africa Squadron. There is no question that there was a significant moral component within British policy, and the long-standing belief that the promotion of 'legitimate' trades would render the slave trade economically redundant means that the promotion of Britain's palm-oil trade and the suppression of slavery could be viewed as complementary policies. There were those within government in London and within the Church Mission Society who had long been of the opinion that Britain should 'acquire' Lagos as a trading post and trading settlement. As one of the early British visitors to the city, G. A. Robertson, had remarked, 'Lagos is one of the most desirable places on this coast for an European settlement'.[67] British missionaries operating from Badagry to the west of Lagos on the Nigerian coast played their part in encouraging the Foreign Office to consider the possibility of annexing Lagos. Rarely reticent when it came to offering policy advice, the missionaries were particularly keen to see Britain take control as the deposed former Oba (King) of the city, Akitoye, had promised to end the slave trade if he was re-installed. In November 1851 a delegation consisting of a British consul and three naval officers presented Kosoko, the current Oba of Lagos and the nephew of Akitoye, with what amounted to an ultimatum from Lord Palmerston. It demanded that Kosoko accept British 'friendship', which would only be extended to him if he abandoned the slave trade. According to a British report of the meeting, Kosoko's representatives defiantly replied 'that the friendship of the English was not wanted'.[68] As diplomatic efforts had clearly failed, and as no costly inland military expedition through malarial forests was required to reach Lagos, the decision was made to seize the city.

Embarrassingly for British power the first attack on Lagos in late November 1851 failed, and there was loss of British life. But on Christmas Eve a more determined attempt was made, when HMS *Bloodhound* and HMS *Teazer*, the latter an advanced modern screw-propeller steamer, crossed the sand bar that defended the city and eased into the shallow waters of Lagos harbour. Behind them followed a flotilla of British ships. On Boxing Day the attack began. Although both the lead British ships ran aground, they were re-floated and able to launch a heavy attack on the palace of the Oba of Lagos. Impressive defensive trenches had been dug and the Oba defended his city with batteries of cannon, around forty in total. The next day the attackers succeeded in hitting the gunpowder magazine in the Oba's palace with a rocket, causing an enormous explosion.[69] When the British landed, the battle was all but over and the city had been evacuated. Lagos belonged to the British; they were to stay for the next hundred and nine years.

The bombardment of the city was, like much of British policy on the slave coasts of Africa, motivated by the twin objectives of suppressing the slave trade and opening up the interior of Africa to 'legitimate trade', that would be of benefit and advantage to Britain, as the anti-slave-trade mission and colonial expansion increasingly dovetailed. With the Oba having fled north to the lands of the Ijebu people, Akitoye was put on the throne, his only tasks to sign an anti-slave-trade treaty with Britain and maintain order. He succeeded in the first but failed disastrously in the second. Akitoye died in 1853 and in 1861 Lagos was annexed and put under the direct political control of a British governor answerable to London, a move that marked the beginning of the colonization of Nigeria.

One of the officers on board HMS *Bloodhound* during the bombard-ment of Lagos was Lieutenant James Pinson Labulo Davies, the son of Recaptives who had attended the Church Mission Society's Grammar School in Freetown. His arrival in Lagos was, despite coming on a hostile British warship, a form of homecoming. Davies was a man of the Yoruba tribe, his parents having been born in the Nigerian cities of Abeokuta and Ogbomoso, and he settled in the city. He became one of a small elite who were critical of the formation of colonial Lagos. This community could trace its story back to 1839 when two men of the Nigerian Hausa tribe, freed from slavery in Trinidad, arrived in Freetown on their way back to their homeland. Inspired by this epic transatlantic voyage a group of Aku Recaptives in Free-town, reasoning that they were only around a thousand miles away from Nigeria, joined together to purchase a ship, which they named the *Queen Victoria*. In 1839 sixty-seven of them returned to their former towns and villages. Their first settlement was ironically at the slave-trading port of Badagry; later they moved inland to the city of Abeokuta and then some went on to Lagos. They embarked upon this whole project without any support or financial assistance from the British government. They became some of the few thousand Africans who managed to return to their original homelands after escaping from slavery. In Lagos they lived alongside former Muslim Yoruba slaves who had returned to their homeland from Brazil following the Malê Slave Revolt of the mid-1830s. In the following years further expeditions left Freetown for Nigeria. Aku Recaptives who had grown relatively wealthy through their activities as traders and shopkeepers in Freetown purchased former slave ships, which were still sold as prizes at auction in the harbour at Freetown, and used them to travel back to their lost homelands.[70] In Nigeria many of them became both traders and self-energized Christian missionaries, spearheading British efforts to spread Christianity in Nigeria in the years before formal colonization. In Lagos they slipped into the same types of urban trading that had built their fortunes in Freetown. Some invested and most had a hand in the palm-oil trade. By the 1870s there were over a thousand of them in the city. British-educated, deeply Christian and as committed to missionary work as they were to establishing them-selves as traders, these returners to their native lands – most of them either former liberated Africans or the children of liberated Africans – became known in Lagos as the Saro, a diminutive corruption of Sierra Leone.[71] As well as James Davies, also resident in Lagos by the 1850s was Samuel Ajayi Crowther, who became the first ever black bishop in the Anglican Church. Another arrival from Freetown was Thomas Babington Macaulay, a CMS reverend of Recaptive Yoruba parents. Born in the Kissy district of Freetown, he was named after the British politician and educated in the Freetown Grammar School. Macaulay was the driving force behind the creation of a similar CMS Grammar School in Lagos, an institution that still exists.

The Saro were members of the Yoruba tribe, and so were not ethnic outsiders, but culturally and religiously they were a hybrid people. They were Africans but also – despite very few of them ever setting foot in Britain – in a sense black Britons, laying claim to such an identity several decades before the 'Scramble for Africa' and a century before the emergence of Britain's post-war black commu-nities. Their hybrid names – mixtures of Yoruba and English – can still be found on a few remaining gravestones and memorials in the older graveyards and churches of Lagos and Freetown.* The Anglican

---

* James Pinson Labulo Davies, Samuel Ajayi Crowther and Thomas Babington Macaulay were buried in Ajele Cemetery in Lagos Island, and there remained until 1971 when the cemetery was needlessly destroyed in order to build an anonymous official building by Mobolaji Johnson, the Military Governor of Lagos State. This act of cultural vandalism was condemned at the time by Wole Soyinka.

architecture of those churches further testifies to their long-forgotten story. Despite their hybrid identity and deep commitment to the Anglican religion and British education, the Saro were at the forefront of the emergence of Nigerian nationalism in the middle of the twentieth century.

When James Pinson Labulo Davies established himself in Lagos in the 1850s he was perfectly placed to take advantage of the enormous boom in the palm-oil trade. This son of Nigerian parents who had been shipped along the African coast as human cargo now bought ships of his own. Like other Saro traders he bought former slave ships at auction in Freetown, refitted them and shipped palm oil and cotton from Lagos to Britain.[72] Davies' shipping line ran from the ports of Lokoja, Lagos and Freetown in West Africa to Liverpool, Plymouth and Portsmouth. He and others also bought goods confiscated from condemned slave ships in Freetown, and shipped them for sale in Lagos. He provided Macaulay with the funds to establish the Church Mission Society Grammar School in Lagos. Other members of the Saro community also contributed funds to the new school. Much of the money came from the expansion of the 'legitimate' trades in African commodities – palm oil, cotton and ivory. This encouraged British firms to pour capital into Lagos. Better situated for trade with Britain and full of experienced Saro businessmen, Lagos overtook Ouidah as the region's chief port and the city became known eventually as 'The Liverpool of West Africa'.[73] Davies became a major employer in the city and sought to constantly expand his business through personal connections with members of the Church Mission Society and British business partners in London, Manchester and Liverpool. His links to Britain became critical to his trading activities and in the early 1860s he was wealthy and established enough to travel to Britain.

By the mid-nineteenth century the interception of slave ships on the high seas and in the rivers and the lagoons of West Africa was only one aspect of Britain's anti-slave-trade strategy. The bombardment of Lagos was a feature of a significant shift in tactics and in late 1849, when Frederick Forbes, a successful anti-slave-trade captain, came ashore in Dahomey, there was a new emphasis on efforts to persuade and pressure local kings and chiefs to abandon the trade. Missions were dispatched to inland kingdoms to cajole regional leaders into signing treaties and encourage them to diversify into what were described at the time as 'legitimate' trades. Heading north from the slave port of Ouidah in Dahomey, Captain Forbes marched through West Africa's forest belt to Abomey, the capital city of Dahomey, and there waited for an audience with King Ghezo.

By 1849 Ghezo was one of the dominant figures in the supply side of the Atlantic slave trade. He had achieved this in virtual partnership with the Brazilian slave-trader Francisco Félix de Sousa. An infamous figure in the history of West Africa, de Sousa based himself and his business in Ouidah, adopted many local customs including aspects of the vodun religion and is reputed to have maintained a harem of slave women with whom he fathered a hundred and three children.[74] De Sousa had supported Ghezo's rise to power during the 1820s. When the Nigerian Oyo empire collapsed in the 1830s, following an internal rebellion – effectively a jihad by its Muslim subjects – Ghezo broke away from his overlords and formed Dahomey into an independent state. With de Sousa as his slave factor at the coast he exploited the regional chaos and through wars and slave-raiding took over the region's slave trade. In doing so, however, he placed himself and his kingdom in direct conflict with British ambitions and the stated mission of the West Africa Squadron. Ships of the squadron had regularly intercepted slave ships from Ouidah and, after bilateral suppression treaties had been signed with Portugal and Brazil, even seized slave ships lying at anchor there, to Ghezo's fury.[75] In 1849, the year Forbes arrived for his audience with Ghezo, Francisco Félix de Sousa died, but his son Izidoro de Sousa took over his father's concession, a move which did not indicate any willingness on the part of King Ghezo to abandon the slave trade.

Dahomey in the 1840s was famous in Europe, not only as a slave-trading state but as a highly militarized society – though hardly more militarized in cultural terms than mid-Victorian Britain. The military prowess of Dahomians was a favoured subject of travel writers and journalists, and Dahomey had come to be known as the 'Black Sparta'. What most fascinated Europeans was the presence of a feared regiment of female soldiers within the Dahomian army.

Women from other ethnic groups captured in battle as well as the daughters of Dahomian families were recruited into the King's army; the indigenous women were drafted through a levy system. Forbes, who wrote and published an account of his time in Dahomey, described various aspects of Dahomian culture, but knowing his audience, he dedicated a whole chapter to what he called the 'Amazons of Dahomey'.

As Forbes travelled north and while he awaited his audience with King Ghezo, he must have been well aware that previous delegations had arrived in Abomey and attempted to persuade the King to halt the traffic in slaves. Ghezo had received them all, attempted to impress them with his wealth and military power and dismissed their overtures. The same year that Forbes visited the King, William Winniett, Governor of the British Gold Coast colony, was granted an audience. At their meeting the King informed him that Dahomey sold around nine thousand slaves each year, three thousand of which were sold privately by the King himself. The King also imposed a tax on each slave sold. After two decades in which slave ships dispatched from Ouidah had been pursued and intercepted by the ships of the Royal Navy, Ghezo conceded to Winniett that he was willing to adhere to any demand the British government might make of him, 'except to give up the slave trade'. The trade, he said, 'has been the ruling principle of my people. It is the source of their glory and wealth. Their songs celebrate their victories and the mother lulls the child to sleep with notes of triumph over an enemy reduced to slavery. Can I, by signing . . . a treaty, change the sentiments of the whole people?'[76]

Forbes was granted his audience with King Ghezo in May 1850. He carried with him letters that outlined Britain's official opposition to the slave trade and one from Queen Victoria that expressed her personal opposition to the trade.[77] Forbes also brought gifts of silks and cloths from Queen Victoria. We only have Forbes' version of events, gleaned from his published account. In it he describes how, after being presented to crowds of Dahomians, he and his entourage entered the royal palace. They then passed through the 'palace-square', where 'at the foot of the ladder leading to the palaver-house, on each side were three human heads, recently decapitated, the blood still oozing', while 'about the yard were many flags, of all colours . . . amongst which . . . were several union-jacks'.[78] When presented before the King, Forbes recounts how he made the then all too familiar anti-slave-trade case, suggesting that if Ghezo 'retained the slaves and made them cultivate the soil, Dahomey . . . would become a great nation, and himself a great king'.[79] In truth Forbes was well aware of the futility of attempting to cajole African monarchs to abandon the slave trade. In his previous book, *Six Months' Service in the African Blockade*, published in 1849, he had admitted that, 'To expect an African king to keep a treaty, and offer him nothing but a dazzling present – to do this is idle. It is only placing him under the mercies of his subjects, who, assisted by the Slave-Merchants, would assuredly murder him'.[80]

By the 1850s Ghezo had in fact already established a flourishing and 'legitimate' trade in palm oil, a key ingredient of soap. For two decades the trade had existed alongside the slave trade in Dahomey, very slowly becoming a major source of the King's income.[81] In the 1840s he had passed laws making it illegal for his subjects to cut down any palm trees that he declared sacred, and most tellingly he had introduced taxes on the sale of private palm oil. While this policy was – in the long term – to offer the rulers of Dahomey an alternative to the international slave trade, it was not without its own moral problems, as palm oil was produced by slaves on plantations in Africa rather than in the New World. But at the time of Forbes' visit, Ghezo remained unwilling to countenance abandoning the slave trade or yielding to British diplomatic pressure. He also reminded his guests that, as his own father had informed him, while it had been the French who had first established the trade in slaves with Dahomey, the British had later come to dominate that trade, becoming 'the first of white men'. This uncomfortable historical fact added a complicating tone of hypocrisy to British condemnations of Dahomey as a barbarous, slave-trading, rogue state.[82] The extent to which the King was committed to trade in 1850 was emphasized, perhaps unintentionally, by the fact that among the gifts he presented to Forbes was 'a captive girl'. The child was a slave. She had been captured around two years earlier during the Okeadon War of 1848, fought between Ghezo's armies and a people from the Egbado clan of the Yoruba ethnic group, known today as the Yewa.[83] Her parents had been killed in the conflict and she had been taken prisoner. She had not been sold to the slave-traders, which led Forbes to believe that she was of a high-class family, and he believed that to have refused to accept the child 'would have been to have signed her death-warrant, which, probably, would have been carried into execution forthwith.'[84] This was a supposition by Forbes but Dahomey – along with other kingdoms such as the Ashanti and Benin – did engage in human sacrifice to mark the passing of kings and other events.[85] Previous visitors to Abomey had witnessed the ritual killings of slaves and prisoners of war by the King's female corps of bodyguards. King Ghezo, whose commitment to the slave trade was never broken by any British delegation or any offer of subsidies or inducements, had previously offered enslaved slave children as gifts to earlier delegations. Just one year before the arrival of Forbes, Brodie Cruickshank, the Chief Justice of the Cape Coast, had visited the court of Abomey. Cruickshank's report of his visit is, as the historian Philip D. Curtin noted, 'unusually free of cultural bias'. In it Cruickshank reported that the King presented him with two slave girls as a gift, which Ghezo apparently hoped might be offered to Queen Victoria, to do her washing.[86] The historian Joan Amin Addo has speculated as to whether King Ghezo imagined the children to be an appropriate gift to present to the Queen because he presumed that wealthy British households still maintained black child servants as novelties or pets, as they of course had done throughout much of the seventeenth and eighteenth centuries. If this was Ghezo's line of thinking then it was not an unreasonable one.

For Forbes, a highly respected officer of the West Africa Squadron of the Royal Navy and a diplomatic envoy, the gift of the child meant that he, having been tasked with suppressing the Dahomey slave trade, found himself setting sail for Britain from the port of Ouidah with a freed slave child on board his ship. A punctilious record-keeper and chronicler of events, Forbes listed the child among the presents he had received on behalf of the Queen from King Ghezo, 'two magnificent cloths (to me) to present to Her Majesty . . . a rich country cloth, a captive girl, a caboocer's stool, and footstool, ten heads of cowries, and one keg of rum'.[87] Because Forbes had been acting in the service of the state he suspected, or at least speculated, that this might affect the legal status of the child as it was possible that 'the government would consider her as the property of the Crown'.[88] The girl, who was probably seven or eight, was given the name Sarah, but dubbed Sally by the crew who, according to Forbes, grew fond of her on their journey home.

It was upon their return to England that this little girl's life took a quite incredible turn. 'Immediately on arriving', Forbes tells us, 'I applied through the Secretary of the Admiralty, and received for answer that Her Majesty was graciously pleased to arrange for the education and subsequent fate of the child'. Queen Victoria requested that Sally be brought to Windsor Castle and so, on 9 November 1850, the little girl from Abomey, now named Sarah Forbes Bonetta, after Captain Forbes and HMS *Bonetta*, made her first appearance at court, and her first entry in the Queen's journal. Victoria wrote:

> We came home, found Albert still there, waiting for Capt. Forbes & a poor little negro, girl, whom he brought back from the King of Dahomé, her parents & all her relatives having been sacrificed. Capt. Forbes saved her life, by asking for her as a present . . . She is 7 years old, sharp & intelligent, & speaks English. She was dressed as any other girl. When her bonnet was taken off, her little black woolly head & big earrings gave her the true negro type.[89]

Queen Victoria may well have also decided that the circumstances that had brought this young girl to Britain meant that responsibility for her welfare rested with her. The Queen was, after all, the intended recipient of King Ghezo's gift. Whatever Victoria's motivations and sentiments, Sarah Forbes Bonetta's life was transformed by the Queen's willingness to draw her into the extended circle of her court and provide her with an excellent education. But as a black child, a former slave thrust into the heart of Victorian Britain's elite, her life story was also buffeted and shaped by the profound contradictions and confusion about race that the Queen and most of her subjects shared in the middle decades of the nineteenth century.

Queen Victoria was both symbol and woman, monarch and mother. Out on the colonial frontiers, agents of the empire and British merchants invoked her name, image and titles when seeking to legitimize and expand British influence, and in doing so created what has been called the construct of the Great White Queen – a symbolic Victoria who was often little more than a cipher for British power. At home in her palaces, surrounded by her frenetic court and enormous family, Victoria the woman was a very different figure. There is much evidence to support the contention that at a personal and intellectual level the Queen was generally opposed to the racism of the mid-nineteenth century. She had close, interpersonal relationships with the non-white members of her court – her Indian attendant Abdul Karim being perhaps the most significant and controversial – and from the very start of her reign was linked to Britain's anti-slavery mission. This was partly due to her gender – abolitionism had long been regarded as a political issue in which it was appropriate for women to play an important role – and partly because her accession coincided with the final manumission of the slaves in the West Indies. But her husband Prince Albert's vocal denouncement of slavery and support for the doomed Niger expedition of 1840 was taken as a reflection of views held by both the prince and his wife. The Queen also held several audiences over her long reign with people of African descent, many of them African kings, chiefs and missionaries, others former slaves turned abolitionists from the United States and the British Empire. In 1851, the year after Sarah Forbes Bonetta came into her life, the Queen discussed the struggle against the slave trade with Samuel Ajayi Crowther, who met her at Windsor, and did not at first realize that the lady with whom he was in conversation was the Great White Queen herself. As noted earlier Victoria was also said to have been emotionally affected by her reading of *Uncle Tom's Cabin* and went out of her way, even contravening diplomatic protocol, to meet the book's author. Yet Victoria ruled over an empire that in the latter decades of the nineteenth century was increasingly influenced by racial thinking and new 'scientific' racial theories and Victoria, like most Victorians, thought in terms of racial 'types', and may well have believed, to some extent, that the races of mankind possessed innate, inner characteristics.

The life of Sarah Forbes Bonetta, like that of so many of the black people who became caught up in Britain's imperial project, is one that can only be told through the words of others. Her own voice is largely silent. We do not know how she understood or rationalized the strange journey she underwent, from being a victim of the slave trade to a ward of the queen of the most powerful nation on earth. Being so young and having already been orphaned in war and held as a slave in the court of Abomey, she must have been traumatized by her experiences, but there is nothing to allow us to do more than speculate as to her emotional well-being. Frederick Forbes tells us that, 'Of her own history she has only a confused idea. Her parents were decapitated; her brothers and sisters, she knows not what their fate might have been.'[90]

Mid-Victorian ideas about race were to combine with the Queen's own wishes and ideas that emerged from Britain's anti-slavery and 'civilizing' missions to give shape to the strange life of Sarah Forbes Bonetta, for while she was placed under the protection of the Queen the question as to where she might best be cared for arose. There was in the mid-nineteenth century a common belief in Britain that the European climate was injurious to the health of Africans and other non-European peoples. The damp as much as the cold, it was thought, could prove fatal and in the interests of her health it was decided that the infant Sarah should be returned to Africa as quickly as possible. In January 1851, just two months after she had first met the Queen, the Keeper of the Queen's Privy Purse, Charles Phipps, wrote to the Rev. Henry Venn asking him to assist the palace in finding a location in coastal Africa where Sarah might be educated and cared for. The optimal location was obvious to Henry Venn. In 1851 he was secretary of the Church Mission Society, a post he held for thirty-two years. Sarah's future he judged could be secured in Freetown, Sierra Leone. Seventy years of British missionary work and waves of settlement, each more unlikely than last, had by 1851 turned the pestilential peninsula that had snuffed out the lives of the 'Black Poor' of late Georgian London into a bustling African town surrounded by villages. The efforts of the West Africa Squadron had populated Freetown and the Church Mission Society had built, within its environs, a whole network of educational and religious institutions; a boys' school, a girls' school, a number of churches, hospitals and a prestigious grammar school – the oldest in Africa. Many of the African teachers and missionaries who manned those institutions had been trained in Britain, and sent back to Freetown to spread the twin virtues of education and Christianity. The ill-health that had afflicted some of them had helped perpetuate the myth that Africans could never thrive in European climates.

The long-term hope was that from Freetown these black missionaries and teachers would move eastwards establishing new missions,
churches and schools along the coast of West Africa, transforming
a region that anti-slavery campaigners hoped would soon no longer
be known as the Slave Coast. Freetown was to become the base
camp for the continental civilizing mission, but civilization was not
all that the missionaries from Freetown would bring to their fellow
Africans. These British-educated, Christianized Africans, some of
whom had been liberated from slave ships by the West Africa
Squadron, or were the children of Recaptives, would open up the
region to British trade and British culture. Transplanting Sarah to
Freetown would, it was said, protect her health from the cold of
England, while at the same time placing her on the path towards a
future as a black missionary. Sarah's intelligence, which had been
noted by Forbes and by the Queen herself, made this future vocation
seem both probable and appropriate.

While arrangements for her return to Africa were reaching a
conclusion she came again to visit her benefactor. The Queen's
journal entry for 11 January 1851 describes her thoughts on the
child she was now calling by the less formal Sally. 'After luncheon,
Sally Bonita [sic], the little African girl came with Mrs. Phipps &
showed me some of her work. This is the 4th time I have seen the
poor child, who is really an intelligent little thing . . . '[91] That year
Sarah Forbes Bonetta became known to the Victorian public when
Forbes published *Dahomey and the Dahomans*, which told some of her
back story and informed the public that she was under the care and
protection of the Queen. Forbes wrote effusively about Sarah's
talents, describing her as 'a perfect genius' who 'now speaks English
well, and has a great talent for music . . . She is far in advance of
any white child of her age, in aptness of learning, and strength of
mind and affection'. Being what Forbes described as 'an excellent
specimen of the negro race' he speculated as to whether her talents
and later development might be used to test the 'capability of the
intellect of the Black: it being generally and erroneously supposed
that after a certain age the intellect becomes impaired, and the
pursuit of knowledge impossible — that though the negro child
may be clever, the adult will be dull and stupid.'[92]

Sarah's education in Freetown at the Church Mission Society's girls' school did not become a test case in the dubious study for the intellect of the human races. It is not known exactly how long she remained in Sierra Leone but by the mid-1850s she had returned to England, seemingly unconcerned about any imagined risks to her health. In December 1855 she appears again in Queen Victoria's journal. Sarah, whom Queen Victoria almost always referred to using the more informal name 'Sally', had come to visit her bene-factor at Windsor Castle. Victoria's journal entry for the day reads, 'Saw Sally Forbes, the negro girl whom I have had educated: she is immensely grown and has a nice slim figure'.[93] Three years later Sarah was again in attendance at court, as a guest at the wedding of the Queen's eldest daughter, Victoria the Princess Royal. Histo-rians have suggested that her presence at this event, both highly public and acutely personal to the Queen and the royal family, demonstrates the Queen's high regard and personal affection for the child she had by then known and provided for almost a decade.

By the late 1850s Sarah had settled in the seaside town of Brighton, then a highly fashionable resort, popular with the expanding middle classes and the aristocracy and royalty of Europe. One of the few crowned heads who disliked the town was Queen Victoria herself, who had abandoned the Royal Pavilion as it was unable to provide her growing family with the privacy she demanded for them. Queen Victoria selected Miss Sophia Welsh, an elderly lady with experience of life in India, to care for Sarah in Brighton and assist with her introduction into polite society.[94] Sarah lived at 17 Clifton Hill, with Miss Welsh and her sister Mary. Well known in the town, she was an accomplished, educated and eligible young woman. Some time in 1862 it appears that she became known to James Pinson Labulo Davies, who, having built up his wealth from shipping and the palm-oil business in Lagos, was visiting Britain. Davies sought an introduction to her and the two were engaged to be married, the match apparently approved of by Queen Victoria.

The wedding of two wealthy, highly educated and well-connected British Africans, one of whom had strong links to the Queen, was of huge interest to the press and the public. Hundreds of people – some reports say thousands – turned out on the streets of Brighton on the day to cheer the couple. Months afterwards reports of the event were still appearing in the colonial press, which reproduced the reports from the British newspapers. Two days after the wedding the *Leeds Mercury* ran one under the headline, 'Interesting Marriage in Brighton' describing the bride and groom as 'a lady and gentleman of colour, whose previous history gives to the ceremony a peculiar interest, chiefly to those who have been so long and so deeply interested in the African race and who have watched the progress of civilisation caused by the influence of Christianity on the negro'. In an unsubtle attack on the racial attitudes of the United States, in the midst of the American Civil War, the paper also proudly pronounced that 'the ceremony will also tell our brethren on the other side of the Atlantic that British ladies and gentlemen consider it a pleasure and a privilege to do honour to those of the African race who will prove themselves capable of appreciating the advantages of a Liberal education'.[95] The *Brighton Herald* agreed that the wedding demonstrated the liberal and enlightened attitudes that it suggested prevailed in Britain, among the educated and religiously minded. The newspaper described 'the spectacle of the natives of a distant Continent, separated from us by strong natural barriers, assembled under the wing of the Church of England, partaking of its rites, and recognised to all its privileges by a large party of fellow-subjects and fellow-Christians, differing indeed in the colour of their skin, but asserting no social, religious, or natural superiority on that account'.[96] The same publication concluded that the wedding was testimony to 'the labours of the philanthropists and the missionary over prejudices of pride and blood which [even the] most sanguine followers of Wilberforce could scarcely have looked forward to!' The *Brighton Gazette* similarly delighted in reporting that the wedding party that entered St Nicholas' Church consisted of 'white ladies with African gentlemen, and African ladies with white gentlemen until all the space was filled'.[97] That the same report repeatedly fixated on the contrasts in skin colour between the white and black guests amply demonstrated that Britain in 1862 was not the colour-blind and relaxed nation they claimed it had become.

As a few of the newspaper reports from 1862 reveal, somewhere along the line Forbes' belief that Sarah had been spared being sold into the Atlantic trade because 'she was of a good family' had become inflated and exaggerated.[98] She was described as the daughter of an

African chief and ultimately as an orphaned 'African Princess'. At their wedding reception Henry Venn gave a speech honouring the newly married couple and expressing his delight that Sarah 'had received such an education as was calculated to be of the greatest benefit to the African natives, amongst whom she was so shortly to reside'.[99] To Venn, Sarah's short life – she was still only nineteen – had been spent in preparation not for her wedding but for her return to Africa, where she could begin her work as a black missionary. Venn expressed his earnest hope that Sarah's marriage would help cement links between England and Africa, 'which latter country has been so much civilized, chiefly with her connection with England'.[100]

The couple's marriage certificate told a more sombre story, cataloguing the broken family backgrounds and atomized families of a woman who had been a child slave and a man whose parents had been liberated from a slave ship. The certificate notes Sarah's parents as 'unknown' and in place of their names it describes Sarah as 'a Negress of Dahomey, West Africa'. James Davies is listed as the son of Labulo, 'a Negro of Sierra Leone'. His occupation is recorded as African merchant. The document also gives Sarah's full name, for the first time, as Ina Sarah Forbes Bonetta. The historian Caroline Bressey has suggested that 'Ina' might have been Sarah's lost African name, which, standing on the threshold of a new phase in her life, she perhaps felt able to reclaim.[101]

On 15 September the couple attended the studio of Camille Silvy, portrait photographer to the rich and famous. This precocious Frenchman of aristocratic lineage, still in his twenties, had photographed much of the British aristocracy and all the royal family, with the exception of the Queen herself, and a Silvy portrait was a real statement of wealth and position in mid-Victorian Britain.

Sarah Forbes Bonetta is next recorded in Britain in 1867. She came with her eldest daughter, Victoria, to whom the Queen was godmother. On 9 December mother and daughter visited the Queen, who recorded the meeting in her voluminous diary. 'Saw Sally, now Mrs Davis, & her dear little child, far blacker than herself, called Victoria & aged 4 a lively intelligent child, with big melancholy eyes'.[102] When Sarah's daughter was christened the Queen sent her new goddaughter a gold cup, salver, knife, fork and spoon as gifts.

The inscription on the cup and salver read 'To Victoria Davies, from her godmother, Victoria, Queen of Great Britain and Ireland, 1863'.[103] By the late 1860s Sarah was seriously unwell, her health having been damaged by tuberculosis. Her husband's finances were similarly ailing. His shipping company was in trouble and his debts were mounting. By 1873 he owed his European trading partners around £11,000.[104] Four years later his debts had risen to £20,500. Sarah moved to Madeira; like those who had sought to care for her in the 1850s, she concluded that a gentler climate would allow her to recover her health, but in 1880, aged thirty-seven, she died. On the day Queen Victoria received the news she was expecting a visit from Sarah's daughter Victoria. The Queen later decided to ensure that her goddaughter, like her mother before her, would be protected and provided for: 'I shall give her an annuity', she wrote in her journal.[105] Victoria Davies was educated at Cheltenham Ladies' College with all fees paid by the palace.

NINE

'Cotton is King'

Over the summer of 1851 around six million visitors flocked to London to visit the Great Exhibition, held in the Crystal Palace, which had been specially built in Hyde Park. There they marvelled at the wealth and the wonders of Britain and her colonies. In the midst of this great pageant of national and imperial self-confidence *The Times* carried an article describing the relationship between Britain and a former colony. 'For all practical purposes', it stated, 'the United States are far more closely united with this kingdom than any one of our colonies, and keep up a perpetual interchange of the most important good offices: taking our manufactures and our surplus population and giving us in return the materials, of revenue and of life.'[1] When it came to trade and investment the United States, the colony that had been so disastrously lost in the 1770s, mattered more than any of the territories over which the Union flag still fluttered. Even India, then under the proxy rule of the East India Company, counted less than America. In the age of free trade, British goods poured into America's booming cities and American raw materials streamed across the Atlantic to Britain. These flows were mirrored by pulsating surges of money. The United States was the favoured destination for British capital and British banks were instrumental in financing the construction of the cities and factories of the rapidly industrializing Northern states. Many of the same banks and credit houses were active in financing the great agricultural boom that had moved along the Mississippi Valley, a booming monoculture economy that had hugely enriched the Southern states. Britain's banks possessed such vast reserves of investment capital in the 1850s partly because Britain's factories and industrial regions were so far in advance of her competitors. Britain in the middle of the nineteenth century accounted for around a quarter of all world exports, and that enormous share of world trade was set to increase. While most commentators revelled in the nation's industrial predominance, more cautious voices pointed to the dependence of a worryingly high number of the nation's factories on raw materials imported from America. The industrial revolution that had enabled Victorian Britain to become an economic superpower is often imagined as a great burst of heavy industry, an orgy of smelting, hammering, riveting and forging. Yet in the North-West of England the sounds that wafted over the valleys of industrialized Lancashire and Cheshire were not the thuds of heavy machinery or the roars of the blast furnace but the rhythmic chatter of the power loom and spinning jenny. Here industry and wealth rested upon the mastery of fine precision movement and repeatability. In that region and in smaller clusters elsewhere in the British Isles, mass production on an unprecedented scale had been perfected and new ways of life, new relationships to time and new family structures had all yielded to the discipline of the factory and the factory clock. The most important and profitable of all the goods that flowed out of the coal-blackened cities of northern England in the middle of the nineteenth century were cotton cloth, chintzy fabrics, thread and finished clothing. By 1860 cotton goods accounted for 40 per cent of all British exports.[2] The geography of the Industrial Revolution was shaped by the requirements of cotton. The North-West of England, the region that came to dominate the industry, was blessed with numerous fast-flowing rivers in which waterwheels could be built and from which power could be drawn. Those rivers were fast-flowing because of the North-West's high rainfall and humidity. The humidity proved critical in another respect, as the damp atmosphere prevented the cotton threads and fibres from drying out and snapping. Later, when 'the iron muscles of the steam-engine' were harnessed to accelerate and further mechanize the production of cotton thread and the weaving of cotton fabric, Lancashire once again seemed to have been blessed. Almost providentially all the great mill towns of the region, with the sole exception of Preston, had by chance been built near or in some cases on the Lancashire coalfields.[3] One of the by-products of burning coal was coal gas: it rapidly replaced candles in the mills, providing the mill owners with a far cheaper source of artificial light that allowed them to profitably extend the working day and increase returns.

The cotton industry had started in earnest in Lancashire in the middle decades of the eighteenth century. Some of the initial capital invested in the cotton trade had been accumulated through Britain's triangular slave trade, as had much of the business acumen that was a feature of the early cotton entrepreneurs. Decades of slave-trading and sugar-trading had brought into being complex networks of finance and credit that helped the cotton industry advance at a rapid speed. As cotton moved from a cottage industry that fitted around older rhythms of rural life into factories and mills, other lessons learnt from New World slavery were applicable. Management techniques and methods of labour accounting drew their inspiration from the plantations of the West Indies. The cotton goods produced in the mills that grew up around Manchester were themselves commodities within the Atlantic economy. Raw cotton, some of it grown by enslaved Africans in the West Indies, was processed into cloth and clothes in English mills and was then sold to the slave-traders of Liverpool. Some of these 'Manchester Cottons' were then shipped to the slave coasts of Africa on the first leg of the slave-traders' triangular journeys. There they were offered to the African and Afro-European coastal slave-traders in exchange for captive Africans. Some of the cheaper Manchester cotton was dyed and patterned to resemble higher quality Indian cotton cloth that had long been sought after in Africa.[4] Other Manchester cloth, recognizable by its coarse checked pattern, was sold in vast quantities right across the slave-trading regions. By the middle of the eighteenth century Manchester cotton had become so firmly associated with the slave trade that producers in Lancashire were supplying their cotton textiles not just to British slave-traders but to French slavers based in Nantes, Rouen and Bordeaux.[5] In 1792, the year that Parliament rejected William Wilberforce's second Abolition Bill, an event three thousand miles away set the stage for the next step in the expansion of the Lancashire cotton industry. That year Eli Whitney, a school teacher in Savannah, Georgia, invented a simple hand-cranked machine that separated the useless cotton seeds from the valuable cotton fibres. Two simple metal rollers, each mounted with rows of metal teeth, drew out the seeds with astonishing ease. This process had previously been done by hand and was one of the bottlenecks that slowed down the cultivation and harvesting of raw cotton. Whitney's cotton-gin – 'gin' being short for engine – increased the speed at which seeds could be separated from fibres by a factor of eight. When the machine was further refined, and a series of later adaptations and modifications made, speeds increased even further. Almost at a stroke the economics of cotton cultivation had been transformed, as therefore had the economics of slavery. Before the cotton-gin the slave system had appeared to many observers to be doomed to a slow and inevitable decline, as it was gradually outmoded by the dynamism of free labour. Eli Whitney's cotton-gin gave American cotton slavery a terrible second wind. Just as the climate and geography of the North-West of England were ideal for the processing of cotton into thread and cloth, the Mississippi Valley was ideally suited to cotton cultivation. As cotton brushed aside other crops and more and more land was given over to it, Mississippi, Louisiana, Alabama, the Carolinas, west Texas, Georgia, Arkansas and Tennessee became known as the 'Cotton Kingdom'. The climate of Mississippi was in effect the inverse of Lancashire's; early rains gave way to a long dry season of hot weather with little humidity, allowing cotton balls to split and ripen for picking. Geography had also provided the region with a transport super-highway. On the waters and the banks of the Mississippi River another great burst of industrial expansion and steam power took place. Paddle steamers carried the cotton from the fields to the ports of Mobile and New Orleans. By the 1850s there were seven hundred of them working the Mississippi. Along with land and slaves they were the most profitable investments in the Southern states.[6] As the historian Walter Johnson has powerfully argued, these five-hundred-ton giants represented a far greater concentration of industrial power than the mills and factories of the Northern states. In New Orleans the whole cotton economy was supplied with slave labour through the largest slave market in North America.[7] From there and other Southern ports another great fleet of steam-powered vessels shipped the precious cargoes across the Atlantic. Millions of bales were transported by steam trains on a rail system that was expanding at an astonishing rate. By the 1860s the network had radiated out across the nation and was nudging up towards the frontier, which itself was moving ever westwards into new lands, territories that to politicians and businessmen in the Southern states appeared ideally suited to the needs of the cotton plant and perfect also for the expansion of slavery. The new efficiencies made possible by the cotton-gin and booming demand from the mills and factories of Lancashire fuelled an unprecedented cotton boom. Between 1820 and 1830 American cotton production doubled. By 1840 America was producing more than a million bales of cotton a year. By 1860 cotton accounted for more than half of all American exports. From the 1820s onwards slave owners in the states of the Upper South had begun to sell their slaves to traders and plantation owners in the Deep South where they were more valuable and where their labour would be far more profitable. This was the economic rationale for the internal, inter-state slave trade, mentioned in an earlier chapter, and that the historian Ira Berlin has described as a 'second middle passage'.[8] The slave ships of this domestic trade carried Africans from Virginia and the Carolinas to New Orleans and other Southern ports. The *Creole*, the American ship that a group of slaves seized and diverted to the British Bahamas in 1843, was on its way to New Orleans as part of this internal slave trade. Around a million slaves were moved from North to South. Others were marched across America, chained together in coffles, in the same way that their ancestors had been marched to the slave-trading rivers on the African coast. As more and more Upper South slave owners cashed in on the cotton boom, many thousands of slaves were shipped to the slave markets of Louisiana on Mississippi river boats. These slaves were literally 'sold down the river' to work on Deep South plantations. It was exactly this phenomenon that provided Harriet Beecher Stowe with much of the drama and dislocation around which she structured *Uncle Tom's Cabin*. When we first meet Uncle Tom he is a slave living in rural Kentucky, where he has spent most of his life, but he is sold by his owners to a Southern slave-trader and shipped on a paddle steamer to Louisiana, the very heart of the Cotton Kingdom. On the eve of the Civil War the most valuable commodity within the whole American economy was the four million enslaved

Africans. The majority were in the Deep South and almost half of them were employed in the cultivation of cotton. The South had grown so rich from its cotton boom that by the 1860s it enjoyed the highest per capita income on earth − $16.66.[9] There were more millionaires in the Mississippi Valley in 1860 than anywhere else in the United States.[10] At that moment the white population of the 'slave states' stood at around 2.1 million, their wealth, 'way of life' and economy dependent upon the cotton trade and slavery.

After forty years of expansion, the Deep South in the 1860s represented one half of a global, transatlantic industrial economy. The Cotton Kingdom was the economic twin of Manchester, or 'Cottonopolis' as it had come to be known. Manchester, the shock city of the Industrial Revolution, was the centre of a vast constellation of British mills and factories − around two and a half thousand cotton mills and factories in Lancashire. Broadly speaking spinning was based to the south of Manchester and the weaving of the spun thread into cloth was centred to the north, and certain cities had acquired specialisms for various types of cloth. The cotton industry was directly employing 430,000 people, the majority of whom were women. Around 500,000 people worked in the ancillary industries, producing hosiery and other cotton goods, working in the docks where the cotton bales were unloaded and in the warehouses where they were stored. An army of mechanics kept the looms and spindles oiled and correctly calibrated, small dealers of innumerable types fed and supplied the workers and in Manchester itself the local Cotton Exchange kept a cabal of traders and speculators constantly busy. For each worker employed directly in the mills there were said to be another three who were to some extent dependent upon cotton. *The Economist* wrote that 'the cotton manufacture, from the first manipulation of the raw material to the last finish bestowed upon it, constitutes the employment and furnishes the sustenance of the largest proportion of the population of Lancashire, North Cheshire, and Lanarkshire . . . if we take into account the subsidiary trading occupations and add the dependent members of their families we may safely assume that nearer four than three million are dependent for their daily bread on this branch of our industry'.[11] Four million people was a fifth of the entire population of Britain.

The rise of cotton had forged what one American journalist described as 'a fusion of interests' between 'The planters of the United States . . . and the manufacturers of Great Britain'.[12] The Cotton Kingdom and Cottonopolis lived in a state of economic co-dependency; disruption in one region risked bringing ruin upon the other. In 1853 *The Economist* warned portentously that should 'any great social or physical convulsion visit the United States', then 'England would feel the shock from Land's End to John O'Groats.'[13]

The shop window for the cotton industry was Manchester itself, known as the city that clothed the world. Manchester was supplied with the cotton that was her economic lifeblood by the city that is today her great rival but that was then her closest ally – Liverpool. Just thirty miles apart, Liverpool and Manchester were critical to one another's economic development and advanced together in a state of mutual co-dependence. Both underwent enormous population booms made possible, in large part, by the rise of the cotton economy. The two cities began the nineteenth century with populations of less than 100,000 but by the middle of the 1860s had become comparative megacities with populations of more than 500,000. Liverpool, the dominant port of the eighteenth-century triangular slave trade, became the great nineteenth-century port for the importation of slave-produced cotton. One commentator noted that, 'When the Whigs . . . effected its abolition there were many who thought that the sun of Liverpool's prosperity had set. [but] The cotton trade was to do a vast deal more for the great port of the Mersey than the trade in human flesh'.[14] This was because, as was explained, 'The same wind which bore a vessel from the Mersey would waft her across the Atlantic to the rich Sea Islands, or to New Orleans, the great emporium of the Cotton States of America.'[15] The Liverpool banks and trading houses that had financed the slave trade diversified into the cotton business. The string of docks along the Mersey rapidly expanded.

The roots of much of this wealth stretched across the ocean and into Southern society, feeding off the lives and labour of 1.8 million American slaves. Their bodies were commodities within the global cotton economy, their sweat and their suffering integral to Britain's industrial power. Although cotton was drawn into Liverpool from Brazil, Egypt, India and elsewhere, the proportion of that critical commodity which came into Britain from the United States never fell below 73.4 per cent between 1840 and 1858. In the peak year, 97.1 per cent of all the cotton landed on the Mersey came from the US.[16] Three decades after abolishing slavery and half a century after abolishing the slave trade Britain was, economically speaking, up to her neck in Southern cotton slavery. Here the barriers between black British history and mainstream history break down. The Africans who grew and picked the cotton that landed in enormous bales on the docks of Liverpool, although they never set foot on British soil, are as much a part of our story as any black migrant. They were as much caught up in British power and the Atlantic economy as the West Indian slaves who just two decades earlier had been freed from bondage on British plantations. When Karl Marx looked at Britain as she was in the early 1860s, he saw the nation dependent upon two systems of slavery. 'As long as the English cotton manufacturers depended on slave-grown cotton,' he wrote, 'it could truthfully be asserted that they rested on a twofold slavery, the indirect slavery of the white man in England and the direct slavery of the black men on the other side of the Atlantic'.[17]

In March 1858, James Henry Hammond, a Senator for South Carolina who owned a plantation with more than three hundred enslaved Africans, gave from the floor of the US Senate a speech that would become infamous. Speaking for much of the ruling elite of the South he outlined what became known as his 'Mudsill Theory', a doctrine that said slavery was justifiable, ancient and economically essential. 'In all social systems', Hammond explained, 'there must be a class to do the menial duties, to perform the drudgery of life. That is, a class requiring but a low order of intellect and but little skill. Its requisites are vigour, docility, fidelity. Such a class you must have, or you would not have that other class which leads progress, civilization, and refinement. It constitutes the very mud-sill of society . . . . Fortunately for the South, she found a race adapted to that purpose to her hand. A race inferior to her own, but eminently qualified in temper, in vigour, in docility, in capacity to stand the climate, to answer all her purposes. We use them for our purpose, and call them slaves.'[18] Many Southerners not only agreed with Hammond, they believed that American slavery and the American cotton industry had developed together in perfect unison and in accordance to 'Nature's law'. This confluence of events, the development of this hyper-profitable mono-crop and the system of 'negro slavery', was taken by some as proof of God's benevolence and perhaps even of some higher plan. In a collection of letters published some years earlier Hammond had stated that in his view 'American slavery is not only not a sin, but especially commanded by God through Moses, and approved by Christ through his apostles.'[19]

In his Mudsill Theory speech, Hammond denounced a 'Senator from New York' who had attacked Southern slavery. In defence of slavery Hammond not only dismissed calls for abolition, he compared the slaves who laboured in the cotton fields of the South to the white men and women who worked in the factories of the North. 'Your whole hireling class of manual laborers and "operatives," as you call them, are essentially slaves', Hammond claimed. 'The difference between us is, that our slaves are hired for life and well compensated; there is no starvation, no begging, no want of employment among our people, and not too much employment either. Yours are hired by the day, not cared for, and scantily compensated, which may be proved in the most painful manner, at any hour in any street of your large towns. Why, you meet more beggars in one day, in any single street of the city of New York, than you would meet in a lifetime in the whole South . . . Our slaves are black, of another and inferior race. The status in which we have placed them is an elevation. They are elevated from the condition in which God first created them, by being made our slaves. None of that race on the whole face of the globe can be compared with the slaves of the South. They are happy, content, unaspiring, and utterly incapable, from intellectual weakness, ever to give us any trouble by their aspirations. Yours are white, of your own race; you are brothers of one blood. They are your equals in natural endowment of intellect, and they feel galled by their degradation.'[20] James Henry Hammond's speech, perhaps more than any other, explains why it was that in 1861 the United States of America went to war against herself. The House was, as Abraham Lincoln later said, 'divided against itself' and could not and did not stand, but those who brought about its collapse always intended to draw the world into the conflict, for a civil war was a global affair.

James Henry Hammond remarkably defended slavery not only

from Northern Senators but also, when he felt it necessary, from British abolitionists. In 1845 he published a collected volume of his letters, which he claimed had never been 'originally intended for publication', as a riposte to the international campaign of American and British abolitionists, an unjustified assault of the slave-holding South, which according to Hammond, had seen 'Clergymen lay aside their Bibles, and Females unsex themselves to carry on this horrid warfare against Slave-holders'.[21] This compendium of letters was addressed to 'Thomas Clarkson, the English Abolitionist'. Hammond and many other Southerners regarded Clarkson as an enemy because of his role in the World Anti-Slavery Convention of 1840. At that gathering, which had been well reported in the United States, Clarkson had reasoned that the planters of the American South and their supporters were essentially amoral and as such immune to Christian sentiment or appeals to their moral consciences. The only strategy when opposing such an enemy, he had suggested, was to appeal to their material interests. Clarkson and others had therefore called for a boycott of slave-produced Southern cotton and its substitution in the mills of England with cotton produced by free labourers in India. That way, Clarkson suggested, Britain and her factories would no longer be contaminated by America's 'blood stained produce', and the economic foundations of the slave economy of the Mississippi Valley would be swept away. In the two decades since the World Anti-Slavery Convention the opposite had happened. The Cotton kingdom had expanded and Britain had become even more dependent upon Southern cotton. In 1855 the pro-slavery American journalist David Christy had published one of the most famous books of the century, *Cotton is king*, which like many books of the age had a long but telling subtitle – *The culture of cotton, and its relation to agriculture, manufactures and commerce; to the free colored people; and to those who hold that slavery is in itself sinful*. In his opening chapter Christy argued that the opportunity Thomas Clarkson and the abolitionists had identified in 1840 had been missed. Slavery in America, he conceded, might perhaps have been abolished in earlier decades as 'There was a time when American slave labor sustained no such relations to the manufactures and commerce of the world as it now so firmly holds; and when, by the adoption of proper measures, on the part of the free colored people and their friends, the emancipation of the slaves, in all the States, might have been effected. But that period has passed forever away'.[22] By the mid-1850s, after what Christy called 'nearly a "thirty years' war"' fought by a transatlantic alliance of free black people and their abolitionist supporters, 'causes, unforeseen, have come into operation, which are too powerful to be overcome . . . What Divine Providence may have in store for the future, we know not; but, at present, the institution of Slavery is sustained by numberless pillars, too massive for human power and wisdom to overthrow'.[23] Abolition of American slavery, Christy assured his readers, was an economic impossibility because, 'Cotton IS King, and his enemies are vanquished'.[24]

James Henry Hammond's 1858 speech to the US Senate is infamous today not for its unabashed defence of slavery, or its dismissal of black people as an 'inferior race'. His words – like those of David Christy – are remembered for their hubris. In the most provocative part of his address Hammond had suggested that the economic power of cotton was so formidable that it rendered the South and Southern slavery invulnerable.

If the Northern states of the Union were to make war on the slave-holding Southern states then 'King Cotton' would come to their defence. Cotton would force the owners of cotton mills in the Northern states to support their Southern business partners and it would reach out across the Atlantic and compel the merchants and the working people of abolitionist, anti-slavery Britain to recognize Southern independence, and perhaps even offer the South material aid. If Britain's leaders were to follow any other policy, Hammond reasoned, they would be condemning half a million Lancashire mill workers, and 3.5 million of their dependants and fellow countrymen, to destitution. He was far from alone in believing that in cotton the South had found an economic super-weapon. Three months before the outbreak of the Civil War, *The Times* grew alarmed at the growing clamour for war in the South. In near-apocalyptic tones it warned its British readers that an American war would leave '4,000,000 people in trepidation and distress.' Appreciating the danger earlier than many of the mill owners, *The Times* thundered, 'one-third of our trade is in jeopardy and the earnings of one-sixth of our population may be rendered precarious . . . We look upon the prospect with an affected horror . . . We ask whether any man in the kingdom can contemplate it without terror?'[25]

When war did finally come it arrived first in Hammond's home state of South Carolina. On 28 April 1861 South Carolinian rebels launched a bombardment on the federal garrison at Fort Sumter in Charleston Harbor, claiming the federal soldiers garrisoned there constituted 'a foreign entity' upon South Carolinian territory. In his speech of 1858 Hammond had warned that in order to unleash the full, war-winning power of King Cotton, 'The South is willing to go one, two or three years without planting a seed'. In the event Southern plantation owners were not called upon to leave their fields fallow or hoard their cotton seeds. Six days after the attack on Fort Sumter, Abraham Lincoln's government declared a blockade of all Southern ports, and for the next four years the planters of the Deep South, rather than boycotting production, were desperately seeking out means of breaching the Northern blockade and shipping even a fraction of their precious cotton to the factories of England.

Yet even before the imposition of the Northern blockade the Cotton is King strategy had been undermined. Years of sabre-rattling and secessionist posturing had not gone unnoticed in Europe. Mill owners in Britain had been given fair warning of the coming war, and ample time to consider their options. Lancashire's cotton manufacturers had stockpiled supplies and sought out new sources of raw cotton. Stockpiles had been built especially high as the years immediately prior to the Civil War had provided bumper crops. Between 1859 and 1860 America cotton producers had exceeded world demand. The overproduction of raw cotton had fed through into the supply of finished goods and at the end of 1860 there were vast stocks of unsold cotton clothing on the world market. Although most observers believed that the war would be brief, and that the stockpiled raw cotton would be enough to see Lancashire's mills through the crisis, efforts had been made to expand production elsewhere. Production of Egyptian and Indian cotton had been increased and additional supplies of Brazilian cotton were also coming online. A group of opportunistic British investors had also pumped money into the cotton-cultivating regions of Ottoman Anatolia. The outbreak of hostilities in Charleston Harbor was therefore not seen as a reason for immediate panic and those who had for years talked up the idea of 'King Cotton' as a war-winning weapon were momentarily dumbfounded. When prices began to rise it was not entirely as a result of scarcity but also because across the world cotton merchants had engaged in an orgy of price speculation and hoarding. Cotton was bought, sold and resold, passing through the hands of every known species of speculator, trader, broker, warehouseman and shipping agent on its laborious progress from field to factory, and at each stage a commission was charged or a profit drawn. By the time the cotton reached the loom it had risen in price several fold. By early 1862 the stockpiles had begun to dwindle and the unsold stocks of cotton goods had found buyers. Although additional supplies of raw cotton were arriving from India and elsewhere, Britain's imports of cotton in 1862 were half what they had been in the last year of peace. Imports from the United States stood at 4 per cent of their pre-war levels. By October 1862, around 58 per cent of all Lancashire looms stood idle for want of cotton. The smaller mills, which were often owned by operators who were heavily mortgaged, were the first affected and the first to close their doors and lay off workers. The wealthier mill owners, many of whom remained convinced even in 1862 that the war would soon be over, had the financial reserves to weather more of the storm. Looking to the long term they were desperate to avoid seeing their relatively skilled workforce, with its specialized skills, broken up and scattered. To prevent workers from migrating to other regions in search of new employment some negotiated cuts in pay and a few agreed to shorter hours. Where they could, mill owners attempted to process alternative, non-American cottons, but there was not enough to go round and not all machines were compatible with the most common Indian 'short staple' variety, which was far less profitable as its fibres easily snapped and frayed during both the spinning and weaving processes. This demanded constant intervention from machine operators, slowing down production and shrinking profits.

At the end of 1862 around 70 per cent of the labour force, 312,200 men and women, were without work. The Lancashire Cotton Famine, as it had become known, impoverished both mill workers and men and women employed in related trades and industries. With some irony the mill workers began to pawn the last of their possessions, which included their cotton goods, shirts and dresses, bed sheets and tablecloths. The poet Edwin Waugh visited Preston in 1862 and saw the effects of the cotton famine at close quarters.

> I was astonished at the dismal succession of destitute homes and the number of struggling owners of little shops, who were watching their stocks sink gradually down to nothing and looking despondingly at the cold approach of pauperism. I was astonished at the strings of dwellings, side by side, stript, more or less, of the commonest household utensils . . . sometimes crowded, three or four families of decent working people in a cottage of half-a-crown a week rental; sleeping anywhere, on benches or on straw, and afraid to doff their clothes at night because they had no other covering.[26]

Thousands of destitute mill workers, rather than await the approach of pauperism, moved away to find new employment. Journalists who visited the region reported the roads packed with footsore men, trudging between the towns looking for work or heading off to other regions. Some left to find work in the wool industries of Yorkshire and some of those who had savings used them to purchase cheap, steerage-class tickets to New York.

To provide for those who did not or could not leave, the creaking architecture of the Poor Law was brought into operation. The Poor Law, a hated system that ran the workhouses, was administered by local Poor Law Guardians but was utterly unsuited to a crisis on the scale of the cotton famine. The Poor Law Guardians were tasked with finding employment on public-works schemes for those men able to labour and provide relief for those who could not. Among the many aspects of the system that were deeply resented was its inability to draw a distinction between respectable working men who found themselves unemployed due to no fault of their own, and the feckless and the drunkards. All forms of unemployment were seemingly tarred with the same judgemental brush. The Poor Law demanded the men work for their bread and thousands were sent to the stone yards or quarries to break stones. One unexpected complication of this practice was that men and women accustomed to working as machine operators in the almost tropically hot conditions of the cotton mills suffered desperately when forced to labour in the open air of cold northern England. Large numbers of men were made sick as their lungs, corrupted and contaminated by years of cotton dust, failed them in the stone yards.

To augment the funds made available to the Poor Law Guardians, local relief committees were established. In May 1862 the Lancashire and Cheshire Operatives Relief Fund was born and a month later the Cotton Districts Relief Fund was created. Around the same time a Central Committee brought together the mayors of the worst-suffering mill towns. Seventeen local relief committees were formed, one in each of the major mill towns. Appeals for private donations were made to better-off parts of the country as well as to Britons living in the empire. In 1863 the government pushed through the Public Works Act, which allowed local authorities to raise funds to pay for public-works schemes that would provide paid work for the unemployed mill workers. Across Lancashire today are their physical remains. Sewers were constructed, canals dug, parks created, roads resurfaced or constructed from scratch. One of the most bizarre relics of the cotton famine can be found above Rochdale. Running across the Pennines through Rooley Moor is the Cotton Famine Road, a substantial, well-built, Victorian cobblestone highway. It shoots incongruously across the heather going to nowhere in particular. It was the labour of thousands of men who would much rather have been earning the high industrial wages available in the cotton mills. Despite these efforts the cotton famine devastated Lancashire. Soup kitchens had to be opened; some were almost immediately overwhelmed and ran out of funds and food to distribute. In December 1862 at the very height of the cotton famine the Guardians who oversaw the Poor Law, along with the various relief committees, were between them supporting 485,434 people in Lancashire.[27] In the town of Stalybridge, in which all but five of the sixty-three factories had been forced to close, a riot broke out and soldiers with fixed bayonets patrolled the streets. Although commonly remembered as the Lancashire Cotton Famine the distress spread to all the regions of the country in which cotton was processed. There was comparable suffering but on a smaller scale in Cheshire and Derbyshire as well as in parts of Scotland and Northern Ireland.

Hundreds of thousands of working-class Britons had been cast into destitution, new forms of poor relief had been hurriedly put in place and the British economy had been dealt a thunderous blow, all because an ocean away the forced labour of four million enslaved, black Americans had been disrupted. The mill workers of Lancashire and the slaves of the Mississippi Valley were unknowingly trapped within what historians call the First Age of Globalization – which began in the middle of the nineteenth century and was brought to an end by World War One and its isolationist aftermath. The mills of Lancashire, and the towns that had been built around them, were particularly exposed to shocks elsewhere in the system not merely because the cotton they processed was vulnerable to naval blockade, but because it was produced by enslaved people. Everywhere in the Atlantic world the enslavement of Africans had been met not with passive acceptance but with war and revolution. Slavery was an inherently unstable institution; we understandably focus on its brutality rather than its inefficiency. British abolition had been achieved largely peacefully, but had come about only after a succession of West Indian slave rebellions, and the fear of further impending revolts that drove all sides to the negotiating table in 1833. Slavery in America was extinguished not through slave rebellions but by a war, fought predominantly by white men, over the future of slavery in the South and in the as yet unconquered West. For all her 'moral prestige', post-emancipation, anti-slavery Britain had ignored the calls of abolitionists like Thomas Clarkson and remained economically complicit in American slavery. In the 1860s the poor people in the English North-West paid a heavy price for that hypocrisy.

In 1861, during the early months of the Civil War, the British genre painter Richard Ansdell completed *The Hunted Slaves*, one of his most effective, if less well-known, works which depicted a potent and highly topical subject – the fugitive slave. By 1861 numerous artists, along with a number of writers and poets in both Britain and America, had explored the theme. When Ansdell's painting was first exhibited at the Royal Academy in 1861 its catalogue entry included a quote from Henry Longfellow's abolitionist poem *The Slave In the Dismal Swamp*, which told of the plight of a slave fugitive being pursued through the swamps of Virginia. Ansdell's painting may well have been a painterly realization of another literary work. It has been suggested that it was inspired by a passage in *Uncle Tom's Cabin*. The scene in question tells the story of Scipio, described by Harriet Beecher Stowe as 'a native-born African' man who had the 'rude instinct of freedom in him to an uncommon degree'. Having escaped his slave-masters, Scipio is hunted down, pursued across a swamp and eventually surrounded by the bloodhounds of the local slave-catchers. We find Ansdell's fugitives – a man and a woman, presumably husband and wife – trapped in the same predicament. Driven into the far right of the canvas by a pack of snarling mastiffs, the husband raises an axe to strike at one of the fearsome hounds as it rushes at them through the reeds. Around his wrist hang the broken chains of slavery and at his feet another of the attack dogs lies stricken, reeling from a blow delivered by the axe. Near the bare ankles of his wife a snake coils itself menacingly around a log, adding to the sense of imminent and inevitable disaster. The sky is tinged with pink, hinting that this slave hunt has lasted all day, and behind the desperate couple the swamp stretches off to the horizon.

Any Victorian viewer of the painting who knew something of the workings of the Southern slave system – which, by 1861, would have included anyone who had read *Uncle Tom's Cabin* – would have understood that the couple's predicament was dire. The informed viewer would have known that the hounds – whose collars are clearly visible – had, moments earlier, been released by the slave-hunters and that they themselves would soon be on the scene to disarm and capture the fugitive couple. The art critic of *The Times* described *The Hunted Slaves* as a painting with '*vigour* enough, and subject enough, for those who like such strong meat'. Aware that its subject was controversial and its execution perfectly calibrated to evoke sympathy and moral condemnation, he noted that, 'The present circumstances of the South will enhance its interest'.[28] Such was the painting's impact that prints were made and sold to the public.[29] In September 1862, as the dreadful scale of the cotton famine was becoming apparent, Richard Ansdell donated *The Hunted Slaves* to the Lancashire Cotton Relief Committee. It was offered as a prize in a lottery and raised £700 for the nearby mill towns. The winner was one Gilbert Moss of Liverpool, who gave it to the

City Corporation. Today it hangs in Liverpool's International Slavery Museum, a memorial to both the passion of British anti-slavery sentiment and as a relic of the great outpouring of charity and relief that helped save the people of Lancashire from hunger and destitution. Yet Ansdell's evident sympathy for the American slave was not indicative of the attitudes that prevailed in his native city. Liverpool in the 1860s was a city that had little sympathy for fugitive slaves or for anyone whose actions disrupted the transatlantic flow of American cotton. More than any British city, Liverpool stood by and sided with the pro-slavery Confederate states during the Civil War. While there was considerable Confederate lobbying in London, and while both arms and ships were supplied to the South from Glasgow, Liverpool was the Confederate's most steadfast ally and for four years became, in effect, the European headquarters of the Confederate states, and was described as such by its supporters. It was in Liverpool's Rumford Place that the Confederate Government of Jefferson Davis established an unofficial embassy and a Liverpool firm, Fraser Trenholm and Co., became the company through which the business affairs of the Confederate government were organized in England. The South's greatest champion on Merseyside, and one of their chief propagandists in Britain, was James Spence, a member of the city's Exchange and a moderately successful merchant in tinplate. Spence helped found the Liverpool Southern Club and helped propagate support for the South among the mill towns of Lancashire. It was said that more Confederate flags fluttered over the Mersey than the Mississippi and under those banners the city's merchants met Southern representatives and businessmen in mansions in the more expensive and fashionable districts of the city to plot how they could support the South and turn the crisis into a business opportunity. In May 1861 Britain declared herself neutral in the American Civil War. That month the new Foreign Enlistment Act prohibited British citizens from serving in either Lincoln's Union Army or Jefferson Davis' Confederate Army, nor in the navies or on the merchant ships of either North or South. British shipbuilders were officially prohibited from building warships for either side, and from arming or supplying ships that were intent on making war on the navies or merchant fleets of North or South. The Liverpool merchant Thomas E. Taylor described how the Liverpool merchants reacted to the news of the British neutrality:

> The proclamation awakened no respect whatever for the blockade . . . it was received in the spirit in which it was issued – as a piece of mere international courtesy; and those of her Majesty's loyal subjects who were most affected by the new situation at once took steps to make the best of it . . . Firm after firm, with an entirely free conscience, set about endeavouring to recoup itself for the loss of legitimate trade by the high profits to be made out of successful evasions of the Federal cruisers; and in Liverpool was awakened a spirit the like of which had not been known since the palmy days of the slave trade.[30]

For the traders of Liverpool their nation's official policy of strict neutrality meant nothing and they set about thwarting the restrictions and breaking the rules, not that the government went far out of its way to enforce British neutrality. Goods bound for the Confederacy were shipped to British ports in the Bahamas and there transferred to fast, specially-built American ships known as blockade-runners. The British vessels then loaded up with Southern cotton and sailed back to Liverpool with their illicit cargo, which attracted high prices in the cotton exchanges of Liverpool and Manchester. Such brazen disregard for national policy was only possible with official collusion. The British officials and local governors in those far-off outposts tended to be pro-Confederacy and willing to turn blind eyes to blockade-running.[31] Liverpool's shipyards built at least thirty-six blockade-runners for the South during the Civil War and most of them were manned by crews that included large numbers of British officers and men willing to risk the dangers for the fortunes to be made bringing guns to the Confederates and shipping back cotton to the 'hungry mills' of Lancashire. The British officers, both Royal Navy and merchant, who ran the blockade tended to do so under *noms de guerre*. Some went on to have notable naval careers and were never censured for having contravened national policy and broken international law.

In March 1862 a newly constructed ship, the *Oreto*, left Liverpool to begin life as a merchant ship for new owners. Some months later she appeared in American waters as a fully armed Confederate steam-ship, CSS *Florida*. On board was a crew that consisted mainly of British sailors and officers. After this, suspicion was aroused in London about a vessel then being built in Birkenhead by the firm John Laird and Sons. Ship no. 290 was clearly a warship and yet even after the government had been alerted, and even though both Prime Minister Lord Palmerston and Foreign Secretary John Russell had been warned that ship no. 290 was a Confederate warship, she was allowed to set sail. Ship no. 290 was next sighted in the Caribbean having trans-formed herself into the armed screw sloop the CSS *Alabama*. She bristled with British-made armaments and like the *Florida* was manned by British sailors. John Laird and Sons were evidently a company able to bend to the prevailing winds of politics. Twenty years earlier they had built the steamers *Albert*, *Soudan* and *Wilberforce* in which anti-slavery missionaries had, with royal support, embarked upon a doomed expedition up the River Niger to develop legitimate trades and thereby undermine the economics of the slave trade. Despite having openly built the *Alabama* in blatant breach of the law the firm was never prosecuted. The British government however were. After the Civil War the United States government pursued legal claims against Britain demanding damages arising from the ships that the CSS *Alabama* had sunk during the war. In 1872 the British government settled the so-called *Alabama* claims by payments to the United States of $15.5 million. During the Civil War Liverpool's newspapers followed the merchants' lead. Three out of four of them sided with the South. The fourth, the *Liverpool Daily Post*, admitted in an editorial that its pro-neutrality stance was bound to prove unpopular in the city.[32] On more than one occasion in the early years of the war abolitionist meetings were disrupted and anti-slavery speakers heckled and even assaulted – incidents that would have been almost incon-ceivable in the 1840s. The American abolitionist Henry Ward Beecher, the brother of Harriet Beecher Stowe, spoke in Liverpool in October 1863, after an invitation from the Union Emancipation Society; he was harangued and heckled by members of the crowd. These voices were later dismissed as the impotent 'bellowings and howlings' of 'Southern hirelings' who were attempting to 'stifle the voice of Liver-pool for freedom'.[33] But it was not an isolated incident and Beecher came away convinced that all classes of Liverpudlians favoured the

Confederacy. In this atmosphere, and in a city that was home to numerous Southern businessmen and Confederate agents, the anti-slavery traditions upon which Britain had set such store gave way during the Civil War to open advocacy of slavery.

Southerners like Senator James Henry Hammond who had convinced both themselves and others that 'Cotton IS King' had disastrously misunderstood the scale and the complexity of Victorian Britain's economy. Although the suffering and distress of the people of Lanca-shire was real and damaging, the predictions of economic collapse made before the war, in both Britain and America, had been over-blown. Cotton was not the only material from which cloth could be woven: the wool and linen industries underwent minor revivals. Britain's arsenals and foundries supplied arms and munitions to both sides – both legally and illicitly. British factories manufactured uniforms, boots and other materials of war and the financiers of the City of London loaned money to and drew profits from the wartime economies of both North and South. In these ways and others, the wider British economy was able to make up for some of the losses suffered by the cotton industry. If the reasons why 'King Cotton' did not bring Britain's economy down are increasingly clear to historians, a more complex and vexing question remains: why did Britain choose neutrality? While the government's policy can be put down to cold pragmatism and cautious self-interest, the popular reaction is harder to understand. Why did a people who had flocked to buy 1.5 million copies of *Uncle Tom's Cabin*, and who had welcomed Frederick Doug-lass and the whole pantheon of African American abolitionists into their assembly rooms and town halls, not rush to support the North? Why did the anti-slavery impulse that was still strong among large sectors of the population not inspire immediate condemnation of the South and praise for Lincoln and the North? British attitudes confused commentators at the time and have puzzled historians since. Harriet Beecher Stowe struggled to make sense of this very contra-diction. In 1863 she wrote *A reply to "The affectionate and Christian address of many thousands of women of Great Britain and Ireland, to their sisters, the women of the United states of America"* in which she reminded British women of the strong anti-slavery sentiment they had demonstrated during her visit a decade earlier. Stowe expressed her alarm and surprise that in the ten intervening years there appeared to have been a 'decline of the noble anti-slavery fire in England'.[34] In the hope of rekindling those flames she deployed all the rhetorical flourish that might be expected of a woman who had spent her life among the fiery speeches of the anti-slavery circuit. Addressing the 'Sisters of England' she explained how many in the North felt betrayed by the factions within Britain who were actively supporting the Confederacy. 'We have heard on the high seas the voice of a war-steamer, built for a man-stealing Confederacy with English gold in an English dockyard, going out of an English harbour, manned by English sailors, with the full knowledge of English Government-officers, in defiance of the Queen's proclamation of neutrality.'[35] The war-steamers that preyed on Northern shipping and weighed on Harriet Beecher Stowe's mind were the products of Liverpool's pro-Confederacy merchant elite, but what did the people of the cotton-producing towns themselves think about the war and the terrible predicament it had placed them in? It was once simplistically believed that support for North and South was split on the basis of class, with the mill owners and the merchants supporting the South, and the mill workers supporting the North. In truth the patterns of support for North and South across the country and across the four years of the war are complex and no simple narrative emerges.[36] Memories of the cotton famine are also clouded by folklore and by later misrepresentations. But in the first two years of the war there was unquestionably a tendency among all classes in Britain to support the South rather than the North. More pro-South societies than pro-North ones were formed in the towns and most of the newspapers supported the cause of the region's trading partners in the Mississippi Valley.

There were many among the propertied classes of Britain who saw in the South a latent nation of landowners and proto-aristocrats with whom they felt a natural affinity. Some among the wealthy elite, in business and in Parliament, who supported the South camouflaged their real motivations behind an insincere concern for the fate of the cotton workers of Lancashire. Yet there were also members of the propertied classes who had long opposed slavery for moral reasons, and who were opposed to the South and disturbed by what one writer called 'The Slaveholders' War'. Some industrialists and politicians supported the North because they regarded slave labour as inferior to free labour, as they regarded free trade as superior to protectionism. They viewed slavery as a highly unstable system upon which Britain had unwisely, if only by proxy, become economically dependent.[37] But there was also considerable support for the South among the mill workers of Lancashire. Letters to local newspapers and reports of the meetings of pro-Southern clubs reveal that many of the mill workers viewed democratic America as a land where white working-class men were awarded full citizenship and given opportunities that were denied them in class-riven Britain. Many supported the South partly out of a sense of racial solidarity. To them the South was a nation full of 'little white men', like themselves. Some regarded the Northern blockade as an assault upon the principle of free trade and others distrusted the government of Abraham Lincoln, seeing it as centralizing and perhaps even authoritarian. In all the mill towns, pro-Confederate 'Southern Clubs' were formed. Lectures were given in defence of the South and its right to secure its freedom outside the United States. Some of this was the work of Southern agitators and their British supporters, men like James Spence, a Liverpool tin merchant, but these agents of the Confederacy were able to tap into sympathies that pre-existed their propagandizing. The majority of the local MPs in Lancashire either favoured the South or kept their opinions to themselves. In April 1862 in the cotton-producing town of Ashton-under-Lyne, six thousand unemployed mill workers gathered together in an enormous public meeting to condemn the Northern blockade. The following year eight thousand people gathered in Oldham to support the South. In October 1862 a minister from one of Oldham's Congregationalist churches was shouted down when he called upon the people of the town to support the North. A Southern Independence Association was formed in the town, and at a meeting called by the deputy mayor, the Confederacy was described as 'heroic', and a motion passed stating that its recognition by England was the best way of ending both the Civil War and the suffering of the Oldham mill workers. Pro-North, anti-slavery meetings were held and counter-demonstrations did assemble, many of them organized by the energetic members of the Union and Emancipation Society, but

more voices were raised in support of the South and in favour of
its recognition than in opposition to slavery and support of President
Lincoln's government. Perhaps it is not surprising that hungry,
fearful people supported a political strategy that would alleviate
their sufferings and revive their economic fortunes. The pioneering
work of the historian Mary Ellison shows how in the face of distress
some of the workers of Lancashire acted out of self-interest and
sided with the Confederacy, or at least favoured its recognition by
the British government.[38] Her analysis suggests that the areas worst
affected by the cotton famine tended to be those most committed
to supporting the South's right to secede from the Union. This is
not to say that the people of Oldham or Preston were pro-slavery
but merely that they were desperate for their government to intervene on their behalf, recognize the Confederacy and restore the
flow of cotton. Yet many workers, the men and women with the
least to gain and the most to lose, did support the North and doing
so acted counter to their immediate economic interests. There were
men and women in all the mill towns who even during the worst
months of the cotton famine regarded themselves as the guardians
and inheritors of Britain's anti-slavery traditions and acted accordingly. To them anti-slavery was so intertwined with Britishness that
support for the South was unthinkable. Viewing the conflict through
the prism of class they also saw in the plantation owners of the
Deep South a propertied class that reminded them of the mill
owners and the aristocrats of Britain.

Some of the men and women who were impoverished by the cotton
famine understood that the last hands to have touched the bales of
cotton that arrived in the mills were those of the black slaves who
had loaded them onto ships on the docks of Mobile and New Orleans.
The Lancashire towns from which unions and cooperative societies
emerged were those that most firmly supported the North and its
advocacy of free labour. The town most strongly pro-North and most
passionately anti-slavery was Rochdale, where abolitionist and anti-
slavery societies had been vocally active long before the outbreak of
the American Civil War. Since the 1850s the town had been able to
look for inspiration to the figure of John Bright, the Quaker, Liberal
Party MP who was from a Rochdale, mill-owning family. The Bright
family's own Rochdale mills ran out of cotton in late 1861, yet John

33. A famous and horrific image of the scars left by the whip. By the 1860s, 1.8 million enslaved Americans were engaged in the cultivation of cotton, the bulk of which was exported to Britain.

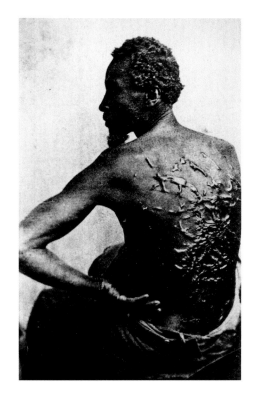

34. There were around 4,500 mills in Lancashire processing cotton. The American Civil War plunged the region into an economic crisis known as the Cotton Famine.

35. A wedding photograph of James Davies and Sarah Forbes Bonetta. Captured in war as an infant, she was presented to a British naval officer by King Ghezo of Dahomey as a gift for Queen Victoria. Brought up under the protection of the Queen, her wedding in 1862 was a society event.

36. Cetshwayo kaMpande, the king of the Zulu who famously led his people to victory over British forces at the Battle of Isandlwana. After being deposed he toured Britain in 1882, had an audience with Queen Victoria and was partially restored to the throne.

37. The 'Congo conference' of 1884–1885. Held in Berlin, this gathering of great powers set the terms by which the late-Victorian 'Scramble for Africa' was organized. No Africans were present.

38. There are few images of the West Africa Squadron but later photographs taken of slavery-suppression missions in the Indian Ocean capture the drama. Here enslaved East Africans sit on the deck of HMS *Daphne* in November 1868.

39. Children released from an intercepted dhow aboard HMS *Daphne* in 1868.

40. The three kings of Bechuanaland travelled to Britain in 1895 in order to appeal to British public opinion and escape the clutches of Cecil Rhodes and the British South Africa Company. From left to right: Sebele I of the Bakwena, Bathoen I of the Bangwaketse, and Khama III of the Bamangwato. To the far right stands their ally, the Reverend William Charles Willoughby of the London Missionary Society.

41. Khama III (c. 1837–1923), king of the Bamangwato people of Bechuanaland, now Botswana. Under his reign the country became a British protectorate.

42. 'The Conquest of Africa', a children's board game based on the travels of the African explorer and journalists Henry Morton Stanley.

Village Sénégalais. – Porte Maillot.　　　　　　Les Lutteurs

43. Senegalese wrestlers perform for visitors at a French colonial exhibition in a mock-African village specially constructed for the event in Paris.

44. 'A Peek at the Natives'. This contemporary and highly racialized illustration shows visitors to the infamous 'Savage South Africa' show at Earl's Court in 1899. The show promised visitors 'a sight never seen previously in Europe, a horde of savages direct from their kraals'.

45. A postcard of Abomah the African Giantess, from around 1911. Believed to be around seven feet tall, she was billed in the music halls and theatres of Britain as an 'African Amazon', a female warrior of Dahomey. Her real name was Ella Williams, the daughter of liberated slaves from South Carolina.

46. Pablo Fanque, the black circus performer and entrepreneur depicted in the *Illustrated London News*, 20 March 1847. A poster for one of his performances inspired the Beatles to write the song 'Being For the Benefit of Mr Kite', which appeared on *Sgt. Pepper's Lonely Hearts Club Band*.

Souvenir of Abomah the African Giantess

47. Walter Tull, c. 1910. Born in Folkestone, Kent in 1888, Tull was one of the the first black footballers in Britain. At outbreak of World War I, he joined the 1st Footballers' Battalion of the Middlesex Regiment. Despite military rules that barred black men from becoming officers, he was commissioned in May 1917 but died on the Somme in March 1918.

48. Men of the British West Indies Regiment in camp on the Albert–Amiens Road, September 1916.

Bright continued to pay his workers two-thirds of their salaries through the cotton famine. A friend of Frederick Douglass and a correspondent of William H. Seward, US Secretary of State, Bright was passionately opposed to Southern slavery and so committed to the defence of American democracy that his letters on those subjects were read out in meetings of Abraham Lincoln's inner circle.[39]

From the beginning of the conflict, Southern propagandists working in Britain sensed the depths of British anti-slavery sentiment and feared its potential. They were consistently careful never to openly identify the South with slavery and tended to present the South as a new nation seeking its freedom from the grip of a more powerful neighbour. When the issue of slavery could not be sidestepped, the more sophisticated defenders of the South played to British notions of gradualism and conservatism. They presented Lincoln's government as reckless, bent on immediate emancipation of millions of slaves, and suggested that such a course of action would lead inevitably to insurrection and racial war. Confederate propagandists and their supporters warned that Lincoln's policies risked igniting a conflict that would place white women and children in dreadful jeopardy and would lead to the extermination of the former slaves. There were those in Britain who, by following this line of thinking, found themselves occupying a position that was at the same time anti-slavery and pro-Confederate. They accepted the Southern fiction that once independence was granted to the new Confederate States of America, they would inevitably abolish slavery of their volition, but cautiously and gradually, rather as Britain herself had done in the 1830s.

While some Britons remained loyal to the Confederacy right up until the final days of the war, the tide of popular opinion and political sympathy turned decisively in late 1862. The critical moment that re-drew the battle lines came in September when Abraham Lincoln issued the Emancipation Proclamation, which promised to free Southern slaves on 1 January 1863. Until that moment Lincoln's official position had been that the war was waged to preserve the Union and not to end the institution of slavery: after it the war was understood in Britain as an armed struggle against slavery. While fears of an American slave uprising lingered on in some quarters, much of the indifference and confusion that had characterized British popular reactions evaporated over the course of 1863 as the emancipation of the Southern slaves was seen as the final realization of British abolitionist dreams. In the mind of the radical Newcastle journalist W. E. Adams, the Emancipation Proclamation cut 'the ground from under the feet of those who profess to sympathise with the South on the grounds that slavery was likely to be sooner abolished by it, than by the North. It is now more evident than ever the pro-Southern sentiments are proslavery sentiments also.'[40] British anti-slavery fervour re-emerged and aligned itself to the Northern cause. The popular force that Southern agents and diplomats had long feared might be aroused began to assert itself. In the last weeks of 1862, pro-North, anti-slavery meetings were held across the country. The most dramatic took place in Manchester on 31 December, the day before the Emancipation Proclamation legally freed the Southern slaves – they became physically free only by abandoning their owners and coming over the Union lines, or at the end of the war when the Confederacy was dissolved. That day a crowd gathered for a 'Manchester Meeting of working-Men' in the Free Trade Hall. The grand public meeting adopted an immediate set of resolutions and drafted an address to be sent to President Lincoln himself. The first resolution recorded that 'this meeting, recognising the common brotherhood of mankind and the sacred and inalienable right of every human being to personal freedom and equal protection, records its detestation of negro slavery in America . . .' The Address to the President stated that 'As the citizens of Manchester, assembled at the Free Trade Hall, we beg to express our fraternal sentiments towards you and your country . . . One thing alone has in the past lessened our sympathy with your country and our confidence in it, we mean the ascendancy of politicians who not merely maintained negro slavery but desired to extend and root it more firmly. Since we have discerned however that the victory of the Free States in the war which has so severely distressed us as well as afflicted you will strike off the fetters of the slave, you have attracted our warm and earnest sympathy . . . Heartily do we congratulate you and your country on this your humane and righteous course'.[41] On 19 January 1863 Lincoln replied, in his address 'To the Working men of Manchester'.

I know and deeply deplore the sufferings which the working people of Manchester and in all Europe are called to endure in this crisis. It has been often and studiously represented that the attempt to overthrow this Government which was built on the foundation of human rights, and to substitute for it one which should rest exclusively on the basis of slavery, was unlikely to obtain the favour of Europe. Through the action of disloyal citizens, the working people of Europe have been subjected to a severe trial for the purpose of forcing their sanction to that attempt. Under the circumstances I cannot but regard your decisive utterances on the question as an instance of sublime Christian heroism which has not been surpassed in any age or in any country. It is indeed an energetic and re-inspiring assurance of the inherent truth and of the ultimate and universal triumph of justice, humanity and freedom. I hail this interchange of sentiments, therefore, as an augury that, whatever else may happen, whatever misfortune may befall your country or my own, the peace and friendship which now exists between the two nations will be, as it shall be my desire to make them, perpetual.

At the end of January an enormous pro-North meeting was held at Exeter Hall in London, the historic centre of abolitionist activity in Britain, a building that was sadly long ago demolished. In February the extent to which pro-North anti-slavery sentiment was on the rise was demonstrated by a gathering of between three and four thousand people in Liverpool, the self-declared 'headquarters of Southern sentiment'. The Liverpool assembly, like the other fifty that were held in towns and cities across Britain in 1863, affirmed its support for President Lincoln and emancipation. While there was some pro-Southern heckling this gathering in the Confederacy's former stronghold was a clear indication that the South's supporters had failed.[42] In July 1863 the Union Army defeated Robert E. Lee's forces at Gettysburg and on the same day the city of Vicksburg fell to President Lincoln's forces after a long and terrible siege. The tide of the war turned as decisively as the tide of British public opinion. In January 1865 Congress passed the 13th Amendment to the Constitution abolishing slavery throughout the United States of America.

TEN

'Mercy in a Massacre'

The pro-Southern, pro-slavery sentiment that had taken hold of Liverpool and seeped out to the mill towns of Lancashire during the first two years of the American Civil War would not have surprised Frederick Douglass. Soon after arriving for his second speaking tour, in late November 1859, he sensed a new mood in Britain. He noted that since his visit in the 1840s sections of the British population had become conspicuously more racist in their attitudes towards black people and notably less sympathetic to the plight of the American slave. Douglass put this alarming change down to the importation into Britain of what he described as 'American prejudice', a mindset which he found to be particularly entrenched in Liverpool; a city which long before the Civil War was firmly on the side of the South and the Southern slave owner. However the chill wind that so disturbed and disappointed him in 1859 had blown in from the West Indies rather than from the Mississippi Valley.

By the late 1850s it had become acceptable, if not exactly respectable, in Britain to openly and publicly question whether the abolition of British slavery had been a successful enterprise and the right decision. Increasing numbers of people felt able to make public assertions about the capacities and humanity of black people in terms that many would have found unacceptable in the 1830s and 1840s. Patriotic pride in abolition and continuing anti-slavery sentiment remained defining elements of British political and cultural identity, as would be shown by the surge in support for the North following Abraham Lincoln's Emancipation Proclamation in 1862, but by the middle of the century abolition and philanthropy had a growing army of vocal detractors, and new and highly virulent strains of 'scientific racism' were gaining ground. In the opinion of these new sceptics abolition had been a mistake because the whole endeavour had been based upon a mistaken set of assumptions about the nature of Africans. Proponents of this standpoint pointed to the West Indies, where there had been a precipitous decline in the economic fortunes of the plantations in most of the former slave colonies – especially Jamaica. The waning prosperity of the sugar islands was a consequence of numerous factors, most notably the removal of the preferential tariff protections behind which the slave-owning planters had long sheltered. Exposed to the open market, many British producers found it impossible to compete with the sugar producers of Cuba and Brazil – where cane sugar was still produced by enslaved Africans. In addition, decades of over-planting during the boom years of the sugar economy had left the soil exhausted, and in the case of Jamaica her economic decline had begun even before the end of the eighteenth century. The faltering profitability of Jamaican plantations had been reflected in the compensation offered to the planters for slaves on that island, which were valued at around £44, around 38 per cent of the value ascribed to slaves in Guyana, where prime estates built on fresh soil were capable of generating far greater profits. Wiser heads had seen the decline of Jamaica coming decades earlier and had sold up. Those who had remained were in the market for a scapegoat on which to pin the blame and exercise their frustrations.

An alternative interpretation of events in the West Indies saw everything through the prism of race, arguing that the plantations were no longer so profitable because from the moment they were emancipated the former slaves sank into idleness and moral corruption – exactly in keeping with the true nature of Africans. Advocates of this way of thinking suggested that without coercion, the whip and the regimentation of plantation life Africans refused to work – for their former masters or for their own betterment – and that their innate idleness was ruining their prospects and those of their former masters. The white plantation owners, some of whom had returned to Britain when their estates had failed, were repeatedly portrayed as the victims of abolition. From the 1840s onwards they had lobbied energetically, presenting their case before Parliament and in the press. To whoever would listen they repeated their mantra: abolition had ruined their businesses because without slavery the 'blacks' simply would not work.[1]

All of this, it was said, had been foreseen in the late eighteenth and early nineteenth centuries by pro-slavery writers like Edward Long, but those sober warnings, made by men who had lived among Africans and had claimed to know their true nature, had been drowned out by the hysterical clamour of the abolitionists. William Wilberforce, Thomas Clarkson, Thomas Fowell Buxton and their like had, it was claimed, been wrong about slavery and wrong about the character, capacities and humanity of the African. Promoters of this new, darker, supposedly scientific racial interpretation of the recent past asserted that the central message of the abolitionists had been disastrously flawed; the African was neither fully a man nor a brother. Not only had Britain ruined her own colonies by believing otherwise, she was actively engaged in spreading this false philosophy around the world.

The first apostle of this new racism was the critic and essayist Thomas Carlyle, a hugely influential figure in the mid-nineteenth century whose writings helped set the tenor of his times, influencing novelists as much as scholars and philosophers. In 1849, less than a decade after the World Anti-Slavery Convention and eleven years after emancipation in the West Indies, Carlyle published an essay in *Fraser's Magazine* entitled 'Occasional Discourse on the Negro Question'. At that time Carlyle judged that his views were so controversial that it was prudent to publish the essay under a pseudonym, and from behind the veil of anonymity he laid out his views on slavery, the decline of the West Indies and the inner nature of Africans. In part the 'Occasional Discourse' was an unoriginal regurgitation of the familiar, well-worn arguments deployed by the pamphleteers of the pro-slavery lobby half a century earlier. Like them Carlyle camouflaged his profound contempt for black people behind a passionately expressed – and in his case far from disingenuous – declaration of compassion for poor white people, particularly the Irish. Their sufferings, Carlyle suggested, were no less severe and much more important than the rights and lives of inferior, racial outsiders. Like a number of the writers who had trod the same intellectual pathways before him Carlyle also maintained that slavery had not been as brutal and inhumane as the abolitionists had suggested and that conditions on the slave ships of the Middle Passage had been nowhere near as atrocious as figures like Thomas Clarkson had suggested. Carlyle then took a moment to interrogate the mission of the West Africa Squadron, asking if a 'blockade [of] the continent of Africa itself . . . along the extremely extensive and unwholesome coast' was a sensible policy given that, as Carlyle put it, the 'nefarious populations' of Cuba and Brazil 'will not, for love or fear, watching or entreaty, respect the rights of the negro'.[2] But it was in analysing the situation in the post-emancipation West Indies that Thomas Carlyle was at his most venomous and vitriolic. Brushing aside the effects of tariff reform and global competition, he heaped all blame for the economic misfortunes of the sugar islands onto the heads of the former slaves. All of the islands' difficulties were a consequence of the racial inferiority of the Africans and the refusal of their allies among the missionaries and abolitionists to accept that incontrovertible reality. At the core of his argument was a rabid denouncement of the former slaves whose ultimate crime was to have attempted to attain some degree of communal and economic independence.

The phenomenon that so outraged Carlyle had begun almost immediately after abolition. When freed from bondage at the end of the hated apprenticeship system in 1838, around half of the four hundred thousand former slaves abandoned the plantations – the scene of crime of slavery – and set off to establish small farms of their own. In 1832, before emancipation, there were 2,014 freehold farms in Jamaica, by 1840 there were 7,848.[3] As most of the prime land was in the hands of the former slave owners these new settlements tended to be in the hills or on marginal land away from areas of white control. These independent black settlements were on occasions attacked by whites and the philanthropists of the British and Foreign Anti-Slavery Society attempted to assist the former slaves found these 'free villages' by raising funds, much as they would do in 1865 to help the freedmen of the American South.

Carlyle characterized these free villages as 'pumpkin farms'. He saw the fact that the former slaves had abandoned the plantations upon which they had been whipped and beaten not as evidence of their desperate desire to be economically independent but as proof of their intrinsic and essential laziness. Rather than endure hard and disciplined labour on plantations, they had fallen back into what Carlyle ridiculed as a form of basic subsistence agriculture, a way of life that enabled them to spend the bulk of their time in idleness. In the crudest racialized terms Carlyle derided the former slaves as 'pumpkin-eating Quashees', and with the abolitionists also in his sights he described the West Indies as islands upon which 'our beautiful black darlings are at last happy; with little labor except to the teeth, which, surely, in those excellent horse-jaws of theirs, will not fail'.[4]

In truth the poor black people of Jamaica had worked industriously to forge their new settlements, clear and cultivate their plots and establish a market-garden economy, the remnants of which exist in Jamaica to this day. Carlyle chose to close his eyes to that reality. By abolishing slavery, he contended, the British had broken one of the immutable laws of nature. In language that still has the capacity to shock, over one and a half centuries later, he asserted that black people were, in his words, a form of 'two legged cattle', and in freeing them from slavery and sparing them from the whip the critical relationship between master and slave, higher-people and lower-race, had been ruptured. In one of his most infamous passages he spelt out how the laws of race and nature, as he saw them, had been contravened by the abolition of slavery and the slave trade. As if speaking directly to the free black people of the West Indies, he wrote, 'my obscure black friends . . . You are not "slaves" now; nor do I wish, if it can be avoided, to see you slaves again; but decidedly you will have to be servants to those that are born wiser than you, that are born lords of you – servants to the whites, if they are (as what mortal can doubt they are?) born wiser than you. That, you may depend upon it, my obscure black friends, is and was always the law of the world, for you and for all men; to be servants, the more foolish of us to the more wise; and only sorrow, futility and disappointment will betide both, till both, in some approximate degree, get to conform to the same.'[5]

The position that Carlyle articulated in 1849 was condemned by some. The liberal philosopher John Stuart Mill wrote a scathing riposte and one commentator in the United States suggested that the essay 'would do credit to a Mississippi slave driver'.[6] But, four years later, when he re-published the essay in pamphlet form, Carlyle judged that the mood had turned against abolition and against the former slaves to such an extent, that he felt able to claim authorship and – most tellingly – make a change to the title. The 1853 pamphlet was entitled *Occasional Discourse on the Nigger Question*. That change of word – as the historian Catherine Hall has pointed out – both reflected and contributed to the hardening of attitudes and the rise of new forms of racism on both sides of the Atlantic.[7]

On 24 November 1859, the day that Frederick Douglass landed in Liverpool to begin his second tour of Britain, Charles Darwin's *On the Origin of Species* went on sale to the public.[8] The religious scandal that erupted soon after the publication of Darwin's master-work has had the effect of disguising the fact that to many of Darwin's contemporaries – scientists, philosophers and politicians – his theory of evolution by natural selection was largely in keeping with observations that were already being made and social theories that were already in the ascendancy. The intellectual movement that became known as Social Darwinism – of which Darwin himself was not an advocate – offered potential explanations of the mech-anisms that were at work behind phenomena that others had identified. For example, many of those who supported Carlyle's views on the inner nature of Africans had begun to suggest that black people were uniquely suited, or adapted, to labouring in the tropics. Long before the publication of *On the Origin of Species* it had been suggested that Africans were natural slaves because they were supposedly stronger and more vigorous than other races yet lacked the gifts of intellect and invention that might have made other forms of work appropriate. Others contended that black people felt pain less acutely than other races, which was surely a trait that further demonstrated their unique suitability for slavery. Slavery was also a fitting institution for Africans as they supposedly would only work when compelled to do so. Slavery was therefore a system appropriate to both their physical make-up and inner nature. The writer Anthony Trollope spoke for many when, after a short trip to the West Indies in 1859, he resolved that black people were an inherently 'servile race' lacking in initiative and enterprise. 'The negro's idea of emancipation', wrote Trollope, 'was and is emancipation not from slavery but from work. To lie in the sun and eat breadfruit and yams is his idea of being free.'[9]

It had also been noted that unlike some of the aboriginal peoples that Europeans had encountered on the frontiers of their expanding empires, Africans tended to survive contact with whites. It was therefore suggested that for millennia supposedly 'doomed races' like the Tasmanian aboriginals – almost exterminated within fifty years of the arrival of Europeans on their island – had held their regions of the globe in trust, in providential anticipation of the eventual arrival of the higher white race. No longer needed, now that the 'higher' white race had arrived to take up its birth right these fragile peoples seemed to the Reverend and amateur ethnographer Frederic W. Farrar to 'disappear from before' European civilization, 'as surely and as perceptibly as the snow retreats before the advancing line of sunbeams'.[10] The more sturdy and resilient Africans did not melt away in the face of Europeans. They had therefore surely been brought into existence to act as servants to the whites. If the natural and inevitable fate of the Tasmanians was their extinction at the hands of British farmers and convict settlers then the evident and unavoidable destiny of the African was perpetual slavery. It was Carlyle himself who most clearly articulated this theory in 1867, writing that, 'One always rather likes the Nigger; evidently a poor blockhead with good dispositions, with affections, attachments – with a turn for Nigger Melodies, and the like – he is the only Savage of all the coloured races that doesn't die out on sight of the White Man; but can actually live beside him, and work and increase and be merry. The Almighty Maker has appointed him to be a Servant.' Unable to resist another tangential swipe at the abolitionists he added, 'Under penalty of Heaven's curse, neither party to this pre-appointment shall neglect or misdo his duties therein.'[11] While much of this could be explained as a divine plan in which God had assigned specific roles and tasks to the various races of mankind, Social Darwinism appeared to offer an alternative scientific explanation for the same distorted observations. It was not a prerequisite for beliefs but another strand to them.

The urgent intensity of Social Darwinism led to a revolution within science and schisms within scientific movements and institutions, as enthusiastic converts to the new and rapidly developing

Darwinian world-view sought to break free from older, more
conservative and morally cautious voices – which on some questions
included Charles Darwin himself. In the study of race and human
difference these divisions came on top of existing disagreements
over the origins of mankind. In January 1863, the month that the
Emancipation Proclamation came into legal effect in the Southern
states, a faction of the Ethnological Society of London broke away
and established the Anthropological Society of London. Its founders
were all eminent men: the Africa explorer Richard Burton, the poet
A. C. Swinburne, the anthropologist Dr James Hunt and Henry
Hotze, who was the editor of the pro-slavery pro-Confederate newspaper *The Index*, and arguably the leading propagandist for the
Southern cause in Britain. There is evidence to suggest that Dr James
Hunt may also have been a paid agent of the Confederacy during
the Civil War.[12] The members of the Anthropological Society of
London were predominantly men who believed in polygenism, the
theory that the various human races are so anatomically and intellectually divergent from one another that they constitute different
and distinct species, with either no common ancestor or one so
distant as to be irrelevant. Many were advocates of the pseudo-
science of phrenology – the utterly erroneous but fashionable belief
that the dimensions of the various features of the human skull were
indicators of the intellectual capacities of both individuals and races.
The society was openly and adamantly hostile towards abolitionism
and anti-slavery and its members were mockingly condescending
towards missionaries, deriding them for working among African
peoples whom the anthropologists believed could not advance or
be 'civilized'. In one needlessly provocative gesture the society
publicly taunted the Christian Union by displaying, in the front
window of the premises opposite them, an articulated skeleton of
a so-called 'savage'.[13]

In private the members of the society gave full flight to their
fanatical anti-theism and rampant racism. A group of members
centred around Richard Burton formed the 'Cannibal Club', an
all-male dining club that met in the private banquet room of Barto-
lini's Dining Rooms off Fleet Street. Its official symbol was a mace
that had been carved to resemble the head of an African man, his
jaws gnawing at a human thighbone.[14] To entertain his fellow diners

the poet Swinburne composed a 'cannibal catechism' that lampooned the rites of the Church. The activities of the Cannibal Club have long been the subject of both lurid speculation and academic study but what seems clear is that it was bacchanalian, fanatically antagonistic towards Christianity and fixated with sex, male sexuality and pornography. Its supposed function was to provide its members with a space in which views and theories that were generally regarded as socially unacceptable could be aired and debated. Given the venomous nature of the beliefs that members of the society were willing to openly state and publicly promote, in academic papers and in speeches, we can only speculate as to the opinions so controversial they had to be kept in the private circle of their hedonistic dining club.

In 1863 key members of the London Anthropological Society, including Dr Hunt, travelled north to attend the annual meeting of the British Association for the Advancement of Science in Newcastle upon Tyne. During the event, which 'the good people of Newcastle' somewhat optimistically dubbed the 'wise week', Hunt presented a paper, entitled 'On the Physical and Mental Character of the Negro'. The paper laid out Hunt's view that Africans were a separate species, closer to apes than Europeans.[15] Hunt's paper was not out of step with others that were delivered during the conference. He was preceded on the podium by John Crawfurd, a former colonial governor and another convert to polygenism, whose lecture was entitled 'The Comixture of the Races of Man as Affecting the Progress of Civilisation'. Dr Hunt's paper was a fulsome denouncement of the intellectual abilities of Africans. Serving up an old dish reheated, he suggested that while African children showed intellectual promise in their early years a form of intellectual lethargy soon overtook them, inhibiting and restraining their later development. Numerous pro-slavery writers had said much the same in the late eighteenth century. Speaking as a scientist rather than a slave-owning propagandist, Dr Hunt explained that, 'In the West Indian Islands it has frequently been observed that all the Negroes in places of trust which require intelligence have European features. Negro children are precocious; but no advance in education can be made after they arrive at the age of puberty – they still continue mentally children.' He added that as adult Africans were so lacking in invention and initiative 'the present slave-holders of America no more think of rebellion amongst their full-blooded slaves than they do of rebellion amongst their cows and horses.' This remark, the newspaper reports of the meeting tell us, was met with 'hisses' from the audience. Hunt then went on to discount all reports of intelligence and talent among black people, claiming that 'civilized blacks are not pure negroes, but in nearly every case they have European blood in their veins'. Any skills, capacities or aptitudes that a black person might demonstrate, Hunt submitted, could therefore be put down to the white blood that surely flowed in their veins. What Hunt called the 'full-blooded, woolly-headed, typical negro' was in all cases and at all times a being without intellectual gifts.

In the hope of injecting some wisdom and some balance into 'wise week' the Newcastle journalist W. E. Adams and his employer Joseph Cowen – both supporters of the Union and American aboli-tion – had arranged for a smattering of dissenting voices in the audience. With the help of George Holyoake, another Newcastle newspaper man and a pioneer of secularism, they had asked William Craft, the African American anti-slavery speaker and fugitive slave, to attend the meeting and confront Dr Hunt. William Craft had been living in Britain with his wife Ellen since the early 1850s.[16] Both were powerful speakers and had toured extensively on the anti-slavery circuit. In 1863 William Craft had, by chance, recently returned from a trip to Dahomey, a state that was undergoing major convulsions following the death – some sources say assassination – of the infamous slave-trading King Ghezo. Craft was a gifted and celebrated public speaker and a dangerous debating opponent, and the prospect of a public confrontation between a famous scientist and an equally well-known African American abolitionist drew an expectant audience.

The conclusion of Dr Hunt's speech, the newspapers inform us, was 'received with mingled cheers and hisses'.[17] William Craft then rose to respond. He began by rejecting Hunt's suggestion that the physical attributes of Africans were markers of any innate inferiority, remarking that, 'The thickness of the skull of the negro had been wisely arranged by Providence to defend the brain from the tropical climate in which he lived. If God had not given them thick skulls, their brains would probably have become very much like those of many scientific gentlemen of the present day.'[18] This quip elicited much laughter and applause. Craft then denounced Dr Hunt's paper as a debasement of science motivated by a desire to legitimize old racial prejudices. When confronting Hunt on his claim that black children made no 'advance in education' after puberty he brought up the case of Sarah Forbes Bonetta, whose very public wedding had taken place just one year earlier. Craft recommended that Dr Hunt, 'refer to the instance of the little girl brought to this country by Captain Forbes. This child was presented to the Queen, who had her carefully educated. When she grew up she mingled in good society, and interested everyone by her proficiency in music, and recently she had been married to a commercial gentleman of colour at Lagos.'[19] At the conclusion of his rebuttal the crowd was said to be loudly applauding the fugitive slave.

Momentarily wrong-footed, Dr Hunt and his supporters found their composure and responded with a toxic mixture of anger and ridicule. Feeling the need to account for William Craft's evident eloquence and intellect, as well as denounce his arguments, Dr Hunt confronted him on his own racial background. 'Anyone at all acquainted with the subject', Hunt suggested, would be able to deduce from the oration he had just delivered that Craft 'was not a pure Negro', although Hunt feared that 'there were many present who were deluded with the idea that he was'.[20] Even some weeks after the gathering in Newcastle, supporters of Dr Hunt felt compelled to labour this point: a letter to the President of the society by one Dr Philip Carpenter demanded that it be recorded that 'Mr. Craft is not an African but an American gentleman, having been born in the Southern States of America.' The *Journal of the Anthropological Society* itself regarded William Craft's identification of himself as 'an Englishman of African parentage, unfortunately born in America' as 'not quite satisfactory, as Mr. Craft knows himself that one of his parents is a Euro-American, and the other he has never alleged to be of really pure African blood'.[21]

After explaining away his opponent's talents and oratory Dr Hunt then accused him of meeting 'scientific argument' with 'poetical clap-trap', and 'worthless assumptions'. Hunt concluded that he would 'leave his scientific friends to judge of the value of Mr. Craft's remarks'.[22] While the Honorary Secretary of the society Mr Carter

Blake warned that unless Craft could explain 'the seal which nature had impressed on the physical character of the Negro, his breath was all spent in vain when he contended for the equality of the African and European races.'[23] Using the sort of twisted reasoning that would not have disgraced a witch-trial, William Craft, Sarah Forbes Bonetta, Frederick Douglass and all other notable and celebrated black figures were dismissed as either beneficiaries of their European heritage or mere aberrations. Dr Hunt was not alone when he called upon his countrymen to recognize 'the absolute impossibility of applying the civilisation and laws of one race of man to another'.[24]

The tiny town of Morant Bay, capital of the parish of St Thomas in east Jamaica, is as much a backwater today as it was in 1865. Far from the wealthy hotels and busy tourist beaches of the north coast, it is Jamaica's poorest parish. The gnawing, remediless poverty that hangs over St Thomas has long been a push factor that has scattered its people across the world. Successive generations have emigrated to Britain and the United States, abandoning the cane fields and struggling sugar estates, with their crumbling great houses, austere relics of slavery. St Thomas is one of the last parts of Jamaica in which vague traces of the African cultures that were carried to the island by the former slaves still survive. In rural St Thomas the Kumina funeral rights are still performed. On the death of a relative family members and friends gather together in the home of the deceased. For nine days and nights those who knew the dead man or woman visit the home, which is symbolically transformed into the 'dead yard'. During this 'Nine Nights' ceremony they gather around the body, laid out and iced, to appease the ghost or 'Duppy' of the deceased. On the ninth and final night, the Duppy is asked to leave. Only then is the body buried. Failure to follow this custom, some believe, will result in the spirit of the dead re-emerging to 'ride' the night and stalk the places it knew in life.[25] These traditions, that survived their passage from Africa, morphed and changed in Jamaica under the crushing heel of plantation slavery, and offer solace to the people of St Thomas, many of whom feel neglected by their rulers in Kingston and held in suspicion by the authorities.

The roads to St Thomas are among the worst in the country and the parish was the last part of the island to be able to offer school places to all its children. Some of the people of St Thomas believe they are neglected because they are warily mistrusted by the authorities. The suspicion among some is that this distrust stems from an event that took place in St Thomas a hundred and fifty years ago. Although few people outside Jamaica or beyond the Jamaican diaspora have ever heard of Morant Bay what happened there, and what spilled out into the villages of St Thomas in late 1865, is known to all Jamaicans. Like slavery itself memories of the Morant Bay Uprising – also known as the 'Morant Bay War' – remain an open wound and a burning grievance.

The story began six months after the end of the American Civil War when a crowd of local black people marched on Morant Bay. They attacked the police station, took possession of a small arsenal of weapons and confronted the local volunteer militia. Later there were outbreaks of violence in the surrounding parishes, but the trouble spread no further. The uprising had been led by a charismatic Baptist lay-preacher named Paul Bogle.

Blood had been spilt, including that of white people, government property had been destroyed and the law contravened, and a rigorous reaction from the colonial authorities was inevitable. However, what had taken place was still a small event in a backwater region of an island colony that, by 1865, was of little real importance to the vast and sprawling British Empire.[26] When the reaction from the colonial authorities came it was so brutal and disproportionate that by the end of the year events in Jamaica had scandalized Victorian Britain, driven the cultural and intellectual elite of the empire into two hostile camps and exposed the full virulence of the new scientific forms of racism. Britain's relationships with black people in the West Indies, in Africa and in Britain itself, for the rest of the nineteenth century and much of the twentieth, were influenced by the racial debates that exploded out of the Morant Bay Rebellion and its brutal aftermath.

The causes of the rebellion had been put in place decades earlier. Although slavery had been abolished black Jamaicans had remained powerless and impoverished. The population of the island in the 1860s comprised around 14,000 whites and around 430,000 black people – former slaves and their freeborn children. There was also a small mixed-race community of so-called Creoles, and up in the hills lived the Maroons, the descendants of runaway slaves. Although the black population were the overwhelming majority they had almost no political voice. In the election of 1863 only 1,457 people on the entire island met the property qualifications required to vote, and the Jamaican Assembly was controlled by a white elite made up of the same old families and plantation owners who had run the island before emancipation.[27] There were a smattering of black and mixed-race officials in minor positions but the white elite were in a position to wield their political power without serious challenge and use it to pass laws beneficial to their interests. During the period of so-called apprenticeship, 1832–38, they had pushed through vagrancy laws and other measures designed to confine the former slaves to the plantations upon which they had been enslaved, or inhibit their ability to travel beyond their local parishes – laws that were not dissimilar to the later Pass Laws of Apartheid South Africa. Other measures had been passed that were intended to restrict free black people's access to farm land. The price of land was exaggerated, extortionately high land rents were charged and systems of credit were developed that looked suspiciously like forms of debt slavery.

The white population were protected by a garrison of 900 soldiers but their presence did little to liberate them from their fears. The whites were troubled by lingering memories of the Jamaican slave rebellion of 1831–32 (also known as the Baptist War). Others were haunted by the more distant spectre of the Haitian Revolution, the legendary and successful slave rebellion of the early nineteenth century that was still within living memory, if only just. The Haitian Revolution dwelt in the minds and lingered in the nightmares of white populations across the English- and French-speaking West Indies. Slaveholders in Brazil and Cuba had their own bleak history of slave risings and repression to fully occupy their sleeping hours.

The disruption to global trade and the unnatural fluctuations in world commodity prices caused by the American Civil War were felt among the poor black people of Jamaica almost as acutely as among the mill workers of Lancashire. Despite its verdant fertility so much of the colony had been turned over to the production of sugar that Jamaica, by the middle of the nineteenth century, was heavily reliant upon imported American foodstuffs. Their cost had increased enormously during the war, as had cotton clothing, a basic essential on a tropical island. Between 1859 and 1865 the cost of living in Jamaica rose by around 60 per cent.[28] These adversities had fallen upon Jamaica when she was already reeling from a succession of seemingly biblical disasters. A three-year drought had devastated parts of the island while a succession of floods had washed away crops elsewhere. These misfortunes had been accompanied by plagues of smallpox and cholera.[29] But the distress caused by the American Civil War merely added to economic difficulties whose roots were in the employment crisis that had confronted Jamaica ever since 1838.

This island, upon which slaves had once been driven by the whip to work around the clock, keeping boiling-houses fed with raw cane under the light of flaming torches, had by the 1840s been plunged into unemployment and underemployment. By the 1850s and 1860s economic push-factors not dissimilar to those that would encourage Caribbean immigrants to head to Britain and the United States in the twentieth century were already at play. As the soil grew thin and unproductive the wealthier plantation owners returned to Britain, leaving their estates untended but still out of bounds to poor, landless black families. Work became scarce and what little there was on the surviving plantations was back-breaking and low paid. The only alternative was subsistence agriculture in independent farms and villages, and the majority of Jamaicans would have far preferred to farm for themselves, but this was only possible if land could be bought or rented. Yet as the situation grew more desperate in the 1850s and early 1860s the Jamaica Assembly and the Colonial Office in London went out of their way to inhibit the availability of land on Jamaica. When black people attempted to settle on empty Crown lands, which were owned by the state, or form settlements on abandoned sugar plantations they were classified as 'squatters' and taken before the magistrates or driven off. By the 1860s reports were coming in from Jamaica of hundreds of people taking to the roads, wandering for miles between the villages and plantations in search of work. Landless, poor Jamaicans were known to walk thirty-five miles for a single day's work on a distant plantation. Their plight and their desperation mirrored that of the mill workers of Lancashire during the same years.

By the mid-1860s the situation in Jamaica was this: a free people who were blithely and routinely accused of being congenitally lazy were being prevented from gaining access to the land upon which they might demonstrate their industriousness and self-reliance, as well as provide for themselves and their families. At the same time West India landowners whose businesses had failed were returning to Britain and pinning responsibility for their financial failure on the former slaves. Behind all of these sweeping assertions and unthinking stereotypes were old racial myths that now mixed and fused with new strains of racial thinking.

In April 1865 the landless poor of St Ann's parish in the north of Jamaica attempted to break the impasse by drafting a petition which they hoped to send to Queen Victoria herself. 'The humble petition of the poor people of Jamaica and parish of St Ann's' outlined their plight and described how high food prices had left them hungry and the cost of cotton clothing had left 'numbers of our people half naked'. Worst of all, mass unemployment had left them without hope. The petitioners requested access to Crown lands upon which they might forge new free communities, demonstrate their capacity for work and become productive farmers. The Crown owned huge tracts of land on Jamaica, which included upland areas that had never been settled and prime farm land on former sugar estates that had failed to pay their quitrents and thus been forfeited. As the petitioners explained, what they sought was the opportunity to 'put our hands and heart to work, and cultivate coffee, corn, canes, cotton and tobacco, and other produce.' They proposed to 'form a company for that purpose, if our Gracious Lady Victoria our Queen will also appoint an agent to receive such produce as we may culti-vate, and give us means of subsistence while at work.' The petitioners proposed that the profits generated by their labour would allow them to pay for their land. They were not expecting it to be gifted to them and they assured their monarch that they, 'will thankfully repay our Sovereign Lady by instalments of such produce as we may cultivate. Your humble servants is [sic] willing to work so that we may be comfortable'. The authors of the petition understood their times. The petition was steeped in the language of self-help, self-improvement and the Victorian cult of work. Just two years earlier, on the same day that Darwin had published *On the Origin of Species*, the same publishers had released Samuel Smiles' book *Self Help*, a manual for self-reliance that perfectly caught the spirit of the age. Channelling that zeitgeist the Jamaican petitioners explained that 'If our Gracious Sovereign will be pleased to grant our request in a few years time our Sovereign Lady Queen will see the improvement of our Island, and the benefit that your humble servant will derive'.[30] The petition was signed by a hundred and eight of the people of St Ann's, most of whom were only able to sign with an 'X'.

The peasant-based agricultural economy that the free black people of Jamaica were proposing might well have been the answer to the island's economic plight. However the governor and the men of the Colonial Office were wilfully blind to their proposition and incapable of envisaging Jamaica's future as lying outside the production of sugar on great estates. Their priority was to maintain on the island a large pliable landless workforce ready to be deployed once the sugar economy began to revive – a day which never came. All other alternatives, especially those that involved some degree of black autonomy, were discounted out of hand and what little investment that was in the island went into providing new roads linking the great estates to one another and to the ports.

It is testimony to the power of mid-Victorian racial stereotypes that the governor and the Colonial Office were incapable of recognizing that the petition of the poor black people of St Ann's amply demonstrated them to be fully in possession of all the character traits and moral virtues that they were alleged to lack. The Jamaican poor had proposed to the government a well-thought-through plan for economic revival that might well have provided the island with an alternative to the perpetually ailing sugar industry. The business plan contained within the 'Humble Petition' was a long-term proposal for what we would today call economic diversification, and was founded upon a firm understanding of the market economy, the workings of credit and the time value of money. It was also predicated on the commitment of the people of St Ann's to hard work, delayed gratification and self-sacrifice. All of this was seemingly invisible to those in power, who portrayed this appeal as evidence of the unwanted influence of the Baptist missionaries and as a naive and grasping demand for welfare and free land made by an undeserving people.

Long before the petition reached Queen Victoria it passed across the desk of Governor Eyre, who appended to it a note that reinforced the myth that black economic distress had its roots in the racial inferiority and immoral and imprudent habits of the former slaves, and not in the economic difficulties that had assailed much of the post-emancipation West Indies. The petition and Eyre's dismissive note were then dispatched to the Colonial Office, where Henry Taylor, head of the West India Department and a close friend of Thomas Carlyle, drafted a response on behalf of the Queen. In the most condescending terms this told the poor black people of St Ann's that their prosperity depended upon them abandoning their dreams of land and independence and returning to the plantations where their labour would, supposedly, 'thereby render the Plantations productive'. In what was perhaps the most callous and patronizing passage it informed the poor that, 'they may be assured, that it is from their own industry and prudence . . . that they must look for an improvement in their condition; and that her Majesty will regard with interest and satisfaction their advancement through their own merits and efforts.'[31] Eyre was so inordinately satisfied with the response that he ordered fifty thousand copies to be printed. He had them distributed across the island under the title 'the Queens advice'. They were posted in public places and instructions were given that they were to be read aloud from the pulpit and at public meetings. Many Jamaicans rightly suspected the advice came from British officials and not from the Queen herself. *The Anti-Slavery Reporter*, the house magazine of British anti-slavery, denounced the document, suspecting that, 'The writer of the Queen's Advice must have been under the immediate teaching of a member of the West India body, full of the inveterate prejudices of his class, and glad of an opportunity to reiterate planter theory, that the negro in Jamaica has nothing to complain of, and that the West-India planter is the best and fairest of task-masters.' The magazine conceded that 'although there may be cases of indolence – as there are in all communities – the Jamaica labourer is at all times willing to work for fair wages, regularly paid.'[32] Yet whoever the author of the response, it was evident that a formal and respectful approach by a desperate people to the legitimate authorities had been met with insouciance and condescension. The official response not only rejected their pleas, it implicitly reinforced the racialized assumption that the poverty of the former slaves was a consequence of their own inherent indolence.

Throughout the summer of 1865 the crisis continued, thousands were unemployed and the magistrates continued to enforce evictions of those accused of squatting abandoned estates and empty farm land.

The event that ignited tensions in Jamaica occurred in early October, when a court case over the eviction of a man who had been farming on an abandoned estate led to a minor disturbance in the court house at Morant Bay. This led to charges being issued for the arrest of the lay-preacher Paul Bogle and a number of other men. When the police came to the village of Stony Gut to make their arrests they were attacked by the local populace. This act of rebellion quickly escalated, the white militia were called up, troops were mobilized and the next day the two sides confronted one another at the court house. The crowd threw stones at the militia, the Riot Act was read and then suddenly the soldiers opened fire, killing seven people. After the initial shock of the salvo receded, a wave of anger overtook the crowd, who attacked and burnt down the court house killing eighteen whites including the local magistrate, the Anglo-German Baron von Ketelhodt. The events of the Morant Bay Rebellion remain legendary in Jamaica and have been described in detail elsewhere; what concerns us here is the response of the governor to the scandal that followed.

On the day of the killings in Morant Bay, the Governor of Jamaica, Edward Eyre, declared martial law. Ships were sent from Kingston to evacuate the white population of the town and the surrounding estates and soldiers were dispatched to the region. The troops arrived the following day and within three days had put down the unrest in the parishes around Morant Bay. Within a week they had pacified the whole region and this violent but relatively minor rebellion was effectively over. However, from 12 October onwards exaggerated and fanciful reports of what had happened in the east of the island were sent to the governor who, rather rapidly it seems, convinced himself that Morant Bay was the opening act in a general rising of the black population. Eyre was urged on in his paranoia by sections of the white population. He evidently became entrapped in a mindset in which all other interpretations of the violence were discounted. At its height it has been estimated that the number of people involved in the disturbances around Morant Bay totalled between fifteen hundred and two thousand. Accepting the higher figure and presuming that all those involved were actively engaged in rebellion, this was less than half of one per cent of the total black population. Yet Eyre, within the first few days of the rebellion, concluded that the black population of Jamaica were engaged in a 'systematic conspiracy'.[33] When no evidence of this conspiracy could be found, Eyre made do with rumour. When later pressed to provide evidence for his conspiracy theory he explained, in a dispatch to London, that 'It could not be expected that there should be any documentary evidence amongst the negroes themselves of a conspiracy to overthrow the Queen's authority, and to massacre the white and coloured people of the Island, nor could it reasonably be supposed that people like the negroes should have established any very complete organisation, or have made any perfect arrangements to act in combination.'[34] In his most expansive fantasy Eyre convinced himself that an island-wide war of ethnic cleansing had been planned. His paranoia was a reflection of his views of black people much more than it was an analysis of the information he was receiving in the governor's mansion. Utterly persuaded that a race war would spread across the island if not immediately and decisively checked he launched a campaign of extraordinarily and utterly disproportionate violence and retribution.

For six weeks units of the West India Regiment, accompanied by the local militia, were let loose upon the rural population of St Thomas parish. Additional troops were drafted into the island and the Maroons – who sided with the British – were armed, equipped and deployed to the areas under martial law. In an orgy of bloodletting 439 black Jamaicans were killed. Sick men were dragged from their homes and shot and as events spiralled out of control soldiers deployed to east Jamaica, some of them hardened veterans of the Indian Mutiny, were given the opportunity to express their individual sadism. Six hundred men and women caught by the troops were flogged; some men were lashed with wire whips, leaving them with egregious injuries. In addition to these crimes against the person over a thousand homes were burnt and men and women who had worked themselves out of absolute poverty, having left the plantations penniless and homeless, were again reduced to destitution.

While individual officers were later said to have acted illegally and beyond their orders what took place in Jamaica during October and November 1865 was not a case of military excess, in which soldiers or their officers slipped the bonds of official control and ran out of control. As well as the atrocities and arbitrary killings in the fields and villages there were calculated and deliberate acts of judicial murder. Hundreds of people were arrested and put on trial. Of them around three hundred and fifty were hanged, including Paul Bogle, who was caught by the Maroons and executed the next day. The highest authorities were not only fully aware of these excesses; they directed them. Of those summarily executed the most shocking case was that of George William Gordon, a wealthy, mixed-race Baptist who was a member of the Jamaica Assembly and a close associate of Paul Bogle. Gordon was also a man whom Eyre considered a political enemy, and the governor was directly involved in his arrest and trial. Gordon was arrested in late October in Kingston, which lies thirty miles from the areas under martial law. But in one of the most outrageous incidents the governor had him transported to Morant Bay by ship, and personally accompanied it. There, within the zone which fell under martial law, Gordon was put on trial. Eyre had it seems been determined to hold Gordon personally responsible for the rebellion. The trial was riven with procedural irregularities and Gordon was denied counsel. After a hearing that lasted only six hours he was found guilty of high treason and sentenced to death. Two days after his arrest Gordon was hanged from the central arch of the court house; a very public killing intended to humiliate the dead man and intimidate his supporters.

This six-week rampage of killing and destruction, which left a great scar across the east of Jamaica, was brutal even by the standards of the mid-nineteenth century. The governor of a British colony oversaw the killing and executions of hundreds (some unofficial sources suggested perhaps a thousand) of the people he had been appointed, supposedly, to protect. At least a thousand homes were destroyed, most of them belonging to innocent people. Eyre's actions had clearly been excessive and some questioned if they had even been legal.

News of the rebellion reached Britain in mid-November 1865. Initially Governor Eyre was congratulated by his superiors at the Colonial Office for his prompt action. In the light of those initial reports the conservative press supported not only the governor's actions but the racial suppositions that had informed and inspired them. On 13 November *The Times* ran an article that concluded that events in Morant Bay had demonstrated that it was 'impossible to eradicate the original savageness of African blood.' For 'as long as the black man has a strong white Government and a numerous white population to control him he is capable of living as a respectable member of society. He can be made quiet and even industrious by the fear of the supreme power, and by the example of those to whom he necessarily looks up. But wherever he attains a certain degree of independence there is the fear that he will resume the barbarous life and the fierce habits of his African ancestors.'[35]

Some observers considered it highly significant that this explosion of black racial violence – which is how many were determined to view events in Morant Bay – had come just seven months after the United States had passed the 13th Amendment, abolishing slavery. Those in Britain and America who during the Civil War had suggested that the liberation of the enslaved peoples of the American South would result in a racial conflict fought on a continental scale believed that in Jamaica they had seen a portent of things to come. Most worryingly the rebellion had occurred on an island upon which the black population had been slowly and gradually emancipated, through a system of apprenticeship that British politicians of all political stripes had arrogantly suggested the Americans would be wise to copy. If, as it was now insinuated, the inner nature of black people was so barbaric that even former slaves who had been gradually introduced to freedom through the intermediary stage of appren-ticeship were capable of rising up and attacking the white population, then even the most apocalyptic predictions of war and chaos in the post-war South had not been overstated. The London papers noted that when news of the Morant Bay Rebellion reached the South alarm spread through the white population, which now prepared itself for a 'general insurrection' from among the freedmen.[36]

However, in the second half of November and early December, as more details of what had happened in Jamaica filtered back to Britain, an alternative picture of events began to emerge. The notion that Governor Eyre had saved the island from a hellish racial conflagration was exposed as a fiction. Days after the first accounts of the rebellion reached London new reports arrived on ships that had left Jamaica during the retribution that had followed. These fresh accounts described the brutality with which the rebellion was suppressed and contained shocking details of the arbitrary killing of unarmed civilians and of summary executions following military hearings that were little more than show trials. As reports containing these details began to appear in the press and circulate around the corridors of power the mood changed. The government was particularly concerned to learn of the circumstances leading up to the execution of George William Gordon, which even when viewed from a distance of three thousand miles appeared highly dubious. As eyewitnesses returned to Britain, and the reports from the Jamaican newspapers were reprinted in British publications, it became evident that the actions of the rebels – if that is indeed what they were – did not match the patterns expected if they had been engaged in a 'systematic conspiracy' to foment racial conflict and seize the island from the whites. As the *Spectator* magazine noted on 18 November, 'These men, it is clear, were not prosecuting a crusade against the white race, but taking vengeance on persons whom they chose to think their political enemies. Even the massacre at Morant Bay, a sufficiently bloody affair, did not begin till after the mob had been fired on from the court-house and blood so spilt by the besieged, and even then the two physicians' lives were spared, and many instances of attempts on the part of the faithful negroes to save individual lives among the upper class are related, while no instances of outrages on women and children are given at all.'[37]

The extent to which, even at this early stage in the scandal, the country was divided over Morant Bay and the actions of Governor Eyre is illustrated by an article that appeared in *The Times* on the day that the *Spectator* had concluded that the black people of Morant

Bay were evidently 'not prosecuting a crusade against the white race'. The leader writer of the paper chose not to question Eyre's version of events and was firm in his belief that 'the noble governor of the island' had 'deemed it necessary to act, in the recent emergency, with promptness and decision, knowing, from his experience, that hesitation would have been fatal.'[38] After all, thundered *The Popular Magazine of Anthropology*, 'the decisive measures taken by Governor Eyre' were informed by his 'most thorough insight into the negro character.' He had presided over an island that, as Eyre himself had said, had been 'sleeping on a volcano'. In a dispatch that was dutifully quoted, Governor Eyre had claimed that 'One moment's hesitation, one single reverse, might have lit the torch which would have blazed in rebellion from one end of the island to another.'[39]

The Times was then the semi-official organ of conservative opinion and was therefore hugely influential. It was this newspaper that had staunchly supported the South during the Civil War. Eyre had apparently saved not just Jamaica but the whole of the British Caribbean from descending into a rebellion that might have led to the creation of a new Haiti. Jamaica was, as the article explained in ominous tones, only 'a day's sail' from that 'Black Republic.' *The Times* did not attempt to piece together timelines or compare official dispatches to other sources in order to determine whether the reported actions of the so-called rebels fitted with the accounts offered by the governor. Confident in Eyre's judgement, his understanding of the 'negro character' and the wisdom of his actions, *The Times* concluded that 'The rebellion of the negroes comes very home to the national soul'. Although what had taken place in Jamaica was a mere 'fleabite compared with the Indian mutiny, it touches our pride more and is more in the nature of a disappointment.' In the tone of injured suitor the writer considered the rebellion of former slaves to be a greater injury to Britain than the Indian rebellion because it was a greater betrayal. 'Jamaica is our pet institution. Its inhabitants are our spoilt children. We had it always in our eye when we talked to America and all the slaveholding Powers. It seemed to be proved in Jamaica that the negro could become fit for self-government; that he could be a planter, a magistrate, a member of the Legislative Assembly; that he could preach and pray with unction and even decorum; that he could behave like a gentleman, and even pay taxes.'

While her external appearance seemed to have suggested that this great project of British moral philanthropy and racial improvement was progressing well, on the inside Jamaica was rotten. The plantation owners, *The Times* recalled, had repeatedly warned the British people that 'the negro was incurably idle, intractable, insolent, that he needed a strong master, and was incapable of either self-control or gentle management . . . But very little of this came out.' The Jamaica planters, who were of course the former slave owners, had not been listened to when they had counselled the nation on the true nature of black people, and now Britain was paying the price for her refusal to accept their forewarnings. The rebellion, *The Times* suggested, was a catastrophic blow for those who believed in the 'grand triumphs of humanity, and the improvement of races, and the removal of primeval curses'.[40]

The Times was far from alone in adopting this tone of weary resignation and feigned injury. Newspaper reports and private letters from 1865 and 1866 repeatedly refer to a sense of 'humiliation' among those who were determined to view the rebellion as an explosion of black racial violence. To them the free black people of the island had embarrassed Britain and made fools of the abolitionists. According to their line of thinking the 'blacks' had been indulged and pampered. The belief, propagated by the abolitionists and the missionaries, that they could be advanced, civilized and made respectable had blinded the country to their true racial character. All the while, as Britain had preached to the Americans and the Royal Navy had pursued the slave ships of other powers, the ungrateful former slaves had been slowly sliding backwards, the evidently thin veneer of civilization unable to conceal their true nature and atavistic barbarism. That at least 793 people lay dead in their graves across east Jamaica, and that hundreds of Jamaicans had been left homeless and physically scarred by a wave of almost random, militarized retribution, made little impact upon the minds of the outraged and humiliated. The conclusion of many British observers was that the British were the true victims of the rebellion.

While *The Times* and other newspapers, which included *The Bee Hive*, the journal of the trades union movement, supported Governor Eyre's prompt action in putting down the rebellion the full picture was emerging of the six-week orgy of violence that had followed.

The reports from Jamaica grew ever more shocking and new questions emerged. Had the initial proclamation of martial law been legal? Even if it was, had the powers provided under martial law been exceeded? Had the killings of unarmed men in the villages been extra-judicial? Had the trials of the men found guilty of treason and subsequently executed followed due process? Why had George William Gordon been shipped into the zone of martial law from his home in Kingston? Most troubling of all, had the rebellion been the island-wide insurrection Eyre had convinced himself that it was? Among the many troubling reports was a dispatch from a 'special correspondent' of the *Jamaica Standard* that was reprinted in the *Spectator*. It described how innocent men caught up in the dragnet of the army and the militia were subjected to arbitrary and collective punishments. Some of them, the report claimed, had been exposed to the whims and personal vindictiveness of individual British officials. Describing the retribution that had followed the initial violence and focusing on one infamous case it noted that 'as nothing could be proved against a lot of *supposed* rebels, except that they were "stragglers"—does he mean vagrants ?—thirty of them were *only* lashed to a gun, and catted with fifty lashes each on the bare back. Among these rebels "was George Marshall, a brown man of about twenty-five years old, who, on receiving forty-seven lashes, ground his teeth and gave a ferocious look of defiance at the provost-marshal. He was immediately ordered to be taken from the gun and hanged," and he was hanged. If this is true, it was most likely a worse crime in the sight of God than that of the rebels themselves.'[41] It was apparent the reputation in question was not only that of the Governor of Jamaica but that of the British Empire.

The reports that had emerged from Jamaica were so profoundly shocking that a coalition of those demanding an official inquiry was quickly assembled. The Jamaica Committee coalesced around the figures of the abolitionist Charles Buxton and the eminent philosopher John Stuart Mill. They were supported by a group of notable figures, many of them leading lights of the Ethnological Society, who had been abandoned and ridiculed by James Hunt and Richard Burton two years earlier when they had broken away to form the

Anthropological Society of London. This grouping included Charles Darwin and Thomas Huxley. They were joined on the committee by the philosopher and biologist Herbert Spencer, the author of *Tom Brown's Schooldays* Thomas Hughes and John Bright, the radical Rochdale MP who had done so much to promote the Union cause and support the Lancashire mill workers during the American Civil War. Indeed most of the members of the committee had been involved in campaigning for the North during the Civil War. The Jamaica Committee pressured the government to launch an inquiry and later demanded that Eyre be put on trial. Some believed that the charge against the governor should be murder.

In December 1865 the Colonial Office established the Jamaica Royal Commission of Inquiry to investigate Eyre's conduct and the governor was relieved of his duties. In April 1866, after fifty-two days of hearings held in Spanish Town, the Commission published its conclusions. In a report that was over five hundred pages long the Commissioners found that 'the punishments inflicted were excessive.' The floggings and beatings were 'positively barbarous', and was the burning of a thousand homes were 'wanton and cruel'.[42] Eyre was dismissed and ordered back to Britain, but on his return, far from being ostracized, was feted and lionized by his supporters. Despite being found guilty of outrageous breaches of authority and his actions condemned in the most forthright manner by a Royal Commission, Eyre was painted as a national hero and defender of the white race. Those who had committed themselves to defending his actions in the first few weeks of the scandal remained unmoved by later evidence and even by the conclusions of the Royal Commission. Banquets were held in his honour, newspaper and magazine reports portrayed him as the victim of conspiracy led by what one publication called 'pseudo-philanthropists', 'political demagogues', 'evil-minded men' and 'worthless persons without either character or property to lose'.[43] The divisions around the scandal ran so deep that a dinner in Southampton held in Eyre's honour was picketed by protestors and there were disturbances in the street.[44] Further demonstrations against him took place in London and the governor was even burnt in effigy in Hyde Park.[45]

Those who supported the former governor formed themselves into the Eyre Defence Committee. This movement was led, perhaps inevitably, by Thomas Carlyle. What to modern eyes seems incongruous is that in the age of the scientific racism it was not the scientists but the novelists and poets who defended the massacres in Jamaica and the pseudo-scientific racism that was deployed to defend Eyre's actions. On the Eyre Defence Committee were some of the most eminent of the Victorians: Charles Dickens, the poets Alfred, Lord Tennyson and Matthew Arnold and Charles Kingsley, author of *The Water-Babies* and *Westward Ho!*. Also supporting Eyre was John Ruskin, the critic and virtual arbiter of artistic taste in mid-Victorian Britain.

Throughout 1866 the two groupings confronted one another in a battle for public opinion. The Eyre Defence Committee raised at least £10,000 and its list of supporters swelled to over thirty thousand individuals. Those who sided with Eyre included numerous members of Parliament, several bishops and members of the aristocracy. In July 1866 the Jamaica Committee brought a lawsuit against Eyre. John Stuart Mill, in a statement published in the *Daily News*, explained that behind the suit lay their determination 'to establish, by a judicial sentence, the principle that the illegal execution of a British subject, by a person in authority, is not merely an error which superiors in office may at their discretion visit with displeasure or condone, but a crime which will certainly be punished by the law.'[46] Shocked at the level of support for Eyre, John Stuart Mill and the other members of the Jamaica Committee considered themselves obliged to use the law to 'uphold the obligation of justice and humanity towards all races beneath the Queen's sway'.[47] Beyond the issue of race the members of the committee also regarded the prosecution as an essential defence of basic civil liberties. They were deeply concerned at the way in which martial law had been extended and used to convict and condemn civilians in Jamaica, disturbed by the highly dubious nature of many of the trials and regarded George William Gordon as a political prisoner who had been put to death after a perfunctory and politically motivated trial. When this private prosecution failed, the committee, the following year, sought a warrant for the arrest of Eyre to stand trial charged with being an accessory to the murder of George William Gordon. Eyre was tried in 1868 only for the jury to find there to be insufficient evidence to convict. At the conclusion of his final prosecution the *Spectator* made a stark admission as to how little value some in Britain had come to place on the lives of black people. In an article entitled 'The End of the Jamaica Prosecution', it summarized the three years of the Morant Bay scandal and concluded that Britain had been willing to 'pardon him, because his error of judgment involves only negro blood', his actions would have 'otherwise been in our nation's eyes simply unpardonable.'[48]

The Morant Bay Rebellion devastated a community of free black people in the rural east of Jamaica; the army and militia left what witnesses described as 'eight miles of dead bodies'.[49] The scandal that followed, the so-called Jamaica Prosecution, exposed the deep fault lines that ran through mid-Victorian Britain demonstrating with graphic clarity that the abolitionist, anti-slavery consensus that had been a fundamental feature of British politics and culture during the 1830s and into the 1850s was over, and that new and toxic forms of racial thinking had emerged. The opinion to which Thomas Carlyle had, in 1849, been reluctant to attach his name were, by 1866, widely held and increasingly legitimized by the men of science.

In November 1865, the *Popular Magazine of Anthropology*, in an attempt to rise above the increasingly hysterical clamour of outrage, offered an appraisal of how, after the disaster of Morant Bay, Britain ought to regard her colonial mission. Although the newspaper refused to 'join in the outcry against attempting the improvement of such races as the negro' it was of the view that in light of the supposedly barbaric behaviour of the free black people of Jamaica there was now a new 'necessity of re-opening the whole question'. Britain's future treatment of black people should from now on 'start with this premise, that if the improvement of races is to take place, it must be conducted calmly on scientific principles, apart from philanthropic sentimentality.'[50] The same publication claimed that while 'The revolution in Jamaica has come like a thunderclap upon the English people', it had not surprised 'those who have made even a partial study of the psychological character of the negro'. To the authors of the magazine the 'Negro Revolt in Jamaica' had perhaps finally woken the British from their long-held misconceptions about the nature of the African. 'For the last half century', the magazine asserted, 'the negro has been an idol to the masses of the British public, and all classes of society have refused to listen to any depreciation of this chosen race . . . Nearly all classes in England have . . . agreed that the negro is a being very little (if at all) inferior, either mentally or morally, to the European. Men of science, even, have joined in the same chorus, and . . . come forward to defend this fashionable idol from any assaults his dignity may have sustained at the hands of the few who have declined to swell the strain of adulation.' Finally, however, in the members of the Anthropological Society of London and their supporters there was 'a small party in England, which within the last three years . . . has done something to stem this current of popular delusion'.[51] During those three years since its foundation they had attracted a growing list of members, including Governor Eyre himself. As the Morant Bay scandal expanded, and the Royal Commission investigated the governor's actions, Dr James Hunt and the society rushed to defend their disgraced colleague.

In February 1866 the society held a meeting at St James's Hall in London. The gathering was originally scheduled to take place at a venue in St Martin's Place, off the Strand, but 'the demand for tickets of admission was so great that it was found necessary to secure [the larger] St. James's Hall'. The main speaker at the meeting was Bedford Pim, an Arctic explorer and officer in the Royal Navy, whose father had served in the West Africa Squadron and died of yellow fever off the African coast while taking part in an anti-slave-trade patrol. To a room packed with supporters of Governor Eyre, Pim delivered a long paper entitled 'The Negro at Home and Abroad'. In the published account of the meeting Pim confessed that 'When the news of the Jamaica rebellion arrived in this country I felt that at last my countrymen, whether they liked it or not, were brought face to face with the negro, and that a clear view of his peculiarities should be laid before them, so as to assist in properly handling this most important subject, whether politically or religiously, in such a manner as to aid in settling the question. The only scientific tribunal before which this could be done with effect was that vigorous and fearless body, the Anthropological Society of London, whose labours will be better appreciated when it is understood that the numerous races composing our vast empire can only be governed properly by studying their anthropological character-istics.'[52] The negro was to be understood in anthropological terms but there was to be no debate over the actions of Governor Eyre. 'One thing is certain', Pim proposed, 'a public servant of whom any country might be proud — "one of the very finest types of English manhood" — has been deposed and degraded for making the safety of his trust the supreme law.'[53]

Among those who were asked to comment on the Eyre Scandal was Winwood Reade. A racial theorist, Africa explorer and philos-opher-mystic, Reade was one of a new breed of imperialists. He was heavily influenced by Social Darwinism, and knew Darwin personally. But by the 1860s the two men's views had radically diverged. Reade had become aggressively dismissive of the Christian morality that informed abolitionism and that animated what Pim called the 'negrophilists of Exeter Hall'.

Speaking to the society, Reade admitted that he had 'more expe-rience of the savage than of the semi-civilized or missionarized negro', into which category he placed the black population of Jamaica. But he had no doubt that the punitive expeditions and exemplary violence that he had witnessed in the colonial wars of Europe's expanding African colonies offered lessons for the future. Rapidly gaining a reputation as an African 'expert', Reade suggested that recent events in Jamaica, and Governor Eyre's murderous response to the Morant Bay disturbances, had to be understood within that wider colonial context. What Reade had seen of how the French controlled their territories in Senegal and what he had witnessed of British actions in Gambia led him to conclude that the utmost severity was necessary when dealing with black people: 'in the Senegal . . . the French were feared and respected . . . in the late Badaboo war the English had shown great indulgence to their enemies, while the French had always acted upon the contrary principle . . . We spared them from benevolence; they supposed that it was from fear.' Summing up, Reade's advice when dealing with black people in Africa or the West Indies was this: 'if you must fight with natives, kill them down. Kill them down not only for self-protection, but from a philanthropic principle. It seems para-doxical to say so, but there may be mercy in a massacre . . . had not Governor Eyre shown such prompt severity, we should now be sending out troops to save white men's lives, instead of a Commission to sit upon black men's carcases.'[54]

The beliefs that Winwood Reade expressed in 1866 were identical to those he had published two years earlier. In 1864 he gave his dark imagination full rein when considering how his principle of philanthropic massacre might be applied to the peoples of Africa. In his book *Savage Africa*, Reade accepted that he would inevitably be 'blamed by ignorant persons' when he stated that 'if war is waged against savages, it must be a massacre'. Yet in his view, 'Cruel as this maxim may appear, it would, if followed out, be the cause of less misery and blood shed afterward.'[55] The misery that Reade sought to avoid and the blood he was determined to safeguard was that of white settlers, no massacre of the Africans was too extreme and no war of extermination too vast if it was undertaken in the spirit of 'self-protection' of the white race. In the closing chapter of his long and rambling book Reade called upon Europeans to accept his assertion that as the white race expanded across the African continent the African peoples themselves 'may possibly become exterminated'. This process might be the result of philanthropic murder but deeper forces were also at work. The extinction of Africans would come as it was in accordance with the 'beneficent law of Nature, that the weak must be devoured by the strong'. In chilling terms Reade foresaw a not too distant future in which 'young ladies on campstools under palm-trees will read with tears "*The Last of the Negroes*", and the Niger will become as romantic as the Rhine.'[56]

ELEVEN

'Darkest Africa'

In August 1884, the British and Foreign Anti-Slavery Society held what was to be the last of the great anti-slavery meetings that had punctuated British history since the 1780s. The gathering, held at the Guildhall in the City of London, was billed as an 'Anti-slavery Jubilee' and was timed to mark the fiftieth anniversary of the abolition of British slavery.[1] Reporting on the celebrations, *The Times* proudly declared: 'There is no nobler chapter in the history of English freedom than that which ended fifty years ago in the emancipation of every slave within the Imperial dominions of the British Crown.' The memory of the great abolitionist struggles of half a century earlier that had so divided the late Georgian British was, by the 1880s, a largely uncontentious source of national unity and pride. Abolition was a parable held aloft as proof of Britain's moral leadership and exceptionalism. The collective pride over abolition, 'stir[s] us all, without distinction of party, sect, or creed to continued perseverance in the same noble work' asserted *The Times*. After all, 'fifty years are an interval all too short to permit Englishmen to forget one of the greatest deeds of mercy and justice ever accomplished by the nation'.[2] Among the speakers at the Guildhall in 1884 was the Prince of Wales, who, to constant cheering, declared himself to be 'sure that in time all countries will follow in the footsteps of England. The best chance of a complete abolition of slavery will lie in civilization, in opening up those great countries, Asia and Africa, many parts of which are now known to but few Europeans'.[3]

Three months later, at another gathering in another European capital, politicians and diplomats from what were then called the

Great Powers assembled to plan how this 'opening up' of the African continent might be realized. British anti-slavery activists may have commemorated 1884 as an anniversary of emancipation but history would better remember it as the year of the Berlin Conference, the meeting that marked the formal beginning of what people both at the time and ever since have called the 'Scramble for Africa'. The delegates who convened in the old Reich's Chancellery on Wilhelm-straße included representatives of all the imperial powers of Europe as well as diplomats from the Ottoman Empire and the United States. No representatives, diplomats or leaders from any African state or people were invited. It is often said that it was at the Berlin Conference that the continent of Africa was carved up by Europeans. In reality, the conference was where the European powers agreed the rules of engagement by which they would bring the continent under their legal control, resulting in a period that would become known as 'New Imperialism'.

Europeans had been in contact with sub-Saharan Africa since Henry the Navigator had commanded his Portuguese caravels to explore the West African coast in search of gold during the Age of Discovery four centuries earlier. Yet right until the last quarter of the nineteenth century the continent remained largely unexplored, 'known to but few Europeans', as the Prince of Wales put it in 1884. While the coastline of West Africa was familiar to European traders, and the Cape and other bridgeheads had been colonized, the rest was poorly understood. Africa was famously the 'dark conti-nent'. It existed only in silhouette and European ignorance of what lay in its great interior – the peoples, raw materials, rivers and mountains – felt to some, at that time of vast and rapid progress, a challenge to be conquered.

For Britain, the Scramble meant that the era of informal anti-slavery imperialism on the coast of Africa was over, and the phase of annexation and control of the interior began. In the minds of a number of statesmen and colonial theorists, Africa's new role was to act as a safety valve for Europe. It was to be an outlet for Europe's energies, ambitions and manufactured goods and an arena in which Europe's internal rivalries could also be played out at a safe distance. In effect, the freedoms of one continent and its people were to be forgone in the economic and security interests of another. To protect peace in Europe, Africa was to be divided and colonized. She was to provide new markets and raw materials. Where her climate was appropriate she was to offer up her soil to white settlers. In Africa, those new colonists would find what German theorists were, in the late nineteenth century, already beginning to call 'Lebensraum' – living space. In those regions that were habitable to Europeans the local Africans were to be divested of their ancestral lands and forcibly converted into a class of landless labourers. The exploration, conquest and colonization of Africa – the last continent to hold out against Europeans – was the great project of the age.

The sheer speed of the Scramble for Africa was breathtaking. In 1870, 10 per cent of Africa was under European control and 90 per cent of the continent was ruled by Africans. By 1900 that situation had been reversed. Ultimately only Ethiopia and Liberia resisted the European onslaught. Within three decades, nine million square miles of territory were added to the empires of Europe, one-fifth of the land area of the globe. Britain had, by some criteria, won the Scramble. One in three Africans became British colonial subjects; forty-five million people, more than the entire population of the UK at the time.

This great transition was largely made possible by new technologies. Africa, unlike the Americas, had never been unknown to Europeans. The British, as we have seen, traded with sub-Saharan Africans from the middle of the sixteenth century but the conquest of equatorial Africa remained impossible until the final quarter of the nineteenth century when the barriers that had kept the Europeans out for centuries were overcome one by one. Shallow-draughted, steam-powered riverboats were, not long after their invention, adapted to become gunboats, and rivers became highways for European military power, direct to Africa's heart. Medical advances allowed Europeans not just to conquer Africa but to occupy it. The prophylactic use of quinine enabled Victorian soldiers and explorers to survive in regions of tropical Africa that their predecessors had known as 'white men's graveyards'. Many zones were still not safe enough to be colonized by British settlers but quinine at least made it possible for administrators and soldiers to be posted to enforce British control and aid the flow of trade and commerce. The final piece of the jigsaw was the Maxim machine gun, a piece of military technology that enabled tiny numbers of European soldiers to overwhelm enormous armies of Africans, although fast, accurate breech-loading rifles were often just as important in many of the 'small wars' that regularly punctuated the Scramble. These new industrial weapons, produced in factories rather than by blacksmiths in workshops, were of a different order to older firearms. The West African armies' ancient muskets, many of which had been sold to them by European slave-traders in earlier centuries, were now disastrously defunct and ineffective.

Colonial theorists promised that Africa would supply Europe with new markets and materials, yet the colonies carved out of the continent in the late Victorian age were, in truth, of little economic significance. Until the First World War few ran at a profit, the cost of administration and infrastructural development usually outweighing the benefits of trade or mineral exploitation. In some places charter companies led the way and took the financial risks, in others strategic concerns encouraged the state to invest directly, which it often did only reluctantly, and there were always some politicians who, from time to time, asked if the whole thing was worth the candle. In 1910 Britain's only significant trading partner on the continent was South Africa, where the bulk of her white settlers lived. The real impact of the Scramble upon Britain was not economic but cultural. While the Scramble transformed the lives of millions of Africans there were others who lived through this great transition unaware that any of it had taken place, little affected by having become subjects of Britain. They toiled their fields never hearing of the distant island that claimed sovereignty over so much of their continent and never encountering a British soldier or administrator. The British public, however, tended to be far more aware of the great change that had taken place and many were deeply intrigued by the new peoples drawn into the empire.

Recent historical debates about the extent to which British people knew or cared about the empire to some extent miss the point. The public might not have regarded Africa as the key to national wealth and security, or as a project that affected their day-to-day lives in material or measurable ways, but they were often fascinated by its sheer drama and exoticism. It was the people of Africa rather than the land, rivers or mountains that gripped the imagination most tightly in the late nineteenth century. Millions of Victorians were just as fascinated by the mysterious people of the African interior as their Elizabethan forebears had been when they read Richard Hakluyt's accounts of the Age of Discovery. Renewed interest in the continent began earlier in the century thanks in large part to a generation of explorers whose exploits, adventures and privations captivated millions across Europe. African exploration caught the popular imagination before the process of colonization got under way, and was one of the great success stories of the booming newspaper industry of the 1860s and 1870s. A number of the explorers were themselves savvy self-publicists. Henry Morton Stanley, the author of the bestselling *In Darkest Africa,* and the man who 'found Livingstone', was a journalist as much as an explorer.

The Victorians were enthralled by military victory and there were great emotional surges of righteous outrage when British blood was spilt or the forward progress of British power temporarily halted by some insignificant tribe who had dared to stand in the way, or attempted to cling on to their own modes of life or their territory. The late Victorian age was regularly scandalized by imperial outrages, such as the Zulu victory over a British force at the Battle of Isandlwana in 1879, the death of Charles George Gordon at the hands of the Mahdi in Khartoum six years later and the 'Benin Massacre' of 1896 that led to the punitive destruction, by a British force, of the Oba's palace in Benin, which the English explorer John Lok had visited in the 1550s. Soldiers, explorers, hunters, missionaries or men who were dynamic combinations of all of the above became national 'heroes'. There was even room in the scramble for Africa for female heroes. The explorer and ethnographer Mary Kingsley undertook two expeditions to Africa and wrote the bestselling *Travels in West Africa.* In the last quarter of the century, the British press were very happy to report every triumph or setback. The daily newspapers, most of them conservative in outlook and targeted at the middle classes, specialized in breathless reports from the African bush or veldt. The age of the New Imperialism coincided with the age of the New Journalism; a tabloid revolution of campaigning, nationalistic, popular press that was always in need of a cause.

The expansion of the British Empire into Africa might have failed to deliver on the promise of wealth and new markets but it succeeded in offering spectacle. In doing so it contributed to a change in how people in Britain viewed the outside world, in particular the new peoples and races brought under British rule; hundreds of tribes each different and distinct were an enormous attraction and one of the great novelties of the age. All manner of stereotypes and judgements were blithely made about the various peoples of Africa in such texts. The Ndebele people were said to be savage warriors; the Yoruba were greedy and money-minded; the Zulu had a history of 'superstitious madness and blood-stained grandeur', in the view of the Victorian novelist Henry Rider Haggard.[4]

These observations were tainted by rapidly evolving forms of racism that emerged in the second half of the nineteenth century. Older ideas from the eighteenth century had held that the various races could be placed on a 'scale of humanity' or 'chain of being' with the white race at the top and the darker races at the bottom. Darwin's ideas and discoveries in the 1860s were understood by many as scientific explanation for this scale. It was, said the Social Darwinists, a consequence of ancient struggles for survival in which the strongest and most worthy races had risen to the top, and rightly so. From around the middle of the century craniometry – the study and measurement of human skulls – became another frontier of racial science. The discovery that there were tiny variations between the 'races' in the size of their skulls and the prominence of various features was presented as physical evidence for the alleged inferiority of the darker races. These dubious calibrations and the conclusions drawn from them went almost unchallenged during the last decades of the nineteenth century and were the foundations for many of the most dangerous racial theories of the twentieth. Another theory which gained ground in the second half of Victoria's reign was the idea that black children were lively and bright when young but after puberty lapsed into a lethargy, making no further intellectual progress. The view that Africans were, in effect, overgrown infants with the same predilections, weaknesses and irrationality had first emerged during the eighteenth century in slave owners' propaganda but it was given a second wind during the Scramble for Africa. It was perhaps best expressed by

Lord Lugard, a colonial soldier who rose to become Governor-General of Nigeria, and described 'the typical African':

> a happy, thriftless, excitable person, lacking in self-control, discipline and foresight, naturally courageous, and naturally courteous and polite, full of personal vanity, with little sense of veracity, fond of music and loving weapons as an oriental loves jewelry. His thoughts are concentrated on the events and feelings of the moment, and he suffers little from apprehension for the future, or grief for the past. His mind is far nearer to the animal world than that of the European or Asiatic, and exhibits something of the animal's placidity and want of desire to rise beyond the state he has reached . . . in brief, the virtues and defects of this race-type are those of attractive children . . . [5]

Imperial conquest put the builders of the British Empire in a position to make such judgements, and Social Darwinism enabled these influencers to regard the act of conquest itself as proof that they were superior to the 'dark races'. That the Africans had been conquered meant that they were inferior, so the argument went, and as inferiors their inevitable fate was to be ruled over by a wiser and stronger race. The belief that the British were such a people became more deeply ingrained and widespread in the later nineteenth century, as the humanitarianism of the abolitionist and anti-slavery eras – hypocritical and paternalistic though it was – evaporated. In its place came this harder, more biological view of race. A growing sense of white superiority and British exceptionalism spread, and came to influence even how many poorer Britons viewed Africans and other racial outsiders, even though the poor lived beyond the reach of the middle-class newspapers and the expensively produced memoirs of the explorers. They imbibed the new racism and racial hierarchies through the visual culture of their age and, after 1870, through elementary education that was made compulsory up to the age of thirteen. The late Victorian generation were the first to be presented with the famous map of the British Empire, blocked out in colonial British red, reduced to a less than masculine pink by cartographers to make the cities and rivers of the colonies and dominions more easy to read. Such racial views were by no means universal, and there were always Britons of all classes who, even in the most jingoistic and racist periods, rejected or distrusted the racial assumptions and were happy to welcome black people into their communities. But a widespread disdain for foreigners and sense of superiority over people of African heritage did become increasingly a feature of Britain in the second half of the nineteenth century, just as opposition to slavery had been a key feature of the national self-image in the middle decades.

This increasing belief in the hierarchy of races and the civilizing mission in Africa fused with a popular urge to encounter exotic peoples. This found its expression in the colonial exhibitions of the late nineteenth and early twentieth centuries which have, with good reason, been described as 'people shows' and 'human zoos'. Some of these were private affairs run by impresarios, others were vast exhibitions with a degree of state sanction and official recognition, with local councils becoming increasingly eager to secure the services of troupes of the most exotic Africans. The scale of some of these events and the efforts organizers made to provide audiences with supposedly authentic encounters with African peoples was previously unheard of, but the phenomenon of the African transported to Europe and displayed as a human exhibit was not. Africans had been exhibited before paying audiences throughout the nineteenth century.

Saartjie Baartman, also known as Sarah and as the Hottentot Venus, was a woman of the Khoikhoi people of southern Africa. She was born in the Eastern Cape around 1789. When white colonists murdered her fiancé, she was sold as a slave to Hendrik Cesars, a mixed-race Cape farmer, who made her work as a domestic servant in Cape Town. In 1810 she was brought to Britain by Cesars and a ship's surgeon named Alexander Dunlop, both of whom later claimed that she had signed a contract allowing herself to be put on public exhibition. In London Saartjie Baartman was displayed almost naked in a cage. Her physical appearance, and in particular her large buttocks, was examined and prodded by the men and some women who came to view her. She was eventually transported to France and sold again, this time to an exhibitor in the French capital. In 1815 she was studied by the French naturalist Georges Cuvier, one of the earliest proponents of the theory of extinction in the natural world. In the middle of the century more Khoikhoi and Khoisan people were exhibited in Britain, usually in temporary exhibitions and unsavoury sideshows that described them as 'Bushmen'. They were followed by a number of Zulu people.

The development of photography brought images of the people of the 'dark continent' to a wider European audience, yet this, perhaps, only made the yearning for real contact all the greater. The black population of Victorian Britain, tiny and concentrated in London and a handful of port towns, consisted mainly of people from the West Indies, the USA or Sierra Leone, who had no connection with exotic tribes from the inner, dark heart of Africa. They were novelties, and many of them took to the stage – as we shall see – but they were no substitute for people brought directly from Africa.

The earliest human exhibits from Africa were presented to the public in music halls and travelling circuses, usually as individuals or small groups. But later in the century far larger imperial exhibitions were staged. The Great Exhibition at the Crystal Palace in 1851 marked the advent of an age of 'International Exhibitions', 'World Fairs' and 'Expositions'. Between the 1860s and the First World War, the decades just after the creation of mass rail-transport networks and just before the advent of cinema, these events were an important aspect of European mass culture. All major European cities, and a number of minor ones, that had aspirations to or pretentions of grandeur and world status put on international exhibitions. London and Paris dominated but by holding an international exhibition smaller cities were able to momentarily burst upon the world stage, as Wolverhampton and Cork did in 1902, with Bradford following in 1904. The age of the international exhibitions coincided with the Scramble for Africa and the event organizers were happy to promote and celebrate the great imperial project. It was perhaps inevitable that the newly conquered peoples of Africa would be drawn into this new culture of mass spectacle. Imperial pavilions and 'native villages' which warehoused troupes of the supposedly savage peoples of Africa became an accepted and expected feature of the exhibitions. Millions of Britons living in the late nineteenth and early twentieth centuries visited and so had contact, often for the first time in their life, with people from Africa in such circumstances; for visitors from rural areas or smaller towns the African 'exhibits' were in many cases the first black people they had encountered.

These 'native villages' purported to be authentic arenas for genuine representations of African life, and were contrasted in the official programmes with the displays of European industry and technology in the pavilions that surrounded them.[6] The human exhibits were instructed to re-enact village life, produce the 'hand-icrafts associated with their existence', and perform tribal and even sacred customs.[7] The 'villagers' were separated from the white audiences by fences and were often commanded to perform their simulations to a timetable that could be advertised in advance. A village at the Franco-British Exhibition in Earls Court in 1908 housing around a hundred and thirty allegedly Senegalese Africans attracted three-quarters of a million visitors, who were promised that they would 'penetrate the mysteries of the sunlit Continent, to transport yourself at a moment from the prosaic world in which you live to a land of mystery and romance.'[8] It was slightly less popular than the Ceylon Village and the Irish Village, both of which were more successful than the Our Indian Empire pavilion. Many of the more spectacular shows exhibited animals in similar surroundings that also had their 'natural' habitats recreated for them by the organizers.

While they were intended to be celebrations of the triumphs of the imperial project, such exhibitions were also a reaffirmation of European racial supremacy over Africans, and other supposedly lesser peoples. In the later decades of the nineteenth century, the new sciences of ethnography and anthropology were deployed to provide exhibitions with the veneer of scientific respectability and to suggest that they had some purpose beyond entertainment and titillation. Yet the exploitation of the Africans placed on public display in faux African villages, imperial pavilions and music-hall sideshows was not altogether unnoted. The misuse of a man known as Klikko the Wild Dancing Bushman, who was put on display in a stage show that ran between 1912 and 1913, was so blatant and distasteful that an appalled stagehand, working at the Palace Theatre in Maidstone, reported the show to the Aborigines Protection Society.[9]

While all of these exhibitions and shows were undoubtedly exploitative, not all were as they seemed, and in some cases, the paying public were exposed to a lesser form of exploitation. In a number of shows there were, among the human exhibits, African performers. These were men and women who had effectively become professional ethnographic re-enactors, and who moved from city to city performing as required, taking some share of the profits. The Bradford Exhibition in 1904 had attempted to secure the services of a troupe of Ashanti people from the Gold Coast. When they were unavailable, the organizers booked a group of around a hundred men, women and children from Somalia, a country in which British forces had recently been engaged. Led by a chief and a mullah, the Somalis constructed their own, allegedly authentic African village and there they lived for the duration of the exhibition, which lasted from May until October 1904. The enormous Yorkshire crowds who visited the exhibition could observe various aspects of their traditional modes of life; there were demonstrations of traditional wrestling and spear-throwing, traditional metal workers produced authentic weapons and other implements, and weavers produced handicraft items. One of the most popular events was 'washing day', which predictably was dominated by the women. However, the savage authenticity of the Somalis was called into question by a report in the *Bradford Daily Telegraph*, which noted that on their departure a number of the men were seen wearing English suits. Many of them also spoke English, and when a fire at the showground damaged the troupe leader's accommodation, his personal belongings were valued at almost £300, enough in 1904 to purchase a small house.[10] It was also observed that the Somalis were in no particular hurry to return to their homeland and throw themselves back into the traditional modes of life they had spent the summer of 1904 re-enacting in a public park in Yorkshire. Their next stop was not the Horn of Africa but the Belgian town of Liège. It was clear that the Somalis were a professional outfit whose leaders had done financially very well by touring the European circuit of colonial exhibitions and African shows, thereby making a mockery of the popular notion of Africans as naive and unworldly. It was noted too that the Africans who occupied the Senegalese village at the Franco-British Exhibition in 1908 had arrived in London from France rather than Senegal. From there, they continued their progress across Europe. Other troupes of Africans were similarly professionalized and well travelled.

The African villages at some exhibitions (including the Somali and Senegalese Villages at Bradford and the Franco-British

Exhibition) included schools or workshops which were intended to demonstrate that the process of European colonization had brought immeasurable advantages to primitive peoples. The official guide to the Franco-British Exhibition described the Senegalese Village as a 'cruel-looking stockade' where 'over a hundred men and women from the borders of the desert are now living exactly as they do in their native Africa'. The presence of the school was proof, said the guide, 'that France cares for her far-away children with as much solicitude as Great Britain, and seeks as energetically and successfully to raise the standard of their lives'.[11]

The imperial exhibitions often attempted to draw anatomical and cultural comparisons between the various African peoples on display. The International Horticulture Exhibition held in London in 1892 included a number of people from the Zulu tribe and contained a Sudanese village. Attempts to contrast the qualities of the two peoples were somewhat undermined by the fact that the Sudanese were in reality from Senegal. Undeterred, the programme suggested the 'Sudanese' had attained a higher level of civilization than the Zulu as some of their number had been converted to Christianity.[12] The appearance of a Zulu choir was presented by the organizers as proof that efforts to similarly 'civilize' the Zulu were under way and bearing fruit.

During the Scramble for Africa, audiences were especially keen to view Africans who came from tribes against whom British forces had fought. Decades of intermittent colonial warfare, ceaselessly relayed to the public in sensationalized newspaper accounts and *Boy's Own* colonial adventure books had accustomed millions to think of tribes such as the Zulu of South Africa or the Ashanti of the Gold Coast as particularly warlike and savage. The opportunity of seeing, in the flesh, the warriors who had fought against British troops on the colonial frontier and, in the case of the Zulu, comprehensively defeated them at the 1879 Battle of Isandlwana was not to be missed. The impresarios who organized and profited from such exhibitions discovered that the effect could be further heightened if their African 'exhibits' were made to re-enact famous frontier battles that had, just years or in some cases months earlier, been the subject of fevered press coverage. These displays of colonial warfare, pitting British forces against 'savage' Africans in mock combat, were enormously popular, and never more so than when they portrayed white soldiers holding the 'thin red line' against men from tribes whose martial reputations were unquestioned and widely understood. That the Europeans, played by re-enactors or former soldiers, wore uniforms and the Africans appeared semi-naked all added to the sense of spectacle and exoticism.

At the turn of the century the most extravagant of all the imperial exhibitions arrived in Britain. The legendary 'Savage South Africa' show was the invention of Frank Fillis, an Anglo-South African circus owner. The show promised the public 'a sight never seen previously in Europe, a horde of savages direct from their kraals'.[13] Savage South Africa landed at Southampton docks with six elephants, seven lions and, somewhat incongruously for an African show, eight tigers. Travelling with the wild beasts were ten Boer families and, according to the *Bristol Mercury*, 'several members of the Cape Town Rifles, Bechuanaland Police and South African Police' all of whom were to perform in the show.[14] The other stars of 'Savage South Africa' were two hundred Africans, said to be made up of a hundred and fifty 'Swazi' and 'Basotho' people, and a group of 'Shangane mine-workers'. There were also fifty Zulu men, who had been recruited not to further demonstrate the fearsome reputation of their people, but to impersonate the Ndebele, against whom Cecil Rhodes's British South Africa Company had recently fought the Second Matabele War. The Ndebele people are an ethnic offshoot of the Zulu and it was presumed that the London audiences would be none the wiser. A film camera was sent to Southampton docks to meet the ship. The minute-long reel shows the 'Zulu' men gathered under the shadow of a giant crane, performing for the camera, encouraged by a white man in a frock coat and top hat. From Southampton 'the natives and animals' were transported to Earls Court on 'three special trains'.[15]

The show ran for a year between 1899 and 1900, and during this time the Anglo-Boer War broke out. Fillis seized the opportunity to approach the British army which, rather remarkably, loaned him six hundred soldiers. Fillis's new show, hosted in London's Olympia, staged re-enactments of episodes from the conflict.[16] Among the African 'performers' was Peter Lobengula, the son of the late King Lobengula Khumalo, the Ndebele leader who had been defeated by the British South Africa Company in the First Matabele War, 1893–94.

However, this most extravagant of shows brought to a head a disapproval that had been rumbling since the exhibitions had begun. In 1899, the Aborigines Protection Society condemned it for exploiting Africans and in Parliament, one MP asked the Secretary of State for the Colonies, Joseph Chamberlain, to take 'steps to procure the return of these Natives to their own country'.[17] While *The Times* did worry about the ethics of turning Africans into human exhibits, it ultimately concluded that 'whatever view one may take of the action of the organizers in bringing over a large number of natives to be stared at and to take their chance of being demoralized in such strange and unedifying surroundings, there is nothing to be said against the entertainment itself. It is a capital circus performance with a special interest lent to it by the representation of famous scenes in recent South African history'.[18]

But what disturbed a number of Victorian and Edwardian commentators more than the exploitation of African people was that such exhibitions brought African men into contact with white British women, and not only that, but there were rumours of sexual contact between the black men and white female visitors. These claims led the organizers of 'Savage South Africa', the London Exhibition Company, to bar all white women from the area housing the Africans – the so-called 'Kaffir kraal'. When it was revealed that Peter Lobengula had married an English woman, Kitty Jewell, even the most lurid rumours were recounted as fact. American newspapers took great delight in reporting that in London 'fashionable women go into the black men's huts and give them presents'. These encounters, they maintained, were merely the overtures to the 'vilest orgies'.[19] The Texan newspaper the *Galveston Daily News* suggested that by allowing 'this little band of savages' into their capital city the episode had 'brought home to the English people for the first time the seriousness of mixed marriages'.[20] In 1917, a writer in the popular magazine *Tit-Bits* commented that, 'some years ago we used to have large bodies of natives sent from Africa on military service or in some travelling show, and it was the revelation of horror and disgust to the whole the manner in which English women would flock to see these men, whilst to watch them fawning over these black creatures and fondling them and embracing them, as I have seen dozens of times, was a scandal and a disgrace to English womanhood.' Racial mixing did not just offend the author, he believed it was a real and direct threat to the control of the empire and the preservation of racial hierarchies. If, as he was convinced, such events permitted the barriers that separated the races to be crossed, 'how then', he asked, 'is it possible to maintain as the one stern creed in the policy of the Empire the eternal supremacy of the white over black?'[21]

British administrators in the colonies similarly disliked the imperial exhibitions. There were reports in 1899 that the South African authorities had attempted to prevent Africans being taken to London for 'Savage South Africa'. What the authorities there and elsewhere in the African empire feared was that those who had taken part in such events, having travelled to Europe and met thousands of Europeans, would return home with a new understanding of their colonial rulers, which would undermine white racial prestige, and that contact between white women and African men would put white women in Africa at risk. One of the ways in which the organizers attempted to limit the damage – as they saw it – was to control how much of Britain the African 'exhibits' and performers were able to see. This was achieved, on occasion, by containing them within the exhibition grounds, or at least attempting to do so. When Africans travelled as self-contained and self-organized troupes, who moved independently from city to city, this was, of course, impossible and there was another type of visiting African even more difficult to control and corral.

Throughout the later decades of Queen Victoria's reign, a number of royal delegations containing African kings and chiefs visited Britain. These were often arranged by the Colonial Office, which liked to use them to impress upon African rulers the military and economic power of Britain. Others were arranged in order for African leaders to negotiate with officials at the Colonial Office, and some were the initiative of Africans themselves. These visits subverted the racial hierarchies of empire in ways that fascinated the hierarchical and class-based British public. African kings were both black and royal – and therefore doubly exotic. Some had attained fame before they set foot on British soil and their arrival in the country was a national event. Cetshwayo kaMpande, the deposed King of the Zulu people, visited Britain in 1882, just three years after his victory over British forces at the Battle of Isandlwana. The British press, which had reported the defeat in lurid detail, was fascinated by the King's visit. The shock of Isandlwana had inspired a wave of hatred against the Zulus; however, once British military dominance in southern Africa had been reasserted and the natural order of things – as the British viewed it – restored, the mood changed. Deposed and exiled, Cetshwayo was no longer a military threat and could thus be feted as a 'noble savage' and leader of an exotic warrior people. The Zulu king used his visit to meet Queen Victoria and officials at the Colonial Office, with whom he negotiated his partial reinstatement as King of the Zulu. Rather unsubtly, the Colonial Office included in his itinerary a tour of Woolwich Arsenal, during which he saw enormous artillery pieces being forged, and of the Royal Naval Dockyard at Portsmouth.

The most remarkable of the many royal African visits of the Victorian age took place in 1895. It was initiated by King Khama of the BagammaNgwato people, who lived in the Bechuanaland Protectorate, modern Botswana. In 1893, the Ndebele King Lobengula (whose son had been a human exhibit in the 'Savage South Africa' show) had been defeated by Cecil Rhodes, the Prime Minister of the Cape Colony and diamond-mining millionaire whose British South Africa Company ruthlessly used its own private army to expand British control in southern Africa. The Ndebele had then been largely corralled onto two 'native reserves' and huge swathes of land had been distributed to white settlers by what was called the 'Loot Committee'. By 1895, Cecil Rhodes had decided on his next target. His aim was to draw the Bechuanaland Crown Colony into the Cape Colony, then to bring the Bechuanaland Protectorate under the control of his British South Africa Company, rather than the British government. Threatened by Cecil Rhodes's plans, King Khama protested to the Cape Colony government, where he had a number of supporters who regarded him as a loyal ally of the British. Though he had fewer supporters in London, the new government of Lord Salisbury was far more sympathetic to Cecil Rhodes and his ambitions than the Liberal Party administration it had toppled. When

Rhodes succeeded in annexing the Bechuanaland Crown Colony it was inevitable that the Bechuanaland Protectorate and the lands of King Khama would be next.

In September 1895, Khama travelled to Britain with two other kings from the Bechuanaland Protectorate, Sebele I of the Kwêna people and Bathoen I of the Bangwaketse. Their unlikely plan to protect their land from Rhodes was to appeal directly to the British people. In 1894 Khama had written to a sympathetic supporter in the government of the Cape Colony, explaining that he intended to 'seek another way of approach which I can speak to the Queen and the people of England'.[22] Their great ally in this venture was the Reverend William Willoughby and his colleagues in the London Missionary Society. Once they arrived in Britain, Khama, Sebele and Bathoen attended a meeting with Joseph Chamberlain, Secretary of State for the Colonies, in which they made a plea for their lands to be maintained under the protection of the Crown and not incorporated into the territories administered by the British South Africa Company. They then embarked upon one of the best organized and most effective public-relations operations in British history and visited every major city in the country, clustering their appearances by region for greater efficiency. During September they toured the Midlands, visiting Wellingborough, Leicester, Enderby and Birmingham. In October they went to Stockport, Liverpool, Manchester, Dewsbury, Bradford, Leeds and Halifax. Another tour later that month saw them appear in Manchester, Edinburgh, Glasgow, Sheffield and Hanley. Upon the instruction of the kings, professionally produced books of press cuttings containing articles taken from a hundred and thirty-five British newspapers and New York dailies were distributed.

A glimpse at the itinerary for just one stop in the tour shows how each day was a whirl of events, meetings, speeches and dinners, and reveals the warmth of reception they received. The visit of Khama, Bathoen and Sebele to Birmingham on 27 September 1895 began at nine thirty with a special breakfast in the mayor's parlour in the Council House. In his invitation for the breakfast the Deputy Mayor of Birmingham requested the pleasure of the company of those Birmingham citizens who were 'To Have The Honour of Meeting Khama, the chief of the Bamangwato; Sebele, Chief of the

Bakwena; and Bathoen, Chief of the Bangwaketse'.[23] A special 'Royal Programme, and a Descriptive Sketch', of the 'Visit of King Khama, ruler of Bechuanaland Accompanied by Native African Chiefs to Birmingham September 1895' was also printed.[24] It promised to reveal 'King Khama's Life, Character, and Career: A Most Interesting And Graphic Account of African Habits and Customs.'[25] The schedule of events explained that after a busy day meeting local manufacturers, having lunch with Mr R. Cadbury of the Bournville chocolate factory and speaking at the Council House with the Deputy Mayor, the kings were to 'attend a reception at the Town Hall (for which 2,500 invitations have been issued) afterwards KHAMA will be presented with an illuminated address; and in the same building be present at a meeting of the London Missionary Society, at which the KING will speak'.[26] The three kings were to stay at the Cobden Hotel and leave Birmingham New Street Station the following morning for their next set of engagements, in Brighton.

It was a hectic, inventive and brilliantly stage-managed tour that turned three unknown African kings from minor southern tribes into national celebrities and unleashed a great torrent of press coverage in which Rhodes and the British South Africa Company were largely vilified. The three kings and their missionary allies ensured that every positive aspect of their characters and back stories was emphasized and publicized, and that the people they ruled over were portrayed as the innocent victims of Rhodes and his limitless ambition. Readers of British newspapers in the autumn of 1895, like any of the thousands of people who attended the numerous meetings, talks and audiences at which the three kings were present, were reminded that King Khama had refused to take a second wife, as had been customary, and had repressed polygamy among his people. They were also informed that King Khama personally eschewed alcohol and campaigned tirelessly for the eradication of hard liquor from his kingdom. As the temperance movement was the largest mass-participation social movement in late Victorian Britain, Khama's abstemiousness won him a great many friends and admirers. The public were constantly and repeatedly reminded of the depth of the three kings' Christian faith, and their strong links to the men of the London Missionary Society. It helped that Sebele's father had been baptized by David Livingstone. Khama,

Sebele and Bathoen and their missionary supporters were also able to tap into Britain's long anti-slavery tradition by suggesting that Rhodes's ultimate intention was to force the people of the Bechuanaland Protectorate to work in the Kimberley gold mines, where they would be reduced to something akin to a state of slavery. The effect was dramatic. The British press, which by 1895 had supported numerous colonial wars and annexations, and presented its readers with many sensationalist and exaggerated portraits of various African tribes, proved infinitely flexible. Sensing the public mood and knowing a good story when it saw one, it poured praise upon the three kings of Bechuanaland, never tiring of playing on the obvious symbolism of this 'trinity' of kings who had arrived from a distant land. The *Yorkshire Daily Post* was not untypical in its effusive praise for Khama: 'The African Chief Khama is the best example of what a black man can become by means of good disposition and Christianity, a British officer described him as a man far in advance of his people in Africa ruling by generosity instead of fear, cool in danger and self possessed at all times. It has been said that his manners would win golden opinion in any society.'[27]

Throughout all of this Khama, Sebele and Bathoen were able to present themselves to the British people as grateful beneficiaries of the Victorian 'civilizing mission'. They were, after all, not seeking to escape the empire but had willingly submitted to its embrace and hoped only for that embrace to endure. Here were Africans who wanted to live under the rule of Queen Victoria and under the protection of the empire. Instead, their dispute was with Cecil Rhodes and the British South Africa Company, whose harsh rule they desperately sought to avoid. Throughout their tour they were, therefore, able to lay two opposing visions of the empire alongside one another. The 'civilizing mission' vision of British trusteeship, which, although paternalistic, patronizing and groaning under the weight of racial supposition, was infinitely more benign than the brutal, rapacious, land-grabbing form of settler capitalism practised by Cecil Rhodes and the British South Africa Company. Khama, Sebele and Bathoen fully understood the difference between the two. In June 1895, Khama had sent a petition to Joseph Chamberlain which rightly appraised the methods and priorities of the British South Africa Company. '[We] see that the Company does not love black people', he wrote, 'it loves only to take the country of the black people and sell it to others that it may see gain.'[28]

As there had been during previous royal African visits, there were some attempts by the Colonial Office to control the schedule and determine which aspects of British life the kings were permitted to see. When it was suggested, for example, that they might visit a prison the request was refused on the grounds that it would be a 'humiliation' for the prisoners 'to be looked upon by Kaffirs'.[29] The kings did, however, go to the Crystal Palace, which by 1895 was no longer located in Hyde Park but in Sydenham, south London. There they visited an imperial exhibition entitled 'The East African Village and Great Display by the Natives of Somaliland under the Direction of Herr Carl Hagenbeck'.[30] Hagenbeck was a near-legendary supplier of exotic animals and 'savage' peoples to the colonial exhibitions and zoos of Europe. His East African Village came replete with sixty-five Somali 'villagers', who, as was customary by 1895, re-enacted their daily routines and tribal customs for the paying public. Alongside the village was an ostrich farm, for which admission was two shillings. Khama, Sebele and Bathoen went to both and were all said to have been 'greatly pleased by their entertainment'.[31] What they thought of the morality of placing fellow Africans on display in an ersatz village on the edge of London was not recorded.

Repeatedly throughout their tour, as the three kings built up popular support, they held negotiations with Cecil Rhodes's agents in Britain. In November 1895 they rejected what the British South Africa Company called its 'maximum offer' on the status of their territories and the amount of land they were expected to cede to the company for the construction of a new railway. In a letter of 4 November they wrote to Rhodes and his company:

> You speak to us as if you had taken our land in war and we had to beg it from you. The land is ours, not yours, and we cannot speak of giving the best parts to you. We occupy the waters with our cattle and our gardens, and we cannot remove our people for the sake of letting you sell our country.[32]

That month, the kings met Chamberlain. They agreed to cede land to the government for the construction of the railway but were promised compensation. More importantly, they were assured that they were to 'live as hitherto under the protection of the Queen' and that they were to 'rule their own people much as at present'.[33] Rhodes responded to the government's recognition of the rights of the kings to rule over their own land and people by complaining that it was a humiliation to have been 'utterly beaten by these niggers'.[34] On 20 November, at Windsor Castle, Khama, Sebele and Bathoen were finally granted an audience with Queen Victoria, who they knew as *MmaMosadinyana* – 'the little woman of many days'.[35] They returned to Bechuanaland in 1896 and the protectorate remained under direct British administration until 1960 when it became the modern state of Botswana. Khama, Sebele I and Bathoen I are recognized by Botswanans as founders of their nation. Had they not embarked upon their tour of Britain it is probable that Cecil Rhodes would have annexed the protectorate and incorporated it into what became Rhodesia.

Through all this – the Scramble for Africa, the rise of the imperial exhibitions, the visits of African kings and the emergence of new forms of racism – there were, at the centre of the empire itself, communities of black Britons: ordinary people living ordinary lives. There were black Victorians and black Edwardians, as there had been black Georgians and black Tudors. The new colonial project, like the slave trade before it, brought black people to Britain while at the same time older links, such as those between Britain and Sierra Leone, developed, evolved and in some ways deepened. There was often, as the historian Douglas Lorimer suggests, a divergence between attitudes and behaviour. While racism undoubtedly affected the lives of all black Victorians and Edwardians, some were able to navigate within British society and often move around within the empire and within certain British institutions – the churches, universities, the army and the professions. They found and created roles for themselves in which they were accepted, at least by some, and entered new arenas when allowed to become black 'firsts'. As in all societies those with money and education fared best, and there continued to be a black underclass of beggars and the destitute, but luck sometimes counted for much.

Africans, West Indians and African Americans arrived in Britain in the latter half of the nineteenth century not as pageboys and domestic slaves as in the Georgian era but as students, as sailors and simply as migrants. Others were born in Britain, the products of generations of contact, migration and Christian missionary work. A disproportionate number of students came from Sierra Leone, as the Krio people built upon their unique links to Britain, which ran deeper than those of any other African people, except perhaps for some of the old coastal people of the South African Cape. The University of Durham developed particularly strong ties with both the West Indies and West Africa, and became one of the few centres for the education of black men in Britain through the late nineteenth and early twentieth centuries. A few black women were sent to Britain, by family or by the Church, to receive a higher education. Young people from both colonies trained and studied in the cold North-East. Other British institutions focused on training Africans as missionaries and by the end of the century London University and the universities of Cambridge and Liverpool had begun to attract and accept African students, most in medicine or the law. Thanks to these programmes there were African doctors working in British hospitals half a century before the advent of the National Health Service, which would so heavily rely upon the efforts of black migrants. Among the first black doctors in Britain were John Alcindor from Trinidad and the Jamaican Harold Moody, who studied medicine at King's College but was denied a hospital position on account of his race. In the 1930s Moody formed the League of Coloured Peoples, a civil rights movement aimed at advancing the life chances of black Britons by attacking the inter-war colour bar and improving what later became known as race relations.

Some of the black students who studied in Britain stayed and became members of a black British middle class. Photographs of well-to-do black Victorians show the men in starched black frock coats, the women in respectable high-necked and embroidered gowns. They carry pocket watches, wear top hats and pose with Bibles in hand. They appear in family groups or as individuals, in front of painted backdrops of Arcadian scenes or sitting on heavy and overly ornate chairs. They look unmistakably Victorian, and yet as they have so often been written out of our vision of that period they can appear incongruous and out of place, as if a modern photographer has used an old camera to photograph twenty-first-century black Britons in costume.

Many of the more famous black Victorians and Edwardians came from Freetown families. Samuel Coleridge-Taylor, the celebrated composer of *The Song of Hiawatha*, who was once described as the 'African Mahler', was born in London, the son of a Freetown Krio man who had trained as a doctor in Britain. Others came from West Indian families. John Richard Archer was born in Britain but from West Indian stock; his father came from Barbados and his mother was Irish. Archer attended Coleridge-Taylor's funeral and was politically active from a young age, becoming one of the first Africans to win public office in Britain and becoming a councillor for Battersea in 1906. In 1913, after a campaign marked by racial aspersions and questions over his nationality, he became mayor. As well as municipal politics he was active in Pan-Africanist and Labour politics, and corresponded with black political leaders in the United States.

As in the eighteenth century men of African descent played a role in Britain's imperial ventures during the nineteenth century, serving in the army and navy. Most occupied lowly ranks as army regulations stipulated that officers had to be of 'pure European descent' – we shall hear more about this later. Yet exceptions were made. J. A. Horton and W. B. Davis, both from Sierra Leone, became commissioned medical officers in the British army in the late 1850s. Horton was the son of an Igbo man who was liberated from a slave ship, landed at Freetown and later married a woman who was descended from the Nova Scotian settlers. Horton wrote four medical books, based on his experiences serving as a medical officer in West Africa, but is better remembered for his greatest political work, *West African Countries and Peoples, British and Native: A Vindication of the African Race* (1868). This eloquent denouncement of the pseudo-scientific racism of the Victorian age is a forgotten classic. Horton described his masterpiece as 'An endeavour . . . to disprove many of the fallacious doctrines and statements (detrimental to the interests of the African race)'.[36] Among the ordinary soldiers who served in the Victorian army was Jimmy Durham, who was found as an infant by soldiers of the Durham Light Infantry abandoned on a battlefield in Sudan, in 1885. Renamed and brought to Britain he became an informal regimental mascot, then a bugle boy and finally, at fourteen, a boy soldier, his application being approved by Queen Victoria herself. He served with the Durham Light Infantry in India and after returning with his regiment to the North-East of England married a local woman. His mixed-race descendants lived in County Durham until the 1990s.

Since the sixteenth century and the life of the royal trumpeter John Blanke, black people in Britain had been involved in the world of performance: music, dance and the stage. Over the intervening centuries racial stereotypes about black musicality and physicality had reinforced the notional links between blackness and performance. In the second half of the nineteenth century, when black people were fewer than during the slave-trading seventeenth and eighteenth centuries, their rareness made them an exotic draw for audiences, and hundreds of black Britons and black migrants from Africa and the Americas joined the Victorian entertainment industry, a vast and sprawling network of theatres, music halls and travelling shows that performed to millions of people each week.

The most celebrated black performers of the late nineteenth century were not black Britons but African Americans. The Fisk Jubilee Singers originated in Nashville, Tennessee, then in the early 1870s introduced the British public to black American gospel music, bringing new songs into British churches, including 'Swing Low, Sweet Chariot'. Their tour of Europe was one of the greatest musical events of the century. Lord Shaftesbury arranged for them to perform in London for six hundred specially selected guests and in 1873 they sang for Queen Victoria, who was said to have been affected by their rendition of the song 'John Brown's Body'. According to one report, the Prince of Wales, who had been given lessons on the minstrel banjo from the black Bohee brothers, requested they sing the harrowingly tragic slave lament 'No More Auction Block For Me'.[37] The impact of the Fisk Jubilee Singers was all the greater because black music performed by black people was a novelty to British audiences who, ever since the 1830s, had become accustomed to minstrel tunes – a distorted and appropriated form of black music – being sung by white men in blackface. When the Fisk Jubilee Singers toured there were reportedly difficulties with a number of inn-keepers who had accepted their accommodation booking presuming that the 'minstrels' were white and were unhappy to discover otherwise.[38] Although their music was far closer to what we would today categorize as spiritual or gospel music and they themselves were largely responsible for the rethinking of some of these categories, the Fisk Jubilee Singers were, at the time, regarded as performers of 'Negro Minstrelsy'.

The story of the Fisk Jubilee Singers is today becoming better known but most of the black entertainers who performed in Britain in the nineteenth and early twentieth centuries are long forgotten. Ella Williams, the daughter of South Carolina slaves, took to the stage under the name Abomah the African Giantess; on her second tour of Britain, she was billed as the Living Colossus. Many reports claimed she was seven feet six inches tall, although her height varied from billing to billing. An article in the never-reliable London magazine *Tit-Bits* declared her to be eight feet tall. It's now suggested that she was around six feet eleven. To add topicality to her stage persona she was, during the 1890s, said to be the daughter of a female general who had, supposedly, commanded the 'African Amazons' of Dahomey. *Tit-Bits* went further, claiming that Ella Williams from South Carolina had formerly been 'one of the attendants and body guard of the barbaric King of Dahomey, whose Amazonian warriors have been famous alike for their prowess and cruelty. Trained for her bloodthirsty calling from early childhood, she was inured to hardship and pain. Her stature increasing out of proportion to her years, she became a particular favorite of the monarch, and led his army. This extraordinary woman stands over eight feet in height, and can easily support the weight of a man on her outstretched hand. The dusky beauty, having recently evinced a strong desire to travel, and particularly to visit England, will no doubt soon pay a visit to some of our principal cities.'[39] On stage, she narrated interesting incidents from her life and sang music-hall and minstrel numbers, including (sadly) a song by Ernest Hogan (who was himself an African American) entitled 'All Coons Look Alike to Me'. She toured across Britain and the empire until 1915 when she returned to the United States, where she ended up performing in sideshows.

The circus proprietor Pablo Fanque, another of the most successful black entertainers of the Victorian age, was born in Norwich under the more mundane name of William Darby. His father was said, vaguely, to have come to Britain from Africa. The young Darby was apprenticed in the circus, and specialized in horsemanship and rope vaulting. He rapidly rose up the bill to become a star performer, adopting the flamboyant stage name Pablo Fanque. He later added to his celebrity by performing on the trapeze alongside his infant son, 'Master Pablo Fanque', who was described by one newspaper as 'the youngest performer in the world, his precious talents have obtained for him the appellation of the gem of Africa', although is unlikely that he ever set foot on the African continent.[40] What is striking about the surviving advertisements and reviews of Pablo Fanque's circus is how few of them make mention of his race. The *Caledonian Mercury* in November 1838 described him as 'a gentleman of colour' but dedicated far more column inches to describing his various 'feats' and 'leaps' than his complexion.[41] Neither *Blackwood's Lady's Magazine* nor the *Illustrated London News* in 1847 saw any difficulty in describing this black British entrepreneur 'as a native of Norwich'.[42]

By the 1840s, Pablo Fanque had struck out independently to form his own circus and had become an established feature of the entertainment world. An entrepreneur, philanthropist and star of the circus ring he was one of the great entertainers of his age. His legendary acts of horsemanship were performed before Queen Victoria and for thirty years his circus toured Britain. An advertisement from the *Preston Chronicle* reported that 'PABLO FANQUE'S CIRCUS in the orchard NIGHTLY OVERFLOWS'. Among the acts listed on the bill were 'Mr Pablo Fanque's leaping over a number of difficult objects', 'Principal Acts of Horsemanship' by a Mr Moffatt and further down the bill an act described as 'Serious Pantomime – Three Fingered Jack – Mr Moffatt and the whole company'.[43] In wonderfully evocative Victorian prose the advertisement also informed readers that 'It is Mr P. F.'s intention to give the proceeds of one night to some charitable institution in Preston; due notice of which will be given'. This was not unusual. Fanque gave numerous benefit performances in aid of local charities or even individuals who found themselves in distress, including an 1843 performance in Town-Meadows Rochdale that was billed as 'BEING FOR THE BENEFIT OF MR. KITE'. Despite the fame he enjoyed in the mid-nineteenth century, Pablo Fanque would be almost completely forgotten today were it not for a bizarre, chance happening. In 1967 a poster advertising the 1843 Rochdale performance of 'Pablo Fanque's Circus Royal' was bought from an antique shop in Sevenoaks, Kent, by John Lennon, who was there to film a video for the Beatles' songs 'Penny Lane' and 'Strawberry Fields Forever'. Lennon and Paul McCartney took the text of that poster, which listed the various acts due to appear alongside Pablo Fanque, and transformed them, sometimes verbatim, into the lyrics of the song 'Being For the Benefit of Mr Kite' which appears on the album *Sgt. Pepper's Lonely Hearts Club Band*. Pablo Fanque himself is mentioned in the song.

Despite the enormous appeal of the imperial exhibitions and people shows, the images of Africans that developed during the Scramble for Africa and in the years that followed had to compete for space within British popular culture and the popular imagination with stereotypes and archetypes from the blackface minstrelsy and *Uncle Tom's Cabin*. This world of 'Bibles, Banjos and Bones', as one historian called it, remained a perennial feature of British cultural landscape and was no longer, strictly speaking, an American import.[44] Uncle Tom lived to the century's end and on into the twentieth century long after American slavery was dead in its grave.

Just as persistent were minstrelsy and minstrel tunes. The minstrel song book was still being played on the street, minstrel acts still took to the stage, and the minstrel tradition along with *Uncle Tom's Cabin* were both able to transition into emerging new mediums. In the spring of 1896, just a few months after King Khama and the other kings of Bechuanaland had left for home, the Lumière Brothers, the inventors of cinema, opened their Cinématographe at the Empire Theatre at 7 Leicester Square, London. While filming street scenes in London the Lumière cinematographers stumbled across a troupe of blackface minstrels performing for a small crowd in front of Le Solferino Restaurant in Rupert Street. The silent film of that encounter, entitled *Nègres dansant dans la rue*, shows a group of six men in blackface. They are wearing white trousers, dark jackets and waistcoats; two have top hats and the rest straw boaters. Two play banjos, one man a guitar and another the penny whistle. There is a tambourine player and a troupe leader. They all dance the comic, exaggerated, swaying dance that had become part of the minstrel tradition, as they sang what one nineteenth-century journalist described as 'ultra-sentimental ditties', and 'songs that affect a nonsensical jocosity'.[45] The audience consists mainly of men and young boys, who smile and laugh, perhaps as amused by the novel presence of the film camera as by the minstrels' performance. The minstrels filmed in Rupert Street, white British men working in a trade that was never secure or particularly well paid, presumably spent much of their professional lives taking part in this bizarre, almost ritualized form of racial impersonation, a daily lampooning of a people they did not know and who lived in a country they would never visit. By 1896 minstrelsy had been part of British culture for sixty years, ever since Thomas D. Rice had performed his Jumpin' Jim Crow act at London's Surrey Theatre. It was almost half a century, in 1896, since Henry Mayhew had encountered men from an earlier generation of blackface performers on the London street, with burnt cork framing their poorly washed faces. In the last years of the nineteenth century minstrelsy was still going strong but by then the men in blackface competed for custom and coins with other troupes performing other musical forms. Among their main rivals in the 1890s and during the first decade of the twentieth century were the popular German 'Oompah' bands that – for obvious reasons – abruptly disappeared from the British street in early August 1914, never to return.

TWELVE

'We are a Coloured Empire'

On 12 August 1914, hundreds of thousands of French soldiers in uniforms of blue jackets and red trousers surged across the German border. To their north, in Belgium, German cuirassiers launched a thunderous cavalry attack on the little town of Haelen. Three thousand miles away, little noticed or commented upon at the time, a small British force headed through the African bush towards Lomé, the capital of the German colony of Togoland. That day, far from the battlefields of France and Belgium, Lance Corporal Alhaji Grunshi of the British West African Frontier Force became the first soldier in British service to fire a shot in the land war. Ten days later Edward Thomas, of the 4th (Royal Irish) Dragoon Guards, became the first white British soldier to fire his rifle in anger in Europe. The First World War began in Africa and it was to end there on 14 November 1918, when the last German units surrendered, three days after the armistice in Europe.

For black people in Britain and many other parts of the empire, the First World War changed their understanding of the empire and their place within it. It was during wartime that black people from parts of Africa and the West Indies gained new and first-hand experience of the racism and racial hierarchies that both informed and, for many, justified colonial rule. In ways that were not easily foreseeable when the armies marched to battle in the summer of 1914, the First World War led to the temporary lowering of the physical, cultural and legal barriers that had been erected between the races and between the subject peoples of the empire. During the war one million Africans were recruited to work as carriers in Africa. At least a hundred thousand of them died; some suspect the actual figure is at least double that. Thousands of men from modern Ghana were recruited for the Gold Coast Regiment; they were sent to fight the Germans in East Africa, alongside four regiments of the West African Frontier Force, men from British Nigeria. Africans from Sudan, Rhodesia, Ethiopia and Nyasaland were recruited into the King's African Rifles and shipped across eastern Africa in pursuit of the German forces. These men encountered soldiers from the West Indian islands who served in the specially formed British West Indies Regiment. Fifteen thousand West Indians served in the war, labouring on the Western Front and fighting in the Middle East as well as in Africa. When these black subjects of the empire encountered one another, and other non-white peoples in the hyper-globalized military zones that existed behind the lines, in port cities of the Allied nations and on board the ships that linked Britain to her empire, they were able to discuss their experiences and gain a new, deeper understanding of the inner workings of empire. This, combined with deep resentment at the unequal and unjust treatment black soldiers and sailors experienced during the conflict, ensured that many returned to their homes profoundly disillusioned. Just as disenchanted were those who had been victims of the violence that erupted in numerous British cities in the months after the war. Yet at the outbreak of hostilities, what is striking is how little of this was foreseen and how strong the sense of unity within the empire was, even across the barriers of race. Also unanticipated was just how much enthusiasm there was for the war among black people in both African and West Indian colonies.

Few parts of the empire greeted the outbreak of war with such passion as the islands of the British West Indies. In the Bahamas, Grenada, British Honduras (now Belize), British Guiana (now Guyana), the Leeward Islands, St Vincent, St Lucia, Barbados, Trinidad and Tobago and most of all in Jamaica there was a feeling that the people of the West Indies had to do their bit in the impending struggle. The 'war fever' that took hold of the West Indies in 1914 and 1915 was as contagious and as virulent a strain as that which swept through the industrial towns of Edwardian Britain. In Jamaica, public meetings and open-air rallies in support of the war were held in Kingston and a number of smaller towns. The threat of German invasion, a rather far-fetched notion, was debated in the newspapers and patriotic, pro-imperial euphoria gripped the island. This great surge of affection for the 'mother country' stemmed from the regard in which many older Jamaicans had held Queen Victoria, the monarch whose coronation had been celebrated just weeks before Emancipation in 1838 and to whom the poor of St Ann's parish had written their appeal in 1865. This bond of loyalty and respect had survived Victoria's death in 1902 and had – to a certain extent – been transferred to her successors Edward VII and then George V.

In both public meetings and in the press the British Empire was presented in Jamaica as a paragon of morality and virtue. A highly idealized interpretation of the British 'civilizing mission' was contrasted with the unwavering and unreasoning brutality of 'Prussian militarism' and 'German tyranny'. Repeatedly in 1914 and 1915, the British Empire was portrayed in the local newspapers and in rallies held in support of the war as an empire of emancipation, a commonwealth of justice, freedom, and even equality. Jamaica, the former slave colony, had been the crucible of the great experiment of emancipation. The island and her free, if largely impoverished, people were cited as living proof of British virtue, as they had been between 1838 and the outbreak of the Morant Bay Rebellion in 1865. In the patriotic mood of 1914 the memory of abolition was repeatedly underscored and the story of slavery consistently obscured. Jamaica's terrible history of slavery, rebellion and repression was for the moment set aside and the descendants of the enslaved encouraged to imagine themselves members of an imaginary British Empire of sympathetic paternalism and racial equality.

Soon after hostilities commenced there were calls from colonial governors and the public at large for a new regiment of the British army made up of islanders who were willing to fight in France. At war rallies, unofficial self-appointed recruiting sergeants challenged young Jamaican men to commit themselves to the defence of the nation and called upon them to fight for the empire that had emancipated their ancestors. At one rally, Brigadier General Blackden, general officer in command of local forces in Jamaica, asked, with remarkable tactlessness, if the men in the audience – the grandchildren and great-grandchildren of slaves – were willing to fight for freedom and liberty, or were going 'to sit down and be slaves'[1].

A letter from a Jamaican patriot that appeared in the *Jamaica Times* on 5 September 1914 read,

> As a British subject, I feel called upon to express myself . . . we as loyal citizens, for the love that we hold for the British flag, should be so patriotically inspired as to stand beside her if need be. We should fight as brave men and die as heroes. So that the enemy may see that we are not made of common stuff or are in any way inferior to those who have already sacrificed their lives in this appalling struggle . . . Men of the island of Jamaica . . . be honourable; be not branded as cowards if you're needed for active service. Be courageous, be firm, be resolute, prepared to defend your country with your life's blood.[2]

Responding to the popular mood, colonial administrators across the West Indies, and elsewhere in the empire, transmitted offers of service to the Colonial Office – the government department that administered the huge sprawling empire – and to the War Office, then rapidly expanding: but the clamour among West Indian men to serve in the British army at the very moment it faced a German army vastly superior in numbers and, as it turned out, also in tactics and leadership, was greeted with deep alarm. On 28 August 1914, just three weeks after the war began, officials from the Colonial Office asked their colleagues in the War Office to consider the possibility that a contingent of troops raised in the British West Indies might be permitted to serve abroad. The War Office responded first by questioning the fighting quality of black West Indian men, suggesting they would be ineffectual in the cold of a European winter, and then by proposing that they might be put to better use 'maintaining order if necessary, in the islands' of the West Indies.[3]

Popular support for the war cannot be explained only as a temporary outbreak of 'war fever'. Since the end in the 1840s of the protective sugar tariffs, the West Indies had been blighted by suffocating poverty. That poverty had been the underlying cause of the Morant Bay uprising. In 1914, war was understood as both a chance for the islands to demonstrate their loyalty to the empire and as an employment opportunity for their unemployed and underemployed men. In such an atmosphere there was inevitably a clamour among young West Indians to join up and get to France before the Germans were defeated – as most people blithely agreed that they soon would be. Some West Indians, fearing they would miss their chance to be part of the great adventure, sold their belongings to buy tickets to Britain or stowed away on ships bound for British ports, aiming to enlist in the British army immediately upon their arrival in the 'mother country'. The War Office regarded West Indians in the British army as highly undesirable and in late 1914 they called upon the Colonial Office to discourage volunteers from believing that if they travelled to Britain they would be welcomed into the army.

From the very start of the conflict there was the view in Britain and the 'white dominions' of the empire (Australia, Canada, New Zealand and especially South Africa) that this was to be a 'white man's' war – a European conflict from which the non-white subject peoples were to be excluded. The great exception was the British Indian Army, an institution that had emerged out of the lessons learnt from the Indian Mutiny of the 1850s and that occupied a unique place in the empire. There was a determination within the War Office, and among white settlers in Africa, that black Africans and black West Indians were not to be permitted to fight against white men, as this, it was feared, would undermine white racial prestige, and threaten the security of white settlers in the colonies. For decades colonial administrators had striven to ensure that modern weapons were kept out of the hands of their black subjects, and it was impressed upon them that the lives of white men (and even more so white women) were sacrosanct. Violence against white people in the empire elicited extraordinarily violent responses – punitive raids and exemplary punishments. The informal rules of imperial government determined that black men were armed only when formed into colonial regiments (often known as askari) and used to fight Africans, under the guidance and watchful eyes of white officers.

At the Colonial Office, the rejection of the proposal for the formation of a black West Indian regiment was regarded with deep concern. It was feared that the War Office's high-handed dismissal of earnest offers of service would be deeply resented by the patriotically minded people of the West Indies and other rejected proposals would equally offend the coastal elites of West Africa. A number of colonial governments expressed similar alarm at the decision. This led to a long and protracted series of discussions between the War Office and the Colonial Office. King George V took an early and genuine interest in the issue and probably did most to force a change of policy. On 22 April 1915 he met Lord Kitchener, Secretary for War, who, when pressed, expressed his support for the creation of a West Indian unit, so long as there were restrictions imposed upon where it could be deployed. Further wrangling between the War Office and Colonial Office followed but on 19 May approval was finally given for a new West Indian regiment.

That same day, nine men from the West Indies who had stowed away on the SS *Danube* landed at the docks of the East End. They had planned to volunteer for the British army upon arrival but were promptly arrested and taken to the West Ham Police Court, charged with being stowaways, to which they all pleaded guilty, and detained in the warren of cells beneath the building. Their names appear grouped together as 'stowaways' in the court registers: Thomas Bayley, thirty-six; Sidney Redmond, just nineteen; Alan Thornhill, Leo Yarwood, George Cousins, and Eric Blakely, twenty; Albert Goppy, twenty-one, and Arthur Ford and George Walker, twenty-three.[4] A newspaper report describing their appearance in court reveals that the nine were charged by the Royal Mail Steam Packet Company. Mr J. W. Richards, prosecuting on behalf of the company, told the court that 'the day after leaving Trinidad the ship called at Barbados. It was presumed that the men came aboard there for the day.' When Richards said that the West Indians were 'found on the vessel' the magistrate Mr Gillespie interjected, 'In a dark corner, I suppose?' – to which there was laughter in the court. Mr Richards then explained that after their discovery 'the men were put to work, and they did not cause any trouble'. They were, he noted, 'desirous of enlisting in the army'. At which point Mr Gillespie quipped, 'What, do they want to enlist in the Black Guards?' Again, the court erupted into laughter. Local police officer Detective Sergeant Holby informed the court that 'he had made enquiries at the local recruiting office, and they told him they [the stowaways] could not enlist there because of their colour, but if application was made to the War office, no doubt they would be enlisted in some regiment of black men'.[5] Mr Gillespie then ordered the nine stowaways be detained for a week.

On 24 May the stowaways were brought before a second hearing. Under the headline 'The Docks – Spoiling for a Fight', the *Stratford Express* reported that the court clerk Mr Jackson informed the men that he had heard a 'coloured Battalion' was being formed in Cardiff.[6] The article carried a comment by Sir Algernon Edward Aspinall, secretary to the West India Committee, an organization of businessmen that had emerged from the London Society of West India planters and merchants and the eighteenth-century lobby group that had defended slavery and fought to secure compensation for the slave owners in 1834. Aspinall said that 'he would send them back to the West Indies. The men, however, said they would not go. They had come to fight, and they were going to fight.' At this hearing, the men were discharged. What became of them afterwards is difficult to ascertain, but for three of them we have Royal Navy service records. They tell us that Eric Blakely from Trinidad survived the war. The last record of him was in April 1920. Arthur Ford, another Trinidadian, also survived and at the end of the war both he and Blakely received the Mercantile Marine Medal, awarded for service in hostile waters. Albert Goppy also made it through, but died young, at only thirty-two. He had been living in Manhattan. Whether any of the West Ham stowaways were permitted to enlist in the British army, which had been their ambition, is not known.

When Mr Jackson, the West Ham court clerk, had heard that a 'coloured Battalion' was being formed in Cardiff he was probably reporting inaccurate rumours. However, on 26 October, a supplement to the *London Gazette* carried an announcement of the formation of a new unit in which black men from the West Indies would be permitted to serve. It was to be known as the British West Indies Regiment (BWIR) – not to be confused with the West India Regiment, into which men liberated from slave ships by the West Africa Squadron had been conscripted in the nineteenth century. That same week King George V, who had played so critical a role in the creation of the BWIR, issued an *Appeal to the Empire*, which on Sunday 31 October was read out in church services in the West Indies.

At this grave moment in the struggle between my people and a
highly organized enemy who has transgressed the Laws of Nations
and changed the ordinance that binds civilized Europe together, I
appeal to you. I rejoice in my Empire's effort, and I feel pride in
the voluntary response from my Subjects all over the world who
have sacrificed home, fortune, and life itself, in order that another
may not inherit the free Empire which their ancestors and mine
have built. I ask you to make good those sacrifices. The end is not
in sight. More men and yet more are wanted to keep my Armies
in the Field, and through them to secure Victory and enduring
Peace. In ancient days the darkest moment has ever produced in
men of our race the sternest resolve. I ask you, men of all classes,
to come forward voluntarily and take your share in the fight. In
freely responding to my appeal, you will be giving your support
to our brothers, who, for long months, have nobly upheld Britain's
past traditions, and the glory of her Arms.[7]

The notion of a 'free empire', forged through the sacrifices of many
generations, was a vision of the past that was blind to the memory
of slavery and ignored racial hierarchies but was taken by many to
imply that those who came 'forward voluntarily' and took a 'share
in the fight' would be treated equally, irrespective of race. Yet even
those who had supported the creation of a West Indian regiment,
and pushed the reluctant War Office in that direction, had never
intended that the black volunteers be treated equally or permitted
to fight in France alongside white soldiers and against a white enemy.
While the Colonial Office had worried that the rejection of West
Indian volunteers would damage morale in the colonies they too
saw the conflict in Europe as a 'white man's war', and envisaged
West Indian volunteers serving elsewhere in the empire. On this
the two government departments were united, black men were not
to be permitted to fight and kill white men.

Over the course of the First World War twelve battalions of the
BWIR were raised, consisting of 397 officers and 15,204 men. The
first battalions began their training in October 1915, at the Seaford
army camp in Sussex. The recruits came from across the West Indies
but the majority, 10,280 (66 per cent) were Jamaicans.[8] In all,
26,637 Jamaican men volunteered to serve in the new regiment

but 13,940 were rejected on medical grounds, testimony to the hardship and poverty that blighted that island in the early twentieth century. Brigadier General Blackden, who had called upon the men of Jamaica to meet the challenge of their times, now grumbled about the physical health of the soldiers he had encouraged to enlist, complaining that too many of the volunteers were an 'undersized, ragged, bare-footed set of fellows, who came forward probably to get a meal'.[9] The British public and the press, however, were impressed with the health and vigour of the men of the regiment when they had finished their training. When the BWIR were invited to march in the Lord Mayor's Show in London in November 1915, the *Daily Chronicle* reported that 'a very special cheer greeted the appearance of the small detachment of the British West Indies Regiment. And the pleasure of the occasion was reciprocal. The dusky faces of the smiling West Indians made one forget that colour had ever been a racial barrier.'[10] The *Belfast Evening Telegraph* described the BWIR as 'sturdy West Indian troops' and the *Daily News* plumped for 'huge and mighty men of valor'.[11]

Once trained all four of the initial BWIR battalions were deployed to Egypt, as it was presumed that men from the West Indies would be able to cope with the heat more easily than soldiers from Britain. Units of the BWIR served in Egypt and the Middle East until the end of the war, and fought in the Palestine campaign. The machine-gun section of the BWIR took part in a series of raids on Turkish trenches in July 1917. However when the 3rd and 4th Battalions were transferred to France in 1916 they arrived expecting to fight. Instead they were largely segregated from white British troops and became – in practice if not in name – a labour battalion. They dug, repaired, and worked in the munitions depots; critical work but not what they had been trained to do and not what they had hoped for. The men of the BWIR were also subjected to racial taunts from white troops. A BWIR soldier from Trinidad complained that he and his comrades were 'treated neither as Christians nor as British citizens, but as West Indian "Niggers", without anybody to be interested in or look after us.'[12]

It was at this point that the men from the West Indies were drawn into the wider logic of imperial racial politics. Enormous efforts were made to maintain the men in their lowly position at the foot of the imagined hierarchy of races. Only in the unique conditions of the African theatre of operations were black British soldiers – both African troops and units of the BWIR – put into combat against the Germans. The German forces in Africa consisted of local African recruits and thousands of press-ganged carriers, who outnumbered the German colonial troops. Even when faced with an acute manpower shortage the British, unlike their French allies, put racial considerations above all other factors, and refused to recruit black Africans and West Indians for combat service in Europe, to the outraged opposition of one small section of the political elite. The policy was that black men would serve as labourers or in other support roles, a policy in stark contrast to that adopted towards their Indian soldiers who arrived in France in the autumn of 1914, even before the inception of the Western Front, where they were tolerated and even welcomed. However, by the end of 1915 the Indian infantry had been redeployed outside of Europe, although the cavalry remained in France – the 20th Deccan Horse famously charged the German lines during the Battle of the Somme. Despite relying so heavily upon Indian soldiers in 1914 and 1915 and despite having at their disposal vast reservoirs of potential manpower from Africa and the West Indies, the generals and politicians remained determined that war on the Western Front was to be 'a white man's war'. That determination, confidently expressed in the early stages of the conflict, was more difficult to adhere to and harder to explain as the horrific scale and murderous nature of the conflict became apparent.

As losses on the Western Front began to mount alarmingly in 1915, it was proposed in the House of Commons that a regiment of Zulu men (who were still famed as great warriors and remembered for the battles they had fought against the British during the Scramble for Africa) from southern Africa be raised and deployed in Europe. The War Office blocked this proposal. Even before the war there had been those within colonial circles who had proposed that units of new black African troops could be formed for colonial service in Africa, and perhaps elsewhere in the empire. The British Empire in Africa, far more populous than those of France or Germany, was home to a number of African peoples, in particular the Zulu and the Hausa of northern Nigeria, regarded as 'martial races' by various colonial 'experts'. Indeed,

France's policy of mass recruitment of men from her West and North African colonies, in accordance with a military and demographic theory known as the 'Force Noir' principle, was looked upon by British advocates of African recruitment as irrefutable evidence of the potential of the African soldier. Despite recruiting from her more sparsely populated African territories France, by 1916, had raised seventeen battalions of Tirailleurs Sénégalais, who served on the Western Front. By 1918 ninety-two African battalions had been deployed in Europe, taking part in the French attacks during the Battle of the Somme and fighting in the Battle of Verdun.

However in 1915 Andrew Bonar Law, Secretary of State for the Colonies, wrote a secret memorandum in which he concluded that the recruitment of Africans would pose too great a threat to British rule in Africa after the war – particularly in South Africa as there 'a large body of trained and disciplined black men would create obvious difficulties, and might seriously menace the supremacy of the white.'[13] Like many others Bonar Law was also convinced that 'no South African native could stand a European winter'. This refrain – that was to be constantly repeated by British politicians and colonial administrators right up until the 1940s – grew harder to sustain over time as the black soldiers of France, the Tirailleurs Sénégalais, proved themselves as capable as any other troops of weathering the most terrible winters of the war – albeit with appalling casualties.

By the end of 1916, theoretic musings as to the potential military capacities of Africans and vague proposals for recruitment of men from that continent gave way to urgent political debate. During the six terrible months of the Battle of the Somme, engagement after engagement generated casualty lists far longer than the General Staff had expected or prepared for. After just the first day of fighting, sixty thousand of Lord Kitchener's eager volunteers were killed, wounded or missing. The Battle of the Somme was to rage on for another hundred and forty days. The volunteers who had swelled the ranks of Britain's army in 1915 had been decimated and new levies were required. Although the Indian Army had already served courageously, and despite the acute manpower crisis, neither the War Office nor the Chief of Staff were yet willing to consider the recruitment of Africans into the army for service on the Western Front.

In the face of shocking British losses, those who believed that the recruitment and perhaps even conscription of Africans into the ranks of the British army was a matter of urgency, and perhaps even national survival, found their voice. As did those among the elites of British West Africa, who were largely in favour of local recruitment, hoping it would allow them to negotiate a better deal in the post-war empire, and presuming, perhaps, that it would be the sons of the poor and not their own young men who would be sent to the battlefields. In December 1916, the *Lagos Weekly Record* encouraged the British to adopt French methods of recruitment in Africa.[14] 'What France has done on such an appreciable scale, Great Britain could do on a more extensive scale', the paper suggested in an editorial.[15]

The loudest voice in Britain was that of Major Darnley Stuart-Stephens, a former commander of the Lagos Battalion who had served in Nigeria during the Scramble for Africa and penned a controversial article for the *English Review*. In 'Our Million Black Army', Stuart-Stephens presented the continent as an 'almost unlimited reservoir of African man-power', from which twenty thousand men could be drawn almost immediately. In northern Nigeria he suggested were more than seven hundred thousand martial warriors. These 'bonny fetchers', he wrote, 'are now engaged in the pastoral arts of peace. But I would make bold to assert that a couple of hundred thousand could, after six months' training, be usefully employed in daredevil charges into German trenches.' In what to the modern reader is extraordinary language he advocated 'placing at once in the trenches . . . 70,000 big, lusty coal-black devils, the time of whose life is the wielding of the bayonet, and whose advent would not be regarded by the Boches as a pleasing omen of more to come of the same sort.'[16]

In the minds of some observers the portrait of the African soldier that Major Stuart-Stephens painted, of a muscular warrior-athlete, made their potential deployment in Europe more, not less, problematic. This popular and highly racialized image of the black African or West Indian man as a child of nature, unencumbered by the burdens of civilization or intellect and endowed with natural strength and innate health stood in stark contrast to the picture emerging from the front and from the recruiting offices of Britain. Thousands of British men who volunteered for service in 1914 and 1915 were underweight, physically frail and in general poor health. These men, many of whom had been happy to abandon the damp terraces of the industrial cities, bore the bodily stamp of intergenerational malnutrition and were afflicted by various diseases and conditions that blighted Britain's poorest urban communities in the early twentieth century. Captain J. C. Dunn, a medical officer and Boer War veteran, whose memoir *The War the Infantry Knew* is one of the great social histories of the trenches, lamented the 'astonishing number of men whose narrow and misshapen chests, and other deformities or defects, unfitted them to stay the more exacting requirements of service in the field'.[17] And Captain Dunn was speaking only of men who had been passed fit for service. A shocking number of would-be British recruits had failed the rudimentary medical examination that was undertaken in the recruiting offices. The poor health of so many British men had been similarly exposed fifteen years earlier in a recruitment crisis during the Boer War, when it had been estimated that 60 per cent of the male population were unfit for active military service. In 1914 and 1915 the authorities discovered that little had changed, despite the work of eight separate Royal Commissions between 1904 and 1914, all of which had been tasked with investigating these issues.[18]

The formation in November 1914 of the first 'bantam' battalions was indicative of the malnutrition and sickliness that had blighted the health and development of millions of Britons. These were units made up of men under five feet three inches, the minimum height for a soldier at the start of the war. The bantam battalions were even issued with a special version of the standard-issue Lee Enfield rifle that had a shorter stock. Over the six terrible months of the Battle of the Somme the physical frailties of many British soldiers was made bleakly apparent, as was their psychological vulnerability. By the end of 1916, fifty thousand British troops were being treated for shell-shock. These rates were no higher than those experienced by other armies but the Australians, alongside whom the Tommies had fought at Gallipoli and on the Somme, had come to regard the British as poor fighters, generally lacking in courage and deficient in manliness. Thus in 1916, at the very moment when the recruitment of black men from the West Indies and Africa for deployment on the Western Front would have been most advantageous and most militarily appropriate, there was something approaching a crisis of British masculinity. Black men, while regarded by many to be intellectually inferior and therefore unsuited to modern technological warfare, were at the same time viewed by others as potentially physically superior to the malnourished and diminutive British men from the industrial cities. There was, in certain circles, a fear that if the black troops were deployed on the Western Front, their supposed primitive vitality would be set alongside the emasculated sickliness of many British recruits in a way that would damage white racial prestige. Thus national paranoia and long-established racial stereotypes conspired to form new, if largely unspoken, justifications for the exclusion of black men from the European theatre. In this atmosphere the imperial authorities went so far as to ensure that sporting competitions held behind the lines, in which black men took on their white compatriots, were not played before a civilian public. While victories by black men on the field of sport could and often were explained away by reference to their much-purported animalistic strength and natural vigour, *The Times* cautioned that 'the black man's victory' would be 'hailed as proof that the hegemony of the white race is approaching the end.'[19]

Yet Stuart-Stephens' article of 1916 not only reignited the debates of the previous year, it spawned a 'Million Black Army' movement. Among its supporters were a number of men with experience in the colonies.[20] One of the most vocal and significant of them was Sir Harry Johnston, the explorer and former associate of Cecil Rhodes, who was to later pen *The Backward Peoples and Our Relations with Them,* a dispiritingly racist and ceaselessly patronizing tract which included a map of Africa shaded to convey the degree to which Johnston believed the local people were 'backwards'. Sir Harry accepted an invitation from the French government to visit the camps of the Tirailleurs Sénégalais. He came away convinced that the men of Britain's African Empire could be formed into just as effective a fighting force.[21] Many others agreed with his assessment. From July 1917, the parliamentary campaign for the 'Million Black Army' movement was led by the Liberal MP Josiah Wedgwood, the great-great-grandson of Josiah Wedgwood I, who in the eighteenth century had been a key member of the Society for Effecting the Abolition of the Slave Trade. It was the elder Wedgwood who had had his Staffordshire potteries produce the famous abolitionist medal bearing the figure of the kneeling slave and the slogan 'Am I Not a Man and a Brother?'. Having served in the Dardanelles Campaign and recently returned from active service in East Africa the younger Wedgwood presented himself in 1917 as a man of authority on military matters. Addressing Parliament, he too advocated the adoption of the French system to raise black soldiers for European service. This should be done, he stated with shocking candour, 'because we do not want all the whites killed – to put it bluntly. To slow down the rate of killing of our men and to eke out the finest race on earth'.[22] He went on to explain that his support of African recruitment stemmed from his wish 'to see the coloured man gets his due honour, and that self-esteem and self-respect which comes from overcoming fear . . . They want to show themselves the equal in courage to the white – to break once for all the colour bar. Comradeship in danger will do what the education of centuries would never effect.'[23]

The most strident and inevitably the most eloquent supporter of the 'Million Black Army' movement was yet another old colonial soldier – Winston Churchill. In May 1916, before the Battle of the Somme had begun, Churchill spoke in Parliament. 'What part is Africa going to play in the present struggle?' he asked. 'The French African Empire is much smaller than that over which we rule . . . yet I am told – of course, it is a purely unofficial figure – that the French are employing, or intend to employ, in the line in France nearly 100,000 men from Africa. What the French can do,' he argued, 'we can do.'[24] Speaking like the historian he was, Churchill called upon MPs to imagine posterity's judgement. 'Let us project our minds ahead and think what historians of the future would write if they were writing a history of the present time and had to record that Great Britain was forced to make an inconclusive peace because she forgot Africa; that at a time when every man counted, when every man was needed and the greatest hardships were imposed, the Government of Great Britain was unable to make any use of a mighty continent which sea power had placed at the disposal of herself and her Allies.' Churchill offered a vision for how the manpower of Africa might be tapped at source and history's judgement averted: 'Imagine a great place of arms being created in Egypt,' he explained, 'where the climate is suitable, where African troops raised in various parts of the Continent would be assembled, drilled and trained, and then passed into the war as individuals or as units in whatever capacity they were best fitted for, and in whatever theatre of war and against whatever enemies the climate and their religion rendered it most suitable for them to be employed.' These measures were necessary, Churchill reasoned, because of 'the grave situation' facing the nation. 'What is going on while we sit here, while we go away to dinner, or home to bed? Nearly 1,000 men – Englishmen, Britishers, men of our own race – are knocked into bundles of bloody rags every twenty-four hours, and carried away to hasty graves or to field ambulances . . . every measure must be considered, and none put aside while there is hope of obtaining something from it'.[25] Supporters of the 'Million Black Army' movement proposed that another fact-finding mission be sent to determine how the French Army managed its recruitment polices in Africa in order to learn from their experiences.

Opposition came from multiple directions. Firstly from a number of serving and former colonial officers who strongly disagreed with their colleagues. One wrote, 'It must not be forgotten that a West African native trained to use of arms and filled with a new degree of self-confidence by successful encounters with forces armed and led by Europeans was not likely to be more amenable to discipline in peace time.'[26] Almost every pretext and plausible argument was employed to counter the suggestion that the wartime manpower shortage necessitated the recruitment of black soldiers to fight against a white enemy on European soil. It was suggested – yet again – that Africans could not endure or even perhaps survive European winters and it was claimed that they were intellectually incapable of using of complicated modern weapons and would be unable to grasp contemporary military tactics. Another argument argument against African recruitment was that there were said to be an insufficient supply of white officers fluent in their languages. The government of the Union of South Africa consistently reiterated their view that training black soldiers to fight against a white enemy would, in the longer term, threaten white dominance in Southern Africa.[27] From June 1917 onwards, the President of the Union of South Africa, Jan Smuts, sat as a member of the Imperial War Cabinet and from that position was able to block the 'Million Black Army' concept. Resistance from the Colonial Office also remained steadfast. So resolute was this wall of opposition that in May 1918 – when there were few signs that the war had entered its final year – an inter-departmental conference that agreed to the formation of a West African Service Brigade for deployment in the Middle East or Africa added the stipulation, 'but not against Germans in Europe'.[28]

Despite vociferous opposition there were black men who outmanoeuvred the colour bar and fought on the Western Front. A number of men from the West Indies made their way to Britain and – unlike the West Ham stowaways of 1915 – successfully enlisted in British army units. Among them was Lionel Fitz Herbert Turpin from British Guyana, who rejected the opportunity to serve with the BWIR and joined the Royal Warwickshire Regiment. Turpin fought in France and survived the war, although had to endure the effects of exposure to poison gas for the rest of his life.[29] Another group who were even better placed were West Indians and Africans who were resident in Britain at the outbreak of the conflict. When the mixed-race Jamaican brothers Roy and Norman Manley, who were studying in Britain in 1915, attempted to join the Royal Flying Corps, they were refused. However, both were later accepted into the Royal Field Artillery. An Oxford Rhodes scholar, Norman Manley manned guns on the Somme and was promoted during the war. He was, however, appalled by the routine racism and prejudice. Roy Manley was killed near Ypres in 1917. Norman went on to become Jamaica's first chief minister and never forgot his experiences during the war. He is recognized today as one of the National Heroes of Jamaica.

The other group able to cross the colour line to service in the regular army were men from Britain's pre-war black population, many of whom had been born in Britain. The number of black people in Britain before the First World War was very small, probably just a few thousand, and a fraction of the size of the eighteenth-century black population that had been constantly refreshed by the ceaseless arrival of enslaved African servants. In 1914 there was a tiny black middle class mainly living in London, many of whom had connections to Sierra Leone. Most of the rest were African and West Indian sailors in Liverpool, Cardiff and London. Finally there were smaller clusters elsewhere and an unknown number of black and mixed-race families descended from individuals who had found themselves in Britain and settled down. Their status, when it came to military recruitment, was something of a quandary. This was in part because there existed a great deal of confusion among recruiting officers as to the status and rights of black residents of Britain but also because the acceptability or otherwise of a young man presenting himself at the recruiting office was determined not solely by military regulations, but by the opinions of the recruiting officer who processed his application. Between 1914 and 1918 there were recruiting officers who refused to admit black men into the British army. There were others, evidently, who disregarded the issue of race. Just as there were recruiters who accepted men who were below the minimum height and boys who were under age, there were those who believed that race should be no bar to military service. Furthermore the recruiting sergeants, just as much as the men stood in front of them, were at times swept up in 'war fever', and regarded it as their patriotic duty to accept as many volunteers as possible. Gilbert Grindle, a principal clerk at the Colonial Office, wrote in December 1914, 'I hear privately that some recruiting officers will pass coloureds. Others, will not, and we must discourage coloured volunteers.'[30]

Ernest Marke, who left his native Sierra Leone during the war and worked on merchant ships, recalled in his autobiography that he and another man from Sierra Leone were accepted into the army without any difficulties at a Liverpool recruiting office in 1918.[31] Marke's acceptance was all the more remarkable given that in 1918 he was not only a black African but just fifteen years old.

So confused were recruiting officers by the question of race that some black British men who had been conscripted into the army, after the 1916 Military Service Act, were rejected from service, or prevented from gaining admission to recruiting offices even though they had their call-up papers in their hands.[32] Some black Britons were posted to the BWIR, and served with that unit for the duration of the war, while others were placed within the Royal Engineers

(Coloured Section), which had been specially created to receive them. However some did serve in regular units, training and fighting alongside white recruits. It was largely a matter of chance as to which type of unit a black soldier was dispatched.

The most celebrated of the black Britons who fought on the Western Front is Walter Tull. The mixed-race son of the son of a slave, he was three generations away from the plantations of Barbados. At the outbreak of war, Tull was a professional footballer playing in the midfield for Northampton Town FC. In the first weeks of the war he was considering a transfer offer from Glasgow Rangers but instead, on 14 December, presented himself at the army recruiting office in Holborn in London, and joined the Middlesex Regiment. Tull's unit was known as the 1st Footballers' Battalion, as it was made up of players and fans. His commanding officer, Major Frank Buckley, was a former Manchester United player and veteran of the Boer War. When he presented himself to the recruiting sergeant, there could have been little doubt that this twenty-six-year-old professional football player was fit for active service. He was also famous, having appeared in the newspapers and in front of huge football crowds. Tull was rapidly promoted to sergeant and – in a concession granted to the footballers' battalion – travelled across the country at weekends playing for his club until the end of the professional season. Then, in November 1915, the battalion headed for France.

In 1916, he became one of the fifty thousand British men to be treated that year alone for what was then called 'acute mania' and would today be diagnosed as post-traumatic stress disorder. After a short recuperation in England he returned to the front in September and took part in the later offences of the Battle of the Somme. In February 1917, however, he travelled to Scotland and there began training to become an officer, after having been recommended for officer training the previous November. This, in theory, should have been impossible and under normal circumstances would almost certainly not have been allowed. The 1914 *Manual of Military Law* prohibited what it termed 'alien soldiers' from 'exercising any actual command or power', stipulating that 'Commissions in the Special Reserve of Officers are given to qualified candidates who are natural born or naturalised British subjects of pure European descent', a vague term (perhaps deliberately so) that was often taken to mean

individuals who appeared to be Caucasian.[33] Another army document, the *Short Guide to Obtaining a Commission in the Special Reserve
of Officers*, published by HM Stationery Office in 1912, reiterated
that all candidates 'must be of pure European descent'. Nevertheless,
Tull was recommended by his commanding officers. The manpower
crisis of 1917, after the disastrous losses of the Somme, was not
deemed severe enough for recommendations of the 'Million Black
Army' movement to be put into operation but it did encourage the
army to waive or suspend some of its rules and regulations regarding
the race of officers and men, regulations that in many cases had
always been open to some degree of interpretation and discretion.
In May 1917, Walter Tull won his commission as second lieutenant.
Not only had he been permitted to fight in Europe against a European enemy, he was now to lead white British troops into action.
Later, in 1917, Second Lieutenant Tull took part in operations on
the Italian Front, for which he was mentioned in dispatches. He was
also recommended for the Military Cross. In March 1918, during
the German spring offensive, he was killed in action near the French
village of Favreuil. His body was never recovered from the battlefield, despite attempts by men of his unit to do so. He is listed as
one of the missing, among the 34,785 names engraved into the
Arras Memorial in Nord-Pas-de-Calais.

The opponents of the 'Million Black Army' movement, having
largely succeeded in preventing the deployment of black men on
the European battlefield, were equally determined to ensure that
the role Africans and West Indians had played in the war was
airbrushed out of the developing national memory of the conflict.
On the morning of Saturday 19 July 1919, a month after the Treaty
of Versailles was signed by the reluctant German delegation, an
official Victory Parade was held in London. The parade was the
sombre centrepiece of a whole programme of official celebrations
and London was fittingly bedecked with bunting and the flags of
the victorious Allied nations. Military bands played across the city
and in London's parks performers entertained the huge crowds. It
was for these celebrations that Sir Edwin Lutyens designed the
Cenotaph, which, as it had been originally envisaged as a temporary

structure, had been erected on Whitehall in wood and plaster rather than Portland limestone. When the Allied troops selected to take part in the parade marched past the Cenotaph they saluted in memory of their fallen comrades – around a million of them from Britain and the empire. But by the summer of 1919 the memory of the black men from Africa and the West Indies who had fought or laboured in the war was already being expunged from the official record and popular memory. The Victory Parade was part of that process of conscious and deliberate forgetting.

Fifteen thousand soldiers, sailors and airmen took part. Each of the Allied commanders, General Pershing, who had led the US Expeditionary Force, Marshal Foch, the supreme Allied commander, and Field Marshal Douglas Haig, the British commander-in-chief, had led armies that were multi-racial. Each of the generals saluted their fallen comrades in the London Victory Parade at the head of columns from which all black men had been excluded. Within the British columns were men from Canada, Australia, South Africa and India. No troops from the West Indies were permitted to march; neither were any black African units. When asked to explain why the Nigeria Regiment, which had fought against German forces in the East African campaign, had not been invited to take part in any of the official victory celebrations the Colonial Office responded by suggesting that it would be 'impolitic to bring [to England] coloured detachments to participate in the peace processions'.[34] This was later said to have been because the cost of their transportation to London would have been prohibitive, despite the fact that Indian troops had been shipped to London specifically to take part in the celebrations. Just six years earlier, the organizers of the Royal and Military Tournament of 1908 had not found the cost of shipping a hundred soldiers of the West African Regiment to Britain from Sierra Leone to be an impediment to their commercial plans. An African correspondent who wrote to *West Africa,* the Lagos-based newspaper, found that explanation unbelievable.

> In your issue published the week after the Victory march in London, you asserted that Africans could not be in the march because there was no time to get them to England owing to lack of transport. You do not mean to say that Great Britain could not afford to send

out two men-of-war to bring them if they had been wanted? . . .
They were fit to assist in breaking the aggression of Germany but
they were not fit to be in the Victory march . . . [35]

The determination of the authorities to write the role of black
sailors and soldiers out of the official memory and memorialization
of the war was noticed by black people living in Britain as much
as by those in the colonies. In London, the Society of Peoples of
African Origin (SPAO), in its newspaper the *African Telegraph*,
wrote 'we can only conclude that it is the policy of His Majesty's
Ministers to ignore the services of the black subjects of the
Empire.'[36] Not only were the Africans and West Indians excluded
from the Victory Parade of 19 May, they were also excluded from
another Victory Parade for dominion troops held on 3 May. The
exemplary service and heavy sacrifice of the Nigerian and other
African units was recalled in the war memoirs of their white officers,
but not in the official celebrations. Likewise, the hundreds of thousands of Africans who had laboured in the Carrier Corps were largely
forgotten. In Jamaica and the other West Indian islands the mistreatment of the men of the BWIR, the refusal to permit them to fight
on the Western Front and the slights and abuses that were poured
upon them, led to considerable bitterness.

In 1919, most units of the BWIR were concentrated in an army
camp near the coastal Italian city of Taranto. There around eight
thousand soldiers awaited demobilization. After four years of
mistreatment it was in Italy that the humiliation of the men of the
BWIR was the most systematic and deliberate. The sense of joint
enterprise that had, to some extent, eased racial tensions during the
war disappeared, and any lingering sense of comradeship evaporated.
Gershom Browne, a Guyanese soldier who served in 'C' Company
of the 1st BWIR recalled, 'Since we came here, we couldn't understand why these British soldiers they didn't seem to want any
attachment with us. We had always seemed to get on good together
in Egypt.'[37] BWIR troops reported being ostracized and segregated
from white soldiers. When a pay rise was given to other imperial
troops, it was denied to the West Indians on the grounds that they
were 'natives'. In December 1918, the West Indians, who had volunteered to fight and seen action in the Middle East, were ordered to

do the laundry of both white British troops and civilian Italian labourers, and then to clean the latrines of the white troops. Once again, they were tacitly and deliberately demoted from soldiers to labourers. Their dissatisfaction eventually tipped over into a refusal to carry out orders, and then a full-blown mutiny, the leaders of which were sentenced to between three and five years' imprisonment. Another was sentenced to twenty-one years and one man was executed by firing squad. After the mutiny the army relented and awarded the black troops the pay increase that had been denied to them. During the war, 185 soldiers from the BWIR died in action or of wounds and 1,071 fell prey to disease. The Colonial Office rightly observed that the troops who returned to Jamaica from Taranto were politicized and disillusioned. Two generations on from Morant Bay, the mistreatment of the men of the BWIR starkly demonstrated to the people of the West Indies the reality of their place in the empire, and exactly where they stood in the racial hierarchy.

In 1919, the American race theorist Madison Grant published his now infamous book *The Passing of the Great Race*, a clarion call for the isolation and preservation of what he called the 'Nordic Race'. The Nordic, Aryan or Anglo-Saxon peoples were to be further purified, in Grant's vision, by a rigid programme of eugenics. As the soldiers of Britain, India and the white dominions marched through London, the American journalist Lothrop Stoddard was busy drafting *The Rising Tide of Color Against White World-Supremacy*, in which he lambasted those in Europe who had permitted black men to serve in the war in any capacity. Grant and Stoddard had discussed their ideas while writing their respective tomes. In Stoddard's view, the war had represented an egregious breach in the barriers that separated the races and kept the dark-skinned peoples of the world in a subservient position. 'White solidarity', he wrote, had been 'literally blown from the muzzles of the guns.' The great betrayal of the white race had come when 'The Allies poured into white Europe colored hordes of every pigment under the sun.' Stoddard criticized Major Darnley Stuart-Stephens and his 'Million Black Army' concept and believed that the war in Africa had been just as dangerous. 'Far and wide over the Dark Continent,' he wrote, 'black armies fought for their respective masters – and learned the hidden weakness of the white man's power . . . The psychological effect of these colored auxiliaries in deepening the hatred of the white combatants was deplorable.'[38] In the view of race theorists like Stoddard the use of black soldiers during the war had undermined the security of the white race, and it was therefore critical in the post-war period for black men and other non-whites to be put back in their proper place and more firmly segregated. Grant and Stoddard spoke for many in 1919 who surveyed the world and were appalled by the emergence of new black communities in the cities of Europe and the Northern states of the US. Just as disturbing was the sight of black men and women in relatively well-paid industrial jobs. Most outrageous of all were the mixed relationships and marriages between black men and white women.

At around ten o'clock on the evening of 5 June 1919, a month before the Victory Parade snaked its way through the broad boulevards of central London, a twenty-four-year-old sailor from Bermuda, who had served in the Royal Navy during the war, was chased through the streets of Liverpool. He was pursued by a mob that was between two and three hundred strong. His name was Charles Wootton and he was eventually chased down to the Queen's Dock and surrounded on the water's edge by a hostile crowd. One of the police officers on the scene estimated that by this point the crowd was about two thousand strong. In the chaos that followed Wootton was at one point seized by a policeman, but was ripped out of the officer's grasp by the mob. Stones were thrown, driving Wootton into the water. Some reports say that members of the crowd, at this point, shouted, 'Let him drown.'[39] The *Liverpool Echo* reported that as Wootton floundered in the water, 'a detective climbed down a ship's rope and was about to pull the man out of the water when a stone thrown from the middle of the crowd struck Wootton on the head and he sank. His body was later recovered by means of grappling irons.'[40]

   Although a number of police officers were at the scene on the night of the murder of Charles Wootton no arrests were made. The *Liverpool Evening Express* informed its readers that the coroner's inquest determined that there was insufficient evidence to determine how 'he got into the Queen's Dock'. Yet the report carried statements from a number of witnesses and a police officer who had all been present that evening.[41] Wootton had died publicly, in front of perhaps as many as two thousand people, yet no one could 'positively say whether the negro was thrown into the dock or jumped in'.[42] The inquest returned the near-meaningless verdict of 'Found drowned'.[43] Various terms have been used to describe the killing of Charles Wootton, in the heart of a British city a century ago. But the most appropriate term is also the most disturbing – his death was a lynching.[44]

1919 had been welcomed in as the first year of peace after four years of terrible conflict, but the year was anything but peaceful. Overshadowed by the memory of the war, it was one of the most febrile and violent years of the twentieth century. In Britain, there were riots and violent disturbances in nine cities as returning soldiers and local men turned upon the country's black population, which had considerably increased in size during the war years. Five people were killed in the riots of 1919, including Charles Wootton. Hundreds were injured and around two hundred and fifty arrested.

At the end of the war there were probably around twenty thousand black people living in Britain. Most could be found in the major port towns – Liverpool, Glasgow, Cardiff and London's East End. But there were also clusters in Barry and Newport in Wales, Hull, Manchester and South Shields in the North-East. The war years and the immediate post-war period were perhaps the first time in British history in which the majority of black Britons lived outside the capital. Liverpool's black population stood at around five thousand at the end of the war and was unusually diverse, consisting of men from across the West Indies as well as a large number from West Africa – a reflection of the city's role in shipping and the palm-oil trade that had been so energetically promoted by the British at the height of their nineteenth-century anti-slave-trade crusade.

The size and make-up of black Britain in 1919 was a reflection of centuries of contact between Britain and Africa but also of the global nature of the conflict the nation had just endured. Although Britain's arsenals and munitions factories had risen to the challenge, the nation had also relied upon imported weapons and munitions.

Imported food had helped nourish the population, sparing them the terrible privations that befell German civilians during the so-called 'hunger blockade'. The merchant shipping that had been Britain's lifeline and the fleet that had enforced the blockade of her enemies had been manned by seamen from across the empire, including Africa and the West Indies. Men from those regions had also come to Britain in search of work in the booming wartime factories, and in doing so became part of the great engine of industrial war that had made victory possible. Black sailors landed in war-time Britain and, on discovering that work was available in such abundance in the factories and ports, decided to stay rather than sign on to a new ship. Other black sailors ended up in Britain because the ships they were on in 1914 were requisitioned by the government and put to war service. Britain's expanded black population was disproportionately male, as had been the black British population during the age of Atlantic slavery in the eighteenth century. Although thousands of Africans and West Indians had settled in the country, or found themselves there at the end of the conflict, they represented only a small fraction of the vast international army of workers and sailors from across the world who had come to Britain to find work in the booming war economy. As well as men from the British Empire, thousands of Europeans had also arrived. Particularly well represented were Danes, Swedes, Poles and Russians, many of whom had been working on British ships, and between periods of shipboard employment they settled in the poorer districts around the ports, often near the clusters of black populations. Men of African descent from the Caribbean and from West Africa were therefore merely the most visible of the new immigrants. The colour of their skin made them an easy and obvious target for resentment and ultimately violence.

The end of the war marked the end of the labour emergency. Peace brought with it sudden and severe competition for work. Two million soldiers, sailors and airmen were rapidly demobilized in the months after November 1918. British men returned home to discover that the country's economy could find no place for them. The 'Land fit for Heroes' that the Prime Minister, Lloyd George, had promised had failed to materialize and the lack of work was aggravated by an acute housing shortage. Huge numbers of white

British workers and former soldiers – men who only months earlier had risked their lives in the name of their country – felt a powerful sense of economic betrayal. Some, perhaps only a minority, were on the lookout for a scapegoat.

During the conflict, the colonial authorities, the British army, Royal Navy, merchant navy and innumerable private firms had been willing to employ black men. At the cessation of hostilities there was a demand, from labour and the unions, that Africans and West Indians hired during the war be dismissed to make way for demobilized white men. Similar demands were made with regards to women who had been brought into the factories and the trades during the war years, and were now expected to return to their pre-war domestic roles. Within weeks of the end of the war white sailors who had served alongside black seamen during the conflict had begun to inform their employers that they were now unwilling to work with them. Ship-masters and factory managers tended to respond by dismissing the black men. The *Liverpool Courier* reported, in June 1919, that one hundred and twenty black men who worked in the sugar refineries and making oilcake (a form of cattle feed) were dismissed over the space of a week when white colleagues refused to work beside them.[45] Ernest Marke, the Sierra Leonean teenager who had managed join the British army in 1918, noted that in Liverpool 'things became different with the demobilisation of thousands of men from the armed forces and the closing down of munitions factories. It now became scarcity of jobs, not men, with the demobbed men wanting their old jobs back and Negroes being sacked to make room for them.'[46]

A profound divergence developed between how black people regarded themselves and how they came to be seen by sections of the public. Black men who had volunteered for military service had done so in the firm belief that they were members of the empire and British subjects – not aliens. They had joined up to defend the empire but also to ensure their position within it by demonstrating loyalty and competence. Black men who had fought for Britain in the First World War were also aware of the fact that they had fought as volunteers and not conscripts. Conscription had never been introduced into Africa or the West Indies and this reinforced their sense of commitment to the national cause. There were reports from 1919 and into the early 1920s of black men wearing their uniforms or their medal ribbons to prove that they had shared in the dangers and privations of the conflict.

The colonial soldiers and sailors who lived in Britain did so alongside members of longer established and more settled black communities, who had even greater reason to consider themselves British, but in 1919, both the more recent arrivals and the black Edwardians discovered that they were all viewed with suspicion and considered, by some, as aliens. The existence of black communities was suddenly regarded as evidence for the existence, in Britain, of a 'colour problem'.

The racial tensions of 1919 first metastasized into violence in Glasgow. On 23 January, both black and white sailors assembled in the yard of Glasgow's mercantile marine office hoping to be signed on to ships. Gathered together, and in direct competition for the same limited supply of jobs, groups of white sailors who resented the presence of black colonial seamen began to shout abuse. This led to scuffles and eventually to an eruption of serious fighting.[47] The white sailors were joined by locals who together pursued and attacked the black seamen, thirty of whom were taken into protective custody by the police. Pistols, knives and improvised weapons were used and three people were seriously injured – two white sailors and one black. No charges were brought.

The next to be attacked were a community of Arab sailors – men mostly from Yemen and Somalia – who had settled in South Shields by the Tyne, and whose descendants still live in the same Tyneside terraces. Their numbers had quadrupled during the war years when employment had been plentiful. Within months of the end of the war the Arab sailors, despite being British subjects and union members, were abruptly refused work on British ships. They then became the focus of an attack by a white mob that included a number of white sailors from other European nations. After a chase through the town, the Arab seamen and their pursuers confronted one another in the Holborn district. The homes of the Arab men were attacked and in the chaos revolvers were fired over the heads of the mob by some of the Arabs, who then chased their attackers back to the shipping office where the trouble had begun. Bitterness over relations between white women and Arab men was said to have been one of the causes of the riot.

Two months later there were riots in London's dockland when black sailors were attacked on Cable Street, later the site of a much more famous riot in the 1930s, fought against Sir Oswald Mosley's black-shirted fascists. The following month, hostels housing black sailors were attacked in Limehouse, a part of the capital in which there had been an intermittent black population since the eighteenth century. The police estimated that between three and five thousand people took part in those riots.[48] In May, Asian and Chinese communities were also targeted, as were white women who lived with or who had married black men. The next month there was an incident involving black sailors by the docks at Hull, and violence erupted in Newport, in Wales, with black men targeted in the wake of a meeting by one of the seamen's unions. Once again, black men's hostels and black families' homes were attacked and ransacked. Racial violence next exploded in the Welsh port of Barry, and by 11 June, the disturbances had spread to Tiger Bay in Cardiff. The riots in Cardiff lasted a week and cost three men their lives. Troops were secretly put on standby as huge gangs patrolled the streets on the hunt for black men and Arabs. The Cardiff riots were as ferocious, if shorter in duration, as those that took place in Liverpool.

The events that led up to the death of Charles Wootton in Liverpool began in May, when it was estimated that between five and six hundred black men in Liverpool were out of work and on the breadline. Many were former soldiers or sailors and some actively wanted to return to their homelands in the West Indies and Africa, but could find no ship on which they could work their passage and had no money to pay for a journey home. They were stranded in a country in which they could no longer find employment and in which – despite their war service – they were unwanted and increasingly resented. The army's decision to demobilize a number of men from the British West Indies Regiment in Britain rather than in their home islands exacerbated the problem in Liverpool. The city's Head Constable, Francis Caldwell, told the local council that 'Since the Armistice the demobilisation of so many negroes into Liverpool has caused this feeling to develop more rapidly.'[49] The Liverpool Ethiopian Association, a Pan-Africanist self-help group dedicated to defending the interests of Africans in Britain, suggested to the Lord Mayor of Liverpool that the Colonial Office should come to the assistance of the stranded men, and pay them £5 as a bounty, in recognition of their war service and for their repatriation. This was relayed by the Mayor to the Colonial Office but abruptly dismissed as a 'bribe'. That said, if the Colonial Office had agreed to the £5 bounty it would have been too late to prevent disaster; even as the proposal was being debated the situation had begun to spiral out of control.

In a move that in the circumstances was probably ill advised, the Liverpool police had, in May, attempted to close down an illegal gaming house run by black men. The result was a pitched battle in the streets. However, the real violence erupted in June, when disturbances broke out between black sailors and a group of white men that included locals and a number of foreign sailors, many of them Scandinavians. On the 4th, the night before the murder of Charles Wootton, a West Indian sailor named John Johnson was stabbed by group of Scandinavian sailors for refusing them a cigarette, or at least that was the pretext for the assault. The victim's wounds were severe and news of his condition sparked anger. The following night, a group of black sailors, associates of Johnson, threw beer over a group of Scandinavian sailors in a bar. According to the *Liverpool Daily Post*, the Scandinavians were then 'assailed by the coloured men with sticks, knives, razors and pieces of iron taken from lampposts; eight Scandinavians were taken to hospital and the coloureds headed for the Scandinavians' home in Great George Square.'[50]

The violence continued the next night. There were reports of disturbances in Great George Square where both Scandinavians and black sailors lodged. When the police arrived at the scene they decided that the correct course of action was to raid a boarding house where a number of black men were living at 18 Upper Pitt Street, which formed the western side of the square. With an angry crowd gathered in the square the police entered the hostel but encountered considerable resistance. Four policemen were injured; two sustained gunshot wounds, apparently struck by the same glancing bullet, for after four years of war Britain in 1919 was awash with illegally held firearms. During the raid, six black seamen were arrested but Charles Wootton (also known as Wootten) escaped through a rear entrance, before being spotted by the crowd. Wootton was then chased for over half a mile and finally caught and murdered at the Queen's Dock. His lynching was, however, not the end of the 1919 riots in Liverpool. In no other city was the violence so sustained. Black men were also attacked in Stanhope and Hill Streets, where they lived in a huge boarding house run by the Elder Dempster Shipping Company. This facility, large enough to house between three and four hundred men, was destroyed. Across the city the homes of black men and black families were targeted by the mob. Many were ransacked, their contents dragged out into the street and set on fire. Ernest Marke, the young Sierra Leonean, recalled encountering a mob of men on Brownlow Hill.

> They started chasing us the moment we were spotted, shouting, 'Niggers, niggers, stop them niggers.' A lady heard the shout, looked through her window and saw the mob after us. She beckoned to us, ran downstairs and opened the door to us and then let us out quickly into the back alley, from where we maneuvered ourselves through other back lanes to the bottom of the hill by the Adelphi hotel. No sooner had we reach the main thoroughfare when we were spotted by another mob. A tram car was going southward where we lived; we ran for it, the mob on our heels. I caught it but my friend was unlucky. That was the last time I saw him. I learned later that he was beaten unconscious and left for dead.[51]

The violence in Liverpool was orchestrated by well-organized gangs, hundreds and sometimes thousands strong, who hunted black men on the streets. On 8 June, three days after Charles Wootton was murdered, three West African men were stabbed in Liverpool. By 10 June, around seven hundred black people were sheltering from white gangs in the local bridewells (petty offenders' prisons). Others took refuge in the Ethiopian Hall, the headquarters of the Liverpool Ethiopian Society. That day in Liverpool, reported *The Times*, 'White men appeared determined to clear out the blacks who have been advised to stay indoors. This counsel many of them disregarded . . . Whenever a negro was seen he was chased and if caught severely beaten.'[52] The *Liverpool Evening Express* described the situation the following day:

> Wrecked houses, despoiled of their furniture, gaping holes in plate glass windows, shops which have been broken open by hooligans and emptied of their contents by thieves, and charred patches on the road to donate a bonfire made by some innocent person's furniture are visible evidence of the result of rioting in the negro colony of Liverpool last night . . . The Negroes by their hundred have thrown themselves upon the mercy of the authorities. In dozens they presented themselves at the bridewell yesterday afternoon and evening, and before today's dawn broke there were between 600 and 700 Black men safely housed at their own request in the main bridewell at Cheapside. During the day this number has been considerably increased. Four hundred were marched through the streets by the police.[53]

Alongside the lynching of Charles Wootton, this was perhaps the most heartrending of the many tragic spectacles of 1919; the sight of four hundred black people, men, women and children, being marched through the streets of Liverpool under police escort — some of them made refugees in their own city. To make matters even worse in August, in the latter stages of Liverpool's summer of riots, the men tasked with defending the city and — in theory at least — its black residents went on strike. The Liverpool police strike of 1919 was only ended when three battalions of soldiers, supported by tanks, were deployed in the city and a battleship accompanied by destroyers sailed up the Mersey — an overreaction by a British government grown twitchy and paranoid in the aftermath of the Russian Bolshevik revolution of 1917.[54]

The factors that in 1919 induced thousands of men in the port towns of Britain to turn upon local black communities were numerous and complex. There is no question that profound anxieties over the scarcity of work were critical. Some of the opposition towards black seamen stemmed from the simple fact that they were perceived as unwelcome competition for work, but an old colonial practice aggravated the situation. Black seamen who signed on to

49. The London Victory Parade, 19 July 1919. Flags of the Allied nations flew from windows along Whitehall and crowds lined the street by the Cenotaph. Black soldiers were not permitted to march among the ranks of the victorious armies.

50. 130,000 African American GIs were stationed in Britain during the Second World War. By 1944 they represented the largest black population Britain had ever known.

51. An African American GI dances with a white British woman at Frisco's International Club, Piccadilly, London.

52. Trinidadian-British cricketer Learie Constantine being congratulated by his solicitor outside court in June 1944, having successfully sued Imperial London Hotels for refusing him a room on the grounds of race.

53. Dick Turpin, the first black British boxing champion. His father Lionel Turpin fought for Britain on the Western Front during the First World War.

54. The *Empire Windrush* brought 492 West Indians to Britain in June 1948, and became a symbol of the start of post-war migration.

55. Some of the 492 West Indians preparing to disembark from the *Empire Windrush* in 1948.

56. West Indian migrants temporarily housed in the deep-level air-raid shelter under Clapham Common in south London.

57. Racism in post-war Britain drove black migrants into the hands of slum landlords. Here a West Indian family struggle in squalid and overcrowded conditions, July 1949.

58. Notting Hill, 3 September 1958. The police search a black man on Talbot Road during the so-called 'race riots'. The violence was caused by racist thugs from across London who descended on Notting Hill, intent on attacking black residents.

59. The East End of London in the 1960s. Racist graffiti scrawled on the front door of a black family's home.

60. Britain on 1 May 1968, eleven days after Enoch Powell's infamous 'Rivers of Blood' speech.

61. Grieving protesters march from New Cross to the House of Commons in 1981 on the 'Black People's Day of Action', after thirteen young black people were killed in a fire at Deptford in south London.

62. Toxteth in 1981. Liverpool's Chief Constable, Kenneth Oxford, later suggested the riots were caused by 'the problem of half-castes in Liverpool'. There had been previous 'race riots' in Liverpool in 1948 and 1919.

63. The Brixton riots erupted after the Metropolitan Police launched operation Swamp 81, which used the so-called 'sus laws' to stop and search young black people. The underlying causes of the riots were racism, unemployment and victimization by the police of British-born black youths.

64. A mock-up of the *Empire Windrush* at the Opening Ceremony of the 2012 Olympics.

work on ships in Africa or the Caribbean had customarily been paid at lower rates than British sailors. Indeed, whole communities had developed in West Africa that were reliant upon employment on British ships, and who were regarded by the shipping companies as reservoirs of cheap maritime labour. The Kru community of Free-town, Sierra Leone, was seen as one such reservoir, and in the early twentieth century there was a transient community of Kru men resident in Liverpool.[55] Africans were recruited to work in the boiler rooms of steamships in the latter half of the nineteenth and early twentieth centuries in part because it was believed they could better withstand the heat, rather as it had been believed in the seventeenth and eighteenth centuries that they were uniquely capable of with-standing the heat of the West Indian plantations. Drawn to work on ships by tradition and to the sea by ceaseless poverty, in both the West Indies and West Africa thousands of the black men who found themselves in Britain in 1919 stood accused of competing unfairly for maritime work and driving down wages. These tensions had long existed but they were amplified by the war, as the number of black seamen in Britain and on British ships increased enormously.

Another resentment that fuelled the racism behind the violence of 1919 was opposition to inter-racial relationships and marriages. *The Times* reported that 'In the post war situation many [blacks] married Liverpool women and while it is admitted that some of them made good husbands the intermarriage of black men and white women, not to mention other relationships, has excited much feeling.'[56] In a far less sober editorial the *Liverpool Courier* maintained that 'one of the chief reasons of popular anger behind the present disturbances lies in the fact that the average negro is closer to the animal than is the average white man, and that there are women in Liverpool who had no self-respect.'[58] In another near-hysterical and racially charged article the newspaper suggested that the heightened opposition to racial mixing was, somehow, the work of enemy agents, 'dangerous foreigners . . . plotting the break up of the British empire . . . They believe that if only they can stir up British men by showing up in the most disgusting fashion all intercourse between black men and white women, then they will be on a fair road to accomplishing their objects.'[58] The same month, the *Morning Post* published an article entitled 'The Negro Riots. A Lesson for England', that demonstrated the extent to which scientific racism, with its emphasis on notions of racial purity, pollution and degeneration, had diverted Britain from the idealism that had been expressed (though not always believed) by the abolitionists of the late eighteenth and early nineteenth centuries. Paraphrasing Josiah Wedgwood I's great abolitionist slogan 'Am I not a Man and a Brother', the *Post* warned that Britain 'cannot give full privileges as "a man and a brother" to other racial types without accepting them also as brothers-in-law; and that path leads to racial degeneration'.[59]

Sir Ralph Williams, the former Resident Commissioner in the Bechuanaland Protectorate, a man who had had considerable dealings with King Khama and who regarded himself as an expert on colonial matters, explained to *The Times* that inter-racial marriages were bound to lead to social tensions, as in the minds of most Britons such unions were repugnant. 'Every one of us', he wrote, 'has, probably, many friends among the coloured people, whom we bear in our kindliest remembrance . . . [hostility to inter-racial relations] does not, either, I think, arise from any feeling of social superiority. The cause is far deeper. It is an instinctive certainty that sexual relations between white women and coloured men revolts our very nature.'[60] Rather typically for a former colonial administrator, Williams offered no opinions upon morality or social desirability of relationships between white men and black women, for which he was criticized by F. E. M. Hercules, the General Secretary of the Society of Peoples of African Origin. By the early twentieth century, black people in Britain had their own organizations and spokespeople who were able to counter the racial attacks that were poured upon them, not that such voices were heard above the clamour of racial denouncement and victim-blaming that characterized much of 1919.

It was in the midst of the Liverpool riots and while the press was in this agitated mood that F. E. M. Hercules received the news that no black soldiers were to be permitted to march in the London Victory Parade of July. He caught the resulting tone of anger and betrayal in an article for the *Africa Telegraph*. He wrote:

Every ounce of strength was put into the struggle by the black man . . . He fought with the white man to save the white man's home and the war was won. Black men all the world over are asking to-day: 'What have we got? What are we going to get out of it all?' The answer, in effect, comes clear, convincing and conclusive: 'Get back to your kennel you damned dog of a nigger!'[61]

Underlying the hostility towards inter-racial relations in 1919 was a deeper sense of racial superiority in Britain that had arisen out of the Scramble for Africa and the growth and propagation of Victorian racial science. Decades of colonial propaganda had conditioned many people in Britain to view men and women of African descent as lesser peoples who had been defeated and subdued by British power. The war had increased the size of the black population at the very moment in which forms of racism that affirmed and celebrated white, Anglo-Saxon racial supremacy were on the rise. Regurgitating the mantra of white racial supremacy that had emerged from the era of the Scramble for Africa, the Liverpool Courier reminded its readers that 'The white man . . . regards [the black] as part child, part animal and part savage'.[62]

There was also a view among the mobs that patrolled the streets of Liverpool that blackness and Britishness were mutually exclusive. To them, black people were both aliens and racial inferiors; they should therefore be at the very back of the queues for jobs and homes and be regarded as legitimate targets for violent assault. Yet newspaper reports of the Liverpool and Cardiff disturbances repeatedly make mention of the fact that among the black victims of the attacks were veterans who had served in France or on Atlantic convoys. Of the seven hundred black people who were forced to take shelter from white mobs in the Liverpool bridewells in the summer of 1919, around eighty were soldiers or sailors recently discharged from their war service.[63] Many of these black men were viewed by the mobs as foreigners with no legitimate claims to Britishness or British residency, but were nothing of the sort: they were men who had volunteered for service and put themselves at risk of injury or death only to find themselves assaulted on the streets and in their homes by other Britons who regarded their skin colour as incontrovertible evidence that they were not and could never be British. Those who were British-born were also notionally stripped of their nationality and identity by the racial thinking that informed and fuelled the indiscriminate racial violence of 1919.

On 23 June, three weeks after the murder of Charles Wootton, the Colonial Secretary, Lord Milner, issued a 'Memorandum on the Repatriation of Coloured Men'. It read:

> I am seriously concerned at the continued disturbances due to racial ill feeling against coloured men in our large sea ports. These riots are serious enough from the point of view of the maintenance of order in this country, but they are even more serious in regard to their possible effect in the colonies . . . I have every reason to fear that when these men get back to their own colonies they might be tempted to revenge themselves on the white minorities there, unless we can do something to show that His Majesty's Government is not insensible to their complaints . . . I am convinced that if we wish to get rid of the coloured population whose presence here is causing so much trouble we must pay the expense of doing so ourselves. It will not be great.[64]

The Lord Mayor of Liverpool, together with the Chief Constable and officials from the Ministry of Labour, began to draw up plans for the evacuation of the entire black population of the city to abandoned army camps outside the city. There they would be interned while a scheme for their repatriation to their homelands in Africa and the West Indies could be worked out and put into action. The fact that many of the black people driven from their homes were black Britons with no other homeland to which they might be repatriated was just one of the flaws in the scheme. Another was that a proportion of those who might feasibly be returned to their countries of origin were married with British wives, and in many cases mixed-race children. Repatriation under those circumstances would have entailed the break-up of British families and in the impoverishment of women and children. Ultimately this plan to intern and repatriate black Liverpudlians was recognized as impractical and incendiary and nothing came of it.

Surveying the global picture, the Colonial Office noted that across the world racial tensions, heightened by the dislocations of the war years and by the spread of new forms of racism, had sparked terrible outbreaks of violence in 1919. While white gangs patrolled the streets of Liverpool, black men were murdered and lynched in the United States. In what James Weldon Johnson, of the National Association for the Advancement of Colored People (NAACP), called the Red Summer, attacks on black people took place in twenty-five American cities. Twenty-three black Americans were killed in Chicago, hunted down and murdered by white gangs. Perhaps as many as two hundred black people died in the Elaine, Arkansas massacre in September and October 1919. A further six black people were killed in Washington DC while the death toll among the black community of Knoxville, Tennessee still remains unknown, with estimates ranging from twenty-five to a hundred people. As in Britain during that terrible summer, tensions over employment were a major underlying cause as poorer white Northerners resented the influx of black people from the South who had moved north to find jobs in the factories producing war materials.

In Britain, a large number of black men did voluntarily return to their homes in the West Indies and West Africa, taking with them eyewitness accounts of the riots and racial attacks of 1919. They were joined by others who had grievances arising from their mistreatment while serving in the BWIR or the navy during the war. The Colonial Office was conscious of the levels of disillusionment among black servicemen and aware that there would be outrage when news of the riots and the murder of Charles Wootton reached the colonies.

On 18 July, exactly at the moment that thousands of white soldiers in London were gathering for the London Victory Parade, making their last-minute preparations in the vast tented village that had been set up to accommodate them in Kensington Gardens, there was a riot in Freetown, Sierra Leone. The immediate targets were Syrian and Lebanese immigrants who had built their businesses there.[65] Black residents of Freetown were enraged at the imposition of a colour bar in the colony which prevented them gaining access to civil service positions and posts in British companies. Soldiers and sailors who had served in the war found, like their comrades in Britain, that they had been discharged and effectively discarded at the coming of peace. They were also deeply affronted when the government refused to pay war gratuities that had been promised to returning soldiers. But the violence was also linked to the riots in Britain. Members of Freetown's Krio community, the descendants of the Nova Scotian settlers and the liberated Africans who had passed through the gates of the King's Yard, organized a petition in which one of the signatories complained that 'there was considerable indignation in some parts of the city at the report of racial disturbances in Liverpool, Cardiff and a few other places in England and Wales which gave rise to considerable apprehension that the "sea-boys" repatriated from those places with a deep sense of injury would instigate reprisals in Sierra Leone against the white residents'.[66]

Just four days later, riots broke out in British Honduras, now Belize. There, the sudden and unexpected increases in the price of food brought people out onto the streets. Former soldiers, the most notable of whom was Samuel Haynes, who had served in the BWIR, led the riots. A poet and founder of the local branch of Marcus Garvey's Universal Negro Improvement Association, Haynes later wrote 'Land of the Free', the national anthem of independent Belize. One of the slogans used by the rioters in Belize was 'This is our country and we want to get the white man out. The white man has no right here'.[67] There were further riots and disturbances during 1919 in Trinidad and Guyana.[68] Beyond the British Empire and United States, disturbances occurred in the Belgian Congo, Panama and Costa Rica.

Among those who commented upon the events of 1919 was Mr John Hobbis Harris, a Baptist missionary who had lived in the Congo Free State. Harris was the secretary of the Anti-Slavery and Aborigines' Protection Society, an organization that could trace its roots back to the British and Foreign Anti-Slavery Society, the body that had called the World Anti-Slavery Convention of 1840. In June 1919, before the murder of Charles Wootton and before it had been announced that black soldiers would be excluded from the London Victory Parade, Harris was interviewed about the riots, and the predicament in which black Britons and former servicemen from the West Indies and Africa had been placed:

> The mass of the British public are intensely appreciative of all the
> coloured races have done in the war – and that is the story yet to
> be told in full – that they will insist on justice, which is all that

the black man wants. It is well to recognise, however that the question of the colour bar is going to be the great post-war problem in all the overseas territories. The thing the British public does not realise adequately is that we are a coloured empire . . . We are an Empire of 435,000,000, and 350,000,000 are coloured. What we have got to make our mind up on is whether we're going to solidify our empire or disrupt it. Ours being a coloured Empire, legislation resting solely on colour is unthinkable except at the risk of dissolution of the Empire . . . You cannot prevent the black man from coming here, because this is the centre of his Empire. You could no more tell him that he must not come to London, Liverpool or Cardiff than he has the right to tell you that you must not go to Lagos or Durban or Johannesburg. After many years' study of this difficult question, I have definitively come to the conclusion that colour in itself must be no bar in any sphere of human activity . . . The colour bar is the last rampart of slavery.[69]

After 1919, and for much of the rest of the twentieth century, Britain struggled with exactly these questions. How was it possible to be a 'coloured Empire', ruling over tens of millions of black people on West Indian islands and across great swathes of Africa, while at the same time seeking to prevent people from those regions from visiting the nation that they were told was their 'mother country' and the centre of *their* empire? How could Britain call upon black men and women from the West Indies and Africa to fight and labour in war and then exclude them from the fruits of victory — such as they were? Irrespective of these questions, in the inter-war years legislation based on colour was passed into law and pre-existing ordinances were subverted and targeted against black seamen and their families.

During the riots of 1919, the police undertook interviews with the black people who had been sheltered in the Liverpool bridewells. They and other members of the black community were registered, their details recorded, to produce a relatively detailed picture of the black population of the city, with the origins, trades and family backgrounds of hundreds of people. This was used after the riots to develop a system of observation and monitoring in Liverpool. Black seamen were issued with registration cards that contained photographs and fingerprints that had to be produced to sign on for ships, a system copied and adopted by other ports. The Aliens Order of 1920 and Special Restrictions (Coloured Alien Seamen) Order of 1925 further required all black seamen domiciled in Britain, including British subjects, to register with the police and then prove their nationality. An initiative of the Home Office Aliens Department, this legislation has been described as 'the first instance of state-sanctioned race discrimination inside Britain to come to widespread notice'.[70] The 1925 order gave the police powers to stop black seamen as they landed in British ports and demand to see their documentation. However, sailors did not always carry passports and were not required to and so many black seamen had no means of proving their nationality. Those unable to demonstrate their status as British subjects, and those whose documentation was regarded by the police as unsatisfactory, were required to register as aliens, which made their potential deportation a far simpler process. Black British subjects, along with Indians and Arabs from the empire, were in this way exposed to the threat of deportation under a legislation that had been intended to control and limit the numbers of aliens.[71] In Cardiff in the 1920s, men with passports, discharge papers from war service in the army or navy and even birth certificates, all demonstrating their status as British subjects, were forced by the police to register as aliens. One seaman who had his passport confiscated and issued with an Aliens Card was threatened with arrest when he refused to accept it.[72] These restrictions and the spread of a colour bar in inter-war Britain meant that in one narrow sense the mobs of 1919 had succeeded in their efforts to strip black people of their status as full British citizens.

THIRTEEN

'We Prefer their Company'

There were more black people in Britain in 1944 than there were in 1948, the year the *Empire Windrush* docked at Tilbury and 492 West Indians landed in the imperial 'mother country'. The black population in the summer of 1944 was somewhere around a hundred and fifty thousand.[1] In 1948, there were probably fewer than twenty thousand. Britain's black population may well not have returned to its 1944 peak until around 1958, after ten years of post-war immigration from the West Indies and Africa.[2]

This change is accounted for by a single factor. On the eve of D-Day, in June 1944, there were a hundred and thirty thousand African American GIs, both army and air force, stationed in Britain. The wartime influx of black American soldiers was unprecedented in multiple ways. Never before had the black population been so large, yet the majority of this wartime population were neither migrants nor settlers. Nor were they black Britons or even black subjects of the British Empire, but soldiers and citizens of another state – albeit mistreated soldiers and second-class citizens. Their arrival in Britain, their interactions with the British public and the strategies and policies adopted by both the British government and the American authorities to manage those interactions revealed much about Britain and the British in the middle of the twentieth century.

Racially segregated America sent a racially segregated army to Britain in 1942. In the Southern states, that segregation was upheld through a system of organized repression, political disenfranchisement and

economic marginalization known as the Jim Crow laws, named after
the blackface minstrel character that Thomas D. Rice brought to
London in the 1830s. Except for the white officers commanding
black Americans, the two 'races' lived as separately in Britain as they
had at home. They were billeted in separate camps, often ate in
separate canteens, and spent their free time in separate army clubs.
Within its camps and bases, the US Army (which included the
USAAF) was at liberty to replicate on British soil all the divisions,
inequalities and injustices that characterized relations between black
and white Americans in the middle of the twentieth century.

The question for the British authorities, who had opened up their
country to their new ally, was whether American segregation and
American racism would be permitted beyond their fences. Would
Jim Crow style segregation be allowed in the towns and villages of
Britain? Would bars, dance halls and restaurants refuse to admit
black men; would railway carriages be reserved for whites only?
Would racial discrimination become formalized and officially sanctioned, and, if so, would the British public comply? Furthermore,
how could Britain be seen as a reasonable, rational, paternalistic
colonial master, who had the best interests of her subject peoples
at heart at all times, if she was also complicit in the establishment
of a formal colour bar? And what of the thousands of black Britons,
born and bred in the country? What of the black soldiers, airmen
and workers who had left the colonies to serve the empire in its
hour of need and were now resident in Britain? How would they
and their families react if news of such laws in Britain reached the
islands of the West Indies and the port cities of West Africa?

If they had been in a position to choose, Britain's political leaders
surely would have been glad to sidestep all of these questions. Their
preference would have been for the American army deployed to
Britain in 1942 to be all-white. This would not have been out of
step with official wartime policies towards black people from the
British Empire. To accept or reject the labour of black men from
the British Empire was a decision within the gift of the British
government, and the demands for skilled men did force the government to recruit men and women from both the West Indies and
Africa, but perhaps with the memories of 1919 influencing their
decision-making, an interdepartmental consultation, held in January

1942, concluded that despite Britain's pressing wartime labour needs the 'recruitment to the United Kingdom of coloured British subjects, whose remaining in the United Kingdom after the war might create a social problem, was not considered desirable.'[3]

However, the racial composition of the army America sent to Britain was, of course, a matter for the Americans, and one over which the British had little influence. Not that this stopped the government from attempting to persuade the Americans to send a racially monotone force. In a War Cabinet meeting of July 1942, Anthony Eden, the Foreign Secretary, expressed his concern that if black troops were sent, tensions would arise between the British public and white American soldiers because there was a likelihood of 'certain sections of our people showing more effusiveness to the coloured troops than the Americans would readily understand'.[4] Desperately fumbling for further reasons as to why black troops should be excluded, Eden fell back on a familiar trope. Forgetting, perhaps, that he was discussing men from North America, rather than equatorial Africa, he wheeled out the now customary contention that the African Americans would struggle to cope with the supposedly extreme conditions of winter in southern England. Unsurprisingly, black GIs from cities like Chicago, New York and Washington DC found the rigours of the English winter entirely tolerable.

Eden's Private Secretary, Oliver Hardy, later laid out the dilemma he and Eden believed the country would face if, as was expected, around 10 per cent of the American force deployed to Britain was black. 'If we treat them naturally as equals, there will be trouble with the Southern officers. If we treat them differently, there will be trouble with the "North Americans"', by which he meant men from the Northern states.[5] Despite polite, diplomatic protestations by the British the Americans were not swayed. For their own domestic political reasons, and in response to pressure from black American civil rights groups, they insisted that the American army dispatched to England contained African Americans. But the Allies did agree that the African American proportion of the US force would be representative of the proportion of black people in the American population as a whole, hence the figure of 10 per cent.

Anthony Eden, Winston Churchill and the British government

could no more determine the ethnic make-up of the US Army than they could control how the British public reacted to the rather sudden arrival of tens of thousands of African American soldiers. After the isolation of 1940 and 1941 the British were overjoyed to be joined on their island by their American allies. As the GIs began to land and occupy their new bases *The Times* commented, 'We feel stronger, not only physically but even more in spirit, for their presence among us.'[6] Deployment began in May 1942, and by the autumn there were around eleven thousand black troops in the UK. Most were in the South-West of England and in the port towns of the south coast; some were in Wales, East Anglia and on Merseyside. With the exception of Bristol and Liverpool, which both had small black populations of their own and long links to the Atlantic slave trade, in most of the areas black people were almost unknown. Their inhabitants, as well as the more worldly citizens of the ports, proved extraordinarily welcoming to the African American troops. In the rural areas and market towns of a Britain that had only a tiny black population, they were an exciting novelty and rather rapidly became particularly popular among the British public.

Britain had, of course, experienced serious racial violence in 1919, and in the 1920s passed laws targeting 'coloured seamen'. Yet little over two decades later, black GIs were welcomed with open arms. But this did not mean that racial prejudice had somehow disappeared. The black Americans were not immigrating, had not come to stay and were not suspected of 'taking British jobs' or houses; rather the opposite, the influx of 1.5 million well-paid GIs, both black and white, was a great boon to Britain's battered wartime economy.

The black Americans were popular with the British public, in part, as they appear to have accepted their deployment to Britain with better grace and fewer complaints than many of their white compatriots. Many white Americans were accustomed to a number of everyday luxuries that were unknown to the British, and they grumbled endlessly about their absence. African Americans, by contrast, especially those from the rural South, had lived pre-war lives of comparative poverty. In material terms, their living standards were far closer to those of their British hosts. Having never known the 'comforts of home' that the white GIs so sorely missed, the black GIs complained less about life in Britain. They were paid the same as their white countrymen, and many black GIs had more money in Britain than they had had as civilians. All GIs were extremely well-paid by British standards, but the black troops were seen as less flashy and overt in their consumption. They were repeatedly described by British civilians as 'self-controlled', 'reserved' and 'disciplined'. 'Everybody here adores the Negro troops, all the girls go to their dances, but nobody likes the white Americans. They swagger about us as if they were the only people fighting this war. They all get so drunk and look so untidy while the negroes are very polite, much smarter and everybody's pets',[7] wrote a British woman from Marlborough in Wiltshire in March 1943. This politeness, of course, was a trait that generations of black men had learnt in the post-Civil War South, as such attributes were essential for survival in the regions in which black communities lived under the shadow of the Jim Crow laws.

Before the American deployment, Oliver Hardy had feared that the 'North Americans', white men from the Northern states, would take offence if the British treated the black GIs in a discriminatory manner. During the summer of 1942, it became apparent that it was the British public who most vehemently objected to the mistreatment of black GIs in Britain. Exposed for the first time to the sheer vindictiveness of American racial prejudice, it was they who took greatest offence, and they who were most repelled by the violence meted out to black GIs. In reaction to a ceaseless stream of abuses and incidents in which white Americans attacked, assaulted or abused the black GIs, there was a wave of revulsion and resentment, which developed into a great upsurge of anti-American sentiment. The reputation of the Americans was particularly tarnished within local communities who witnessed the abuse of black GIs at first hand, and despite careful attempts to control the press, reports of some incidents did appear in British newspapers. In December 1943 George Orwell noted that 'The general consensus of opinion seems to be that the only American soldiers with decent manners are the Negroes.'[8] A pub in Bristol displayed a notice that read 'Only blacks served here' and when the landlady in another bar was confronted by white Americans who were angry that coloured customers were served their drinks and treated as equals, she responded, 'Their money is as good as yours, and we prefer their company.'[9]

Acts of violence against black GIs by white American soldiers had been predicted by Hugh Dalton, the President of the Board of Trade, who in conversation with an official from the Ministry of Information in July 1942, had warned that the British public would take the side of black GIs if they were assaulted by white Americans in the street or pubs.[10] In one such incident, in Cosham near Portsmouth in the summer of 1943, a group of black GIs who had gathered outside the pub were ordered to disperse by a group of white American Military Police. When an argument erupted the Military Police were surrounded by British civilians, one of whom shouted, 'Why don't you leave them alone?' One of the black GIs shouted down the Military Police, saying, 'We ain't no slaves, this is England'.[11] Members of Britain's small black population and the cohort of West Indian servicemen and women in the country also sided with the black GIs when the latter faced attacks or abuse from white Americans. The traditional British love of the underdog may have played a part here, as many Britons almost instinctually took the side of the oppressed minority.[12] One strategy adopted by the Americans to reduce tension was the policy of 'rotating passes', a subtler form of segregation whereby black troops would be allowed to visit the approved pubs and dance halls on one night, and whites on another.

An incident reported in *The Times* in October 1942 exposed how American racial views were seen as not only at odds with those that prevailed in Britain but as directly contrary to the stated aims of the war itself. The incident involved the manager of a snack bar in Oxford who – more in sadness than anger – wrote to *The Times*:

> The other night a coloured US soldier came into our establishment and very diffidently presented me with an open letter from his commanding officer, explaining that "Pte. — is a soldier in the US Army, and it is necessary that he sometimes has a meal, which he has, on occasion, found it difficult to obtain. I would be grateful if you would look after him." Naturally we looked after him to the best of our ability, but I could not help feeling ashamed that in a country where even stray dogs are "looked after" by special societies, a citizen of the world, who is fighting the world's battle for freedom and equality, should have found it necessary to place himself in this humiliating position. Had there been the slightest

objection from other customers, I should not have any hesitation in asking them all to leave.[13]

In 1943, the American Office of War Information and the British War Office commissioned the public information film *Welcome to Britain*, which was shown to American soldiers but not the British public.[14] Bizarrely, it starred the Hollywood actor Burgess Meredith (best known today for playing the role of 'the Penguin' in the 1960s *Batman* television series). Meredith played the role of the soldier everyman, who wandered around wartime England having meaningful encounters with British civilians, railway workers, American generals and, at one point, Bob Hope. He was by turns naive and lost, and worldly and knowledgeable. Repeatedly, he spoke straight to camera, offering advice on how to navigate the cultural differences between Britain and the United States. In one scene, set in an English railway station, a black GI from Birmingham, Alabama, is invited to tea by an elderly British lady. 'If you come to my Birmingham you must come to my home and have a cup of tea with me,' she says, shaking the black soldier warmly by the hand. At this point, the black GI conveniently heads off to buy cigarettes allowing Meredith to turn to camera and speak directly to his GI audience. 'Now look, men,' he begins, 'you heard that conversation. That's not unusual here, it's the sort of thing that happens quite a lot. Now let's be frank about it, there are coloured soldiers as well as white here and there are less social restrictions in this country – just what you heard an English woman asking a coloured boy to tea, she was polite about it and he was polite about it. Now that might not happen at home, but the point is we're not at home.' He continued, 'If we bring a lot of prejudices here what are we gonna do about 'em?' In a second scene Meredith and the black GI happen, as if by accident, upon Major General John C. H. Lee, Commander of the Services of Supply (SOS), the unglamorous labour and logistics corps of the US Army, to which the majority of the black GIs had been assigned. In a staged and mawkish conversation the general, whose ancestors had fought for the Confederacy during the Civil War, is allowed to eulogize at length about the promise of 'real citizenship' that America had supposedly offered 'the Negro'. Disturbingly, the general promises that 'everyone is treated the same when it comes to dying.' He then pontificates about the war and the opportunity it offers the nation to 'try to live up to our American promises'. As General Lee finally finishes his impromptu lecture, the music swells, the white GI shares a cigarette with his black comrade and the military audience is left to reflect. Laughably unsubtle and clumsy by modern standards, *Welcome to Britain* nonetheless went down extremely well with the white US troops and with the British press. The *Daily Mail* said that the film 'should do more than any other single factor to create a genuine Anglo-American understanding'.[15] A number of British newspapers joined together and called for the film to be put on general release to British civilians. The military authorities politely rejected that proposal.

During the First World War, Winston Churchill, as we have seen, campaigned in support of the 'Million Black Army' movement and spoke powerfully in Parliament in favour of the recruitment of black African soldiers for deployment on the Western Front. As Prime Minister in another conflict, two decades later, he was far more reticent on the subject of race. In September 1942, by which time there were around eleven thousand black troops in Britain out of a total of a hundred and seventy thousand US personnel, the racial attitudes of many white US soldiers had already led to outbreaks of violence and public disturbances. Through the work of Mass Observation, a social research organization founded in 1937, the government was well aware that black soldiers were being attacked on the streets and driven out of pubs and dance halls. On 29 September, Labour MP Tom Driberg tackled Churchill on the issue in the House of Commons, asking if he was 'aware that an unfortunate result of the presence here of American Forces has been the introduction in some parts of Britain of discrimination against negro troops; and whether he will make friendly representations to the American military authorities asking them to instruct their men that the colour bar is not a custom of this country and that its non-observance by British troops or civilians should be regarded with equanimity?'[16] Churchill responded evasively, 'The question is certainly unfortunate. I am hopeful that without any action on my part the points of view of all concerned will be mutually understood and respected.'[17] The communist MP William Gallacher then rose to ask the Prime Minister whether he was aware of 'a letter, a copy of which I have sent to him, from a number of [British] serving men informing me that an officer has given them a lecture advising them on the necessity for discrimination in connection with negroes who are in London.' Gallacher received no answer from the Prime Minister, who would not be drawn on such a sensitive issue dividing the wartime allies.

The lecture William Gallacher was referring to was probably connected to a document by Major General Arthur Dowler in August 1942. Dowler was the Senior British Administrative Officer in the Southern Command, which covered the English South-West, the region to which most of the black GIs had been deployed. In the absence of guidance from his superiors, Dowler, after consulting the Americans, had drafted a document that he entitled *Notes on Relations with Coloured Troops*. It began, 'Among the American troops in this country are a number of units whose personnel are coloured troops.' While Dowler admitted that 'they contribute a valuable service to the prosecution of the war by the provision of labour both skilled and unskilled', he warned that 'their presence in England presents a new problem to British men and women brought in contact with them . . . The racial problem is there and cannot be ignored. It is necessary, therefore, for the British, both men and women, to realize the problem and to adjust their attitude so that it conforms to that of the white American citizen.' Dowler's assessment of the character of the African American GI was influenced by his conversations with the American authorities, but it could just as easily have been assembled from the various caricatures and stereotypes that had been burnt onto the British psyche by a century of reading *Uncle Tom's Cabin* and listening to minstrel songs. Dowler wrote that 'While there are many coloured men of high mentality and cultural distinction, the generality are of a simple mental outlook. They work hard when they have no money and when they have money prefer to do nothing until it is gone. In short they have not the white man's ability to think and act to a plan. Their spiritual outlook is well known and their songs give a clue to their nature.'[18] The British public had to be especially careful, said the general, because black men 'are natural psychologists in that they can size up the white man's character and can take advantage of a weakness. Too much freedom, too wide associations with white men tend to make them lose their heads and have on occasions led to civil strife.'[19] He concluded that it was critical that 'white women should not associate with coloured men. It follows then that they should not walk out, dance, or drink with them. Do not think such action hard or unsociable. They do not expect your companionship and such relations would in the end only result in strife.'[20]

Notes on Relations with Coloured Troops was drafted without permission from the War Office or the War Cabinet and raised enormous concerns within the Colonial Office, where officials were attempting to soothe racial tensions within the empire and advocate a policy of broad racial equality. In a memorandum written in early October, the Under-Secretary of State for the Colonies, Viscount Cranbourne, warned of the dangers to Britain's reputation among the black people of the empire if the government was seen to be going along with the Americans in the establishment of formal segregation in Britain. The Ministry of War, however, was broadly in favour of supporting the American policies of racial segregation and the Secretary of State for War, Sir James Grigg, prepared an official paper in which he described the nation as being 'on a razor's edge', caught between the racial attitudes of its American allies and the British public's revulsion at segregation and the violence that it led to. Grigg argued that in order to control the situation it was imperative that British soldiers be supplied with 'the facts and history of the colour question' in the US Army.

On 13 October 1942, the War Cabinet met to discuss the treatment and segregation of black GIs in Britain, and determine whether British service personnel were to be educated in American racial attitudes as in *Notes on Relations with Coloured Troops*. Viscount Cranbourne, nervous as to how British policies would look to black people in the colonies, argued as Sir James Grigg had that British soldiers should be made aware of the racial issues that existed in the United States, to allow them to understand why white Americans were so fervently opposed to interaction between the races. After a fractious meeting, it decided that Britain would not oppose the American army's policy of segregation but would not permit British authorities, military or civilian, to play a part in enforcing it. However, it also concluded that 'it was desirable that the people of this country should avoid becoming too friendly with coloured American troops',[21] but there were to be no formal instructions on how to treat black American GIs.

The Cabinet also discussed the disruption that racial segregation had caused in the UK. One American general had observed that 'the Negro British nationals are rightly incensed. They undoubtedly have been cursed, made to get off the sidewalk, leave eating places and separated from their white wives by American soldiers.'[22] While Churchill could be circumspect on his views on race in Parliament, he was often flippant in private. When Viscount Cranbourne told him of a black Colonial Office official who had been barred from eating at his usual lunchtime restaurant because it had become a favourite with white American officers, Churchill quipped, 'That's all right. if he takes his banjo with him they'll think he's one of the band.'[23]

Churchill was by no means alone among politicians of the age in his propensity to fall back upon racial stereotypes. In the 1920s, David Lloyd George – who once insisted that Britain 'reserve the right to bomb the niggers' – suggested that Churchill's personality might be a result of racial mixing among his ancestors. With no evidence to substantiate his claims, Lloyd George privately expressed the view that the half-American Churchill 'undoubtedly had nigger blood in him. Look at his build and slouch. The Marlboroughs [Churchill's family] were a poor type physically, but Winston was strong. Another characteristic of Winston is that when he gets excited he shrieks: again the nigger comes out.'[24]

As a result of the Cabinet meeting, a guidance memo, *Instructions as to the advice which should be given to British service personnel*, was completed and approved by both the Cabinet and the Supreme Commander of the Allied Forces, General Eisenhower, a few months later. Although far less frank than Dowler's *Notes on Relations with Coloured Troops* its message was not dissimilar, suggesting that Britons 'should be sympathetic towards coloured American troops – but remember that they are not accustomed in their own country to close and intimate relations with white people'. The instructions also explained that 'for a white woman to go about in the company of a Negro American is likely to lead to controversy and ill feeling. It may also be misunderstood by the Negro troops themselves'. It continued, 'This does not mean that friendly hospitality in the home or in social gatherings need be ruled out, though in such cases care should be taken not to invite white and coloured troops at the same time.'[25]

*

The warmth with which the British public embraced the black GIs was profoundly difficult for many white GIs from the Southern states to accept. Information films like *Welcome to Britain* partially persuaded them that the warmth of the British and the lack of racial segregation in pubs and cafes could be attributed to a quirk of cultural difference. However, when it came to inter-race relations, the gulf between the views of the Americans and their British hosts was so wide that at times it threatened to seriously damage inter-Allied relations.

Many white GIs refused to tolerate inter-racial relations point blank. For them, relationships between black GIs and British women were morally intolerable, and contacts between black GIs and British white women, however platonic, were liable to elicit violent reactions. One lieutenant wrote home that 'one thing I noticed here which I don't like is the fact that the English don't draw any color line . . . the English must be pretty ignorant. I can't see how a white girl could associate with a negro.'[26] Another white GI revealed how he and others reacted: 'Every time so far that we have seen a nigger with a white girl we have run him away. I would like to shoot the whole bunch of them.'[27]

There was some British sympathy with the American position on inter-racial relationships. Both the *Notes on Relations with Coloured Troops* and the *Instructions as to the advice which should be given to British service personnel* had taken great pains to emphasize how sensitive the Americans were on this issue, and offered historical background to contextualize and, to some extent, excuse American racism. Some Britons recoiled at the sight of mixed-race couples. In October 1942 the novelist Ann Meader was horrified to see two black soldiers with two blonde white girls in Weston-super-Mare, where large numbers of GIs were stationed. Meader confessed to her diary that she felt the British girls should be 'shot' for taking the risk of introducing 'coloured blood' into their children.[28] The Conservative MP Maurice Petherick wrote, disgruntledly, to Anthony Eden at the Foreign Office in December 1943, appalled that a number of black GIs had been stationed in his Falmouth constituency. Deploying a racial term rarely used in England since the seventeenth century, he complained that in Falmouth 'as in other parts of England women of the lowest order are consorting with the blackamoors . . . There is very strong feeling about this', he warned Eden, before suggesting that the Foreign Secretary should ask the Americans 'to send those we have to North Africa, where the poor devils, they would be much more happy and warm.'[29] He also recommended that the black GIs be transferred to the Italian front where they would be free to 'go and fertilize the Italians who are used to it anyhow'.[30]

The same year, Maurice Dale Colbourne, an official of the British Information Service in New York, published *America and Britain: a Mutual Introduction*. Having travelled extensively within the United States, Colbourne recognized that white American and British views on inter-racial relationships overlapped far more than their views on segregation. He complained of 'Britons with no colour problem, and imagining themselves free from colour prejudice,' who 'easily slip into violent denunciations of the American colour bar as a disgrace to and denial of democracy . . . Whenever I encounter a Briton waxing eloquent along that line,' Colbourne continued, 'I ask him, preferably in front of others: "Would you like your sister to marry a Negro?" '[31] It was on this point, he suggested, that the Allies could unite. Later, the Army Military History Institute in Pennsylvania surveyed soldiers who had served in the Second World War, drafting a series of questionnaires. When asked, 'Did you note any instances of ethnic, racial or religious discrimination? Please explain . . . ?', Sergeant Theodore G. Aufort, from southern California, answered 'yes', recalling the tensions among the white GIs as a conflict of 'North against the South'. Aufort explained, 'The southern boys were always using the argument, "would you want your sister to marry one".'[32]

The British authorities were well aware of the potential for inter-racial relationships to inflame anger among white American soldiers, and of the propensity for that anger to spill over into violence. Throughout the summer of 1942 and into 1943, white GIs kept up a sustained campaign of violence against black GIs who met or dated white British women. In Bristol, a city in which a large number of black GIs were stationed, one well-to-do resident reported that 'every open space . . . is full of black Americans with their white girls.'[33] Black GIs in the city had become so accustomed to being attacked by their white countrymen that they had even taken to stationing lookouts. In December 1942 there was a series of fights and stabbings in the Old Market area of the city, which began when a group of white Southerners decided to stamp out relationships between black GIs and local women.

A journalist from the *New Statesman and Nation* spoke to a number of the white GIs and painted a horrific picture of their attitudes and behaviours. He reported meeting white Southerners 'who seemed rational enough until the Negro problem was mentioned, and who would then show a terrifying lynching spirit, which was about the ugliest thing imaginable.'[34] He concluded that at the heart of the problem was the fact that white GIs from the 'deep south . . . take it for granted that it is their duty to interfere if they see black troops with white girls.' He suggested that the American authorities were duty-bound to 'use every device of persuasion to let white southern troops know that it is against discipline to treat Negro soldiers in a way to which their training and education has accustomed them'. Such a process of 'discipline and education' could not of course be put in place overnight but, 'If things are left to drift very unhappy incidents' were bound to occur, he warned.[35] In one of these unhappy incidents a white GI from the South who had been invited into an English home for the evening was enraged to discover that his fellow guest was an African American soldier, whom he proceeded to physically attack in front of his horrified hosts. General Eisenhower had some sympathy with the actions of his white troops and suspected that some English girls did not understand the gravity of their relationships with black troops. In a letter to Washington in September 1942, he wrote:

> To most English people, including the village girls – even those of perfectly fine character – the negro soldier is just another man, rather fascinating because he is unique in their experience, a jolly good fellow and with money to spend. Our own white soldiers, seeing a girl walk down the street with a negro, frequently see themselves as protectors of the weaker sex and believe it necessary to intervene to the extent of using force, to let her know what she's doing.[36]

That month, tensions over relationships between black GIs and British women were exposed in the British press through the actions of an unlikely figure. Mrs May, the wife of the vicar in the village of Worle, near Weston-super-Mare, took it upon herself to draw up a six-point code designed to limit contact between white women and black soldiers.

1. If a local woman keeps a shop and a coloured soldier enters, she must serve him, but she must do it as quickly as possible and indicate as quickly that she does not desire him to come there again.
2. If she is in a cinema and notices a coloured soldier next to her, she moves to another seat immediately.
3. If she is walking on the pavement and a coloured soldier is coming towards her, she crosses to the other pavement.
4. If she is in a shop and a coloured soldier enters, she leaves as soon as she has made her purchase or before that if she is in a queue.
5. White women, of course, must have no social relationship with coloured troops.
6. On no account must coloured troops be invited to the homes of white women.

Mrs May then held a series of public meetings at which copies of her new code were distributed, and she addressed the ladies of Worle, alerting them to their new responsibilities. The result was a scandal in the national press as the women of Worle turned, not against the black GIs, but against Mrs May. One local woman told the *Sunday Pictorial*, 'I was disgusted, and so were most of the women there. We have no intention of agreeing to her decree.'[37] Another commented, 'If the woman is talking like this in the name of the Church I should be interested to know what her husband's bishop thinks of it.'[38] In a quite remarkable editorial comment, which appeared under the headline 'Vicar's Wife Insults Our Allies', the *Sunday Pictorial* attempted to offer comfort to the arriving black GI by assuring him 'that there is no colour bar in this country and that he is as welcome as any other allied soldier. He will find the vast majority of people here have nothing but repugnance for the narrow-minded, uninformed prejudices expressed by the vicar's wife. There is – and will be – no persecution of coloured people in Britain.'[39]

They were fine words, but black Britons who could recall 1919, or who had experienced the colour bar and the prejudice of the inter-war years, knew that they offered a highly idealized view of Britain and British race relations. Yet the attempts – both official and impromptu – by the Americans to enforce racial segregation, and the unabashed and overt prejudice that the US Army brought with it to Britain, allowed the press and public to adopt a position of moral superiority on the issue of race, as their ancestors had done over the issue of slavery in the 1840s and 1850s. Racial prejudice was considered an American vice that the more civilized and culturally sophisticated British rejected.

The British authorities were particularly active in the matter of inter-racial relationships. As well as issuing the *Instructions as to the advice which should be given to British service personnel*, they took part in direct attempts to limit contact between British women and black GIs, and in this way became complicit in American-led efforts to enforce segregation. In some cases the law and the police were used to target British women known to be associating with black American troops. In the summer of 1943, police in Derbyshire used the wartime Defence Regulations to launch prosecutions aimed at stopping 'The association of U.S.A. coloured troops with British women', while in Melton Mowbray five women were prosecuted 'for trespassing on premises in the occupation of coloured troops'.[40] Another group of women were charged by the magistrates in in Newton Abbot, in 1944, for violating the security of a nearby military area. All five were married and were said to have been caught attempting to visit their black boyfriends. The local newspaper decided to name and shame them, going as far as to inform readers that the husband of one woman was 'serving abroad' and that she had two children, aged four and seven.[41] The heavy-handed and moralistic approach taken by the police, magistrates and the press in these cases was indicative of a wider concern about wartime extramarital activity. Many of the women who became the sweethearts of both black and white GIs were married. The enormous levels of social dislocation caused by the war, almost unimaginable to generations who did not live through the conflict, enormously disrupted normal patterns of familial relationships. The affairs and flirtations between white British women and black American GIs was, in one sense, merely a highly visible and more morally dubious manifestation of these deeper social ruptures.

A series of changes in US Army deployment and police tactics began to bring the situation under control. In 1943, when there was a second influx of black GIs, the army came to terms with the fact that the cause of the violence was racist white soldiers. A discipline regime was introduced, as were Military Police patrols that included both black and white officers. However what ended the crisis was D-Day, and the transfer of the vast majority of the black GIs to the Continent.

The debate about black GIs and their relationships with white women, though, continued long after the war. In the years after 1945, thousands of British women who had or would become engaged or married to white GIs, or had children with them out of wedlock, went to the United States under the GI bride scheme, but the white sweethearts of black GIs had the significant obstacle that inter-racial marriage was banned in around twenty states.

In 1947, a woman from the Midlands named Margaret Goosey travelled to Virginia, and there married her black GI sweetheart Thomas Johnson, in contravention of Virginia law. The groom was arrested and sent to the state industrial farm; the bride was jailed for six months and deported. The case was reported in the British press and raised in Parliament by Tom Driberg, the MP who had confronted Churchill on the abuse of black GIs in 1942. Driberg asked Ernest Bevin, then Foreign Secretary, if he would agree that it did not matter how 'undesirable a particular marriage may seem to be to many people, or to the local legislator', it is 'an elementary human right that men and women should be allowed to get married, irrespective of race or creed.'[42] Bevin, however, could 'see no ground for action' as the 'case was in accordance with Virginia State Law' and because 'Miss Goosey was warned by the State Authorities beforehand.'[43] Driberg asked that 'this very difficult subject' be referred to the Working Group on the Convention on Human Rights.[44]

Hanging over all the debates and official protestations around the issue of inter-racial relations during the years of American deployment was a deep-seated but often unspoken concern about mixed-race children, or 'brown babies', as they were often called at the time. In November 1942, the Home Secretary, Herbert

Morrison, wrote that he was 'fully conscious that a difficult sex problem might be created if there were a substantial number of cases of sex relations between white women and coloured troops and the procreation of half-caste children.'[45] Unlike many of his colleagues, Morrison did not believe the solution lay in some form of public education, which in his opinion would be unlikely 'to have any influence on the class of women who are attracted by coloured men'.[46] *The Colour Problem As The American Sees It*, an Army Bureau of Current Affairs educational pamphlet that was distributed in December 1942, suggested that the problem of mixed-race children was not just an American concern but a British one too. Produced for British service personnel, it was intended as a document that would open up group discussions. In strikingly Darwinian language, the pamphlet stated that while it was not necessary to go into 'a long discussion as to whether mixed marriages between white and coloured are good or bad. What is fairly obvious is that in our present society such unions are not desirable, since the children resulting from them are neither one thing nor the other and are thus badly handicapped in the struggle for life'.[47]

In October 1943, Churchill was informed by the Duke of Marlborough, the Military Liaison Officer to US forces, that ten brown babies had already been born and that it was 'quite conceivable that there are many others which are on the way'.[48] When Eleanor Roosevelt asked her husband, President Franklin D. Roosevelt, about the matter, he said, 'I think this is a British problem – not American.'[49]

By the end of the war, twenty-two thousand children had been born to British mothers and white American soldiers. The number of 'brown babies' was not known but became the subject of feverish speculation, with estimates ranging from a plausible five hundred and fifty to a ludicrously exaggerated twenty thousand. The most reliable estimates were carried out by the black British civil rights organization The League of Coloured Peoples, which was founded by Dr Harold Moody in 1931. Their 1946 estimate was five hundred and fifty-three. By 1948 that figure had grown to seven hundred and seventy-five.

The warmth and hospitality that had characterized the war years evaporated. Many children were abandoned by their mothers, who had themselves been ostracized by their communities and even families. Most were sent to children's homes, from which very few were successfully placed for adoption. Schemes for their adoption by black families in the United States were considered but never put into action as innumerable legal hurdles stood in the way. Furthermore Britain's politicians worried about how it looked to the non-white peoples of the colonies if Britain demonstrated herself incapable or unwilling to care for and educate a mere few hundred mixed-race children, and saw the only solution to be their mass deportation. There was more strident and ugly opposition from within the United States. Mississippi Congressman John E. Rankin, who was infamous for using the word 'nigger' in debates in the House of Representatives, expressed, in the House, his rabid opposition 'to bringing to this country a lot of illegitimate half-breed Negro children from England' whose mothers, he said, were 'the scum of the British Isles'.[50]

Black GIs were not the only newcomers to Britain during the war. Although Churchill had flippantly dismissed concerns about discrimination against the black colonial officials, there were those in Whitehall who feared that the abuse of black Britons and black subjects of the British by white Americans would threaten morale in the colonies and among the black servicemen and women in Britain. By 1942, there was a large number of black colonial servicemen and women, whose rights and morale were an issue of material importance to the war effort. At the start of the war the government had yielded to pressure from black organizations and the colonies and announced that black men who were 'not of pure European descent' would be permitted to serve in the British armed forces, overthrowing the policy of the First World War. Black men were also to be allowed to put themselves forward for commissions and be judged on an allegedly equal basis alongside white candidates, although this policy was only to last for the duration of 'the present emergency'.[51] However, the War Office and Colonial Office, using almost the same words as they had done during the First World War, once again concluded that black men from the West Indies 'would be of doubtful military value for combat service overseas, especially against German troops in Europe'.[52]

The fall of France in the early spring of 1940 left Britain alone against the might of the Nazi war machine and cleared the mind of British politicians, who were inspired to take a more pragmatic approach to the deployment of colonial manpower and expertise. Policies were relaxed and men from the West Indies arrived in Britain to carry out essential war work. Six hundred foresters were sent to Scotland from British Honduras, as were three hundred and fifty engineers and electricians to Liverpool. More men followed. Unlike in the First World War, black colonial subjects were deployed in skilled combat roles in the European theatre of operations, and not merely as labourers. More than twelve thousand West Indians served in the British forces during the war, many of them highly skilled specialists. Some were trained and served with the Royal Canadian Air Force, and were deployed to Britain as part of that contingent. Over a hundred men from the West Indies who served with the RAF and Royal Canadian Air Force were decorated during the conflict. Women from the West Indies also served, eighty in the Women's Auxiliary Air Force and thirty in the Auxiliary Territorial Service (the ATS). These black men and women, who were based in Britain and wore uniforms, reported very little racism from white Britons, although a 1945 edition of the patriotically British magazine *John Bull* noted in an editorial that 'Rudeness to colonial service girls in this country is surprisingly common . . . a West Indian girl in the ATS was refused a new issue of shoes by her officer who added: "at home you don't wear shoes anyway".' The editorial lamented that 'Colonial troops came to this country to help us win the war. But they are bitter because the colour bar still exists in Britain.'[53]

In the majority of racist incidents in which black service personnel were assaulted or insulted, the perpetrators were white American GIs. Such incidents began to occur within weeks of the Americans' arrival. In August 1942, a West Indian musician playing in a band during a dance in an English village hall attracted no hostility from a group of white Southern American soldiers so long as he remained on stage – white Americans being accustomed to being entertained by black musicians. However, as a newspaper report revealed, the moment he 'took to the floor with the wife of one of his [white] colleagues in the band, one of the southern American boys probably went across the room and struck him.'[54]

On 23 June 1943, Sergeant Arthur Walrond, an RAFVR wireless operator and gunner from Barbados, was attacked by two white GIs at a dance after asking a white woman to dance. Walrond, who was a journalist by profession, complained to the Colonial Office, stating, 'I came to this country from the British West Indies as a volunteer for Air Crew Duties under the protection of the British Government, and I demand as far as humanly possible that I get that protection and its corresponding consideration.' With striking eloquence, he demanded that the perpetrators of the attack be punished and asked 'that action be taken to ensure the non-recurrence of such an affair as this either with myself or other coloured people in this country . . . I have never been trained to think in terms of nations or races and I had hoped that four years of war would at least have taught the world this lesson. But the long standing underlying prejudice for coloured people despite their value, ability or achievement still remains to rear its ugly head, and leaves the most distasteful gap to be bridged. To say time will remove these ills is not good enough'.[55] That day, Walrond's Stirling bomber was shot down in a mission over Cologne and he was killed.[56]

Black civilians from the colonies were also affected by the imported racism of the white GIs. In the summer of 1944, the West Indian cricketer Learie Constantine booked a room at the Imperial Hotel in Russell Square. Before arriving Constantine took the precaution – thankfully unimaginable today – of asking the hotel if his race would pose any impediment to him staying, and was assured that there would be no problems on that account. When Constantine and his family arrived, on the evening of 30 July, they were informed by the manageress, Margaret O'Sullivan, that they could stay for one night, not the four that he had booked. During the ensuing argument O'Sullivan was heard to say 'he is a nigger . . . We won't have niggers in this hotel.'[57] This, it later transpired, was because also staying in the hotel were a number of white American soldiers, who O'Sullivan believed would object to the presence of a black family. O'Sullivan later claimed that she feared there would be a quarrel between Constantine – who was travelling with his wife and daughter – and the Americans. When the case of *Constantine v. Imperial Hotels Ltd* came to court in 1944 one witness explained that Constantine had reminded the management that 'he was a British subject, and that he saw no reason why Americans, who were aliens, should have any preference at the hotel over a British subject.'[58] Questions about the incident were asked in Parliament and in June 1944, Constantine took the case to the High Court. As racial discrimination was not legally prohibited in Britain at the time, the case rested on contract law. The judge found in Constantine's favour and awarded damages. The case was widely publicized and in certain circles was regarded as a national embarrassment.

The vast majority of the black men and women who served in the British forces during the Second World War did not experience racism of the sort experienced by Learie Constantine. While the number of black people in Britain grew in relative terms, in keeping with the racial policies of the First World War, most of the black people who served in the Second never even set foot in Britain and were deployed either in Africa or in other colonial regions. There were three hundred and seventy-two thousand Africans. The Royal West African Frontier Force (RWAFF) recruited in Nigeria, the Gold Coast and Sierra Leone, their soldiers fighting in the Abyssinian campaign against the Italians between 1940 and 1941, and in Burma against the Japanese. The King's African Rifles (KAR) comprised men from Kenya, Uganda, Tanganyika (now Tanzania), Somaliland and Nyasaland (now Malawi); it took part in the defeat of the Italians in Abyssinia and the capture of the Vichy French colony of Madagascar. Africans too fought against the Japanese in the Burma campaign, which was the first time the KAR and RWAFF had been permitted to fight outside their home continent. Significantly, their opponent was a non-white enemy. The deployment was regarded as a phenomenal success and several of the African troops were decorated, including one who received the British Empire Medal. All of the customary pseudoscientific-racial theories were put forward to explain the Africans' prowess at jungle combat; they were said to be miraculously immune to the diseases of the south-east Asian jungles and somehow naturally adept at fighting in dense tropical undergrowth. Among those who served in the KAR was Hussein Onyango Obama, the grandfather of the 44th President of United States, who was deployed in both Ceylon (now Sri Lanka) and Burma.

FOURTEEN

'Swamped'

In 1942, when black American GIs were being assaulted in British pubs and dance halls, the Colonial Secretary, Viscount Cranbourne, argued that if British military personnel were to be given information to help them appreciate American views on race then American troops should be given similar information to help them understand that the British people did not share their views. But how enlightened were British racial attitudes by the end of the Second World War? Exposure to the full virulence of American racism had powerfully demonstrated that British sentiments were profoundly different from those that prevailed in the American South, but the war had also shown that on the issue of racial mixing, some Britons were less enlightened. The abandonment of many of the mixed-race children fathered by black GIs illustrated the strength of the social stigma surrounding it. That said, it is hard to imagine post-war Britain passing anti-miscegenation laws similar to those that prohibited inter-racial marriage in Virginia at the time. What is certain is that British attitudes were changed by the war, not just from the experience of living alongside the black GIs and fighting alongside airmen and soldiers from the black colonies, but through what had been learnt during the conflict about Nazi racial policies.

One of the most significant outcomes of the Second World War was that it made racism less acceptable, not everywhere and not instantly, but in ways that in the long term proved hugely significant. The biological, Social Darwinian racism that had emerged in the latter half of the nineteenth century, out of which the Nazis' racial theories had arisen, was widely repudiated after 1945, as was the view that race was an appropriate or even meaningful concept around which societies could be organized. The view that race was the 'key to history', as the British Prime Minister Benjamin Disraeli had claimed in the 1850s, lay in tatters. Not only was Social Darwinian racism discredited, so too were the racial pseudo-sciences of eugenics and 'racial-hygiene' that had later emerged. In the post-war years people began to talk of the 'myth of race', and the idea that any of the world's ethnic groups were 'racially pure', a concept that had been absolutely central to the Nazi world-view, was dismissed as a fantasy. The inescapable reality that racism had led to Auschwitz permeated the national consciousness.

Throughout the war, the newsreels and the newspapers had constantly reminded soldiers and civilians alike that a war against Nazi racism was a conflict for freedom, equality and a more inclusive view of humanity. However, the intellectual demolition of race could not undo centuries of racial thinking. Millions of people had become habituated to the idea of race, and instinctively viewed the world in racial terms. This, after all, was how they had been taught to make sense of the world, explain the rise of the European empires and rationalize their injustices. The idea of race, and the practice of racism, had emerged over centuries. It was deeply rooted and to some extent and in some quarters impervious to factual rebuttal. As the dark skin of Africans had for many generations been accepted as a marker of their supposed inferiority, the revelation that there was no scientific basis for this could not be easily assimilated into everyday thinking. For many in Britain the ideologies of imperialism and racial supremacy, along with the visual landscape of racist cartoons, *Boy's Own* adventure stories, gollywogs, 'Little Black Sambo' and a now misremembered cultural echo of Uncle Tom, remained far more potent than reports from the frontiers of the human sciences.

In 1945, soon after the Labour Party's landslide victory in the general election, the British Pan-Africanist leader George Padmore attempted to build on post-war antipathy to racism by writing an open letter to Clement Attlee. Padmore was part of the burgeoning independence movement that was spreading across Africa and the West Indies. His *Open Letter to the Prime Minister* included a forthright condemnation of imperialism but also contained a call for racial discrimination in Britain to be outlawed and made a 'punishable offence'. Attlee did not respond to Padmore, nor did his government address the problem of discrimination or seek to end the colour bar that since at least 1919 had kept black people out of certain British trades and workplaces. The far more pressing issue for the new government was Britain's acute labour shortage, which Attlee and his Cabinet colleagues were determined would be solved using white foreign workers and not black subjects of the British Empire.

In June 1946 the British Cabinet Manpower Working Party determined that in order to meet her post-war target, Britain would need 940,000 additional workers. By the end of the year they had raised their estimate to 1,346,000.[1] To help fill this enormous shortfall, over 100,000 members of the Polish armed forces and their families, who had lived in Britain during the war and fought against the Nazis, were given the right to settle permanently. A further 80,000 European 'Displaced Persons', mostly Ukrainians, Latvians and Poles, who were being housed in miserable camps in Germany and Austria, were also recruited under the European Voluntary Workers scheme (EVW). Throughout the immediate post-war decades the British labour force was further expanded through an influx of Irish immigrants.[2] However, the government actively discouraged immigration by black West Indians.

In early 1947 the Colonial Office dispatched an official to the West Indies to dispel rumours that there were thousands of job vacancies in Britain.[3] One glaring problem with this strategy was that the newsagents of the islands stocked copies of British newspapers like the *South London Daily Press*, and West Indians were able to see for themselves the pages of classified advertisements for positions in British firms. Incredulous local governors and journalists were informed that these were not real openings but 'paper vacancies'. That June, an official from the Ministry of Labour rightly warned that 'It may become extremely embarrassing if at a time of labour shortage there should be nothing but discouragement for British subjects from the West Indies while we go to great trouble

to get foreign workers.'[4] Yet the Ministry of Labour remained stridently opposed to recruitment in the West Indies.

In 1947 the Ministry embarked upon an evaluation exercise
that was ostensibly designed to determine the potential of what
officials described as 'surplus male West Indians'. The findings were
predictably negative. The report suggested – yet again – that black
West Indians would be 'unsuitable for outdoor work in winter
owing to their susceptibility to colds and more serious chest and
lung ailments'.[5] However, it simultaneously concluded that West
Indians, despite being accustomed to the tropics, would be unable
to work in British coal mines as they would find the conditions
underground 'too hot'. In the view of the Ministry of Labour the
temperature range within which black people were capable of
working was extraordinarily narrow, despite the fact that in 1940
Britain had dispatched six hundred men from tropical British
Honduras to work as foresters in the frozen north of Scotland,
and that thousands of West Indian airmen had successfully endured
sub-zero nights in unpressurized RAF bombers on missions over
Germany.

That same year, a hundred and ten Jamaican workers arrived,
unexpectedly, in Britain on the former troopship the *Ormonde*,
having ignored the Colonial Office's untruths about 'paper vacancies'. Among their number were ten stowaways. Rather than being
welcomed to labour-starved post-war Britain, as thousands of European Voluntary Workers had been, the Jamaicans were categorized
as a problem. The next year, British governors in the West Indies
warned London that thousands more West Indians were applying
for passports. The new Colonial Secretary, Arthur Creech Jones,
did his best to inform his colleagues that 'West Indians are well
aware of the labour shortage in Great Britain, and it is known to
them that it is proposed to employ thousands of [European]
Displaced Persons . . . In these circumstances there has been a
natural and immediate demand for the employment of British West
Indians, who are British subjects and many of whom have had
experience of work in Britain during the war years, to relieve the
labour shortage in Britain'.[6] The demand among West Indians for
the chance of employment in Britain was made more acute by the
fact that when the thousands of men who fought for Britain during

the war returned home, they found that their homelands' economies had been devastated. In Jamaica a hurricane in 1944 had caused devastating floods. The destruction had been especially severe in St Thomas parish, which in the 1940s, as it had been in the 1840s, was the island's poorest. It was also the parish in which the Morant Bay Rebellion had broken out and from which a high proportion of the post-war migrants to Britain were to come. The labour shortage in Britain and the economic crisis in the West Indies were the pull and push factors that inspired a wave of West Indian migration that the British government proved unable to prevent, though not for want of trying.

On 22 June 1948 the *Empire Windrush* arrived at Tilbury docks and four hundred and ninety-two men from the West Indies came ashore. A report of their arrival in the imperial 'mother country', in the *London Evening Standard*, carried the headline 'WELCOME HOME'.[7] As the Trinidadian calypso singer Lord Kitchener (real name Aldwyn Roberts) disembarked he was met by a film crew from Pathé News, who asked him to perform his newly composed song, 'London is the Place to Be'. The arrival of the *Empire Windrush* is widely and rightly understood as a great watershed in the black history of Britain and the year she arrived has come to be seen as the symbolic beginning of the modern phase in the relationship between Britain and the West Indies. The government, however, regarded her as an embarrassment. There were instant recriminations in Whitehall and behind the scenes attempts were made to ensure that the *Windrush* did not set a precedent and inspire further migration. Arthur Creech Jones was heavily criticized for having allowed her to set sail. He stood accused of failing to have 'kept a lid on things' and permitting this 'invasion' of Britain by West Indians.[8] The Minister of Labour, George Isaacs, was quick to stress that the West Indians had not been officially invited to Britain, and warned colleagues that 'the arrival of these substantial numbers of men under no organised arrangement is bound to result in considerable difficulty and disappointment . . . I hope no encouragement will be given to others to follow their example.'[9] There had even been attempts to prevent the *Windrush* from leaving Jamaica; Attlee, the Prime Minister, had made enquiries as to whether she might be diverted to East Africa, and the West Indian migrants offered work on groundnut farming projects there.[10] When it became clear that the government was unable to prevent the *Empire Windrush* from docking, or to prevent the migrants from coming ashore – given that they were British subjects carrying British passports – they changed their strategy. The *Windrush* migrants were to be dispersed across the country and while this was being arranged they were warehoused in an old deep-level air-raid shelter near Clapham South underground station, which was reopened to accommodate them. While the government certainly did not welcome their arrival, British industry evidently did. Within a month the government had found work for all but twelve. The rest were hard at work in undermanned and essential industries across the country, from Scotland to Gloucester.[11]

Around half of the migrants on the *Empire Windrush* had been in Britain during the war, serving in the RAF or the army or working in munitions factories, and might therefore be better thought of as being returnees than immigrants. Three days after their arrival the Labour MP Tom Driberg, who had challenged Winston Churchill over the abuse of black GIs in 1942, warned the men from the islands that Britain was 'not a paradise. There may be difficulties', he told them, 'caused through ignorance and prejudice, but don't let it get you down. Try and stand on your own as soon as you can.'[12] That Saturday around forty thousand spectators packed into Villa Park in Birmingham to watch the middleweight boxer Dick Turpin defeat Vince Hawkins and become Britain's first black boxing champion. Turpin was the mixed-race product of an earlier wave of West Indian migration. His father, Lionel Fitzherbert Turpin, from British Guiana (now Guyana), had travelled to Britain in 1914 and joined the Royal Warwickshire Regiment, which ironically was the regiment in which Enoch Powell enlisted during the Second World War. Having side-stepped the First World War colour bar, Turpin served on the Western Front. After being gassed on the Somme he returned to Britain, married a British woman, and raised his mixed-race children.

On the day the *Empire Windrush* reached Tilbury, eleven Labour MPs sent a letter to Attlee requesting that he put in place controls to limit black immigration to Britain. They wrote:

The British people fortunately enjoy a profound unity without uniformity in their way of life, and are blessed by the absence of a colour racial problem. An influx of coloured people domiciled here is likely to impair the harmony, strength and cohesion of our people and social life and cause discord and unhappiness among all concerned.

In our opinion colonial governments are responsible for the welfare of their peoples and Britain is giving these governments great financial assistance to enable them to solve their population problems. We venture to suggest that the British government should, like foreign countries, the dominions and even some of the colonies, by legislation if necessary, control immigration in the political, social, economic and fiscal interests of our people.[13]

These suggestions were profoundly at odds with a bill that was at that moment was making its way through Parliament. During the summer of 1948, as the *Empire Windrush* was crossing the Atlantic, the British Nationality Act was in the latter stages of becoming law. It received Royal Assent on 31 July, five weeks after the West Indians landed at Tilbury. The act, which was in part a response to Canada's introduction of Canadian citizenship, gave the people of the empire who had formerly held the status of British Subject the new status of Commonwealth Citizen. This gave them the right to enter and settle in Britain, which was seen as the necessary continuation of a long British tradition of open borders, which was deemed fitting for a nation at the centre of a vast (if rapidly collapsing) empire. By modern standards, post-war Britain's immigration laws and her reaffirmation of citizenship rights to hundreds of millions of her colonial subjects were incredibly liberal.

Yet MPs of all parties imagined the act would simply enable the continued flow of two-way traffic between Britain and the 'old dominions' – Canada, South Africa, Australia and New Zealand – which were sometimes called the 'white dominions' or the 'old commonwealth'. The act was intended to ensure that British people remained free to settle in the colonies and commonwealth citizens were free to reside in Britain. The people the government envisaged making use of the rights of entry and residence enshrined in the 1948 Act were white people of 'British stock', to use the common phrase of the time, who were coming 'home' to Britain. Their rights of entry and residence in Britain were regarded as exceptionally valuable bonds that held the empire together, and were essential if Britain was to maintain her position as the lode star around which the colonies orbited. Furthermore the traffic between Britain and the old dominions flowed both ways. Most of the seven hundred and twenty thousand Britons who left their war-ravaged homeland between 1946 and 1950 headed for new lives in the old dominions. Australia was the most popular post-war destination for Britons weary of austerity and frustrated by continued rationing.[14] Like many political decisions made in the immediate post-war years the underlying objective was to ensure Britain remained a significant world power, but the emotional appeal of the idea of the old dominions and their deep historical bonds to the 'mother country' was immensely powerful in the 1940s and 1950s.

However, as all commonwealth subjects were theoretically equal, the same rights of entry and residence applied to the non-white peoples of what was called the 'new commonwealth', which included Africa and the West Indies, as well as Asia. Few politicians believed that large numbers of non-white people from the 'new commonwealth' would make use of their new rights to reside in Britain, yet that is exactly what they did. Quite unintentionally, the post-war government that had been busily discouraging immigration by non-white people from the West Indies had signed the warrant for exactly the sort of mass migration they so vehemently opposed. As the bill was debated, men across the West Indies, who had fought for Britain during the war, applied for the British passports to which they were entitled and which, after 1 January 1949, when the Nationality Act came into force, guaranteed them right of entry and residence in Britain.

In August 1948, while the West Indians from the *Empire Windrush* were settling into their new jobs and lodgings, *The Times* reported on disturbances that had broken out in Liverpool. As the next chapter in the black history of Britain was beginning, Liverpool was reliving the nightmare of 1919. What *The Times* reported as 'Liverpool Racial Disturbances' were in fact organized attacks on the homes and clubs of black people.[15] As in 1919, the unions were involved, this time the National Union of Seamen, which had been working hard to prevent black sailors finding employment on British ships. At the union's 1948 annual conference one of the themes for discussion was 'the colour question'.[16] The Assistant General Secretary was happy to boast from the podium that 'In quite a few instances we have been successful in changing ships from coloured to white, and in many instances in persuading masters and engineers that white men should be carried in preference to coloured.'[17] On other occasions 'committees had been set up in the main ports to vet all "coloured" entrants to the country who claimed to be seamen.'[18] When the violence began in 1948, the hostels in which black sailors lived were once again targeted. When, on the second day of the disturbances, a mob two thousand strong attacked one hostel, the police responded exactly as they had done thirty years earlier during the disturbances in Great George Square that led to the death of Charles Wootton: they raided the hostel and arrested the black men trapped inside. What followed in Liverpool was intergenerational distrust of the police by the black community that lingered on into the 1980s.

Between 1945 and 1950 only five thousand migrants from the West Indies arrived in Britain but two unexpected events in the early 1950s contributed to this number increasing significantly. In 1951, Jamaica was struck by Hurricane Charlie, the most ferocious storm to hit the island since 1903. On 16 August, the day before it struck, forecasters predicted Charlie would miss Jamaica, but at 8.30 pm, with winds reaching 130 mph, it shifted course and headed straight for the south-eastern shore. It made landfall at Morant Bay, crashing into that poor blighted town. So strong were the winds that an avenue of palm trees that had been planted along the shoreline were ripped out of the ground. Not even their stumps remained. To the west of Morant Bay, around Kingston, thousands of houses were destroyed and ships from the harbour were flung onto the shore around Port Royal. In Spanish Town every single one of the nine thousand structures, including the old Jamaica Assembly building and the Governor's Residence, from which the announcement of emancipation had been read in August 1838, were damaged. Across the east of the island, fifty thousand people lost their homes and a hundred and sixty-two lost their lives. When hundreds of power lines came down, those who had been thrown into the flood waters were electrocuted. In St Thomas parish, around Morant Bay, crops were uprooted and the topsoil washed away by a storm surge that brought the sea rushing inland.[19] Thousands of people who had been barely able to subsist before the hurricane had even fewer reasons to remain and many looked to emigrate.

The following year, their options were suddenly curtailed when the United States Congress passed the Immigration and Nationality Act (also known as the McCarran–Walter Act). The 1952 act placed new restrictions on entry, reducing the flow of West Indian migrants to a trickle. The number of visas allocated to the British West Indies as a whole was slashed to a mere eight hundred per year and no more than one hundred could be awarded to Jamaicans.[20] The new American restrictions channelled thousands of prospective emigrants towards Britain – the 'mother country'. The numbers arriving in the UK in the 1950s reflected the ambitions of thousands of people to better their lives, and the continued poverty that blighted the islands, but it was also a reflection of the lack of alternatives. From 1948 to 1952 the number of West Indians entering Britain each year was between 1,000 and 2,000. In 1953, the first year after the American Immigration and Nationality Act, the total reached 3,000. It then leaped to 10,000 in 1954, more than quadrupled in 1955 to 42,000 and then, for the next two years, stabilized. The 1956 total was 46,000 and 42,000 came in 1957. There was then a tailing off in 1958 and 1959, for which the respective totals were 30,000 and 22,000.[21]

The general election that returned Winston Churchill to 10 Downing Street in October 1951 resulted in a Conservative government that was every bit as uncomfortable with West Indian migration as the Labour government of Clement Attlee. One member of Churchill's Cabinet, the Marquess of Salisbury (formerly Viscount Cranbourne), warned of the risk that the arrival of large numbers of black people posed a threat to 'the racial character of the English people'.[22] In 1954, during lunch at Chequers with the Governor of Jamaica, Sir Hugh Foot, Churchill expressed his concern that if West Indian migration continued 'we would have a magpie society: that would never do'.[23] A year later Harold Macmillan reported in his diary, with some incredulity, that Churchill thought 'Keep Britain White' might make an appropriate slogan with which to fight the upcoming election.[24] In the aftermath of the Second World War such appeals to racial sentiment were widely regarded as unacceptable.

In the early 1950s, Churchill asked government officials in various departments to devise mechanisms by which West Indians might be kept out of the country, contrary to the rights of entry and residence they enjoyed under the 1948 Nationality Act. The challenge was to draft legislation that specifically targeted non-white immigrants while not appearing to be motivated by racial considerations. Any new law that was overtly racial risked a backlash from sections of the press and public and would damage Britain's standing in the world. Most importantly, such legislation would cause deep resentment among the nations of the multi-racial and then still fledgling British Commonwealth.[25] In 1955 Churchill's government considered introducing a five-year limit on the right of settlement to non-white immigrants from the new Commonwealth but thought better of it at the last minute. The legally simpler option of a blanket withdrawal of the rights of entry and residence bequeathed to all Commonwealth citizens under the 1948 Nationality Act would have antagonized the governments of the old dominions at the very moment that Britain wanted to draw those new nations closer to her, rather than push them further away.

In order to change the public mood and prepare the British people for new legislation that would, in effect, strip non-white immigrants of their rights of entry and settlement, successive British governments set about gathering information that was intended to prove that the black settlers represented a social problem. Five internal investigative studies were launched in the 1950s, by both Labour and Conservative politicians, all of which set out to delineate and define the problems caused to the country by the presence of black migrants and demonstrate the negative effects the host population might face if black people continued to arrive in significant numbers. No comparable investigations were established to discover if the arrival of European Voluntary Workers from the Displaced

Persons camps of post-war Europe might pose similar threats to the social fabric of the nation. The final investigation, set up by the Cabinet in December 1953, was carried out by the Working Party on Coloured People Seeking Employment in The United Kingdom. Within the working party were representatives from the Home Office, the Colonial Office, the Commonwealth Relations Office, the Ministry of Labour and National Service, the Scottish Home Department, the Ministry of Transport and Civil Aviation, and the National Assistance Board. Its report of 17 December 1953 makes for shocking reading today. It suggested that 'coloured workers' struggled to find employment because of their 'irresponsibility, quarrelsomeness and lack of discipline' and stated that black men were 'slow mentally' and in general 'not up to the standards required by British employers'.[26] These claims were made despite the fact that thousands of West Indians were already working in Britain and several major British employers were actively recruiting workers from the West Indies. By 1956, London Transport had begun recruitment in Jamaica and Barbados. British Rail was advertising in the Barbados Labour Office. The British Hotels and Restaurant Association was also in the West Indies seeking to attract new workers and the National Health Service was appealing for West Indian women to come to Britain and train as nurses. Enoch Powell, who was Minister of Health between 1960 and 1963, was among those involved in that recruitment campaign. Cheaper and faster travel, by sea and increasingly by air, was lowering the cost of immigration. British firms including the National Health Service and London Transport were happy to pay to transport new migrants and recoup the money once they began work.

Yet in the same years the language of immigration in Britain was slowly shifting to reflect the changing mood. Whereas migrants from Europe had in the immediate post-war years been described as people full of 'the spirit and stuff of which we can make Britons' and people who would be 'of great benefit to our stock', black men from the colonies were said to be 'unreliable and lazy' and regarded as part of an 'immigration problem'.[27] These terms and other coded phrases became a means through which the racially motivated hostility towards black people could be publicly discussed in ways that did not highlight race or skin colour.[28] By the 1970s

the words 'immigrant' and 'coloured' were being used almost interchangeably, even though only one in three immigrants entering
Britain came from the new Commonwealth.[29] British sociologist
Sheila Patterson undertook a study of West Indian migrants in
Brixton during the 1950s. Asking white residents to describe the
traits that differentiated them from the West Indian migrants, some
complained of their supposed 'primitiveness, savagery, violence,
sexuality, general lack of control, sloth, irresponsibility – all these
are part of the image'.[30] These terms and stereotypes that by the
1950s were firmly and resolutely associated with black people living
in Britain had their roots in the racial theories that had been born
out of the slavery of the eighteenth century and the imperialism of
the nineteenth.

Britain's great post-war imperial dilemma was also largely a
product of the eighteenth and nineteenth centuries. While the
post-war governments fretted about the arrival of West Indian immigrants they also looked on in dismay as the empire built by their
Georgian and Victorian forebears began to collapse. Government
opposition to the immigration of black Commonwealth citizens was
profoundly at odds with the mood of universalism and anti-racialism
in which the multi-racial Commonwealth had been born. Those in
government who favoured imposing immigration controls specifically targeting non-white migrants understood that such laws risked
damaging the Commonwealth and would inevitably give succour to
the Pan-Africanist and independence movements in the West Indies
and Africa. The possibility of drafting legislation that drew a distinction between the white British subjects of the 'old dominions' and
the black citizens of the 'new commonwealth', which included
Africa, the West Indies and the Indian subcontinent, was considered,
but all governments understood that such a move would have been
seen as a blatant attempt to keep black people out. Such a racially
specific immigration act would have been a de facto admission that
the old imperial claims of universal equality and freely given British nationality, irrespective of race, were a charade. Post-war British
governments therefore walked the tightrope between damaging the
Commonwealth project and their general opposition to non-white
migration into Britain. Speaking some years later, Sir David Hunt,
Winston Churchill's Private Secretary, paraphrased the dilemma.

'The minute we said we've got to keep these black chaps out, the whole Commonwealth lark would have blown up.'[31]

The post-war governments were also wary of introducing racially targeted immigration control as they feared a backlash from the sections of the British public who since the war had set their minds against all forms of racial prejudice and welcomed the increasing diversity of their country. Opinion polls on racial attitudes were not conducted until after the Notting Hill riots in 1958, by which time there had already been ten years of official discouragement of immigration and vilification of non-white migrants from the non-white commonwealth.[32] The trajectory of racism in Britain in the post-war years is therefore difficult to ascertain. Sheila Patterson, the author of the sociological study *Dark Strangers*, found that while many white people in Brixton had fixed and negative views of their black neighbours, these prejudiced opinions were not universal.

The common view, which is reflected in the memories of some West Indian migrants from the era, was that the country was split three ways. In his book *The Colour Problem* Anthony Richmond argued that one-third of the population were 'Extremely prejudiced people' who 'strongly resist the idea of having any degree of contact or communication with coloured people. They object vehemently to mixed marriages, but are almost as strongly opposed to having coloured people in their homes, or to working with them in a factory or office. In fact they are generally of the opinion that coloured people should not be allowed in Britain at all.'[33] Jamaican-born Sam King, who served in Britain with the RAF during the Second World War, came back on the *Empire Windrush* and, in 1983, became the first black mayor of the London borough of Southwark, agreed. He defined Anthony Richmond's 'Extremely prejudiced' proportion of the population as the 'third of people in Britain [who] still had imperialist ideas' and felt that 'People from the colonies should be planting bananas and chocolate and whatever it is.' The middle third King regarded as being mildly hostile to black migration and the final third, he thought of as 'just nice, ordinary people' who did not hold racist views.[34]

That final third are often forgotten in our telling of the dispiriting story of the rise of British racism in the 1950s and 1960s, but opposition came from within Britain as well as from without, from white people as well as from black and brown people. Millions of Britons opposed racism, and campaigned against apartheid in South Africa and white-only rule in Rhodesia; they and their votes mattered. It was also likely that many millions of white Britons in the period struggled to reconcile the racial hierarchies and unquestioned white supremacy of the age of empire with which they had been brought up, with the post-war view that racism and racial intolerance were socially unacceptable. Anthony Richmond noted that 'One remarkable fact which emerges from almost all studies of prejudice in Britain is that most people think others more prejudiced than themselves. In so far as their behaviour is largely determined by what they believe to be the expectations of others, discriminatory practices consequent upon prejudices are nearly always attributed to a need for deference to the views of others.'[35] Richmond believed that 'a judicious educational campaign will have little influence on the minority who are severely prejudiced, but could make considerable headway with others. At the present time landladies refuse accommodation because of what their husbands or the neighbours might think; employers refuse accommodation to coloured workers because of what their white employees might say and do; hotel and restaurant managers worry what their clients will think if they admit Negroes; and people make derogatory remarks about coloured people because it seems the thing to do'.[36] There was unquestionably a paradox. Why, asked another British social scientist, were 'coloured people so often . . . shabbily treated when the vast majority of individual Britons are favourably disposed towards them?'[37]

The view from the other side of the 'colour problem' was little examined by sociologists or journalists. The word repeatedly used in the memoirs of the West Indian and African migrants who came to Britain in the post-war decades is 'disappointed'. They were disappointed that the nation they had been told was their 'mother country' treated them so badly, disappointed that skills and talents which the nation had found useful during the war years were disregarded in peacetime and they were ushered into low status or menial jobs. They were deeply disappointed and wounded when they discovered how difficult it was to fulfil the most basic human need and find somewhere to live. Thousands of post-war black migrants were consigned to the poorest parts of Britain's cities and there left prey to predatory landlords such as West London's infamous Peter Rachman. The migrants would have felt an even deeper sense of disappointment had they known the help that was offered to the European Voluntary Workers and denied to them, and that behind closed doors successive governments had plotted to portray them as indolent, immoral and backward. Many felt they been lied to, not just by prospective employers who had actively recruited in the West Indies, but by the British Empire.

The issue that continued to cause the deepest ruptures in Britain in the post-war era, as it had done during the war years, was inter-racial relationships and marriages. Many who regarded themselves as not racist or even anti-racist were opposed to inter-racial rela-tions. Yet, again, there was more tolerance than we might imagine today. The British social scientist Michael Banton, who in the late 1950s was studying social attitudes towards black migrants in Britain, conducted a series of sample interviews which formed part of the research behind his 1959 book *White and Coloured: The Behaviour of British People Towards Coloured Immigrants*. His research revealed that many Britons were largely relaxed about the immigration of non-white people. 76 per cent of his sample agreed with the state-ment 'Coloured people are just as good as us when they have the same training and opportunities', 68 per cent agreed with 'A lot of the coloured people here are very clever' and 67 per cent agreed with, 'If we all behaved in a more Christian way there would not be any colour problem.'[38] Banton regarded 'Responses to the state-ment disapproving of intermarriage' as being 'of particular interest.' He reported that when presented with the statement 'It would be a good thing if people of different races mixed with one another more', 62 per cent of his interviewees approved. Those in favour of mixed marriages made comments such as 'How can anyone stop them if they love each other?', or 'If there's one way of breaking down the colour bar it's through marriage', while 'Those who argued against intermarriage confined themselves to stating what they felt – "it's not right", "looks peculiar", "not natural" ', etc.'

Some people, Banton discovered, still subscribed to the pseudo-scientific ideas that had emerged from the racial eugenics of the early twentieth century, and which suggested that mixed-race children were mentally deficient or prone to other congenital defects. Banton noted that 'When people are asked their views about inter-marriage in general, and are not considering a concrete problem posed by a member of their own family, they are apt to reply that they object to intermarriage "because of the children" . . . people believe that the children of such unions are biologically handicapped. The notion that the children of racially mixed marriages inherit the worst features of both races still lingers.'[39] One of Banton's interviewees remarked, 'Everything about the colour bar comes back to this – the children suffer'. Another said 'It's hard luck on the children being half-castes.' Mixed-race children were seen as a social problem in other ways. They were regarded by some as being neither one thing nor another; as Banton wrote, 'Mixed-blood populations often are in a precarious position; born in poverty and raised among the disinherited, they are ill-prepared for the difficult role they have to play.'[40]

The range of opinion on inter-racial relationships that Banton's research exposed was reflected in a 1958 episode of *People in Trouble*, a topical news discussion programme. The programme-makers unthinkingly categorized inter-racial marriage as a social problem in need of journalistic exploration, and by the very nature of the programme they labelled those in mixed marriages or the products of mixed marriages as 'people in trouble'. Yet the guests they brought together to speak on the subject covered a broad range of opinion and experience. They included a very happily married inter-racial couple and their mixed-race infant son; a privately educated mixed-race half-Nigerian British army officer; and a white British woman unhappily estranged from her apparently abusive Nigerian husband. That Nigerians featured in two of the interviews was testament to the increase in immigration from Africa, as well as the West Indies.

In addition to the 'people in trouble', the programme included interviews with two political figures, who topped and tailed the show, as per the established format. The first was James Wentworth Day, then a prospective parliamentary candidate for the Conservatives. The second was Lord Altrincham, the historian and journalist

John Grigg, who later renounced his title and became a key figure in the Anti-Apartheid Movement. Having interviewed the blissfully content mixed-race family, host Daniel Farson turned to the camera and asserted that 'Many widely travelled and intelligent people in this country would be against mixed marriages'. He then introduced Wentworth Day, describing him as a man who had worked as 'an advisor to the Egyptian government and the Sudan, so you know what you are talking about.' To which Wentworth Day responded, 'Well I've been there and seen them in their own home surroundings. And as a parliamentary candidate I've been into a good many working class houses . . . where there have been many mixed marriages and I've seen the children; and my view is this. That no first class nation can afford to produce a race of mongrels. Now that is what we're doing. Sooner or later that's going to come back on the children. Those children are unfair hostages to the future; it's unfair on the children; it's unfair on the nation. It's one of the reasons why France is a third class nation today. Too much mixed blood. Look at the other angle: the black man, and I refuse this humbug of talking about the "coloured" man; he's black and we're white – has a different set of standards, morals, values and principles. In many cases their grandfathers were eating each other! The lion [sic] doesn't change his spots in all that time!'

After being diverted into general discussion of the supposed character failings of black people, Farson eventually brought Wentworth Day back to the subject of mixed marriages. 'Are you implying' he asked 'that a half-caste is in any way mentally deficient?'

WENTWORTH DAY: Definitely.

FARSON: You've nothing to prove this at all!

WENTWORTH DAY: That unfortunate child is born with an inferiority complex; if it isn't born with it it grows up with it.

FARSON: You can't possibly say that it's 'born' with an inferiority complex. That's something that we instil into it later.

WENTWORTH DAY: We may instil it and also, the pure black people may do it themselves because they have an instinctive contempt you know for what they call 'white trash'.

FARSON: But if conditions were different; there was not this social prejudice, such as you have, and there were not the practical difficulties, then if two people were in love then wouldn't you recommend them to get married?

WENTWORTH DAY: Love is a very curious thing; it depends on how you define it. I think a lot of these mixed marriages are caused purely by downright sex. Or sloppy sentimentality.

FARSON: Have you got a daughter yourself?

WENTWORTH DAY: I have a daughter who is young, charming, intelligent, with taste and discrimination.

FARSON: Well what would you feel if she said she was going to marry a coloured man?

WENTWORTH DAY: I should strongly advise her against it. I should give her all the practical reasons why not. I should ask her if she wanted to wake up in the morning and see a coffee-coloured little imp on the pillow beside her, calling her mummy. If she did marry him I should be bitterly disappointed.

After this extraordinary exchange there followed an interview with Michael Savage, a rather suave and insouciant Scottish-Nigerian ex-public schoolboy. An officer in the British army, Savage explained, in his upper-class Scottish accent, that he had not 'suffered very much' from racial prejudice. When asked by Farson if he would 'consider marrying a white girl', he responded without hesitation, 'If I wanted to marry a white girl I should marry a white girl.'

The final interview was no less remarkable than that with Wentworth Day. In 1958, Lord Altrincham was the editor of the *National and English Review*, and famous in Britain for having recently criticized the Queen's advisers and speech writers, whom he accused of writing speeches that left the monarch sounding like 'a priggish schoolgirl, captain of the hockey team, a prefect, and a recent candidate for Confirmation'.[41] Farson understatedly introduced the controversial peer as 'Someone with strong views on many subjects, including the colour problem' and who was 'completely in favour of mixed marriages, in spite of all the obvious disadvantages'. The interview continued:

LORD ALTRINCHAM: I'm sure that I would never be prejudiced on grounds of colour when it came to marrying, I can't imagine being prejudiced on that ground, it seems to me quite ridiculous that anybody should be.

FARSON: But you might not be but perhaps your friends would and your neighbours, and people who would influence your children?

LORD ALTRINCHAM: That's the whole trouble you see, it's this social atmosphere against mixed marriages which creates the problem. It's because people have got a – a complete bugbear in their minds, a completely unreal idea that mixed marriages are bad that they create a climate in which it is difficult for children of mixed parentage but if there weren't the atmosphere then it would be perfectly normal, just like people with fair hair and dark hair intermarrying.

FARSON: But at the moment this atmosphere is so strong one would hesitate to recommend a mixed marriage even to two people who are in love.

LORD ALTRINCHAM: Well if they're really in love they won't need to have any recommendation, they'll actually do it. And the more people who do it the quicker this beastly atmosphere will be removed.

FARSON: Well how do you think we can help remove it?

LORD ALTRINCHAM: Well I think to just those of us who believe in it to say so as often as possible and those of us who fall in love with coloured people get married as quickly as possible.

FARSON: Now do you think that this atmosphere will change in fifty years, or a hundred years?

LORD ALTRINCHAM: Oh certainly, certainly, I think it is changing now, I think there's certainly a very different atmosphere now from say, before the war, what I remember. And I'm sure in the next fifty years it will have changed dramatically, in fact it will be quite normal. The idea of pure race is nonsense; there isn't such a thing as pure race. We're all the result of mixed marriage in the past and that's why the human race is fairly exciting and fairly interesting.

Farson then wrapped the programme up, characterizing Lord Altrincham's support for inter-racial marriages as one of the two 'extreme points of view' that the programme had aired. 'One has to face the fact', he solemnly concluded, 'that there is this great social prejudice and all the practical difficulties; in fact I cannot honestly say that I am really in favour of mixed marriages but that is because things are as they are and I can only hope that they will change.' At this the screen faded to black and the credits rolled.

That the inter-racial couple and the mixed-race army officer featured in *People in Trouble* reported having encountered very little racial prejudice may, perhaps, have been an effort on their part to make the best of a difficult situation, but they may well have been honestly reporting their genuine experiences, which would concur with Michael Banton's findings that 62 per cent of Britons in the mid-1950s were generally comfortable with the idea of racial mixing – or at least said they were when asked by a researcher. There were certainly many people who were not just comfortable with, but actively in favour of, inter-racial marriages, as Michael Banton's later work suggested. Yet there was also operating in post-war Britain what he called a 'colour scale' through which individuals were ranked not just by their race and skin colour, but also by their socio-economic status.[42] The better off and better educated were, to some extent, insulated from the worst aspects of British racism. But by the late 1950s there were a small number of Britons who were so irreconcilably opposed to racial mixing that the mere sight of mixed-race couples was enough to rouse them to violence.

In 1958, violence broke out in Nottingham and later in the Notting Hill area of London. The disturbances were called riots, but were in reality attacks launched against black people and their homes by white mobs. As is the case with all mass social disturbances, there were multiple causes, and the 'riots' of 1958 have to be seen within the context of the post-war economic downturn, the tradition of inner-city gang violence and the post-war Teddy boy phenomenon.[43] However, one of the sparks for the violence was a strong antipathy among a small number of young white working-class men to inter-racial relationships. In this respect, the 1958 'riots' were not dissimilar to some of the disturbances of 1919.

In Nottingham, the trouble began when white drinkers objected to a black man and a white woman talking together in a bar in the St Ann's area. In only a few hours, a thousand white men were involved in attacks on West Indians, and eight people were hospitalized. When, a week later, a mob of young white men gathered again in Nottingham, intent on inciting further violence, they were disappointed to discover no black people on the streets. After unsuccessfully attempting to break into a lodging house in which black people were thought to live the mob turned against itself. In the aftermath, one regional bus company began offering tours of the parts of the city in which the fighting had taken place, forcing the Lord Mayor of Nottingham to make an appeal for people not to go to the area 'for sightseeing purposes'.

One week later, in Notting Hill, four hundred mainly young, working-class white men carrying improvised weapons launched two successive nights of attacks on local black people and their homes. They were at first unopposed but by the third and fourth nights black residents of Notting Hill, some of whom were former servicemen, had organized and armed themselves. They defended their community vigorously. It was at this point that the police finally stepped in to regain control. In the defence of their homes and communities the West Indians were assisted by some of their white neighbours, who resented the fact that most of the white 'rioters' were thugs and troublemakers who had flocked to Notting Hill from other parts of the capital.

There are two schools of thought about what happened in Britain in 1958. The first is that a succession of liberal post-war governments, obsessed with making a success of the multi-racial Commonwealth, sensitive to foreign opinion and uncertain about Britain's role in the world, finally caught up with a British public who, by 1958, had enough of coloured immigration. The alternative view is that in 1958, sections of the British public caught up with a political class that had never wanted mass coloured immigration and that ever since Clement Attlee had attempted to divert the *Empire Windrush* to East Africa had been attempting to discourage black migrants from coming to the country and devise legislation to refuse them entry.[44] Whichever the case, the 'riots' of 1958 were a watershed moment.

Within a week of the riots in Nottingham, and before the Notting Hill disturbances had hit the news, two Nottingham MPs used the violence as the pretext to call for immigration controls, despite the fact that black people had been the victims rather than the perpetrators of the disturbances. One writer in the *Contemporary Review* argued that the underlying cause of the riots had been the presence of black immigrants. In this perverse reading of events, proximity to members of a 'lesser race' had triggered a moral decline among white working-class Londoners that had inspired them to attack their black neighbours.[45] In the weeks after Notting Hill, small groups of backbench MPs from both major parties felt emboldened enough to demand new immigration controls and link the black populations to crime. The Conservative Martin Lindsey warned of the damage that would be done to the national character if Britain were allowed to become a 'multiracial' society.[46] Norman Manley, the Prime Minister of Jamaica, who alongside his brother Roy had served with the British army on the Western Front during the First World War, travelled to Britain to assess the situation in the aftermath of the riots. While walking the affected area he was, at one point, moved on by police officers after a gang of white youths gathered nearby. Manley defiantly rejected calls being made at the time for a moratorium on passports being issued to West Indian migrants who were planning to travel to Britain and spoke to a large crowd of black Londoners, urging them to stand up for their rights.

But even some of those in Westminster and Fleet Street who understood that these 'race riots' had in fact been thuggish attacks on black people by white gangs went along with the debates about the 'social problems' and 'economic difficulties' that were said to arise from black migration. British subjects who travelled to their imperial mother country on British passports, often at the invitation of British companies, were cast by parts of the press and political class as aliens who, under the right circumstances, might be 'repatriated', a demand that was echoed by the mobs that had terrorized black people on the streets of Nottingham, shouting 'go home' and 'go back to your own country'.[47] Significantly, a poll conducted by Gallup in the summer of 1961 discovered that 67 per cent of the population supported restrictions on immigration from the new Commonwealth. Only 21 per cent of respondents supported a continuation of the liberal arrangements that existed under the 1948 Nationality Act.

The next year, the 1962 Commonwealth Immigrants Act determined that Commonwealth citizens carrying passports that were not issued directly by the UK government, but rather by a British colonial government or governor, would be subject to immigration controls upon entering Britain. The act also placed restrictions on the number of black people from the new Commonwealth permitted to enter the country each year. The Labour Leader of the Opposition, Hugh Gaitskell, decried the act as 'cruel and brutal anti-colour legislation'.[48] It was also pointed out in Parliament that white immigrants from the old dominions would be largely unaffected by the act, and it was suggested that if the government's genuine aim was to reduce the flow of unskilled labour from abroad then the same conditions should be applied to workers from Ireland, who were free to enter the country irrespective of their skills or qualifications. For those on the extreme right, the act did not go far enough.

In 1964, Peter Griffiths, the Conservative candidate in a by-election in Smethwick in the West Midlands, fought on the slogan 'If you want a nigger neighbour vote Labour'. From the hustings, Griffiths advocated not just an end to non-white immigration but the repatriation of those who had already arrived. He won, with a swing of over 7 per cent, and in doing so demonstrated that race and immigration were issues that could win votes. The Labour Prime Minister, Harold Wilson, denounced Griffiths as a 'parliamentary leper' for having run such an openly racist campaign yet the effect on both major parties was considerable. Richard Crossman, Labour Minister for Housing and Local Government, wrote in his diary in 1965,

> Ever since the Smethwick election it has been quite clear that immigration can be the greatest potential vote-loser for the Labour Party if we are seen to be permitting a flood of immigrants to come in and blight the central areas of our cities . . . We have become illiberal and lowered the quotas at a time when we have an acute shortage of labour . . . We felt we had to out-trump the Tories by doing what they would have done and so transforming their policy into a bipartisan policy.[49]

The same year, the Race Relations Act brought in measures to outlaw discrimination on the grounds of race and made incitement to racial hatred a criminal offence. It is today regarded as a landmark in race relations in Britain. However, further Immigration

Acts from 1968 to 1971 removed the last remnants of the rights of entry and residence that had been awarded to Commonwealth citizens by the 1948 Nationality Act and the 1960s ended with perhaps the most infamous speech in British twentieth-century political history.

Enoch Powell's 'Rivers of Blood' speech has been analysed extensively, but what was perhaps most significant about it in the context of the times was that Powell did not couch his opposition to black migration behind numbers, as so many others had done. Powell asserted not that excessive levels of black and Asian people might force too rapid a change on Britain as they took time to assimilate, but that they could never assimilate, by dint of their race and skin colour. Powell directed his fury just not against the immigrants but against their children. In toxically racist language he described British-born children of West Indian origin as 'wide-grinning piccaninnies'. This was an unsubtle but precisely calibrated attack on the younger generation, the British-born children of the immigrants who Powell believed could never become British despite knowing no other homeland. 'The West Indian or Asian does not, by being born in England become an Englishman', he said seven months after the 'Rivers of Blood' speech. 'Time is running against us and them', he warned ominously.[50] In another speech he described skin colour as being like a 'uniform' that could not be removed.

Within a day of the 'Rivers of Blood' speech Powell was sacked from the shadow Cabinet by the Leader of the Opposition, Edward Heath, a fact that is too often overlooked but that stands as evidence of the genuine and principled opposition to racism that existed within both the Conservative and Labour Parties in the post-war period. Just as genuine was the scale of public support for immigration control to limit the numbers of new Commonwealth immigrants. Powell, now in the political wilderness, received 110,000 letters, only 2,300 of which disapproved of the 'Rivers of Blood' speech. A Gallup poll taken at the end of April 1968 reported that 74 per cent of those questioned agreed with him. On 23 April, as the House of Commons debated a second Race Relations Bill, 2,000 London dock workers downed their tools in protest at his sacking. The next day the meat porters of Smithfield market submitted a petition containing ninety-two pages of signatures in his support.

While Powell discussed the possibility of new legislation, some of his followers embarked upon a wave of attacks against black people that those who lived through them have never forgotten. In one of the bleakest chapters in British history, homes were attacked, and there was a wave of racial assaults, some of them serious. Chillingly, wooden crosses were burnt outside the homes of black people in Britain. Martin Luther King had been murdered by a white racist in Memphis just a few months earlier, and the iconography of American racism and the KKK was in the newspapers and in people's minds.[51]

Powell had been characteristically precise in the language of his 'Rivers of Blood' speech and had inverted the symbolism of history by describing the black man as having the 'whip hand over the white man'. His later speeches were equally precise. Powell spoke not just of immigrants and immigration control but of the 'immigrant-descended population'. His targets were the children of the men and women who had left their homes in the West Indies and Africa in the 1940s and 50s. Powell warned on more than one occasion that even a complete halt to the immigration of non-white people into the country would not prevent the expansion of the non-white population. What was needed, he later stated, was a 'Ministry of Repatriation'. Yet by the mid-1970s 40 per cent of the black population were British-born. They had no other country to which they felt a strong bond. They also lacked the immigrants' sense of being outsiders and their willingness to accept rejection and tolerate shabby treatment. Powell called them 'the immigrant-descended population', while even those who claimed to be impartial and objective defined them using the term 'second-generation immigrants', a glaring contradiction that is commonly used today.

Between 1979 and 1989, unemployment in Britain averaged 9.1 per cent, a significant increase. Homelessness was on the rise, as was child poverty and crime. In parts of Britain's inner cities black people were accused of placing even greater strains on already over-stretched public services. They were, at the same time, one of the groups worst affected by the economic downturn; victims of the economic crisis for which they were held partly responsible.[52] By every social indicator – unemployment, overcrowded housing, educational attainment, criminal convictions – black people were profoundly disadvantaged.

In 1978 Margaret Thatcher, then Leader of the Opposition, gave an interview to Granada Television's *World in Action* programme, in which she spoke on the issue of immigration. The future Prime Minister stated that 'people are rather afraid that this country might be rather swamped by people with a different culture and, you know, the British character has done so much for democracy, for law and done so much throughout the world that if there is any fear that it might be swamped people are going to react and be rather hostile to those coming in'.[53] A year later in early 1979 in a newspaper interview she again suggested that 'some people have felt swamped by immigrants. They've seen the whole character of their neighbourhoods change.'[54] While neighbourhoods across Britain had changed since the war for all sorts of reasons, immigration certainly being one of them, immigrants accounted for a mere 4 per cent of the British population in 1979. Yet the word 'swamped' struck home with voters and shocked some commentators. Intentionally or not it was an echo of Enoch Powell's 'Rivers of Blood' speech, redolent of when he had spoken, a decade earlier, of English people who found 'their homes and neighbourhoods changed beyond recognition' and parts of the country that had become 'alien territory'.[55] Thatcher's words were denounced by black British groups and by her political opponents, and criticized by some in her own party including Bernard Levin, a sometime supporter of hers who wrote in *The Times* that, 'If you talk and behave as though black men were some kind of virus that must be kept out of the body politic then it is the shabbiest hypocrisy to preach racial harmony at the same time.'[56]

1981 began with an appalling tragedy. Thirteen young people, all of them black, died when a house in the New Cross area of London was consumed by fire. They were celebrating a birthday party. The police ruled out the possibility that the fire had been started deliberately and, when pushed by the families, dismissed suggestions that if it was an arson attack there might have been racial motives. There was silence from the political class and a strong sense among black Londoners that the authorities were not interested in the deaths of black people. When, in March, around twenty thousand black people marched from Deptford to central London to demand a thorough investigation, sections of the press reported the predominantly peaceful march as a day of riots. When, the next month, the Metropolitan Police began an operation against violent street crime in Brixton, they entered a community that had run out of patience with official indifference, ceaseless harassment and vilification. That police operation, launched in April 1981, made use of the hated 'sus' law (section 4 of the Vagrancy Act 1824, which allowed police officers to stop and search anyone merely on the suspicion that they had intent to commit an offence) and was an exercise in what at the time was called 'hard policing'. The operation was undertaken by the Special Patrol Group, a unit with a terrible reputation among London's black communities. With breathtaking insensitivity that revealed the depth of racism within the force, the Metropolitan Police chose to name the operation 'Swamp 81'. Over two days, 120 plainclothes officers stopped and searched 943 people, arresting 118 on various charges. This heavy-handed operation came on top of a series of incidents that had gradually ratcheted up tensions between young black people and the police, resulting in a complete breakdown of trust, an explosion of anger and a wave of destruction.

The riots of 1981 spread beyond London to other inner-city areas in which young black people, the children of the *Windrush* generation, felt themselves marginalized and persecuted by the police. Riots broke out in Handsworth in Birmingham, Moss Side in Manchester and Toxteth in Liverpool, where deep tensions between the black population and the police had long been festering. Liverpool Chief Constable Kenneth Oxford, almost as if seeking to emphasize and highlight the historical continuities, suggested that the underlying cause of the riots was 'the problem of half-castes in Liverpool.' Mixed-race residents of the city – many of whose families had lived in Liverpool since before the First World War – were described by their own chief constable as 'the product of liaisons between black seamen and white prostitutes in Liverpool 8 [Toxteth]'.[57]

There was a terrible symmetry to the fact that the most serious and sustained of the early 1980s riots took place in the cities from which the slave-traders had set sail in the seventeenth and eighteenth centuries: Liverpool, Bristol and London. Cities that had been enriched by the slave trade and the sugar business saw fires set and barricades erected by young people who were the distant descendants of human cargo. Not far from the flickering flames of the Bristol riots, a statue of Edward Colston, a slave-trader and member of the Royal African Company in the seventeenth century, looked on as the police were driven out of the black St Pauls district.

The riots of the early 1980s were profoundly different from the disturbances of 1919, 1948 and 1958, all of which were at various times described as 'race riots' but were mostly outbursts of violence in which white gangs targeted black people and communities. This was not the case in the 1980s. These riots have been called 'uprisings'. They were fought by young black people in response to years of systematic persecution and prejudice. They were destructive and damaging but they were understandable. While it is clear today that the riots marked the beginning of the end of one chapter, the nature of the new age that followed remains to be seen. The 1990s and the 2000s were, in many ways, better days. Survey after survey plotted the decline of racist sentiment as a younger generation emerged who had not experienced the racism of the post-war period nor been brought up to view the world in racial terms. Yet this period was the era in which the name of Stephen Lawrence was added to the long list of black Britons who have been murdered by racists.

Historians tend to be cautious when it comes to commentating on the modern age, the period through which we are currently living. For me, the period from the 1980s onwards is the one I know from personal memory as well as through historical study, which probably clouds more than it clarifies judgement. But I strongly recall that in the 1980s there was a strong sense among black people of being under siege, and of feeling the need to fight for a place and a future in the country.

One of the ways in which black people, and their white allies, attempted to secure that future was by reclaiming their lost past. The uncovering of black British history was so important because the present was so contested. Black history became critical to the generation whom Enoch Powell could not bring himself to see as British. A history was needed to demonstrate to all that black British children, born of immigrant parents, were part of a longer story that stretched back to the Afro-Romans whose remains are only now being properly identified. It was in the 1980s that the concept of Black History Month was brought to Britain – an idea that been pioneered in the United States back in the 1920s, as 'Negro History Week.'[58] The black past had been largely buried and the task of exhumation took on real urgency during the 1980s. Unusually, history became critical to a whole community, while at the same time being highly personal to those who discovered it. To look at the portrait of Olaudah Equiano for the first time, and stare into the eyes of a black Georgian, was, for me as for many thousands of black Britons, a profound experience. To see Equiano, with his cravat and scarlet coat, was to feel the embrace of the past and of a deeper belonging. The black British history that was written in the 1980s was built on the foundations of earlier scholars like James Walvin, and was expanded by hundreds of committed volunteers; local historians, community historians and brilliant, determined, some-times obsessive amateurs. Most worked and still work outside of academia, producing bottom-up, community-facing local history or uncovering the presence of black people in parts of the British story from which they have been expunged – the world wars, the history of seafaring, the world of entertainment and many others. It is hard to believe that without the recent decades of black history research and writing, the nation, in 2007, would have committed £20 million to commemorate the bicentenary of the abolition of the slave trade. A sum that matched, by chance, the price the nation had paid the slave owners in compensation for the loss of their human property in 1838.

The next step, I contend, is to expand the horizon, and reimagine black British history as not just a story that took place in Britain, and not just as the story of settlement, although it matters enormously. From the sixteenth century onwards, Britain exploded like a supernova, radiating its power and influence across the world. Black people were placed at the centre of that revolution. Our history is global, transnational, triangular, and much of it is still to be written.

Conclusion

The opening ceremony of the 2012 London Olympic Games, a vast, globally televised pageant that celebrated the British national story, and that revelled in the nation's diversity, music and pop culture, included a mock-up, miniature *Empire Windrush*. This replica was made of a metal frame around which had been stretched fabric printed with the covers of hundreds of post-war British newspapers. She appeared in the Olympic stadium as one among a series of symbolic representations of the pivotal events in British history: the Industrial Revolution, the First World War, the campaigns of the Suffragettes, the Jarrow March of 1936 and the creation of the NHS in 1948 – the year the *Windrush* docked at Tilbury.

An average, unremarkable passenger ship, the *Windrush* had a short but remarkable life. She was built in 1930, in Hamburg, by the German firm Blohm & Voss. Her original name was the MV *Monte Rosa*. From 1933 until 1939 she carried working-class German families on cheap holiday cruises, arranged and subsidized by the Nazi Party's Strength Through Joy organization.[1] In 1939, the MV *Monte Rosa* went to war and was requisitioned as a troopship to carry German soldiers to battle in the invasion of Norway. Later, she transported Norwegian Jews from their homeland to Denmark. Most were later deported to Auschwitz, and there murdered. In 1944, the *Monte Rosa* was bombed by the RAF and had limpet mines attached to her hull by members of the Norwegian Resistance, but survived both attacks.[2] She was captured by British forces in 1945, and seized as a prize of war.

In 1954, carrying the name we know her by today, the *Windrush* once again became a troopship. She was carrying British soldiers of the Duke of Wellington's Regiment home from action in the Korean War when an explosion in her engine room killed four of her crew and started a fire. All her passengers were saved but the *Windrush* sank and today lies under the waters of the Mediterranean. After so dramatic a life it is strange that what has made the *Empire Windrush* one of the icons of modern British history is a single, mundane Atlantic crossing she made during the summer of 1948.

The metal-framed, cloth-covered *Windrush* of the 2012 Olympics, replete with ersatz smoke billowing from her two funnels, was accompanied on her procession around the Olympic stadium by a group of twenty-first-century black Londoners. Dressed in baggy 1940s style suits and trilby hats, they carried leather suitcases of the sort their ancestors had arrived with sixty years earlier, and which can be seen stacked up on porter's trolleys and on the platforms of English railway stations in many of the black-and-white photographs of the time.

The London of 1948, to which the *Empire Windrush* brought those early settlers, was busily preparing to host another Olympics. A month and a week after the *Windrush* docked at Tilbury, the 1948 games got under way in London's old Wembley stadium, a relic of the 1924 British Empire Exhibition.[3] The opening ceremony began with the traditional parade of the teams from each competing country. The athletes then were mainly male and the audience that cheered them on almost entirely white, as was case when Arthur Wint, the six-foot-four-inch black Jamaican sprinter, won the 400 metres. Wint took to the podium to receive Jamaica's first ever Olympic gold medal to the strains of 'God Save the King', as Jamaica was then a British Crown Colony so had no anthem of her own. Like half of the men who arrived in London on the *Empire Windrush*, Arthur Wint had served in the Second World War. Having trained in Canada he became a Spitfire pilot for the RAF, rising to become Flight Lieutenant Wint. Fittingly, it was the band of the RAF that played the national anthem as the gold medal was hung around his neck.

Despite the military bands, the pageantry and the appearance of the royal family there are fleeting moments in the official colour film shot to record the 1948 Olympics that hint at the true state of post-war Britain. The Olympic marathon took the runners and the film cameras through a shattered, exhausted, bomb-ravaged London. The runners streaked past bombsites, long since colonized by weeds and saplings. These little background details reveal a country that had barely got back on its feet after the war; that was still counting the pennies and assessing the damage. The need to rebuild the nation and its industries was palpable, and lay behind the post-war labour crisis, which in turn had motivated the men on board *Empire Windrush* to embark upon their journey. Despite the bunting and the jubilant crowds it was clear that London in 1948 was a city in decline. By the 1980s she would have lost two million of her inhabitants. London did not return to her 1939 population peak of 8.6 million until the beginning of 2015, by which point 44 per cent of the Londoners would be officially classified as Black or Minority Ethnic, many of them immigrants or the descendants of immigrants. From among them came some of the dancers and musicians who performed in the opening ceremony of the 2012 Olympics. Many of them were grandchildren of the immigrants of the *Windrush* generation, others were the children of later immigrants from Africa and Asia.

Britain's black population today stands at around 2 million, a little more than 3 per cent of the national total. Over a million black people had made their homes in London by the time of the 2012 Olympics. There had been, at most, a few thousand black Londoners in 1948. The history symbolized by the *Empire Windrush* has become a part of the British story, in a way that no one who attended the 1948 Olympic Games could have possibly imagined. The *Empire Windrush* herself has entered the folklore and vocabulary of the nation. There is a Windrush Square in Brixton, a heritage plaque in Tilbury marks the spot where the ship docked and the West Indian migrants came ashore, and a musical based on the lives and ambitions of the *Windrush* migrants enjoyed a successful run in London's West End.

There is however a potential paradox in all this. The *Windrush* story has the capacity to obscure another deeper history. Those involved in black British history talk of the dangers of the 'Windrush Myth', the widespread misconception that black history began with the coming of that one ship. Yet this idea in turn perpetu- ates the notion that black British history is exclusively a history of black settlement in Britain, rather than a global story of Britain's interaction with Africans on three continents. The 'Windrush Myth' raises the possibility that the story of post-war immigration might overshadow the black British history that the post-war migrants themselves were so eager to see exhumed and have celebrated.

As well as losing sight of the more distant past our focus on the post-war story has meant that, at times, we have been slow to recognize more recent changes. Since the start of the 1980s Britain has undergone a second great wave of black migration, one that has largely gone unnoticed. This new influx lacked a single iconic moment, comparable to the docking of the Windrush in 1948, and it took place in the far less romantic settings of Gatwick and Heathrow airports, but it was in those great hubs of modern air travel that thousands of Africans arrived – despite ever stricter immigration laws. At the turn of the century West Indians still made up the majority of the UK's black population. But, as the 2011 census revealed, between 2001 and 2011 the British African population doubled, through both migration and natural increase. For the first time, probably, since the age of the Atlantic slave trade, the majority of black Britons or their parents have come to this country directly from Africa, rather than from somewhere in the Americas.

The migrants from West Africa were mostly Nigerians and Ghanaians, and tended to be a little wealthier than the West Indians who had come before them, but were certainly not wealthy by global standards. Some came initially to study but ended up staying. Others migrated to join family and set up home, or to take up employment in a Britain that was still hungry for skilled workers. Many of those who arrived from Somalia, Zimbabwe and Sudan came as refugees. The long queues at Britain's airports of British Africans travelling to Accra, Freetown or Lagos, to attend family reunions, weddings or funerals, speak to the strengths of the new connections between Britain and Africa. The great post-war project to build an English-speaking multi-racial Commonwealth with London at its heart, a community of willing nations led by statesmen and businessmen, has, in a sense, been overtaken by globalization and unprecedented levels of world migration. In a form that the politicians of the 1940s did not envisage London remains at the centre of the former empire. The capital has become a node in a vast global network of family connections, remittances, investment and mobility. Despite the questionable attractions of nearer Dubai, millions of Africans still feel powerfully drawn to London.

While the British African population expands, the West Indian population – longer established and more fully integrated – has amalgamated and assimilated more successfully than perhaps any other immigrant group of modern times. The remarkable capacity of West Indian immigrant families to assimilate can be seen in the marriage statistics. Less than half of British West Indians have partners who are also West Indian. According to the *Economist*, 'A child under ten who has a Caribbean parent is more than twice as likely as not to have a white parent.'[4] While West Indians have drawn millions of white British people into their family networks, they and the African migrants have drawn the whole nation towards their cultures and music. Through sports, music, cinema, fashion and (only latterly) television, black Britons have become the standard-bearers of a new cultural and national identity, the globalized hybrid version of Britishness that was so successfully and confidently expressed in 2012. These successes and achievements have been remarkable and in many ways unexpected. The problem is that these good news stories can at times become window-dressing and inspire wishful thinking.

The reality is that disadvantages are still entrenched and discrimination remains rife. A report by the Equality and Human Rights Commission published in August 2016 showed that black graduates in Britain were paid an average 23.1 per cent less than similarly qualified white workers. It revealed that since 2010 there had been a 49 per cent increase in the number of ethnic-minority sixteen- to twenty-four-year-olds who were long-term unemployed, while in the same period there had been a fall of 2 per cent in long-term unemployment among white people in the same age category. Black workers are also more than twice as likely to be in insecure forms of employment such as temporary contracts or working for an agency. Black people are far more often the victims of crime. 'You are more than twice as likely to be murdered if you are Black in England and Wales', said the report, starkly.[5] When accused of crimes, black people are three times more likely to be prosecuted and sentenced than white people.

*

When, as a young man, I began to study history I came to see it as
a way to understand the forces that had brought my parents together,
shaping my own experiences. Like millions of others, I am a product
of Britain's long involvement with Africa: a history of slave-trading
and colonization; but also of traders, missionaries and the Saro
people who, having been liberated from slave ships, returned to
Nigeria from Sierra Leone bringing to Lagos – the city of my birth
– their Anglican faith and their hybrid Anglo-African identity. My
parents were able to meet in the Britain of the 1960s due to links
that had been established in the late nineteenth century between
communities, schools and churches in Lagos, Sierra Leone and other
parts of West Africa and universities in the North of England. The
racist attacks that, two decades later, led to me and my family being
driven from our home by thugs inspired by the National Front were
a feature of another inescapable aspect of that same history – the
development and spread of British racism. The walls of disadvantage
that today block the paths of young black Britons are a mutated
product of the same racism. Knowing this history better, understanding the forces it has unleashed, and seeing oneself as part of a
longer story, is one of the ways in which we can keep trying to
move forward.

ACKNOWLEDGEMENTS

I am indebted to the research, diligence and insights of James Walvin, Peter Fryer, Catherine Hall, Stuart Hall, Paul Gilroy, Folarin Shyllon, Kenneth Little, Kathleen Chater, Marika Sherwood, Phillip D. Curtin, Basil Davidson, Ray Costello, Gretchen Gerzina, Joan Amin Addo, Joseph Opala, Hakim Adi, Marika Sherwood, Eric Williams, Caroline Bressey, Onyeka Nubia, William Pettigrew, Richard Huzzey, Imtiaz Habib, Adam Hochschild, Hugh Thomas, Simon Schama, Vincent Carretta, Richard Blackett, Robert Nowatzki, Christopher Fyfe, Seymour Drescher, David Brion Davis, Miranda Kaufmann, Phillip D. Curtin, Norma Myers, Maya Jasanoff, Matthew Parker, Luke G. Williams, and many others.

I am grateful also to Georgina Morley, Zennor Compton and Nicholas Blake at Pan Macmillan for their incredible patience, instructive insights, numerous corrections and amendments. Thanks as ever to my agent Charles Walker at United Agents. As the writing of any book takes its toll on those around the writer I would like to offer my thanks to my partner, Susie Painter, whose patience, tolerance and gentle criticisms were essential to the writing of this book. To our baby daughter I offer my sincere thanks for sleeping every night and smiling every day. I am eternally grateful to Mrs Marion Olusoga-Ndebele without whose guidance and love I could never have aspired to any sort of literary or intellectual life. I am indebted to my beloved sister Kemi Kilburn of Stadt Creative who designed the black history heritage plaques that were at the heart of this project and which now adorn buildings and monuments on three continents.

This book accompanies a four-part BBC television series that has been the work and passion of a group of remarkable people. I'd like to thank our brilliant series producer James van der Pool and talented producer

528 BLACK AND BRITISH

and director Naomi Austin. The production has been kept on track and repeatedly championed by our formidable Executive Producer Chris Granlund. Thanks also to Producer Shabnam Grewal, Researchers Jyoti Mehta, Mireia O'Prey and Steve Tappin, Production Manager Susan Creighton, and Production Coordinator Temi Suberu. The sumptuous photography for the series was the made possible by the talents of Jon Sayers, Geoffrey Sentamu and Oliver Schofield while the visceral sound-scapes were the work of sound reformists Ian Maclagan and Lucy Pickering. The films were formed and sculpted by Film Editors Darren Jonusas and Sam Billinge.

I am extremely grateful to Martin Davidson and Janice Hadlow, whose idea this project was and whose support empowered me and my colleagues to bring this and other marginalized histories to a wider audience. Additional thanks to Fatima Salaria, whose passion for and commitment to this project went beyond the call of professional duty. Thanks are due also to former Controller of BBC 2 Kim Shillinglaw, who urged me to devise news ways in which black history could be presented to our audiences. The support of BBC Director of Content Charlotte Moore has also been enormously appreciated, as has been that of Head of Commissioning Tom McDonald. Other thanks go to Adam Barker, whose measured advice was gratefully received, and to Judith Nichol Partnerships Manager at the BBC.

In addition to my colleagues at the BBC I would like also to thank our Series Consultant Professor James Walvin, a historian whose work I had admired for a decade before I have the pleasure of getting to know him. We are also thankful to Miranda Kaufman, author of the upcoming book *Black Tudors*, who intellectually held my hand as I ventured into areas beyond my specialisms. Special thanks go to Paul Reid and his team at the Black Cultural Archives, our partners in this endeavour. Our other partners were Heritage Lottery Fund and Historic England.

In addition to these close friends of the production I would like to thank individuals across the world who offered their time and assistance to allow us to tell often difficult chapters in our collective history and who opened up their communities and resources to us. They include William Pettigrew, Joe Alle, Dr Richard Benjamin, Mary Beard, Janina Ramirez, Jo Seaman, Hella Eckhart, Helen Rappaport, Celine Luppo McDaid, Michael Bundock, Michael Ohajuru, Humphrey Welfare, Carolyne Chorachan, Ray Costello and Madeline Heneghan.

Black British history, more than any other area of history I have ever worked in, has been built upon the efforts, labours and passions of committed amateurs – journalists, teachers, community-leaders and local historians. To those pioneers I offer my gratitude and admiration.

BIBLIOGRAPHY

PRIMARY SOURCES

1915 West Ham Police Court Register Charges Court Ledgers 1915,
    West Ham Magistrate Court Records, Newham Archives and Local
    Studies Library.
Jamaica Disturbances: Papers Laid Before The Royal Commission of Inquiry by
    Governor Eyre (London, 1866), p. 3: Despatch from Governor Eyre
    to the Right Hon. Edward Cardwell, M.P. Flamstead, January 1866.
National Maritime Museum, Greenwich, London, Macpherson
    Collection (PAH8184).
TNA: CAB 67/WP(G) 4015.
TNA: CO 1028/22, *Draft Report of Working Party on Coloured People*
    Seeking Employment in The United Kingdom, 17 December 1953.
TNA: E 101/417/2, no. 150.
TNA: E 101/417/6, no. 50.
TNA: FO 371/26206, F. E. Evans, minute, 22 January 1942, Foreign
    Office General Political correspondence, A 10036/257/45.

NEWSPAPERS AND JOURNALS

Anti-slavery Reporter
Anti-Slavery Reporter and Aborigines' Friend
Bath Chronicle
Blackwood's Lady's Magazine
Brighton Gazette
Brighton Herald

Bristol Mercury and Daily Post
Daily Advertiser
Diplomatic Review
Era
Fraser's Magazine for Town and Country
General Evening Post
Gentleman's Magazine
Hansard
Illustrated London News
Independent
Leeds Mercury
Leeds Times
Legal Observer
Liverpool Courier
Liverpool Daily Post
Liverpool Echo
Liverpool Evening Express
Liverpool Weekly Post
London Chronicle
Morning Post
New Statesman and Nation
New York Herald-Tribune
Spectator
Stratford Express
Sunday Pictorial
The Times
Tit-Bits
Virginia Gazette
Wolverhampton Chronicle
York Herald

SECONDARY SOURCES

Addison, Paul, *Churchill: The Unexpected Hero* (2005)
Aldgate, Anthony, Jeffrey Richards, *Britain Can Take It: The British Cinema in the Second World War*, second edition (2007)
Almeida, Dr Joselyn M., *Reimagining the Transatlantic, 1780–1890* (2013)
Ames, Eric, *Carl Hagenbeck's Empire of Entertainments* (2008)

Andrews, Kenneth R., *Trade, Plunder and Settlement: Maritime Enterprise and the Genesis of the British Empire, 1480–1630* (1984)

Anon., 'African Man-Power', *Sun*, Christchurch, vol. III, issue 924, 26 January 1917

Anon., *American slavery: report of a public meeting held at Finsbury Chapel, Moorfields, to receive Frederick Douglass, the American slave, on Friday, May 22, 1846: with a full report of his speech* (1846)

Anon., *Farewell Speech of Mr. Frederick Douglass, Previously to Embarking on Board the Cambria, Upon His Return to America, Delivered at the Valedictory Soiree Given to Him at the London Tavern, on March 30, 1847* (1847)

Anon., *Franco-British Exhibition 1908 Official Guide Section III: The Visible Empire* (1908)

Anon., *Instructions for the Guidance of Her Majesty's Naval Officers Employed in the Suppression of the Slave Trade* (1844)

Anon., *Proceedings of the General Anti-Slavery Convention, Called by the Committee of the British and Foreign Anti-Slavery Society, Held in London, Friday, June 12th, to Tuesday, June 23rd* (1840)

Anon., *The Anti-Slavery Reporter and Aborigines' Friend* (1865)

Arnold, Arthur R., *The History of the Cotton Famine, from the Fall of Sumter to the Passing of the Public Works Act* (2013). (Original work published 1864.)

Arrowsmith, Sarah, *Mappa Mundi: Hereford's Curious Map* (2015)

Baikie, William Balfour, *Narrative of an exploring voyage up the rivers Kwo'ra and Bi'nue (Commonly known as the Niger and Tsádda) in 1854* (1856)

Ball, Edward, *Slaves in the Family* (1998)

Banton, Michael, *White and Coloured: The Behaviour of British People Towards Coloured Immigrants* (1959)

Barkarn, Elazar, *The Retreat of Scientific Racism: Changing Concepts of Race in Britain and the United States Between the World Wars* (1992)

Bennett, G. H., *Destination Normandy: Three American Regiments on D-Day* (2009)

Berlin, Ira, *Generations of Captivity: A History of African-American Slaves* (2009)

Bethell, Leslie, *The Abolition of the Brazilian Slave Trade: Britain, Brazil and the Slave Trade Question, 1807–1869* (2009)

Bindman, David, Henry Louis Gates and Karen C. C. Dalton, *The Image of the Black in Western Art: From the Early Christian Era to the 'Age of Discovery': from the demonic threat to the incarnation of sainthood* (2010)

Black, Jeremy, *A Brief History of Slavery* (2011)

——, *The Atlantic Slave Trade in World History* (2015)

Blackburn, Robin, *The Making of New World Slavery: From the Baroque to the Modern, 1492–1800* (1998)

Blackett, R. J. M., *Building an Antislavery Wall: Black Americans in the Atlantic Abolitionist Movement 1830–1860* (1983)

——, *Divided Hearts: Britain in the American Civil War* (2001)

——, *Making Freedom: The Underground Railroad and the Politics of Slavery* (2013)

Bloom, Harold, *William Shakespeare's Othello* (1987)

Blyth, Robert J., 'Britain, The Royal Navy and the Suppression of Slave Traders in the Nineteenth Century' in Douglas Hamilton and Robert J. Blyth (eds), *Representing Slavery* (2007)

Boime, Albert, *Art in an Age of Counterrevolution, 1815–1848* (2004)

Bolt, Christine, *Victorian Attitudes to Race* (1971)

Bourne, Stephen, *Black Poppies: Britain's Black Community and the Great War* (2014)

Bousquet, Ben, and Colin Douglas, *West Indian Women at War: British Racism in World War II* (1991)

Braidwood, Stephen J., *Black Poor and White Philanthropists: London's Blacks and the Foundation of the Sierra Leone Settlement, 1786–91* (1994)

Bressey, Caroline, 'Of Africa's brightest ornaments: a short biography of Sarah Forbes Bonetta', *Social and Cultural Geography*, vol. 6, no. 2, April 2005

Bressey, Caroline, and Hakim Adi, *Belonging in Europe – The African Diaspora and Work* (2013)

Brown, Jacqueline Nassy, *Dropping Anchor, Setting Sail: Geographies of Race in Black Liverpool* (1994)

Brown, William Wells, *Three Years in Europe; or, Places I have Seen and People I have Met* (1852)

Browne, Janet, *Charles Darwin: The Power of Place* (2003)

Bruder, Edith, *The Black Jews of Africa: History, Religion, Identity* (2008)

Buckner, Phillip Alfred, *Rediscovering the British World* (2005)

Bundock, Michael, *The Fortunes of Francis Barber: The True Story of the Jamaican Slave Who Became Samuel Johnson's Heir* (2015)

Burkhardt, Frederick, Sydney Smith (eds), *The Correspondence of Charles*

Darwin: volume 1, 1821–1836 (1985); volume 2, 1837–1843 (1986); volume 4, 1847–1850 (1985)

Burton, J., and A. Loomba, Race in Early Modern England: A Documentary Companion (2007)

Bynum, W. F., Roy Porter (eds), Companion Encyclopedia of the History of Medicine, vol. 2 (1993)

Campbell, Kofi Omoniyi Sylvanus, Literature and Culture in the Black Atlantic: From Pre- to Postcolonial (2006)

Campbell, Neil, Jude Davies, George McKay, Issues in Americanisation and Culture (2004)

Carlyle, Thomas, 'Occasional Discourse on the Negro Question', Fraser's Magazine for Town and Country (London, vol. XL, February 1849)

——, The Works of Thomas Carlyle: vol. 30, Critical and Miscellaneous Essays, volume 6 (2010)

——, The Selected Works of Thomas Carlyle (2014)

Carretta, Vincent, Unchained Voices: An Anthology of Black Authors in the English-Speaking World of the Eighteenth Century (2004)

——, Equiano, the African: Biography of a Self-made Man (2005)

——, Phillis Wheatley: Biography of a Genius in Bondage (2011)

Cash, Bill, John Bright: Statesman, Orator, Agitator (2011)

Cashmore, E., United Kingdom?: Class, Race and Gender since the War (1989)

Cecil, Richard, The Works of the Rev. John Newton, To which are Prefixed Memoirs of his Life, vol. 2 (1844)

Centre for Contemporary Cultural Studies, EMPIRE STRIKES BACK: Race and Racism in 70's Britain (2004), p. 62

Chamberlin, J. Edward, Come Back to Me My Language: Poetry and the West Indies (1993)

Chater, Kathleen, Untold Histories: Black people in England and Wales during the period of the British slave trade c.1660–1807 (2009)

Christopher, Emma, A Merciless Place: The Fate of Britain's Convicts after the American Revolution (2011)

Christy, David, Cotton is king: or, The culture of cotton, and its relation to agriculture, manufactures and commerce; to the free colored people; and to those who hold that slavery is in itself sinful (1855)

Clarkson, Thomas, The history of the rise, progress, and accomplishment of the abolition of the African slave-trade, by the British Parliament (1836)

Clifford, Mary Louise, *From Slavery to Freetown: Black Loyalists After the American Revolution* (2006)

Cobb, Thomas Read Rootes, *An Historical Sketch of Slavery: From the Earliest Period* (1858)

Coffman, D'Maris, Adrian Leonard and William O'Reilly, *The Atlantic World* (2014)

Colaiaco, James A., *Frederick Douglass and the Fourth of July* (2015)

Coleman, Deirdre, *Romantic Colonization and British Anti-Slavery* (2009)

Conneau, Theophilus, *A Slaver's Log Book: Or 20 Years' Residence in Africa: the Original Manuscript* (1853)

Coombes, Annie E., *Reinventing Africa: Museums, Material Culture and Popular Imagination in Late Victorian and Edwardian England* (1997)

Copley, Esther, *A History of Slavery and Its Abolition* (1839)

Costello, Ray, *Black Tommies: British Soldiers of African Descent in the First World War* (2015)

Cumming, Mark (ed.), *The Carlyle Encyclopedia* (2004)

Curtin, Philip D., *The Image of Africa: British Ideas and Action, 1780–1850*, vol. 2 (1964)

d'Anghiera, Peter Martyr, *The decades of the newe worlde or west India conteynyng the nauigations and conquestes of the Spanyardes, with the particular description of the moste ryche and large landes and ilandes lately founde in the west ocean perteynyng to the inheritaunce of the kinges of Spayne. Wrytten in the Latine tounge by Peter Martyr of Angleria, and translated into Englysshe by Rycharde Eden* (1555)

Dabydeen, David, *Hogarth's Blacks: Images of Blacks in Eighteenth Century English Art* (1987)

Dalton, Karen C. C., 'Art for the Sake of Dynasty: The Black Emperor in the Drake Jewel and Elizabethan Imperial Imagery', in Peter Erickson, Clark Hulse, *Early Modern Visual Culture: Representation, Race, and Empire in Renaissance England* (2000)

Daniels, Roger, *Guarding the Golden Door: American Immigration Policy and Immigrants since 1882* (2004)

Dattel, Gene, *Cotton and Race in the Making of America: The Human Costs of Economic Power* (2011)

Davies, K. G., *The Royal African Company* (1957)

Davis, Lance E., Stanley L. Engerman, *Naval Blockades in Peace and War: An Economic History since 1750* (2006)

Davis, Lee Allyn, *Natural Disasters* (2008)

Delumeau, Jean (trans. Matthew O'Connell), *History of Paradise: The Garden of Eden in Myth and Tradition* (2000)

Desmond, Adrian, and James Moore, *Darwin's Sacred Cause: Race, Slavery and the Quest for Human Origins* (2010)

Dickerson, Vanessa D., *Dark Victorians* (2008)

Douglass, Frederick, *The Frederick Douglass Papers: 1842–1852* (2009)

Dowler, Major General Arthur, *Notes on Relations with Coloured Troops* (1942)

Doy, Gen, *Black Visual Culture: Modernity and Post-Modernity* (1999)

Drescher, Seymour, *Capitalism and Antislavery: British Mobilization in Comparative Perspective* (1987)

——, *The Mighty Experiment: Free Labor Versus Slavery in British Emancipation* (2004)

——, *Abolition: A History of Slavery and Antislavery* (2009)

——, *Econocide: British Slavery in the Era of Abolition* (2012)

Dunn, Richard S., *Sugar and Slaves: The Rise of the Planter Class in the English West Indies, 1624–1713* (2000)

Dyde, Brian, *The Empty Sleeve: The story of the West India Regiments of the British Army* (1997)

Eckardt, Hella, *Objects and Identities: Roman Britain and the North-western Provinces* (2014)

Edwards, Rosalind, Suki Ali, Chamion Caballero, Miri Song (eds), *International Perspectives on Racial and Ethnic Mixedness and Mixing* (2012)

Ellison, Mary, *Support for Secession: Lancashire and the American Civil War* (1973)

Eltis, David, David Richardson, *Atlas of the Transatlantic Slave Trade* (2015)

Equiano, Olaudah, and Vincent Carretta (eds), *The Interesting Narrative and Other Writings: Revised Edition* (2003)

Erickson, Peter, Clark Hulse, *Early Modern Visual Culture: Representation, Race, and Empire in Renaissance England* (2000)

Falconbridge, Anna Maria, *Two voyages to Sierra Leone, during the years 1791-2-3, in a series of letters: By Anna Maria Falconbridge. To which is added, a letter from the author, to Henry Thornton, Esq. M.P. and chairman of the Court of Directors of the Sierra Leone Company* (1794)

Falola, Toyin, and Matthew M. Heaton, *A History of Nigeria* (2008)

Farrar, The Rev. Frederic W., 'Aptitudes of Races', *Transactions of the Ethnological Society of London*, 27 March 1866

File, Nigel, and Chris Power, *Black Settlers in Britain 1555–1958* (1981)

Floyd-Wilson, Mary, *English Ethnicity and Race in Early Modern Drama* (2003)

Forbes, F. E., *Dahomey and the Dahomans: Being the Journals of Two Missions to the King of Dahomey, and Residence at His Capital, in the Year 1849 and 1850* (1851)

Forbes, Lieutenant Frederick Edwyn, *Six Months' Service in the African Blockade, from April to October, 1848, in Command of HMS Bonetta* (1849)

Fox, William, *An Address to the People of Great Britain, on the Propriety of Refraining from the Use of West India Sugar and Rum* (1791)

Frost, Diane, 'Diasporan West African Communities: the Kru in Freetown and Liverpool', *Review of African Political Economy* 29:92 (2002), pp. 285–300

Frost, Diane, and Richard Phillips, *Liverpool '81: Remembering the Riots* (2011)

Fryer, Peter, *Staying Power: The History of Black People in Britain* (1984)

——, *Aspects of British Black History* (1993)

Fury, Cheryl A., *The Social History of English Seamen, 1485–1649* (2012)

Fyfe, Christopher, *History of Sierra Leone* (1962)

Geppert, A., *Fleeting Cities: Imperial Expositions in Fin-de-Siècle Europe* (2010)

Gerzina, Gretchen, *Black London: Life before Emancipation* (1995)

Gilbert, Alan, *Black Patriots and Loyalists: Fighting for Emancipation in the War for Independence* (2012)

Gilroy, Paul, *The Black Atlantic: Modernity and Double Consciousness* (1995)

——, *Postcolonial Melancholia* (2004)

Glasson, Travis, *Mastering Christianity: Missionary Anglicanism and Slavery in the Atlantic World* (2011)

Goodwin, Stefan, *Africa in Europe: Antiquity into the Age of Global Exploration* (2008)

Gott, Richard, *Britain's Empire: Resistance, Repression and Revolt* (2011)

Grant, Ben, *Postcolonialism, Psychoanalysis and Burton: Power Play of Empire* (2008)

Green, Jeffrey, *Black Edwardians: Black People in Britain 1901–1914* (1998)

Guasco, Michael, *Slaves and Englishmen: Human Bondage in the Early Modern Atlantic World* (2014)

Habib, Imtiaz, *Black Lives in the English Archives, 1500–1677: Imprints of the Invisible* (2008)

Hadfield, Andrew, and Paul Hammond (eds.), *Shakespeare and Renaissance Europe* (2004)

Hakluyt, Richard, *The Principal Navigations, Voyages, Traffiques and Discoveries of the English Nation*, 'The second voyage to Guinea set out by Sir George Barne, Sir John Yorke, Thomas Lok, Anthonie Hickman and Edward Castelin, in the yere 1554. The Captaine where of was M. John Lok' (1904 edn)

Hall, Catherine, *Civilising Subjects: Metropole and Colony in the English Imagination 1830–1867* (2002)

——, 'The Lords of Humankind Re-Visited', in *Bulletin of the School of Oriental and African Studies*, University of London, vol. 66, no. 3 (2003), pp. 472–85

Hall, Edith, Richard Alston, Justine McConnell, *Ancient Slavery and Abolition: From Hobbes to Hollywood* (2011)

Hall, Kim F., *Things of Darkness: Economies of Race and Gender in Early Modern England* (1995)

Hamilton, Douglas, and Robert J. Blyth, *Representing Slavery* (2007)

Hammond, James Henry, *Gov. Hammond's Letters on Southern Slavery: Addressed to Thomas Clarkson, the English Abolitionist* (1845)

Hammond, John Craig, Matthew Mason (eds), *Contesting Slavery: The Politics of Bondage and Freedom in the New American Nation* (2011)

Hammond, Richard James, *Portugal and Africa, 1815–1910: A Study in Uneconomic Imperialism* (1967)

Hancock, David, *Citizens of the World: London Merchants and the Integration of the British Atlantic Community, 1735–1785* (1997)

Hansen, Randall, *Citizenship and Immigration in Postwar Britain* (2000)

Harrison, Brian, *Seeking a Role: The United Kingdom 1951–1970* (2010)

Harvey, Thomas, and William Brewin, *Jamaica in 1866: a narrative of a tour through the island: with remarks on its social, educational and industrial condition* (1867)

Heffer, Simon, *Like the Roman: The Life of Enoch Powell* (2014)

Hennessy, Peter, *Having it So Good: Britain in the Fifties* (2007)

Heuman, Gad, *Killing Time: Morant Bay Rebellion Jamaica* (1995)

Heyrick, Elizabeth, *Immediate, not Gradual Abolition* (1824)

Higgins, Iain Macleod, *Writing East: The 'Travels' of Sir John Mandeville* (1997)

Hill, Errol G., and James V. Hatch, *A History of African American Theatre* (2003)

Hill, Pascoe Grenfell, *Fifty Days on Board a Slave-Vessel in the Mozambique Channel, in April and May, 1843* (1844)

Hinton, John Howard, *Memoir of William Knibb, Missionary in Jamaica* (1849)

Hirschfeld, Fritz, *George Washington and Slavery: A Documentary Portrayal* (1997)

Hitchens, Christopher, *Why Orwell Matters* (2002)

Hoare, Prince, *Memoirs of Granville Sharp, esq.* (1820)

Hochschild, Adam, *Bury the Chains: Prophets and Rebels in the Fight to Free an Empire's Slaves* (2005)

——, *Bury the Chains: The British Struggle to Abolish Slavery* (2005)

Holt, Thomas C., *The Problem of Freedom: Race, Labor, and Politics in Jamaica and Britain, 1832–1938* (1992)

Hopkins, A. G., *An Economic History of West Africa* (2014)

Horton, James Africanus Beale, *West African Countries and Peoples, British and Native: A Vindication of the African Race* (1868)

Hughes, Robert, *Fatal Shore* (1982)

Huzzey, Richard, *Freedom Burning: Anti-Slavery and Empire in Victorian Britain* (2012)

Hynes, Samuel Lynn, *Reporting World War II: American journalism, 1938–1944* (1995)

Inikori, Joseph E., Stanley L. Engerman (eds), *The Atlantic Slave Trade: Effects on Economies, Societies and Peoples in Africa, the Americas, and Europe* (1992)

Jackson, Ben, and Robert Saunders, *Making Thatcher's Britain* (2012)

James, Winston, 'The Black Experience in Twentieth Century Britain', in Philip D. Morgan and Sean Hawkins, *The Oxford History of the British Empire Companion Series: Black Experience and the Empire* (2004)

James, Winston, Clive Harris, *Inside Babylon: The Caribbean Diaspora in Britain* (1993)

Jasanoff, Maya, *Liberty's Exiles: The Loss of America and the Remaking of the British Empire* (2011)

Jay, Nancy, *Throughout Your Generations Forever: Sacrifice, Religion, and Paternity* (1992)

Jenkinson, Jacqueline, ' "All in the Same Uniform"? The Participation of Black Colonial Residents in the British Armed Forces in the First World War', *Journal of Imperial and Commonwealth History*, 40:2, pp. 207–30

———, 'Black Sailors on Red Clyteside: rioting, reactionary trade unionism and conflicting notions of "Britishness" following the First World War', *Twentieth Century British History* 19 (1) (2008), pp. 29–60

———, *Black 1919: Riots, Racism and Resistance in Imperial Britain* (2009)

Jobson, Richard, *The Golden Trade* (1623)

Johnson, Walter, *River of Dark Dreams: Slavery and Empire in the Cotton Kingdom* (2013)

Joseph Rowntree Foundation, *Contemporary Social Evils* (2009)

Kaufmann, Miranda, 'Caspar van Senden, Sir Thomas Sherley and the "Blackamoor" Project', *Historical Research*, vol. 81, no. 212 (May 2008), pp. 366–71

———, *Black Tudors* (2017)

Keese, Alexander, *Ethnicity and the Colonial State: Finding and Representing Group Identifications in a Coastal West African and Global Perspective (1850–1960)* (2015)

Kelsey, Harry, *Sir John Hawkins: Queen Elizabeth's Slave Trader* (2003)

Kennedy, Dane, *The Highly Civilized Man: Richard Burton and the Victorian World* (2005)

Kennedy, Greg, Keith Neilson, *Far-flung Lines: Studies in Imperial Defence in Honour of Donald Mackenzie Schurman* (2013)

Kent, Susan Kingsley, *Gender and Power in Britain 1640–1990* (1991)

———, *Aftershocks: Politics and Trauma in Britain, 1918–1931* (2009)

Killingray, David (ed.), *Africans in Britain* (1994)

———, ' "All the King's Men?" British Blacks in the First World War', in R. Lotz and I. Pegg (eds), *Under the Imperial Carpet. Essays in Black British History 1780–1950* (1986)

———, 'The Idea of a British Imperial African Army', *Journal of African History*, vol. 20, no. 3 (1979)

Knight, Ian, *Companion to the Anglo-Zulu War* (2008)

Knight-Bruce, G. W. H., *Memories of Mashonaland* (1895)

Knowles, Mark, *Tap Roots: The Early History of Tap Dancing* (2002)

Koester, Nancy, *Harriet Beecher Stowe: A Spiritual Life* (2014)

Krenn, Michael L., *Race and U.S. Foreign Policy from 1900 Through World War II* (1998)

Kynaston, David, *Austerity Britain, 1945–1951* (2008)

——, *Modernity Britain: Book One: Opening the Box, 1957–1959* (2013)

Langley, J. Ayodele, *Pan-Africanism and Nationalism in West Africa, 1900–1945: a study in ideology and social classes* (1973)

Last, Dick van Galen, Ralf Futselaar, *Black Shame: African Soldiers in Europe, 1914–1922* (2015)

Latimer, John, *The Annals of Bristol in the Eighteenth Century* (1893)

Laurens, Henry, David R. Chesnutt, *The Papers of Henry Laurens*, vol. 16, *September 1, 1782–December 17, 1792* (2002)

Law, Robin, *From Slave Trade to 'Legitimate' Commerce: The Commercial Transition in Nineteenth-Century West Africa* (1998)

——, *Ouidah: The Social History of a West African Slaving 'Port', 1727–1892* (2004)

Lawrance, Benjamin Nicholas, *Amistad's Orphans: An Atlantic Story of Children, Slavery, and Smuggling* (2015)

Layton-Henry, Zig, Paul B. Rich, *Race, Government and Politics in Britain* (2016)

Lee, Jo-Anne, John Lutz, *Situating: Critical Essays for Activists and Scholars* (2005)

Lee, Julia Sun-Joo, *The American Slave Narrative and the Victorian Novel* (2010)

Levy, David M., *How the Dismal Science Got Its Name: Classical Economics and the Ur-Text of Racial Politics* (2002)

Little, K. L., *Negroes in Britain: A Study of Racial Relations in English Society* (1948)

Lloyd, Christopher, *The Navy and the Slave Trade* (1949)

Long, Edward, *Candid Reflections Upon the Judgment Lately Awarded by the Court of King's Bench, in Westminster-Hall, on What Is Commonly Called the Negroe-Cause by a Planter* (1772)

——, *The History of Jamaica. Or, General Survey of the Antient and Modern State of that Island: with Reflections on its Situation, Settlements, Inhabitants, Climate, Products, Commerce, Laws, and Government*, 3 vols (1774)

Longmate, Norman, *The Hungry Mills. The story of the Lancashire cotton famine 1861–5* (1978)

Lorimer, Douglas A., *Colour, Class and the Victorians: English attitudes to the Negro in the mid-nineteenth century* (1978)

Lovejoy, Paul, 'The Volume of the Atlantic Slave Trade: a Synthesis', in *Journal of African History*, no. 23, 1982

Lowther, Kevin G., *The African American Odyssey of John Kizell: A South Carolina Slave Returns to Fight the Slave Trade in His African Homeland* (2012)

McGlynn, Frank, and Seymour Drescher (eds), *The Meaning of Freedom: Economics, Politics, and Culture after Slavery* (1992)

McInnis, Maurie D., *Slaves Waiting for Sale: Abolitionist Art and the American Slave Trade* (2011)

MacKenzie, John (ed.), *Imperialism and Popular Culture* (1986)

MacMaster, Neil, *Racism in Europe: 1870–2000* (2001)

Mancall, Peter C. (ed.), *The Atlantic World and Virginia, 1550–1624* (2007)

Mann, Kristin, *Slavery and the Birth of an African City: Lagos, 1760–1900* (2007)

Marke, Ernest, *In Troubled Waters: Memoirs of My Seventy Years in England* (1975)

Martone, Eric, *Encyclopedia of Blacks in European History and Culture* (2008)

May, Roy, and Robin Cohen, 'The Interaction Between Race and Colonialism: A Case Study of the Liverpool Race Riots of 1919', *Race & Class*, 10/15/1974, vol. 16, issue 2, pp. 111–26

Mayhew, Henry, *London Labour and the London Poor* (1861)

——, *Mayhew's London, Being Selections from London Labour and the London Poor* (1970)

——, *The London Underworld in the Victorian Period: Authentic First-Person Accounts by Beggars, Thieves and Prostitutes* (2012)

Maynard, Douglas H., 'The World's Anti-Slavery Convention of 1840', *Mississippi Valley Historical Review*, vol. 47, no. 3 (December 1960)

Meer, Sarah, *Uncle Tom Mania: Slavery, Minstrelsy, and Transatlantic Culture in the 1850s* (2005)

Miller, Monica L., *Slaves to Fashion: Black Dandyism and the Styling of Black Diasporic Identity* (2010)

Mintz, Steven (ed.), *African American Voices: A Documentary Reader, 1619–1877* (2009)

Mitchell, William Harry, Leonard Arthur Sawyer, *The Empire Ships: A Record of British-built and Acquired Merchant Ships During the Second World War* (1990)

Moody, Harold, *The Colour Bar* (1944)

Moore, Christopher Paul, *Fighting for America: Black Soldiers – the Unsung Heroes of World War II* (2005)

Morgan, Kenneth, *Slavery and the British Empire: From Africa to America* (2007)

Morgan, Philip D., and Sean Hawkins, *The Oxford History of the British Empire Companion Series: Black Experience and the Empire* (2004)

Murphy, Richard, *The Limits of Law: British Efforts to Suppress the Slave Trade, 1818–1850* (Unpublished thesis, University of Colorado at Boulder, History)

Myers, Norma, *Reconstructing the Black Past: Blacks in Britain, c. 1780–1830* (1996)

Myers, Walter Dean, *At Her Majesty's Request: An African Princess in Victorian England* (1999)

Neely, Mark E., Jr., *The Boundaries of American Political Culture in the Civil War Era* (2015)

Nowatzki, Robert, *Representing African Americans in Transatlantic Abolitionism and Blackface Minstrelsy* (2010)

Nussbaum, Felicity A., *The Limits of the Human: Fictions of Anomaly, Race and Gender in the Long Eighteenth Century* (2003)

O'Keeffe, Paul, *A Genius for Failure: The Life of Benjamin Robert Haydon* (2009)

O'Quinn, Daniel, *Staging Governance: Theatrical Imperialism in London, 1770–1800* (2005)

Oldfield, J. R., *Chords of Freedom: Commemoration, Ritual and British Transatlantic Slavery* (2008)

Oldham, James, *English Common Law in the Age of Mansfield* (2004)

Olusoga, David, and Casper W. Erichsen, *The Kaiser's Holocaust: Germany's Forgotten Genocide and the Colonial Roots of Nazism* (2010)

Osuntokun, Akinjide, *Nigeria in the First World War* (1979)

Parsons, Neil, *King Khama, Emperor Joe, and the Great White Queen: Victorian Britain through African Eyes* (1998)

Patterson, Orlando, *Slavery and Social Death* (1982)

Paul, Kathleen, *Whitewashing Britain: Race and Citizenship in the Postwar Era* (1997)

Peach, Ceri, *The Caribbean in Europe: Contrasting Patterns of Migration ond Settlement in Britain, France and The Netherlands*, Research Paper in Ethnic Relations No. 15, October 1991

Pearce, Malcolm, Geoffrey Stewart, *British Political History, 1867–2001: Democracy and Decline* (2002)

Peters, Laura, *Dickens and Race* (2013)

Pettigrew, William A., *Freedom's Debt: The Royal African Company and the Politics of the Atlantic Slave Trade, 1672–1752* (2013)

Phillips, Mike, Trevor Phillips, *Windrush: The Irresistible Rise of Multi-racial Britain* (1998)

Pieterse, Jan Nederveen, *White on Black: Images of Africa and Blacks in Western Popular Culture* (1992)

Pim, Commander Bedford, *The Negro and Jamaica: Read Before the Anthropological Society of London, February 1, 1866, at St. James's Hall, London* (1866)

Poser, Norman S., *Lord Mansfield: Justice in the Age of Reason* (2015)

Potter, Harry, *Law, Liberty and the Constitution: A Brief History of the Common Law* (2015), p. 176

Pybus, Cassandra, *Black Founders: The Unknown Story of Australia's First Black Settlers* (2006)

Rankin, F. Harrison, *The White Man's Grave: A Visit to Sierra Leone, in 1834*, vol. 2 (1834)

Rappaport, Helen, *Queen Victoria: A Biographical Companion* (2003)

Rawley, James A. and Stephen D. Behrendt, *The Transatlantic Slave Trade: A History* (2005)

Reade, Winwood, *Savage Africa; being the narrative of a tour in equatorial, southwestern, and northwestern Africa; with notes on the habits of the gorilla; on the existence of unicorns and tailed men; on the slave-trade; on the origin, character, and capabilities of the negro, and on the future civilization of western Africa* (1863)

Rees, Siân, *Sweet Water and Bitter: The Ships that Stopped the Slave Trade* (2009)

Reynolds, David, 'The Churchill Government and the Black American Troops in Britain During World War II', *Transactions of the Royal Historical Society*, vol. 35 (1985), pp. 113–33

——, *Rich Relations: The American Occupation of Britain, 1942–1945* (2000)

Rice, Alan, *Creating Memorials, Building Identities: The Politics of Memory in the Black Atlantic* (2011)

Rich, Paul B., *Race and Empire in British Politics* (1990)

Richmond, Anthony H., *The Colour Problem* (1955)

Ricketts, Charles, *The Boswells: the story of a South African Circus* (2003)

Rodriguez, Junius P., *Slavery in the United States: A Social, Political, and Historical Encyclopedia, volume 1* (2007)

Rose, Jonathan, *The Intellectual Life of the British Working Classes* (2001)

Rose, Sonya O., *Which People's War?: National Identity and Citizenship in Wartime Britain* (2003)

Rush, Anne Spry, *Bonds of Empire: West Indians and Britishness from Victoria to Decolonization* (2011)

Russell, David Lee, *The American Revolution in the Southern Colonies* (2000)

Ryan, Louise, Wendy Webster, *Gendering Migration: Masculinity, Femininity and Ethnicity in Post-war Britain* (2008)

Samantrai, Ranu, *AlterNatives: Black Feminism in the Postimperial Nation* (2002)

Sandhu, Sukhdev, *London Calling: How Black and Asian Writers Imagined a City* (2004)

Sani, Shehu, *Hatred for Black People* (2013)

Schama, Simon, *Rough Crossings: Britain, the Slaves and the American Revolution* (2009)

Schofield, Camilla, *Enoch Powell and the Making of Postcolonial Britain* (2013)

Schuman, Michael A., *Frederick Douglass: "Truth Is of No Color"* (2009)

Schwarz, Suzanne, 'Extending the African Names Database: New Evidence from Sierra Leone', in *African Economic History*, vol. 38 (2010)

——, 'Reconstructing the Life Histories of Liberated Africans: Sierra Leone in the Early Nineteenth Century', in *History in Africa: A Journal of Method* 39 (January 2012)

Scott, Daryl Michael, 'The Origins of Black History Month', Association for the Study of African American Life and History, *LA Times*, 11 February 2014.

Sharp, Granville, *Extract From A Representation of the Injustice and Dangerous Tendency of Tolerating Slavery, or of Admitting the Least Claim of Private Property in the Persons of Men, in England. In four parts* (1769)

——, *A Short Sketch of Temporary Regulations (until better shall be proposed) for the Intended Settlement on the Grain Coast of Africa, near Sierra Leona* (1786)

Shephard, Ben, 'Showbiz Imperialism: The Case of Peter Lobengula', in John MacKenzie (ed.), *Imperialism and Popular Culture* (1986)

——, *Kitty and the Prince* (2003)

Sherwood, Marika, 'Lynching in Britain', *History Today*, XLIX (1999), pp. 21–3

——, 'Perfidious Albion: Britain, the USA, and Slavery in the 1840s and 1860s', in *Contributions in Black Studies, A Journal of African and Afro-American Studies*, vol. 13, Special Double Issue, 1 January 1995

——, *After Abolition: Britain and the Slave Trade Since 1807* (2007)

Shukla, Sandhya, and Heidi Tinsman, *Imagining Our Americas: Toward a Transnational Frame* (2007)

Smith, Graham, *When Jim Crow met John Bull: Black American soldiers in World War II Britain* (1987)

Smith, Richard, *Jamaican Volunteers in the First World War: Race, Masculinity and the Development of a National Consciousness* (2004)

——, 'Loss and Longing: Emotional Responses to West Indian Soldiers during the First World War', *Round Table* (2014), vol. 103, no. 2, pp. 243–52

Smith, Robert Sydney, *The Lagos Consulate, 1851–1861* (1979)

Snyder, Terri L., *The Power to Die: Slavery and Suicide in British North America* (2015)

Sokol, B., *Shakespeare and Tolerance* (2008)

Soumonni, Elisée, 'The compatibility of the slave and palm oil trades in Dahomey 1818–1858', in Robin Law, *From Slave Trade to 'Legitimate' Commerce: The Commercial Transition in Nineteenth-Century West Africa* (1998)

Stanziani, Alessandro, *Debt and Slavery in the Mediterranean and Atlantic Worlds* (2016)

Starling, John, Ivor Lee, *No Labour, No Battle: Military Labour during the First World War* (2009)

Stephen, Daniel, *The Empire of Progress: West Africans, Indians, and Britons at the British Empire Exhibition, 1924–25* (2013)

Stilwell, Sean, *Slavery and Slaving in African History* (2014)

Stoddard, Lothrop, *The Rising Tide of Color Against White World-Supremacy* (1920)

Stowe, Harriet Beecher, *A Key to Uncle Tom's Cabin; Presenting the Original Facts and Documents Upon Which the Story is Founded Together with Corroborative Statements Verifying the Truth of the Work* (1853)

——, *A reply to "The affectionate and Christian address of many thousands of women of Great Britain and Ireland, to their sisters, the women of the United states of America". By Mrs. Harriet Beecher Stowe, in behalf of many thousands of American women* (1863)

——, *Uncle Tom's Cabin: or, Life Among the Lowly*, Applewood Edition (2001)

Stuart-Stephens, Major Darnley, 'Our Million Black Army', *English Review*, October 1916.

Tabili, Laura, 'The Construction of Racial Difference in Twentieth-Century Britain: The Special Restriction (Coloured Alien Seamen) Order, 1925', *Journal of British Studies* 33 (January 1994), pp. 54–98

Taylor, Miles (ed.), *The Victorian Empire and Britain's Maritime World, 1837–1901: The Sea and Global Power* (2013)

Taylor, Thomas E., *Running the Blockade During the American Civil War* (1896)

Thomas, Hugh, *The Slave Trade: History of the Atlantic Slave Trade, 1440–1870* (1997)

Thomsett, Michael C., *Heresy in the Roman Catholic Church: A History* (2011)

Thomson, Ian, *The Dead Yard: Tales of Modern Jamaica* (2009)

Thorne, Christopher, 'Britain and the black G.I.s: Racial issues and Anglo-American relations in 1942', *Journal of Ethnic and Migration Studies*, vol. 3, issue 3, (1974) pp. 262–71

Tomkins, Stephen, *The Clapham Sect: How Wilberforce's Circle Transformed Britain* (2012)

Trexler, Richard C., *The Journey of the Magi: Meanings in History of a Christian Story* (2014)

Twells, Alison, *British Women's History: A Documentary History from the Enlightenment to World War I* (2007)

Underhill, Edward Bean, *The Tragedy of Morant Bay: A Narrative of the Disturbances in the Island of Jamaica in 1865* (1895)

Ungerer, Gustav, *The Mediterranean Apprenticeship of British Slavery* (2008)

Van Cleve, George William, *A Slaveholders' Union: Slavery, Politics, and the Constitution in the Early American Republic* (2010)

Virdee, Satnam, *Racism, Class and the Racialized Outsider* (2014)

Walvin, James, *Black and White: The Negro and English Society, 1555–1945* (1973)

——, *England, Slaves and Freedom, 1776–1838* (1986)

——, *A Short History of Slavery* (2007)

——, *The Zong: A Massacre, the Law and the End of Slavery* (2011)

Ward, A. W., and G. P. Gooch (eds), *The Cambridge History of British Foreign Policy 1783–1919* (1922–23)

Ward, Steve, *Beneath the Big Top: A Social History of the Circus in Britain* (2014)

Watts, John, *The Facts of the Cotton Famine* (1866)

Waugh, Edwin, *Lancashire Sketches* (1869)

Webster, Wendy, *Imagining Home: Gender, 'Race' and National Identity, 1945–64* (1998)

Williams, Eric, *Capitalism and Slavery* (1944)

Williams, Gomer, *History of the Liverpool Privateers and Letters of Marque: With an Account of the Liverpool Slave Trade* (1897).

Williams, Jack, *Cricket and Race* (2001)

Williams, Joseph John, *Psychic Phenomena of Jamaica* (2011)

Winegard, Timothy C., *Indigenous Peoples of the British Dominions and the First World War* (2014)

Wood, Marcus, *Blind Memory: Visual Representations of Slavery in England and America, 1780–1865* (2000)

Worger, William H., Nancy L. Clark, Edward A. Alpers, *Africa and the West: From the slave trade to conquest, 1441–1905* (2010)

Yafa, Stephen, *Cotton: The Biography of a Revolutionary Fiber* (2006)

Ziegler, Philip, *London at War, 1939–1945* (1995)

NOTES

PREFACE

1 Tim Bale, *The Conservatives Since 1945: The Drivers of Party Change* (2012), p. 127.

INTRODUCTION: 'Years of Distant Wandering'

1 David Hancock, *Citizens of the World: London Merchants and the Integration of the British Atlantic Community, 1735–1785* (1997), p. 1.
2 Anna Maria Falconbridge, *Narratives of Two Voyages to the River Sierra Leone during the years 1791-1792-1793* (1794), p. 23.
3 Hancock, *Citizens of the World*, p. 2.
4 Falconbridge, *Narratives of Two Voyages*.
5 Among the first to work on Bunce Island was Dr M. C. F. Easmon in the 1940s. From the 1970s onwards the American archaeologist Joseph Opala became heavily involved in research into the island and its place in the Atlantic slave trade. It was Opala who made the links between Bunce Island and the Gullah people of South Carolina and Georgia. More recent work has been carried out by the American archaeologist Christopher DeCorse.
6 See Edward Ball, *Slaves in the Family* (1998).
7 Gretchen Gerzina, *Black London: Life before Emancipation* (1995), p. 3.
8 Geoffrey Littlejohns, *Independent*, 7 August 1995, quoted in Sukhdev Sandhu, *London Calling: How Black and Asian Writers Imagined a City* (2004), p. 1.
9 The date for this speech is often given as 1964. Most sources however report that it was delivered on 23 April 1961.
10 Ben Jackson and Robert Saunders, *Making Thatcher's Britain* (2012), p. 239.
11 Quoted in Simon Heffer, *Like the Roman: The Life of Enoch Powell* (2014), p. 335.
12 Jackson and Saunders, *Making Thatcher's Britain*, p. 239.
13 Heffer, *Like the Roman*, p. 337.

14 Ceri Peach, *The Caribbean in Europe: Contrasting Patterns of Migration and Settlement in Britain, France and The Netherlands*, Research Paper in Ethnic Relations No. 15, October 1991.

15 See Paul Gilroy, *Postcolonial Melancholia* (2004).

16 Randall Hansen, *Citizenship and Immigration in Postwar Britain* (2000), p. 188.

17 Satnam Virdee, *Racism, Class and the Racialized Outsider* (2014), p.115.

18 Stuart Hall, 'Black Chronicles II' (2008), http://autograph-abp.co.uk/exhibitions/black-chronicles-ii

19 Kim F. Hall, *Things of Darkness: Economies of Race and Gender in Early Modern England* (1995), p. 222.

20 See Karen C. C. Dalton, 'Art for the Sake of Dynasty: The Black Emperor in the Drake Jewel and Elizabethan Imperial Imagery', in Peter Erickson, Clark Hulse, *Early Modern Visual Culture: Representation, Race, and Empire in Renaissance England* (2000).

21 Quoted in Edith Hall, Richard Alston, Justine McConnell, *Ancient Slavery and Abolition: From Hobbes to Hollywood* (2011), p. 36.

22 The details were supplied by the men; the navy made no attempt to check them. For example, in the *Victory*, the seaman George Ryan is listed as born in Africa, but he is recorded as being born in Monserrat in the *Jalouse*'s muster books in 1809.

23 K. G. Davies, *The Royal African Company* (1957), p. 67.

24 See David M. Levy, *How the Dismal Science Got Its Name: Classical Economics and the Ur-Text of Racial Politics* (2002).

ONE: 'Sons of Ham'

1 Thanks to Dr Richard Benjamin for his guidance on the evidence of the African presence in Cumbria.

2 Hella Eckardt, *Objects and Identities: Roman Britain and the North-western Provinces* (2014), p. 74.

3 Peter Fryer, *Staying Power: The History of Black People in Britain* (1984), p. 2.

4 See *York Herald*, 15 August 1901; and *An Inventory of the Historical Monuments in City of York*, volume 1, *Eburacum, Roman York*. Originally published by Her Majesty's Stationery Office, London, 1962.

5 Eckardt, *Objects and Identities*, p. 86.

6 Edith Bruder, *The Black Jews of Africa: History, Religion, Identity* (2008), p. 25.

7 Bruder, *Black Jews of Africa*, p. 25.

8 J. Burton and A. Loomba, *Race in Early Modern England: A Documentary Companion* (2007), p. 46.

9 Burton and Loomba, *Race in Early Modern England*, p. 46.

10 Iain Macleod Higgins, *Writing East: The 'Travels' of Sir John Mandeville* (1997), pp. 9–12.

11 Quoted in Kofi Omoniyi Sylvanus Campbell, *Literature and Culture in the Black Atlantic: From Pre- to Postcolonial* (2006), p. 72.

12 Sarah Arrowsmith, *Mappa Mundi: Hereford's Curious Map* (2015), p. 53.

13 Jean Delumeau (trans. Matthew O'Connell), *History of Paradise: The Garden of Eden in Myth and Tradition* (2000), p. 72.

14 Michael C. Thomsett, *Heresy in the Roman Catholic Church: A History* (2011), p. 187.

15 Stefan Goodwin, *Africa in Europe: Antiquity into the Age of Global Exploration* (2008), p. 172.

16 Kenneth R. Andrews, *Trade, Plunder and Settlement: Maritime Enterprise and the Genesis of the British Empire, 1480–1630* (1984), p. 106.

17 Andrews, *Trade, Plunder and Settlement*, p. 106.

18 Hugh Thomas, *The Slave Trade: History of the Atlantic Slave Trade, 1440–1870* (1997), p. 154.

19 Richard Hakluyt, *The Principal Navigations, Voyages, Traffiques and Discoveries of the English Nation*, 'The second voyage to Guinea set out by Sir George Barne, Sir John Yorke, Thomas Lok, Anthonie Hickman and Edward Castelin, in the yere 1554. The Captaine where of was M. John Lok'.

20 Hakluyt, *Principal Navigations*, quoted in Burton and Loomba, *Race in Early Modern England*, p. 129.

21 Hakluyt, *Principal Navigations*, vol. 4 (1907), p. 101.

22 Andrews, *Trade, Plunder and Settlement*, p. 109.

23 David Northrup, in Peter C. Mancall (ed.), *The Atlantic World and Virginia, 1550–1624* (2007), p. 177.

24 Peter Martyr d'Anghiera, *The decades of the newe worlde or west India conteynyng the nauigations and conquestes of the Spanyardes, with the particular description of the moste ryche and large landes and ilandes lately founde in the west ocean perteynyng to the inheritaunce of the kinges of Spayne. Wrytten in the Latine tounge by Peter Martyr of Angleria, and translated into Englysshe by Rycharde Eden* (1555), p. 358.

25 Harry Kelsey, *Sir John Hawkins: Queen Elizabeth's Slave Trader* (2003), p. 31.

26 See Gustav Ungerer, *The Mediterranean Apprenticeship of British Slavery* (2008).

27 Cheryl A. Fury, *The Social History of English Seamen, 1485–1649* (2012), p. 76.

28 Hakluyt, *Principal Navigations*, p. 330.

29 Michael Guasco, *Slaves and Englishmen: Human Bondage in the Early Modern Atlantic World* (2014), p. 106.

30 Burton and Loomba, *Race in Early Modern England*, p. 108.

31 Jan Nederveen Pieterse, *White on Black: Images of Africa and Blacks in Western Popular Culture* (1992), p. 18; and Richard C. Trexler, *The Journey of the Magi: Meanings in History of a Christian Story* (2014), p. 102.

32 David Bindman, Henry Louis Gates and Karen C. C. Dalton, *The Image of the Black in Western Art: From the early Christian Era to the 'Age of Discovery': from the demonic threat to the incarnation of sainthood* (2010), p. 4.

33 Burton and Loomba, *Race in Early Modern England*, p. 109.

TWO: 'Blackamoors'

1 The belief that Africans were the descendants of the biblical Ham did not necessarily translate into support for their enslavement. As the historian Robin Blackburn points out, when the English trader Richard Jobson visited West Africa in the 1620s he expressed his confident belief that Africans were the descendants of the disgraced son of Noah, but was adamant in his disdain for the slave trade. See Robin Blackburn, *The Making of New World Slavery: From the Baroque to the Modern, 1492–1800* (1998).

2 See Imtiaz Habib, *Black Lives in the English Archives, 1500–1677: Imprints of the Invisible* (2008); and Miranda Kaufmann, *Black Tudors* (2017).

3 Guasco, *Slaves and Englishmen*, p. 103; Habib, *Black Lives*, p. 198.

4 Peter Fryer, *Staying Power: The History of Black People in Britain* (1984), p. 9.

5 In November 1513 another boy, again given the name Henry, was to be born to Henry and Catherine. That infant lived for only a few hours and was the third of the six pregnancies of Catherine of Aragon, from which only one child, Mary, would survive.

6 TNA: E 101/417/2, no. 150.

7 Miranda Kaufmann, 'Blanke, John (*fl.* 1507–1512)', *Oxford Dictionary of National Biography*, Oxford University Press, Sept 2014.

8 TNA: E 101/417/6, no. 50.

9 Kaufmann, 'Blanke, John'.

10 Fryer, *Staying Power*, p. 2.

11 Fryer, *Staying Power*, p. 9.

12 Miranda Kaufmann, in David Dabydeen, John Gilmore and Cecily Jones, *The Oxford Companion to Black British History* (2010), p. 487.

13 Burton and Loomba, *Race in Early Modern England*, p. 136.

14 TNA, *Tudor Royal Proclamations*, vol. 3, pp. 221–2 (c. January 1601).

15 TNA, *Tudor Royal Proclamations*, vol. 3, pp. 221–2 (c. January 1601).

16 Miranda Kaufmann, 'Caspar van Senden, Sir Thomas Sherley and the "Blackamoor" Project', *Historical Research*, vol. 81, no. 212 (May 2008), pp. 366–71.

17 My thanks go to Dr Miranda Kaufmann for her advice on Casper Van Senden.

18 Eric Martone, *Encyclopedia of Blacks in European History and Culture* (2008), p. 201.

19 Harold Bloom, *William Shakespeare's Othello* (1987), p. 45.

20 Guasco, *Slaves and Englishmen*, p. 105.

21 Mary Floyd-Wilson, *English Ethnicity and Race in Early Modern Drama* (2003), p. 2.

22 B. Sokol, *Shakespeare and Tolerance* (2008), p. 117.

23 Andrew Hadfield and Paul Hammond (eds), *Shakespeare and Renaissance Europe* (2004), p. 5.

24 Richard S. Dunn, *Sugar and Slaves: The Rise of the Planter Class in the English West Indies, 1624–1713* (2000), p. 240.

25 Jeremy Black, *The Atlantic Slave Trade in World History* (2015), p. 46.

26 Dunn, *Sugar and Slaves*, p. 240.

27 Thomas, *The Slave Trade*, p. 176.

28 D'Maris Coffman, Adrian Leonard and William O'Reilly, *The Atlantic World* (2014), p. 446.

29 Coffman et al., *The Atlantic World*, p. 448; and William A. Pettigrew, *Freedom's Debt: The Royal African Company and the Politics of the Atlantic Slave Trade, 1672–1752* (2013), p. 25.

30 Pettigrew, *Freedom's Debt*, p. 11.

31 James A. Rawley and Stephen D. Behrendt, *The Transatlantic Slave Trade: A History* (2005), p. 139.

32 Rawley and Behrendt, *The Transatlantic Slave Trade*, p. 139.

33 Pettigrew, *Freedom's Debt*, p. 11.

34 Fryer, *Staying Power*, p. 18.

THREE: 'For Blacks or Dogs'

1 Robert Hughes, *Fatal Shore* (1982), p. 19.

2 *Nocturnal Revels, or the History of King's-Place and Other Modern Nunneries*, vol. 1 (1779), quoted in Alison Twells, *British Women's History: A Documentary History from the Enlightenment to World War I* (2007), p. 194.

3 Norma Myers, *Reconstructing the Black Past: Blacks in Britain 1780–1830* (1996), p. 48.

4 *Daily Advertiser*, 13 December 1744, reprinted in Nigel File and Chris Power, *Black Settlers in Britain 1555–1958* (1981), p. 8.

5 Kathleen Chater, *Untold Histories: Black people in England and Wales during the period of the British slave trade c.1660–1807* (2009), p. 86.

6 Cited in Gomer Williams, *History of the Liverpool Privateers and Letters of Marque: With an Account of the Liverpool Slave Trade* (1897), p. 78. The *Tatler* of 1709 was a journal founded by Richard Steele. The modern publication is named after this original but is not a successor company.

7 Cited in Williams, *History of the Liverpool Privateers*, p. 478.

8 See David Dabydeen, *Hogarth's Blacks: Images of Blacks in Eighteenth Century English Art* (1987), p. 101.

9 James Walvin, *Black and White: The Negro and English Society 1555–1945* (1973), p. 50.

10 John Latimer, *The Annals of Bristol in the Eighteenth Century* (1893), p. 15.

11 Latimer, *The Annals of Bristol*, p. 147.

12 Latimer, *The Annals of Bristol*, p. 146.

13 Latimer, *The Annals of Bristol*, p. 147.

14 Quoted in K. L. Little, *Negroes in Britain: A Study of Racial Relations in English Society* (1948), p. 198.

15 Quoted in Gretchen Gerzina, *Black London: Life before Emancipation* (1995), p. 42.

16 *Gentleman's Magazine*, October 1764, p. 493.

17 Walvin, *Black and White*, p. 47.

18 Edward Long, *Candid Reflections Upon the Judgment Lately Awarded by the Court of King's Bench, in Westminster-Hall, on What Is Commonly Called the Negroe-Cause by a Planter* (1772).

19 Walvin, *Black and White*, p. 46.

20 See Chater, *Untold Histories*, p. 43.

21 *Notes and Queries*, vol. 6, 1852. Reprint. London: Forgotten Books, 2013. pp. 410–11. Quoted in Walvin, *Black and White*, p. 48.

22 Dabydeen, *Hogarth's Blacks*, p. 30.

23 *Daily Register*, 18 October 1765, reprinted in Nigel File and Chris Power, *Black Settlers in Britain 1555–1958* (1981), p. 12.

24 *British Apollo*, 13 February 1708, reprinted in File and Power, *Black Settlers*, p. 11.

25 Quoted in Dabydeen, *Hogarth's Blacks*, p. 30.

26 Joshua Reynolds, *Portrait of the Prince of Wales*. Arundel Castle.

27 *Elizabeth Murray, Lady Tollemache, later Countess of Dysart and Duchess of Lauderdale (1626–1698) with a Black Servant by Sir Peter Lely* (Soest 1618 – London 1680), circa 1651.

28 *Lady Grace Carteret, Countess of Dysart (1713–1755) with a Child (possibly Lady Frances Tollemache [1738–1807]), a Black Servant, Cockatoo and Spaniel*. Johann Aegidius Eckhardt (d. Chelsea 1779), circa 1740.

29 *The Character of A Town-Miss* (1680), p. 7. Quoted in Fryer, *Staying Power*, p. 31.

30 *Heyday! Is this my daughter Anne!* F. E. Adams invt. et fecit. The Lewis Walpole Library Image ID lwlpr04459.

31 Chater, *Untold Histories*, p. 85.

32 *The Orthodox Gentleman's Magazine*, quoted in Myers, *Reconstructing the Black Past*, p. 71.

33 Chater, *Untold Histories*, p. 93.

34 *Bath Chronicle*, 10 February 1763.

35 *Daily Courant*, 29 March 1719, reprinted in File and Power, *Black Settlers in Britain*, p. 14.

36 Eric Williams, *Capitalism and Slavery* (1944), p. 44.

37 Cited in Williams, *History of the Liverpool Privateers*, p. 477.

38 Fryer, *Staying Power*, p. 22.

39 Thomas Read Rootes Cobb, *An Historical Sketch of Slavery: From the Earliest Period* (1858), p. cxlvi. Quoted in Michael Bundock, *The Fortunes of Francis Barber: The True Story of the Jamaican Slave Who Became Samuel Johnson's Heir* (2015), p. 61 and Monica L. Miller, *Slaves to Fashion: Black Dandyism and the Styling of Black Diasporic Identity* (2010), p. 50.

40 'Fielding's Penal Laws of London', 1768, in *The Retrospective Review*, vol XII, ed. Henry Southern and Sir Nicholas Harris Nicolas (London, 1825), p. 221.

41 *Gentleman's Magazine*, October 1764, p. 493.

42 Quoted in Little, *Negroes in Britain*, p. 198.

43 Seymour Drescher, *Capitalism and Antislavery: British Mobilization in Comparative Perspective* (1987), p. 33.

44 See Chater, *Untold Histories*.

45 Felicity A. Nussbaum, *The Limits of the Human: Fictions of Anomaly, Race and Gender in the Long Eighteenth Century* (2003), p. 167.

46 *London Chronicle*, 16–18 February 1764, quoted in Fryer, *Staying Power*, p. 69.

47 In Bundock, *The Fortunes of Francis Barber*, p. 99.

48 Henry Mayhew, *The London Underworld in the Victorian Period: Authentic First-Person Accounts by Beggars, Thieves and Prostitutes* (2012), pp. 364–5.

49 Chater, *Untold Histories*, p. 94.

50 Drescher, *Capitalism and Antislavery*, p. 34.

51 Drescher, *Capitalism and Antislavery*, p. 35.

52 See Chater, *Untold Histories*.

53 See Terri L. Snyder, *The Power to Die: Slavery and Suicide in British North America* (2015), p. 122.

54 Latimer, *The Annals of Bristol*, p. 492.

55 Latimer, *The Annals of Bristol*, p. 492.

56 Fryer, *Staying Power*, p. 73.

57 Quoted in Gerzina, *Black London*, p. 53.

58 Tim Macquiban, 'Africanus, Scipio (*c.*1702–1720)', *Oxford Dictionary of National Biography*, Oxford University Press, 2004.

59 Quoted in Chater, *Untold Histories*, p. 228.

60 Quoted in Fryer, *Staying Power*, pp. 23–4.

61 Chater, *Untold Histories*, p. 93.

62 Caroline Bressey and Hakim Adi, *Belonging in Europe – The African Diaspora and Work* (2013), p. 16.

63 Lady Mary Coke (*Letters and Journals*, 1.194–5), quoted in Vincent Carretta, 'Soubise, Julius (*c.*1754–1798)', *Oxford Dictionary of National Biography*, Oxford University Press, 2004.

64 Vincent Carretta, *Unchained Voices: An Anthology of Black Authors in the English-Speaking World of the Eighteenth Century* (2004), p. 7.

65 A point made by the music journalist Bernard Gordillo, quoting the *Gentleman's Magazine*, 1780.

FOUR: 'Too Pure an Air for Slaves'

1 Prince Hoare, *Memoirs of Granville Sharp, esq.* (1820), p. 32.

2 Quoted in Adam Hochschild, *Bury the Chains: Prophets and Rebels in the Fight to Free an Empire's Slaves* (2005), p. 43.

3 Hoare, *Memoirs of Granville Sharp*, p. 33.

4 Hoare, *Memoirs of Granville Sharp*, p. 33.

5 Hoare, *Memoirs of Granville Sharp*, p. 34.

6   Hoare, *Memoirs of Granville Sharp*, p. 36.

7   1694, *Gelly v. Cleve*.

8   Quoted in Fryer, *Staying Power*, p. 116.

9   Norman S. Poser, *Lord Mansfield: Justice in the Age of Reason* (2015), p. 288.

10   Travis Glasson, *Mastering Christianity: Missionary Anglicanism and Slavery in the Atlantic World* (2011), p. 79.

11   Quoted in Harry Potter, *Law, Liberty and the Constitution: A Brief History of the Common Law* (2015), p. 176.

12   Quoted in Potter, *Law, Liberty and the Constitution*, p. 176.

13   Quoted in Potter, *Law, Liberty and the Constitution*, p. 176.

14   Quoted in Potter, *Law, Liberty and the Constitution*, p. 176.

15   James Walvin, *England, Slaves and Freedom, 1776–1838* (1986), p. 39.

16   Granville Sharp, *Extract From A Representation of the Injustice and Dangerous Tendency of Tolerating Slavery, or of Admitting the Least Claim of Private Property in the Persons of Men, in England. In four parts* (1769), pp. 20–21.

17   Sharp, *Extract From A Representation*, p. 20.

18   Hoare, *Memoirs of Granville Sharp*, p. 49.

19   Hoare, *Memoirs of Granville Sharp*, p. 49.

20   Hoare, *Memoirs of Granville Sharp*, p. 52.

21   Esther Copley, *A History of Slavery and Its Abolition* (1839), p. 212.

22   Hoare, *Memoirs of Granville Sharp*, pp. 53–4.

23   Fryer, *Staying Power*, p. 119.

24   Hoare, *Memoirs of Granville Sharp*, pp. 53–4.

25   James Walvin, *Black and White: The Negro and English Society, 1555–1945* (1973), p. 120.

26   Thomas Clarkson, *The history of the rise, progress, and accomplishment of the abolition of the African slave-trade, by the British Parliament* (1836), p. 62.

27   Hoare, *Memoirs of Granville Sharp*, p. 60.

28   Hoare, *Memoirs of Granville Sharp*, p. 70.

29   Poser, *Lord Mansfield*, p. 293.

30   James Oldham, *English Common Law in the Age of Mansfield* (2004), p. 308.

31   Quoted in Fryer, *Staying Power*, p. 123.

32   Gretchen Gerzina, *Black London: Life before Emancipation* (1995), p. 120.

33   Poser, *Lord Mansfield*, p. 293.

34   *The Legal Observer, Or, Journal of Jurisprudence*, vol. 6, p. 64.

35   *The Legal Observer*, p. 64.

36   Hoare, *Memoirs of Granville Sharp*, p. 77.

37   *Arguments on the Negro Cause. Mr. Hargrave's arguments in the case of James Somerset, the Negro lately determined by the court of the Kings bench, The Gentleman's and London Magazine*, December 1772, p. 779.

38   T. B. Howell, *A Complete Collection of State Trials*, vol. XX, 1 January 1816, p. 80.

39   Poser, *Lord Mansfield*, p. 293.

40   Howell, *State Trials*, p. 79.

41 Quoted in Fryer, *Staying Power*, p. 124.

42 Howell, *State Trials*, pp. 79–80.

43 Walvin, *Black and White*, p. 126.

44 Walvin, *Black and White*, p. 126.

45 Quoted in Daniel O'Quinn, *Staging Governance: Theatrical Imperialism in London, 1770–1800* (2005), p. 54.

46 Quoted in Paul Kosmetatos, 'A portrait of a banking calamity', http://www.cam.ac.uk/research/discussion/a-portrait-of-a-banking-calamity From James Boswell, *The Scots Magazine*, vol. 34, p. 312.

47 Quoted version comes from a letter to the *General Evening Post* of 21–23 June 1772.

48 Howell, *State Trials*, p. 82.

49 Quoted in Fryer, *Staying Power*, p. 69 and Vincent Carretta, *Equiano, the African: Biography of a Self-made Man* (2005), p. 208.

50 See Walvin, *Black and white*, p. 127.

51 Poser, *Lord Mansfield*, p. 297.

52 Quoted in Alan Gilbert, *Black Patriots and Loyalists: Fighting for Emancipation in the War for Independence* (2012), p. 8.

53 Quoted in Carretta, *Equiano*, p. 208.

54 Hoare, *Memoirs of Granville Sharp*, p. 91.

55 Quoted in Gilbert, *Black Patriots*, p. 8.

56 Quoted in Fryer, *Staying Power*, p. 126.

FIVE: 'Province of Freedom'

1 George William Van Cleve, *A Slaveholders' Union: Slavery, Politics, and the Constitution in the Early American Republic* (2010), p.35.

2 Norman S. Poser, *Lord Mansfield: Justice in the Age of Reason* (2013), p. 296.

3 Van Cleve, *A Slaveholders' Union*, p. 37.

4 Vincent Carretta, *Phillis Wheatley: Biography of a Genius in Bondage* (2011), p. 130.

5 Alan Gilbert, *Black Patriots and Loyalists: Fighting for Emancipation in the War for Independence* (2012), p. 9.

6 A point expansively and eloquently made by Alan Gilbert in *Black Patriots and Loyalists*.

7 Michael Bundock, *The Fortunes of Francis Barber: The True Story of the Jamaican Slave Who Became Samuel Johnson's Heir* (2015), p. 112.

8 Gilbert, *Black Patriots and Loyalists*, p. 6.

9 Van Cleve, *A Slaveholders' Union*, p. 38.

10 David Lee Russell, *The American Revolution in the Southern Colonies* (2000), p. 69.

11 John Craig Hammond, Matthew Mason (eds), *Contesting Slavery: The Politics of Bondage and Freedom in the New American Nation* (2011), p. 57.

12 *Virginia Gazette*, 25 November 1775.

13 See Orlando Patterson, *Slavery and Social Death* (1982).

14 Quoted in Pybus, *Black Founders*, p. 18.

15 Gilbert, *Black Patriots*, pp. 174–5.

16 Gilbert, *Black Patriots*, p. 175.

17 Kevin G. Lowther, *The African American Odyssey of John Kizell: A South Carolina Slave Returns to Fight the Slave Trade in His African Homeland* (2012), p. 98.

18 Henry Laurens, David R. Chesnutt, *The Papers of Henry Laurens*, vol. 16, *September 1, 1782–December 17, 1792* (2002), p. 79.

19 Quoted in Maya Jasanoff, *Liberty's Exiles: The Loss of America and the Remaking of the British Empire* (2011), p. 80.

20 Quoted in Jasanoff, *Liberty's Exiles*, p. 88.

21 Fritz Hirschfeld, *George Washington and Slavery: A Documentary Portrayal* (1997), p. 26.

22 Pybus, *Black Founders*, p. 37.

23 Stephen J. Braidwood, *Black Poor and White Philanthropists: London's Blacks and the Foundation of the Sierra Leone Settlement, 1786–91* (1994), p. 31.

24 Peter Fryer, *Staying Power: The History of Black People in Britain* (1984), p. 193.

25 Fryer, *Staying Power*, p. 193.

26 Fryer, *Staying Power*, p. 193.

27 Braidwood, *Black Poor*, p. 68.

28 Pybus, *Black Founders*, p. 44.

29 Simon Schama, *Rough Crossings: Britain, the Slaves and the American Revolution* (2009), p. 218.

30 Braidwood, *Black Poor*, p. 85.

31 See Deirdre Coleman, *Romantic Colonization and British Anti-Slavery* (2009), p. 28.

32 Braidwood, *Black Poor*, p. 86.

33 See Emma Christopher, *A Merciless Place: The Fate of Britain's Convicts after the American Revolution* (2011), and David Olusoga and Casper W. Erichsen, *The Kaiser's Holocaust: Germany's Forgotten Genocide and the Colonial Roots of Nazism* (2010).

34 Seymour Drescher, *The Mighty Experiment: Free Labor Versus Slavery in British Emancipation* (2004), p. 91.

35 Braidwood, *Black Poor*, p. 87.

36 Fryer, *Staying Power*, p. 197.

37 Coleman, *Romantic Colonization*, p. 29.

38 Braidwood, *Black Poor*, p. 93.

39 Christopher Fyfe, *A History of Sierra Leone* (1962), p. 16.

40 Adam Hochschild, *Bury the Chains: Prophets and Rebels in the Fight to Free an Empire's Slaves* (2005), p. 152.

41 Braidwood, *Black Poor*, p. 132.

42 Fryer, *Staying Power*, p. 201.

43 *Two voyages to Sierra Leone, during the years 1791-2-3, in a series of letters: By*

Anna Maria Falconbridge. To which is added, a letter from the author, to Henry Thornton, Esq. M.P. and chairman of the Court of Directors of the Sierra Leone Company (1794), pp. 64, 65.

44 Simon Schama, *Rough Crossings: Britain, the Slaves and the American Revolution* (2009), p. 193.

45 Norma Myers, *Reconstructing the Black Past: Blacks in Britain, c. 1780–1830* (1996), p. 127.

46 Prince Hoare, *Memoirs of Granville Sharp, esq.* (1820), p. 317.

47 Hoare, *Memoirs of Granville Sharp*, p. 313.

48 Hoare, *Memoirs of Granville Sharp*, p. 345.

49 Quoted in Fyfe.

50 Granville Sharp, *A Short Sketch of Temporary Regulations (until better shall be proposed) for the Intended Settlement on the Grain Coast of Africa, near Sierra Leona* (1786), p. 22.

51 Sharp, *A Short Sketch*, p. 27.

52 Braidwood, *Black Poor*, p. 86.

53 Hoare, *Memoirs of Granville Sharp*, pp. 320–21.

54 Hoare, *Memoirs of Granville Sharp*, pp. 320–21.

55 Hoare, *Memoirs of Granville Sharp*, pp. 313–14.

56 Hoare, *Memoirs of Granville Sharp*, p. 314.

57 Hoare, *Memoirs of Granville Sharp*, p. 344.

58 Hoare, *Memoirs of Granville Sharp*, pp. 345–6.

59 Hoare, *Memoirs of Granville Sharp*, p. 353.

60 Document made available to author at Sierra Leone Archives, Freetown.

61 Document made available to author at Sierra Leone Archives , Freetown.

62 Hochschild, *Bury the Chains*, p. 178.

63 Hochschild, *Bury the Chains*, p. 202.

64 Hochschild, *Bury the Chains*, p. 203.

65 Hochschild, *Bury the Chains*, p. 206.

66 Mary Louise Clifford, *From Slavery to Freetown: Black Loyalists After the American Revolution* (2006), p. 126.

67 Hochschild, *Bury the Chains*, p. 208.

SIX: 'The Monster is Dead'

1 Richard Jobson, *The Golden Trade* (1623), p. 89.

2 Edward Long, *The History of Jamaica. Or, General Survey of the Antient and Modern State of that Island: with Reflections on its Situation, Settlements, Inhabitants, Climate, Products, Commerce, Laws, and Government*, 3 vols (1774), vol. 1, pp. 493–4.

3 Seymour Drescher, *Econocide: British Slavery in the Era of Abolition* (2012), p. 24.

4 Printed in the *London Chronicle*, 18–20 June 1772.

5 Printed in the *London Chronicle*, 18–20 June 1772.

6 For the most comprehensive account of the *Zong* affair see James Walvin, *The Zong: A Massacre, the Law and the End of Slavery* (2011).

7 Prince Hoare, *Memoirs of Granville Sharp, esq.* Appendix Number VIII SHIP ZONG, p. xviii.

8 James Walvin, *A Short History of Slavery* (2007), p. 152.

9 Kenneth Morgan, *Slavery and the British Empire: From Africa to America* (2007), p. 157.

10 William Fox, *An Address to the People of Great Britain, on the Propriety of Refraining from the Use of West India Sugar and Rum* (1791), p. 4.

11 Morgan, *Slavery and the British Empire*, p. 155.

12 Quoted in Vincent Carretta, *Unchained Voices: An Anthology of Black Authors in the English-Speaking World of the Eighteenth Century* (2013), p. 150.

13 Hoare, *The Memoirs of Granville Sharp*, p. 374.

14 One of the two models of the *Brooks* is held by Hull Museums. See http://www.hullcc.gov.uk/museumcollections/collections/storydetail.php?irn=154

15 Richard Cecil, *The Works of the Rev. John Newton, To which are Prefixed Memoirs of his Life*, vol. 2 (1844), p. 438.

16 Steven Mintz (ed.), *African American Voices: A Documentary Reader, 1619–1877* (2009), p. 69.

17 Stephen Tomkins, *The Clapham Sect: How Wilberforce's Circle Transformed Britain* (2012), p. 98.

18 Adam Hochschild, *Bury the Chains: The British Struggle to Abolish Slavery* (2005), p. 86.

19 John Almon, John Debrett, John Stockdale, *The Parliamentary Register*, vol. XXIII (1788), p. 606.

20 Olaudah Equiano and Vincent Carretta (eds), *The Interesting Narrative and Other Writings: Revised Edition* (2003), p. 343.

21 *British and Foreign State Papers*, vol. V: *1817–1818* (1837), p. 559.

22 These are Seymour Drescher's figures, quoted in Kenneth Morgan, *Slavery and the British Empire: From Africa to America* (2007), p. 168.

23 Elizabeth Heyrick, *Immediate, not Gradual Abolition* (1824), pp. 2–3.

24 Hochschild, *Bury the Chains*, p. 326.

25 Richard Gott, *Britain's Empire: Resistance, Repression and Revolt* (2011), p. 265.

26 Hochschild, *Bury the Chains*, p. 344.

27 John Howard Hinton, *Memoir of William Knibb, Missionary in Jamaica* (1849), p. 49.

28 Hinton, *William Knibb*, p. 261.

29 Hinton, *William Knibb*, p. 262.

SEVEN: Moral Mission

1 For an explanation of the discrepancies between the number of delegates and attendees, see Douglas H. Maynard, 'The World's Anti-Slavery

Convention of 1840', *Mississippi Valley Historical Review*, vol. 47, no. 3 (December 1960).

2 Catherine Hall, 'The Lords of Humankind Re-Visited', in *Bulletin of the School of Oriental and African Studies*, University of London, vol. 66, no. 3 (2003), pp. 472–85.

3 Drescher, *Abolition*, p. 267.

4 Hall, 'The Lords of Humankind Re-Visited', pp. 472–85.

5 *Description of Haydon's picture of the Great Meeting of Delegates held at the Freemasons' Tavern, June 1840, for the abolition of slavery and the slave trade throughout the world* (1840), p. 8.

6 *Description of Haydon's picture*, p. 9.

7 *Proceedings of the General Anti-Slavery Convention, Called by the Committee of the British and Foreign Anti-Slavery Society, Held in London, Friday, June 12th, to Tuesday, June 23rd* (1840), p. iii.

8 *Proceedings of the General Anti-Slavery Convention*, p. 543.

9 Quoted in Maynard, 'The World's Anti-Slavery Convention of 1840', p. 468.

10 *Proceedings of the General Anti-Slavery Convention*, p. 11.

11 *Proceedings of the General Anti-Slavery Convention*, p. 22.

12 Trollope quoted in Richard Huzzey, *Freedom Burning: Anti-Slavery and Empire in Victorian Britain* (2012), p. 18. Darwin quoted in Dr Joselyn M. Almeida, *Reimagining the Transatlantic, 1780–1890* (2013), p. 195.

13 R. J. M. Blackett, *Building an Antislavery Wall: Black Americans in the Atlantic Abolitionist Movement 1830–1860* (1983), p. 7.

14 Blackett, *Building an Antislavery Wall*, p. 10.

15 R. J. M. Blackett, *Making Freedom: The Underground Railroad and the Politics of Slavery* (2013), pp. 22–3.

16 *Proceedings of the General Anti-Slavery Convention*, p. 3.

17 *Proceedings of the General Anti-Slavery Convention*, pp. 12–13.

18 *Proceedings of the General Anti-Slavery Convention*, p. 3.

19 *American slavery: report of a public meeting held at Finsbury Chapel, Moorfields, to receive Frederick Douglass, the American slave, on Friday, May 22, 1846: with a full report of his speech* (1846).

20 Quoted in Sandhya Shukla and Heidi Tinsman, *Imagining Our Americas: Toward a Transnational Frame* (2007), p. 94.

21 Huzzey, *Freedom Burning*, p. 39.

22 Blackett, *Building an Antislavery Wall*, p. 15.

23 *Wolverhampton Chronicle*, March 1852.

24 Suzette Spencer and the *Dictionary of Virginia Biography*, 'Henry Box Brown (1815 or 1816–after February 26, 1889)'. *Encyclopedia Virginia*. Virginia Foundation for the Humanities, 4 Nov. 2014. Web. 10 Jan. 2016.

25 Blackett, *Building an Antislavery Wall*, p. 4.

26 Henry Mayhew, *London Labour and the London Poor* (1861), pp. 425–8.

27 Henry Mayhew, *The London Underworld in the Victorian Period: Authentic First Person Accounts by Beggars, Thieves and Prostitutes* (2012), pp. 364–5.

28 William Wells Brown, *Three Years in Europe; or, Places I have Seen and People I have Met* (1852), pp. 112–13.

29 Cited in James A. Colaiaco, *Frederick Douglass and the Fourth of July* (2015), p. 21.

30 Frederick Douglass, *The Frederick Douglass Papers: 1842–1852* (2009), Douglass to Jonathan D. Carr, 1 November 1847, pp. 267–8.

31 'England Should Lead the Cause of Emancipation: An Address Delivered in Leeds, England, on December 23, 1846', *Leeds Times*, 26 December 1846. Gilder Lehrman Center for the Study of Slavery, Resistance, and Abolition http://glc.yale.edu/england-should-lead-cause-emancipations.

32 Blackett, *Building an Antislavery Wall*, p. 6.

33 Douglass, *The Frederick Douglass Papers*, Henry C. Wright to Frederick Douglass, 12 December 1846.

34 Douglass, *The Frederick Douglass Papers*, Douglass to Wright, 22 December 1846.

35 *Farewell Speech of Mr. Frederick Douglass, Previously to Embarking on Board the Cambria, Upon His Return to America, Delivered at the Valedictory Soiree Given to Him at the London Tavern, on March 30, 1847* (1847). Gilder Lehrman Center for the Study of Slavery, Resistance, and Abolition http://glc.yale.edu/farewell-british-people

36 Quoted in Robert Nowatzki, *Representing African Americans in Transatlantic Abolitionism and Blackface Minstrelsy* (2010), p. 46.

37 Nowatzki, *Representing African Americans*, p. 44.

38 Blackett, *Building an Antislavery Wall*, p. 159.

39 Albert Boime, *Art in an Age of Counterrevolution, 1815–1848* (2004), p. 582.

40 Paul O'Keeffe, *A Genius for Failure: The Life of Benjamin Robert Haydon* (2009), p. 406.

41 Hall, 'The Lords of Humankind Re-Visited', pp. 472–85.

42 Quoted in Laura Peters, *Dickens and Race* (2013), p. 64.

43 Quoted in Julia Sun-Joo Lee, *The American Slave Narrative and the Victorian Novel* (2010), p. 3.

44 *Wolverhampton Chronicle*, March 1852.

45 Jonathan Rose, *The Intellectual Life of the British Working Classes* (2001), p. 383.

46 Huzzey, *Freedom Burning*, p. 22.

47 Marcus Wood, *Blind Memory: Visual Representations of Slavery in England and America, 1780–1865* (2000), p. 147.

48 Wood, *Blind Memory*, p. 146.

49 Harriet Beecher Stowe, *Uncle Tom's Cabin: or, Life Among the Lowly*, Applewood Edition (2001), vol. 2, p. 238.

50 Harriet Beecher Stowe, *A Key to Uncle Tom's Cabin; Presenting the Original Facts and Documents Upon Which the Story is Founded Together with Corroborative Statements Verifying the Truth of the Work* (1853), p. 10.

51 Quoted in Rose, *The Intellectual Life of the British Working Classes*, p. 383.

52 Quoted in Sarah Meer, *Uncle Tom Mania: Slavery, Minstrelsy, and Transatlantic Culture in the 1850s* (2005), p. 21.

53 Meer, *Uncle Tom Mania*, p. 163.

54 Quoted in Meer, *Uncle Tom Mania*, p. 167.

55 Nancy Koester, *Harriet Beecher Stowe: A Spiritual Life* (2014), p. 153.

56 Meer, *Uncle Tom Mania*, p. 140.

57 *The Times*, 12 September 1836.

58 Nowatzki, *Representing African Americans*, p. 60 and Meer, *Uncle Tom Mania*, p. 149.

59 Meer, *Uncle Tom Mania*, p. 161.

60 Nowatzki, *Representing African Americans*, p. 4.

61 Blackett, *Building an Antislavery Wall*, p. 160.

62 Nowatzki, *Representing African Americans*, p. 7.

63 Henry Mayhew, *Mayhew's London, Being Selections from London Labour and the London Poor* (1970), pp. 535–6.

64 *The Morning Chronicle: Labour and the Poor*, 1849–50; Henry Mayhew – Letter LV, Thursday 6 June 1850.

65 *The Morning Chronicle: Labour and the Poor*, 1849–50; Henry Mayhew – Letter LV, Thursday 6 June 1850.

66 Mark Knowles, *Tap Roots: The Early History of Tap Dancing* (2002), p. 118.

67 Errol G. Hill and James V. Hatch, *A History of African American Theatre* (2003), p. 102.

68 Hill and Hatch, *A History of African American Theatre*, p. 102.

69 Frederick Burkhardt, Sydney Smith (eds), *The Correspondence of Charles Darwin: volume 1, 1821–1836* (1985), letter to Caroline Darwin, [9 November 1836]; Frederick Burkhardt, Sydney Smith (eds), *The Correspondence of Charles Darwin: volume 2, 1837–1843* (1986), Appendix IV, 'Darwin's notes on marriage'. Emma Darwin referred to CD as her 'nigger' as a term of endearment (Emma Darwin 2: 104). Darwin, C. R. to Darwin, Emma [25 May 1848].

70 Frederick Burkhardt, Sydney Smith (eds), *The Correspondence of Charles Darwin: volume 4, 1847–1850* (1985), pp. 145–6.

71 Burkhardt, Smith (eds), *The Correspondence of Charles Darwin: volume 1, 1821–1836*, pp. 518–19.

72 See Adrian Desmond and James Moore, *Darwin's Sacred Cause: Race, Slavery and the Quest for Human Origins* (2010), p. 137.

73 Mark E. Neely Jr., *The Boundaries of American Political Culture in the Civil War Era* (2015), p. 127.

EIGHT: 'Liberated Africans'

1 Siân Rees, *Sweet Water and Bitter: The Ships that Stopped the Slave Trade* (2009), p. 3.

2 AN ACT to amend and consolidate the Laws relating to the abolition of the slave trade (24th June 1824).

3 Slave Trade Consolidation Act 1824.

4   Figures from William James, *Naval History of Great Britain*, vol. 5 of the 1837 edn, annexe 167.

5   Marika Sherwood, *After Abolition: Britain and the Slave Trade Since 1807* (2007), pp. 116–17.

6   A. W. Ward and G. P. Gooch (eds)., *The Cambridge History of British Foreign Policy 1783–1919* (1922–23), p. 244.

7   Jeremy Black, *A Brief History of Slavery* (2011), p. 124.

8   Seymour Drescher, *Abolition: A History of Slavery and Antislavery* (2009), p. 267.

9   Christopher Lloyd, *The Navy and the Slave Trade* (1949), p. 4.

10   *Instructions for the Guidance of Her Majesty's Naval Officers Employed in the Suppression of the Slave Trade* (1844), p. 1.

11   *Proceedings of the General Anti-Slavery Convention, Called by the Committee of the British and Foreign Anti-Slavery Society, Held in London, Friday, June 12th, to Tuesday, June 23rd* (1840), pp. 239–40.

12   William Balfour Baikie, *Narrative of an exploring voyage up the rivers Kwo'ra and Bi'nue (Commonly known as the Niger and Tsádda) in 1854* (1856), p. 390.

13   Lieutenant Frederick Edwyn Forbes, *Six Months' Service in the African Blockade, from April to October, 1848, in Command of HMS Bonetta* (1849), p. vii.

14   Baikie, *Narrative of an exploring voyage*, pp. 390–91.

15   *Parliamentary Papers, House of Commons and Command*, volume 45, pp. 3–5.

16   Theophilus Conneau, *A Slaver's Log Book: Or 20 Years' Residence in Africa: the Original Manuscript* (1853), p. 95.

17   F. Harrison Rankin, *The White Man's Grave: A Visit to Sierra Leone, in 1834*, vol. 2 (1834), p. 137.

18   National Maritime Museum, Greenwich, London, Macpherson Collection (PAH8184).

19   Miles Taylor (ed.), *The Victorian Empire and Britain's Maritime World, 1837–1901: The Sea and Global Power* (2013), p. 50.

20   Benjamin Nicholas Lawrance, *Amistad's Orphans: An Atlantic Story of Children, Slavery, and Smuggling* (2015), p. 301.

21   Diane Frost, 'Diasporan West African Communities: the Kru in Freetown and Liverpool', *Review of African Political Economy* 29:92 (2002), pp. 285–300.

22   Taylor, *The Victorian Empire*, p. 49.

23   Richard Huzzey, *Freedom Burning: Anti-Slavery and Empire in Victorian Britain* (2012), p. 42.

24   Leslie Bethell, *The Abolition of the Brazilian Slave Trade: Britain, Brazil and the Slave Trade Question, 1807–1869* (2009), p. 160.

25   Huzzey, *Freedom Burning*, p. 45.

26   Huzzey, *Freedom Burning*, p. 42.

27   Robert J. Blyth, 'Britain, The Royal Navy and the Suppression of Slave Traders in the Nineteenth Century' in Douglas Hamilton and Robert J. Blyth (eds), *Representing Slavery* (2007), p. 81.

28 Seymour Drescher, *Abolition: A History of Slavery and Antislavery* (2009), p. 287.

29 Marika Sherwood, *After Abolition: Britain and the Slave Trade Since 1807* (2007), pp. 187–8.

30 Conneau, *A Slaver's Log Book*, p. 178.

31 *Instructions*, pp. 4–5.

32 *Parliamentary Papers, House of Commons and Command: volume 19, 1831* Great Britain. Parliament. House of Commons Colonies and Slaves One Volume Relating To Colonies; Africans Captured Jamaica; Slave Emancipation; Slave Trade Session 14 June–20 October 1831 H.M. Stationery Office, p. 65. Cited in Richard Murphy, *The Limits of Law: British Efforts to Suppress the Slave Trade, 1818–1850* (Unpublished thesis, University of Colorado at Boulder, History).

33 *Parliamentary Papers, House of Commons and Command: volume 19* Great Britain. Parliament. House of Commons January 1, 1831 H.M. Stationery Office, p. 65.

34 Rankin, *The White Man's Grave*, pp. 119–21.

35 Rankin, *The White Man's Grave*, pp. 121–3.

36 Pascoe Grenfell Hill, *Fifty Days on Board a Slave-Vessel in the Mozambique Channel, in April and May, 1843* (1844), pp. 47–8.

37 Hill, *Fifty Days on Board a Slave-Vessel*, pp. 48–9.

38 Lloyd, *The Navy and the Slave Trade*, p. 99.

39 Huzzey, *Freedom Burning*, p. 46.

40 The illegality of the slave trade in the nineteenth century means that the historical data on the numbers of Africans enslaved is problematic and is subject to an ongoing historical debate. See David Eltis, David Richardson, *Atlas of the Transatlantic Slave Trade* (2015) and Paul Lovejoy, 'The Volume of the Atlantic Slave Trade: a Synthesis', in *Journal of African History* (No. 23, 1982), pp. 473–501.

41 A. G. Hopkins, *An Economic History of West Africa* (2014), p. 113.

42 Suzanne Schwarz, 'Reconstructing the Life Histories of Liberated Africans: Sierra Leone in the Early Nineteenth Century', in *History in Africa: A Journal of Method* 39 (January 2012), p. 2.

43 Rankin, *The White Man's Grave*, p. 106.

44 *Parliamentary Papers, House of Commons and Command: volume 51*, p. 19, His Majesty's Commissioners to Viscount Palmerston, Sierra Leone, 4th June 1834.

45 Rankin, *The White Man's Grave*, pp. 123–5.

46 Rankin, *The White Man's Grave*, p. 108.

47 Rankin, *The White Man's Grave*, p. 113.

48 Suzanne Schwarz, 'Extending the African Names Database: New Evidence from Sierra Leone', in *African Economic History*, vol. 38 (2010), p. 140.

49 Schwarz, 'Extending the African Names Database', p. 143.

50 Brian Dyde, *The Empty Sleeve: The story of the West India Regiments of the British Army* (1997), p. 31.

51 Dyde, *The Empty Sleeve*, p. 124.
52 Rankin, *The White Man's Grave*, p. 108.
53 Rankin, *The White Man's Grave*, p. 92.
54 Christopher Fyfe, *A History of Sierra Leone* (1962), p. 182.
55 Fyfe, *A History of Sierra Leone*, p. 183.
56 Fyfe, *A History of Sierra Leone*, p. 115.
57 Lloyd, *The Navy and the Slave Trade*, p. 16.
58 Rankin, *The White Man's Grave*, pp. 115–16.
59 Fyfe, *A History of Sierra Leone*, p. 171.
60 Fyfe, *A History of Sierra Leone*, p. 131.
61 Fyfe, *A History of Sierra Leone*, p. 204.
62 Seymour Drescher, *The Mighty Experiment: Free Labor Versus Slavery in British Emancipation* (2004), p. 98.
63 Fyfe, *A History of Sierra Leone*, p. 153.
64 William H. Worger, Nancy L. Clark, Edward A. Alpers, *Africa and the West: From the slave trade to conquest, 1441–1905* (2010), p. 110.
65 Kristin Mann, *Slavery and the Birth of an African City: Lagos, 1760–1900* (2007), p. 93.
66 Robert Sydney Smith, *The Lagos Consulate, 1851–1861* (1979), p. 19.
67 Smith, *The Lagos Consulate*, p. 19.
68 Quoted in Smith, *The Lagos Consulate*, p. 25.
69 Smith, *The Lagos Consulate*, p. 30.
70 Fyfe, *A History of Sierra Leone*, p. 212.
71 Toyin Falola and Matthew M. Heaton, *A History of Nigeria* (2008), p. 126.
72 Kristin Mann, *Slavery and the Birth of an African City: Lagos, 1760–1900* (2007), p. 125.
73 Mann, *Slavery and the Birth of an African City*, p. 122.
74 Richard James Hammond, *Portugal and Africa, 1815–1910: A Study in Uneconomic Imperialism* (1967), p. 69.
75 Robin Law, *Ouidah: The Social History of a West African Slaving 'port', 1727–1892* (2004), p. 157.
76 Hugh Thomas, *The Slave Trade: The Story of the Atlantic Slave Trade 1440–1870* (1997), p. 695, and Elisée Soumonni, 'The compatibility of the slave and palm oil trades in Dahomey 1818–1858', in Robin Law, *From Slave Trade to 'Legitimate' Commerce: The Commercial Transition in Nineteenth-Century West Africa* (1998), p. 82.
77 Joan Amin-Addo in Gretchen Gerzina, *Black Victorians / Black Victoriana* (1995), p. 12.
78 F. E. Forbes, *Dahomey and the Dahomans: Being the Journals of Two Missions to the King of Dahomey, and Residence at His Capital, in the Year 1849 and 1850* (1851), vol. 2, pp. 33–5.
79 Forbes, *Dahomey and the Dahomans*, p. 188.
80 Lieutenant Forbes, *Six Months' Service in the African Blockade, from April to October, 1848, in Command of HMS Bonetta* (1849), p. ix.

81 Soumonni, 'The compatibility of the slave and palm oil trades', p. 82.

82 Forbes, *Dahomey and the Dahomans*, p. 187.

83 Forbes, *Dahomey and the Dahomans*, p. 193.

84 Forbes, *Dahomey and the Dahomans*, p. 207.

85 Sean Stilwell, *Slavery and Slaving in African History* (2014), p. 115; and see Nancy Jay, *Throughout Your Generations Forever: Sacrifice, Religion, and Paternity* (1992), Chapter 5.

86 Philip D. Curtin, *The Image of Africa: British Ideas and Action, 1780–1850*, vol. 2 (1964), pp. 407–8 and Thomas, *The Slave Trade*, p. 696.

87 Forbes, *Dahomey and the Dahomans*, p. 193.

88 Forbes, *Dahomey and the Dahomans*, p. 207.

89 Quoted in Walter Dean Myers, *At Her Majesty's Request: An African Princess in Victorian England* (1999), p. 24.

90 Forbes, *Dahomey and the Dahomans*, p. 208.

91 Quoted in Myers, *At Her Majesty's Request*, p. 30.

92 Forbes, *Dahomey and the Dahomans*, p. 208.

93 Helen Rappaport, *Queen Victoria: A Biographical Companion* (2003), p. 307.

94 Caroline Bressey, 'Of Africa's brightest ornaments: a short biography of Sarah Forbes Bonetta', *Social and Cultural Geography*, vol. 6, no. 2, April 2005.

95 *Leeds Mercury*, Saturday 16 August 1862.

96 *Brighton Herald,* 16 August 1862.

97 *Brighton Gazette*, 16 August 1862.

98 Forbes, *Dahomey and the Dahomans*, p. 207.

99 Bressey, 'Of Africa's brightest ornaments'.

100 *Brighton Herald*, 16 August 1862.

101 Bressey, 'Of Africa's brightest ornaments'.

102 Rappaport, *Queen Victoria*, p. 307.

103 Rappaport, *Queen Victoria*, p. 307.

104 Alessandro Stanziani, *Debt and Slavery in the Mediterranean and Atlantic Worlds* (2016), p. 79.

105 Rappaport, *Queen Victoria*, p. 307.

NINE: 'Cotton is King'

1 *The Times*, 4 July 1851.

2 Gene Dattel, *Cotton and Race in the Making of America: The Human Costs of Economic Power* (2011), p. 37.

3 R. Arthur Arnold, *The History of the Cotton Famine, from the Fall of Sumter to the Passing of the Public Works Act* (2013), p. 4. (Original work published 1864.)

4 Peter Fryer, *Staying Power. The History of Black People in Britain* (1984), p. 14.

5 Joseph E. Inikori, Stanley L. Engerman (eds), *The Atlantic Slave Trade: Effects on Economies, Societies and Peoples in Africa, the Americas, and Europe* (1992), p. 167.

6 Walter Johnson, *River of Dark Dreams: Slavery and Empire in the Cotton Kingdom* (2013), p. 6.

7   Johnson, *River of Dark Dreams*, p. 2.
8   Ira Berlin, *Generations of Captivity: A History of African-American Slaves* (2009), p. 14.
9   Stephen Yafa, *Cotton: The Biography of a Revolutionary Fiber* (2006), p. 145.
10 Johnson, *River of Dark Dreams*, p. 5.
11 *The Economist*, 19 January 1861, quoted in Lance E. Davis, Stanley L. Engerman, *Naval Blockades in Peace and War: An Economic History since 1750* (2006), p. 127.
12 David Christy, *Cotton is king: or, The culture of cotton, and its relation to agriculture, manufactures and commerce; to the free colored people; and to those who hold that slavery is in itself sinful* (1855), p. 58.
13 Quoted in Christy, *Cotton is king*, pp. 46–7.
14 Arnold, *The History of the Cotton Famine*, p. 7.
15 Arnold, *The History of the Cotton Famine*, p. 7.
16 Davis and Engerman, *Naval Blockades in Peace and War*, p. 127.
17 *New York Herald-Tribune*, 14 October 1861.
18 Junius P. Rodriguez, *Slavery in the United States: A Social, Political, and Historical Encyclopedia, volume 1* (2007), p. 666.
19 James Henry Hammond, *Gov. Hammond's Letters on Southern Slavery: Addressed to Thomas Clarkson, the English Abolitionist* (1845), p. 5.
20 Wagner, Gallagher, McPherson, *The Library of Congress Civil War Desk Reference*, p. 54.
21 Hammond, *Gov. Hammond's Letters*, p. 32.
22 Christy, *Cotton is king*, p. 11.
23 Christy, *Cotton is king*, p. 48.
24 Christy, *Cotton is king*, p. 11.
25 *The Times*, 22 January 1861, in Norman Longmate, *The Hungry Mills. The story of the Lancashire cotton famine 1861–5* (1978), p. 33.
26 Edwin Waugh, *Lancashire Sketches* (1869), p. 330.
27 John Watts, *The Facts of the Cotton Famine* (1866), p. 129.
28 Maurie D. McInnis, *Slaves Waiting for Sale: Abolitionist Art and the American Slave Trade* (2011), p. 209.
29 R. J. M. Blackett, *Divided Hearts: Britain in the American Civil War* (2001), p. 167.
30 Thomas E. Taylor, *Running the Blockade During the American Civil War* (1896), pp. 10–11 and in Marika Sherwood, *After Abolition: Britain and the Slave Trade Since 1807* (2007), p. 53.
31 Marika Sherwood, 'Perfidious Albion: Britain, the USA, and Slavery in the 1840s and 1860s', in *Contributions in Black Studies, A Journal of African and Afro-American Studies*, vol. 13, Special Double Issue, 1 January 1995, p. 12.
32 Longmate, *The Hungry Mills*, p. 246.
33 *New York Times*, 17 November 1863, 'Rev. Henry Ward Beecher's Final Farewell Speech at Liverpool on Oct. 30'.
34 *A reply to "The affectionate and Christian address of many thousands of women of*

Great Britain and Ireland, to their sisters, the women of the United states of America". By Mrs. Harriet Beecher Stowe, in behalf of many thousands of American women (1863), p. 62.

35 Stowe, *A reply*, p. 53.

36 See Blackett, *Divided Hearts*.

37 Richard Huzzey, *Freedom Burning: Anti-Slavery and Empire in Victorian Britain* (2012) pp. 128–9.

38 See Mary Ellison, *Support for Secession: Lancashire and the American Civil War* (1973).

39 Bill Cash, *John Bright: Statesman, Orator, Agitator* (2011), p. 146.

40 Quoted in Blackett, *Divided Hearts*, p. 32.

41 *The Anti-slavery Reporter*, 5 February 1863, pp. 43–4.

42 Longmate, *The Hungry Mills*, p. 254.

TEN: 'Mercy in a Massacre'

1 Thomas C. Holt, *The Problem of Freedom: Race, Labor, and Politics in Jamaica and Britain, 1832–1938* (1992), p. 280.

2 Thomas Carlyle, 'Occasional Discourse on the Negro Question', *Fraser's Magazine for Town and Country* (London, vol. XL, February 1849).

3 Christine Bolt, *Victorian Attitudes to Race* (1971), p. 79.

4 Thomas Carlyle, *The Selected Works of Thomas Carlyle* (2014), p. 469.

5 Carlyle, 'Occasional Discourse'.

6 John Greenleaf Whittier, a New England, Quaker abolitionist, quoted in Vanessa D. Dickerson, *Dark Victorians* (2008), p. 76.

7 See Catherine Hall, *Civilising Subjects: Metropole and Colony in the English Imagination 1830–1867* (2002).

8 *On the Origin of Species* went on sale to the book trade two days earlier. See Janet Browne, *Charles Darwin: The Power of Place* (2003). For Douglass' arrival see Michael A. Schuman, *Frederick Douglass: "Truth Is of No Color"* (2009), p. 85.

9 J. Edward Chamberlin, *Come Back to Me My Language: Poetry and the West Indies* (1993), p. 23.

10 The Rev. Frederic W. Farrar, 'Aptitudes of Races', *Transactions of the Ethnological Society of London*, 27 March 1866.

11 Thomas Carlyle, *The Works of Thomas Carlyle*: vol. 30, *Critical and Miscellaneous Essays*, volume 6 (2010), p. 5.

12 See *Darwin's Sacred Curse*.

13 W. F. Bynum, Roy Porter (eds), *Companion Encyclopedia of the History of Medicine*, vol. 2 (1993), p. 1,439.

14 Dane Kennedy, *The Highly Civilized Man: Richard Burton and the Victorian World* (2005), p. 168.

15 *Anthropology at the British Association: The Anthropological Review*, vol. 1, no. 3

(Nov. 1863), p. 379 and Ben Grant, *Postcolonialism, Psychoanalysis and Burton: Power Play of Empire* (2008), p. 89.

16 R. J. M. Blackett, *Divided Hearts: Britain in the American Civil War* (2001), p. 42.

17 'The Negro before the Savans', *The Pacific Appeal*, Saturday 31 October 1863.

18 'The Negro before the Savans'.

19 *Anthropology at the British Association*, p. 389.

20 *Anthropology at the British Association*, p. 391.

21 *Anthropology at the British Association*, p. 462.

22 *Anthropology at the British Association*, p. 391.

23 *Anthropology at the British Association*, p. 391.

24 Christine Bolt, *Victorian Attitudes to Race* (1971), p. 93.

25 Joseph John Williams, *Psychic Phenomena of Jamaica* (2011), p. 166.

26 It was arguably chance and circumstance that meant that the Morant Bay Rebellion was the disturbance that brought to a climax the tensions that had been brewing in Jamaica since the 1840s. For accounts of earlier disturbances, riots and violent land disputes that had similar potential see Thomas C. Holt, *The Problem of Freedom: Race, Labor, and Politics in Jamaica and Britain, 1832–1938* (1992).

27 Frank McGlynn and Seymour Drescher (eds), *The Meaning of Freedom: Economics, Politics, and Culture after Slavery* (1992), p. 134.

28 Holt, *The Problem of Freedom*, p. 265.

29 Holt, *The Problem of Freedom*, p. 263.

30 Thomas Harvey and William Brewin, *Jamaica in 1866: a narrative of a tour through the island: with remarks on its social, educational and industrial condition* (1867), pp. 101–2.

31 Mark Cumming (ed.), *The Carlyle Encyclopedia* (2004), p. 461.

32 *The Anti-Slavery Reporter and Aborigines' Friend* (1865), p. 28.

33 Gad Heuman, *Killing Time: Morant Bay Rebellion Jamaica* (1995), p. 171.

34 *Jamaica Disturbances: Papers Laid Before The Royal Commission of Inquiry by Governor Eyre* (London, 1866), p. 3: Despatch from Governor Eyre to the Right Hon. Edward Cardwell, M.P. Flamstead, January 1866.

35 *The Times*, 13 November 1865.

36 Bolt, *Victorian Attitudes*, p. 77.

37 *Spectator*, 18 November 1865.

38 *The Times*, 18 November 1865, quoted in *The Popular Magazine of Anthropology*, vol. 1, issue no. 1, January 1866, p. 16.

39 *The Times*, 18 November 1865, quoted in *The Popular Magazine of Anthropology*, p. 16.

40 *The Times*, 18 November 1865, quoted in *The Popular Magazine of Anthropology*, p. 16.

41 *The Spectator*, 18 November 1865.

42 *Report of the Jamaica Royal Commission 1866*, p. 41.

43 *The Popular Magazine of Anthropology*, p. 17.

44 Gad Heuman, *Killing Time*, p. 171.

45 Ian Thomson, *The Dead Yard: Tales of Modern Jamaica* (2009), p. 140.

46 Edward Bean Underhill, *The Tragedy of Morant Bay: A Narrative of the Disturbances in the Island of Jamaica in 1865* (1895), p. 199.

47 *The Diplomatic Review*, vol. 14, 1886, p. 118.

48 *Spectator*, 6 June 1868.

49 Richard Huzzey, *Freedom Burning: Anti-Slavery and Empire in Victorian Britain* (2012), p. 184.

50 *The Times*, 18 November 1865, quoted in *The Popular Magazine of Anthropology*, p. 16.

51 *The Popular Magazine of Anthropology*, pp. 14–15.

52 Commander Bedford Pim, *The Negro and Jamaica: Read Before the Anthropological Society of London, February 1, 1866, at St. James's Hall, London* (1866), p. v.

53 Pim, *The Negro and Jamaica*, p. vi.

54 Pim, *The Negro and Jamaica*, p. 63.

55 Winwood Reade, *Savage Africa; being the narrative of a tour in equatorial, southwestern, and northwestern Africa; with notes on the habits of the gorilla; on the existence of unicorns and tailed men; on the slave-trade; on the origin, character, and capabilities of the negro, and on the future civilization of western Africa* (1863), p. 327.

56 Reade, *Savage Africa*, p. 452.

ELEVEN: 'Darkest Africa'

1 J. R. Oldfield, *Chords of Freedom: Commemoration, Ritual and British Transatlantic Slavery* (2008), p. 90.

2 *The Times*, 2 August 1884.

3 *The Times*, 2 August 1884.

4 Henry Rider Haggard, *Child of Storm*, quoted in Ian Knight, *Companion to the Anglo-Zulu War* (2008), p. 103.

5 Quoted in Shehu Sani, *Hatred for Black People* (2013), pp. 68–9.

6 Neil MacMaster, *Racism in Europe: 1870–2000* (2001), p. 77.

7 A. Geppert, *Fleeting Cities: Imperial Expositions in Fin-de-Siècle Europe* (2010), p. 124.

8 Quoted in Geppert, *Fleeting Cities*, p. 124.

9 Jeffrey Green, *Black Edwardians: Black People in Britain 1901–1914* (1998), p. 4.

10 Green, *Black Edwardians*, p. 4.

11 *Franco-British Exhibition 1908 Official Guide Section III: The Visible Empire* (1908).

12 Annie E. Coombes, *Reinventing Africa: Museums, Material Culture and Popular Imagination in Late Victorian and Edwardian England* (1997), p. 95.

13 Quoted in Neil MacMaster, p. 75.

14 *Bristol Mercury and Daily Post*, 22 April 1899.

15 *The Era*, 22 April 1899.

16 Charles Ricketts, *The Boswells: the story of a South African Circus* (2003), p. 16.

17 Hansard HC Deb 4 May 1899, vol. 70 cc1302–4.

18 *The Times*, 9 May 1899.

19 *Galveston Daily News*, 20 August 1899, quoted in Ben Shephard, 'Showbiz Imperialism: The Case of Peter Lobengula', in John MacKenzie (ed.), *Imperialism and Popular Culture* (1986). See also Ben Shephard, *Kitty and the Prince* (2003).

20 *Galveston Daily News*, 20 August 1899, quoted in Shephard, 'Showbiz Imperialism'. See also Shephard, *Kitty and the Prince*.

21 *Tit-Bits*, 21 July 1917, quoted In Centre for Contemporary Cultural Studies, *EMPIRE STRIKES BACK: Race and Racism in 70's Britain* (2004), p. 62.

22 Neil Parsons, *King Khama, Emperor Joe, and the Great White Queen: Victorian Britain through African Eyes* (1998), p. 51.

23 Gaborone Archives. Documents made available to the author by kind permission of the Botswana National Archives and Records Service.

24 Gaborone Archives.

25 Gaborone Archives.

26 Gaborone Archives.

27 *Yorkshire Daily Post*, 1895, quoted in G. W. H. Knight-Bruce, *Memories of Mashonaland* (1895).

28 Parsons, *King Khama*, p. 60.

29 Parsons, *King Khama*, p. 214.

30 Eric Ames, *Carl Hagenbeck's Empire of Entertainments* (2008), p. 296.

31 Parsons, *King Khama*, p. 111.

32 Parsons, *King Khama*, p. 196.

33 Parsons, *King Khama*, p. 207.

34 Parsons, *King Khama*, p. 222.

35 Parsons, *King Khama*, p. 80.

36 James Africanus Beale Horton, *West African Countries and Peoples, British and Native: A Vindication of the African Race* (1868), p. v.

37 Paul Gilroy, *The Black Atlantic: Modernity and Double Consciousness* (1995), p. 90.

38 Gilroy, *The Black Atlantic*, p. 89.

39 *Tit-Bits*, 7 September 1900.

40 Quoted in Steve Ward, *Beneath the Big Top: A Social History of the Circus in Britain* (2014), p. 80.

41 Ward, *Beneath the Big Top*, p. 80.

42 *Blackwood's Lady's Magazine*, vol. 22, 1847, p. 162, and *Illustrated London News*, 20 March 1847.

43 Ward, *Beneath the Big Top*, p. 81.

44 Douglas A. Lorimer, *Colour, Class and the Victorians: English attitudes to the Negro in the mid-nineteenth century* (1978).

45 Quoted in K. L. Little, *Negroes in Britain* (1948), p. 191.

TWELVE: 'We are a Coloured Empire'

1 Richard Smith, *Jamaican Volunteers in the First World War: Race, Masculinity and the Development of a National Consciousness* (2004), p. 41.

2 *Jamaica Times*, 5 September 1914, quoted in Anne Spry Rush, *Bonds of Empire: West Indians and Britishness from Victoria to Decolonization* (2011), p. 122.

3 John Starling, Ivor Lee, *No Labour, No Battle: Military Labour during the First World War* (2009), p. 237.

4 1915 West Ham Police Court Register Charges Court Ledgers 1915, West Ham Magistrate Court Records, Newham Archives and Local Studies Library.

5 *Stratford Express*, 19 May 1915, 'The Docks Black Men for the Front At West Ham Police Court to-day'.

6 *Stratford Express*, 29 May 1915, 'The Docks – Spoiling for a Fight'.

7 Quoted in Richard Smith, *Jamaican Volunteers in the First World War,* p. 55.

8 Rush, *Bonds of Empire*, p. 121.

9 Smith, *Jamaican Volunteers in the First World War*, p. 71.

10 *The Times History of the War*, vol. 16 (1918), p. 86.

11 Richard Smith, 'Loss and Longing: Emotional Responses to West Indian Soldiers during the First World War', *Round Table*, 2014, vol. 103, no. 2, pp. 243–52.

12 Quoted in Rush, *Bonds of Empire*, p. 121.

13 Quoted in Timothy C. Winegard, *Indigenous Peoples of the British Dominions and the First World War* (2014), p. 98.

14 Dick van Galen Last, Ralf Futselaar, *Black Shame: African Soldiers in Europe, 1914–1922* (2015), p. 43.

15 David Killingray, 'The Idea of a British Imperial African Army', *Journal of African History*, vol. 20, no. 3 (1979), pp. 421–36.

16 Major Darnley Stuart-Stephens, 'Our Million Black Army', *English Review*, October 1916, quoted in Lothrop Stoddard, *The Rising Tide of Color Against White World-Supremacy* (1920), Preface p. vi.

17 Louise Ryan, Wendy Webster, *Gendering Migration: Masculinity, Femininity and Ethnicity in Post-war Britain* (2008), p. 20.

18 Joseph Rowntree Foundation, *Contemporary Social Evils* (2009), p. 8.

19 Smith, 'Loss and Longing'.

20 Killingray, 'The Idea of a British Imperial African Army'.

21 Last, Futselaar, *Black Shame*, p. 43.

22 Greg Kennedy, Keith Neilson, *Far-flung Lines: Studies in Imperial Defence in Honour of Donald Mackenzie Schurman* (2013), p. 86.

23 'African Man-Power', *Sun*, Christchurch, vol. III, issue 924, 26 January 1917.

24 Hansard HC Deb 23 May 1916 vol. 82 cc2003–69.

25 Hansard HC Deb 23 May 1916 vol. 82 cc2003–69.

26 Akinjide Osuntokun, *Nigeria in the First World War* (1979), p. 45.

27 Kennedy, Neilson, *Far-flung Lines*, p. 86.

28 Killingray, 'The Idea of a British Imperial African Army'.

29 Ray Costello, *Black Tommies: British Soldiers of African Descent in the First World War* (2015), p. 73.

30 Quoted in Costello, *Black Tommies*, p. 26.

31 Ernest Marke, *In Troubled Waters: Memoirs of My Seventy Years in England* (1975), p. 25.

32 David Killingray, ' "All the King's Men?" British Blacks in the First World War', in R. Lotz and I. Pegg (eds), *Under the Imperial Carpet. Essays in Black British History 1780–1950* (1986), pp. 177–8.

33 Tull was commissioned into the Special Reserve because his was a Service battalion.

34 Quoted in David Olusoga, *The World's War* (2014), p. 297.

35 Quoted in Olusoga, *The World's War*, p. 402.

36 Jacqueline Jenkinson, ' "All in the Same Uniform"? The Participation of Black Colonial Residents in the British Armed Forces in the First World War', *Journal of Imperial and Commonwealth History*, 40:2, pp. 207–30.

37 Quoted in Stephen Bourne, *Black Poppies: Britain's Black Community and the Great War* (2014), p. 70.

38 Lothrop Stoddard, *The Rising Tide of Color Against White World-Supremacy* (1920), p. 209.

39 Jacqueline Nassy Brown, *Dropping Anchor, Setting Sail: Geographies of Race in Black Liverpool* (1994), p. 21.

40 *Liverpool Echo*, 6 June 1919, quoted in Jenkinson, 'All in the Same Uniform'.

41 *Liverpool Evening Express*, 10 June 1919, 'Negro in Dock No Evidence How he Got into Water'.

42 *Liverpool Evening Express*, 10 June 1919, 'Negro in Dock'.

43 *Liverpool Evening Express*, 10 June 1919, 'Negro in Dock'.

44 See Marika Sherwood, 'Lynching in Britain', *History Today*, XLIX (1999), pp. 21–3.

45 *Liverpool Courier*, 11 June 1919.

46 Marke, *In Troubled Waters*, p. 32.

47 Jacqueline Jenkinson, 'Black Sailors on Red Clydeside: rioting, reactionary trade unionism and conflicting notions of "Britishness" following the First World War', *Twentieth Century British History* 19 (1) (2008), pp. 29–60.

48 Jacqueline Jenkinson, *Black 1919: Riots, Racism and Resistance in Imperial Britain* (2009), p. 77.

49 Jenkinson, 'All in the Same Uniform'.

50 *Liverpool Daily Post*, 11 June 1919, and *Liverpool Weekly Post*, 21 June 1919, quoted in Roy May and Robin Cohen, 'The Interaction Between Race and Colonialism: A Case Study of the Liverpool Race Riots of 1919', *Race & Class*, 10/15/1974, vol. 16, issue 2, pp. 111–26.

51 Marke, *In Troubled Waters*, pp. 30–31.

52 *The Times*, 10 June 1919.

53 *Liverpool Evening Express*, 11 June 1919.

54 May and Cohen, 'The Interaction Between Race and Colonialism'.

55 David Killingray, *Africans in Britain* (ed) (1994).

56 *The Times*, 10 June 1919, quoted in Elazar Barkarn, *The Retreat of Scientific Racism: Changing Concepts of Race in Britain and the United States Between the World Wars* (1992), p. 58. *The Morning Post*, 13 June 1919, 'The Negro Riots. A Lesson for England'.

57 *Liverpool Courier*, 11 June 1919.

58 *Liverpool Courier*, 16 June 1919, quoted in Susan Kingsley Kent, *Aftershocks: Politics and Trauma in Britain, 1918–1931* (2009), p. 51.

59 *The Morning Post*, 13 June 1919, quoted in Kent, *Aftershocks*, p. 51.

60 Barkarn, *The Retreat of Scientific Racism*, p. 58.

61 Quoted in Peter Fryer, *Staying Power: The History of Black People in Britain* (1984), p. 316.

62 *Liverpool Courier*, 11 June 1919.

63 Costello, *Black Tommies*, p. 140.

64 Quoted in Kent, *Aftershocks*, p.53.

65 Alexander Keese, *Ethnicity and the Colonial State: Finding and Representing Group Identifications in a Coastal West African and Global Perspective (1850–1960)* (2015), p. 67.

66 J. Ayodele Langley, *Pan-Africanism and Nationalism in West Africa, 1900–1945: a study in ideology and social classes* (1973), p. 208.

67 May and Cohen, 'The Interaction Between Race and Colonialism'.

68 Centre for Contemporary Cultural Studies, *EMPIRE STRIKES BACK*, p. 60.

69 *Liverpool Evening Express*, 11 June 1919.

70 Laura Tabili, 'The Construction of Racial Difference in Twentieth-Century Britain: The Special Restriction (Coloured Alien Seamen) Order, 1925', *Journal of British Studies* 33 (January 1994), pp. 54–98.

71 May and Cohen, 'The Interaction Between Race and Colonialism'.

72 K. L. Little, *Negroes in Britain* (1948), p. 65.

THIRTEEN: 'We Prefer their Company'

1 There are various estimates. James Walvin, *Black and White: The Negro and English Society, 1555–1945* (1973); K. L. Little, *Negroes in Britain: A study of racial relations in English society* (1948). In *The Colour Bar* (1944), Harold Moody suggested there were around ten thousand black people in Britain in 1939.

2 Peter Fryer in his *Staying Power: The History of Black People in Britain* (1984) suggests that by 1958, a hundred and twenty-five thousand West Indians had arrived in Britain, and some very modest immigration from Africa. Other estimates put the number who had arrived by 1958 at a hundred and fifteen thousand.

3 TNA: FO 371/26206, F. E. Evans, minute, 22 January 1942, Foreign
   Office General Political correspondence, A 10036/257/45. David
   Reynolds, 'The Churchill Government and the Black American Troops in
   Britain During World War II', *Transactions of the Royal Historical Society*, vol.
   35 (1985), pp. 113–33.
4 Quoted in Reynolds, 'The Churchill Government'.
5 Quoted in Philip Ziegler, *London at War, 1939–1945* (1995), p. 218.
6 Michael L. Krenn, *Race and U.S. Foreign Policy from 1900 Through World War II*
   (1998), p. 343.
7 David Reynolds, *Rich Relations: The American Occupation of Britain, 1942–
   1945* (2000), p. 303.
8 Christopher Hitchens, *Why Orwell Matters* (2002), p. 109.
9 Quoted in K. L. Little, *Negroes in Britain* (1948), p. 240.
10 Krenn, *Race and U.S. Foreign Policy*, p. 344.
11 Reynolds, *Rich Relations*, p. 305.
12 Graham Smith, *When Jim Crow Met John Bull* (1987), p. 180.
13 *The Times*, 2 October 1942, quoted in Little, *Negroes in Britain*,
   pp. 240–41.
14 Anthony Aldgate, Jeffrey Richards, *Britain Can Take It: The British Cinema in
   the Second World War*, second edition (2007), p. 292.
15 Aldgate and Richards, *Britain Can Take It*, p. 292.
16 Hansard HC Deb 29 September 1942, vol. 383 cc670–1.
17 Hansard HC Deb 29 September 1942, vol. 383 cc670–1.
18 Major General Arthur Dowler, *Notes on Relations with Coloured Troops*,
   quoted in Ben Bousquet and Colin Douglas, *West Indian Women at War: British
   Racism in World War II* (1991), pp. 175–7.
19 Dowler, *Notes on Relations*, quoted in Bousquet and Douglas, *West Indian
   Women at War*, pp. 175–7.
20 Dowler, *Notes on Relations*, quoted in Bousquet and Douglas, *West Indian
   Women at War*, pp. 175–7.
21 Peter Fryer, *Staying Power: The History of Black People in Britain* (1984),
   p. 361.
22 Quoted in Reynolds, *Rich Relations*, p. 306.
23 Fryer, *Staying Power*, p. 361.
24 Quoted in Paul Addison, *Churchill: The Unexpected Hero* (2005), p. 104.
25 Christopher Thorne, 'Britain and the black G.I.s: Racial issues and Anglo-
   American relations in 1942', *Journal of Ethnic and Migration Studies*, vol. 3,
   1974, issue 3, pp. 262–71.
26 Quoted in Alan Rice, *Creating Memorials, Building Identities: The Politics of
   Memory in the Black Atlantic* (2011), p. 169.
27 Quoted in Rice, *Creating Memorials*, p. 169.
28 Quoted in Reynolds, *Rich Relations*, p. 307.
29 Smith, *When Jim Crow met John Bull*, p. 190.
30 Smith, *When Jim Crow met John Bull*, p. 190.

31 Smith, *When Jim Crow met John Bull*, p. 94.

32 Army Service Experience Questionnaire Part 1 General Military Service Sergeant Theodore G. Aufort, US Army Military History Institute.

33 Reynolds, *Rich Relations* p. 303.

34 *New Statesman and Nation*, 22 August 1942, quoted in Samuel Lynn Hynes, *Reporting World War II: American journalism, 1938–1944*, p. 222.

35 *New Statesman and Nation*, 22 August 1942.

36 Christopher Paul Moore, *Fighting for America: Black Soldiers – the Unsung Heroes of World War II* (2005), pp. 91–2.

37 *Sunday Pictorial*, no. 1,434, 6 September 1942.

38 *Sunday Pictorial*, no. 1,434, 6 September 1942.

39 *Sunday Pictorial*, no. 1,434, 6 September 1942.

40 Reynolds, 'The Churchill Government'.

41 Quoted in G. H. Bennett, *Destination Normandy: Three American Regiments on D-Day* (2009), p. 45.

42 Hansard HC Deb 11 February 1948, vol. 447 cc369–70.

43 Hansard HC Deb 11 February 1948, vol. 447 cc369–70.

44 Hansard HC Deb 11 February 1948, vol. 447 cc369–70.

45 Quoted in Paul B. Rich, *Race and Empire in British Politics* (1990), p. 152.

46 Quoted in Rich, *Race and Empire*, p. 152.

47 Sonya O. Rose, *Which People's War?: National Identity and Citizenship in Wartime Britain* (2003), p. 262.

48 Smith, *When Jim Crow met John Bull*, p. 207.

49 Quoted in Smith, *When Jim Crow met John Bull*, p. 209.

50 Quoted in Smith, *When Jim Crow met John Bull*, p. 211.

51 Reynolds, 'The Churchill Government'.

52 TNA: CAB 67/WP(G) 4015, quoted in Reynolds, 'The Churchill Government'.

53 Quoted in Gen Doy, *Black Visual Culture: Modernity and Post-Modernity* (1999), p. 66.

54 *New Statesman and Nation*, 22 August 1942, quoted in Neil Campbell, Jude Davies, George McKay, *Issues in Americanisation and Culture* (2004), p. 88.

55 Quoted in Bennett, *Destination Normandy*, p. 43.

56 For Arthur Warlond's service record, see the website 'Caribbean aircrew in the RAF during WW2 A record of West Indian volunteers who served in the Royal Air Force during the Second World War', http://www.caribbeanaircrew-ww2.com/?p=292

57 Jack Williams, *Cricket and Race* (2001), p. 40.

58 Quoted in Phillip Alfred Buckner, *Rediscovering the British World* (2005), p. 335.

FOURTEEN: 'Swamped'

1 Ranu Samantrai, *AlterNatives: Black Feminism in the Postimperial Nation* (2002), p. 73.

2 Satnam Virdee, *Racism, Class and the Racialized Outsider* (2014), p. 100.

3 Winston James and Clive Harris, *Inside Babylon: The Caribbean Diaspora in Britain* (1993), p. 22.

4 James and Harris, *Inside Babylon*, pp. 21–2.

5 James and Harris, *Inside Babylon*, p. 22.

6 James and Harris, *Inside Babylon*, p. 22.

7 Peter Fryer, *Staying Power: The History of Black People in Britain* (1984), p. 372.

8 Quoted in David Kynaston, *Austerity Britain, 1945–1951* (2008), p. 274.

9 Quoted in Kynaston, *Austerity Britain*, p. 274.

10 Jo-Anne Lee, John Lutz, *Situating: Critical Essays for Activists and Scholars* (2005), p. 49.

11 James and Harris, *Inside Babylon*, p. 23.

12 Mike Phillips and Trevor Phillips, *Windrush: The Irresistible Rise of Multi-racial Britain* (1998), p. 87.

13 Wendy Webster, *Imagining Home: Gender, 'Race' and National Identity, 1945–64* (1998), p. 26, and James and Harris, *Inside Babylon*, p. 25.

14 Peter Hennessy, *Having it So Good: Britain in the Fifties* (2007), p. 274.

15 *The Times*, 4 August 1948.

16 E. Cashmore, *United Kingdom?: Class, Race and Gender since the War* (1989), p. 79.

17 Quoted in Fryer, *Staying Power*, p. 367.

18 Quoted in Fryer, *Staying Power*, p. 367.

19 Lee Allyn Davis, *Natural Disasters* (2008), p. 276.

20 Roger Daniels, *Guarding the Golden Door: American Immigration Policy and Immigrants since 1882* (2004), p. 120.

21 Kathleen Paul, *Whitewashing Britain: Race and Citizenship in the Postwar Era* (1997), p. 132.

22 Quoted in Winston James, 'The Black Experience in Twentieth Century Britain', in Philip D. Morgan and Sean Hawkins, *The Oxford History of the British Empire Companion Series: Black Experience and the Empire* (2004), p. 370.

23 Peter Fryer, *Aspects of British Black History* (1993), p. 34.

24 Fryer, *Aspects of British Black History*, p. 33.

25 James, 'The Black Experience', p. 371.

26 TNA: CO 1028/22, *Draft Report of Working Party on Coloured People Seeking Employment in The United Kingdom*, 17 December 1953.

27 Webster, *Imagining Home*, p. 23; James and Harris, *Inside Babylon*, p. 22.

28 Paul, *Whitewashing Britain*, p. 135.

29 Brian Harrison, *Seeking a Role: The United Kingdom 1951–1970* (2010), p. 82.

30 Quoted in Susan Kingsley Kent, *Gender and Power in Britain 1640–1990* (1991), p. 330.

31 Paul, *Whitewashing Britain*, p. 142.

32 Paul, *Whitewashing Britain*, p. 139.

33 Anthony H. Richmond, *The Colour Problem* (1955), p. 240.

34 Phillips and Phillips, *Windrush*, p. 82.

35 Richmond, *The Colour Problem*, p. 241.

36 Richmond, *The Colour Problem*, p. 241.

37 Michael Banton, *White and Coloured: The Behaviour of British People Towards Coloured Immigrants* (1959), p. 9.

38 Banton, *White and Coloured*, p. 203.

39 Banton, *White and Coloured*, p. 136.

40 Banton, *White and Coloured*, p. 137.

41 David Kynaston, *Modernity Britain: Book One: Opening the Box, 1957–1959* (2013), p. 66.

42 Rosalind Edwards, Suki Ali, Chamion Caballero, Miri Song (eds), *International Perspectives on Racial and Ethnic Mixedness and Mixing* (2012), p. 170.

43 Paul Gilroy, *There Ain't No Black in The Union Jack* (1987), p. 99.

44 Paul, *Whitewashing Britain*, p. 132.

45 Camilla Schofield, *Enoch Powell and the Making of Postcolonial Britain* (2013), p. 120.

46 Paul, *Whitewashing Britain*, p. 159.

47 Fryer, *Staying Power*, p. 377.

48 Malcolm Pearce and Geoffrey Stewart, *British Political History, 1867–2001: Democracy and Decline* (2002), p. 483.

49 Quoted in Neil MacMaster, *Racism in Europe: 1870–2000* (2001), p. 180.

50 Randall Hansen, *Citizenship and Immigration in Postwar Britain* (2000), p. 188.

51 Fryer, *Staying Power*, p. 385.

52 Stephanie Barczewski, John Eglin, Stephen Heathorn, Michael Silvestri, Michelle Tusan, *Britain Since 1688: A Nation in the World* (2014), p. 320.

53 Margaret Thatcher Foundation 1978 Jan 27 Fr Margaret Thatcher TV Interview for Granada *World in Action* ('rather swamped') http://www.margaretthatcher.org/document/103485

54 *Observer*, 25 February 1979.

55 Camilla Schofield, *Enoch Powell and the Making of Postcolonial Britain*, p. 234.

56 Zig Layton-Henry, Paul B. Rich, *Race, Government and Politics in Britain* (2016), p. 76.

57 Diane Frost and Richard Phillips, *Liverpool '81: Remembering the Riots* (2011), p. 32.

58 Daryl Michael Scott, 'The Origins of Black History Month', Association

for the Study of African American Life and History, *LA Times*, 11 February 2014.

CONCLUSION

1 William Harry Mitchell, Leonard Arthur Sawyer, *The Empire Ships: A Record of British-built and Acquired Merchant Ships During the Second World War* (1990), p. 477.
2 Michael Tillotson (ed.), *SOE and The Resistance: As Told in The Times Obituaries* (2012), p. 62.
3 See Daniel Stephen, *The Empire of Progress: West Africans, Indians, and Britons at the British Empire Exhibition, 1924–25* (2013).
4 *The Economist*, 28 January 2016, 'The Next Generation'.
5 Equality and Human Rights Commission, *Healing a Divided Britain: The Need for a Comprehensive Race Equality Strategy* (2016), p. 8.

INDEX

INDEX

597

Quakers 208–9
Queensberry, Duchess of (Catherine
        Hyde) 108–9
quinine 401
Quintuple Treaty (1841) 290

Race Relations Act (1964) 512–13
race riots
    (1919) 454–66, 470
    (1958) 509–11
    (1980s) 517
    (1981) 516–17
Rachman, Peter 504
racial mixing 27–8, 412–13
racial stereotypes 105, 109–10, 259, 260,
        265, 274
racism 15, 256–7, 280, 281–2, 462, 502
    and abolitionist movement 257–9
    and black Georgians 110–11
    and black Victorians 256–7, 419
    changing attitudes towards during
            Second World War 489–90
    colonial exhibitions and Africans as
            human exhibits 406–11
    during First World War 427
    experienced by black soldiers during
            First World War 435–6
    hierarchy of races belief 405, 406, 408,
            436
    rise of in 1950s/60s 499–504
    and Scramble for Africa 404–6
    and white supremacy mantra 408, 413,
            461, 490, 503
    see also scientific racism
radioisotope analysis 30–1, 32, 33
Rankin, F. Harrison 302–4, 310, 314, 316
    The White Man's Grave 310–11
Rankin, John E. 485
Reade, Winwood 397–8
    Savage Africa 398
Rebecca (brig) 24
Recaptives (Liberated Africans)
        (Freetown) 309–22
    Aku 318
    apprenticeship of children 314–15
    assembling and assessment of in King's
            Yard 309–11
    business successes of 319
    formation of communities 317–18

and missionaries 317–18, 321
numbers of 316
receptiveness to Christian message
        321
recruitment into army 313–14
recruitment into navy 314
Register of 311–13
return to homelands 324–6
Remond, Charles Lenox 246
Remond, Sarah Parker 246
Restoration (1660) 72
Reynolds, Admiral Sir Barrington 308
Reynolds, Joshua 89
Rhodes, Cecil 411, 414–15, 416, 417,
        418, 419
Rice, Thomas D. 272, 426, 468
Rich, Robert 106
Richardson family 254–5, 248, 281
Richmond, Anthony 503
    The Colour Problem 502
Richmond, Bill 80, 98, 110
Riddell, John 140
riots see race riots
Rochdale 362–3
Roman Empire 18, 29–32, 33 see also
        Afro-Romans
Roper, Moses 244–5
    Narrative 252
Royal African Company 22–3, 73–5, 221,
        238
Royal African Corps 313, 314
Royal Ethiopian Regiment 147, 150, 159
Royal Navy see West Africa Squadron
Royal Society of St George 10
Royal West African Frontier Force
        (RWAFF) 488
Rush, Benjamin 143
Ruskin, John 394

St Domingue (now Haiti) 217–18
St George's Bay Company 187
St John's Maroon Church (Freetown) 196
St Kitts 72, 75, 92
St Thomas parish (Jamaica) 378–9, 493,
        498
San Juan de Ulúa, Battle of (1568) 52
Sancho, Ignatius 80, 108, 110–12, 213
Sano, Buckor 199
Saro people 325–6

Dominique 218
Towerson, William 47, 48, 50
Trafalgar, Battle of 20–1
translators
    recruitment of Africans as 46–7
Travels of Sir John Mandeville, The 36–7, 38,
    40, 56, 201
Trollope, Anthony 238, 372–3
Tudor era
    English explorers and trade with
        Africa 40–9
    mystification of Africa 52–4
    slave trade 16, 50–2, 63
    view of blackness/whiteness 65–6
    see also black Tudors
Tull, Walter 445–6
Turpin, Dick 494
Turpin, Lionel Fitzherbert 443, 494

Umbelina (slave schooner) 301–2
Uncle Tom Penny Offerings 269
Uncle Tom-themed plays 269–70
Ungerer, Gustav 51
Union and Emancipation Society 361
United States 239
    attacks on and lynching of blacks in
        (1919) 462–3
    cotton production 342–3
    Fugitive Slave Act (1850) 248
    Immigration and Nationality Act
        (1952) 498
    Jim Crow laws 468
    railway expansion 343
    relations with Britain 242–3, 339
    segregation of army 467–8
    slavery *see* American slavery
    trade relations with Britain 339, 340
US Army *see* American GIs; black GIs
Utrecht, Treaty of 23, 24

Van Senden, Caspar 62, 63
Venn, Henry 333, 337
Vice Admiralty Courts 295
Victoria, Queen 261, 277, 328, 331–2,
    422, 429
    and anti-slavery mission 332
    opposition to racism 332
    as ward of Sarah Forbes Bonetta 331,
        332–3, 334, 335, 337–8

Victorian era
    blackface minstrelsy 271–8
    see also black Victorians
Victory, HMS 20
Virginia 67, 68–9, 71–2, 74, 76

Wales, Prince of 399, 422
Wallace, William 130
Walpole, Horace 136
Walrond, Sergeant Arthur 486–7
Walvin, James 85, 518
Wanderer, HMS 306, 322
War of Jenkins' Ear (1738–49) 24
War Office 430, 431–2
Washington, George 150, 151, 153, 156,
    157, 191
Washington, Harry 156, 157–8, 191, 195
Waugh, Edwin 352
Webb, Martha 194
Wedgwood, Josiah 206, 220, 440–1, 460
Wedgwood, Josiah (great-great-
    grandson) 440–1
Welcome to Britain (film) 473–4, 478
Wells, Nathaniel 92–3
Wendworth Day, James 505, 506–7
Wesley, John 209, 210, 212
    Thoughts upon Slavery 209
West Africa Squadron 284, 289–308, 370
    Brazilian ships targeted 308
    and Dahomey 327
    expense of running 299
    failure of to protect lives of Africans in
        its care 302–5
    Freetown as base 289
    hampering of and limitation to
        activities 284, 293–4
    lack of resources 298–9
    number of slave ships
        intercepted 306–7
    patrols and capture of slave ships 289,
        291, 295
    payment of bounties 300–1
    risk of disease and death serving
        on 301, 305
    ships 296–8
    suppression of slave trade
        missions 283–5, 287–99, 301
    treaties and legality of searches 291–2,
        294